MEDIEVAL DUBLIN XVI

The lord mayor of Dublin, Mr Oisín Quinn, opens 'Clontarf 1014–2014: National Conference Marking the Millennium of the Battle of Clontarf, 11–12 April 2014', Edmund Burke Theatre, Trinity College Dublin

Medieval Dublin XVI

Proceedings of Clontarf 1014–2014: National Conference Marking the Millennium of the Battle of Clontarf

Seán Duffy

EDITOR

FOUR COURTS PRESS

Typeset in 10.5 pt on 12.5 pt Ehrhardt by
Carrigboy Typesetting Services for
FOUR COURTS PRESS LTD
7 Malpas Street, Dublin 8, Ireland
www.fourcourtspress.ie
and in North America for
FOUR COURTS PRESS
c/o ISBS, 920 NE 58th Avenue, Suite 300, Portland, OR 97213.

A catalogue record for this title is available
from the British Library.

ISBN 978–1–84682–603–0 hbk
ISBN 978–1–84682–604–7 pbk

This book is published with the active support of
Dublin City Council/Comhairle Chathair Átha Cliath.

Dublin City
Baile Átha Cliath

Printed in England
by TJ International, Padstow, Cornwall.

Contents

LIST OF ABBREVIATIONS 7

LIST OF CONTRIBUTORS 11

EDITOR'S PREFACE 13

The (legendary) rise of Dál Cais
BART JASKI 15

Hunting for the genetic legacy of Brian Boru in Irish historical sources
CATHERINE SWIFT 62

The kings of Dublin and Leinster before the battle of Clontarf
EDEL BHREATHNACH 81

Brian and the Uí Néill kingship of Tara
EOIN O'FLYNN 92

Brian Boru, the Book of Armagh and the Irish church in the tenth and eleventh centuries
DENIS CASEY 103

Clontarf 1014: military significance, external dimension and outcome
COLMÁN ETCHINGHAM 122

Brian Bóraime, the Insular Viking world, and the battle of Clontarf
PATRICK WADDEN 144

Glorious by association: the obituary of Brian Boru
MÁIRE NÍ MHAONAIGH 170

The battle of Clontarf: the archaeological evidence
ANDREW HALPIN 188

Dál Cais after Clontarf
PAUL MacCOTTER 210

After Brian Bóraime: the high-kingship and the kings of Connacht
MARIE THERESE FLANAGAN 218

Brian Bóraime's right to rule: an unfinished dialogue
LENORE FISCHER 260

The battle of Clontarf in later Irish tradition
MEIDHBHÍN NÍ ÚRDAIL 280

Writing history in the digital age: the battle of Clontarf goes online
ROMAN BLEIER, SPARKY BOOKER, EOIN O'FLYNN, CHERIE N. PETERS, CHRISTINA WADE, CAOIMHE WHELAN 307

BIBLIOGRAPHY 325

Abbreviations

AC	*Annála Connacht: the annals of Connacht (AD1224–1544)*, ed. A.M. Freeman (DIAS, Dublin, 1944)
AClon	*The annals of Clonmacnoise, being the annals of Ireland from the earliest period to AD1408 translated into English AD1627 by Conell Mageoghagan*, ed. D. Murphy (Dublin, 1896)
ACott	'The annals in Cotton MS Titus A. XXV', ed. A. Martin Freeman, *Revue Celtique*, 41 (1924), 301–30; 42 (1925), 283–305; 43 (1926), 358–84; 44 (1927), 336–61
AFM	*Annála ríoghachta Éireann: annals of the kingdom of Ireland by the Four Masters, from the earliest period to the year 1616*, ed. J. O'Donovan, 7 vols (Dublin, 1851)
AI	*The annals of Inisfallen (MS Rawlinson B. 503)*, ed. S. Mac Airt (DIAS, Dublin, 1951)
ALC	*The annals of Loch Cé: a chronicle of Irish affairs from AD1014 to AD1590*, ed. W.M. Hennessy, 2 vols (RS, London, 1871; repr. IMC, Dublin, 1939)
AMisc	*Miscellaneous Irish annals, AD1114–1437*, ed. S. Ó hInnse (DIAS, Dublin, 1947)
AR	'The annals of Roscrea', ed. Dermot Gleeson and Seán Mac Airt, *PRIA*, 59, C (1957–9), 137–80
AT	'Annals of Tigernach', ed. Whitley Stokes in *Revue Celtique*, 16 (1895) 374–419; 17 (1896) 6–33, 119–263, 337–420; 18 (1897) 9–59, 150–97, 267–303; reprinted in two vols (Felinfach, 1993).
AU	*Annala Uladh ('Annals of Ulster'), otherwise Annala Senait ('Annals of Senat'): a chronicle of Irish Affairs AD431 to AD1540*, ed. W.M. Henessey and B. MacCarthy, 4 vols (Dublin, 1887–1901); *The annals of Ulster (to AD1131)*, ed. S. Mac Airt and G. Mac Niocaill (Dublin, 1983)
BBCS	*Bulletin of the Board of Celtic Studies*
BL	British Library [formerly British Museum], London
Bodl.	Bodleian Library, Oxford
Byrne, *Irish kings*	F.J. Byrne, *Irish kings and high-kings* (London, 1973)
CCT	*Cath Cluana Tarbh. 'The Battle of Clontarf'*, ed. and trans. Meidhbhín Ní Úrdail (ITS, London, 2011)
CGG	*Cogadh Gáedhel re Gallaibh*, ed. and trans. James Henthorn Todd, RS (London, 1867)
CGH	*Corpus genealogiarum Hiberniae*, i, ed. M.A. O'Brien (Dublin, 1962)

CGSH	*Corpus genealogiarum sanctorum Hiberniae*, ed. Pádraig Ó Riain (Dublin, 1985)
CIH	*Corpus iuris hibernici*, ed. D.A. Binchy, 6 vols (Dublin, 1978)
Clarke et al. (eds), *Ireland and Scandinavia*	H.B. Clarke, Máire Ní Mhaonaigh and Raghnall Ó Floinn (eds), *Ireland and Scandinavia in the early Viking Age* (Dublin, 1998)
CMCS	*Cambridge Medieval Celtic Studies* (from Number 26 onwards *Cambrian Medieval Celtic Studies*)
CS	*Chronicum Scotorum*, ed. W.M. Hennessy (RS, London, 1866)
DIAS	Dublin Institute for Advanced Studies
DIB	*Dictionary of Irish biography*, ed. J. McGuire and J. Quinn, 9 vols (Cambridge, 2009)
DIL	*Dictionary of the Irish language and Contributions to a dictionary of the Irish language* (Dublin, 1913–76; compact ed. 1983); see also, *eDIL*
Duffy, *Brian Boru*	Seán Duffy, *Brian Boru and the battle of Clontarf* (Dublin, 2013)
eDIL	*Electronic dictionary of the Irish language*, based on *DIL*, at http://edil.qub.ac.uk/
EHR	*English Historical Review* (1886–)
FAI	*Fragmentary Annals of Ireland*, ed. Joan N. Radner (Dublin, 1978)
FFÉ	*Foras feasa ar Éirinn le Seathrún Céitinn, D.D. The History of Ireland by Geoffrey Keating, D.D.*, ed. and trans. David Comyn, Patrick S. Dinneen (4 vols, ITS, London, 1902–14)
Hogan, *Onomasticon*	Edmond Hogan (ed.), *Onomasticon Goedelicum: locorum et tribuum Hiberniae et Scotiae. An index, with identifications, to the Gaelic names of places and tribes* (Dublin, 1910)
IER	*Irish Ecclesiastical Record*
IHS	*Irish Historical Studies*
IMC	*Coimisiún Láimhscríbhinní na hÉireann* (The Irish Manuscripts Commission)
Ir. mon. deeds, 1200–1600	*Irish monastic and episcopal deeds, AD1200–1600* [...], ed. N.B. White (IMC, Dublin, 1936)
ITS	Irish Texts Society (vol. 1–, London, 1899–)
Jaski, *Early Irish kingship*	Bart Jaski, *Early Irish kingship and succession* (Dublin, 2000)
JCHAS	*Journal of the Cork Historical and Archaeological Society* (1892–)
JGAHS	*Journal of the Galway Archaeological and Historical Society* (1900–)
JKAHS	*Journal of the Kerry Archaeological and Historical Society* (1968–)

JLAHS	*Journal of the County Louth Archaeological and Historical Society* (1904–)
JRSAI	*Journal of the Royal Society of Antiquaries of Ireland*
LGÉ	*Lebor gabála Érenn: The Book of the taking of Ireland*, ed. R.A.S. Macalister, ITS 34, 35, 39, 41, 44, 5 vols (Dublin, 1938–56)
LGP	*Leabhar Gearr na Pailíse*
LL	*The Book of Leinster*, ed. R.I. Best, O. Bergin, M.A. O'Brien and A. O'Sullivan, 6 vols (Dublin, 1954–83)
LM	*An Leabhar Muimneach maraon le suim aguisíní*, ed. Tadhg Ó Donnchadha (IMC, Dublin, 1940)
LMG	*Leabhar Mór na nGenealach: The Great Book of Irish genealogies compiled (1645–66) by Dubhaltach Mac Fhirbhisigh*, ed. Nollaig Ó Muraíle, 5 vols (Dublin, 2003–4)
LU	*Lebor na hUidre / Book of the Dun Cow*, ed. R.I. Best and O. Bergin (Dublin, 1929)
MacL	Edward MacLysaght, *Irish families: their names, arms and origins* (Dublin, 1957; third revised edn, 1972)
MD	*The Metrical Dindshenchas*, ed. E. Gwynn, Todd Lecture Series 8–12 (Dublin, 1903–35)
MMIS	Mediaeval and Modern Irish Series (vol. 1–, Dublin, 1931–)
NAI	National Archives of Ireland [formerly PROI], Dublin
NHI, i	*A new history of Ireland*, i: *prehistoric and early Ireland*, ed. D. Ó Cróinín (Oxford, 1987; repr. with bibliographical supp., 1993)
NHI, ii	*A new history of Ireland*, ii: *medieval Ireland, 1169–1534*, ed. A. Cosgrove (Oxford, 2005)
NHI, ix	*A new history of Ireland*, ix: *maps, genealogies, lists. A companion to Irish history, part II*, ed. T.W. Moody, F.X. Martin and F.J. Byrne (Oxford, 1984)
Ní Mhaonaigh, *Brian Boru*	Máire Ní Mhaonaigh, *Brian Boru: Ireland's greatest king?* (Stroud, 2007)
NLI	National Library of Ireland
NMAJ	*North Munster Antiquarian Journal* (1936–)
Ó Corráin, *Normans*	Donncha[dh] Ó Corráin, *Ireland before the Normans* (Dublin, 1972)
ODNB	*Oxford dictionary of national biography: from the earliest times to the year 2000*, ed. H.C.G. Matthew and B.H. Harrison, 61 vols (Oxford, 2004)
Orpen, *Normans*	G.H. Orpen, *Ireland under the Normans*, 4 vols (Oxford, 1911–20; new ed., 4 vols in 1, Dublin, 2005)
Peritia	*Peritia: Journal of the Medieval Academy of Ireland* (1982–)

PRIA	*Proceedings of the Royal Irish Academy*
RC	*Revue Celtique*
RIA	Royal Irish Academy
RS	*The chronicles and memorials of Great Britain and Ireland during the Middle Ages, published under the direction of the Master of the Rolls* ('Rolls Series'), 99 vols (London, 1858–96)
RSAI	Royal Society of Antiquaries of Ireland
SHR	*Scottish Historical Review* (1903–28; 1947–)
TBC 1	Cecile O'Rahilly, *Táin Bó Cúailnge: Recension I* (Dublin, 1976)
TBC LL	Cecile O'Rahilly, *Táin Bó Cúalnge: from the Book of Leinster* (Dublin, 1967)
TBC St	Cecile O'Rahilly, *The Stowe version of Táin Bó Cuailnge* (Dublin, 1961)
TCD	Trinity College Dublin
TRHS	*Transactions of the Royal Historical Society* (1872–)
UCD	University College Dublin
UJA	*Ulster Journal of Archaeology* (1853–)
WHR	*Welsh History Review; Cylchgrawn Hanes Cymru* (1960–)
ZCP	*Zeitschrift für celtische Philologie* (1896–)

Contributors

EDEL BHREATHNACH is chief executive officer of the Discovery Programme, Dublin.

ROMAN BLEIER is DiXiT/Marie-Curie research fellow at the Centre for Information Modelling, Austrian Centre for Digital Humanities, University of Graz.

SPARKY BOOKER lectures in medieval history at Queen's University, Belfast.

DENIS CASEY holds a PhD from the University of Cambridge and is based at the Centre for Teaching and Learning, Maynooth University.

COLMÁN ETCHINGHAM lectures in medieval history at Maynooth University.

LENORE FISCHER is an independent scholar and holds an MA in medieval history from the University of Limerick.

MARIE THERESE FLANAGAN is professor emerita of medieval history at Queen's University, Belfast.

ANDREW HALPIN is assistant keeper of antiquities at the National Museum of Ireland.

BART JASKI is keeper of manuscripts and curator of printed books (rariora) at Utrecht University Library.

PAUL MacCOTTER holds a PhD in medieval history from University College Cork.

MÁIRE NÍ MHAONAIGH is professor of Celtic and medieval studies at the University of Cambridge.

MEIDHBHÍN NÍ ÚRDAIL is associate professor, School of Irish, Celtic Studies and Folklore, University College Dublin.

EOIN O'FLYNN holds a PhD in medieval history from Trinity College Dublin.

CHERIE N. PETERS holds a PhD in medieval history from Trinity College Dublin.

CATHERINE SWIFT lectures in Irish Studies at Mary Immaculate College, Limerick.

PATRICK WADDEN is assistant professor of history at Belmont Abbey College, North Carolina.

CHRISTINA WADE is a postgraduate research student at Trinity College Dublin.

CAOIMHE WHELAN is an Irish Research Council postdoctoral fellow at Trinity College Dublin.

Editor's preface

There are few more emblematic dates in Irish history than that of the battle of Clontarf, fought on Good Friday, 1014, when the high-king Brian Boru lost his life in the hour of victory against his Scandinavian and Irish foes. To mark the 1000th anniversary of Clontarf and of Brian's death, a major conference of academic experts was held on 11–12 April 2014 in the Edmund Burke Theatre, Trinity College Dublin, bringing together leading experts in the field from universities throughout Ireland (including Queen's Belfast, Trinity College Dublin, University College Dublin, University College Cork, Maynooth University and the University of Limerick), Great Britain (including the Universities of Cambridge, St Andrews and Liverpool), and further afield, as well as specialists from the National Museum of Ireland and elsewhere. This volume gathers together the texts of most papers delivered on the occasion and a number of others besides. The editor is very grateful to the authors for contributing so readily to a volume which, it is hoped, will be a fitting record of the proceedings of the Battle of Clontarf Conference and a lasting legacy of the commemorations to mark the millennium of the battle of Clontarf.

The objectives of the Battle of Clontarf Conference were, by gathering together for the first time the leading authorities on the subject, to bring us closer to establishing what really happened at Clontarf,[1] to reevaluate the origins of Brian Boru,[2] and his career,[3] his dynastic legacy,[4] and his later literary image,[5] in the light of the latest research. It was also hoped to bring into the realm of public discourse recent investigations of the subject of the high-kingship of Ireland,[6] and of the role of the Vikings in medieval Ireland,[7] dispelling (or perhaps reconfirming) myths, shedding new light, and – by no means least – raising public awareness by presenting this scholarship in a forum that was entirely open to the public and admission-free.

Trinity College Dublin was an appropriate venue for the conference, having a unique connection to Brian, being the home of the so-called Brian Boru's Harp whose image is the national symbol of Ireland. Although the harp has no known link to Brian and is considerably later in date, Trinity College does nevertheless house the only artefact surviving today which we can definitively state the high-king saw and perhaps touched – the world-famous Book of Armagh with its inscription generally thought to mark his visit to the primatial city in 1005,[8] in which he is described as *Imperator Scotorum* ('Emperor of the Gaels'). Trinity College also houses the largest collection of medieval

1 See, in particular, Bhreathnach, Etchingham, Halpin, and Wadden, below. 2 See Jaski's important study of his dynasty's rise to power, below. 3 See Bhreathnach, Casey, Etchingham, and O'Flynn, below. 4 See Swift and MacCotter, below. 5 See, in particular, Fischer and Ní Úrdail, below. 6 See the major study by Flanagan, below. 7 A subject at the core of Etchingham's analysis, below. 8 But see Casey, below.

manuscript sources for the battle of Clontarf including the Book of Leinster version of the famous *Cogadh Gáedhel re Gallaibh* ('The War of the Irish with the Foreigners') which, more than anything else, created the later mythical image of Brian Boru and which was analysed in depth at the conference.[9]

These and other priceless artefacts formed the centrepieces of a free exhibition in the Long Room of Trinity's Old Library, opened to coincide with the conference (https://www.tcd.ie/library/exhibitions/boru/). And, to complement the conference, a team of postgraduate research students in Trinity also developed a Battle of Clontarf website,[10] which can be accessed at https://dh.tcd.ie/clontarf/. During the course of the conference, both the *Irish Times* and the *Irish Independent* ran special supplements, while the March–April issue of the best-selling *History Ireland* magazine was also devoted entirely to the subject of Brian Boru and Clontarf (guest editor, Seán Duffy).

The conference was also the 16th in a sequence of annual symposia organized by the Friends of Medieval Dublin, the proceedings of which appear annually in this series, published by Four Courts Press. The Friends of Medieval Dublin remain most grateful to the latter for their collaboration with them on this project and their commitment to the series and to Irish academic publishing in general. With regard to the current volume, the editor would like to thank Claire Fitzgerald and Martin Fanning for the attention to detail that has characterized their work on the papers below.

The 'Friends' is an entirely not-for-profit organization which exists primarily to foster interest in Dublin's medieval heritage. We would not be able to continue without the support, through attendance at our events, of the people of Dublin, but, equally, since most of our activities cost money to mount, we could not do it without the backing in particular of Dublin City Council. The Battle of Clontarf Conference was a major event which cost a considerable amount to stage and simply would not have happened without the financial support provided by the City Heritage Officer, Charles Duggan. The editor in particular is extremely grateful to him for encouraging this project from the start and for the subvention towards the cost of making this volume affordable to the people of Dublin. Likewise, the input and encouragement of the City Archaeologist, Dr Ruth Johnson, is greatly appreciated.

Finally, few successful conferences are organized by one person and the Battle of Clontarf Conference was no exception. I am therefore very thankful to the team of friends (upper- and lower-case) who put the proverbial gallons of blood, sweat and tears into making this particular conference a success, and I know they will not baulk at me singling out in particular the indefatigable efforts of the conference secretary Dr Cherie Peters.

SEÁN DUFFY
Chairman, Friends of Medieval Dublin

9 See, in particular, Etchingham, Fischer, Ní Mhaonaigh, and Ní Úrdail, below. **10** See Bleier et al., below.

The (legendary) rise of Dál Cais

BART JASKI

1. INTRODUCTION

In 997, Brian mac Cennétig (Brian Bóraime), king of Munster, and Máel Sechnaill mac Domnaill, king of Tara, made peace at Port dá Chaineóc, near Clonfert on the Shannon. Their treaty concluded fifteen years of raiding and campaigning on a scale rarely witnessed in Ireland before that time, but all too often afterwards. The two kings agreed to divide Ireland in two: the southern half, called Leth Moga, was given to Brian, and the northern half, Leth Cuinn, to Máel Sechnaill. The latter gave the hostages of Leinster and the Viking settlements there, including Dublin, to Brian, who in turn rounded up the hostages of Connacht and handed them over to his former adversary.[1] The political division of the island was not to last. After the two kings had combined forces and defeated the kings of Leinster and Dublin in 999, Brian consolidated his position, and in 1002 Máel Sechnaill had to submit himself to his power. Brian would spend the next decade establishing his supremacy over the whole of Ireland. His ambitions would finally end at the bloody battlefield of Clontarf. On Good Friday 1014, Dál Cais, augmented by the forces of the rest of Munster and southern Connacht, would overcome the forces of Leinster, Dublin and their overseas allies. Yet they lost their aged king and his oldest son and heir-apparent, Murchad.

So much is well known from the historical sources and numerous textbooks written on Brian and the legendary battle of Clontarf. The propaganda tract *Cogadh Gáedhel re Gallaibh*, written during or even before the reign of Brian's great-grandson Muirchertach Ua Briain (d. 1119),[2] saw Brian's heroic death as the last and ultimate sacrifice of Dál Cais in their ceaseless struggle to rid Ireland of the tyranny of the heathen 'Foreigners'. This served to legitimize their claim to the kingship of Munster and Ireland. Less well known are the earlier endeavours of Brian himself to explain the rise of his dynasty and their claim to the kingship of Munster and domination of Leth Moga. After all, it was only during his father's lifetime that Dál Cais had started to get noted as a force in Thomond, and before that time they rarely appear in the sources, and even then under a different name, that of the Northern Déisi.

1 *AI* 997.2; Bart Jaski, 'The Vikings and the kingship of Tara', *Peritia*, 9 (1995), 310–51, at 348. 2 Máire Ní Mhaonaigh, 'The date of *Cogad Gáedel re Gallaib*', *Peritia*, 9 (1995), 354–77; see further Denis Casey, 'A reconsideration of the authorship and transmission of *Cogadh Gáedhel re Gallaibh*', *PRIA*, 113C (2013), 139–61.

Brian's main vehicle to explain the sudden rise of Dál Cais was a collection of miscellaneous texts called the Psalter of Cashel, in particular the section concerned with the secular genealogical records of Ireland. As far as its contents can be reconstructed at present, these records were first drafted in the time of Cathal mac Finguine around 740, updated by Cormac mac Cuilennáin *c.*900, and again by Brian mac Cennétig at about 1000. All three had been powerful kings of Munster who had challenged the supremacy of the kings of Tara.[3] Hence Brian tapped into an existing literary tradition, but he – or rather

3 Bart Jaski, 'The genealogical section of the Psalter of Cashel', *Peritia*, 17–18 (2003–4), 295–337, at 333. For the involvement of Brian in the Psalter of Cashel, see also Pádraig Ó

his literary agent(s) – left clear marks which bore an unmistakable Dál Cais signature. This was of course mainly the case in the genealogies of the Eóganacht, who had ruled Munster as kings of Cashel for centuries, and those of Dál Cais themselves. The current study is devoted to the question of how Dál Cais justified their claims to rule Munster before *Cogadh Gáedhel re Gallaibh*, and whether there are other (either contemporary or later) sources that are related to the material in the Psalter of Cashel under discussion. In order to do so, we first have to take a look at what the historical sources say about the rise of Dál Cais.

2. IN DÉIS TÚAISCIRT UNTIL *c*.700

'The sudden rise of the Dál Cais to the summit of power in Munster, and shortly thereafter to the overkingship in Ireland, was plainly an event of revolutionary import in Irish history'. In this way John Kelleher begins his essay 'The rise of the Dál Cais', published in *North Munster studies* in 1967.[4] Kelleher was the first to give a detailed exposition of the history of Dál Cais before the advent of Brian Bóraime. He assembled a number of references in the sources, but in the eyes of his contemporaries spoiled his case by suggesting that Dál Cais had been able to rise to such prominence because they were set up as a buffer state by the kings of Mide to check the danger posed by the kings of Cashel.[5] A couple of years later Donnchadh Ó Corráin offered a more balanced description of the matter.[6] In my article 'The Vikings and the kingship of Tara', I compared the rise of Dál Cais at the mouth of the Shannon with that of Fergal ua Ruairc in Bréifne at the sources of the Shannon in the middle of the tenth century, and set this in the context of the crisis that had befallen the Uí Néill of the north and midlands at the time, and the decline of the Eóganachta of Munster.[7] A new sythesis was finally offered by Seán Duffy in his *Brian Boru and the battle of Clontarf*, published to commemorate the millennial anniversary of that event in 2014.[8]

In order to understand the unique position in which Dál Cais would find themselves, it is necessary to go back to the year 629. The annals report a battle at Carn Feradaig, where Failbe Flann, king of Cashel, repulsed the king of

Riain, 'The Psalter of Cashel: a provisional list of contents', *Éigse*, 23 (1989), 107–30, at 127–8. On Cormac, see further Máire Ní Mhaonaigh, 'Cormac mac Cuilennáin: king, bishop and sage', *ZCP*, 58 (2011), 109–28. 4 J.V. Kelleher, 'The rise of the Dál Cais' in Etienne Rynne (ed.), *North Munster studies: essays in commemoration of Monsignor Michael Moloney* (Limerick, 1967), pp 230–41. 5 See the review of Pádraig de Brún in *Studia Hibernica*, 9 (1969), 169–71, at 170; Kathleen Hughes, in her review in *The Antiquaries Journal*, 48:1 (1968), 123–4, regrets that the article is not 'stiff with footnotes'. 6 Ó Corráin, *Normans*, pp 7–9, 114–17; see also Byrne, *Irish kings*, pp 180–1, 214, 239 (both without footnotes). 7 Jaski, 'The Vikings', 339–43. 8 Duffy, *Brian Boru*, pp 61–91.

Connacht, Guaire Aidne, of Uí Fhiachrach Aidne. The latter's ally, Conall mac Máeldub, king of Uí Maine, was killed.[9] The site of the clash between the rulers of Munster and those of southern Connacht is significant. Carn Feradaig is situated a couple of miles to the southwest of Limerick, and marked the border between two branches of the Déisi Becc ('Déisi Minor' or 'Little Déisi'). In Déis Déiscirt were situated to the south of it, around what is now Small County. Their lands extended until the Ballyhoura Hills (including Cenn Abrat or Febrat) and included Áth na nDéise (Athneasy), Brug na nDéise (Bruff) and Ard Pátraic. The important monastery of Emly lay in the lands of the Eóganacht Airthir Cliach to their east. The Uí Fhidgeinte – held to be related to the Eóganacht – ruled the country to their west. The lands to the north of Carn Feradaig became the territory of In Déis Túaiscirt, the older name of Dál Cais. Francis John Byrne has suggested that the battle of Carn Feradaig marked the beginning of the expansion of In Déis Túaiscirt into east Clare.[10]

The first time the sources mention a king of the Northern Déisi is in the defective list of guarantors of the *Cáin Fhuithirbe*, which was promulgated over Munster around 680. The lemma reads: 'To a tryst with Donennach i.e. king of Uí Fhidgeinte, and to the king of In Déis Túaiscirt'.[11] Unfortunately, the name of this king is not given, but in 697 the guarantor list of *Cáin Adomnáin*, Adomnán of Iona's *Lex Innocentium* meant to protect women, children and clerics from the violence of warfare, Andelait is named among the eight Munster kings who signed the law.[12] Andelait was one of the three sons of Dímma, who is called *Superbus* in the genealogies. Dímma was the grandson of Óengus, the eponymous ancestor of the Uí Óengussa, the leading dynasty of the Northern Déisi at this point. The genealogies and regnal lists state that Dímma had been married to Dunlaith, a daughter of Doithnennach, who may have been a dynast of the Cíarraige.[13] Dímma was succeeded by three of his sons, one after the other: Fer Domnach, Andelait and Dub Dúin.

3. RELATIONSHIP WITH THE KINGS OF CASHEL

The above information may imply that the Northern Déisi had been successful in establishing themselves as overkings of Thomond, for the laws were not

9 *AU* 627.2; *AI* 629.1. I give here and elsewhere the editorial years given in the editions of the annals, which may not always be the true year. According to Daniel Mc Carthy, the battle took place in 629; see the schedule at http://www.irish-annals.cs.tcd.ie/ (retrieved 16 June 2016). 10 Byrne, *Irish kings*, p. 239. 11 Liam Breatnach, 'The ecclesiastical element in the Old-Irish legal tract *Cáin Fhuithirbe*', *Peritia*, 5 (1986), 36–52, at 42 §6. 12 Máirín Ní Dhonnchadha, 'The guarantor list of *Cáin Adomnáin*', *Peritia*, 1 (1982), 178–215, at 180 §50, 198. 13 *LM*, p. 318; cf. *CGH*, p. 240 (153a24–28); *CGH*, pp 307–8 (160b20–24). Dunlaith is six generations removed from Imchath, just as Máel Tuile, the father of

sanctioned by all the Munster or Irish kings, only by the overkings. The Old-Irish Munster law-tract *Críth gablach* specifically names *Cáin Adomnáin* as an example of a law of which it is proper that a king binds them on the *túatha* under his rule – meaning his own and those he held in clientship.[14] The kings of Corco Baiscinn and Corco Mruad, later confined to the south-western and north-western parts of Thomond, are not named in either *Cáin Fhuithirbe* or *Cáin Adomnáin*. It thus appears that they had become clients of an overking in the region, perhaps of the Northern Déisi.

At this stage the Northern Déisi were nominally still subject to the king of Munster, but the latter's grip on them was far from secure. In 713, there was another battle at Carn Feradaig, but this time the king of Cashel, in the person of Cormac mac Ailella, was the aggressor. It says something for the strength of the Northern Déisi that they could not only succesfully resist the king of Cashel, but kill him in battle as well – a rare feat during the preceding couple of centuries.[15] The political impact can be gauged from the tract *Frithfolaid rig Caisil fri túatha Muman*, which has been dated to the middle of the eighth century. It deals with the obligations of the king of Cashel towards the peoples of Munster in exchange for their subservience.[16] Of the peoples of Thomond only the Corco Mruad are mentioned.[17] The Northern Déisi are named but once in a curious passage:

> *Tri hocthigeirn rig Muman: na Deissi 7 In Deiss Tuaiscirt 7 Corco Laigde*
>
> (Three *ócthigeirn* of the king of Munster: the Déisi, In Déis Túaiscirt and Corco Loígde).[18]

In the normal sense *ócthigern(a)* means 'young lord' or 'noble of an inferior grade', but this does not seem to fit here. The compound óc can also mean

Rechtabra, who is another guarantor of *Cáin Fhuithirbe*. According to *LM*, p. 317, Dímma was killed by a Máel Tolae son of Máel Tuile. **14** *CIH*, ii, p. 569.10–17; Daniel Binchy (ed.), *Críth gablach*, MMIS 11 (Dublin, 1941), ll. 514–24; Jaski, *Early Irish kingship*, pp 98–9. **15** *AU* 713.6; *AI* 713.2 (where Cormac is called 'son of Máenach', but he was his grandson); *AFM* 710=713; *CGH*, p. 360 (320a36); Myles Dillon (ed.), 'The story of the finding of Cashel', *Ériu*, 16 (1952), 61–73, at 67 l. 120. **16** For discussion of this tract, of which there are two recensions, see Byrne, *Irish kings*, pp 196–9; Jaski, *Early Irish kingship*, p 205; Thomas Charles-Edwards, *Early Christian Ireland* (Cambridge, 2000), pp 534–48, where at p. 534 it is dated. **17** J.G. O'Keeffe (ed.), 'Dál Caladbuig and reciprocal services between the kings of Cashel and various Munster states' in John Fraser, Paul Grosjean and J.G. O'Keeffe (eds), *Irish texts, fasciculus I* (London, 1931), pp 19–21, at p. 21 §13. **18** O'Keeffe, 'Dál Caladbuig', p. 21 §14 (the version in Dublin, Trinity College, MS 1298 (*olim* H.2.7), p. 188a19–21, reads: *Tri hoctigern rig Muman: na Dessi 7 Deis Tuaiscirt 7 Corco Laigde*). The king of Thomond is named in the second recension of the middle of the tenth century, where he receives considerable but rather fanciful privileges (see Donnchadh Ó Corráin in his review of Byrne, *Irish kings*, in *Celtica*, 13 (1980), 150–68, at 162–3), see the Book of Lecan (henceforth Lec), fol. 192va45–51 (compare O'Keeffe, 'Dál Caladbuig', p. 21

'young man' and hence 'warrior', so the sense may be 'warrior lords' here, especially since three population groups are thus named. The same applies to the title *toísech ócthigern Érenn*, 'leader of the *ócthigeirn* of Ireland' given to Conchobar (d. 772?) of Cenél nEógain, the brother of the kings of Tara Áed Allán (d. 743) and Niall Frossach (d. 778).[19] If this translation is accepted, we may infer that the three population groups enjoyed a special status as the primary warriors of the king of Munster.[20]

It is probably no coincidence that none of these three population groups belongs to the Eóganachta. According to the tract, the Déisi and Corco Loígde receive, every seventh year, the highest stipend from the king of Cashel, fifty and forty *cumala* respectively. The Déisi had established the kingship of Cashel first and did not have a tax-collector over them. The Corco Loígde had alternated in the kingship of Cashel until the time of their king Lugaid Mac Con; they are free, without taxation, for this reason.[21] It seems that the king of Cashel had to buy off his nominal suzerainty over these peoples and explain their relative free position by a past connection with Cashel. This also applied to other peoples, but for our discussion it is important to note that naming the Déisi and Corco Loígde among the *ócthigeirn* of the king of Munster points to a similar ploy. We may hence tentatively conclude that the Northern Déisi were in an equal position. And, as we shall see, Dál Cais were to exploit such a construction for their own benefit.

4. SETTLEMENT IN THOMOND

The Northern Déisi were not the only Munster peoples that emigrated to Thomond in the seventh century or before. The most northern branch of the Eóganachta were the Eóganacht Ninussa or Eóganacht Árann who lived on the Aran Islands and the adjacent coastal area of the Burren.[22] The kindred of Fergus Scandal (d. 584) of Eóganacht Airthir Cliach held lands in Corco Mruad.[23] Probably in the decades around 700 the Uí Chonairge, a branch of the Alltraige, who lived to the north of the Cíarraige at the mouth of the Shannon, crossed over to the territory of the Corco Baiscinn. Another branch lived among the Corco Mruad.[24] And in 705 the annals note: 'The battle of

§17; Byrne, *Irish kings*, p. 197). **19** Kuno Meyer (ed.), 'The Laud genealogies and tribal histories', *ZCP*, 8 (1911), 291–338, at 295.27. Note that Conchobar lived in the same period as to which the *Frithfolaid*-tract is dated. See also *AT*, 1063, where Gilla Erraith Ua Maíl Mithig is called *ardóicthigern na nGáedhel*: 'high-*ócthigern* of the Gaels'. **20** *CGG*, p. 75 §51, states that prior to the battle of Sulchóit in 964 warriors of Dál Cais in the armies of the Uí Néill were recalled to participate in the battle. **21** O'Keeffe, 'Dál Caladbuig', pp 20 §10, 21 §13. This alternation is also mentioned in the Old-Irish tract *Scéla Moshauluim* and other sources, see Jaski, *Early Irish kingship*, p. 232, for references. **22** F.J. Byrne, 'The Eóganacht Ninussa', *Éigse*, 9 (1958–61), 18–29. Their genealogies have not been preserved. **23** O'Keeffe, 'Dal Caladbuig', 19 §7. **24** Donnchadh Ó Corráin, 'Alltraighe', *Journal of the*

Corco Mruad, in which Célechair son of Comán fell'. This individual belonged to the Uí Chormaic, who gave their name to the territory to the southwest of modern day Ennis.[25] His lineage belonged to the Uí Fhidgeinte on the other side of the Shannon estuary, and who had colonized this part of Thomond in earlier times. It is not clear if the Northern Déisi were involved in this battle, but considering later events this may well have been the case.

In 741, another battle was fought at Carn Feradaig, but nothing more is known, not even who fought against whom, except that the further unknown Torcán 'Tini Reid' fell therein. Whatever went on, the power of the Northern Déisi did not suffer unduly, for in 744 the annals note: 'Destruction of Corco Mruad by the Déis'. We can take this to mean that the Northern Déisi were well under way to controlling the area which covers the whole of County Clare. This victory was probably the cumulation of decades of struggle. The Northern Déisi were on the rise, and no wonder that the death of their king, Torpaid, is noted in the annals in 765.[26]

From this point onwards, however, the annals are silent until 934. But if we may regard the later genealogical sources and regnal lists about this period as trustworthy,[27] it appears that the Northern Déisi had been ruled by the Uí Óengussa from about the early or middle of the seventh century onwards. The first king of their ranks had been Óengus's grandson Dímma, mentioned above. His son and successor, Fer Domnach, is credited with giving Inis Sibtonn (King's Island in Limerick) to Mainchín and Crónán (see §16 below). Fer Domnach was succeeded by two of his brothers, the aforementioned Andelait (fl. 697) and Dub Dúin. Andelait's son Cernach (from whom the Uí Chernaig are named) was next in line, followed by Cernach's son Torpaid (d. 765). No descendant of Torpaid is recorded, and the kingship was taken by two brothers in succession, Domnall and Finn. They were grandsons of Echthigern (from whom the Uí Echthigirn are named), grandson of Fer Domnach. Finn was succeeded by Domnall's son Cormac, who probably lived in the decades around 900.

The Uí Chernaig had their lands around and north of Limerick, at that time the centre of power of the Northern Déisi. To the north of them were the Uí Echthigirn, whose lands extended until Doon Lough, and even further northwards were the Uí Róngaile, named after Róngal, the son of Dímma's cousin Máel Cáich.[28] It seems that these three branches of the Uí Óengussa

Kerry Archaelogical and Historical Society, 2 (1969), 27–37, at 32–3; idem, *Normans*, pp 30 and 70. **25** *AU* 705.2; *CGH*, p. 231 (152a17); Byrne, 'Ninussa', 7; D. Blair Gibson, 'Chiefdoms, confederacies, and statehood in early Ireland' in Bettina Arnold and D. Blair Gibson (eds), *Celtic chiefdom, Celtic state: the evolution of complex social systems in prehistoric Europe* (Cambridge, 1995), pp 116–28, at p. 121, gives a map with the ringfort Cathair Commáin, which is dated to the late eighth or early ninth century, in the middle of Uí Chormaic. **26** *AU* 741.8 (the Torcán in question is not the one mentioned at *CGH*, p. 243 (153b9), who lived much later); *AT* 744, *AFM* 760=765. **27** *LM*, pp 321–3. **28** See the

had established themselves in this area in the seventh and eighth centuries, and spent their time afterwards consolidating their position, relatively undisturbed by the kings of Cashel and the struggles around them. Yet important changes were in the making to upset the political order in Thomond. These new developments centred around the Uí Thairdelbaig, who lived to the east of the Uí Óengussa, in the lands to the west of the Shannon. They start to get noted in the sources around 900.

5. UÍ THAIRDELBAIG IN *BETHU PHÁTRAIC*

In the Irish Life of Patrick, *Bethu Phátraic*, also known as the Tripartite Life of Patrick, the saint goes on a tour around Ireland. He also pays the Limerick area a memorable visit.[29] He enters Munster at Cashel, where he baptizes Óengus son of Nad Fraích, who is the ancestor of the Eóganacht Glendamnach and Eóganacht Airthir Cliach, and the text states that twenty-seven kings of the descendants of Óengus and his brother Ailill, the ancestor of the Eóganacht Chaisil, were in Cashel until Cenn Gécán. This king reigned between 895 and 901, until he was deposed by Cormac mac Cuilennáin. This gives us the date of the first edition of *Bethu Phátraic* which stood at the basis of the extant versions in the manuscripts.[30]

Patrick proceeds via Múscraige Breogain to the lands of the Arada Cliach, situated to the southeast of Limerick. There he meets Ailill son of Cathbad son of Lugaid, said to be of the Eóganacht Airthir Cliach.[31] Ailill's son was eaten by pigs (*mucca*), and Malach the Briton, a member of the Céli Dé of Patrick's own household, does not dare to ask God to bring him back to life. Hence Malach's church in the north-eastern corner of the Southern Déisi will remain small. With the help of the prayers of Ailbe of Emly and bishop Íbar, Patrick resurrects the boy from the collected bones. The boy is probably the Torc ('Boar') mentioned among Ailill's six sons in the genealogies.[32] Patrick

map in Blair Gibson, 'Chiefdoms', p. 123. **29** Kathleen Mulchrone (ed.), *Bethu Phátraic. The Tripartite Life of Patrick. I: texts and sources* (Dublin, 1939), pp 118–24; Whitley Stokes (ed.), *The Tripartite Life of Patrick with other documents relating to that saint*, 2 vols (London, 1887), i, pp 194–208. See also idem (ed.), *Lives of the saints from the Book of Lismore* (Oxford, 1890), pp 13–16. **30** Mulchrone, *Bethu Phátraic*, pp v–vi. The section discussed here is found in both of the main manuscripts, BL, Egerton 93, and Bodl., Rawlinson B 512. K.H. Jackson, 'The date of the Tripartite Life of St Patrick', *ZCP*, 41 (1986), 5–45, dates at 15–16 the language of both manuscript versions to the tenth century. **31** Mulchrone, *Bethu Phátraic*, p. 119, l. 2320. Lugaid is the son of Ailill Flann Becc, and brother of Dáire Cerbba (*CGH*, p. 195 (148a20)), and also father of Conall Corc, the ancestor of the ruling branches of the Eóganachta. Two genealogies of the Uí Chathbath are found at *CGH*, pp 210 (150a18) and 222 (151a23), both running until *c.*700 (by generation count); cf. Margaret E. Dobbs, 'Miscellany from H.2.7 (TCD)', *ZCP*, 21 (1941), 307–18, at 312 §10. Patrick meets this Ailill at Óchtur Cuillend in Uí Chuanach (Mulchrone, *Bethu Phátraic*, p. 119, l. 2319), which reflects the name of the Uí Chathbath Chuille. **32** *CGH*,

subsequently baptizes in the area and proceeds to the hill of Cláire, which we can situate to the south of Emly, in the territory of the Southern Dési. There he curses Rath Choirpri and Rath Bróccáin, because the Cenél Cholmáin (now unknown) opposed him. Going westwards towards the territory of Uí Fhidgeinte, King Lonán son of the son of Erc makes a feast for the saint at Mullach Cae which, according to the text, is to the south of Carn Feradaig. Men of art (*aesa ceirdd*) come to the feast and ask for food. Obliged to honour their request, Patrick sends them on to Lonán, but the king wants the food to be blessed first. Nessán comes to the feast and offers Patrick a cow, which he gives to the buffoons (*druthaib*), who are at once swallowed up by the earth. They were led by Derc mac Scirire of the Northern Déisi. Patrick says that no king or one fit to be a king or a bishop will be from his (glossed as: Lonán's) descendants. Lonán was evidently from the Uí Fhidgeinte.[33] Patrick blesses Nessán and establishes Mungret, to the west of Limerick, as Nessán's church.

The men of Thomond come to meet Patrick in their seafleets at Domnach Mór Maige Áine (Donaghmore),[34] a few miles to the southeast of Limerick, but he baptizes them from the southeast in Tír Glaiss.[35] Then Patrick goes to Finnine, a hill near Domnach Mór from which one can see the country to the north of Limerick, and blesses it. Cáirthenn son of Blat, ancestor (*sen*) of Clann Thairdelbaig, is baptized at Saingel, a place-name meaning 'Different angel' (*sain aingel*), because it was not the angel Victor but a different angel who talked with Patrick there. Cáirthenn's wife only gave birth to misborns. It is there that Eochu Ballderg ('Redspot') was brought forth. Patrick formed him from a clot of gore, and the red spot was left on his body as a sign of this miracle. Patrick does not enter Thomond, but blesses it and prophesizes that after sixty years Senán of Scattery Island will come.

Then he goes to the Southern Déisi, and desires a monastery at Ard Pátraic. He is opposed by Derball mac Áeda (probably of the Southern Déisi), who says that he would believe if Patrick removes Cenn Abrat from the Ballyhoura Hills, so that he can see the lake in the plain to the south in the lands of the Fir Maige Féine (Fermoy). Patrick starts to melt the mountain, which is now called Belach Lectha, 'the Pass of Melting'.[36] Yet Derball announces that it will

p. 210 (150a18–22). **33** Mulchrone, *Bethu Phátraic*, p. 122, l. 2397. In the edition (l. 2379) the name is given as *Lonán macc Maicc Eirgg*, but in the *Notulae* in the Book of Armagh (written in 807) it is given as *Lonán m(acc) m(aicc) Eircc*, see Ludwig Bieler (ed.), *The Patrician texts in the Book of Armagh* (Dublin, 1979), p. 182, l. 49. I take him to belong to the dynasts of Uí Fhidgeinte mentioned at ll. 50–2 (not identified by Bieler), who are also named in the genealogies at *CGH*, pp 231–2 (152a15–30), including Erc son of Brión, son of Fiachu Fidgenid, who according to some genealogies is the son of Dáire Cerbba mentioned in n. 31 above. **34** Mulchrone, *Bethu Phátraic*, p. 123, l. 2407; Stokes, *Tripartite Life*, i, p. 206. They are identified as the Corco Mruad in the Middle-Irish Life of Senán, see Stokes, *Lives of the saints*, pp 54–5. **35** Probably not Tír dá Glass (Terryglass), at the north-eastern shore of Lough Derg, which would have taken Patrick too far from his route. **36** In 978, Brian defeated his rival Máel Muad of Eóganacht Raithlind here (see §8 below);

do Patrick no good after all, and so the saint curses him: there would be neither king nor bishop of his kindred, and every seven years the men of Munster were allowed to peel his people as an onion – in other words, to tax them severely. Patrick also meets Fer Gair son of Ross (of the Déisi Muman),[37] who, however, tarried because of the rain. So Patrick says that their assemblies will always be showery, and his people are cursed.

The whole section is full of hagiographic commonplaces in which opponents of the community of Patrick at the time of writing are cursed, while supporters owe their prosperity to the saint's good graces. It is important to note that *Bethu Phátraic* contains elements of a (mainly) Latin Life, now lost, which was probably written at the end of the eighth century. Headwords of this Life are found in the *Notulae* in the Book of Armagh, written in 807. Hence the scenes with Óengus son of Nad Fraích, Lonán son of the son of Erc, Thomond (probably Domnach Mór Maige Aine), Cláire (Hill), and (the forts of) Coirpre and Bróccán were in their essence already in the lost Latin Life.[38] This would have included the first passages in which the action takes place in the area of the Southern Déisi, including the buffoons who are led by someone of the Northern Déisi. In the eighth century the Southern and Northern Déisi were apparently not in the good books of Patrick's community. By the end of the ninth century we see that the Southern Déisi are still suffering from Patrick's wrath, if we may regard the scene with Derball as being added between the lost Latin Life and the common core of *Bethu Phátraic* of *c.*895. Yet, among the Northern Déisi, Clann (or Uí) Thairdelbaig have emerged as staunch supporters of Patrician supremacy, as the miraculous creation of Eochu Ballderg testifies – similar to the Uí Chathbath who descend from the resurrected boy. Eochu's father Cáirthenn mac Blait was baptized at Saingel (Singland), to the southeast of Limerick, which with a fanciful etymology is connected to Patrick. The genealogies mention a saint Mo Langa Saingil who was a great-great-grandson of Eochu Ballderg.[39] The latter is the younger brother of Óengus, the ancestor of the Uí Óengussa, rulers of the Northern

see also Diarmuid Ó Murchadha, 'Cenn Ebrat, Sliab Cain, Belach Ebrat, Belach Legtha/Lechta', *Éigse*, 29 (1996), 153–71. Derball is unidentified, and as a male name it is only attested in a late poem as the head of Patrick's household, *CGSH*, p. 121 §672.17.

37 Fer Gair son of Ross son of Brecc son of Art Corp, *CGH*, p. 399 (LL 328b54); Séamus Pender (ed.), *Déssi genealogies* (Dublin, 1937), pp 2 §1 and 10 §49. His descendants, the Uí Fhir Gair, were settled in the territories of the Southern Déisi and gave their name to the barony of Uregare, near the parish of Athneasy.

38 Bieler, *Patrician texts*, p. 182 (nrs 48–53). I give the order as they appear in the *Notulae*, which differs from the order in *Bethu Phátraic*. See further Charles-Edwards, *Early Christian Ireland*, pp 11–13. The scenes with the resurrected boy and Senán are in Patrick's *Vita Quarta* of the ninth century, see F.J. Byrne and Pádraig Francis (tr.), 'Two Lives of Patrick: *Vita Secunda* and *Vita Quarta*', *JRSAI*, 124 (1995), 5–117, at 58–9 §§78–9, 106–7. The scene with Óengus is in Tírechán of *c.*690 (Bieler, *Patrician texts*, p. 162 §51.4) and the *Vita Tertia* of the late eighth century (cf. Byrne and Francis, 'Two Lives', 14–15).

39 *LM*, p. 305; the pedigree at *CGSH*, p. 34 §205 is corrupt, cf. *CGH*, p. 239 (153a21); see §17 below.

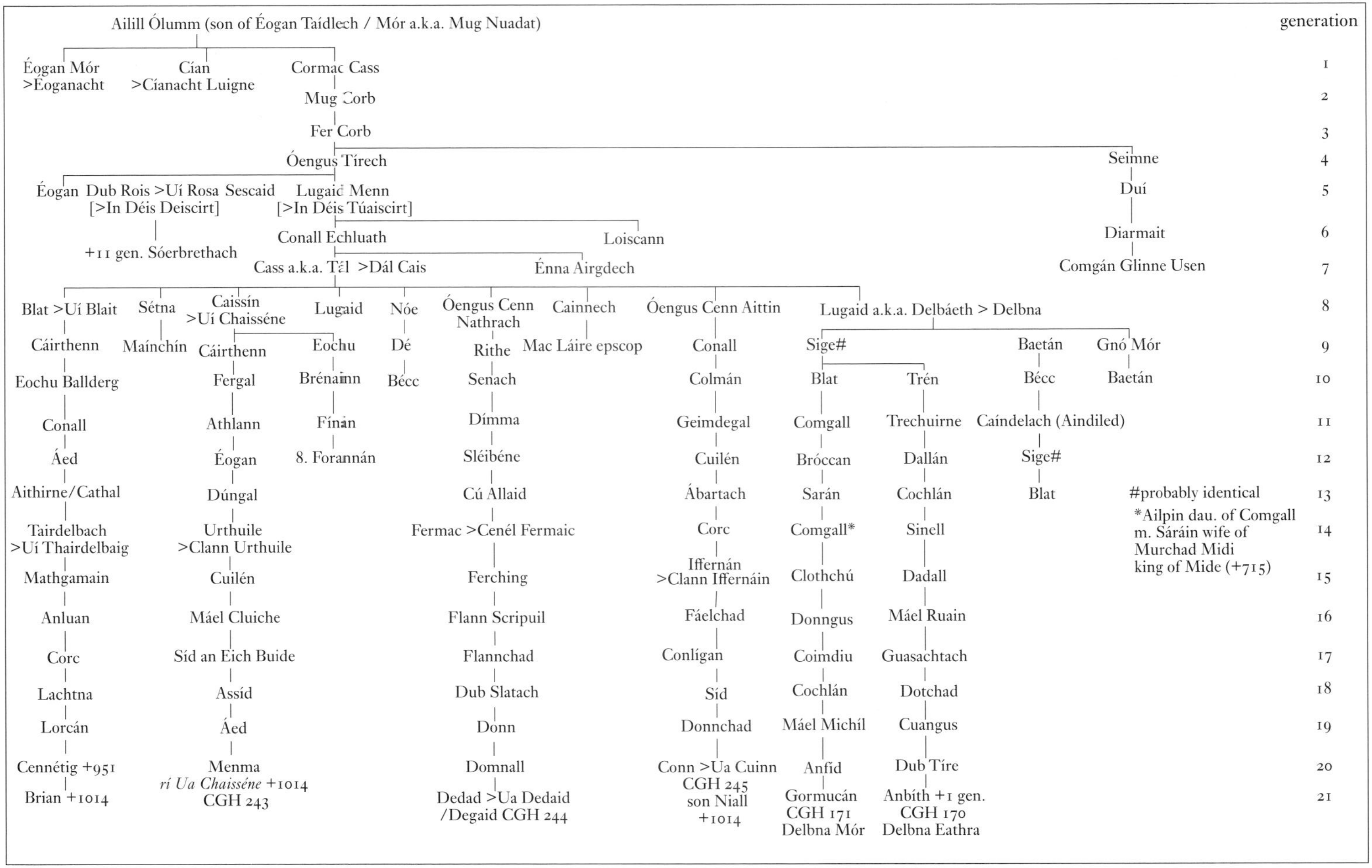

Table 1.1. The main Dál Cais pedigrees according to the long version of the Dál Cais genealogies and related sources

Déisi (see table 1.1).[40] Hence it appears that the passage in *Bethu Phátraic* reflects the fact that the Uí Thairdelbaig were plotting their own ecclesiastical policy at the time, which usually goes hand in hand with an independent political course.

6. ALLIANCES

The role of the Uí Thairdelbaig in *Bethu Phátraic* makes it imperative to investigate the position of the community of Patrick in Munster in the ninth century. There are several indications that the kings of Cashel did not always honour the payment of taxes to the community of Patrick, and it is indeed suggested that this led to the death of King Cormac in 713 – as we have seen, in battle against the Northern Déisi. Hence the promulgation of the *Lex Patricii* in Munster in 823 was a significant event. It was a coordinated effort by Artrí mac Conchobair, erenagh (*airchennech* – lay abbot) and bishop of Armagh, and Feidlimid mac Crimthainn. The latter had become king of Cashel in 820, after succeeding the elderly Artrí mac Cathail, who on two occasions had promulgated the Law of Ailbe, Munster's foremost saint whose successors resided at Emly. Feidlimid was also a member of the Céli Dé, who promoted reform in the Irish church. Feidlimid backed the cause of the bishop of Armagh, but his main target was Clonmacnoise. He led several raids to the monastery and their ecclesiastical lands inhabited by the Delbna Ethra. He may at some stage have controlled the area, as it was plundered by his enemy Niall Caille, king of Tara, in 835 and 840. Yet in 842 Forannan and Diarmait, who had previously struggled for the abbacy of Armagh, promulgated the *Lex Patricii* in Munster anew. Feidlimid died in 847, and the kingship of Cashel was taken by lesser men.[41]

From the sources it is not clear which of the Munster kings supported Feidlimid in his raids in Leth Cuinn. Yet we may note a couple of similarities with the later period. In the ninth century, both Feidlimid and the Uí Thairdelbaig supported the claims to primacy of Patrick's community. This policy was continued by Brian's brother Mathgamain and Brian himself.[42] According to the genealogies the Delbna are related to Dál Cais, with the implication that they are subservient to them and protected by their kings (see §14 below). This fits in with the developments during Feidlimid's reign. When Dál Cais rose to power they devoted much energy to the area around the

40 *LM*, p. 316 (*badh hé sinnsior cloinne Carthainn*), cf. *CGH*, p. 236 (152b3). 41 Byrne, *Irish kings*, pp 211–29; Jaski, *Early Irish kingship*, pp 221–5. 42 *AI* 973.3, where Mathgamain gives Dub dá Leithe, the successor of Patrick (at Armagh), the perpetual right to levy his taxes in Munster, about which the latter quarrelled with the successor of Ailbe at Emly. For Brian's relationship with Armagh, see Ailbhe MacShamráin, 'Brian Bóruma, Armagh and high kingship', *Seanchas Ardmhacha*, 20:2 (2005), 1–21; Duffy, *Brian Boru*,

Shannon to the north of them (see §8 below). Hence we may wonder if the support for Patrick's community did not mean support for Feidlimid as well. If this hypothesis is correct, then it is likely that this caused the rise of Uí Thairdelbaig within the Northern Déisi as they profitted from joining the king of Cashel in his military exploits in Leth Cuin – exploits which they themselves were to lead in the future.

While this hypothesis is out of necessity based on circumstantial evidence, due to the paucity of the sources, we see that subsequent events lend it some support. Máel Sechnaill mac Máele Ruanaid of Clann Cholmáin in Mide was the first king of Tara of whom contemporary sources state that he took the hostages of the king of Cashel. This happened in 855, and in 858 he defeated the Munstermen again and crossed the whole province from east to west and from south to north as far as the Aran Islands. This earned him the title of 'king of all Ireland' at his death in 862. Máel Sechnaill's son Flann Sinna emulated his father. In 880, when he had just become king of Tara, he plundered Munster from Bórama to Cork. Bórama, the fort from which Brian would take his name, is less than two miles north of Killaloe, and apparently marked the northern boundary of Thomond.[43] It was perhaps during this expedition that Flann also came to Mag Adair (Moyare Park), in later sources the inauguration site of Dál Cais, where they held a fair (*óenach*) and where stood their sacred tree. It is likely, however, that Mag Adair did not yet have this status when the Uí Óengussa were in power, but only became the inauguration site of Dál Cais after the Uí Thairdelbaig had obtained the kingship – similar to Tulach Óc becoming the inauguration site of the Ua Néill branch of Cenél nEógain in the eleventh century.[44] According to other genealogies Maicín mac Braín of Uí Thairdelbaig was killed when Flann Sinna was at Mag Adair.[45] For almost two decades Flann dominated Ireland, but his position was challenged when in 901 Bishop Cormac mac Cuilennáin assumed the kingship of Cashel.[46]

As with Feidlimid, it was a cleric and member of the Céli Dé who united Munster, although it is not quite clear why he took on the might of the king of Tara and his allies. In 906, Flann and Cerball, king of Leinster, harried eastern Munster from Gabrán (Gowran, east of Kilkenny) to Limerick. Cormac retaliated the next year by taking a fleet up the Shannon, plundering Mide and taking the hostages of Connacht. In 908 a major battle was fought at Belach

pp 138–44, 186–8. 43 *AFM* 877=880; Duffy, *Brian Boru*, p. 69; see §11 below. It is likely that Flann took the hostages of Munster on that occasion, as in 882 he led an army of Irish and Foreigners to Armagh, just like his father had done in 860, who on that occasion was accompanied by the men of Leinster, Munster and Connacht; Jaski, 'The Vikings', 319–21. 44 Duffy, *Brian Boru*, pp 105–6; Elizabeth FitzPatrick, *Royal inaguration in Gaelic Ireland, c.1100–1600: a cultural landscape study* (Woodbridge, 2004), pp 52–9, 141. 45 *LM*, p. 308. Bráen was the great-great-grandson of Ailgel son Tairdelbach, see table 1.2. On Mag Adair (between Tulla and Quin), see further Duffy, *Brian Boru*, pp 65–6. 46 Jaski, 'The Vikings',

Mugna (Ballaghmoon, Co. Carlow), where Cormac mac Cuilennáin and the cream of Munster royalty were slain. The *Fragmentary annals* list among the casualties Connadar 'of Mag Adair' and Aineslis 'of Bórama' of Uí Thairdelbaig.[47] We do not know these names from the genealogies, but again the Uí Thairdelbaig appear to stand out among the Northern Déisi. Another noteworthy victim of the battle was Eiden mac Cléirig, the exiled king of Uí Fhiachrach Aidne of southern Connacht. This is noteworthy, because Eiden's daughter Mór would become the wife of Brian and mother of his son Murchad. Eiden's grandson Máel Ruanaid would fall at the battle of Clontarf. That Eiden and two members of the Uí Thairdelbaig fought for Cormac mac Cuilennaín may imply that the close bonds between their two dynasties were already established in this period.

7. THE EMERGENCE OF DÁL CAIS

From what scanty evidence there is, and following the above interpretation, it appears that the Uí Thairdelbaig plotted their own course by supporting Patrician primacy in Munster and the aspirations of Cormac mac Cuilennáin. It has been suggested that they likewise may have supported Feidlimid mac Crimthainn in the early ninth century.[48] Both kings were also clerics and affiliated to the Céli Dé, and we have seen that the genealogical connection between the Delbna and Dál Cais may be explained from Feidlimid's exploits in Delbna Ethra. It is also likely that where it is explicitly recorded that the Munster kings used fleets along the Shannon these were provided by the rulers of Dál Cais.

Throughout this period the Uí Óengussa held the kingship, but their control of Uí Thairdelbaig seems to have been limited. Their position was further put under pressure by the presence of a large contigent of Vikings at Limerick, notably in the 920s and 930s, close to their territories.[49] While the Uí Óengussa were thus occupied, the Uí Thairdelbaig continued to extend their influence. In 925 the annals note that Ánrothán son of Máel Gorm assumed the kingship of Corco Mruad, the territory in the north-western part of Co. Clare. Ánrothán was a descendant of Mathgamain son of Tairdelbach,[50] and set

322–3. **47** *FAI*, pp 156 §423 and 160 (poem). This entry also refers to Cormac's teacher Diarmait of the Céli Dé; see further also *CGSH*, p. 162 §713, which also includes Feidlimid mac Crimthainn and Flannán mac Tairdelbaig, for whom see §17 below. **48** For additional support for this interpretation, see §18 below. **49** Ryan, 'Brian Boruma, king of Ireland' in *North Munster studies*, pp 355–74, at pp 356–8; Duffy, *Brian Boru*, pp 71–3; see further Jaski, 'The Vikings', 330; Clare Downham, *Viking kings of Britain and Ireland: the dynasty of Ívarr to AD1014* (Edinburgh, 2007), pp 35–42, 53–5. **50** *CGH*, p. 239 (153a9–13); the identification seems sound, both names are quite rare, and Ánrothán belongs to the same generation as Lorcán, the father of Cennétig (d. 951); see also Ó Corráin, *Normans*, p. 114; Blair Gibson, 'Chiefdoms', p. 122, who is, however, wrong in stating that Brian Bóraime

aside the ruling dynasty of Corco Mruad, whose king Murchad, son of Flann (d. 907) son of Flaithbertach (d. 873), had died in 920. Ánrothán died in 936, and his son Congalach died as king of Corco Mruad in 988, after which the descendants of Flaithbertach regained the kingship.[51] If anything, this intrusion shows again the independent and ambitious course followed by the Uí Thairdelbaig, who by now had extended their sway over the northern part of Thomond. The whole area was becoming unified, and hence we find that in 927 the annals name Máel Corguis ua Conaill as 'bishop of Thomond' (*epscoip Tuadmuman*).[52] He was probably a grandson of Conall son of Eochaid son of Tairdelbach, who is named as the ancestor of the Áes Cluana ('People of the Church') of Dál Cais.[53] It is clear that the Uí Thairdelbaig were dominating Thomond at this stage, and taking the kingship was no doubt on the top of their priority list.

After the death of Cormac of Uí Echthigirn the kingship was taken by an outsider, Rebachán mac Mothla, abbot of Tuaim Gréine (Tuamgraney, near the western shore of Lough Derg). At his death in 934 he is named as 'king of Dál Cais', the first time this dynastic name is used in the extant sources. According to the genealogies, Rebachán was one of the seven kings of Uí Óengussa who ruled Dál Cais, but no record of his ancestry has survived.[54] Yet in the same year his son Dubgilla, 'lord of Uí Chormaic', was killed by Congalach son of Lorcán through treachery.[55] Uí Chormaic is the same territory to the southwest of Ennis we have mentioned in §4 above, and was at least in later times separated from the lands of the Uí Oengussa by those of the Uí Chaisséne and Tradraige.[56] Even if Rebachán indeed belonged to the Uí Oengussa, he was not a member of the principal ruling families of Uí Chernaig, Uí Echthigirn and Uí Róngaile, whose lands were all situated roughly between Limerick and the area around Bridget Lough, west of Lough Derg. These families had lost their grip on the kingship of Dál Cais, and with

later replaced the leaders of Corco Mruad by his kinsman Máel Sechnaill mac Croscrach (*sic*) – this is a misreading of *AI* 983.2. At p. 123 it is said that the names Flaithbertach and Rechtabra were unusual for Corco Mruad, and that they were probably external impositions as well. However, they appear in the genealogies of the rulers of Corco Mruad, see *CGH*, p. 254 (154d44); *LM*, pp 254–5. **51** *AFM* 987=988. At *AI* 983.2, Lochlann son of Máel Sechnaill is still called *rígdomna* ('fit to be a king of') Corco Mruad. **52** *AI* 927.3. **53** *LM*, p. 309. No Máel Corguis is named among the grandsons of Conall, but not all are enumerated. On the Áes Cluana in the eleventh and twelfth centuries, see Donnchadh Ó Corráin, 'Dál Cais – church and dynasty', *Ériu*, 24 (1973), 52–63. The next bishop of Thomond recorded is Diarmait son of Aicher (*AI* 953.3), perhaps a son of Aicher mentioned at *LM*, p. 308 (Uí Ailgile), or at *LM*, p. 302 (Clann Coscraig), both suggested in Ó Corráin, ibid., 54 note 13. **54** *AI* 934.1; *LM*, pp 316–17, 323. The statement in Byrne, *Irish kings*, p. 214, and Duffy, *Brian Boru*, p. 73, that he belonged to the Uí Chernaig is not supported in the sources. **55** *AU* 934.2 (*dux Nepotum Cormaic*); *AFM* 932=934; Duffy, *Brian Boru*, p. 74. **56** No other lordship called Uí Chormaic existed in Thomond, and in the genealogies of Uí Óengussa no Cormac is mentioned (*LM*, pp 316–20). Rebachán may have belonged to the Uí Chaisséne, whose lands were to the east of Uí Chormaic, and perhaps had the killing of Rebachán's son Dubgilla the last potential rival of Uí Thairdelbaig had been eliminated. Significantly, the deed was committed by Congalach, whose father Lorcán now assumed the kingship. The Uí Thairdelbaig had finally arrived into the kingship, and the whole of Ireland would soon feel its impact.

It is unknown when Lorcán was succeeded by his son Cennétig, but this probably happened already before the 930s were over. We know of two wives of Cennétig, of whom Bé Binn, daughter of Aurchad (d. 945), king of Western Connacht, is the best known, as she was the mother of Brian Bóraime and his brothers Flann and Conchobar.[57] Cennétig's other wife was a daughter of Óengus (d. 915), son of Flann Sinna and brother of Donnchad Donn; their son was Donn Cuan (d. 950).[58] There can be little doubt that Donn Cuan was older than Brian, even if we assume that the latter was born in 927 rather than in 941.[59] The alliance with Clann Cholmáin was further strengthened by the marriage between Cennétig's daughter Órlaith with none other than Donnchad Donn, who ruled as king of Tara from 919 to 944. In 941 the annals record that Cennétig's daughter Órlaith was killed after it was discovered that she had a sexual relationship with Óengus, the aged king's own son.[60] We do not know when these two marriages took place. Seán Duffy suggests that the marriage with Órlaith was prompted by a desire to curb the aggressive king of Cashel, Cellachán. This Cellachán sacked Clonmacnoise in 936 and plundered Clonard in 939, and was also an enemy of Dál Cais.[61] Yet Cennétig's marriage had taken place earlier, perhaps to weld an alliance against the Vikings of Limerick. Whatever the case, Cennétig and Dal Cais had arrived on the Irish political scene, even before the annals start to take serious notice of them.

8. THE ROAD TO CASHEL

The reign of Cennétig coincided with political developments that heralded a sweeping change of the political map of Ireland, causing within a few generations the demise of the kingship of Tara as overkingship of the Uí Néill,

taken over its lordship: see n. 64 below. 57 M.E. Dobbs (ed.), 'The Ban-Shenchus', *Revue celtique*, 48 (1931), 163–234, at 188–9, 227; Duffy, *Brian Boru*, pp 74–5. 58 Dobbs, 'The Ban-Shenchus', p. 197, where it is said that she was the daughter of Óengus (d. 1017) son of (Donnchad) Carrach Calma (d. 969), who was the son of Murchad son of Óengus (d. 915) son of Flann Sinna. This is chronologically impossible, and I take it to mean that she was the daughter of Óengus, grandfather of Donnchad Carrach Calma. When this Óengus died in 915 'in ripe old age', he was the most senior son of Flann Sinna then alive, and meant to succeed his father, who died the next year (*AU* 915.1); see further Jaski, 'The Vikings', pp 324–5. 59 On this matter, see Duffy, *Brian Boru*, pp 92–3. 60 *CS* 940=941; Jaski, 'The Vikings', 338. Kelleher, 'The rise', 236, saw this marriage as an indication that Dál Cais had been set up by Clann Cholmáin as a new power to counter the ambitions of the kings of Cashel. Two other wives of Donnchad Donn also came from emerging dynasties, namely of Cenél Conaill and Uí Briúin Bréifne, see Dobbs, 'The Ban-Shenchus', p. 187. 61 Duffy,

and even sooner the kingship of Cashel as the overkingship of the Eóganachta. Several dynasties fell from power and new dynasties emerged, Dál Cais among them. In 944, Donnchad Donn, son of Flann Sinna, died, and there was no agreed candidate to succeed him as king of Tara. As we can extrapolate from the annals, two major alliances rapidly emerged. The one consisted of Congalach Cnogba, king of Brega, plus the up-and-coming Fergal ua Ruairc, king of Bréifne and later of Connacht, plus Cellachán, king of Cashel. The other party was formed by Ruaidri ua Canannáin, king of Cenél Conaill in the north, plus Clann Cholmáin of Mide, Uí Fhiachrach Aidne of southern Connacht, and Dál Cais led by Cennétig.

In 944, Cellachán, king of Cashel, invaded Thomond and defeated Cennétig in battle, killing his sons Finn and Dub.[62] Six years later, in 950, Cennétig suffered another defeat, now at the hands of Congalach, king of Brega, who had just secured the kingship of Tara from his rival Ruaidrí ua Canannáin. Again two of Cennétig's sons were slain, Donn Cuan and Echthigern. Yet although no victory by him is recorded, Cennétig is the first person ever to be styled king of Thomond in the *Annals of Ulster* at his death in 951. Although this may not have been an official title – *Chronicum Scotorum* simply names him king of Dál Cais – it mirrors the title given to the bishop of Thomond mentioned earlier. The area was developing into a new territorial kingship, ruled by Cennétig's family. And such was the impression made by him that the *Annals of Inisfallen* call him *rígdomna Caisil*, a man fit to be king of Cashel, an attribute to which his descendants would certainly live up.[63]

Cennétig was succeeded by his son Lachtna, who was killed three years later by the Uí Fhlainn and Uí Chernaig. The latter belonged to the Uí Óengussa, who may have had a last fling at the kingship. The Uí Fhlainn are named after a cousin of Tairdelbach, and so perhaps the Uí Thairdelbaig were also assailed by closer relatives.[64] However, it was to no avail. Lachtna's brother Mathgamain took the kingship of Dál Cais, and with the death of Cellachán of Cashel in 954 became the leading Munster king of his day. Yet his main interests were, like those of his father, focussed on the north. This brought him into conflict with Fergal ua Ruairc of Uí Briúin Bréifne who, as a complete

Brian Boru, p. 76. **62** *AU* 944.7; *AFM* 942=944; *CGH*, p. 237 (152b37); Mag Dúin was probably in Thomond. *LM*, p. 122, records a battle won by Cennétig over Cellachán near Limerick; see further Duffy, *Brian Boru*, pp 76–7. **63** Jaski, 'The Vikings', 333–9; Duffy, *Brian Boru*, pp 74–81. **64** *LM*, p. 127, and p. 297 for Flann's genealogy. At p. 307 there is a pedigree which turns Congalach (d. 1018), king of Uí Fhailge, into a descendant of this Flann son of Urchlosach son of Congal, rather than his contemporary Flann dá Congal (d. 740). The pedigree probably belongs to the update of the Psalter of Cashel after the battle of Clontarf, and appears to be an attempt by Dál Cais to claim the overlordship of Uí Fhailge in northwest Leinster, cf. §17 below. Note, however, also the Uí Chernaig and Uí Fhlainn of the Uí Chaisséne, both descending from Eochaid mac Cuiléin, and also the Uí Rebacháin from his brother Máel Cluiche, *LM*, p. 313. The last may descend from Rebachán, king of Dál Cais, mentioned in §7 above.

outsider, became king of Connacht in 956. Fergal had already a reputation as a plunderer of churches in the Shannon area, and the west of Mide became rife with fleets eager to profit from the disarray among Clann Cholmáin. In 963 Domnall ua Néill, the new king of Tara since the death of Congalach in 956, arrived in the area to establish his authority. In the same year Dál Cais were vanquished by Fergal ua Ruairc in a naval battle near Clonmacnoise, after which Thomond was plundered.[65]

This was a decisive turning point. Until then, the records suggest that the Uí Thairdelbaig had mainly been seeking opportunities further north along the Shannon. No raid to the south has been recorded, but his defeat in 963 caused Mathgamain's attention to turn into that direction. His eye fell on the vacant kingship of Cashel, where all the four successive kings after Cellachán had suffered a violent death through internal rivalries, the last being Cellachán's son Donnchad. According to *Cogadh Gáedhel re Gallaibh* Mathgamain set up camp at Cashel in 964, and received the acknowledgement of his superiority from the Eóganacht Chaisil (Cellachán's kindred) and the neighbouring Múscraige.[66] In 967, Mathgamain is called 'king of Cashel' for the first time in the annals – and won overnight fame – on the occasion of his demonstrating that he was worthy of the title. He first defeated the Vikings of Limerick at Sulchóit (Solloghod), roughly between Emly and Cashel, and on the next day burned and plundered Limerick. A dynast of the Osraige was killed in the violence, a sign that Mathgamain had hauled in more allies. To round this all up, two years later Mathgamain took the hostages from Máel Muad, king of Eóganacht Raithlinn, in southern Munster, his last remaining competitor. Mathgamain now well and truly dominated Munster, and this was underlined in 972 when a council of Mathgamain, Máel Muad and Fáelán, king of the Déisi, issued an ordinance (*cáin*) to procure the banishment of Viking mercenaries from Munster, of the Vikings from Limerick and the burning of Limerick itself. The next year, no doubt instigated by Mathgamain, the successor of Patrick made a visitation of Munster and established Armagh's ecclesiastical tax over the province.

However, as often happened with such spectacular successes in Irish politics, it did not last. Máel Muad went into opposition, and in 976 Mathgamain was treacherously captured by Donnubán of Uí Fhidgeinte and put to death by Máel Muad, who assumed the kingship of Cashel forthwith. It was a hard blow for Dál Cais to lose such an able king, but it was their fortune that he would be succeeded by an equally capable brother: Brian Bóraime. In 978 Máel Muad and his allies suffered a crushing defeat at Belach Lectha, on the border of the Southern Déisi (see §5 above), which Mathgamain's

65 Jaski, 'The Vikings', 337–41; Duffy, *Brian Boru*, pp 82–5. 66 According to *CGG*, p. 74 §51, Cathal son of Feradach of Delbna Mór, king-soldier of Ireland (*rí amsach*), aided Mathgamain through affection, friendship and kinship. He was killed in battle later on,

murderer did not survive. Brian took the kingship of Cashel, and this set him on the road to the kingship of Ireland.[67]

In three generations the Uí Thairdelbaig had risen to an extraordinary powerful position: Lorcán became king of Dál Cais, Cennétig of Thomond, Mathgamain of Cashel and Munster, and Brian of Ireland. Before we finally assess the factors which gave rise to this development, we first have to consider how Dál Cais themselves explained their own phenomenon. In a culture in which present political relationships were explained by the (remote) past, and new claims are backed up by 'tradition' to show that all was as it should be, it is now time to see how Brian and his scholars set to work to show that Dál Cais had a rightful claim to the kingship of Cashel, to dominate Munster, and were of equal status and ancestry as those they had challenged and ousted from office.

9. THE PSALTER OF CASHEL

To investigate how the newly-won position of Dál Cais was explained in the sources, we have to turn to our primary sources for this topic, the secular genealogies as compiled in the Psalter of Cashel under Brian at around 1000, and of which the section on Dál Cais was updated shortly after his death. For the sake of reference, let us first look at the pedigree of Brian Bóraime himself, who is presented as ultimately descending from Ailill Ólumm, whose son Eógan Mór was the eponymous ancestor of the Eóganachta, the rulers of Munster until the advent of Dál Cais. Brian is twenty generations removed from Cormac Cass, the son of Ailill Ólumm:

> Brian (d. 1014) (21), son of Cennétig (d. 951) (20), son of Lorcán (19), son of Lachtna (18), son of Corc (17), son of Anluan (16), son of Mathgamain (15), son of Tairdelbach (>Uí Thairdelbaig) (14), son of Aithirne (Cadlae; Cathal) (13), son of Áed (12), son of Conall (11), son of Eochu Ballderg (10), son of Cáirthenn Find (9), son of Blat (>Uí Blait) (8), son of Tál *alias* Cass (> Dál Cais) (7), son of Conall Echlúath (6), son of Lugaid Mend (Lámderg) (5), son of Óengus Tírech (4), son of Fer Corb (3), son of Mug Corb (2), son of Cormac Cass (1), son of Ailill Ólumm.

There are six medieval manuscripts that contain the Dál Cais genealogies or a substantive part of it: Oxford, Bodleian Library, MS Rawlinson B 502 (*c.*1130) (R);[68]

p. 82 §56. 67 Jaski, 'The Vikings', 341–3, 348; Downham, *Viking kings*, pp 53–5; Duffy, *Brian Boru*, pp 85–91. 68 Kuno Meyer (ed.), *Rawlinson B. 502* (Oxford, 1909) [facsimile], pp 152a41–153b39 (*CGH*, pp 235–45), which corresponds to fol. 82va41–83rb39. Reference is made to the page-numbers as in the facsimile and *CGH*. On the manuscript, see Brian Ó

the Book of Leinster (*c.*1150–60) (LL);[69] Dublin, Trinity College, MS 1298 (*olim* H.2.7) (*c.*1340–50) (H);[70] the Book of Uí Maine (*c.*1378–94) (UM);[71] the Book of Ballymote (*c.*1383–97) (BB);[72] and the Book of Lecan (*c.*1380–1417) (Lec).[73] A small section of the first part is also in Oxford, Bodleian Library, MS Rawlinson B 486 (R4) (*c.*1369–1400).[74] Of these, the two oldest manuscripts, R and LL, were written in Leinster. H and R4 come from Munster, and UM, BB and Lec from Connacht. In R the caption of the Dál Cais genealogies is: *De genealogia Dal Chais ut inuenitur in psalterio Caissil* 'About the genealogies of Dál Cais as found in the Psalter of Cashel'. Although it is lacking in the other manuscripts,[75] there is no reason to question this attribution. However, when the different manuscripts are compared, it is quicky seen that the oldest ones, R, LL and H (and R4) all contain a short version of the Dál Cais genealogies. UM, BB and Lec have the long version, although UM also still misses several sections, while Lec is more verbose and contains additions and insertions not found in BB or UM. Hence BB is, generally speaking, the most complete version, albeit with modernizations and with translations of phrases which are still in Latin in the short version and UM. As BB remains unedited, it is convenient to refer to a seventeenth-century copy of BB with modernized orthography edited as an appendix in *An Leabhar Muimhnech* (*LM*).[76]

The differences between the short and long version become immediately clear from the beginning. R, LL and H begin with enumerating the thirteen sons of Cass (7) son of Conall Echlúath son of Lugaid Mend, without any

Cuív, *Catalogue of Irish language manuscripts in the Bodleian Library at Oxford and Oxford college libraries*, 2 vols (Dublin, 2001–3), i, pp 163–200. **69** LL pp 322e1–323f4, see the diplomatic edition in *LL*, vi, pp 1392–8 (*LL* refers to the printed edn, LL to the manuscript with page- and line-number). For the latest discussion, see Elizabeth Duncan, 'A reassessment of the script and make-up of *Lebor na Nuachongbála*', *ZCP*, 59 (2012), 27–66. **70** H col. 136a22–141Ba11. For H I have consulted the manuscript on microfilm, and have gratefully used Donnchadh Ó Corráin, Genealogies from H: an electronic edition (in preparation), CELT Project (UCC). **71** R.A.S. Macalister (ed.), *The Book of Uí Maine* (Dublin, 1941) [facsimile], fol. 28va1–33rb4. **72** Robert Atkinson (ed.), *The Book of Ballymote* (Dublin, 1887) [facsimile], pp 182a1–191d54. I refer to the current manuscript foliation, fol. 102va1–107rd54. **73** Kathleen Mulchrone (ed.), *The Book of Lecan* (Dublin, 1937) [facsimile], fol. 224va1–230vb50 (ends defectively). These manuscripts are further discussed in Donnchadh Ó Corráin, 'Creating the past: the early Irish genealogical tradition', *Peritia*, 12 (1998), 177–208, at 178–9. **74** R4, fol. 30vb12–32vb30 (ends with *catha Muige Cobha 7 ni ragaib cland*, which corresponds to *LM*, p. 299.30, cf. §13 below). I have consulted the manuscript on microfilm. On the manuscript, see Ó Cuív, *Catalogue*, i, pp 119–34. **75** See Jaski, 'Genealogical section', 305. **76** *LM*, pp 293–332; see also Paul Walsh, 'Review of *An Leabhar Muimhneach*', *Irish Historical Studies*, 3:10 (1942), 135–43, at 139–40. Other, later genealogical records include Séamus Pender (ed.), *The O Clery book of genealogies. Analecta Hibernica*, 18 (Dublin, 1951), pp 147–54, §1931–2019 (mainly pedigrees from the time of Brian onwards); Nollaig Ó Muraíle (ed.), *Leabhar mór na n-geneleach. The great book of Irish genealogies compiled (1645–66) by Dubhaltach Mac Firbishigh*, 5 vols (Dublin, 2003), ii, pp 598–645, §637.1–659.11.

clear indication where this genealogy should be placed in relation to the foregoing Eóganacht pedigrees. UM precedes this section by a single pedigree from Cass to Cormac Cass (1), whom the title styles the son of Ailill Ólumm. Only BB and Lec contain the full version. A collation of the various manuscripts shows that large parts were left out of the short version, sometimes to summarize, sometimes for unknown reasons, and sometimes apparently due to a loss of leaves in the exemplar of R and LL. Even in the enumeration of the six sons of Brian that did not have any offspring, the short version omits the three at the end, with R even not bothering to write *7rl* to indicate this.[77] Yet the records in R and LL go no further than the period shortly after the battle of Clontarf,[78] whereas the other versions have several updates inserted at various intervals, from the 1160s until the time of their codification.[79]

10. OLD NEW NAMES

The whole lineage from Conall Cass (1) to Tál, nicknamed Cass (8), appears to be a construction to connect the Northern Déisi to the Eóganacht rulers of Munster (see table 1.1). Although remarkable deeds were assigned to these forefathers of Dál Cais, as we shall discuss further on, none of them are mentioned in Old-Irish sources. Conall Cass makes his first appearance in literary sources in the first section of *Cath Maige Mucrama* in the Book of Leinster as one of three sons of Ailill Ólumm and forefather of Dál Cais.[80] This simply follows genealogical doctrine as it was accepted at the time, and nothing more is said about him. In the poem *Clann Ailella Óluimm uill*, found in R, LL and Oxford, Bodleian Library, MS Laud 610, he is mentioned as one of the seven sons Ailill Ólomm had with Sadb, the daughter of Conn Cétchathach.[81]

77 *LL* 322f31 (vi, p. 1393), cf. R 152b34 (*CGH*, p. 237), H 137b5, and compare with Lec 225ra14, cf. BB 102vb34, UM 28va68. Ó Muraíle, *Leabhar mór*, ii, p. 606 §640.3, also gives the short version. 78 R and LL do not have any updates beyond *c.*1014–15 either among the descendants of Brian or the collateral branches, and updates of the pedigrees of the main Munster dynasties are found in separate sections: see Jaski, 'Genealogical section', 300. It does not appear that later updates were edited out in the same way as the three mentioned sons of Brian. 79 BB 102rb43 (*LM*, p. 299), Lec 225ra25. This update is carried on until the great-grandsons of Brian's son Tadc (d. 1023), of whom Donnchad is named as bishop of Síl mBriain (he was bishop of Killaloe, 1161–4) and the last surviving member was Tairdelbach, king of Thomond, who died in 1167. Their sons or successors are not included in this section. At H 137b34 a section with different updates begins, including the pedigree of Tairdelbach's son Domnall (Mór), king from 1167 to 1194. 80 Máirín O'Daly (ed.), *Cath Maige Mucrama*, ITS 50 (Dublin, 1975), p. 38. 81 *CGH*, p. 193 (147b50); Kuno Meyer (ed.), 'Mitteilungen aus irischen Handschriften: Die Nachkommen Ailill Ólomms', *ZCP*, 12 (1918), 377.

Mug Corb (2) and his son Fer Corb (3) are appropriately archaic-sounding names. In the Old-Irish poem *Cú cen Máthair, maith clann*, a Fer Corb is mentioned among the remote forefathers of Ailill Ólumm.[82] In later pedigrees, Munster regnal lists and in *Lebor gabála* and related sources his father is called Mug Corb.[83] This actually appears to derive from the pair in the Dál Cais pedigrees, and the two pairs were hence confused, leading to the prehistoric Mug Corb being called 'from Cláire'.[84] In the Dál Cais genealogies Fer Corb is given two sons: Seimne, the father of St Comgán of Glenn Uissen (see §16 below), and Óengus Tírech, an epithet meaning that he possessed or ruled many lands, and which is also borne by Muiredach Tírech, a forefather of the Uí Néill and Connachta.[85] Óengus Tírech (4) is credited with four sons, about whom more below. One of them is Lugaid Mend (5), who in certain sources receives the epithet Lámderg ('Redhand').[86] Lugaid Lámderg is also one of the prehistoric high-kings of Ireland mentioned in the regnal lists and in *Lebor gabála*. His father is Eochu Uairches.[87] Again the impression is that the Dál Cais forefather found his way into the lists of the high-kings of Ireland of the eleventh and twelfth centuries. Lugaid Mend had two sons, including Conall Echlúath (6), father of Énna Airgdech and Cass (7), who gave his name to Dál Cais.[88] Énna Airgdech is another name found among the remote forefathers of Ailill Ólomm, as son of Echu Mumo.[89]

All in all, it appears that the forefathers of Dál Cais were partially culled from the pedigree of Ailill Ólomm, and that this led to these persons being identified with the Dál Cais forefathers in return. It is yet another example of new inventions causing new confusions, all part of the game medieval Irish genealogists and synthetic historians seemed to love to play.

82 *CGH*, p. 200 (148b40). 83 *CGH*, pp 188 (147a51–52), 198 (148b12, Lec and BB), 250 (154ac51, Lec; with, at 154ab45–46, the Fer Corb son of Mug Corb under discussion here); *LGÉ*, v, pp 279–83 §558–65, p. 514 §99–103; *CGH*, pp 119–20 (135b49–54). 84 See the references in Gisbert Hemprich, *Rí Érenn – "König von Irland": Fiktion und Wirklichkeit*, 2nd edn. 2 vols (Berlin, 2015), i, pp 257–8 §99, who, however, continues the tradition by mixing up the two pairs as well (cf. p. 260 §104). 85 *CGH*, pp 147–8 (142a10–39), cf. p. 131 (138a11), etc. 86 Lugaid Mend at *CGH*, pp 170 (145d39), 209 (149b23), 235 (152a43), 250 (154ab43), 427 (LL 336d58), and *CGSH*, pp 6 §21.2, 32 §190, 33 §198, 33 §202–4, 34 §230, 53 §330.1, 57 §378. For Lugaid Lámderg, see §14 below. This has led to Lugaid mac Óengussa of the Ulaid being named as Lugaid Lámderg at *AFM*, i, s.a. 267, and M.E. Dobbs (ed.), 'La bataille de Leitir Ruibhe', *RC*, 39 (1922), 1–32, at 12 §6. He is also a different person than the Lugaid Mend who appears in Whitley Stokes (ed.), 'Acallamh na senórach' in Ernst Windisch and Whitley Stokes (eds), *Irische Texte mit Wörterbuch* 4.1 (Leipzig, 1900), ll. 357–9, 447, 457. Hemprich, *Rí Érenn*, i, 261 §107, mixes them all up. 87 *LGÉ*, v, p. 256 §543, cf. §544, and at p. 508 (*Ériu ard, inis na ríg*, §79, called *Lugaid luinn* 'the fierce'), *CGH*, pp 117–18 (135a40–45: Lugaid); cf. *CGH*, p. 188 (147a44: Lugaid); at pp 198 (148b17–18) and 251 (154b7–8) he is missing. 88 *LM*, p. 294. 89 His name is also spelled Airgtech; *CGH*, pp 120 (136a3), 124 (136b54), both lists of the high-kings of Ireland, cf. *LGÉ*, v, pp 286 §571 (also spelled Airgnech) and 450 (poem CII, where his epithet 'Silvery' is explained); *CGH*, p. 187 (147a21, 33), cf. pp 250 (154ac43) and 362 (LL 320b42); Hemprich, *Rí Érenn*, i, 229–30; see further §14 below.

11. TERRITORIAL CLAIMS IN *DE RAIND HÉRENN*

The Eóganacht genealogies precede the Dál Cais genealogical records in the manuscripts, but are likewise at least for a part attributed to the Psalter of Cashel. They are rather irregularly updated up to the tenth century, with only a few pedigrees running to *c.*1000 or perhaps 1014–15.[90] The Eóganacht genealogies contain a clearly interpolated section on the division of Ireland and Munster, in which the Dál Cais forefathers Cormac Cass, Lugaid Mend (Lámderg) and Conall Echlúath are also mentioned. It seeks to underpin the claims of Dál Cais to the kingship of Cashel. It has the title *De raind hÉrenn* ('About the division of Ireland'), which will be used here as a way of referring to this section, although the title pertains to the first part of it only.[91]

De raind hÉrenn has not received much attention in scholarly publications to date, but it will be argued here that the manuscript context and content suggest that it was drafted during the reign of Brian Bóraime and included in the Psalter of Cashel. It will also be suggested that *De raind hÉrenn* is for a part culled from a precursor of the so-called 'Book of Thomond' found in the eighteenth-century manuscripts of *An Leabhar Muimneach*, pp 41–128 in the printed edition.[92] This same tract was also used by the author(s) of *Cogadh Gáedhel re Gallaibh*. As this theory has some considerable impact on current views about the propagandistic activities under Brian and the literary history of *Cogadh Gáedhel re Gallaibh*, the whole of *De raind hÉrenn* will be given below, for the most part in a loose translation, at times in summary, and divided into sections A to G. In the footnotes there are references to parallel passages or pieces of information found in the Book of Thomond, which discusses the activities of a number of the forefathers, kings and leaders of Dál Cais until Mathgamain.

The first part of *De raind hÉrenn* begins in Latin and discusses the division of Ireland into two equal parts.

> A) *Diuissa est Hibernia insola in duas partes compares eter Conn Cétchathach et Eógan Már qui et Mug Nuadat mac Dergthene diximus ó Áth Chliath anair siar iar n-Eiscir Riada dar certmedón hÉrenn co Fertais Medraige ri Áth Cliath aniarthuaid 7 rl.*[93]

90 Jaski, 'Genealogical section', 324–6. **91** *CGH*, pp 206–8 (149a55–150a3). It is found in R (*c.*1130), LL, BB and Lec, but it is not found before H 128a11 and UM 26ra60 (=R 150a4, *CGH*, p. 208), both of which also miss the last part of the section on the division of Ireland which precedes *De raind hÉrenn* in the other manuscripts (at *CGH*, pp 206–7). **92** Walsh, 'Review', pp 139 and 143, calls *LM*, pp 41–128, the Book of Thomond I, and regards *LM*, pp 293–332 (i.e. the genealogies of Dál Cais from the Psalter of Cashel) section II, and the later pedigrees at *LM*, pp 332–98 section III. In Dublin, Trinity College, MS 1281 (*olim* H.1.7) they are found in this order. **93** *CGH*, p. 206 (149a55–b5), also in BB and Lec.

The island of Ireland was divided in two comparable parts between Conn Cétchathach and Eógan Mór who is Mug Nuadat son of Dergthene as we have said,[94] from Áth Cliath (Dublin) in the east westwards along Esker Riada to right in the middle of Ireland to the Ridge of Medraige (Maree, to the south of Galway) at Áth Cliath (Clarinbridge) in the northwest,[95] etc.

B) Eógan Mór had two sons, Ailill Ólomm and Lugaid Lága, who killed Art mac Cuind.[96] Ailill Ólomm had nineteen sons as we have said.[97] The 'right-half' (*certleth*, i.e. southern half) of Ireland was divided by Ailill Ólumm between Cormac Cass and Fiachu Mullethan son of Eógan, and the posterity of neither would exceed that of the other by one man, and he imposed a curse on anyone who tried to break it.[98]

C) The part of Cormac Cass in Clíu Máil comprises the area from the summit of Cláire [the south-eastern border of the Southern Déisi] to Berna Trí Carpat at Carn Feradaig [their northern border] and from Cenn Abrat [in the Ballyhoura Hills, the south-western border] to the north to Fochor Mág [near Bruree, the western border] and Limerick,

94 This is the reading in R and LL, BB and Lec have: 'Mug Nuadat son of Mug Néit son of Derg son of Dergthene *dicitur*', which is probably the better reading, seeing that this follows other traditions better (cf. *CGH*, pp 190 (147b20–21), 250 (154ab49), 362 (LL 320b27); *CGG*, p. 58 §43; *CGSH*, p. 27 §157.2). Eógan Mór is better known as Eógan Taídlech, 'the Shining'. The epithet Mór invites confusion with his grandson, Eógan Mór son of Ailill Ólomm, and appears to be relatively late; see Meyer, 'Laud genealogies', 312.10–314.25, with Eógan Mór in the poem at 312.26. See Byrne, *Irish kings*, pp 199–200, for a summary of this tract, *De bunad imthechta Eóganachta*, which he attributes to Cormac mac Cuillenáin. Parts of it are at *LM*, pp 53.21–7 and 54.1–6. The division of Ireland is also related at Lec 167ra28–rb5; see Vernam Hull (ed.), 'Eogan Mór and Conn Cétchathach', *ZCP*, 19 (1933), 59–61, which corresponds to *LM*, pp 56.13–57.5. Note also *LM*, pp 61–4 and *CGH*, p. 190 (147b21) on the battle of Mag Léna where Eógan was slain. Sharon Arbuthnot (ed.), *Cóir anmann. A late Middle-Irish treatise on personal names*, ITS 59–60, 2 vols (London, 2005–7), i, pp 65–7, discusses the close relationship between *LM*, pp 41–67, and the long recension of *Cóir anmann* (CA3), ii, pp 9–12 and 86–8 §36–40 on Eógan. She thinks that *LM* took this over from CA3. Note, however, that for the early Munster kings CA3 derives much information from the Munster genealogies, *CGH*, pp 186–7 (147a1–28), and Meyer, 'Laud genealogies', pp 302.17–303.8. For the development of Eógan Mór as a literary figure, see Kenneth Jackson (ed.), *Cath Maighe Léna* (Dublin, 1938), pp xxiv–xxxi; Hemprich, *Rí Érenn*, i, pp 322–5. This matter needs renewed study, for there were political advantages for Dál Cais in presenting Eógan as a common ancestor of both Eóganachta and Dál Cais, and in expanding the legend of the eponym of Leth Moga; see also §11 below. **95** This shows that the passage was written from a southern perspective. **96** Cf. O'Daly, *Cath Maige Mucrama*, p. 56 §58; *CGH*, pp 246 (153b40–44), 403–5 (*Cath Crinna*, LL 328f1–329a45); *LM*, p. 64.21–23. **97** This refers to *CGH*, p. 192 (147b36), which comes right after the *Imprudens Scottorum* introduction to the Psalter of Cashel, for which see Jaski, 'Genealogical section', 302. **98** Cf. *LM*, p. 93.8–9.

and from the area of Dún Eclais near Emly northwards to Slieve Felim [on the border of Co. Limerick and Co. Tipperary] and [along the Shannon] northwards to the border between the Arad and Múscraige Tíre, southeast of Lough Derg. And also from Berna Trí Carpat to Fidnach Brea (Finavarra) [near the north-western border of Co. Clare] and to Esker Riada, and from Áth Bóraime [north of Killaloe] westwards as far as Cú Chulainn's Leap (*Léim Con Caulaind*, Loop Head, at the northern point where the broad mouth of the Shannon meets the sea).[99]

D) Lugaid Mend defeated the peoples of Fir nOl nÉcmacht (the ancient inhabitants of Connacht) and took their lands by force. Hence it was called 'the Rough Land of Lugaid Lámderg' (*Inde dicitur Garbfherann Lugdach Lámdeirg*), and this land was not counted among the share of Dál Cais from the Men of Munster, and no king in Ireland is entitled to taxation or food-custom or hostages or escort (*cís nó bés nó géill nó comaitecht*) from these lands save the king of Dál Cais.[100]

E) An equal number of the kings of Dál Cais and of the kings of the descendants of Fiachu Mullethan took Munster, from the time of Ailill Ólomm to Óengus son of Nad Fraích.[101]

Dímma son of Rónán (of Uí Óengussa) contended with Faílbe Flann about the kingship of Cashel. The nobility of Munster adjudicated to give Cashel to Faílbe, since he was older than Dímma, and that the rights of the kings of Cashel extended from Cuillend Osraige (to the east of Munster) to Cú Chulainn's Leap [hence probably from Limerick to the east and west in a straight line].[102] The rights to hostages, escort, food-render and tax[103] were given to Dímma and the kings of Dál Cais for eternity.[104] Since they did not take the kingship (of Cashel), that land (to the north of the line, i.e., Thomond) was their special property (*ruidless*).

F1) The share of Dál Cais in Ormond is the grave-mound of Conall Echlúath, Druim Cormaic, half of Cnoc Raphann (Knockgraffon, south of Cashel, near Cahir) and every hereditary land of a *bóaire* (commoner

99 Cf. *LM*, pp 72.26–28 (and for a part the poem that follows it at p. 73) and 79.2–4 (and for a part the poem attributed to Cormac mac Cuilennáin which follows it). Not all the place-names mentioned are identified, and these and a few others are not included in my summary. For a full translation of C from the version in BB, see Mac Neill, 'Vita Tripartita', 36. **100** Cf. *LM*, pp 78–82, on Lugaid Lámderg; see further §13 below. At *LM*, p. 79.1 this is called 'sword land' (*feronn cloidhimh*), and note at p. 79.24–25 *ciana coimhtheacha sin nó go bhfuair bás*. For a full translation of D from the version in BB, see Mac Neill, 'Vita Tripartita', 36. **101** Cf. *LM*, p. 83.8–13. **102** See Diarmuid Ó Murchadha, 'Belach Conglais: one or two?', *Peritia*, 16 (2002), 435–43, at 437. **103** I follow here the reading in BB and Lec. **104** *LM*, p. 92.13–25 has a somewhat longer account about Dímma and Faílbe Flann (d. 639), an ancestor of Cellachán Caisil.

freeman) (*cach ra n-orbba bóhairech*) from Cnámchoill (near Tipperary) to Áth Cliath eastwards.[105]

F2) The share of Dál Cais in Desmond from Belach Conglais east to Carn Uí Néit (Mizen Head in the southwest of Co. Cork).[106] Cormac Cass gave land to Lugaid Mac Con, the son of Cormac Cass's mother, when Lugaid went to Tara.[107] Conall Echlúath fostered (*ro alt*)[108] Eochaid son of Cass son of Corc (i.e., the forefather of Uí Echach Muman) and gave the land to him after the refusal of Eochaid's brothers (to give Eochaid land), for which Corc gave a blessing to Conall, and afterwards he gave the kingship of Cashel to himself (or: his son) and with each turn (*cach ra fechtas*)[109] the kingship to Dál Cais for eternity.[110]

F3) The share of Dál Cais in West Munster, in the half where Cairpre Cruithnechán was situated, for he was the enforcing surety (*naidm*) whom Corc mac Lugdach appointed to Conall Echlúath concerning the ownership rights to Cashel (*fri dílsi cirt Caisil*) of Dál Cais for eternity.[111] In that land were the Uí Thornae. Cóemfhind daughter of Conall Echlúath was the mother of Torna's children, and it is on account of their mother's kin (Dál Cais) that they have maintained their inheritance (patrimonial lands) (*forbbae*).[112]

G) This is the alliance (*combaíd*) between Dál Cais themselves, i.e. the Northern Déisi and the Southern Déisi, i.e. everything they hold in common property when the kingship of Cashel is in the north, its grass-vassalry and its entitlement (*a fhérdes 7 a dliged*) is due to the king of the

105 Cf. *LM*, p. 84, where a poem on Conall Echlúath attributed to Cormac mac Cuilennáin includes the line *fearta Chonaill a Feimhen, Dún Cormaic*. See also Ó Murchadha, 'Belach Conglais', 437–8. At *CGG*, p. 74 §51 Mathgamain marches to Cnámchoill before the battle of Sulchóit. For Cnoc Raphann as the royal seat of Eógan Mór, see *LM*, p. 130.23. **106** On the situation of Belach Conglais, see Anthony Candon, 'Belach Conglais and the diocese of Cork, AD1111', *Peritia*, 5 (1986), 416–18; Ó Murchadha, 'Belach Conglais', situates it in Co. Wicklow. He notes that this boundary is also given in *Lebor gabála* (*LGÉ*, v, p. 44 §405), where Dál Cais are mentioned first among the descendants of Éber. **107** *LM*, p. 93.4–7. **108** *CGH*, p. 207 (149b45): *ro ort* 'killed'; *LM*, p. 93.16: *ro-alt* 'fostered'. The latter is correct. In *LM* this section is followed by the statement that this agreement was kept until Faílbe Flann took the kingship of Cashel away from Dímma (cf. section E), and that it was Dímma with Faílbe Flann who defeated Guaire and the Connachtmen at Carn Feradaig in 629 (see §2 above). **109** Meaning that Corc's descendants and Dál Cais held the kingship of Cashel in alternation (*fechtasugud*). BB and Lec have *dá mac … fadeisin* ('to his own son') instead of *dó … fadeisin*. **110** *LM*, p. 83.16–31, and p. 93.8–22, in a more extensive section. **111** *LM*, p. 83.19–22. On the *naidm*, see Fergus Kelly, *A guide to early Irish law* (Dublin, 1988), pp 171–2. The meaning is that, since Cairpre failed in his duties as a surety to have the right to Cashel returned to Dál Cais, his lands became forfeit. **112** *LM*, p. 93.18–22. In *LM* the section on the descendants of Torna follows that of the fostering of Eochu as in

Southern Déisi: thirty heifers from each inheritance (*cach forbae*) every three years. When there is no king of Cashel from either of them, the horse and outer robe from the king of Northern Déisi are due to the king of the Southern Déisi.

Four wealthy persons possess the king of the south (*cethri saidbri foretat ind ríg thess*): the king of Uí Echdach, the king of Dál Cais, the king of (Cíarraige) Luachra, the king of Uí Chonaill and the fifth the king of Uí Chairpri. They are entitled to dignity (*sochraid*), and there should not be his burden (*áre*) / satire (*áere*) from them (*ná raib a ére ocaib*).[113]

12. TAXATION AND ALTERNATION

De raind hÉrenn revolves around three main issues: the divisions of Ireland and Munster and the share to which the forefathers of Dál Cais were entitled (A–C, F); the freedom from taxation and other impositions for that share (Thomond), since it was theirs by right of conquest (D, E); and their right to the kingship of Cashel which they had held in alternation with the Eóganachta (B, E, F3, G).[114] As said, the whole tract is an insertion in the Eóganacht genealogies, and I take section A on the division of Ireland to be a reflection of the agreement between Brian and Máel Sechnaill mac Domnaill in 997 (see §1 above). The term Leth Cuinn is already found in eighth-century sources, but Leth Moga only gains currency in the later period, and is strongly bound to the claims of Dál Cais to rule Leth Moga (Munster and Leinster) as established by Brian for the first time through this agreement.[115] Cormac Cass then obtains a half of Leth Moga (B), but his share only covers the northern half of Munster (B), roughly equal to the whole of Co. Clare (the area of the Northern Déisi), but including lands east of the Shannon, and the whole eastern part of Co. Limerick (the area of the Southern Déisi). It is clear that this is envisaged as a territorial kingdom, rather than a more scattered and fluid dynastic kingdom amidst peoples such as the Corco Mruad and Corco Baiscinn, even when held in clientship. Due to this division and their kinship and equality with the Eóganachta, this land is unquestionably theirs to rule. Some of the place-names mentioned we have already encountered in the historical sources as situated on the boundary of the Northern and Southern

section F2. 113 For a full translation from the version in BB, see Mac Neill, 'Vita Tripartita', pp 36–7. BB and Lec miss Luachra in the enumeration. 114 Compare also *CGG*, p. 54 §41, which also deals with these matters, and ends with a genealogy of Mathgamain and Brian up to Mug Nuadat who divided Ireland with Conn Cétchathach. On the system of alternation, see Jaski, *Early Irish kingship*, pp 229–36, and Immo Warntjes, 'The alternation of the kingship of Tara between 734 and 944', *Peritia*, 17–18 (2004), 394–432. 115 *AI* 997.2 (see §1 above), 1017.2 (chief poet of Leth Moga Nuadat); *AFM* 1072;

Déisi, notably Carn Feradaig in the south and Bóraime in the north. It may be noted that Brian fortified Cashel in 995, thus underlining his claim to it (cf. F1), and also Dún Fochair Máige (B) or Cnoc Fochair in 1012, and Cenn Abrat, both named in section C.[116] Although Cormac Cass's share ran as far as the Eskar Riada (A, C), between Galway and Dublin, it was inhabited by other peoples, and their conquest by Lugaid Mend meant that these lands were free from taxation from the kings of Cashel (D); the same privilege is obtained by Dímma as a compensation for relinquishing his immediate claim to the kingship of Cashel (E).

This is a construction we have met in the *Frithfholaid* tract (see §3 above), where freedom of taxation and other impositions is ceded to powerful Munster peoples in exchange for their nominal submission. A past alternate right to the kingship is given as one of the reasons for such an arrangement. *De raind hÉrenn* uses the same political rhetoric. Can it be that the freedom from taxation and right to alternation had been a convenient explanation for the kings of Cashel to come to terms with the political independence of the Northern Déisi or Dál Cais? The Middle-Irish tract *Cert ríg Caisil* certainly points in this direction. It lists what the king of Cashel is due from the Munster lands, with the exception of the Eóganachta, who are the free peoples of Cashel. Dál Cais enjoy a similar freedom:

> There is due from them, when one of them is not king in Cashel, only 'his whip over his shoulder' to the king of the Eóganacht, and to be at his side, and his horse and harness and an ounce of gold for every fort, and the breadth of his face in gold.[117]

The whip over the shoulder is here given by the superior king of Cashel to the subordinate king of Dál Cais. The expression is found twice in the Book of Thomond.[118] Again a right to the kingship of Cashel is given as a reason for freedom from taxation, almost on a par with the Eóganachta themselves. It is probably no coincidence that *Cert ríg Caisil* is incorporated in the Dál Cais genealogies in BB and Lec.[119] The tract lists also a number of other peoples free of taxation and obligations, except military service, including the Uí Chormaic and Tradraige, who were both settled in Thomond.[120] Although

AU 1075.2; cf. *CGG*, p. 108 §66. **116** *AI*, 995.6, 1012.5; *CGG*, p. 140 §80; Duffy, *Brian Boru*, pp 158–60. In Jackson, *Cath Maighe Léna*, p. 25 §30, Dún Eochair Máige is the burial place of Ailill Ólumm and his sister Sadb, wife of Conn Cétchathach. **117** Myles Dillon (ed.), 'Three texts related to the *Book of rights*', *Celtica*, 6 (1963), 184–92, at 186 (text) and 189 (translation). See also Vernam Hull (ed.), '*Cert ríg Caisil:* The right of the king of Cashel', *Mediaeval Studies*, 11 (1949), 233–8, at 236 and 238 §16. **118** *LM*, pp 98.18 and 109.23; see Dillon, 'The texts', 189 note 2. **119** BB 106rb31–va16, Lec 230vb18–50; it is also in Dublin, Trinity College, MS 1336 (*olim* H.3.17), col. 767.5–768.7. **120** Dillon, 'The texts', 186–7 and 190; Hull, '*Cert ríg*', 236, 237–8 §17.

difficult to date on linguistic grounds,[121] its (somewhat archaic) outlook seems to fit the political situation of the tenth century.

What is proposed here can be summarized as follows: the kings of Cashel used to explain the relative freedom of certain peoples by their involvement with the kingship of Cashel in the past, including a period of alternation in the kingship. When the Northern Déisi rose to power in Thomond and remained relatively independent, this past right to alternation, freedom of taxation, and probably a kinship with the Eóganachta, was also accorded to them. And since the *Frithfholaid* tract and *Cert ríg Caisil* are basically Cashel documents, the initiative to do so apparently lay with the Eóganacht rulers. If so, they must have been dismayed that this ploy served as an ideal pretext for Mathgamain to (re)claim the kingship of Cashel for Dál Cais, who could now protest that they had unjustly been deprived of this right for generations on end. And sure enough, once Dál Cais were in power, it was the turn of the Eóganachta to press their claims through the system of alternation – even immediately after Brian's death when his son Donnchad led the depleted Dál Cais forces back home.[122] Hence a fictional right of rotation alternated between the two rival dynasties in an effort to come to terms with the political reality.

Talk of freedom from taxation and right to alternation best fits in the period when Dál Cais pressed their claims to rule Munster, and therefore in the time of Mathgamain and Brian. This also applies to the setting out of the boundaries of the territory of Dál Cais, especially because some of them were fortified by Brian. Section F describes their shares in East, South and West Munster. In Ormond, their claims are bolstered by the place-names named after their forefathers Conall Echlúath and Cormac Cass (F1). The half of Cnoc Raphann may reflect the equal division of Munster and Cashel claimed by Dál Cais. Particularly interesting is the piece about the fosterage, blessing and inheritance of Echach (F2). To the Uí Echach belonged Máel Muad, who killed Mathgamain in 976, and his rivals, the descendants of Dub dá Bairenn (king of Cashel, d. 959), whose son Dúnlaing died in Brian's army in 988.[123] It was only during the reigns of Mathgamain and Brian that the Uí Echach were important enough to warrant such attention as given in *De raind hÉrenn*.

In West Munster, Torna's descendants, who lived in the northern part of Cíarraige Luachra, owed their inheritance to Torna's wife, the daughter of Conall Echlúath. The importance of this is revealed when we consider that Torna Éces was held to be the fosterfather of Niall Noígiallach, ancestor of the Uí Néill, and of Corc, forefather of the Eóganachta.[124] In the final section G

121 Hull, '*Cert ríg*', 234–5. Hull's attempt to date it by comparing its content to that of the *Book of rights* (*Lebor na cert*) is unsound. This tract is now dated to the reign of Muirchertach Ua Briain (d. 1119), see Myles Dillon, 'On the date and authorship of the *Book of rights*', *Celtica*, 4 (1958), 239–49. **122** *CGG*, pp 212 and 216 §120; see further Jaski, *Early Irish kingship*, pp 233–4. **123** *AI* 988.2; for their enmity with Donnchad after Clontarf, see *CGG*, pp 212–16 §120; *AU* 1014.4–5; *AI* 1015.2. **124** *CGH*, p. 132 (138a42).

the mutual entitlements of the Northern and Southern Déisi are explored. The latter only profit when the Northern Déisi hold the kingship of Cashel. The last part in not transparent, but again we meet the Uí Echach and (Cíarraige) Luachra. The Uí Chonaill and Uí Chairpri are the two main branches of Uí Fhidgeinte, and in this period the latter were only important in the person of their king Donnubán, who treacherously seized Mathgamain in 976, and was killed by Brian in 980.[125] Until the thirteenth century few of his descendants are mentioned in the annals.

With regard to its content, *De raind hÉrenn* fits like a glove the political circumstances of the reigns of Mathgamain and Brian. A complete edition with a detailed linguistic and contextual analysis of the tract is necessary to substantiate this theory, but for now it is argued that we have identified a Dál Cais tract belonging to the period before the battle of Clontarf. This will serve as a basis for further investigation.

13. LUGAID LÁMDERG

We have seen that *De raind hÉrenn* has so many similarities with the Book of Thomond that we have to postulate a precursor or early version of the Book of Thomond which the author(s) of *De raind hÉrenn* used as a source, and which would also date from the period of Mathgamain and Brian. In *De raind hÉrenn* the conquests of Lugaid Mend are called 'the Rough Land of Lugaid Lámderg' (section D), an epithet otherwise not found in the Munster genealogies deriving from the Psalter of Cashel (see §9 above). In two poems about the origins of place-names the epithet Lámderg is also used, in both cases also in relation to the conquest of Thomond. The two are the only ones in the present known corpus of metrical *dindshenchas* which deal with Dál Cais.[126]

In the *dindshenchas* of Sliab nEchtga (Slieve Oughty, the northern border of Thomond) the poet Mac Liag asks the harper Illbreatach about the origin of Sliab nEchtga, and the latter is visited by the ghost of his former master Flann mac Lonáin (d. 896), who relates the lore about who gave their names to the place. This includes Lugaid Lámderg. Flann states that the warrior Finn (mac Cumaill) already prophesized the strength of the youth (*nert na n-óc*) from the south, and that although the plunder was with the Connachta, the

On Torna and his role as fosterfather, see further Jaski, *Early Irish kingship*, pp 162–9. At p. 164 I call Torna a 'politically neutral poet', but *De raind hÉrenn* clearly claims Torna for Dál Cais. This gives sources on this matter such as the poem *Temair Breg, baile na fian*, attributed to Cúán Ua Lothcháin (d. 1024), potentially a whole new edge. Another poem attributed to Cúán is at *CGG*, pp 54–6 §42. **125** Cf. *CGG*, p. 86 §57, where the Uí Chairpri are alarmed by the power of Mathgamain because 'they were in occupation of the territory of Clann Cormaic (Caiss), i.e. Caille Cormaic, from Oclan to Limerick, and from Cnámchoill to Luachair'. **126** Neither is in the collections of prose *dindshenchas*.

Munstermen would enjoy it. The hills form the border between Leth Cuinn and Leth Moga Nuadat. Flann praised the generous Dál Cais and recited a lay to a poor poet, and when Dál Cais heard it, the poor poet was amply rewarded. He then recites: 'Declare to Brian … he shall be high-king over martial Ireland'.[127]

In her study of the poetry attributed to Flann mac Lonáin, Jeanette Ubink dates this poem on linguistic grounds between the end of the tenth and beginning of the eleventh centuries, which seems to confirm the suggestion by others that Mac Liag himself was actually the poor poet and the composer.[128] In the section about Lorcán, the father of Cennétig, in the Book of Thomond Flann mac Lonáin plays an important role in a tale about a match of *fidchell* between Lorcán and Flann Sinna (king of Tara, 879–916).[129]

In the *dindshenchas* of Sliab nEchtga it is clear that the story of the 'coming of the youth from the south' and what follows, is unintelligible without its proper context. Part of this context can be found in the *dindshenchas* of Mag Femin (the plain to the south of Cashel), which is set out as a dialogue between Cummíne and Mac Dá Cherda.[130] It relates that Femen was once the dwelling place of Lugaid son of Óengus, who drove the Foreigners overseas and defeated the descendants of Iarél Glúnmár.[131] He subdued Ireland after he defeated the Connachta and Leth Cuinn in the battle of Luchut. 'The northern part of Munster, after its partition, is the southern part of his territory'. Lugaid Lámderg seized Munster, set its boundaries and had ships at sea. 'Seven kings held sway over Munster between Ailill (Ólumm) and Lugaid'. The thirty descendants of Corc who were kings were actually strangers in Cashel.[132] One notes that Lugaid has nothing to do with Mag Femin, the poem is simply a vehicle to claim Cashel and Thomond for Dál Cais. Thematically, it is closely related to *De raind hÉrenn*. The emphasis on ships is noteworthy, and the driving away of Foreigners perhaps foreshadows the development of this theme in the *Cogadh*.

The proper context for the two poems and *De raind hÉrenn* is found in the account of Lugaid Lámderg in the Book of Thomond.[133] It relates that Lugaid

127 *MD*, iii, pp 304–13 (Sliab nEchtga II), 531–5, only in LL and the Yellow Book of Lecan, and thus outside the main *dindshenchas* collections. **128** Jeanette Ubink, 'Poems attributed to Flann mac Lonáin, including a critical edition of *Maicni Echach ard a nglé*' (MA, Medieval (Celtic) Studies, Utrecht, 2015), pp 51–60, which includes the text and a new translation. It is digitally available via http://dspace.library. uu.nl/handle/1874/ 320467 (retrieved 4 June 2016). For the attribution to Mac Liag, see *MD*, iii, p. 531. **129** *LM*, pp 104–9, including a poem attributed to Flann mac Lonáin. **130** On these two figures, see Pádraig Ó Riain, *A dictionary of Irish saints* (Dublin, 2011), pp 243–5. **131** A forefather of the Ulaid, who play here a role similar to that of the Fir nOl nÉcmacht in D. **132** *MD*, iii, pp 200–3 (Mag Femin II), 512–13, found in R, LL, BB, Lec., etc. Compare the 27 kings of Cashel mentioned in *Bethú Phátraic*, §5 above. **133** *LM*, pp 78–82. Lugaid Lámderg is a name not found as a forefather in the collections of the genealogies of the saints (*CGSH*).

Lámderg won seven battles against the Connachta and killed seven of their kings with nothing but hirelings and youngsters (*amhsa agus giollanradh*) and won swordland (*feronn cloidhimh*) from Berna Trí Carpat at Carn Feradaig to Luchad and from Áth Bóraime to Cú Chulainn's Leap (cf. *De raind hÉrenn* sections A and D). In a short poem attributed to Cormac mac Cuillenáin, Luchut or Luchad is called Áth Luchaid (Kilkeedy near Tubber, in north Co. Clare), and it is added that Lugaid won this land from Eochaid mac Luchta.[134] Afterwards Lugaid took the hostages of Ireland, Alba, Britain and Saxony, and this is then followed by the *dindshenchas* of Mag Femin. Indeed, the precusor of the Book of Thomond may well have been the source from which the poem was entered into the *dindshenchas* collections.

The deeds of Lugaid seem to have become accepted as part of the pre-Christian history of Ireland. We meet him again in the tale of the death of the Munster king Crimthann mac Fidaig, who according to legend ruled Ireland before Niall Noígiallach. Lugaid Mend was the first to take Thomond by force, and hence it is called 'the Rough swordland of Lugaid Lámderg' (*Gairbfherand claidim Luigdech Laimdeirg*). Munster took Osraige as a compensation (*éraic*) for the killing of Eterscél (the father of Conaire Mór) and Thomond as the compensation for the killing of Crimthann mac Fidaig. But Thomond actually belongs to the Connachta by right, from Limerick to the river Drowes.[135] Here the tables are turned again, and Thomond is reclaimed by the Connachta by using the very tale Dál Cais employed to claim it for themselves.[136]

The use of material related to Lugaid Lámderg and other forefathers of Dál Cais is also found in *Cogadh Gáedhel re Gallaibh*. One long passage describes how Brian persuades Mathgamain not to seek peace with the oppressive 'Foreigners', and admonishes him that their forefathers would never have sought peace. Their grandfather Lorcán did not even submit to Máel Sechnaill mac Máele Ruanaid (king of Tara 846–62) for as much time as it would take to play a game of *fidchell* on the green of Mag Adair;[137] Lugaid Mend would never have yielded even a young hare as tribute to the people of Tlaman Tuathail, and gained seven battles over the Connachta, killed seven kings, and drove them with

134 The Éle and Uaithne, to the east of the Shannnon, were named after two daughters of Eochaid mac Luchta, *CGH*, p. 265 (155b44–51), cf. p. 332 (162g31), and were related to Iarél Glúnmár, the son of the Ulsterman Conall Cernach, *CGH*, p. 264 (155b38). 135 Whitley Stokes (ed.), 'The death of Crimthann son of Fidach, and the adventures of the sons of Eochaid Muigmedón', *RC*, 24 (1903), 172–207, at 186–8 §20 (BB and YBL). At 180 §10, Fiachra son of Eochaid takes the land from Connacht until Carn Feradaig. 136 Donnchadh Ó Corráin, 'Historical need and literary narrative' in D. Ellis Evans et al. (eds), *Proceedings of the Seventh International Congress of Celtic Studies … 1983* (Oxford, 1983), pp 141–58, at 145–6, dates it to *c.*1120, when Tairdelbach Ua Conchobair was undermining the power of Dál Cais in Thomond. 137 See *LM*, pp 104–6, where Máel Sechnaill's son Flann Sinna (king of Tara 879–916) plays *fidchell* at Mag Adair, which is chronologically more plausible. It is followed by a poem attributed to Flann mac Lonáin.

only hirelings and boys from Carn Feradaig to Áth Lucait.[138] And Cormac (Cass) fought eight battles in defence of Munster and Leth Moga.[139]

Although there is not a complete match between the *Cogadh* and the Book of Thomond, the similarities are unmistakable. The *Cogadh* even has a few mistakes which are not in the Book of Thomond, and the same applies to *De raind hÉrenn*. The most obvious explanation is that the author of this section of the *Cogadh* culled his information from a precursor of the Book of Thomond where the careers of the three kings were told in some detail. But there is more, for the triumphant campaign of Lugaid starts at Carn Feradaig, and thus he conquers Thomond as swordland and obtains freedom of taxation from the kings of Cashel. We have seen that according to *De raind hÉrenn* and the Book of Thomond the historical king Dímma (Superbus) obtained the same freedom after the battle of Carn Feradaig against the Connachta. It appears that the legend of Lugaid was partly informed by the deeds of Dímma.

Finally, we find excerpts of the Book of Thomond in the introduction to the Dál Cais genealogies in R4. The whole section begins with *Eoghan Mor mac Mogha Neit, tri meic lais*,[140] the same epithet of Mug Nuadat we find in *De raind hÉrenn* sections A and B in §11 above, and in the Book of Thomond. Other similarities with the latter tract, but also material unique to R4, testify of a complex tradition in which the Book of Thomond plays a central role.[141]

14. TRIPLE LUGAID

From the above we can conclude that the Book of Thomond played a pivitol role in the shaping of Lugaid Lámderg as a character in political narratives, which other sources used and further embellished. Contrary to his immediate predecessors, he is a figure of substance, and it probably the case therefore that the *Cogadh* uses Clann Lugaid or Síl Lugaid as an alternative term for Dál Cais, and particularly for the Northern Déisi.[142] According to the long version of the Dál Cais genealogies the latter descend from Lugaid, and not from his brothers Eógan, Dub Rois and Sescaid. BB adds that the Déisi Becc descend from these three,[143] but Lec misses this addition.[144] Yet at the end of the Dál

138 See *LM*, pp 78–9, which does not mention the part on Tlaman Tuathail, but has the rest of the details, and mentions more placenames as part of the territory Lugaid conquered. It is followed by the *dindshenchas* of Femen. 139 *CGG* has Corc instead of Cormac. See *LM*, p. 67, where the eight battles are also enumerated, including one won against the Danes. For the theme of freedom of taxation and right to alternation, see also *CGG*, p. 54 §51. 140 R4 30va1. 141 These similarities include R4 30vb12–15 = *LM*, p. 68.1–3; 30vb15–22 = *LM*, p. 71.9–15; 31ra5–19 = *LM*, p. 76.2–11. Note also 30va8–13 = *CGSH*, p. 36, §215.1; 30vb29–31 = *CGSH*, p. 39, §233. 142 *CGG*, pp 52 and 54 §41, 74 §51, 84 §57; cf. for example *LM*, p. 95: *cloinn Luighdheach Mind*. 143 BB 102ra3–6: *ata in Deis Beg* (*LM*, p. 294). 144 Lec 224va8–9.

Cais genealogies Lec has the same section about Lugaid and his three brothers under the heading *De hUib Rosa andso .i. In Des Deisceartach i nDail Chais*. Of Dub Rois's offspring there were fourteen kings who ruled the Déisi Bécc and fifty saints and other clergy – including one who dwelt at Saingil – who were blessed by Brénainn. The pedigree of Dub Rois's descendant Sóerbrethach is given, who is of the same generation as Brian's ancestor Anluan (16).[145] This section was probably part of the Psalter of Cashel of *c*.740, when the Southern Déisi were still powerful enough to make such claims, but was never updated afterwards. This agrees with the subservient status the Southern Déisi are accorded in *Bethu Phátraic* (see §5 above). In the annals of the late tenth and eleventh centuries a couple of dynasts of the Déisi Bécc are mentioned, having risen to some distinction under the aegis of Dál Cais of which they were now part.[146] It is clear that in this period Déisi Bécc and the Southern Déisi are terms used for the same people.

The genealogical records thus present us with a neat scheme in which the Northern and Southern Déisi are carefully separated, and they first enter the path of greatness once Lugaid Mend conquers Thomond. If other, earlier genealogical traditions existed, they have been surpassed by what the Psalter of Cashel in its last redaction of *c*.1015 presents us with. There seems to be one important exception, found at the end of the Dál Cais genealogies. It seems to be a regnal list of seven names starting with Énna Téith son of Conall. It is headed *In Déis Deiscirt hUa nÉndae*.[147] No Énna Téith is mentioned in the Dál Cais genealogies in R and LL, but BB, Lec and H include a section in which he also figures. I give the text of the Lecan Miscellany with the additions in H between brackets. It begins with Lugaid *alias* Delbáeth, son of Tál *alias* Cass, the eponymous ancestor of Dál Cais:

> *Delbaeth is e indara Lugaid a quo na .u. Dealbnai in cach du.*[148]
> *.U. meic Lugdach (meic Thail) .i. na da En(n)a .i. Enna Teith 7 Enda Airctheach;*[149] *in da Gno .i. Gno Mor 7 Gno Beg; 7 Dealbeath in mac aile Desi diarbo meic Beg, Art* (H: *hErc*), *Mac Reithi.*[150]

145 Lec 228vb15–vba37, also found at Lec 181vc13–46 (see Toirdhealbhach Ó Raithbheartaigh (ed.), *Genealogical tracts. Vol. 1* (Dublin, 1932), p. 181 §170); see also the text and translation in Mac Neill, 'Vita Tripartita', pp 37–8. **146** *AI* 982.3, 1058.4, cf. 1021.1; *CGG*, p. 92 §61. **147** *CGH*, p. 242 (153a49), also in LL, BB, Lec and H. Lec has Conall son of Eochu Ballderg, but no Énna is mentioned among the two sons of Conall at *CGH*, p. 236 (152b7). **148** Compare *CGH*, p. 235 (152b1), where among the sons of Cass is mentioned: *Delbáeth dano is é indara Lugaid at-berar sunn ó tát na cóic Delbna*. The 'second Lugaid' refers to the fact that there is another Lugaid son of Tál *alias* Cass. H 141Ad2–6 has: *Sil indara Lugaidh meic Cais .i. in Lugaidh nach Dealbaeth uair da airmemair Sil mBaedan roime*, cf. *CGH*, p. 235 (152a48) on the other Lugaid: *Lugaid a quo hUi Mael-Baetain*. Delbáeth also had a son named Báetan (BB 107rb21, Lec 220rc51, UM 32ca52; Dobbs, 'Ban-Shenchus', 224), so it is possible that the Lugaids were duplicated; see further below. **149** H gives his name as *Enna Airgnech* and *Enna Airgnig*. **150** H has after *Gno*

> *Enna Teith i crich na nDesi nDeiscirt (Enna Airgnech a crich na nDessa Tuaiscirt).*
> *Coic meic Enna Airctbich .i. Concraid, Dairi Tuidlech, Cormac, Condla, Cairpre.*[151]
>
> Delbáeth, he is the second Lugaid from whom are the five Delbna wherever they are.
> The five sons of Lugaid (son of Tál), i.e. the two Énnae, i.e. Énna Téith and Énna Airgdech; the two Gnó, i.e. Gnó Mór and Gnó Becc; and Dáelbaeth's other son was Dési whose sons were Becc, Erc, Mac Reithi.
> Énna Téith in the land of the Southern Déisi (Énna Airgdech in the land of the Northern Déisi).
> Five sons of Énna Airgdech, i.e. Conchrad, Dáire Tuidlech, Cormac, Condla, Cairpre.

We may assume that Énna Téith son of Conall is the brother of Énna Airgdech, son of Conall Echlúath, son of Lugaid Mend, whom we find in the early part of the Dál Cais genealogies.[152] Gnó Mór and Gnó Bécc are peoples settled to the west of Lough Corrib, where the most western branches of the Delbna were also situated.[153]

Most curious are Dési and his son Becc, who appear to present the eponymous ancestors of Déisi Becc, an image further strengthened by the settlement of Énna Téith among the Southern Déisi, in concordance with *In Déis Deiscirt hUa nÉndae* cited above, and that of Énna Airgdech among the Northern Déisi. The first part of the long version of the Dál Cais genealogies states that Énna Airgdech son of Lugaid Mend was younger than his brother Cass and that the Uí Énna and the Uí Erc in Osraige descend from him.[154] The latter may be connected to the Erc son of Dési in the section above. Nevertheless, the Becc son of Dési is not an eponymous ancestor but an imposter. He is actually a mistake for the saint and prophet Becc mac Dé, best known from saga literature in connection with the death of Diarmait mac Cerbaill in 565.[155] This is his pedigree in the genealogical collections of Irish saints:

Mor: Deissi cuius filius Bec, hErc, Mac Reithi. **151** Lec 180rb49–rc11 (with mistakes edited and translated in Ó Raithbheartaigh, *Gen. tracts*, p. 168 §139) and H 141Ad6–20. Lec 228vb27–35 has the same section except for the first part, and in a different order. It also has Erc instead of Art and adds after Cairpri *Casgiugrand*, similar to the section at Lec 181vc50–vd9 (Ó Raithbheartaigh, *Gen. Tracts*, pp 181–2 §171); see also R4 31rb8–19. **152** *LM*, p. 294. **153** Ó Corráin, *Normans*, p. 14 and the map at p. 11. **154** BB 102va7–8, with minor variants at Lec 224va11–13. I take *in n-uisair* to mean *in n-ósair*, 'the youngest'. *LM*, p. 294 reads *i Muscraighe*. **155** Ó Riain, *Dictionary*, pp 90–1.

Bec m. De Druad m. Gnoe (m. Mair) m. Lugdach m. Dallain m. Bresail m. Mane m. Neil Noigiallaig.
Nó: Bec m. De Druad m. Noe m. Conaill Echlúaith m. Lugdach Mind di Mumain.[156]

The first reference is corrupt, for Lugaid son of Dallán son of Bresal belongs to the Uí Maine in southern Connacht,[157] not to the Cenél Maine of Tethba of the Uí Néill. The territories of both dynasties were surrounded by those of the Delbna. The second reference agrees with the regular Dál Cais genealogies.[158] What we see is that there are two different traditions, one with Gnó Mór son of Lugaid Delbáeth and one with Nóe son of Conall Echlúath son of Lugaid Mend. In the preceding sections we have seen that Énna Téith and Énna Aigdech, brothers of Gnó Mór, are also either sons of Lugaid Delbáeth or of Conall Echlúath son of Lugaid Mend. Hence Nóe derives from Gnó.

The connection with Lugaid Delbáeth can be further explored in the Delbna genealogies, *Cóir anmann* and the *dindshenchas* on Loch Lugborta.[159] They all refer to the story in which Lugaid mac Táil is banished from his lands by his daughter and her husband, the druid Trat, the eponym of the Tradraige (south Co. Clare). In the lands of Cenél Fiachach, in the southwest of Mide, he kindles a fire (*áeth*), which has a peculiar form (*delb*), and its smoke sends his five sons into different directions, from whom the five Delbna descend. Their names may differ. Gnó Mór, Gnó Becc and Baetán are always among them, the other two being either Énna Airgdech, Énna Téith (who settled among the Northern and Southern Déisi) or Anlenn and Aindiled.[160] As has been noted, according to the Dál Cais genealogies Tál had two sons named Lugaid, Lugaid Delbáeth and Lugaid, the ancestor of the Uí Maíl Baetáin or Síl mBaetáin. The Delbna genealogies contain a late poem in which the seven peoples of Delbna descend from Lugaid Delbáeth, while his brother Lugaid Lannglan has five sons: two Gnó, two Énna and Baetán, from whom the Uí Maíl Baetáin of Munster descend.[161]

The triplication of Lugaid and duplications of Énna Airgdech and Becc son of Dé(si) are nothing unusual in the Irish medieval genealogical records, but in this specific case the partial overlap between the Dál Cais and Delbna genealogies is of interest. It seems to have been the result of the forging of an artificial genealogical relationship between the two peoples, and if the use of the term Northern Déisi instead of Dál Cais is anything to go by, this

156 *CGSH*, p. 6 §21.1–2. I follow the edition, apart from the addition in brackets, which is in two of the four manuscripts; see also R4 31r20–28. **157** *CGH*, pp 172–3 (145f8, 28). **158** *CGH*, p. 235 (152a55): *Nóe a quo Bec mac Déi*; *LM*, p. 295. **159** BB 107rc20–rd54, Lec 220va1–vb36; Ó Muraíle, *Leabhar mór*, ii, pp 632–44, §654.1–659.11; Arbuthnot, *Cóir anmann*, i, pp 95 and 133 §72 (CA2, dated to the late twelfth century, p. 72); *MD*, iv, pp 278–80. **160** Cf. *CGH*, pp 170–1 (145d34, 54). **161** Ó Muraíle, *Leabhar mór*, ii, pp 638–42 §657.1–658.8.

happened in the early tenth century at the latest. Further investigation in this material may yield some more indications as to when this took place.

15. SPLITTING UP

The discussion above raises questions about the historical accuracy of the Dál Cais genealogies beyond the legendary ancestors from Conall Corc to Conall Echlúath who connects them with the Eóganachta. We have to consider this as fiction, but the dearth of earlier traditions makes it difficult to connect Dál Cais or Northern Déisi to another population group. Of course, they are usually said to belong to the Déisi Muman. However, there is no clear link between the genealogies of the Déisi Muman and the Déisi Bécc or Dál Cais. It is wrong to assume that Uí Rosa of Déisi Muman were the same as the Uí Rosa of the Southern Déisi, for they were settled in different lands (the former in Brega) and their descendants have different names.[162] In the various versions of the Old-Irish tale 'The Expulsion of the Déisi' no mention is made of the Déisi Bécc or their branches.[163] Although it may be that the lands of the Déisi along the eastern border of Munster shared a common name and history in the remote past, it does not follow that the peoples that were settled there in the sixth and seventh centuries were necessarily related to each other. Perhaps research into the DNA of the Dál Cais families may throw some light on this matter.[164]

In the Dál Cais genealogies, their eponymous ancestor is Cass, a byname of Tál. According to a late version of the *Banshenchas* he was a son of Conall Echlúath and his wife Coirpthe, daughter of Eochu Muigmedón, and so the sister of Niall Noígiallach and his brothers.[165] *Cóir anmann* relates that Conall Echlúath (lit. 'Horse-swift') was so called from the horses (*ech*) which he drove (*do luaid*) when he was young. Few nicknames in this collection are less heroic, and obviously the origin of the name was unknown. Similarly, we are told that

162 See Mac Neill, 'Vita Tripartita', 38, on this theory. He is followed by Paul MacCotter, 'Túath, manor and parish: kingdom of Fir Maige, cantred of Fermoy', *Peritia*, 22–23 (2011–12), 224–74, at 260–1. Others take this for granted, such as Ryan, 'Brian Boruma', 355–6; Byrne, *Irish kings*, p. 180. **163** Not even in Meyer, 'The Expulsion', 122–30, which contains a long list of peoples who belonged to the Déisi or settled within their territories, although one may note the nine sons of Blat, from whom are the Blatraige, at 126 §23 and 134 §27. On the Uí Fhir Gair of the Déisi Muman among the Southern Déisi, see §5 above. **164** See D.E. Wright, 'A set of distinctive marker values defines a Y-STR signature for Gaelic Dalcassian families', *Journal of Genetic Genealogy*, 5 (2009), 1–7; Bart Jaski, 'Medieval Irish genealogies and genetics' in Seán Duffy (ed.), *Princes, prelates and poets in medieval Ireland. Essays in honour of Katharine Simms* (Dublin, 2013), pp 3–17, at p. 16; see also Catherine Swift, 'Interlaced scholarship: genealogies and genetics in twenty-first-century Ireland' in Duffy (ed.), *Princes, prelates and poets*, pp 18–31. **165** Dobbs, 'Ban-Shenchus', 179 (Lec) and 215 (UM); Conall's father Lugaid is said to be 'of the Déisi (Bécc)'

Cass received his name from his ancestor Cormac Cass ('the Swift') or Cás ('the Cruel'). Cass's nickname was Mac Táil ('Son of Adze'), because he was fostered by a wright (*sáir*).[166] If anything, these late, artificial and unimaginative explanations serve to inderline that these three were without standing in early saga literature, unlike many of their contemporaries from the Eóganachta.

Cass is credited with thirteen sons, of whom four left progeny which were to rise to distinction in Thomond: Blat (8) gave his name to Uí Blait and Caissín to Uí Chaisséne; Óengus Cenn Nathrach was the ancestor of Cenél Fermaic and Óengus Cenn Aittin of Clann Iffernáin. We find the first three names reflected in the later medieval cantreds of Omilid east of the Shannon, Ocassin in the middle of Thomond, and Kilnaverik further west, almost as far as the coast.[167] Such territorial names are often based on a historical ancestor, although this does not necessarily mean that the above genealogical scheme is accurate. Yet it should be noted that the Dál Cais genealogies are on the whole chronologically consistent. This can be illustrated by looking at the main divisions of the Uí Blait. These descend from two sons of Cáirthenn Finn son of Blat, of whom Óengus (10) was the oldest. The eponymous ancestors of the main branches and territories of the Uí Óengussa, the Uí Echthigirn, the Chernaig and Uí Róngaile all lived in the same period, around 750. They are all fourteen or fifteen generations removed from Ailill Ólumm (cf. §9 above and table 1.2). This also applies to Tairdelbach, who gave his name to Uí Thairdelbaig, a descendant from Óengus's younger brother Eochu Ballderg. And the same goes for the eponymous ancestors of Cenél Fermaic and Clann Iffernáin mentioned above, and those of Uí Dobarchon and Clann Urthuile of Uí Chaisséne.

That the main dynastic and territorial divisions happened in the same period, even in approximately the same generation, is surely related to the rapid expansion of the Northern Déisi in exactly this period (§4 above). We see the same process in the time of Brian (21), whose descendants took the surname Ua Briain, and similarly surnames such as Ua Dedaid of Cenél Fermaic and Ua Cuinn of Clann Iffernáin were named after his contemporaries. Although dynastic names and surnames were also formed at other intervals, the formation of the main dynastic and territorial divisions happened at decisive nodes in Dál Cais history. The Dál Cais genealogies allow us to assess this process in some detail, more so than with most other dynasties, and that makes their study all the more important. Most individuals are not mentioned in other historical records, but by generation count we can extrapolate in which period they lived, and on the whole it appears that the Dál

(*do nDes Big*; *do nDéis*); R4 31va17–23. **166** Arbuthnot, *Cóir anmann*, ii, pp 48 and 121–2 §§ 167–9 (CA3, dated to the (first half of the) thirteenth century, i, p. 72); *LM*, p. 294; cf. R4 31va10–14 on Tál. Tál is a rare name, and was mainly current in Munster, *CGH*, p. 741. **167** Paul MacCotter, *Medieval Ireland: territorial, political and economic divisions* (Dublin, 2008), pp 191–6, 260.

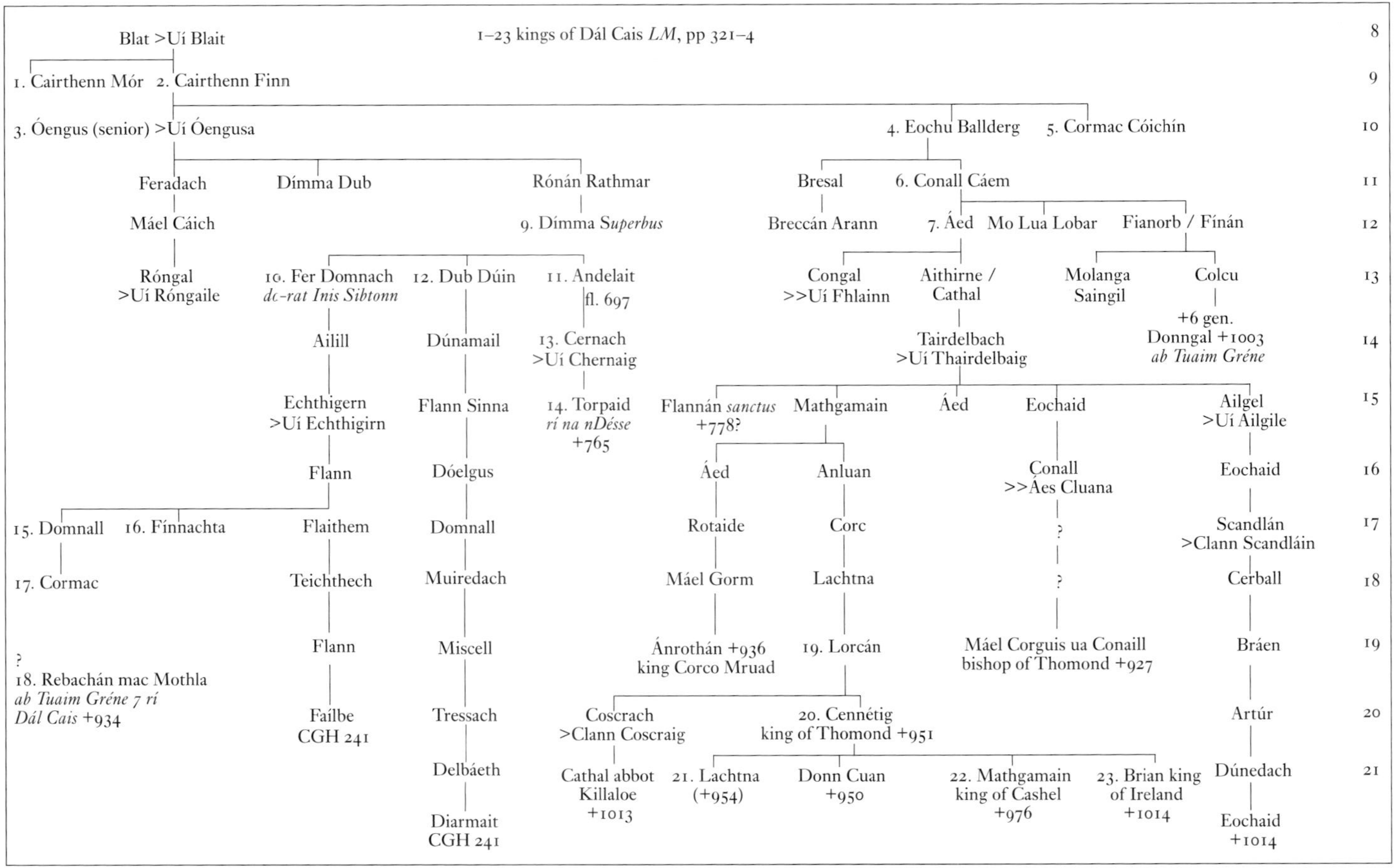

Table 1.2. Uí Blait

Cais genealogies are accurate from at least the eighth century onwards, and those of Uí Óengussa even from at least the seventh century onwards, as they agree with other historical evidence. It was the merit of Brian and his scholars that these records were collected, updated and passed on to future generations.

16. ENCOUNTERS WITH SAINTS

Although the secular genealogies are usually quite sober affairs, merely listing who is related to whom and enumerating pedigrees, occasionally they give some extra information about a person's title or deeds. The Dál Cais genealogies contain references to a number of persons who are also listed in the collections of the genealogies of the Irish saints. Some of these figure in hagiography, although not in the saints' Lives which we can date to the reign of Brian or earlier, in which references to Thomond are extremely rare. The story about Eochu/Eochaid Ballderg in *Bethu Phátraic* is a notable exception, but it does illustrate that such information can be related to ecclesiastical and secular politics.

This generally also applies to information about the Dál Cais saints in the sources. It is therefore important to assess their position in the genealogical collections, as the case of Becc mac Dé has already shown. Another case in point is the genealogy of Comgán of Glenn Uisen (Killeshin, Co. Laois), who is regarded as a grandson of Seimne or Temne son of Fer Corb (3).[168] There is no clear connection between him and Dál Cais, except for a charter from the reign of Muirchertach Ua Briain (1086–1119) which discusses a grant which the community of Killeshin had made to Dál Cais in the past.[169] Of a different cloth is Mac Lai(s)re, either a son of Cainnech son of Blat or Conall Echlúath, who may simply be a local manifestation of the better known Molaise of Devenish.[170] An exceptional case is formed by the pedigree of Bishop Martán of Cúil Breccain in Uí Fhailgi, who even heads the section of Munster saints in LL. Martán is also associated with Donaghmore (Co. Laois). His long pedigree attaches him to Ross son of Colmán son of Cáelchu son of Loarn son of Ruad, who was the son of either a further unknown Corc son of Lugaid Mend (5) or of Cass (7). By generation count Martán would have lived in the tenth century. The version of his pedigree in *Leabhar Breacc* adds that Cáelchu was the first hostage of the men of Munster, whose family lived at Ross (na Ríg) at Tara.[171] This is repeated in a *dindshenchas* of Tara, which also mentions

168 *LM*, p. 294; *CGSH*, p. 39 §233. **169** R.I. Best, 'An early monastic grant in the Book of Durrow', *Ériu*, 10 (1926–8), 135–42; Richard Sharpe, 'Dispute settlement in early Ireland: a preliminary inquiry' in Wendy Davies and Paul Fouracre (eds), *The settlement of disputes in early medieval Europe* (Cambridge, 1986), pp 169–90; Ó Riain, *Dictionary*, pp 220–1. **170** *CGH*, p. 235 (153a49); *CGSH*, p. 34 §202. **171** *CGSH*, p. 32 §190; Ó Riain, *Dictionary*, pp 449–50, who also discusses Fróechnat, a daughter of Martán's father Dúnán

Cáelchu's Grave and his great-grandfather Cormac Cass (1).[172] This is a remarkable connection between Tara and a supposed Dál Cais saint from Leinster, and it may derive from Brian's time, as in most manuscripts the poem is attributed to Cúán ua Lothcháin (d. 1024).[173]

Among the grandsons of Cass we find an undoubtedly historical saint: Mainchín of Mendroichet (d. 652). He is named in the Hiberno-Latin tract *On the miracles of sacred scripture*, written in 655, and also appears in the seventh-century Commentary of the Catholic Epistles and in a Commentary of the Gospels of Mark, in both cases together with one Breccán, perhaps Breccán of the Aran Islands whom we shall meet later on. In the latter tract Mainchín is also associated with Laidcenn, member of the Alltraige, abbot of Clonfertmulloe, author of several Hiberno-Latin tracts, who died in 664. Mainchín may also have acted as successor of Nessán of Mungarit, the saint mentioned in *Bethú Phátraic*.[174] In the middle of the seventh century Fer Domnach (13) of Uí Óengussa gave Inis Sibthonn to Mainchín and Crónán, and was blessed in return. This is King's Island in Limerick where Saint Munchin's church is situated.[175] Mainchín is duly equipped with a chronologically impossible pedigree which states that his father was Sétna (8) son of Cass.[176]

The saintly activity in the Limerick area followed on the battle at Carn Feradaig and the push of the Northern Déisi into Thomond, orchestrated by the Uí Óengussa, the descendants from Óengus (10), the oldest son of Cáirthenn Finn mac Blait. Yet among the latter's four sons the genealogies record the descendants of Eochu Ballderg (10) first, because he was the ancestor of Uí Thairdelbaig.[177] In the short version of the Dál Cais genealogies the records of the Uí Óengussa appear after those of the Uí Thairdelbaig, except the records of the Uí Róngaile, who are found at the end, even after the Uí Chaisséne, Cenél Fermaic and Clann Iffernáin. In the long version all the Uí Óengussa are placed at the end – a significant difference, as we shall see.[178]

Derg, *CGSH*, p. 78 §647. **172** *MD*, i, p. 24. **173** *MD*, i, p. 62 cf. at n. 124 above. **174** Máirín Ní Dhonnchadha, 'The beginnings of vernacular Irish literary tradition', *L'Irlanda e gli irlandesi nell'alto medioevo: Spoleto, 16–21 aprile 2009* (Spoleto, 2010), pp 533–96, at 587–91 (on Mainchín and Lugaid), with references; Ó Riain, *Dictionary*, pp 426–7. On the settlement in Thomond of the Uí Chonairge of the Alltraige, to which Laidcenn belonged, see §4 above. **175** *CGH*, p. 240 (153a29–31); *LM*, p. 295, which adds that Sétna's daughters resided in Cill na nIngen, 'Church of the Nuns' (cf. *CGSH*, p. 160 §711.88); on Crónán of Tuaim Gréine (cf. p. 21 above), see Ó Riain, *Dictionary*, pp 235–6; Ní Dhonnchadha, 'Beginnings', pp 581–3. **176** *CGH*, p. 235 (152a54); *CGSH*, p. 34 §203; Ó Riain, *Dictionary*, pp 417–18. For Liadan daughter of Diarmait son of Duí son of Cáirthenn Mór (*alias* Cáirthenn Finn of Dub?) son of Blat, see *CGSH* pp 33 §198, 159 §711.28, cf. *CGH*, pp 235 (152b2) and 242 (153a50); *LM*, pp 320 and 321 (regnal list); Ó Riain, *Dictionary*, p. 395. **177** As this and subsequent references show, Eochu/Eochaid Ballderg could never have been a contemporary of Patrick as *Bethu Phátraic* relates, see §5 above; but *CGSH*, p. 39 §230 R1 adds: *neach dobaist Patraic.* **178** *LM*, pp 296, 316–20; *CGH*, pp 240–1 (153a25–49), 245 (153b27–39).

A third son of Cáirthenn Finn, Mechair, is listed as the father of Sinech, the mother of Óengus Tuile, who was perhaps a saint.[179]

The fourth son of Cáirthenn Finn is Cormac Cóichín. This Cormac is mentioned in the regnal list of Dál Cais, and in a separate genealogical section we read that he was cursed by St Odrán of the Múscraige because he did not want to grant them a truce for three days and three nights. Cormac's offspring was deprived of the lordship as a result.[180] Eochu Ballderg's sons are Conall Cáem (11) and Bresal, the father of the aforementioned Breccán of the Aran Islands.[181] The long recension states that Conall was blessed by Rúadán of Lorrha (d. 584) in the house of Cairpre Cromm, king of Munster. The same separate genealogical section mentioned above adds that Cairpre's son Áed Fland Cathrach even became the only one of the Eóganachta to be recognized as king of Thomond. He also appears in the regnal list of Dál Cais.[182] Yet in the long version of the genealogies Conall Cáem's son Áed (12) was the first of Dál Cais to go to Cashel, where he took Áed Dub mac Crimthainn (the father of Faílbe Flann) as hostage. He was also blessed by Brénainn of Clonfert. This seems to rely on the Book of Thomond, where several other saints even join the action. And when Áed takes the kingship of Cashel, it is remarked that the Eóganacht historians do not record him.[183] It is clear that this mainly serves to bolster the usual Dál Cais political rhetoric about their claims to Cashel.

17. CHURCH AND DYNASTY

The genealogies credit Conall (Cáem) with two sons, Áed, grandfather of Tairdelbach (14), and Fiannorb.[184] Yet later we find the pedigree of Mo Langa Saingil, where he is named as a son of Fínán (12) son of Conall, to which the long version adds that the last was the son of Eochu Ballderg.[185] According to the genealogies of the saints, Mo Langa lived five generations later, as he

179 This applies equally to some other names, for example, Lasair daughter of Brénainn Bán mac Blait (*LM*, pp 295, 311). **180** *LM*, pp 322, 324; Lec 229rc32–42; Ó Riain, *Dictionary*, p. 519. **181** *CGH*, p. 236 (152b7); *LM*, p. 296; *CSGH*, p. 57 §378; Ó Riain, *Dictionary*, pp 112–13; but differently identified in Ní Dhonnchadha, 'Beginnings', pp 576, 589. For Cumman Cadan son of Cáelchu son of Ramann son of Eochu Ballderg, see *CGSH*, p. 53 §330 (with a reference to a hair given to the king of Dál Cais after he had taken hostages from the king of Cashel); Ó Riain, *Dictionary*, p. 243. **182** *LM*, p. 297, cf. p. 302; Lec 229rc43–va5; Ó Riain, *Dictionary*, pp 541–4. **183** *LM*, pp 296 and 86–92, with at p. 88 *gin go n-áirmhid senchadha Eoganacht é.* At this juncture the Book of Thomond moves to the period of Feidlimid mac Crimthainn (d. 847), with only one section devoted to the dealings between Dímma and Faílbe Flann: see *LM*, pp 92–4; cf. §11 above (*De raind hÉrenn* section E). **184** *CGH*, p. 236 (152b7); *LM*, pp 296–7. The long version of the Dál Cais genealogies mentions a third son of Conall (Cáem), Mo Lua Lobur ('Leper'), a pupil of Mo Chua (Mochuda or Carthach of Lismore, d. 639), *CGSH*, p. 148 §707.563; Ó Riain, *Dictionary*, p. 493. **185** *CGH*, p. 239 (153a21); *LM*, p. 305; cf. §5 above.

is considered as the son of Fínán son of Eochu son of Ailgel son of Tairdelbach.[186] The confusion arises from the ambiguity in the short version of the Dál Cais genealogies, which follows directly on the notion that Eochaid son of Ailgel had seven sons, of whom, however, only one is mentioned. In the short version they are not referred to. The record of the descendants of Fínán's son Colgu breaks off abruptly, and a considerable section is missing which is retained (with updates) in the long version.[187] In the long version the records on Clann Ailgile are also intruded by those of the descendants of Fínán son of Conall son of Eochu Ballderg, and those of Congal son of Áed son of Conall, after which the recording of the seven sons of Eochaid mac Ailgile starts anew – but without a Fínán being named among them.[188]

The conclusion has to be that the long version is the more genuine of the two, and that Fiannorb son of Conall Cáem became Fínán, the great-grandson of Tairdelbach. Of itself it is perhaps a minor matter to know to whom Mo Langa was held to be related, but it should be noted that the mistake in the genealogies of the saints is shared by all the manuscript witnesses. This means that all of them directly or indirectly drew on the common ancestor of the short version of the Dál Cais genealogies, from which R, LL and H all derive.

This is further confirmed by the record that immediately precedes that of Mo Langa in the main manuscripts of the genealogies of the saints, which gives the pedigree of Feidelm and Rónnait as daughters of Rónán son of Óengus Oll son of Urchlosach (16) son of Ailgel son of Tairdelbach, etc.[189] The two women are indeed the daughters of Rónán son of Óengus in the short version, which follows right on the section which names Aurchlosach son of Ailgel. However, no Óengus is mentioned among the direct descendants of Ailgel.[190] The long version makes clear that the Óengus in question is actually the eponymous ancestor of the Uí Óengussa, and that the two women are the sisters of Dímma *Superbus* (12). Their uncle Dímma Dub, brother of Rónán (Rathmar), is also recognized as a saint, and may even appear in hagiography.[191] With their rise in the seventh century, the Uí Óengussa not only interacted with several saints in their vicinity, but also produced a couple themselves. We shall see that the same thing happened among the Uí Thairdelbaig.

It is exactly at the records about the father of Tairdelbach that matters become somewhat confused, again between the short and long version. The versions in R and LL about the decendants of Áed (12) run as follows:

> *Tri meic Aeda: Conall* (LL: *Congal*) *et Aitheirne et Cairthenn.*
> *Dungalach mac Muirgaile meic Cairthind meic Aeda.*

186 *CGSH*, p. 34 §205. 187 This happens at *m. Allamain* at *CGH*, p. 240 (153a24). The part missing corresponds to *LM*, pp 306.5–312.2. 188 At *LM*, p. 307. 189 *CGSH*, p. 34 §204. 190 *CGH*, p. 240 (153a27). 191 *CGSH*, p. 38 §220; Ó Riain, *Dictionary*, p. 266.

Tairdelbach mac Aitreine (LL: *Athirni*) *meic Aeda.*
Da mac Congaile .i. Toltanach 7 Aurchlosach.
Flann mac Aurchlosaich (omitted in LL).[192]

In the first line in the long version the second son of Áed is called Cathal, in the third line Tairdelbach is still a son of Athirne, but then it is repeated that Cathal had one son, Tairdelbach.[193] In several other sources the father of Tairdelbach is called Cathal or Cadlae (gen. Cadléne), so the difference has clearly influences on other sources.[194] On the face of it, the short version is the more consistent, and may in this case preserve the more original reading. It continues with quite detailed records on the descendants of Flann, until they terminate in the same generation as Brian Bóraime (21). The long version only notes that the Uí Fhlainn descend from him, and their records are given after the main branches of Uí Thairdelbaig have all been discussed.[195] Again we see that the long version gives more prominence to the direct forefathers of Brian Bóraime.

Among the sons of Tairdelbach (14) two saints are mentioned, of whom Flannán *sanctus* is the best known. He is associated with the main ecclesiastical foundation of Dál Cais, Killaloe (Cill Da Lua). This was originally a foundation of Mo Lua, and we have seen that a number of Dál Cais saints and their foundations have connections with Mo Lua, who himself belonged to the Corco Óchae, who were settled in the area between West Munster, Cíarraige and Uí Fhidgeinte. This is a matter which deserves further study, as it may be of significance in understanding the earliest ecclesiastical connections of the Northern Déisi. Flannán may be the Flannán of Cell Aird (Killard, on the Atlantic coast of Corco Baiscinn) who died in 778. His brother Áed(án) reputedly founded a church in Leinster.[196] From Flannán's brother Eochaid descend the Áes Cluana we have discussed at §7 above in connection with the bishops of Thomond of the tenth century. It seems that at some stage they settled in the area to the south of Limerick.[197] From another brother of Flannán, Mathgamain, descend Cennétig (d. 951) and his brother Coscrach, whose offspring became one of the most influential ecclesiastical families among Dál Cais.[198]

192 *CGH*, p. 236 (152b8–11), cf. *LM*, p. 297. **193** BB 102vb9–15, Lec 224vb32–8. **194** *CGG*, p. 58 §43, *LM*, p. 329: *m. Cathail*; *CGH*, p. 250 (154a52), *m. Caidléne*, (R and LL), *m. Cathail* (Lec), in the long pedigree of Muirchertach Ua Briain (d. 1119). In LL the father of Áed is called Conall Echlúath, a mistake also found in some records listed at *CGSH*, p. 39 §230, where *m. Caidleni / Cathail / Atrein* are all variants. **195** *LM*, p. 306–7. These are the same Uí Fhlainn who killed Brian's brother Lachtna in 954 (see §7 above), and if the order of names and the place they occupy in the short version is anything to go by, they were the senior branch among the sons of Áed. **196** *CGSH*, p. 39, §230; *AI*, 778.1; Ó Riain, *Dictionary*, pp 346–9, and 490–3 on Mo Lua. **197** MacCotter, *Medieval Ireland*, pp 187, 260. **198** As discussed in detail in Ó Corráin, 'Dál Cais'.

18. CONCLUSION

Tracing the rise of Dál Cais involves a critical scrutiny of all the available sources, which often give only snippits of information about a complex process that covered about four centuries. From obscure and apparently humble beginnings, the northern branch of the Déisi Bécc was at the forefront of the struggles between Munster and Connacht (and later with the Uí Néill), and this gave them the opportunity to enter the strategically important area of Thomond, which they were to dominate from the middle of the eighth century onwards. In this period all their main dynastic branches settled in the territories they were to hold for centuries to come.

This first stage was completed under the leadership of the Uí Óengussa. It was their king Dímma *Superbus*, as we now may deduce, who in 629 won the decisive battle at Carn Feradaig. Situated at the boundary between the Southern and Northern Déisi, and between Munster and Thomond, this landmark is mentioned time and again in the historical and narrative sources. The Uí Óengussa were to produce overkings who endorsed *Cáin Fhuithirbe* and *Cáin Adomnáin* on behalf of the Northern Déisi, who produced saints and donated foundations to other saints. They successfully established a semi-independent kingdom, not unlike the Osraige to the east of Munster, and gained recognition thereof from the kings of Cashel. It has been argued that these gave them freedom from taxation, explained by kinship with the Eóganachta and a past right to alternation in the kingship of Munster.

In the early ninth century Feidlimid mac Crimthainn, member of the Céli Dé, co-promulgator of the Law of Patrick in Munster, and plunderer of Clonmacnoise and Delbna Ethra, may have been supported by Dál Cais in his campaigns. A similar thing happened during the brief reign of Cormac mac Cuilennáin, a name that looms large in Dál Cais sources, and who was of course one of the redactors of the Psalter of Cashel. The Book of Thomond actually relates that Cormac obtained a large fleet from Dál Cais with which Lough Ree was plundered and the hostages of Mide and Connacht were obtained. Cormac even spent Christmas in Clonmacnoise.[199] This no doubt refers to the raid recorded in the annals in 907, and if this is accurate information, we have an important clue as to what further stimulated the advance of Dál Cais. This applies in particular to the Uí Thairdelbaig, whose members were present at the great battle in which Cormac was defeated and killed, and who were also given a prominent place in *Bethú Phátraic* of *c*.895. While the Uí Óengussa suffered from the presence of the Limerick Vikings, the Uí Thairdelbaig extended their lordshiop over Corco Mruad and delivered the first bishops of Thomond mentioned in the annals. After the interregnum of Rebachán (d. 934), whose son, ruler of Uí Chormaic, was killed by the son

199 *LM*, pp 109–10.

of Lorcán of Uí Thairdelbaig, the kingship was theirs. Lorcán's son Cennétig enters the ranks of the major players of the Irish political stage. He is involved in high-status marriage alliances and is active on the Shannon further north. Profiting from the disarray among the Uí Néill and Eóganachta, he establishes himself as king of Thomond. His son Mathgamain, once thwarted in the north, takes the kingship of Cashel and sets his dynasty on the road to further succes.

The spectacular rise of Dál Cais in the tenth century was mainly due to the rise of Uí Thairdelbaig, and they exploited the creation of Dál Cais as a new dynastic identity to the fullest. It is during the reigns of Mathgamain and his brother Brian that the literary propaganda-machine kicks in. It has been argued that the re-editing and updating of the Psalter of Cashel, including the insertion of *De raind hÉrenn*, the stories about Lugaid Lámderg, and the compilation of an early version of the Book of Thomond, were all (nearly) completed during Brian's reign. In all these sources emphasis is placed on the same items: freedom of taxation for Thomond, right to alternation in the kingship of Cashel, the delimination of a territorial kingdom and references to the division of Ireland by Mug Nuadat (Eógan Taídlech, but now also called Eógan Mór), a typology of this division in 997. If it is indeed true that this took place under Brian's guidance, it is one of the most intensive periods of genealogical recording and literary (re)creation ever witnessed in Ireland under a single king. It stimulated a continuation of these activities in generations to come, including the development of a whole new narrative of the pre-Christian past of Munster, cumulating in the texts such as *Cath Maige Léna* on the career of Eógan Mór (Mug Nuadat). And even within Brian's time we see that a number of poems of Cúán ua Lothcháin already accord Dál Cais a place in the new scheme of things.

Much of this argument is based on a detailed assessment of the Dál Cais genealogies. The acceptance of my theory depends on the acknowledgment that these were updated in the Psalter of Cashel in Brian's time (in their final main redaction shortly after his death at Clontarf in 1014), that the long version generally represents this redaction best (including the artifical pedigree from Cormac Cass to Cass), that it contained *De raind hÉrenn*, and that this tract was based on an early version of the Book of Thomond. This is based on textual evidence and the conclusion that the content of the *De raind hÉrenn* fits the concerns during the reigns of Mathgamain and Brian best.

We can also approach this from the other side. We have to take the date of *c.*1130 as the latest possible limit of the writing of *De raind hÉrenn*, since this is the date of R. It should be noted that R lists the pedigrees of the kings of Munster in a separate section, which follows a different textual tradition than the Dál Cais genealogies proper, and runs until Muirchertach, who reigned with some intervals from 1086 to 1119. Hence a possible insertion of *De raind* *hÉrenn* into the common core of the short version could only have taken place during his reign at the latest. This is confirmed by the fact that the *Cogadh* already uses information set out in the Book of Thomond, just like *De raind hÉrenn*. However, *De raind hÉrenn* lacks the overblown literary style we find in the *Cogadh*, and indeed in the Book of Thomond in its present form, perhaps a sign that it was redacted at the same time as the *Cogadh*. *De raind hÉrenn* is also concerned with dynasties who by Muirchertach's time were relatively unimportant. Finally, there are no clear signs of a Munster redaction in the Dál Cais genealogies which can be assigned to *c.*1100.

This said, the differences between the short and long versions of the Dál Cais genealogies need further investigation, as do *De raind hÉrenn* and the Book of Thomond. This last tract especially deserves a thorough analysis, in which its relationship with the *Cogadh* and *De raind hÉrenn* should be explored further. This is beyond the boundaries of the present contribution, but it might give us a true appreciation of the literary activities which Brian stimulated in order to account for his dynasty's extraordinary, not to say legendary, success.

Hunting for the genetic legacy of Brian Boru in Irish historical sources

CATHERINE SWIFT

> Having won an English chariot from an Italian gentleman at play, my uncle had our arms painted on the panels in a more splendid way than ever (surmounted, as we were descended from the ancient kings) with an Irish crown of the most splendid size and gilding. I had this crown in lieu of a coronet engraved on a large amethyst signet-ring worn on my forefinger; and I don't mind confessing that I used to say the jewel had been in my family for several thousand years, having originally belonged to my direct ancestor, his late Majesty, King Brian Boru or Barry. I warrant the legends of the Heralds' College are not more authentic than mine was.[1]

In his travels in Ireland in 1842, Thackeray followed the course of the Shannon upriver from Tarbert to Limerick and then travelled through Clare to Galway, visiting 'a decent little library' in Ennis where he bought 'six volumes of works strictly Irish'. As he describes them subsequently, 'these yellow-covered books are prepared for the people chiefly' and included tales of a highwayman entitled *Adventures of Mr James Freeny*, legends in *Hibernian Tales*,[2] and 'the lamentable tragedy of the "Battle of Aughrim" writ in the most doleful Anglo-Irish verse'. He does not refer explicitly in his *Irish sketchbook* to Brian Boru but it seems fair to assume that his description of Barry Lyndon's ancestry was based, at least in part, on stories he had heard when travelling through Thomond or, perhaps, even elsewhere in Ireland. Certainly his views on Irish pretensions to nobility, as expressed in the *Sketchbook*, can be scathing:

> There is no aristocracy in Dublin. Its magnates are tradesmen – Sir Fiat Haustus, Sir Blacker Dosy, Mr Sergeant Bluebag or Mr Counsellor O'Fee. Brass plates are their titles of honour and they live by their boluses or their briefs. What call have these worthy people to be dangling and grinning at Lord-Lieutenants' levees and playing sham aristocracy before a sham sovereign? Oh, that old humbug of a Castle! It is the greatest sham of all the shams in Ireland.[3]

1 William M. Thackeray, *The luck of Barry Lyndon: a romance of the last century* (New York, 1853), p. 214. 2 This volume was subsequently identified by Séamus Ó Duilearga as a chap-book from before 1825 and was reprinted in *Béaloideas*, 10 (1940), 148–203. 3 William M. Thackeray, *The Irish sketchbook, 1842, by Mr M.A. Titmouse* (London, 1857),

Despite the slightly tiresome tone of derision that marks the *Sketchbook* throughout, there is no reason to believe that Thackeray was misrepresenting the realities of much Irish genealogical aspiration in his own day. Barry Lyndon's claims to royal descent can be paralleled in real accounts of seventeenth- and eighteenth-century Irish seeking to establish themselves on the Continent,[4] and, as early as 1561, Thomas Smyth, as an apothecary in Dublin, was pointing out that professional Irish pedigree-writers were hawking their wares amongst a very wide section of Irish society:

> Their is in Irland four shepts in maner all Rimers ... The seconde sorte is the Shankee [*seanchaidh*], which is to saye in English, the petigrer. They have also great plaintye of cattell, wherewithall they do sucker the rebells. They make the ignoraunt men of the country to belyve that they be discended of Alexander the Great or of Darius or of Caesar, or of some other notable prince, which makes the ignorant people to run madde and cerieth not what they do; the which is very hurtfull to the realme.[5]

In a colonial world marked by frequent reversal of personal fortunes, it was often hard to distinguish between new *arrivistes*, seeking to better themselves and old families, fallen on hard times. John O'Donovan gives a vivid description of one of the latter:

> I had the very good luck to meet O'Flyn [*sic*] (Edmond son of Kellach) himself, who walked with me to the source of the Suck from the Esker over which he shewed me his ancient principality of which he now holds but a few townlands in fee-tail. He knows the names of every bush in the parish of Kiltullagh, the names of which he pronounced for me sitting on Eiscir Ui Mhaonagain over Bun-Suicin in the townland of Cul fearna, the parish of Annagh and county of Mayo, from which we had an extensive view of O'Flyn's country of Loch Ui Fhloinn, Sliabh Ui Fhloinn and of the parish of Kiltullagh. As soon as O'Flyn learned that I was one of the oulde stock, he commenced to give me a most curious account of his own family and of himself; the poor fellow is very much embarrassed and when I met him, was hiding from the sheriff who will arrest him for debt as soon as he can.[6]

p. 362. 4 John Barry, *The study of family history in Ireland* (O'Donnell Lectures, Cork, 1967), pp 13–18. 5 H.F. Hore, 'Irish bardism in 1561', *UJA*, 6 (1858), 165–7, at 166. 6 Castlereagh, 5th July 1837, in Michael O'Flanagan (ed.), *Letters containing information relative to the antiquities of the County of Roscommon collected during the progress of the Ordnance Survey in 1837*, 2 vols (Bray, 1927), quoted in Catherine Swift, 'John O'Donovan and the framing of early medieval Ireland in the nineteenth century', *Bullán*, 1 (1994), 91–103.

In such a context, the popularity of an extensive collection of Munster genealogies, now entitled *An Leabhar Muimneach*, in eighteenth-century Cork, is worthy of note. Its modern editor, Tadhg Ó Donnchadha, has identified thirteen manuscripts, most of which are excerpts, only two being complete. In one, RIA MS 23 E 26, the scribe Richard Tiber states that the collection was put together by Domhnall Ó Duinnín and Tadhg mac Dáire Mhic Bhruaideadha. These were both members of traditional bardic families working for the Meic Charthaigh and the Uí Bhriain respectively and the individuals concerned can both be dated to the late sixteenth or early seventeenth centuries.[7]

Because the *Leabhar Muimneach* genealogies are written in the Irish language, there has, perhaps, been a tendency to assume that they have an ancient ancestral validity which belies their seventeenth-century authorship. However, comparison of the *Leabhar Muimneach* statements on the Dál Cais with twelfth-century counterparts such as the genealogies published in *Corpus Genealogiarum Hiberniae* by M.A. O'Brien, makes it clear that, in some important respects, the nature of the records is very different. If one looks at the apical figure of Cass and his twelve sons, for example, the earlier records refer to descendants who are individuals or to kindred groups (often described by the Irish word *Uí*) who only rarely survive into the modern era. In *An Leabhar Muimneach*, by contrast, Cass's sons have descendants who are described by the word muinter and are clearly linked to modern surnames. Thus *An Leabhar Muimneach* has the O'Deas descending from Óengus Cenn Nathrach (Óengus Snake-Head) son of Cass, the Heffernans and the Naughtons from Óengus Cenn Aittin (Óengus Furze-head), the Hayeses from Áed and the Coughlans from Delbáeth.[8] These statements are made in summary form, only occasionally backed up by lengthy father-to-son lines of descent. Similarly, descendants from Cass's eldest son Blat (ancestor of Brian Boru's line) and yet another brother Caissín can also be described in terms of modern surnames:

> *Dearbhráthair don Bhlod so, Caisín, Ó dtangadar Síol Aodha .i. Clann Mhic Con Mara; agus is uatha sin tángadar Síol gClannchadha. Mac don Bhlod so fós, Bréanainn Bán ó dtáinig Muinnter Urthuile, Muinnter Mhaol Domhnaigh, Muinnter Ghráda; agus Clann Chaisin.*
>
> True brothers of that Blat are Caissín from whom come the Síl Aodha that is the Clann Mhic Con Mara [McNamaras] and it is from those noble men come the Síl gClannchadha [Clancys]. A son of that same Blat is Brénainn Bán from whom come the Muinter Urthaile [Hurleys], the Muinter Mhaol Domnaigh [Muldowneys], the Muinter Ghráda [O'Gradys] and the Clann Chaisín [Cashins/Kissanes].[9]

7 *LM*, pp xi–xv; Luke McInerney, 'Lettermoylan of Clann Bhruaideadha', *NMAJ*, 52 (2012), 93–9. 8 *LM*, p. 237. 9 *LM*, p. 237; translation and identification of English

Other families are said to be descended from the grandsons and great-grandsons of Blat, Cass's eldest son and ancestor of Brian Boru's own lineage:

> *Mic Aodha Caoimh, mic Conaill mic Eochach Baillldeirg; Dearbhráthair d'Eochaidh Bhailldeirg, Fearghal, ó dtangadar Muinnter Íceadha. Dearbhráthair eile d'Eochaidh Bhailldearg so, Aonghus, ó bhfuilid na sloinnte so síos: Muinnter Loingsigh, Muinnter Uaithnidhe, Muinnter Bhreachtgha, Muinnter Bhréanuinn; Muinnter Sheasnáin, Muinnter Riada; Muinnter Shamhradh; agus Muinnter Chorcmacáin.*
>
> Sons of Áed Cáem son of Conall son of Eochu Ballderg – a true brother of Eochu Ballderg is Fergal from whom come the Muinnter Íceadha [Hickeys]. Another true brother of that Eochu Ballderg is Óengus from whom are the following divisions – Muinter Loingsigh [Lynch], Muinter Uaithnidhe [Greene], Muinter Bhreachtgha [?Bracken], Muinter Bhréanuinn [Brennan], Muinter Sheasnáin [Sexton], Muinter Riada [Reidy], Muinter Shamradh [Somers], and Muinter Chormacán [Cormican].[10]

(To put these claims in context, Eochu Ballderg was contemporaneous with St Patrick in medieval Irish tradition and so the authors are suggesting that these families originated in the fifth to seventh centuries, long before Irish surnames actually developed.)[11]

Quite apart from prestigious families such as the McNamaras (to whom there are frequent reference in the Irish annals as well as in other texts), many of these surnames can be traced in Thomond, using sources in both English and Irish (and occasionally Latin) from the later medieval period. Brian Hodkinson's prosopography of medieval Limerick lists an Adam Grene from 1300 and John and Philip Grene from 1311 as well as a Loghlyn Brak (of the Muinter Bhreachtgha?) in 1313 and a William FitzRalph Brak hanged for burglary and murder in 1311.[12] Perhaps most interesting of all, however, is the account of the member of the Muinter Sheasnáin who is said to have been the first Irish mayor of Limerick in the 1530s:

> Edmund Sexten, alias Sesnan, sewer of the Chamber, Humphrey, Nicholas, George and Robert Sexten, alias Sesnan … , all merchants of Limerick. Making them and their posterity capable of bearing offices as mayors, sheriffs, bailiffs, constables, &c. in any part of Ireland, especially in Limerick …[13]

language equivalents of the Irish surnames are my own. 10 *LM*, pp 236–7. 11 Kathleen Mulchrone, *Bethu Phátraic* (Dublin, 1939), p. 123, ll.2415–20. 12 Hodkinson, 'Who was who in medieval Limerick; from manuscript sources' (http://www.limerickcity.ie/media/Who%20was%20who%20in%20medieval%20Limerick.pdf), *s.n.* 13 *Letters and papers,*

> [The citizens of Limerick] beare him displeasure and, as they saie, they moche abhorre him, because he is an Irishman of blode, and (as they saie) he usethe him self according [to] his nature. Howbeit, he is made denizon and free by the King, so as he hathe been Mayour there, contrary to Inglishe statutes, and there liberties.[14]

Apart from the statement on the family's origins in *An Leabhar Muimneach*, the Muinter Sheasnáin is also listed as a branch of the Dál Cais in the mid-seventeenth-century genealogical collection entitled *Leabhar Mór na nGenealach* by Dubhaltach Mac Fhirbisigh.[15] Here the family is further identified as descended from Óengus (brother of Eochu Ballderg), through his grandson Máel Cáech son of Rónán/Róngal son of Óengus and, once again, they share this ancestry with the Muinter Bhreachtgha, the Muinter Bhrenanáin and the Muintir Riada. This version provides us with an even more convincing Hibernization of the English word 'Sexton' as *Seastnán* with medial *t*. On the basis of information about the Uí Róngaile (descendants of Róngal) in a rental of the McNamaras dating back to the fourteenth century, this text gives us the possibility of locating the family in the parishes of Killuran and Kilnoe in East Clare.[16] On the other hand, this East Clare land is territory later associated with the Shanahans (Uí Shanacháin) rather than the Sextons (Uí Sheastnáin) and it might be worth considering instead the only instance of Seastnán as a personal name in *Leabhar Mór* which occurs rather further to the east in a genealogy of a family based in Uaithne Thíre (the barony of Owny), on the eastern side of Lough Derg.[17]

The precise location of the landholdings of the Sesnan/Sexton family may thus be impossible to tie down definitively but the scarcity of the name in Irish-language sources and its fairly clear derivation from English does suggest that, in the case of the seventeenth-century Irish sources, that we are dealing with an assumed Dál Cais pedigree. The earliest ancestor identified in the Sexton papers in the National Library of Ireland may be that of Simon Sastuane from 1437,[18] and this spelling suggests that the family may well have

foreign and domestic, of the reign of Henry VIII, ed. J.S. Brewer et al., 21 vols (London, 1862–1932), vii, p. 443. 14 *State papers published under the authority of his majesty's commission*, 5 pts in 11 vols (London, 1830–52), Henry VIII, pt 3, p. 107; discussed by Brian Hodkinson, 'Edmund Sexton, the first Irish mayor of Limerick' in David Lee (ed.), *Remembering Limerick* (Limerick, 1997), pp 107–11; Clodagh Tait, 'A trusty and well beloved servant : the career and disinterment of Edmund Sexton of Limerick, d. 1554', *Archivium Hibernicum*, 41 (2000), 51–64; Colm Lennon, 'Religious and social change in early modern Limerick: the testimony of the Sexton family papers' in Liam Irwin and Gearóid Ó Tuathaigh (eds), *Limerick history and society* (Dublin, 2009), pp 113–27. 15 *LMG*, iv, p. 688 (§1341.2). 16 James Hardiman (ed.), 'Ancient Irish deeds and writings chiefly related to landed property from the twelfth to the seventeenth century', *RIA Trans.*, 15 (1828), 3–96, at 48. 17 *LMG*, iii, p. 713 §1362.3; for examples of Seasnán without the medial *t*, see further the genealogy of the Munster-based Fir Múscraige, *LMG*, ii, p. 132 and of the Síol Ír (Ulster), *LMG*, ii, p. 392. 18 Hodkinson, 'Who was who in medieval

been Irish-speaking at that date. The condemnation of the Elizabethan Edmund Sexton of Limerick as an Irishman, therefore, is rather more complicated than at first appears. Rather than being mere Gaelic interlopers in an isolated bastion of English settlement, it would seem instead that the family may have been a typical product of a colonial frontier, operating within two different language-spheres and anxious to advance their interests by whatever means most suited the immediate cultural context. A claim to Dál Cais descent, expressed in Irish, certainly would seem to imply that they wished to be considered within the ranks of the *flaith* or lordly class of Irish-speaking Thomond as well as operating as the clients and allies of Henry VII of England.

The case of the Sextons highlights the problems involved not only in linking owners of modern surnames to medieval pedigrees but also to the unexpressed assumptions which often underlie such exercises. While the modern scholarship on Irish families compiled by MacLysaght, Quinn, De Bhulbh, Grenham[19] and others often repeats the seventeenth-century attributions of ancestors to Irish-language surnames, they are rather more cautious when repeating the attributions in the same texts which refer to families bearing names originally coined in other languages. For example, another prominent merchant family in Limerick were the Arthurs who controlled the mayoralty of the city for much of the later Middle Ages and whose family history traces them back to a John Martin Arthur born *c.*1350 who had three sons, Thomas, William and Richard.[20] *An Leabhar Muimneach*, on the other hand, derives the family from a brother of St Flannán of Killaloe and thus from Dál Cais:

> *Mac oile don Toirdhealbhach so Ailgeinén ó dtáinig Ó Meádhra. Agus mac Ailgeinén Eochaidh ó dtáinig Artúr (a quo Artúraigh); Artúr umorro, mac Braoin, mic Cearbhaill mic Sgannláin mic Eochach mic Ailgeinéin.*
>
> Another son of that Tairdelbach is Ailgenán from whom come the Uí Mheadhra. And the son of Ailgenán is Eochu from whom is Arthur from whence come the Arthurs – that is Arthur son of Bróen son of Cerball son of Scannlán son of Eochu son of Ailgenán.[21]

Limerick', *s.n.*, quoting NLI MS 41, 673/4; Colm Lennon, 'Religious and social change', p. 114 quotes G.O. MS 169, f.57 to suggest that the first enfranchised citizen of Limerick may have been a Morris Sexton, father of Edmund. **19** See, for example, Edward MacLysaght, *Irish families: their names, arms and origins*, 4th ed. (Dublin, 1985); Seán E. Quinn, *Surnames in Ireland* (Bray, 2000); Seán de Bhulbh, *Sloinnte uile Éireann: all Ireland surnames* (Dublin, 2002), John Grenham, *Grenham's Irish surnames*, CD (Dublin, 2003). **20** Hodkinson, 'Who was who in medieval Limerick', *s.n.*, quoting the Arthur manuscript; see also E.A. MacLysaght and James Ainsworth, 'The Arthur manuscript', *NMAJ*, 8:1 (1958), 2–19. **21** *LM*, p. 236.

This derivation is still known in the Mid-West[22] (though not ascribed to *An Leabhar Muimneach*) but MacLysaght identified the family as originally Norse and this is currently the most favoured origin locally.[23] MacLysaght's view on the inherent unlikelihood of the *Leabhar Muimneach* ascription has, in turn, impacted on the use of Dál Cais genealogies in modern genetic studies in which the Arthurs' DNA has been investigated as part of a study of Viking-period migration into Ireland.[24] The same group was also involved in a more detailed study of the genetics of Dál Cais (to be considered further below) but the data they themselves had gathered on the Arthurs was not considered relevant to the latter. The conclusion of their study was that genetics indicated a very small likelihood of substantial Viking migration to Ireland; given the ambiguities of the genealogical evidence, one can speculate that the typical Irish genetic profile may, in fact, reveal an Arthur ancestor who chose to give himself a surname which was particularly prestigious in Welsh and Anglo-Norman cultures and who also turns up as an important figure in thirteenth-century Irish literary texts.[25]

One of the problems involved in linking medieval genealogies to modern surnames is, of course, the unfortunate reality that many Irish surnames do not appear until relatively late in the chronological span of historical sources. Around the end of the first millennium AD, the Irish annals begin to describe a certain number of leading dynasties by reference to an apical ancestor and these 'progenitors of various important native families' were originally tabulated by John O'Donovan in the mid-nineteenth century.[26] Subsequent scholarship has attempted to decide at what point the annalists' use of the word *ua* ('grandson') ceases to be a literal description of patrilineal descent and becomes instead a hereditary form leading ultimately to surnames beginning with Ó (*Anglice O'*).[27] This appears to have occurred in at least some cases by the surprisingly early date of the mid-tenth century; the first so far identified include an Ua Cannanáin of 943 (referring to a great-grandfather) and an Ua Cléirig of 923 – surprisingly, because surnames in England and Normandy are said to begin in the post-Conquest period where they are linked, not to patronymics, but to landholdings.[28] The history of surname development in

22 See http://thearthurfamilyoflimerickandclare.com/chapter1history arthurname.html. **23** MacLysaght, *Irish families*, p. 204. **24** Brian McEvoy, Claire Brady, Laoise T. Moore and Daniel Bradley, 'The scale and nature of Viking settlement in Ireland from Y-chromosome admixture analysis', *European Journal of Human Genetics*, 14 (2006), 1288–94. **25** Standish H. O'Grady (ed.), *Silva Gadelica: a collection of tales in Irish*, 2 vols (London, 1892), i, pp 94–232, at pp 99–100; Ann Dooley and Harry Roe (eds), *Tales of the elders of Ireland* (Oxford, 1999), pp 8–9. **26** John O'Donovan (ed.), *The topographical poems of O'Dubhagain and O'Huidhrin* (Dublin, 1862), pp 9–10. **27** Brian Ó Cuív, *Aspects of Irish personal names*, Statutory Lecture, School of Celtic Studies, Dublin Institute for Advanced Studies (Dublin, 1986), pp 32–6; Tomás G. Ó Canann, 'Aspects of an early Irish surname: Ua Cannanáin', *Studia Hibernica*, 27 (1993), 113–44, at 113–14; Diarmuid Ó Murchadha, 'The formation of Gaelic surnames in Ireland; choosing an eponym', *Nomina*, 22 (1999), 25–44. **28** R.A.

Ireland is an under-researched field and the impetus which led Irish dynasties to develop their own hereditary system of surname nomenclature at approximately the same period remains to be determined.[29]

Among Dál Cais, the most prestigious ancestral figure was, of course, Brian Bóraime (Brian Boru) although other ancestors were clearly also of interest to high-medieval contemporaries. The *Annals of the Four Masters* refers to the district west of Killaloe as *Magh Ua t-Toirrdhealbhaigh* in 1192, referring to Brian's ancestor Tairdelbach who is also the key figure in the contemporary life of St Flannán (identified as Tairdelbach's son). The obit in the *Annals of Ulster* under 1054 of an officeholder called Áed mac Cennétig mic Duinn Cuan describes him as *muire Clainne Tairdhelbaig*. The early thirteenth-century account of St Patrick's encounters with the Fianna, *Acallam na Senórach*, gives prominence to Cass himself whose grave is identified with a megalithic tomb at Duntryleague overlooking the peaks of the Galtees and at the southernmost edge of the lands claimed by the later Thomond kings.[30] In their accounts, the twelfth-century genealogies identify the wider kin-group as *Dál Chais* or 'progeny of Cass' and, while placing most emphasis on Brian's ancestry as the key figure of this grouping, do not yet identify his descendants as Uí Bhriain.

It has been suggested by Aubrey Gwynn that the *Annals of Inisfallen* were being compiled in Killaloe in the period in which Brian and his immediate descendants were ruling,[31] and thus they provide our most accurate reflection of how the Uí Briain surname may have come to be used by the family themselves. In 1051, a murderous feud between Brian's grandsons identifies them as Diarmait and Murchad Ua Briain;[32] further grandsons were identified as Domnall Bán Ua Briain in 1052, Domnall Ruad Ua Briain in 1155, Murchad Ua Briain in 1068 while his most successful grandson, Tairdelbach Ua Briain, is normally identified by this title throughout his long career.[33] In 1071, there is reference to *crech mór la U Briain* or a great raid by Ua/Uí Briain – but it is not clear whether this refers to Tairdelbach or to the family more generally. In 1072, Diarmait mac Máil na mBó is killed by Ua Máel Sechnaill and Ua Briain (presumably Tairdelbach, possibly in his role as leader

McKinley, *A history of British surnames* (Abingdon and New York, 2013). **29** Works currently available generally describe the various formulae adopted and their chronological timespan but do not speculate as to the causes of their adoption (for the most interpretative, see F.J. Byrne, 'A note on the emergence of Irish surnames' in Byrne, *Irish kings*, 2nd ed., pp xxxi–xliii); O'Donovan (ed.), *Topographical poems*, pp 17–51; Pádraig de Woulfe, *Sloinnte Gaedhael is Gall: Irish names and surnames* (Dublin, 1922); G.B. Adams, 'Prolegomena to a study of surnames in Ireland', *Nomina*, 3 (1979), 81–94. **30** Catherine Swift, 'Brian Boru's origins and the kingdom of north Munster', *History Ireland*, 22:2 (2014), 18–22; see also entry in *AFM* s.a. 1054 which refers to the burning of Duntryleague by the Uí Briain. **31** Aubrey Gwynn, 'Were the "Annals of Inisfallen" written at Killaloe?', *NMAJ*, 8 (1958), 20–33. **32** Diarmait son of Domnall son of Brian and Murchad son of Donnchad son of Brian. **33** See *AI* 1053, 1058, 1062, 1063, 1067, 1068, 1070, 1071, 1072, 1075, 1076, 1078, 1079 1081, 1086 versus entries where he is simply referred to as Tairdelbach in *AI* 1055,

of a troop) and in 1077, there is reference to *tech Uí Briain a Cind Chorad* (or the house of Ua Briain at Kincora). Brian's great-grandson, Conchobor, is identified as Conchobar Ua Briain in 1078 while two other great-grandsons are termed *da maic Thoirdelbaig* in 1084 but in the latter entry, Muirchertach (who became ruler of Thomond) is also identified as Muirchertach Ua Briain, mac Tairdelbaich. The same entry finishes with a reference to '*.u. h-Ui Briain … im Chennetich h-Ua m-Briain & alii multi* (five of the Uí Briain … around Cennétig Ua Briain and many others)'. Thus Ua Briain/Uí Briain, as a surname formula, was used both of the ruling king and more widely of Brian's descendants by the third quarter of the eleventh century and it may even have spread at this stage to refer to followers who were not genetically descended from Brian.

While the Uí Briain leadership are reasonably well attested as such in contemporary records for the later eleventh century, the same is not equally true of other, subsidiary families which have also been linked to the figure of Brian Boru. One such are the Uí Londgargáin, said to be descended from Brian Boru's grandson Londgargán, son of Donn Cuan who are attested as abbots at Terryglass.[34] Muirchertach mac Londgargáin of Terryglass who is listed in the genealogies circa the 1040s appears to be this man's son while Annud Ua Londgargáin, also of Terryglass, listed in 1099 (in the *Annals of the Four Masters*) may well be his literal grandson. However, Londgargán's grandson, Carthach, was listed in 1045 and his great-grandson is identified as 'Domnall h-Úa Lonngargan, *aird-espoc Dal Cais* (pre-eminent bishop of the Dal Cais)' in 1158 in the *Annals of Tigernach* and his brother Tadg as 'Tadhg O Longargan *espoc Tuadmuman* (bishop of Thomond)' in 1161 in the same text. This section of the *Annals of Tigernach* survives in a transcript of what is taken to be a probable contemporary chronicle (put together by various annalists) from Clonmacnoise and study has shown that some genealogical and locational data was added to basic entries.[35] On balance, however, it seems reasonable to accept that the surname Uí Londgargáin was probably in usage by the mid-twelfth century.

Another family of roughly the same era are the Uí Chennétig (O'Kennedys), descended from a Cennétig who was a brother of Londgargán (and thus another grandson of Brian Boru). A man who may be a son of this man dies in 1054, according to the *Annals of the Four Masters* as 'Aodh mac Cindéittigh, mic Duinn Cuan, *muirn & ordan Dal c-Caís* (Áed, son of Cennétig, son of Donn Cuan, the love and glory of Dál Cais)', probably the same man who, as

1064, 1073, 1079 1080. **34** Donnchadh Ó Corráin, 'Dál Cais – church and dynasty', *Ériu*, 24 (1973), 52–63, at 56, 59. **35** John [Eoin] MacNeill, 'The structure and authorship of the *Annals of Tigernach*', *Ériu*, 7 (1913), 30–113, at 95, 108; Kathryn Grabowski and David Dumville, *Chronicles and annals of medieval Ireland and Wales: the Clonmacnoise group of texts* (Woodbridge, 1984), pp 153–226; Nicholas Evans, *The present and the past in medieval*

Áed mac Cennétig, was killed in another entry under the same year in Thomond. Cennétig's grandson, Céilechar Ua Cennétig of Terryglass died in 1081, according to the *Annals of the Four Masters* while his great-great-grandson, Finn Ua Cennétig, also of Terryglass, died in 1152. However, the *Annals of Inisfallen* list a Donn Cuan Ua Cennétig who died in 1123 while the *Annals of Tigernach* record *da hUa Cendeídigh* (two members of the Uí Chennétig) who died in a clash with the Connachta in 1117. Like their relatives, the Uí Longargáin, therefore, the evidence appears to be that this family surname was in existence by the first half of the twelfth century. By the second half of the twelfth century, if not before, they were rulers east of the Shannon with an obit for 'Amlaim mac Gilla Chaemghen hUí Chendeidigh, *rí Urmuman* (king of Ormond)' in the *Annals of the Four Masters* under 1164.

A family with a slightly later ancestor was Consaidín Ua Briain who was bishop of Killaloe while his Ua Briain brothers, Muirchertach (died 1168) and Domnall (died 1194) were rulers of Thomond in the later twelfth century. Despite being a bishop, he is remembered as ancestor of the *Cland Chonsaidín* whose name survives in Clare as the surname Considine.[36] This family is of particular interest in that, by the time of Pender's seventeenth-century *Census*, they are solely recorded in Clare where nine families of Considin existed in the barony of Bunratty on the north bank of the Shannon and a further nineteen (as Considn and MacConsidn) in the barony of Islands, around Ennis.[37] This contrasts sharply with the Uí Chennétig (O'Kennedys) who, under various spellings, were found scattered through the baronies of Connello, Coonagh (Co. Limerick), Slieveardagh, Lower & Upper Ormond, Kilnamanagh, Middle Third, Eliogarty & Ikerrin, Owney & Arra, Clanwilliam (Co. Tipperary) and Bunratty (Co. Clare). The Lonergans were listed in the baronies of Middle Third and Iffa & Offa in Tipperary while the O'Briens, again under various spellings, were found throughout the modern counties of Clare, Limerick and Tipperary.[38] The processes by which these surnames might have spread in the era between the twelfth century and the seventeenth and the chronological period at which it happened have still to be investigated by modern scholars. Nor is it clear why royal lines such as the O'Briens or O'Kennedys might have been much more successful than others in doing so, though it is tempting to link such success to the known habit of Brian's dynasty of placing close relatives in charge of newly acquired territories.[39] As

Irish chronicles (Cambridge, 2010), pp 45–66. 36 *LM*, pp 325, 342. 37 Séamus Pender (ed.), *A 'Census' of Ireland circa 1659 with supplementary material from the poll money ordinances 1660–1661*, with a new introduction by W.J. Smyth, 2nd ed., IMC (Dublin, 2002), pp 168, 179. 38 Pender (ed.), *Census* (O'Kennedys under various spellings), pp 168, 284, 288, 297, 302, 304, 309, 319, 322, 324, 328; (Lonergans), pp 309, 314; (O'Briens) pp 163–88, 269–91, 295–328. 39 Anthony Candon, 'Tealach Óc and Emain Macha *c.*1100', *Emania*, 15 (1996), 39–46; also Katharine Simms, 'Nomadry in medieval Ireland; the origins of the creaght or caoraigheacht', *Peritia*, 5 (1986), 379–91; eadem, 'The origins of

an interim, however, Hodkinson's prosopography for medieval Limerick indicates that MacBriens were linked to Aherlow in the 1280s and again in 1341 when they are burgesses there, to Esgren (possibly Carrigogunnell) in 1306 and to Caherconlish in 1338 (when they are tenants), and so some degree of spread appears to have occurred in this particular family from a royal line to a considerably larger and more dispersed grouping by the mid-fourteenth century at the latest. (It is worth noting, here that *An Leabhar Muimneach* links the family of the Mac Briain Ó gCuanach or Coonagh and Mac Briain Eatharla (of Aherlow) to the figure of Donnchad, son of Brian Boru, suggesting perhaps that these families were established outside Clare as early as the eleventh century.)[40]

When attempting to trace the genetic legacy of the O'Briens one has also to bear in mind that Brian Boru's fame meant that the personal name Brian, rare or indeed non-existent, before his reign,[41] became popular following his rise. In the *Annals of Inisfallen*, we find a Brian mac Maíle Ruanaid of Uí Briúin Chonnacht (south Roscommon and north Galway) who died in 1004, a Brian Ua Dubda (north Mayo) who died in 1025 and in the *Annals of Ulster*, we find two men called Brian Ua Conchobair (of central Roscommon) who died in 1159 and 1184 respectively. The modern edition of *Leabhar Mór na nGenealach* in the mid-seventeenth century, lists a total of 263 different individual Brians in its index. Given the extremely common practice of patrilineal surname formation in Ireland, this indicates that many modern O'Briens could well be descended from individuals other than Brian Boru himself.

Modern genetic studies of Brian's descendants began in 2008 with a study, not of the O'Briens as such, but rather of the question of whether Irish kingdom names such as Connacht reflected élite dynasties who ruled such territories or whether one could identify the population of a primeval 'tribal' group who may have existed in the era prior to our historical documentation.[42] An earlier study by the same group had identified a DNA haplotype which they equated with the ancestral figure of Niall Noígiallach of the fifth century,[43] and this formed the backdrop to the article: they were seeking to

the creaght: farming system or social unit?' in Margaret Murphy and Matthew Stout (eds), *Agriculture and settlement in Ireland* (Dublin, 2015), pp 101–18; John Ryan, 'The O'Briens in Munster after Clontarf', *NMAJ*, 2 (1941–2), 141–52; 3 (1942), 1–52. **40** *LM*, pp 235, 354, 366–72. **41** Kuno Meyer, 'Brian Borumha', *Ériu*, 4 (1910), 68–73. **42** Brian McEvoy, Katharine Simms and D.G. Bradley, 'Genetic investigation of the patrilineal kinship structure of early medieval Ireland', *American Journal of Physical Anthropology*, 136 (2008), 415–22. **43** L.T. Moore, B. McEvoy, Eleanor Cape, Katharine Simms and D.G. Bradley, 'A Y-chromosome signature of hegemony in Gaelic Ireland', *American Journal of Human Genetics*, 78 (2006), 334–8. Subsequent investigation, by citizen scientists and commercial groups, has indicated that this haplotype is as well attested in Lowland Scotland as it is in northwest Ireland; see https://www.familytreedna.com/groups/r-1b-1c-7/about/background. For discussion of the intersections between history and genetics in the Uí Néill study, see Catherine Swift, 'Interlaced scholarship: genealogies and genetics in twenty-first century Ireland' in Seán Duffy (ed.), *Princes, prelates and poets in medieval Ireland: essays in honour of Katharine Simms* (Dublin, 2013), pp 18–31.

establish whether the pattern which they had identified for Niall's descendants could be paralleled in Munster. The focus of the article was, therefore, not primarily on the families descended from Brian Boru as identified from the later eleventh century but rather on attempting to establish the nature of Dál Cais as a proto-historical grouping of families with a shared genetic inheritance.

The first stage in the study was to identify a group of 247 modern individuals from Munster whose surnames were divided into those names belonging to Eóganacht descendants,[44] Dál Cais descendants, and a collection of random Munster surnames. (Because Y-chromosome DNA mutates slowly, testing modern men is thought to reveal early genetic groupings – a theory which was first articulated in relation to the descendants of the thirteenth-century Mongolian war-leader, Genghis Khan.)[45] The results from these individuals were separated from a control group of 184 Munster samples without surname data; this control group was termed the Munster geographic group.

The Dál Cais descendants consisted of 80 individuals who bore the surnames Cahill (10 samples), Clancy (8), Heffernan (7), Hickey (6), Kennedy (7), McGrath (6), McMahon (5), McNamara (4), O'Brien (14), O'Dea (6) and O'Grady (7). From the evidence outlined above, it can be seen that this list is ultimately derived from the seventeenth-century *Leabhar Muimneach* genealogies rather than from the earliest attested surnames within the O'Brien family tree.[46] Furthermore, in line with the objectives of the article, it includes names such as Clancy, Hickey, McGrath and McNamara who are descended from Caissín son of Cass rather than Brian's own lineage through Blat son of Cass. The Eóganacht descendants numbered 95 in total (distributed amongst 14 surnames) and the random Munster surnames were 72 (involving ten surnames).

The next stage of the 2008 study was to examine the Munster geographic group to see if a dominant Y-chromosome signature could be identified in the region in the way which had previously been done in the northwest. This investigation, however, revealed considerably more diversity than in the northwest, suggesting that the population in Munster is less homogeneous than had been proposed for Donegal and north Connacht and the authors argued that

> it is possible that greater migration to Munster relative to the Northwest over the past 1,000 years (associated with Norman and English conquest) may dilute such a signature in the Munster geographic sample.[47]

44 The Eóganacht were rulers of Cashel with sub-branches in Tipperary, north Cork, Limerick and Kerry in the era prior to the growth to power of Brian Boru's immediate family in the mid tenth century and later; Byrne, *Irish kings*, pp 165–229. 45 Tatiana Zerjal et al., 'The genetic legacy of the Mongols', *American Journal of Human Genetics*, 72 (2003), 717–21. 46 The bibliography cites *LM*; *CGH*; MacLysaght, *Irish families*; idem, *More Irish families* (Dublin, 1982). 47 McEvoy et al., 'Patrilineal kinship structure', 411.

The surname data was then investigated for evidence of important founding lineages, and two potential founding male signatures (frequent Y-chromosomes surrounded by subsidiary diversity) are apparent, centred on what were termed haplotypes A and B. However, these two clusters of leading Y-chromosome signatures were scattered between individuals of the three groups used, e.g., Eóganacht, Dál Cais and random Munster surnames and thus could not be firmly identified with either a Dál Cais or an Eóganacht ancestor:

> It is none-the-less curious that haplotypes A and B, the joint second and third most common Y-chromosomes in the geographic Munster sample (at 2.2% and 1.6%, respectively), are enriched in the surname sample (Dal Cais, Eoganacht and Munster surnames) at 12.9% and 6.5%, respectively.

The authors were unable to point to any precise argument to explain this but they suggested that since a very large percentage of Cluster A haplotypes had surnames indicating a paternal origin in south Munster while a considerably smaller majority of Cluster B surnames came from the north, it was possible that there was some geographic rationale for the distribution of haplotypes A and B.

Overall, they concluded that while

> our analysis cannot exclude the possibility that some level of patrilineal kinship underlaid the Munster Eóganacht and Dál Cais entities, it does seem that if any existed it was not comparable in extent to the widespread kinship in the contemporaneous Uí Néill grouping from the North of the Island, presumably the descendants of the ancestral eponym 'Niall of the Nine Hostages' and his clan.

Their final statement reiterated the fact that they were primarily concerned with attempting to investigate proto-historical realities long predating the development of surnames in Irish families:

> Although the Uí Néill and Eóganacht are often thought of as major contemporary rivals from the North and South of the island respectively, genetic evidence combined with surname information suggest they were founded, established and perhaps led by different means and this may reflect wider differences in organization of Irish tribal societies.[48]

Despite their relative lack of interest in Dál Cais names, as such, this article suggests certain conclusions about the genetic evidence for the surnames

48 Ibid., 414.

studied. The most important is the argument that there is a historical reality linking surnames which *An Leabhar Muimneach* claims were descended from two different sons of Cass. This is said to have no real genetic support. In the light of the case studies above, this does not appear particularly surprising; the *Leabhar Muimneach* claims are often summary in nature and it seems very clear that the prestige of Brian Boru led to a number of individuals making genealogical claims which are now difficult to substantiate and which, in the case of Limerick merchant families such as the Sextons or the Arthurs, seem somewhat unlikely. The figure of Cass himself is depicted as a unifying one for the kingdom of Thomond in the early thirteenth-century *Acallam na Senórach*; it is possible that he also played this role in the twelfth-century genealogies. It seems, at the very least, conceivable that the dynasty of Brian Boru may have deliberately emphasized this remote ancestor as a way of fostering a sense of community within the larger area of modern Clare in which they themselves had made important conquests only during the course of the tenth century.[49] Their expansion beyond modern Clare to Limerick was argued by John Ryan to have taken place in a context where an ancestor dating back to the time of St Patrick, Óengus, grandson of Blat, son of Cass, had established himself and his descendants on the south bank of the Shannon, many years prior to the conquest of Viking Limerick by Brian and his brother Mathgamain in 967 but there is little contemporary evidence to corroborate this.[50] Similarly, their expansion into northern Tipperary can clearly be documented (at least in relation to ecclesiastical sites such as Terryglass) in the period of Brian's own kingship;[51] it is impossible to show that the dynasty or its ancestors were already extant on the eastern shores of Lough Derg long before that date. Thus the lack of genetic evidence for a Dál Cais grouping should, perhaps, be tied more closely to the possibility that the rapid rise to power of Brian Boru's family and his prestige throughout the late medieval period has resulted in the wholesale construction of a genealogical edifice which requires far more detailed investigation than it has received hitherto.

The genetic study of proto-historic kinships within Munster was part of a much wider attempt to identify the diagnostic DNA of the modern Irish

49 *AFM* 932; *AI* 983, 984; Donnchad mac Briain's sons were taking spoil from Corcomroe in *AI* 1054. 50 John Ryan, 'The Dalcassians', *NMAJ*, 3/4 (1943), 189–202, at 195–7, where they are identified as Áes Cluana Findabar; however, he indicates that members of the family who ruled in the later *Topographical poems*, the O Cétfada, are identified as Uí Cétfada who were cited as prestigious members of Dál Cais in 1033, 1045 and 1084. He also cites an alternative genealogy for the family, stemming from the rather later figure of Tairdelbach, father of St Flannán which occurs in the Book of Ballymote and concludes with the statement: 'I suspect that … the Aes Cluana were not originally connected with the Uí Thoirdelbaig, save possibly in the very remote past … and that the ancestors of the Uí Cétfada and Uí Eanna families were introduced into that territory as overlords when the Uí Thoirdelbaig power had grown out of all proportion to what it had been in the old Déis Tuaiscirt or Dál Chais state.' 51 Ó Corráin, 'Dál Cais', 56.

population as a whole. For this exercise, some 1,125 samples were collected from volunteers with surnames geographically distributed throughout Ireland with a further 795 as a general Irish population control group. This wider project found that the incidence of shared DNA between surnames could vary widely:

> the average probability of a man sharing an identical 17 STR Y-chromosome haplotype with another man of the same surname is 8.15%. This value is over 30 times greater than the background Irish population Y-chromosome match possibility of 0.2%. However, the extent of sharing differs widely between surnames. Amongst the most extensively sampled names (with a sample size of >50) it ranged from a 47-fold higher probability over background levels in Ryan to a more modest 4.5 fold increase in Kelly.[52]

In other words, if a man has the surname Ryan, he is far more likely to share a genetic signature with other Ryans than if he had the surname Kelly. (From the point of view of the Irish surname historian, this is not particularly surprising as Brian Ó Cuív has already made the point that there was a relatively small pool of Irish personal names in common use and some were considerably more popular than others; thus the statistical probability of having a Cellach as a potential ancestor was far greater than that of Rian.)[53] This Irish variation within surnames shows a different pattern from that observed in Britain where there appears to be a correlation between the relative rarity of a surname and the diversity of Y-chromosomes found within it.[54] It has been suggested that this difference was linked to a greater ability of Irish lords to reproduce successfully but a simpler explanation may be that Irish surnames are mainly (though not exclusively) patrilineal in origin while the most common English surnames are either locational or occupational. It is also true, as originally pointed out by King and Jobling, that subsequent events such as the Famine have eliminated the genetic evidence for many medieval Irish families while the work of William Smyth and others has highlighted the geographic variability in subsequent birth-rates among the surviving nineteenth-century population.[55]

52 Brian McEvoy and Daniel Bradley, 'Y-chromosomes and the extent of patrilineal ancestry in Irish surnames', *Human Genetics*, 119 (2006), 212–19. 53 Ó Cuív, *Aspects of Irish personal names*, p. 8; idem, 'Personal names as an indicator of relations between the native Irish and settlers in the Viking period' in John Bradley (ed.), *Settlement and society in medieval Ireland* (Kilkenny, 1988), pp 79–88, at p. 79. 54 T.E. King and M.A. Jobling, 'What's in a name? Y chromosomes, surnames, and the genetic genealogy revolution', *Trends in Genetics*, 25 (2009), 351–60; subsequently revised by authors and available at http://www.le.ac.uk/ge/maj4/KingJoblingRevisedWeb.pdf (accessed 13 Jan. 2017). 55 William J. Smyth, 'Mapping the people: the growth and distribution of the population'; idem, 'Variations in vulnerability: understanding where and why people died'; idem, 'Exodus from Ireland – patterns of emigration' in John Crowley, W.J. Smyth and Mike

It should be borne in mind that in much of the research described above, investigations were limited to 17 markers (entitled Short Tandem Repeats or STRs) or even fewer. Some of these markers can be commonly found; in one 2007 study, a sample of 1,814 men carrying 164 names, the commonest 17-STR haplotype was shared across 16 different surnames.[56] The ongoing rise of commercial companies and the reduction in the costs involved has completely changed the basis on which such genetic studies are now carried out; investigation of 111 markers is now relatively commonplace. Furthermore, it is now possible to test single nucleotide polymorphisms or SNPs which allows one to investigate at what point a branch (perhaps containing multiple STR signatures) left the parental genetic tree. (The SNP for the typical signature associated with the descendants of Niall Noígiallach, for example, has been identified and called M-222; it is now possible for Irishmen with this signature to be tested specifically to see not only how many SNPs they have in common with others within the group and thus how many potential lineages there might be but also to see whether they themselves belong to ancestral figures predating the chronological horizon of Niall himself.) Current investigations of the links between surnames and genetic signatures have largely been abandoned by the university sector and are now largely carried out by groups of interested citizens, coming together via the internet and facilitated by groups such as the International Society of Genetic Genealogy. The results of this research are increasingly found, not in the larger academic journals, but on websites run by administrators for particular surname groups and in conference papers published as YouTube videos.[57]

One of the most notable of such investigations has been the work published by Dennis M. Wright.[58] As a long-term investigator of the DNA databases available publically, he was struck by the fact that three particular markers, which had been identified as a common variant of the signature termed the

Murphy (eds), *Atlas of the Great Irish Famine* (Cork, 2012), pp 13–22, 180–98, 494–503; for a graphic depiction of relative birth-rates in different parts of Ireland at the time of Matheson's survey of 1892, see Kenneth Field and Linda Beale, 'Geo-genealogy of Irish surnames', *Journal of Maps*, 6.1 (2010), 651–6. **56** T.E. King, 'The relationship between British surnames and Y chromosomal haplotypes' (PhD, University of Leicester, 2007). A chromosome contains sequences of repeating nucleotides known as short tandem repeats (STRs). The number of repetitions varies from one person to another and a particular number of repetitions is known as an allele of the marker. When someone purchases a test, the STR markers are listed as DYS numbers and the figures given under each represent the specific alleles of that person. When two or more people share the same sequences of allele numbers for the same DYS numbers (or STRs), this is known as a signature. **57** See, in particular, the website run by Maurice Gleeson: https://www.youtube.com/channel/UCHnW2NAfPIA2KUipZ_PlUlw. **58** Dennis M. Wright, 'A set of distinctive marker values defines a Y-STR signature for Gaelic Dalcassian families', *Journal of Genetic Genealogy*, 5 (2007), 1–5; see also Wright's 2016 conference paper: 'The DNA of the Dál gCais & subclades discovered with Big-Y', at www.youtube.com/watch?v=IoNNHRWIXQo and the project website, http://www.irishtype3dna.org/.

Irish Modal Haplotype,[59] were not amongst those investigated in the 2008 study of Munster DNA. Using 25 markers (as opposed to 17), he identified a distinctive genetic profile to be found in the counties of Limerick, Clare and Tipperary and he argued that 'Dalcassian surnames are more strongly represented with this signature [which he termed Irish type III] than other surnames'. By deploying public databases and the information compiled by the commercial testing firms, he identified a group of 7 distinctive STR markers which were replicated in 105 haplotypes (with 191 haplotypes in total belonging to the cluster when those defined as being within a genetic distance of two (GD=2) were also included). Using a smaller number of tests which had examined up to 96 markers per individual, he was also able to identify eight further markers which also belonged to this same distinctive group.

Seventy-eight within the tested samples examined by Wright had identified the country of origin of their earliest known ancestor as Ireland with the next largest number being 13 from Scotland. Of the 78 who knew the county of origin of their ancestors within Ireland, 11 (26%) came from Clare, 10 (23%) came from Tipperary and 7 (16%) came from Limerick, amounting to 65% from the area of Thomond. Using a list of surnames extracted from John Hart's 1892 *Irish pedigrees*, Wright identified the following twenty-eight as Dalcassian:

> MacArthur, O'Beollan/Boland, O'Brien, O'Casey, McConsidine, O'Cormacan, Cosgrave, MacCraith, O'Curry, Eustace, Glinn/Glynn, Hearne, O'Hogan, O'Hurley, O'Kelleher, O'Kennedy, Magan, Maglinn, MacMahon, O'Meara, Muldowney, O'Noonan, Power, Quirk, O'Regan, Scanlon, O'Seasnain and Twomey.[60]

When compared with the names in his database of men with the distinctive group of markers, 24 of the latter were O'Briens, 12 were Caseys, 10 were McGrath/McCraith and 10, surprisingly, were Butlers. There were also five each of Hogans and Kennedys. (He suggests that the entry of this signature into the Butler lineage may have occurred when Murrough O'Brien of Ballyphilip, Co. Limerick married Eleanor Butler of Bansha in the 1690s and took her name.) Checking these results against all entries in the database with these surnames (as opposed to those who had the distinctive genetic signature), he found that 24 of 68 O'Briens shared the Irish Type III signature; 12 of 20 O'Caseys; 10 of 21 McGrath/Mac Craith and 5 of 15 O'Hogan. The exception

59 This was noted by Dennis Wright and Dr Kenneth Nordvedt working together and was emailed to the Rootsweb Genealogy-DNA List on 6 Apr. 2006: http://archiver.rootsweb.ancestry.com/th/read/GENEALOGY-DNA/2006-04/1144414111. 60 Some of these have already appeared above while others such as Power seem distinctly dubious and would merit more detailed investigation.

were the O'Kennedys who had a mere 5 Type III signatures from a total of 44 O'Kennedys tested.

Since the development of SNP testing, which allows the relationship of branches to each other and to the original genetic tree be identified, Wright's original work has been updated. Irish Type III is now thought to branch off from the larger Irish phylogenetic tree at an SNP which is called L226. Sir Conor O'Brien, the present Lord Inchiquin (with a genealogical claim to be 32nd in descent from Brian Boru) has been tested and in a lecture delivered at the Royal Dublin Society in 2016, Denis Wright has summarized Sir Conor's ancestry as including the following sequence of SNPs:

L 226 > FGC5660 > Z17669 > ZZ 31_1 > FGC 5628 > FGC 5659 > ZZ 34_1 > DC 33 > DC 1 > YFS 231286 > FGC 1348.

On the basis of the very detailed tests now available (that the largest company working on Irish genetic genealogy refers to as Big Y), which looks at literally thousands of markers and which were undertaken by 50 men sharing the Irish Type III signature, Wright is currently arguing that Brian Boru may perhaps have shared this list of SNPs from L226 to FGC 5628 with the other SNPs developing in the eras after his reign.

Wright's conclusions can be compared with those of Dennis O'Brien with whom he often collaborates and who is administrator of the O'Brien surname project,[61] which currently has over 500 members of whom 403 have had their Y-chromosome tested. He states that of 305 'O'Brien related surnames' in the project, 52 share L226 and a further 18 share FGC 5659. This means that only 18 in his project apparently share the signature that Wright identifies as probably being that possessed by Brian Boru himself. In fact, the O'Brien project suggests considerable diversity within the O'Brien surname with 102/105 distinct haplogroups currently identified within it.[62] Of particular interest in trying to trace the O'Briens who settled elsewhere in medieval Thomond is the genetic lineage which shares the SNP BY4092 which appears to be associated particularly with Abingdon and which the project currently identifies as having separated from the main family tree in the years 1300–1500;[63] they also have lineages which they think may be associated with the Viscounts Clare. In addition, there are 41 individuals or 13.5% who do not appear to belong to the typical Irish groups at all, having more in common with other Europeans such as Scandinavians.[64] This work is ongoing and the combination of STR and SNP results means that those involved expect that,

61 Dennis O'Brien, 'The DNA of Clan O'Brien', https://www.youtube.com/watch?v=wp-1bfxaXYs (accessed 20 Nov. 2016). **62** The PowerPoint slide accompanying the lecture has 102; orally, it was 105. **63** See n. 39 above. **64** In other words, these signatures do not belong to the typical R1b found in Ireland but instead to other haplogroups such as I which are linked to Germanic groups, especially Scandinavians.

sooner rather than later, research will produce a genetic history which can be clearly linked to specific lineages within surnames. It is already clear, however, that because of the many incidents which can affect the progression of a particular surname through time, we are unlikely ever to end up with a single genetic ancestry for a particular surname.

A point stressed more than once by Dennis O'Brien in his 2016 lecture is the element of choice involved in declaring oneself to be a member of the clan of O'Brien: 'There's the O'Brien as far as the name goes and then, there's the O'Brien as far as the DNA goes.' The group does not require permission to join and fundamentally, if you self-identify as an O'Brien, for whatever reason, the project is happy to accept you. Sometimes, following testing, the individual may find the DNA results do not agree with the accepted oral tradition within a family but that is seen as all being part of the historical investigation:

> A clan is a clan. We're quite happy to have people who believe they're members of the clan. The DNA is not to us that important. What we want to do is provide – so there's the O'Brien clan – and then on top of that, if you want to know a bit more and put yourself in a group and – you know – if you're not descended from Brian Boru – if you descend from another Irish significant figure or a Viking significant figure or something – well, that's alright, you're still an O'Brien.

Barry Lyndon and the Heralds' College would surely agree.

The kings of Dublin and Leinster before the battle of Clontarf

EDEL BHREATHNACH

> *Sochaidi tuc i n-écin aided Bríain meic Cennétig, riasin ngass nglórda co ngail, ria Máel Mórda mac Murchaid, ria slúag Gall mbrogach mbuada i cath torach Tarbchluana.*[1]
>
> A troop brought about with difficulty the death of Brian son of Cennétig, against the loud valorous young warrior, against Máelmórda son of Murchad, against the strong, victorious Gaill in the crowded battle of Tarbchluain (Clontarf).
>
> *Máel Mórda mac Murchada .xiii. A thesbaid i cath Briain. Ac(h)t atberat araile is é Gilla Barrini mac Gillai Rigni (Gota?) de muintir Lifechair ros báid oc Drochuit Dubgaill oc tintód ón chath.*[2]
>
> Máelmórda son of Murchad thirteen years [as king of Leinster]. He died in Brian's battle. But others say that it was Gilla Barrini mac Gillai Rigni of the people of Lifechair who drowned him at Droichet Dubgaill escaping from the battle.

The standard narrative of the battle of Clontarf – based on the annalistic record and the narrative *Cogadh Gáedhel re Gallaibh*[3] – is that Brian Bóraime was slain but that he and his allies were victorious, and that Máelmórda son of Murchad, king of Leinster, was killed in a single combat with Conaing son of Donncuan, Brian's nephew, who also died in the fight. However, as evident from the texts quoted above, the tradition of the Laigin (Leinstermen) differed from the prevailing story in that they claimed to have killed Brian and that Máelmórda was killed by a fellow Leinsterman.[4] This contribution offers a brief view of Brian's career and the battle of Clontarf from the Leinster perspective and that of the villains of the piece, Máelmórda, king of Leinster (d. 1014) and his nephew Sitriuc 'Silkenbeard', Norse king of Dublin

1 The original text quoted here is from the Middle Irish poem *Fíanna bátar i nEmain* most of which is attributed to the poet Cináed ua hArtacáin (d. 976). It is preserved in a number of manuscripts among them the Book of Leinster (LL32a4153–8); an edition and translation was published by Whitley Stokes, 'On the deaths of some Irish heroes', *Revue Celtique*, 23 (1902), 303–48, at 314–15 §45. 2 *LL*, i, p. 183 (LL39c5471–3). 3 *CGG*. 4 The verse quoted from *Fíanna bátar i nEmain* on the battle of Clontarf is one of a number of verses added to Cináed ua hArtacáin's original poem and is attributed to the late twelfth-century Finn, bishop of Kildare.

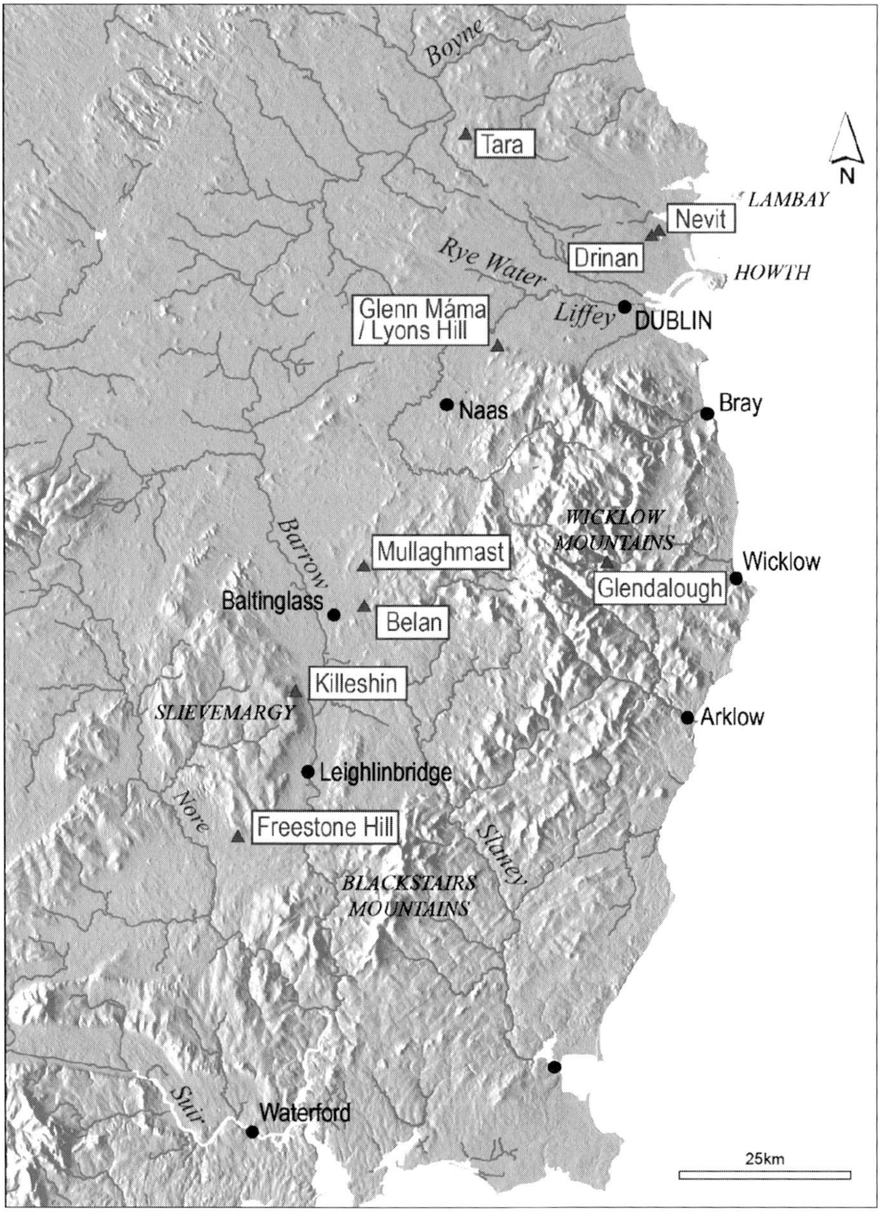

3.1 Locations mentioned in the text

(d. 1042).[5] This is a well-rehearsed history and any new angle presented here is but a footnote to more expansive histories written about the battle of Clontarf in recent years.[6]

THE IMPORTANT STRATEGIC PLACES OF LEINSTER

A consideration of the geographical extent and important places of Leinster is essential to understanding Brian Bóraime's strategy in the region and the response to that strategy. The province of Leinster was dominated by certain geographical features that determined the region's political divisions and economic wealth.[7] The Wicklow Mountains effectively created a north–south and east–west division: to the west were the good lands of the Liffey valley (west Co. Dublin and Co. Kildare) which from around the seventh century to the early eleventh century was divided between the three dominant dynasties of the province: collectively known as the Uí Dúnlainge, their three main dynasties being the Uí Fáeláin, Uí Dúnchada and Uí Muiredaig.[8] Further to the west were the extensive midland bogs dominated by the Uí Failgi. South of the Wicklow Mountains and around the Blackstairs Mountains were the various dynasties of the Uí Chennselaig whose star rose dramatically following the battle of Clontarf.[9] Four rivers created other divisions in Leinster: the Slaney, Barrow, Nore and Liffey. The Barrow valley was the land of the Uí Bairrche, a dynasty that had claimed not only the kingship of Leinster until the seventh century, but the kingship of Tara until that same period. And the lands north of the Liffey to Tara and beyond at that early stage had been lost by the Laigin, and with it any claim to the title of king of Tara.[10] A key natural and contended boundary between north Leinster and the neighbouring kingdom of Brega was the River Rye (Rige), a tributary of the Liffey that flows north of Kilcock and Maynooth and joins the greater river at Leixlip.[11]

One of the main inland entrances from Munster into Leinster was through the kingdom of Osraige at Belach Gabráin (Gowran, Co. Kilkenny) and across the Barrow at Leighlinbridge, Co. Carlow – a route that brought an army into

5 Sitric's mother Gormlaith (d. 1030) was Máelmórda's sister and one of Brian Bóraime's wives. 6 For the most recent and reliable studies of Brian Bóraime's career and the battle of Clontarf, see Ní Mhaonaigh, *Brian Boru*; Duffy, *Brian Boru*. 7 Alfred P. Smyth, *Celtic Leinster: towards an historical geography of early Irish civilization, AD500–1600* (Dublin, 1982). 8 Byrne, *Irish kings*, pp 130–64; Jaski, *Early Irish kingship*, pp 130–3, 310 (genealogy). 9 Doncha[dh] Ó Corráin, 'The Uí Chennselaig kingship of Leinster, 1072–1126. Part I', *Journal of the Old Wexford Society*, 5 (1974–5), 26–31. 10 Byrne, *Irish kings*, pp 136–7; Alfred P. Smyth, 'The Húi Néill and the Leinstermen in the Annals of Ulster', *Études Celtiques*, 14 (1974–5), 121–43; idem, 'Húi Failgi relations with the Húi Néill in the century after the loss of the plain of Mide', *Études Celtiques*, 14 (1974–5), 502–23. 11 Ailbhe Mac Shamhráin, *Church and polity in pre-Norman Ireland: the case of Glendalough* (Maynooth Mongraphs 7, Maynooth, 1996).

the heartland of the province. Another strategic corridor between north and south Leinster was around Baltinglass, Co. Wicklow – its importance is evident from the rich archaeological remains that suggest that this was a highly fortified territory from prehistory.[12] Such strategic places need to be kept in mind when discussing Brian Bóraime's progress through Leinster at various stages during his career. The main coastal entry-point into Leinster from prehistory was the maritime region from Lambay south to Bray with other harbours at Inber Dea (possibly Wicklow or Arklow),[13] Wexford and Waterford. All these places were settled by the Vikings and these settlements, especially Dublin, had a huge impact on the economy and polity of the province as they grew and expanded to create their own hinterlands at the expense of existing kingdoms.

THE KINGS AND DYNASTIES OF LEINSTER, 960–1014

From the eighth century to this period the provincial kingship of Leinster alternated (not always peacefully) between Uí Dúnlainge's three rival dynasties, the Uí Fáeláin, Uí Dúnchada and Uí Muiredaig.[14] Their lands skirted the Wicklow Mountains and the location of their ceremonial capitals at Maistiu (the archaeological complex Mullaghmast, Co. Kildare), Nás (Naas, Co. Kildare) and Liamain (Lyons Hill above Newcastlelyons, Co. Dublin) point to the position of their respective kingdoms relative to one another. To the southeast was the kingdom of the Uí Chennselaig, who were excluded from the kingship of Leinster in the early eighth century, and guarding the Barrow valley were the Uí Bairrche.

This paper's narrative begins when Brian's brother Mathgamain was in the ascendant. In 966, Cellach son of Fáelán, king of Leinster (of Uí Dúnchada) died and his dynasty descended into internal conflict that drew the attention of the ambitious king of Dublin, Amlaíb (Óláfr) Cúarán. Muiredach son of Fáelán, abbot of Kildare and brother of the deceased king, was killed by his nephew Cerball son of Lorcán with the support of Amlaíb Cúarán. In this incident alone, we can see the forces that were at play in Leinster. Presumably Muiredach had wished to become a king-abbot as had been achieved by his illustrious grandfather Muiredach son of Bran (d. 885). However, the Dublin Norse king Amlaíb Cúarán, as I have argued elsewhere, acted like an Irish king and held the ambitions of an Irish king.[15] Not only did he rule Dublin – and

12 Tom Condit, 'Ireland's hillfort capital: Baltinglass, Co. Wicklow', *Archaeology Ireland*, 6:3 (1992), 16–20; see also the project based in the UCC School of Archaeology under the direction of Professor William O'Brien, 'Hillforts, warfare and society in later prehistoric Ireland'. 13 Colmán Etchingham, 'Evidence of Scandinavian settlement in Wicklow' in Ken Hannigan and William Nolan (eds), *Wicklow history and society* (Dublin, 2005), pp 113–38, at p. 114. 14 Mac Shamhráin, *Church and polity*. 15 Edel Bhreathnach, 'The

attempted the same in York – but he aspired to extend his rule into Leinster and the kingdom of Brega, perhaps even to claim the kingship of Tara. Amlaíb was a king-maker in Leinster and a threat to northern and midland Uí Néill kings. The unfortunate Cerball son of Lorcán, who had killed his uncle Muiredach, the abbot of Kildare, was wounded and subsequently died in 967 when he accompanied his ally Amlaíb on an attack of the kingdom of Brega. The kingship of Leinster then passed to Murchad son of Finn of the Uí Fáeláin, and he was sufficiently powerful and politically astute to move against the kingdom of Osraige, the strategic buffer kingdom between Munster and Leinster that was pivotal to the balance of power between the two provinces. Murchad may have foreseen the impending threat from Dál Cais in Munster. He went to Osraige and plundered its core demesne at Mag Raigne (south of Kilkenny city). Despite this action the threat from Munster materialized in the guise of Mathgamain son of Cennétig, Brian's brother, who defeated Murchad and took his hostages in 969. Mathgamain was supported by the Osraige and also by the Déisi whose kingdom lay to the south of Osraige and Leinster. And so began the long and chequered relationship between the Uí Fáeláin kings of Leinster and the Dál Cais kings of Munster which culminated in the death of Murchad's son, Máelmórda, at the battle of Clontarf.

Leinster and Dublin were under constant pressure from the northern and midland kings of Uí Néill and this pressure intensified as a result of Amlaíb Cúarán's expansionist aspirations. For example, the king of Tara, Domnall ua Néill, plundered from the Barrow to the sea in 968, besieged north Leinster and Dublin for two months, and took a tribute of cattle away with him. This tribute was the *bórama Laigen*, continuing a long-standing tradition of Uí Néill kings exacting a cattle tribute from the Laigin although in this case extended to Dublin. Two years later, in 970, Amlaíb Cúarán had the audacity to attack the monastery of Kells and to defeat the king of Tara at the battle of Cell Móna (?Kilmoon, Co. Meath). In Leinster the provincial kingship entered an unsettled phase. Just as the Uí Dúnchada had descended into internal rivalry in the early 960s, the same fate befell the Uí Fáeláin and the provincial kingship almost passed back to the Uí Dúnchada in 972 when their king Domnall Clóen son of Lorcán killed Murchad son of Finn. The third contending dynasty for the provincial kingship, the Uí Muiredaig, now loomed into the picture with a claimant in Augaire son of Tuathal and it would seem that he rather than Domnall was successful in being recognized as king of Leinster in 972. But Augaire was captured by the Norse of Dublin and in 978 they struck at the heart of his kingdom, defeated and killed him at Bithlann (probably Belan in b. Moone/Kilkea) – along the strategic corridor into their

documentary evidence for pre-Norman Skreen, County Meath', *Ríocht na Midhe*, 9:2 (1996), 37–45; eadem, 'Columban churches in Brega and Leinster: relations with the Norse and Anglo-Normans', *JRSAI*, 129 (1999), 5–18.

kingdom and the heartlands of the Leinster kings. And not only did Amlaíb kill Augaire but he also captured his successor Domnall Clóen in 979.

THE BATTLE OF TARA IN 980 AND ITS SIGNIFICANCE

The year 980 was hugely important for the kingship of Tara, for Dublin and Amlaíb Cúarán, and for the kings of Leinster. The year's events must have been keenly followed by Brian Bóraime as he set about moving in the direction of Osraige and Leinster. First, Domnall ua Néill, the northern king of Tara, died in Armagh – not in battle but in penance. This meant that Máel Sechnaill son of Domnall of the midland Uí Néill dynasty was now king of Tara, and in a sense he as much as Brian very rapidly checked the extent of Viking power in Ireland, and most especially of Amlaíb king of Dublin, the Norse intruder into the kingdom of Brega. Máel Sechnaill took on Amlaíb and his allies at the battle of Tara and won. Even the sober Annals of Ulster and Annals of Inisfallen mark this battle as a decisive event:

> The battle of Tara was won by Máel Sechnaill son of Domnall against the Foreigners of Dublin and the Isles, and very great slaughter was inflicted on the Foreigners therein, and Foreign power ejected from Ireland as a result. There fell therein Ragnall son of Amlaíb, the son of the king of the Foreigners, and Conamal, son of a tributary king of the Foreigners, and many others.[16]
>
> A great battle between Máel Sechnaill and the son of Amlaíb, and a slaughter of Foreigners including Ragnall, son of Ímar, at Tara, a measuring rod being required everywhere.[17]

The Annals of Tigernach provide us with a more expansive version and, if a true record, tell us something about the role of the Leinstermen in the battle of Tara:

> The battle of Tara gained by Máel Seachnaill the Great son of Domnall son of Donnchad son of Flann, by the king of Ireland, over the Foreigners of Dublin, over the sons of Amlaíb specially, wherein many fell, including Ragnall son of Amlaíb, crown prince of the Foreigners, and Conmael, son of Giolla (Airi) and the Orator of Dublin, and many others. Bróen son of Murchad, crown prince of Leinster, and Congalach son of Flann, king of the Gailenga, and his son Maelán, and Fiachra and Cú Duilig, two sons of Dublaech, two kings of the Fir Tulach, and Lachtna, king of Mughdoirn Maigen, fell in the counterblow of that battle.[18]

16 *AU* 980. 17 *AI* 980. 18 *AT* 980.

An alternative fate for Bróen is recorded in the Annals of Ulster:

> Bróen son of Murchad, king of Laigin, was taken prisoner by the Foreigners and afterwards put to death.[19]

Bróen son of Murchad belonged to the Uí Fáeláin dynasty. The Annals of Tigernach appear to suggest that he and the other kings named fought with Máel Sechnaill against Amlaíb Cúarán. This would make sense as Amlaíb Cúarán had expanded into their territories and Máel Sechnaill was the only king who could deter the Norse king. That he did, and his next move was to besiege Dublin, take a large tribute from the Dubliners and free Domnall Clóen, king of Leinster (Uí Dúnchada) who had been held hostage. If the Annals of Ulster text is correct, Bróen son of Murchad, Domnall's potential rival, was not so lucky. Perhaps he was brought back to Dublin after the battle of Tara and executed?

Máel Sechnaill's victory at Tara might have stabilized Leinster and contained the Norse of Dublin but the Laigin – and Máel Sechnaill – had to face a looming parallel movement from the Norse of Waterford, represented by their leader Ímar (Ívarr), and Brian Bóraime.[20] Ímar attacked Kildare while Brian attacked Osraige in 982. In a typical change of allegiance, the following year Domnall Clóen, king of Leinster and Ímar were defeated by Máel Sechnaill and his ally, Amlaíb Cúarán's son Glún Iairn (who was Máel Sechnaill's half-brother as they had the same mother, Dúnlaith, sister of Domnall ua Néill, king of Tara). Máel Sechnaill then took spoils from Leinster 'as far as the sea'.[21] Thus by 983 Máel Sechnaill was master of Dublin and of Leinster but his rival Brian had entered the fray and, as so often happened, the contention for control of the kingship of Tara was played out in Leinster. Brian's first step in 983 was to venture into the kingdom of Osraige where he took the hostages of its king, Gilla Pátraic son of Donnchad. Next step was into Mag Ailbe in Leinster where he took the hostages of Leinster, thus putting him on a collision course with Máel Sechnaill. As for the Laigin themselves, all was not well in the province: the southern dynasty of Uí Chennselaig, increasingly playing a part in provincial politics, were taken up with an internal feud in which Domnall Clóen, king of Leinster, intervened and was killed in the process in 984. At this point Leinster was overwhelmed from all sides. The Munster Annals of Inisfallen record for 984:

> A great naval expedition(?) by the sons of Aralt to Waterford, and they and [Brian] the son of Cennétig exchanged hostages there as a guarantee

19 *AU* 980. **20** For a comprehensive account of this Viking dynasty, see Clare Downham, *Viking kings of Britain and Ireland: the dynasty of Ívarr to AD1014* (Edinburgh, 2007), pp 56–62. **21** *AFM* 982.

> of both together providing a hosting to attack Dublin. The men of Munster assembled and proceeded to Mairg Laigen, and the Foreigners overcame the Uí Chennselaig and went by sea; and the men of Munster, moreover, devastated Osraige in the same year, and its churches, and the churches of Laigin, and the fortifications of both were laid waste, and Gilla Pátraic son of Donnchad was released.[22]

Viewing the situation at this point from the Leinster perspective, the future did not augur well: the Waterford Norse had gained a foothold in south Leinster by taking over the kingdom of the Uí Chennselaig, who are weakened by internal feuds, and hence their fleet could use the rivers Barrow and Slaney, and have access to landing points between Waterford and Dublin. Brian Bóraime went to Mairg Laigen, the Slievemargy Mountains to the northwest of Carlow town. Evidence that Brian's strategy was not only a military one, but that he also implemented a strategy of taking over Leinster churches, as he had in Munster, is suggested by the imposition of a Dál Cais saint, Comgán, and even of Dál Cais authority over Killeshin, the main church of this region.[23] Neither the Annals of Inisfallen nor the other annals indicate that Brian and the Norse of Waterford attacked Dublin during this expedition. The main reason would have been that Máel Sechnaill was keeping them in check: he attacked Leinster in 987 and took a tribute of cattle away with him – another echo of *bórama Laigen* – and more significantly, in 989 he besieged Dublin and brought the town under his full authority. The Annals of Tigernach describe his victory in the following rather bleak terms:

> The battle of Dublin gained over the Foreigners by Máel sechnaill son of Domnall, wherein many were slain and the siege of their fortress afterwards for twenty nights, and during it they drank no water save brine. Wherefore they gave him his own award so long as he should be king, and an ounce of gold for every garden to be paid on every Christmas eve forever.[24]

At the same time Máel Sechnaill took Donnchad son of Domnall Clóen, king of Leinster, as a hostage. Between 989 and 995, all these incursions took their toll on the sons of Amlaíb Cúarán: in 989, Glún Iairn was killed by his own slave in drunkenness (and probably at the instigation of rivals) and his brother Sitriuc was expelled from his kingship in 994 by Ímar of Waterford. Yet, in the following year Sitriuc's position was restored by the Uí Fáeláin king, and also his uncle, Máelmórda son of Murchad, next provincial king of Leinster. This was a vital alliance that was to dominate Dublin and Leinster until 1014.

22 *AI* 984. 23 Edel Bhreathnach, 'Killeshin: an Irish monastery surveyed', *CMCS*, 27 (1994), 33–47. 24 *AT* 989.

It is notable that Brian Bóraime's policy towards Dublin and Leinster was cautious. He edged slowly towards Dublin: in 996, for example, he took the hostages of the Uí Chennselaig and of the kingdom of Iarthar Liphi (west Liffey), located in Mag Ailbe. These careful and cautious moves probably give us a more genuine insight into the man than the swashbuckling hero the sagas portray. He was as much a political strategist as he was a man of military force: he built power on making alliances – political, marital and ecclesiastical. His alliance with the primatial church at Armagh, for example, was one of the most significant of his career.[25] His agreement with Máel Sechnaill in 997 is indicative of his shrewd strategy: they divided Ireland between them, Leth Cuinn (the northern half) to Máelsechnaill, Leth Moga (the southern half) to Brian and 'the hostages of the Laigin and of the Foreigners which Máel Sechnaill had, were given to Brian'.[26] From this point onwards, Leinster and Dublin were to become the battleground where the rivalry between Brian and Máel Sechnaill was played out. In 999, Brian and Máel Sechnaill defeated the Laigin and the Dubliners decisively at Glenn Máma west of Dublin and possibly near the ceremonial capital of Liamain.[27] Brian's next step was to enter Dublin and take their hostages, their silver and gold and banish Sitriuc, while Máel Sechnaill took a tribute again from the Laigin.

But what of the provincial kingship of Leinster? Donnchad son of Domnall Clóen was taken prisoner by Sitriuc and Máelmórda and, in the words of the Annals of Ulster, 'the kingship of Laigin was afterwards given to Máelmórda'. Brian's hand was behind all this drama: he banished Sitriuc who headed off to the north-eastern kingdom of Ulaid, returning and submitting to him in 1000. Brian officially deposed Donnchad, king of Leinster and handed the kingship to Máelmórda in 1003 who then submitted to him.

Moving briefly from the chronological and tactical narrative of Brian and his relationship with the Laigin and the Dubliners, it is worth imagining the effect that all this activity had on Leinster and the wider population. The nobles and general populace of Dublin would seem to have suffered most during this conflict: at Glenn Máma another son of Amlaíb Cúarán, Aralt, was killed along with other nobles. The town was subject to constant burnings and sieges, and their wealth was looted. One interesting detail recorded in the annals is the reference to an act of vengeance against the town perpetrated both by Máel Sechnaill and Brian: they destroyed the special wood associated with Dublin, called *Caill Tomair* 'Thor's forest' to the north of the town.[28] Where was this and why was it so important that it should be cut down or burned? As has been suggested by others, this was some form of ceremonial grove, the significance of which both Brian and Máel Sechnaill would have well

25 Duffy, *Brian Boru*, 138–44. 26 *AI* 997. 27 Ailbhe Mac Shamhráin, 'The battle of Glenn Máma, Dublin and the high-kingship of Ireland' in Seán Duffy (ed.), *Medieval Dublin II* (Dublin, 2000), pp 53–64. 28 *AT* 975; *AI* 1000.

understood.[29] After all, Máel Sechnaill cut down Dál Cais's own sacred tree at Mag Adair in 982, and clearly Brian in his attempt to reach Tara in 1000 did so following some ceremonial ritual as, once he was blocked from doing so by Máel Sechnaill, he proceeded to a place called *Ferta Neimid*, an ancestral grave of some significance in Mag Breg (perhaps Nevitt, b. Balrothery East, Co. Dublin). Máel Sechnaill was particularly aware of the symbolic significance of such sites and objects. During his reign he revived the great assembly Óenach Tailten (Teltown, Co. Meath) and caused poems to be composed about Tailtiu and Tara. These kings were acting out old traditions in ceremonial landscapes and were fully conscious of their import.

LEINSTER, THE BATTLE OF CLONTARF AND ITS AFTERMATH

Although Brian concentrated his energies from 1000 on his efforts to bring the powerful kings of Cenél nEógain and Cenél Conaill in the north to heal, conflict between him and the Laigin and Dublin, and between the latter and Máel Sechnaill, escalated as the decade progressed. This was despite the participation of Laigin and Dublin companies in Brian's northern campaigns. The *Cogadh* depicts this through the personal strife between Brian and Máelmórda, fuelled by the latter's mischievous sister Gormlaith. However, if one follows the military incidents in the years leading up to 1014, it can be perceived that the alliance of the Laigin and Dublin could range far and wide, and was strong enough to cause considerable mayhem. For example, in 1013, they retaliated against Máel Sechnaill's invasion as far as Howth. Máelmórda and Sitriuc caught up with his army and killed his son Flaithbertach at a place called In Draignén (Drinan, b. Coolock, Co. Dublin). They moved deeply into Máel Sechnaill's kingdom and reached the settlement of Fore, Co. Westmeath, carrying off captives and cattle. The Dublin fleet dared to attack Cork and in that attack they lost Sitriuc's son Amlaíb and his nephew, Mathgamain son of Dubgilla. An effort was made by Murchad son of Brian to quell this activity when he raided as far as Glendalough and then Kilmainham near Dublin, while Brian himself once more encamped at Slievemargy, and used it as a base to attack Dublin. Whatever about containing external forces and their ambitions in regard to Ireland, a context for the battle of Clontarf recently proposed by Seán Duffy,[30] Brian and Máel Sechnaill had to contain Sitriuc and Máelmórda and, however they shared it, they always had their eye on Dublin's economic wealth.

29 Poul Holm, 'Viking Dublin and the city-state concept. Parameters and significance of the Hiberno-Norse settlement' in Mogens Herman Hansen (ed.), *A comparative study of thirty city-state cultures* (Copenhagen, 2000), pp 251–62, at p. 257. **30** Duffy, *Brian Boru*, pp 242–8.

In conclusion, one might suggest a further scenario for the context of the battle of Clontarf. The battle of Tara in 980 was decisive in that the ambitions of Sitriuc's father Amlaíb Cúarán, which extended beyond Dublin into Brega and even to Tara, were dashed. What if his son Sitriuc had similar ambitions and that there were three kings in contention for the kingship of Tara (or even Ireland) by the early eleventh century? After all, Sitriuc had a fleet that could range as far as Ulaid or Cork. He minted coins in the late 990s, which were based on the coins of the king Æðelræd II of England. After the battle of Clontarf, he continued to reign for two decades – often in conflict with his neighbours in Leinster and in Brega. In the manner of so many other kings across Europe at the time, he went on a pilgrimage to Rome and returned with the foundation relics for a new cathedral, Christ Church.[31] This was more than Máel Sechnaill ever achieved.

And what of the Laigin? Their dynasties were very divided and weakened by constant conflict. In reality, Maelmórda depended on Sitriuc to hold his kingship and Sitriuc continued to interfere in the politics of Leinster after Murchad's death in Clontarf. He blinded and deposed Máelmórda's son Bran in 1018. Bran left Ireland and died in Cologne in 1052. Sitriuc was defeated by the next king of Leinster, Augaire son of Dúnlaing, at Delgany, Co. Wicklow, in 1021. The year 1024 was calamitous for the established Uí Dúnlainge dynasties of Leinster and it led to their loss of the provincial kingship:

> Augaire son of Dúnlaing, king of Laigin, and Máelmórda son of Lorcán, king of Uí Chennselaig, had a house in which they were at Dubloch captured from them by Donn Slébe son of Máelmórda, king of Uí Faeláin, and they fell there. Donn Slébe was afterwards killed by the Uí Muiredaig.[32]

By 1033, the kingship of Leinster was in the hands of the Osraige and then it was secured by the southern dynasty of Uí Chennselaig whose king, Diarmait mac Maíl na mBó, contended for the high-kingship, and as part of his attempt to do so, sought to control Dublin by installing his son Murchad as king there and expelling its Norse king. It is likely that it was in such circumstances that the Laigin revised history and trumpeted that they had won the battle of Clontarf and killed Brian Bóraime.

31 Raghnall Ó Floinn, 'The foundation relics of Christ Church cathedrals and the origins of the diocese of Dublin' in Seán Duffy (ed.), *Medieval Dublin VII* (Dublin, 2006), pp 89–102. 32 *AU* 1024.

Brian and the Uí Néill kingship of Tara

EOIN O'FLYNN

INTRODUCTION

The spectacular rise of the Dál Cais dynasty during the tenth century came at the expense of the Eóganachta kings in Munster but as Brian Bóraime (Boru) extended Dál Cais influence still further it would lead to an inevitable clash with the Uí Néill kings of Tara. The notion of an Irish king with wide-ranging, even island-wide political authority had been around for a long time: it was intimately bound up with the kingship of Tara and its elaboration owed a great deal to the Uí Néill kings who had come to monopolize that kingship. Brian Bóraime would break that link and come closer than any Uí Néill king of Tara to making the notional real. He would eventually eclipse the storied Uí Néill dynasty and recast Ireland's political order.

Tara was certainly the most prestigious kingship in early medieval Ireland. While the place itself was not ordinarily occupied as a royal residence or fortress – indeed it may not have looked all that different from what we see there today – it developed huge symbolic significance as a place of sovereignty and extraordinary kingship in medieval Ireland. Tara's special, privileged position was elaborated on in a series of texts surviving from the seventh century, where it was closely linked to the Uí Néill, a group of related dynasties, or at the very least a group of dynasties claiming to be related. With an elaborately worked out legendary past the Uí Néill would have us believe that they and their ancestors had long dominated the kingship of Tara. While a good deal of this backstory can be dismissed by the historian, the claim was designed to legitimize a situation where by the late seventh century the Uí Néill *were* tightening their grip on the kingship of Tara and did come to monopolize it.[1] They were to hold it right down to Brian's day in an unbroken sequence. Of course within that we must note that the various constituent branches of the Uí Néill, grouped broadly into northern and southern subsections (see fig. 4.1), were often in bitter conflict with one another for pre-eminence. But whoever came out on top in these struggles, the overking of the various Uí Néill branches held the kingship of Tara. And not only that, the holder of this uniquely prestigious kingship claimed a special position of authority over Ireland's other major kings, even if he was not always in a position to back up these claims.

1 *NHI*, i, pp 187, 212; Thomas Charles-Edwards, *Early Christian Ireland* (Cambridge, 2000), pp 453–5, 495; Byrne, *Irish kings*, p. 137; A.P. Smyth, *Celtic Leinster* (Dublin, 1982), p. 8.

4.1 Regions, dynasties and sites mentioned in the text (including Cenél Conaill and Cenél nEógain of the northern Uí Néill, and Clann Cholmáin of the southern Uí Néill).

By securing the submission of the Airgialla, a group of vassal dynasties found stretching from central Ulster down into the midlands, and also by enjoying generally friendly relations with the Connachta, distant cousins of the Uí Néill in the west, the Uí Néill king of Tara could expect to be the dominant player in the northern half of Ireland (Leth Cuinn or 'Conn's Half', a reference to Conn of the Hundred Battles, a legendary Uí Néill ancestor). When possible the Uí Néill king of Tara also sought to impose himself in the southern half of Ireland and was on occasion able to force the submission of the Laigin (the Leinstermen) as well as the territory of Osraige which was wedged between Leinster and Munster.[2] But influence in this southern sphere was contested by the overkings of Munster, the kings of Cashel. The southern half of Ireland, called Leth Moga (Mug's Half), referred after all to a heroic ancestor of the Eóganachta grouping which had long been dominant in Munster. Indeed, a small number of Munster kings were able not only to contest the extension of Uí Néill authority into the southern half of Ireland but, on a few rare occasions, take the fight to them in the north. But not even the most successful Eóganachta kings had provided anything like the challenge to the Uí Néill kings of Tara that was to come from Dál Cais and Brian Bóraime.

Brian came up against a king of Tara who belonged to the southern or midland Uí Néill branch known as Clann Cholmáin, a branch based in Mide with its main royal site at Lough Ennell in today's County Westmeath. This Clann Cholmáin king was Máel Sechnaill son of Domnall (or Máel Sechnaill II as he appears in some of the history books to distinguish him from his great great-grandfather (Máel Sechnaill I) who had also been a king of Tara back in the ninth century). Indeed, the second Máel Sechnaill could claim that over the previous centuries six of his Clann Cholmáin ancestors had held the kingship of Tara. And indeed by reference to the common Uí Néill origin myth and legendary past he could also claim such famous ancestors as Niall of the Nine Hostages, Cormac mac Airt and Conn of the Hundred Battles.

For Máel Sechnaill, the aim was to gain the power and resources necessary to emulate his more successful Uí Néill predecessors, and his political career certainly started well. He emerged as king of his own Clann Cholmáin branch of the Uí Néill in the later 970s. By 980 he was king of Tara having established himself as the leading Uí Néill king and having defeated the ambitious Hiberno-Norse king of Dublin, Amlaíb Cúarán (Óláfr Kváran), in a major battle *at* Tara that year. The location of that battle in 980 must of course be significant. It seems that Amlaíb had attempted to put himself in the mix but

2 For example, the Uí Néill king of Tara Donnchad Midi (d. 797) briefly occupied several royal sites in Leinster and was generally able to dominate it while the territory of Osraige was brought into the northern sphere of influence during the reign of the ninth-century king of Tara Máel Sechnaill I (d. 862).

he was defeated amidst 'very great slaughter' as the Annals of Ulster put it. And Máel Sechnaill immediately followed up his victory at Tara with an attack on Dublin itself. Following a short siege, he secured its submission, extracted a large tribute in cattle and other valuables and released the king of Leinster (Domnall Clóen) who was being held hostage there.[3] While it seems that Amlaíb had been Máel Sechnaill's greatest early challenger, the defeats of 980 marked the end of his political career. His successor as king of Dublin, his son Glún Iairn (r.980–89), would be submissive to the new Uí Néill king of Tara.[4]

THE STRUGGLE FOR THE HIGH-KINGSHIP

So far so good for Máel Sechnaill. He had made a spectacular start to his career and no doubt planned the further expansion of his power. He also very quickly identified the threat posed by Brian Bóraime, who had by now built on the position established by his older brother Mathgamain, taken a firm grip of Norse Limerick and dealt with his rivals for the kingship of Munster. In 982 Máel Sechnaill attacked. He entered Dál Cais territory having marched south from Mide or perhaps having sailed down the Shannon. As part of the attack Máel Sechnaill cut down the tree of Mag Adair. This seems to have been a sacred tree intimately connected with the Dál Cais dynasty's claims to sovereignty and kingship and was probably located at their inauguration site.[5] By cutting down this sacred symbolic tree Máel Sechnaill was doubtless attempting to put Brian in his place and undermine his legitimacy to rule. An attack by a Munster force on Osraige that same year, which at least one of the annalistic sources claims Brian led personally,[6] may have been the initial trigger for this dramatic intervention in the territory of Dál Cais by the Uí Néill king of Tara. The successes that Brian was enjoying in the southern half of Ireland at the time would have marked him out as worthy of Máel Sechnaill's attention anyway.[7] But Brian was not overawed by Máel Sechnaill. He continued to target Osraige over the next few years as this territory again became an area of dispute between an Uí Néill king of Tara and a king of

3 *AU* 980.1; *AT* 979 [980]; *CS* 978 [980]; *AI* 980.4. Alex Woolf, 'Amlaíb Cuarán and the Gael, 941–81' in Seán Duffy (ed.), *Medieval Dublin III* (Dublin, 2002), pp 34–44; Colmán Etchingham, 'North Wales, Ireland and the Isles: the Insular Viking zone', *Peritia*, 15 (2001), 145–87, at 173–5. 4 As we know, many of the leading political figures from this period were closely related and we have an example here because Glún Iairn was Máel Sechnaill's half-brother. When Máel Sechnaill's father (Domnall) had died, his mother (Dúnlaith) went on to marry Amlaíb of Dublin and Glún Iairn was their son. 5 *AT* 981 [982]; *CS* 980 [982]; *AI* 982.4. After 'being dug from the earth with its roots' according to *AFM* 981 [982] which also says this was the site of an óenach (*bile Aonaigh Maighe hAdhar*); see A.T. Lucas, 'The sacred trees of Ireland', *JCHAS*, 68 (1963), 25. 6 *AFM* 981 [982]. 7 *AI* 982.2; *AFM* 981 [982]; for the family background and career of Brian Bóraime, see Duffy, *Brian Boru*; Ní Mhaonaigh, *Brian Boru*.

Munster. In the year 983, Máel Sechnaill defeated the king of Leinster (Domnall Clóen), and Ímar, the Norse ruler of Waterford in battle. He was supported in this by Glún Iairn, king of Dublin.[8] He could of course rely on Glún Iairn's support having only recently secured Dublin's submission. In the same year Brian again attacked Osraige capturing the king Gilla Pátraic and the Annals of Inisfallen tell us that he also took the hostages of Leinster.[9] There were personal ties involved here since Gilla Pátraic of Osraige was Máel Sechnaill's brother-in-law.[10] The Uí Néill king had tried to consolidate his influence in this part of the country by forming a marriage-alliance with the ruling dynasty. But despite this close connection to the rulers of Osraige, Máel Sechnaill's influence in the region was steadily undermined by Brian in the early 980s while Leinster found itself subject to the competing claims of these two great rivals. The year 983 also saw Brian active in the west. According to the Annals of Inisfallen, he brought a large fleet (*coblach mór*) into Connacht and while he had mixed results and sustained some losses it was a statement of intent.[11]

The following year Brian Bóraime also entered into an alliance with the Norse of Waterford and they were active in the southeast but with, it seems, the ultimate aim of increasing the pressure on the rival Dublin Vikings.[12] According to the Annals of the Four Masters, in 984 Brian was also in a position to attack the west of Mide itself, presumably from the Shannon, which was a most daring assault on the king of Tara's home territory.[13] But in 985 he had to put down a rebellion by the Déisi of Waterford.[14] He was also forced shortly afterwards to imprison his nephew, Áed son of Mathgamain, which suggests some internal opposition.[15] The year 985 also saw Máel Sechnaill attacking the Connachta, his attack including the destruction of 'its islands' (*do thogail a n-innseadh*) suggesting access to a naval capability. They were however able to respond immediately and strike Clann Cholmáin's Lough Ennell heartland.[16]

Brian Bóraime was on the Shannon again in 988, appearing on Lough Ree with a fleet of three hundred vessels which included a contingent of Waterford Norse.[17] While this Munster force suffered a reverse in Connacht, Brian had

8 *AU* 983.2; *AT* 982 [983]; *CS* 981 [983]. 9 *AU* 983.4; *AI* 984.2. It is open to debate whether Brian Bóraime secured the submission of Leinster at this stage; see Duffy, *Brian Boru*, p. 107. 10 Máel Sechnaill was married to Gilla Pátraic's sister Mór, who died in 986: *AFM* 985 [986]. A union between Máel Sechnaill and Gormlaith daughter of Murchad (d. 972), king of the Laigin, is also suggested in some sources but is quite uncertain: see Máire Ní Mhaonaigh, 'Tales of three Gormlaiths in medieval Irish literature', *Ériu*, 52 (2002), 1–24, at 19; Ní Mhaonaigh, *Brian Boru*, p. 31. Máel Maire, daughter of Amlaíb, was another of Máel Sechnaill's wives; we only have her obit. but it would suggest an effort by Máel Sechnaill to strengthen links with Dublin. *AT* 1021; *AFM* 1021. 11 *AI* 983.2. 12 *AI* 984.2. For the rivalry between the Dublin and Waterford Vikings, see Clare Downham, *Viking kings of Britain and Ireland: the dynasty of Ívarr to AD1014* (Edinburgh, 2007, repr. 2012), pp 56ff. 13 *AFM* 983 [984]. 14 *AI* 985.2. 15 *AI* 986.2. 16 *AU*, 985.2; *AT* 984 [985]; *CS* 983 [985]. 17 *AI* 988.2; see also, *AU* 988.1; *AT* 987 [988]; *CS* 986

greater success on entering Mide. In a very provocative move he appeared at the hill of Uisnech during this campaign, a site regarded as the centre of Ireland. Uisnech had been a place of significance in the Irish midlands for millennia and it certainly had royal associations in the medieval period as a symbolically important site for the Uí Néill of Mide.[18] Brian's appearance at the site was clearly designed as another challenge to Máel Sechnaill's authority in the region.

The following year, 989, saw the death of Glún Iairn of Dublin at which point Máel Sechnaill reacted quickly to confirm his authority over the Norse settlement. He laid siege to it again and extracted a substantial tribute.[19] In 990 he went south and defeated a North Munster force, though it may be that Brian Bóraime and Dál Cais were not the primary targets on this occasion.[20] But this period did see Brian and Máel Sechnaill again vie for influence in Leinster.[21] Worryingly from Máel Sechnaill's point of view, while he was away campaigning successfully in Connacht in 992, Brian was able to enter Mide and penetrate as far as the Clann Cholmáin royal complex itself at Lough Ennell.[22] This complex consisted of a large ringfort on the western shore of the lake, Dún na Sciath, and a crannog, Cró Inis, on the water nearby. While Brian soon retreated – something the partisan Clonmacnoise annals note with a degree of relish – his appearance at Máel Sechnaill's home was his most daring and provocative act to date and showed the extent of his confidence and ambition. The fact that Brian's army included a contingent from Connacht also suggests that he had drawn away at least some of the king of Tara's support in the west. This was something of a breakthrough for Brian in Leth Cuinn.

In 993, Brian Bóraime again entered Leth Cuinn, reaching Bréifne by way of Lough Ree with another fleet.[23] As well as this threat, Máel Sechnaill was also attacked by Gilla Pátraic of Osraige in the same year.[24] The links established by marriage-alliance were now proving to be of little practical benefit for Máel Sechnaill. He met Brian directly in battle soon after, and while the king of Tara won that particular encounter, it seems to have been a victory of limited long-term significance.[25] Indeed the general impression we

[988]; *AFM* 987 [988]; mention of the Foreigners of Waterford is found only in *CS* and *AFM*. **18** *AI* 988.2. It may be that an impressive conjoined ringfort built in the late seventh or eighth century and sited prominently at Uisnech was the work of Clann Cholmáin: Roseanne Schot, '*Uisneach Midi a medón Érenn*: a prehistoric cult centre and "royal site" in Co. Westmeath', *Journal of Irish Archaeology*, 15 (2006), 47–63. **19** *AT* 988 [989]; *CS* 987 [989]. *AFM* also records a raid 'as far as Loch Ainninn' by a force of 'Foreigners, Danes, and Leinstermen' the year after Máel Sechnaill's assault on Dublin perhaps suggesting that the settlement had recovered sufficiently to retaliate: *AFM* 989 [990]. **20** *AU* 990.3; *AT* 989 [990]; *CS* 988 [990]; *AFM* 989 [990]. **21** *AFM* 989 [990]; *AI* 991.2. **22** *AU* 992.3; *AT* 991 [992]; *CS* 990 [992]; *AFM* 991 [992]. **23** *AI* 993.2; *AFM* 992 [993]. **24** *AU* 993.4; *AT* 992 [993]; *AI* 993.4; Máel Sechnaill also had to deal with some internal unrest in the midlands about this time. **25** *AT* 993 [994]; *CS* 992 [994].

get from this period is of Brian having greater success in extending and maintaining his influence over the lesser kings.

This shift in power is confirmed by the outcome of a *rígdál* (royal conference) held in 997 near Lough Ree where Máel Sechnaill and Brian sat down to establish their respective spheres of influence. While details about this *rígdál* are found only in sources we might suspect as being biased in favour of Brian (the Annals of Inisfallen and the *Cogadh*) and not included in the annal-texts compiled further north, we need not doubt them because the relationship between these two kings really was transformed in the years after the meeting and that transformation is reflected across the range of sources.[26] It seems it was agreed at this *rígdál* to formally divide authority on the island, Leth Cuinn going to Máel Sechnaill and Leth Moga to Brian Bóraime.[27]

Before the meeting, on paper at least, Brian was subordinate to Máel Sechnaill. After it, he had secured recognition of his parity in Ireland. This was a major concession for the king of Tara to make but he had been forced to come to the negotiating table. The agreement reached at the *rígdál* gave official recognition to the shift in the balance of power between these two kings evident on the ground for some time. As a result of this agreement, the following year the two great rivals are recorded campaigning *together*.[28] As we have seen, Máel Sechnaill had, like previous Uí Néill kings of Tara, periodically extended his influence over Dublin, Leinster and Osraige in the southern half. However, he now handed over the hostages of the Laigin and of Dublin to Brian confirming that they now owed submission to him. In turn Brian delivered the hostages of Connacht, which he had recently secured, to Máel Sechnaill in recognition that he was the dominant king of the northern half.

A NEW HIGH-KING

In 999, Brian Bóraime led his forces towards Dublin to enforce his authority in the region. At the important battle of Glenn Máma fought southwest of Dublin (perhaps near Newcastle Lyons on the Dublin–Kildare border) he defeated Sitriuc, king of Dublin, and Máelmórda the Uí Fáeláin king of Leinster, two kings who were closely related and acting in alliance.[29] There is some question whether Máel Sechnaill took part in this battle and the biases and concerns of the various surviving annal-collections are again a factor here. Considering Brian's growing power there would appear to be little incentive

26 See Ailbhe mac Shamhráin, 'The battle of Glenn Máma, Dublin and the high-kingship of Ireland, a millennial commemoration' in Seán Duffy (ed.), *Medieval Dublin II* (Dublin, 2001), p. 59. **27** *AI* 997.2; Duffy, *Brian Boru*, pp 116–19. **28** *AU* 998.1; *AFM* 997 [998]; *AU* 998.5; *CS* 996 [998]; *AI* 998.2. **29** *AU* 999.8; *AT* 997 [999]; *CS* 997 [999]; *AI* 999.4; MacShamhráin, 'Battle of Glenn Máma', pp 53–65.

for Máel Sechnaill to help him. That said, if the spheres of influence agreed at the 997 *rígdál* were still in force it is possible that Máel Sechnaill played a supporting role, acknowledging Brian's rights over Dublin. Following victory in the battle Brian Bóraime entered Dublin. Sitriuc fled north but soon returned and once he had given hostages to Brian he was granted the kingship of Dublin again.[30] This was certainly an important moment for Brian who had firmly established his authority over Dublin and over the Laigin. Perhaps unsurprisingly he now began to apply renewed pressure on Máel Sechnaill. The uneasy agreement reached with the king of Tara would no longer accommodate his ambition.

In the year 1000, Brian Bóraime set off north with the intention of appearing at Tara itself. He led an impressive army now including the recently subdued Leintermen and the Dublin Norse. But his force also included a contingent from south Connacht, i.e., from Leth Cuinn, suggesting he had put aside the agreement reached at the *rígdál*. While he withdrew from Brega with some losses this was a further demonstration of Brian's determination to eclipse the king of Tara.[31] The Clonmacnoise annals describe the events of this year as 'the first revolt, through treachery, of Brian and the Connacht men against Máel Sechlainn the Great'.[32] This characterization of events is not surprising from partisan texts that sought to portray Brian Bóraime as an illegitimate usurper and which were generally sympathetic to Máel Sechnaill and the Uí Néill old order he represented. On the other hand, the *Cogadh Gáedhel re Gallaibh*, commissioned by Brian's descendants, goes so far as to suggest that an agreement was reached around this time by which Máel Sechnaill was given time by Brian to try to secure the active support of Leth Cuinn including his northern Uí Néill cousins and therefore avoid an immediate submission to Brian.[33] This claim seems unverifiable and is perhaps best regarded as an example of the text depicting its hero, Brian Bóraime, as the magnanimous statesman. But it is clear that by this period Brian Bóraime's power and confidence had grown to such an extent that he was intent on eclipsing the king of Tara. The following year saw Munster forces attacking Mide directly and Máel Sechnaill responded to the intensified aggression by working with Cathal, the overking of Connacht, to frustrate Brian's plans.[34] While several of the annal-texts suggest they built a causeway (tóchar) at Athlone, perhaps intended to facilitate communications between Mide and Connacht, maybe the Annals of Inisfallen are more accurate in claiming they placed an obstruction on the Shannon no doubt intended to disrupt the very successful activities of Brian's fleet. But ultimately these schemes were of no avail.[35]

30 *AU* 1000.4; *AT* 999 [1000]; *CS* 998 [1000]; *AI* 1000.2. 31 *AU* 1000.7; *AT* 999 [1000]; *CS* 998 [1000]. Duffy, *Brian Boru*, pp 129–33. 32 *AT* 999 [1000]; *CS* 998 [1000]. 33 *CGG*, pp 119–31. 34 *AU* 1001.5. 35 *AU* 1001.6; *AT* 1000 [1001]; *AI* 1001.5; *CS* 999 [1001].

Even the Uí Néill friendly annals being kept at Clonmacnoise now acknowledged the momentous changes taking place, slipping in the line, 'Brian begins to reign', at the end of their 1001 entry.[36] The following year he came to Athlone and took the hostages of Mide and Connacht.[37] Máel Sechnaill, unable to continue the struggle, submitted to Brian. Máel Sechnaill would remain as the king of Tara but the ancient title now rang hollow. For centuries the most powerful king in Ireland had been the king of Tara but this was now no longer the case. Instead, over the next few years the Uí Néill king of Tara often accompanied Brian on his circuits around the country in a supporting role as the Dál Cais king sought to secure and maintain the submission of Ireland's most powerful kings, particularly those in the north among the Northern Uí Néill and the Ulaid, something Máel Sechnaill had himself struggled to do.[38] There were setbacks for Brian and he was not immediately successful in his ventures north but his military strength grew and grew as he added to his existing resources the forces of those who submitted, making it ever more difficult for those kings still holding out to remain aloof and deny him their submission.

A sure sign of his growing confidence at this point was his appearance at Tailtiu in 1005 while on the way to Armagh. Tailtiu was another ancient site with strong royal associations and was intimately connected with Tara. Tailtiu was the venue for the famous Óenach Tailten, the annual 'Assembly of Tailtiu' which, among other things, had an important political dimension and was long associated with the Uí Néill.[39] For Brian Bóraime to appear at what was one of the most prestigious sites in Leth Cuinn was clearly no accident but rather, just as with his appearance at Uisnech previously, a move designed to further highlight the extent of his power and underline his claims to wide-ranging political authority in Ireland. And it was perhaps also a move designed to highlight the king of Tara's reduced position.

As well as his famous circuit taking in Armagh in 1005, Brian went on several more around Ireland over the next few years and in the year 1011 he finally forced the submission of Cenél Conaill, the major Uí Néill branch in the far northwest.[40] The king of Cenél Conaill was brought south to the Dál

36 *AT* 1000 [1001]; *CS* 999 [1001]. **37** *AU* 1002.1; *AT* 1001 [1002]; *CS* 1000 [1002]; *AI* 1002.2; *AFM* 1001[1002]; as well as his wife Echrad already mentioned, Brian Bóraime also married Dub Choblaig, daughter of Cathal king of Connacht, a marriage which probably dates from this period. **38** *AU* 1002.8; *AT* 1001 [1002]; *CS* 1000 [1002]; *AI* 1002.4; *AFM* 1001 [1002]; *AU* 1004.7; *AFM* 1003 [1004]. **39** *AU* 1005.7; *CS* 1003 [1005]; *AI* 1005.6. See Aubrey Gwynn, 'Brian in Armagh (1005)', *Seanchas Ard Mhacha*, 9:1 (1978), 42. Máel Sechnaill made a concerted effort to reconnect with Tailtiu, reviving the Óenach Tailten himself in 1007. But his efforts failed in political terms at least, something even admitted by Cúán ua Lothcháin who wrote a poem about Tailtiu at this time: *MD*, iv, p. 163; Jaski, *Early Irish kingship*, p. 53, n. 89; Clodagh Downey, 'The life and work of Cúán ua Lothcháin', *Ríocht na Midhe*, 19 (2008), 55–78. **40** *AU* 1006.4; *AI* 1006.2; *CS* 1004 [1006]; *AU* 1007.7; *AI* 1007.3; *AU* 1010.4; *AI* 1010.4; *CS* 1008 [1010].

Cais royal residence of Cenn Corad (Kincora, Co. Clare) to submit to Brian in person. A small number of raids by Máel Sechnaill into Leth Moga from this period, against the Laigin in 1009 for example, might be interpreted as the king of Tara attempting to revive his own position, but in the overall context this seems unlikely.[41] Rather, having exhausted all options for opposition, once Máel Sechnaill submitted to him he appears to have supported Brian.[42]

In an attempt to buttress his new-found authority in the north it seems Brian Bóraime arranged a marriage-alliance with the Northern Uí Néill, sending a daughter (Bé Binn) off to Flaithbertach, king of Cenél nEógain.[43] But Flaithbertach had reason to resent the rise of Brian. If the ancient Uí Néill-dominated political order had endured, he could have expected to succeed Máel Sechnaill as the king of Tara. Perhaps not surprisingly then, in 1012 he attacked his Northern Uí Néill neighbours Cenél Conaill, doubtless attempting to reassert his own authority in the north. But while doing so Máel Sechnaill went north and burned the Cenél nEógain inauguration site at Tulach Óc (Tullaghogue, Co. Tyrone).[44] Máel Sechnaill was no doubt concerned to preserve his own standing in Leth Cuinn as much as to preserve Brian's authority in the north. But the fact that he had to back down when challenged by Flaithbertach in the midlands the following year is perhaps symptomatic of the king of Tara's declining authority.[45]

A RETURN TO POWER?

The political power carefully built up by Brian Bóraime over the course of his long career began to totter in 1013 as some of those kings who had submitted to him began to rebel. The most serious development from his point of view was the revolt of the Dublin Norse and the Laigin. Máel Sechnaill responded by raiding the hinterland north of Dublin but he lost two hundred men including his son Flann in what was a major defeat for the men of Mide.[46] Though perhaps only designed to flatter Brian, the *Cogadh Gáedhel re Gallaibh* tells us that Máel Sechnaill was reduced to asking for his help and protection.[47] It was clear, however, that Brian would need to come north to confront this challenge to his authority in person.

It seems unclear to me from the various accounts of the battle of Clontarf what role the king of Tara played. The *Cogadh*'s claim that he deserted Brian before the battle started can probably be dismissed as a scurrilous attack on the king of Tara. While we cannot rule out opportunism on Máel Sechnaill's part – perhaps he saw Brian's predicament as a chance to revive his own fortunes –

41 *AU* 1009.1. **42** *AU* 1011; *CS* 1009 [1011]; *AI* 1011.5. **43** *RC*, 48 (1931), 228; her obit is at *AU* 1073.1. **44** *AU* 1012.2. **45** *AU* 1013.3; *AFM* 1012 [1013]. **46** *AU* 1013.5; *AI* 1013.2; *CS* 1011 [1013]. **47** *CGG*, pp 148–51.

this would be out of character after years of apparent loyalty, however grudging. Much depends on the weight we give to the claim in the Annals of the Four Masters that Máel Sechnaill played an important role fighting on Brian's side by inflicting heavy losses on the fleeing Vikings and Leinstermen in a secondary engagement.[48]

CONCLUSION

What is clear is that following Brian Bóraime's death at Clontarf Máel Sechnaill reclaimed his former position of authority. He had reasonable success in securing the submission of Ireland's other major kings until his own death in 1022.[49] But the old order was not to be restored. Despite his best efforts, which included commissioning a good deal of literary material which hammered home the message of ancient and rightful Uí Néill dominance in Ireland, the prestige of the Uí Néill kingship of Tara was by now seriously damaged. While a host of Máel Sechnaill's descendants would also hold the title 'king of Tara', these Uí Máel Sechnaill from Mide were never again the most powerful kings in Ireland. Brian had opened the door for non-Uí Néill contenders who would pursue an ideal of high-kingship which, though elaborated by the Uí Néill, he himself had realized. He had eventually built up an authority, albeit fleeting, greater than anything previously achieved by the Uí Néill kings of Tara. The ancient link between the Uí Néill kingship of Tara and the claim to be the most powerful king in Ireland began to unravel.

48 *CGG*, pp 153–69; *AI* 1014.2; *AU* 1014.2; *ALC* 1014; *CS* 1012 [1014]; *AFM* 1013 [1014].
49 *AU* 1022.3; *AT* 1022; *CS* 1020 [1022]; *AI* 1022.4.

Brian Boru, the Book of Armagh and the Irish church in the tenth and eleventh centuries

DENIS CASEY

Considering the level of attention that has been given to the career of Brian Bóraime (Brian Boru), and to his dealings with the church, it is somewhat surprising that the only surviving text that can confidently be said to contain his input has not been the subject of detailed analysis. That short text – entered into the ninth-century Book of Armagh (TCD MS 52) – famously declares Brian to be *imperator scotorum* ('Emperor of the Scots/Irish'), and may be summarized as an agreement between Brian and the church of Armagh; it is frequently associated (on questionable grounds) with Brian's first recorded visit to that church, in 1005. The text is most commonly referred to in passing, to the effect that it represents a confluence of the aggrandizing interests of the would-be secular and ecclesiastical rulers of Ireland (Brian and the clergy of Armagh respectively), or is noted with regard to the aforementioned neologistic royal title (in consideration of which it will hereafter be referred to as the 'IS-text'). The provisions of the agreement have not been subject to detailed scrutiny, nor has the entry in the manuscript received any significant palaeographical or codicological attention, and the aim of this article is to go some way toward addressing these deficiencies. In doing so, it will begin by looking at Brian's chequered relations with various Irish churches, particularly in the years before the probable composition of the agreement. After that, an edition and translation of the IS-text will be provided, with a discussion of various palaeographic features that impact upon its interpretation. Following on from that, the identity of the scribes will be examined, before ending with a discussion of the text's provisions (in which the codicological context will be shown to have a bearing upon its interpretation).

BRIAN'S MIXED RELATIONS WITH THE CHURCHES OF IRELAND

Brian – like so many successful medieval kings – had blood on his hands. Although he is not recorded as having indulged in the sadistic tendencies of his contemporary Gilla Mo Chonna mac Fogartaig of Southern Brega (who yoked a group of Vikings to a plough and forced two of them to pull a harrow by their scrotums), contemporary and slightly later sources nonetheless imply that Brian had a more ruthless and perhaps darker side to him than is commonly acknowledged.[1] For example, the famous eleventh-/twelfth-century text *Cogadh Gáedhel re Gallaibh* ('The War of the Irish with the Foreigners') claimed that Brian was an enslaver, and that after the battle of Sulchóit and the sack of Limerick in 967:

> *Rothinoil uli in brait sin co cnocanaib Sangail, ro marbait cach oen rob inéchta dib, ocus ro dairait cach oen rob indairtha.*
>
> The whole of the captives were collected on the hills of Saingel. Every one of them that was fit for war was killed, and every one that was fit for a slave was enslaved.[2]

On the same occasion the *Cogadh* claims that Brian's and his brother's men engaged in an act entitled *Grafaing mic Feradaich* ('The races of the son of Feradach'), which appears to have been an organized mass rape of female prisoners:

> *Is and, tra, do ronta grafaing mic Feradaich, accu .i. lini mór do gailsechaib nangall i cnocanaib Sangail imacuart, ocus siat croma, ocus a lama ar lar, ocus gilli na sluag ga mairescuid inandegaid, do rait anma nangall ro marbait isin cath.*
>
> It was then they celebrated also the races of the son of Feradach, viz., a great line of the women of the foreigners was placed on the hills of Saingel in a circle, and they were stooped with their hands on the ground, and marshalled by the horseboys of the army behind them, for the good of the souls of the foreigners who were killed in the battle.[3]

Whatever doubts one may have concerning the reliability of the sources detailing these episodes (they are, after all, recorded over a century after the supposed events), they were nonetheless claimed for Brian by the propagandists of his own descendants, and were not the slanders of enemies. In addition, this darker and more disagreeable side to Brian is not restricted to vanquished battle-opponents and their families, but also comes across in his dealings with the church, or rather with individual churches. Even if all the evidence of the *Cogadh* was to be dismissed out of hand and focus instead

1 *AU* 1013.4: *Gilla Mo-Chonna m. Foghartaigh, ri Deiscirt Bregh, do éc ina chotlud i tigh Mael Sechlainn iar n-ol. Leis do·rata na Gaill fon arathar 7 da Ghall ic foirsed asa tiaghaibh 'na ndiaigh* ('Gilla Mo-Chonna son of Fogartach, king of southern Brega, died in his sleep at Mael Sechnaill's house after a drinking-bout. By him the foreigners were yoked to the plough, and two of them made to harrow after them [and sow seed] from their satchels'). For the interpretation of the final clause to the effect that they were forced to pull the harrow by their scrotums, see Pádraig Ó Súilleabháin, 'Nótaí ar thrí fhocal ó na hAnnála', *Éigse*, 15:1 (1973), 22–3, at 23. 2 *CGG*, pp 80–1 (§53). 3 Ibid., pp 82–3 (§55).

turned upon the somewhat more trustworthy annals, we find that Brian first enters the historical record when violating the church of Inis Cathaig (Scattery Island, in the Shannon estuary), where he killed Ímar, king of Limerick, and Ímar's two sons.[4] An even later account in the Annals of Loch Cé claims that Brian eventually paid dearly for this crime. The night before the battle of Clontarf one of Brian's servants is said to have been troubled by a vision of Senán, patron saint of the church of Inis Cathaig. The servant was told that Senán had come to claim debts owed to him, and ominously that *Ammarach tig amm a niocad re Sénan [...] ocus is eigin friss* ('To-morrow the time for paying them to Senan arrives [...] and they must be paid').[5] Revenge is a dish best served cold, and the patron saint of Inis Cathaig had apparently waited thirty-seven years for his.[6] This highly fanciful story is a reminder that even sources that portrayed Brian positively did not convert his every gyve to a grace, especially when they involved violating ecclesiastical rights.

The following snapshots from other points in Brian's career also demonstrate his chequered dealings with contemporary churches. In 984, his forces devastated the churches of Osraige and Laigin,[7] and three years later he took hostages from the Munster churches of Lismore, Cork and Emly (a sure sign that he was not on good terms with them).[8] Other churches he may have viewed more favourably, such as Ros Ailithir (Rosscarbery, Co. Cork), whose lector he ransomed in 990.[9] Likewise, churches associated with Armagh were granted immunity during a military expedition in 1012 (implying that other churches were fair game for plunder).[10] Furthermore, Brian had close familial links to important churchmen, most notably his brother Marcán held high ecclesiastical offices at a number of churches in Munster, including Emly, with which his Dál Cais dynasty appear to have had a fractious relationship.[11]

4 *AI* 977.2. I have taken Ímar's epithet, *rí Gall* ('king of the Foreigners'), to indicate that he was king of Limerick. The different recensions of *Cogadh Gáedhel re Gallaibh* disagree as to who was responsible for the deaths. The version found in the possibly fourteenth-century manuscript TCD 1319 (formerly H. 2. 17) claims that Brian killed Ímar and his two sons (but omits the location), whereas the version found in the seventeenth-century Brussels MS 2569–2572 claims that it was Uí Dhomhnaill of Corco Baiscinn who committed the deed. For the TCD manuscript reading, see *CGG*, pp 102–3 (§64) and for a translation (but not text) of the Brussels manuscript, see *CGG*, p. cxxxv. **5** *ALC* 1014. This interpretation was made by Hennessy: *ALC*, p. 7, f. 6. **6** A reflection of Inis Cathaig as a place of sanctuary (and possibly this incident?) may be found in the Middle Irish *Betha Senáin* ('Life of Senán'), in which Senán is shown the island and informed by the Archangel Raphael that *Bid dín attaig do Gallaib 7 do Gœdealaib* ('It will be a protection of prayer to foreigners and to Gael'): Whitley Stokes (ed. and trans.), *Lives of the saints from the Book of Lismore* (Oxford, 1890), pp 66 (text) and 213 (translation). **7** *AI* 984.2. **8** *AI* 987.2; *CGG*, pp 106–7 (§66). **9** *AI* 990.2. **10** *AU* 1012.3; for a further discussion of this entry, see below. **11** See, in particular, Donnchadh Ó Corráin, 'Dál Cais – church and dynasty', *Ériu*, 24 (1973), 52–63.

AN EDITION AND TRANSLATION OF THE IS-TEXT

Clearly to speak of Brian's relationship with a monolithic Irish church would be inaccurate, but there was one church that liked to think of itself as the embodiment of ecclesiastical authority in Ireland, namely Armagh. Armagh claimed precedence over all other Irish churches partly by virtue of supposedly being the chief church of St Patrick, the possibly fifth-century Romano-British missionary and so-called 'apostle of the Irish'. Since the seventh century it had attempted to claim primacy over – and a range of jurisdictional rights among – the churches of Ireland.[12] Much of our detailed knowledge for these claims comes from a selection of seventh-century Latin documents recorded in the Book of Armagh, which itself is an early ninth-century manuscript consisting primarily of a complete New Testament, material relating to St Martin of Tours and documents concerning St Patrick.[13] A short Latin text was added to this manuscript (most likely in the early eleventh century) – the IS-text – which is central to interpreting Brian's relationship with Armagh. The close analysis of this text and its contexts that follows is intended to shed light on Brian's dealing with Armagh, and with Irish churches in general.[14] An edition and translation is as follows:[15]

S*anctus* patri[ci]us iens ad c*a*elv*m*	Saint Patrick, while going to heaven,
mandauit totum fructv*m*	ordered that the entire fruit
laboris sui ta*m* babtismi	of his labour, so of baptism
ta*m* causar*um* q*uam* elemoisina-	so of legal suits as of alms,
rum deferendum e*ss*e apos-	to be conveyed to the
tolicæ urbi q*uae* scotice	apostolic city which in Scottic
nominat*ur* ardd macha.	is called Ardd macha.
Síc reperi i*n* bebliot*h*ic[i]s	Thus have I found in the libraries
scotor*um* ego scripsi	of the Scots. I have written,
id *est* caluus P*e*rennis i*n* con-	i.e. Calvus Perennis, in
spectu briain imp*er*ato-	the sight of Brian, Emperor
ris scotor*um* *et* q*uod* scripsi	of the Scots and what I have written
fini<t>uit p*ro* omnib*us* regib*us*	he has determined on behalf of all the
maceriæ	kings of Cashel.

12 A vast amount has been written on this topic; one of the most succinct summaries of Armagh's promotion of the cult of Patrick may be found in Charles Doherty, 'The problem of Patrick', *History Ireland*, 3:1 (1995), 15–18. 13 A diplomatic edition of this Patrician material may be found in *Liber Ardmachanus: the Book of Armagh*, ed. John Gwynn (Dublin, 1913), pp 3–48 (fos 2r–24v). Most of those documents are edited and translated (from this and other manuscripts) in Ludwig Bieler (ed. and trans.), *The Patrician texts in the Book of Armagh*, Scriptores Latini Hiberniae 10 (Dublin, 1979). In addition to the lengthy discussion of the manuscript in the introduction to Gwynn's diplomatic edition, it is discussed briefly in Timothy O'Neill, *The Irish hand: scribes and their manuscripts from the earliest times* (2nd ed. Cork, 2014), pp 20–1, 82 and in Denis Casey and Bernard Meehan,

The last four lines of the text are partly obscured, due to the application of a reagent to the manuscript to make its text more legible. This was a common practice in the nineteenth and early twentieth centuries, but while the application of such chemical solutions makes text more distinct in the short term, they actually cause long-term damage to the manuscript and ultimately darken and obscure the text.[16] Within this reagent-stained section there lies something of a conundrum, in the first word of the penultimate line. In the manuscript the word is written *finituit*, with the first 't' encased by two puncta (one above and one below), which suggests that this 't' was earmarked for deletion; the second 't' also has a punctum above it, which could likewise suggest that it was to be deleted. In the early twentieth century John Gwynn – in his widely accepted reading of the text – believed that the first 't' (but not the final 't') was to be deleted.[17] This gave him *finiuit*, which is the perfect third

'Brian Boru and the Book of Armagh', *History Ireland*, 22:2 (2014), 28–9. **14** Useful discussions of this text may be found in Duffy, *Brian Boru*, pp 138–51; Ní Mhaonaigh, *Brian Boru*, pp 30, 46–7; Casey and Meehan, 'Brian Boru and the Book of Armagh'; Aubrey Gwynn, 'Brian in Armagh (1005)', *Seanchas Ard Mhacha*, 9:1 (1978), 35–50, at 41–8; *Liber Ardmachanus*, ed. Gwynn, pp cii–civ; William Reeves, 'On the Book of Armagh', *PRIA (1889–1901)*, 2 (1891–3), 77–99, at 81–4. For previous editions and translations of the text, see Eugene O'Curry, *Lectures on the manuscript materials of ancient Irish history* (Dublin, 1861), pp 653–4 (Explanation of the Fac-similes: Facsimile R) and Facsimile R (p. 7 (separate pagination for the facsimiles at the end of the volume)); Whitley Stokes (ed. and trans.), *The tripartite Life of Patrick, with other documents relating to that saint*, RS, 2 vols (London, 1887), ii, p. 336 (edition only); *Liber Ardmachanus*, ed. Gwynn, p. ciii (translation; a diplomatic edition of the text is at p. 32 (fo. 16v)); David Howlett (ed. and trans.), *Sealed from within: self-authenticating Insular charters* (Dublin, 1999), pp 79–81 (edition and translation). For a facsimile reproduction of the text, see *Book of Armagh: the Patrician documents*, ed. Edward Gwynn, Facsimiles in collotype of Irish manuscripts 3 (Dublin, 1937), fo. 16v; an online image of fo. 16v may be found at www.confessio.ie/manuscripts/dublincodex#30, accessed 19 Apr. 2016. The text has a brief entry in Michael Lapidge and Richard Sharpe (eds), *A bibliography of Celtic-Latin literature, 400–1200*, Royal Irish Academy Dictionary of Medieval Latin from Celtic Sources: Ancillary Publications 1 (Dublin, 1985), p. 158 (§616). **15** The following editorial practices have been observed: all expanded letters are italicized, square parenthesis enclose editorially supplied letters [ ], angled parenthesis mark a possible scribal deletion < >, manuscript line-endings are maintained but hyphens are introduced for run-on words, word separation has been introduced but punctuation and capitalization reflects that found in the manuscript (in so far as possible). **16** A partial mirror image of the stain is found on the facing folio (fo. 17r), which indicates that the reagent was applied to the *imperator scotorum* text and transferred across when the manuscript was closed. A small patch just above the text has a similar stain (and mirror stain on fo. 17r); the applier may originally have intended to cover the entire text but had a change of heart. It is possible that the reagent stain on the IS-text was the work of Charles Graves in the first half of the nineteenth century, who had applied 'a weak solution of gallic acid in spirits of wine' to improve the legibility of colophons elsewhere in the manuscript: Charles Graves, 'On the date of the MS. called the Book of Armagh', *PRIA (1836–69)*, 3 (1844–7), 316–24 and 356–9, at 319. Gwynn's observations indicate that the treated leaves had already become discoloured by the early twentieth century: *Liber Ardmachanus*, ed. Gwynn, p. xiv. **17** *Liber Ardmachanus*, ed. Gwynn, p. ciii. Gwynn's translation is found in an introductory chapter (on the history of the manuscript) of his

singular of the Latin verb *finio/finere*, whose range of meanings can include both 'determine' and 'finish'.[18] In the 1990s, David Howlett suggested expunging both 't's, leaving *finiui*, the perfect first singular of the same verb.[19]

The deletion and/or retention of one or both of the 't's fundamentally alters how the text is read. If Gwynn is followed, the translation will read 'and what I have written *he* has determined on behalf of all the Kings of Maceria', but if Howlett is followed the translation reads 'and what I have written *I* have completed before all the kings of Maceria'.[20] Leaving aside the final word (discussed below), the significance of the different readings lies in the active or passive roles played by Brian and the scribe. According to Gwynn's reading, Brian appears in a judicial capacity pronouncing upon the agreement; according to Howlett's version the scribe was the active agent and Brian almost a background figure. In my edition, translation and analysis, I have chosen to follow Gwynn's interpretation, primarily for palaeographical reasons, as it seems unlikely to me that a scribe would use two different forms of deletion within the same word.[21]

The scribe in question named himself as Calvus Perennis (a direct translation of the Irish name Máel Suthain, meaning 'Ever-tonsured'; an uncommon name, perhaps implying perpetual religious devotion), and although it is often stated that the whole text was written by Máel Suthain, it actually appears to have been written by two different individuals; the second one (Máel Suthain) starting at the beginning of the eighth line (at *Síc*). This was noted by R.I. Best in the 1920s and again independently by Elizabeth Duncan in 2004.[22] This can be deduced from looking at how various individual

diplomatic edition, which is largely based upon two papers by William Reeves, and his additions to Reeves's work are normally indicated by smaller type and signed '—[ED.]'; ibid., p. xiii, n. 1. Nonetheless, in this instance he appears to have revised Reeves's translation. Reeves's two papers are: 'Memoir of the Book of Armagh', *Swords Parish Magazine* (Mar. and Apr. 1861), 1–12 and 'On the Book of Armagh'. **18** In this he may have been following Reeves, who (although he has *finituit* in his edition) translates the passage as 'and what I have written he decreed for all the kings of *Maceria*': 'On the Book of Armagh', 82. Gwynn may also have been influenced by Stokes who has *finiuit*: Stokes, *Tripartite Life of Patrick*, ii, p. 336. Earlier still, Eugene O'Curry thought that the medial 't' was a 'g', and that the final 't' should stand, and consequently he translated the relevant clause as 'and what I have written he determined for all the kings of Maceriæ'. It is evident from his accompanying note that even at that point in time the text was not clear: 'The word "*finiguit*" in the passage is also a difficulty. The *g* has been also read a *t*. It is indistinct, and in fact looks like a *t* with a dot above and a dot below. If so, these dots would represent the scribe's mark of an erasure, and the letter is to be passed over. The word will then stand "*finivit*"': O'Curry, *Lectures on the manuscript materials*, p. 654. **19** Howlett, *Sealed from within*, p. 79. **20** *Liber Ardmachanus*, ed. Gwynn, p. ciii; Howlett, *Sealed from within*, p. 80: my emphasis (on both occasions). **21** Of course this means that the status of the final punctum is left unresolved. Furthermore, it is not impossible that some or all of these puncta may only have been added considerably later. **22** R.I. Best, 'An early monastic grant in the Book of Durrow', *Ériu*, 10 (1926–8), 135–42, at 135, n. 5: 'It has escaped observation hitherto that this entry has been written by two hands, Mael Suthain's being

letters were written, such as 'd' and 'r'. For example, in their 'd's the first scribe uses a forty-five-degree ascender: *ad* (l. 1), *mandauit* (l. 2), *deferendum* (l. 5) and *ardd* (l. 7), compared to Máel Suthain's squat 'd' with a parallel stroke: *id* (l. 10). The letter 'r' also differs. The first scribe's 'r' is more splayed at the top: *laboris* (l. 3), *causarum* (l. 4) and *deferendum* (l. 5); Máel Suthain's 'r' is much tighter, with the right-hand stroke beginning higher up the shaft: *reperi* (l. 8), *scripsi* (l. 9) and *briain* (l. 11). To these may be added (with less certainty): the first scribe's 'u' is generally closed at the bottom (with the second minim often descending slightly (but perceptively) lower), and the second scribe's 'p' generally tends to round up at the end of the bow (whereas the first scribe's is somewhat flatter).[23] The first scribe also uses the angular form ('v' form) of 'u', which is absent from the second scribe's repertoire. However, since the first scribe only uses the angular 'u' in conjunction with a suspension stroke (for 'm'), and the second scribe does not place a suspension stroke over any of his 'u's, this feature is of limited value for diagnostic purposes.

Like the deletions in *finituit* (discussed above), these palaeographic features have implications for interpreting the text. In short, the text written by the first scribe (ll. 1–7) is essentially a statement of Armagh's claims; the text written by Máel Suthain (ll. 8–14) is an endorsement of those claims, most likely written in the presence of Brian and his retinue. Taken as a whole the text indicates a negotiated settlement rather than a unilateral grant. The change between the two sections is also marked by a shift in voice, from impersonal to first person singular, although the first person singular voice does claim 'ownership' of the preceding text (or perhaps 'joint ownership' along with Brian). These two sections need not even have been written at the same time; the first half could have been written in agreement between Armagh and Brian's advisors and then Máel Suthain could have endorsed it subsequently, in his thicker and less elegant script.

THE IDENTITIES OF THE SCRIBES

The identity of the first scribe will almost certainly never be known, but the second has at least named himself: Calvus Perennis or Máel Suthain in Irish.[24] Although compound-names in the form *Máel-* were extremely common, the

rather heavy and ill-formed'. See also, Elizabeth Duncan, *The Southampton Psalter: a palaeographical and codicological exploration*, Anglo-Saxon, Norse and Celtic Manuscript-Studies 4 (Cambridge, 2004), pp 13–14. **23** These are broad generalizations and there is some variation in the forms of these letters within each hand. **24** Although the first scribe cannot be identified, a detailed discussion and list of the personnel of the church of Armagh may be found in Hérold Pettiau, 'The officials of the church of Armagh in the early and central middle ages, to A.D. 1200' in A.J. Hughes and William Nolan (eds), *Armagh: history and society: interdisciplinary essays on the history of an Irish county* (Dublin, 2001), pp 121–86.

name Máel Suthain is actually quite rare; the earliest suggested attestation is from tenth-century England (in the form 'Mæglsothen'), in the record of a grant of land by King Eadwig, in 956.[25] In the published corpus of secular genealogies there is only one Máel Suthain; he was a member of the Uí Chairpri branch of Uí Fhidgente (a people who occupied part of modern Co. Limerick).[26] In the annals only three individuals possibly bore this name, two of whom are discussed below.[27] Other scattered references include a mention in the twelfth-century Irish *Liber hymnorum*, which mentions a Máel Suthain as an authority for an identification of the place in which Dallán Forgaill composed *Amra Coluim Cille*, but it does not give him a patronymic or link him with Brian.[28]

It is sometimes claimed that the Máel Suthain who authored the IS-text (or at least the second half of it) was Brian's *anmchara* ('confessor'; lit. 'soul friend'). Of that Máel Suthain, the only thing known for certain is the date of his death (1031), which is recorded in the seventeenth-century Annals of the Four Masters and possibly in the eleventh-century Annals of Inisfallen too. The entries are as follows:

> *Maolsuthain, anmchara Briain, mic Ceindeittigh, 7 Conaincc Ua Cerbhaill, airchinnech Glinne dá locha, ceann crábhaidh, 7 déirce na nGaoidhel, décc.*
>
> Maelsuthain, anmchara of Brian, son of Ceinneidigh; and Conaing Ua Cearbhaill, airchinneach of Gleann-da-locha, head of the piety and charity of the Gaeidhil, died.[29]

25 Andrew Breeze, 'Mael Suthain and a charter of King Eadwig', *Notes and Queries*, 53:1 (2006), 23–4. I owe this reference to Dr Pádraic Moran. For details of the charter, see *The electronic Sawyer: online catalogue of Anglo-Saxon charters* (§628): www.esawyer.org.uk/charter/628.html, accessed 11 May 2016. **26** *CGH*, p. 252. That particular genealogy records the floruit of one Cenn Fáelad, eight generations prior to its Máel Suthain. That Cenn Fáelad died in 774 (*AI* 774) and following the standard (albeit imprecise) practice of allotting each generation a span of thirty years, Máel Suthain of Uí Chairpri should have died around 1014. There is no Máel Suthain recorded in the published saints' genealogies: *CGSH*. **27** The third is recorded only incidentally in the seventeenth-century Annals of the Four Masters; he had a son who died in the twelfth century: *Mac Maoilesuthain, áird fhear-leighinn iarthair Ereann décc i tTamhlachta* ('Mac Maeilesuthain, chief lector of the west of Ireland, died at Tamhlacht'): *AFM* 1125 (*AFM* here and hereafter refers to the second edition (Dublin, 1856) of that text). Although his association with the west of Ireland is suggestive, this son would have lived to an extreme age (and be born very late in his father's lifetime or posthumously) in order to be a son of either of the Máel Suthains described below, and so it is likely that this entry testifies to the existence of a third Máel Suthain. **28** J.H. Bernard and Robert Atkinson (eds and trans.), *The Irish Liber hymnorum*, Henry Bradshaw Society 13–14, 2 vols (London, 1898), i, p. 164 (text) and ii, p. 56 (translation). **29** *AFM* 1031.

> *Máel Suthain, sruithsenóir Herend, quieuit in Christo; ocus Macc Uíge ánchara in hóc anno.*
>
> Mael Suthain, venerable senior of Ireland, rested in Christ, and Mac Uige the anchorite, rested this year.[30]

Interestingly, in the near-contemporary Annals of Inisfallen this Máel Suthain was not linked with Brian; it is only in the seventeenth-century Annals of the Four Masters that the connection is made. The inclusion of a different co-deceased in the Annals of the Four Masters entry would suggest that if both texts are referring to the same person then the entry in the Annals of the Four Masters does not draw upon the Annals of Inisfallen or on a closely related text at this point.

There is, however, another (and perhaps better) candidate for the authorship of the IS-text. Four annalistic collections record the death of a prominent man of learning named Máel Suthain, who appears to have been a member of Eóganacht Locha Léin (in the vicinity of Killarney, Co. Kerry), under the year 1010:

> *Moel Suthain Hua Cerbaill {do Eoganacht,} ardshui na Herend, quieuit in Christo i nAchud Deo.*
>
> Mael Suthain Ua Cerbaill {of Eóganacht}, eminent sage of Ireland, rested in Christ in Achad Deó.[31]

> *Mael Suthain H. Cerbaill, ardshui Erenn 7 ri Eoganachta Locha Lein, Marcan m. Cenneitigh comarba Coluim m. Cremhthainn 7 Innsi Celtra 7 Cille Da Lua, Muiredach m. Mochloingsi airchinnech Mucnama, in Christo dormierunt.*
>
> Mael Suthain ua Cerbaill, chief sage of Ireland, and king of Eóganacht of Loch Léin, Marcán son of Ceinnéitig, successor of Colum son of Cremthann and [superior] of Inis Celtra and Cell dá Lua, [and] Muiredach son of Mochloingse, superior of Mucnám, fell asleep in Christ.[32]

30 *AI* 1031.4. 31 *AI* 1010.5. The words *do Eoganacht* ('of Eóganacht') were added to the entry by a later hand. Máel Suthain's death in Achad Deó (Aghadoe, on the shore of Lough Leane) does lend credence to claims for his membership of Eóganacht Locha Léin. A cross has also been added next to Máel Suthain's name in the margin of the manuscript of the Annals of Inisfallen (Bodl. Rawlinson B 503, fo. 20v), which may indicate interest in him on the part of the church of Inisfallen (an island in Lough Leane) where the manuscript was kept in the later Middle Ages, thus reinforcing the suggestion that he was indeed a member of the Eóganachta Locha Léin. 32 *AU* 1010.2. The words *7 ri Eoganachta Locha Lein* ('and king of Eóganacht of Loch Léin') were additions to the main text (in both manuscripts of the text). As Kathleen Hughes demonstrated (using a number of tenth-century examples, including one from Brian's Dál Cais dynasty), Máel Suthain was not unique in combining

> *Maolsuthain Ua Cerbhaill do mhuinntir Insi Faithlend, primh saoi iarthair domhain ina aimsir, 7 tigherna Eoghanachta Locha Léin, décc iar ndeighbhethaidh.*
>
> Maelsuthain Ua Cearbhaill, [one] of the family of Inis-Faithleann, chief doctor of the western world in his time, and lord of Eoghanacht of Loch-Lein, died after a good life.[33]

> *Sé bliadhna iar sin co bas Cathail meic Concabair righ Connacht & Maoilsuthain hI Cerbaill airdecnaid hErenn.*
>
> Six years after that to the death of Cathal son of Conchobar, king of Connacht, and Máel Suthain Ua Cerbaill, chief sage of Ireland.[34]

It is possible that the 1031 obit in the Annals of Inisfallen may replicate the earlier (1010) obit in that text, but there is nothing to suggest a duplication (except the extremely common phrase *quieuit in Christo*), nor would this explain parallel duplications in the unconnected Annals of the Four Masters. Consequently, it is more likely that there were two prominent individuals of the same name. I suggest that the earlier Máel Suthain (who died in 1010) is more likely to be the Máel Suthain of the Book of Armagh than the later one, for reasons relating to the respective titles accorded to the two men. The later Máel Suthain was *sruithsenóir Herend* ('venerable senior of Ireland') (*AI*) or *anmchara Briain, mic Ceindeittigh* ('anmchara of Brian, son of Ceinneidigh') (*AFM*). The role of *anmchara* was that of a 'confessor' or 'spiritual director'. According to various earlier ecclesiastical sources from the first millennium, the *anmchara* was charged with providing spiritual guidance and overseeing penance, and this was a function that could be exercised by prominent ecclesiasts; for example, the eighth-century text *Ríagal Phátraic* suggests that the chief bishop should act as an *anmchara* to prominent laymen and ecclesiasts.[35] In terms of financial considerations, the *anmchara* was potentially a recipient of rewards from those to whom he gave direction, and this led to warnings that people were likely to reward their confessors in lieu of doing as they were instructed.[36] Overall, the position of *anmchara* does not appear to be linked to administrative matters such as those dealt with in the IS-text. The term *sruithsenóir* accorded to Máel Suthain in the Annals of Inisfallen does not have very precise connotations and may mean nothing more specific than Mac Airt's translation ('venerable senior') allows.[37]

ecclesiastical and secular office: Kathleen Hughes, *The church in early Irish society* (London, 1966), pp 221–3. 33 *AFM* 1009. 34 Gearóid Mac Niocaill (ed.), 'Annála gearra as proibhinse Ard Macha', *Seanchas Ardmhacha*, 3:2 (1958–9), 337–40, at 330. My translation. Alone among the four entries, this one does not provide any indication either of where Máel Suthain was from or where he died. 35 Colmán Etchingham, *Church organisation in Ireland A.D. 650 to 1000* (Maynooth, 1999), pp 63–4. 36 Ibid., pp 260–1. 37 For examples of the

In contrast, the earlier Máel Suthain (Máel Suthain Ua Cerbaill) is accorded the title *ardshui na Herend* ('eminent sage of Ireland') (*AI*), *ardshui Erenn* ('chief sage of Ireland') (*AU*), *primh saoi iarthair domhain ina aimsir* ('chief doctor of the western world in his time') (*AFM*) and *airdecnaid hErenn* ('chief sage of Ireland') (*Annála Gearra*). Despite the variations in the translations, all but the last of these incorporate the same word, *suí*, in his title. The term *suí* could be applied to a master of either poetic or ecclesiastical learning, and on occasion the *suí* exercised judicial functions.[38] With regard to this combination of learning and official position, Colmán Etchingham has summarized: '*Suí* refers not simply to learning or professional accomplishment in a general sense, but to the pinnacle of achievement in the class or profession concerned'.[39] Thus the title of *suí* was not a vague honorary one, but was awarded to someone who held an official and definite position at the top of the scholarly hierarchy.[40] *Annála Gearra*'s *airdecnaid* ('chief sage') seems slightly different from *ardshui* in that although it refers to one extremely skilled in human or divine learning, it does not have definite career connotations like *suí*, and *ecnae* is used of ecclesiastical scholars in general, in legal texts discussing scholars' status.[41] Other evidence pointing to Máel Suthain Ua Cerbaill's learned status includes a poem on ecclesiastical grades ascribed to him in the fifteenth-century manuscript Bodl. Laud 610 (again with no mention of Brian).[42] Since the IS-text is concerned with important ecclesiastical financial matters, Brian may well have employed the services of a learned individual when negotiating them, such as a *suí* like Máel Suthain Ua Cerbaill. The style of Latin used by the Máel Suthain of the Book of Armagh offers circumstantial support to the identification of him with the *suí* Máel Suthain Ua Cerbaill, as he apparently enjoyed showing off his learning through translating his own name, claiming to have consulted 'the libraries of the

usage of the two elements individually, see ibid., pp 65 (*senóir*) and 207 (*sruith*). However, it is possible that *senóir* may reflect the Latin *seniores* of the *Collectio canonum Hibernensis*, who appear to have had some judicial or arbitration functions; ibid., pp 167 and 206. **38** Ibid., pp 70 and 142. **39** Ibid., p. 185. **40** T.M. Charles-Edwards, *Early Christian Ireland* (Cambridge, 2000), p. 267. For a more recent discussion of the *suí*, see Elva Johnston, *Literacy and identity in early medieval Ireland*, Studies in Celtic History 33 (Woodbridge, 2013), pp 99–101 and 109–12. In the eleventh century, the title *suí* is found in the obits of notable scholars, e.g., Eochaid ua Flannacáin, the father of Máel Muire (*comarba Pátraic* in Brian's time), was called *sui fhilidechta 7 senchusa* ('a master of poetry and historical lore'): *AU* 1004.2. The ecclesiastical hierarchies (including the scholarly hierarchy) were discussed in depth in Liam Breatnach, 'The church in the laws of early medieval Ireland', Statutory Public Lecture, School of Celtic Studies, DIAS, 2014. That lecture was podcast on https://youtu.be/vmHd7WD2EPQ, accessed 19 Apr. 2016; the accompanying handout is available at http://dias.ie/images/stories/celtics/STAT Lecture2014handout.pdf, accessed 19 Apr. 2016. **41** Charles-Edwards, *Early Christian Ireland*, p. 267. For some of the difficulties in interpreting the role of the *ecnae* (Middle Irish *ecnaid*), see Johnston, *Literacy and identity*, pp 106–7. **42** Kuno Meyer (ed.), 'Mitteilungen aus Irischen Handschriften', *ZCP*, 5 (1905), 21–5 and 495–504, at 498–9.

Scots', coining a new and grandiose title for Brian, and cleverly using the somewhat obscure word *maceriæ* to denote the place-name 'Cashel'.[43]

If there were two Máel Suthains – the earlier of whom was the second scribe of the IS-text and the later Brian's *anmchara* – then it appears that they were compounded at least by the time a later story was written in the fifteenth-century manuscript known as *Liber Flavus Fergusiorum*, in which Máel Suthain Ua Cerbaill was called *anmchara* of Brian.[44] That story is not entirely flattering to Máel Suthain, depicting him as potentially hell-bound on account of placing his own interpretations on the scriptures, sexual adventurism and neglecting to recite the hymn *Altus Prosator*, although he does make good these defects in order to ensure his eventual salvation.[45] Nonetheless, as O'Curry notes, the value of the tale is in highlighting (the compound) Máel Suthain's reputation for learning and for indicating that his manuscripts were believed to have been kept in Inisfallen after his death.[46]

THE PROVISIONS OF THE AGREEMENT

According to the agreement, Armagh specifically claimed 'the entire fruit of his [Patrick's] labour, so of baptism so of legal suits as of alms', which Etchingham has characterized as 'the fruits of pastoral care, the profits of justice and discretionary endowments'.[47] There is some ambiguity in the phrase 'the entire fruit of his labour'; this is not a comprehensive list of all possible church dues, as tithes, first fruits and firstlings were all occasionally advocated dues (whatever about the reality of their payment), but they are not mentioned in the IS-text. Among those claimed in the text, some may have been limited in extent, for example, *elemosina* ('alms') is generally used in the early canon law texts to specify offerings made in conjunction with the performance of penance, rather than alms in general.[48] The profits of *causae* ('legal suits') may also have been restricted, and derive from cases concerning

43 This place-name identification was first made in O'Curry, *Lectures on the manuscript materials*, p. 654. 44 Ibid., pp 76–9 (partial and interpolated translation) and 529–31 (Appendix XL; text). It was later reedited (and translated into French) by Joseph Vendryes (ed. and trans.), 'L'aventure de Maelsuthain', *Revue Celtique*, 35 (1914), 203–11. The language of this story suggests that it cannot be earlier than the thirteenth century. 45 In the reference to *Altus prosator* we may note a slight Columban link with the Máel Suthain mentioned in the *Liber hymnorum* as an authority on Dallán Forgaill's composition of *Amra Coluim Cille*. 46 O'Curry, *Lectures on the manuscript materials*, p. 79. In contrast, William Reeves believed that the Máel Suthain who wrote the IS-text was the *anmchara* of Brian who died in 1031, and that O'Curry had compounded the two Máel Suthains: Reeves, 'On the Book of Armagh', 83, n. 2. He also made this identification in his earlier 'Memoir of the Book of Armagh', 4–5. 47 Etchingham, *Church organisation*, p. 217. 48 Ibid., pp 240, 242–3. There are also references to *elemosina* for the souls of the dead; ibid., pp 246–7.

inheritance, and specifically inheritances that may have been tied to perpetual ecclesiastical service. This is the only context in which *causae* is found in the Patrician Lives in the Book of Armagh. According to Tírechán, Patrick and Lóegaire sat in judgment on a matter of inheritance between seven brothers from Tírechán's own territory, *et inuestigauerunt causam hereditatis illorum* ('and they examined the case of their inheritance'), which was subsequently divided in seven.[49] Consequently, the brother closest to Patrick declared: *'filium meum et partem hereditatis meae ego immolo Deo Patricii et Patricio'. Per hoc dicunt alii quia serui sumus Patricii usque in praesentem diem* ('"I offer my son and my share in the inheritance to Patrick's God and to Patrick". It is for this reason, some say, that we are servants of Patrick to the present day.')[50] This example may suggest that the legal cases in which Armagh was interested may have had a direct bearing upon their own property and long-term interests (rather than legal cases in general).

That Patrick is said to have made his declaration 'on the way to heaven' may have been intended to give it added force. Early Irish law indicates a number of instances where statements made at the point of death (or potentially the point of death) were considered especially binding. For example, an oath of paternity sworn by a woman in danger of dying during labour was considered incontrovertible (despite the general inadmissibility of female oaths),[51] and likewise an *audacht* ('bequest') made before death was considered the most noble type of speech, owing to the uncertain fate of the soul.[52] Naturally, there was no question-mark hanging over the fate of Patrick's soul, but in Muirchú's Life of Patrick, the saint made four demands immediately prior to death, all of which were granted by God, and the IS-text may have been worded to evoke the potency of his authoritative near-death demands.[53]

In addition to possible influence from Tírechán's and Muirchú's Lives of Patrick, the position of the IS-text within the Book of Armagh may also have significance for understanding the provisions of the agreement; it was probably placed on fo. 16v in order that it be read with an eye to the surrounding texts. Máel Suthain claimed to have consulted various, unnamed records before completing it, and John Gwynn was in little doubt that the records alluded to in the eighth and ninth lines of the text were from the *Liber Angeli* ('The Book of the Angel'), a seventh-century composite document that advanced various claims of Armagh.[54] It seems, however, that in addition to influence from Muirchú and Tírechán, the IS-text may actually draw directly on the texts that

49 Bieler, *Patrician texts*, pp 134–5 (Tírechán, §15). 50 Ibid. 51 Fergus Kelly, *A guide to early Irish law*, Early Irish Law Series 3 (Dublin, 1988), p. 202. 52 Ibid., p. 123. The sacrosanct nature of an oath sworn at death seems to be implied in an incident in which a member of Clonmacnoise was put to death in a revenge killing and swore at the point of death that he was innocent: *CS* 896. The Four Masters regarded his death as a martyrdom: *AFM* 891. 53 Bieler, *Patrician texts*, pp 116–17 (Muirchú, §§II.5–6). 54 *Liber Ardmachanus*, ed. Gwynn, pp lxviii and ciii, n. 3.

immediately surround it; those are the eighth-century *Additamenta* to Tírechán's Life of Patrick, which begin on column two of fo. 16v (before the IS-text) and end on column two of fo. 18v (after the IS-text). In essence, these *Additamenta* are 'a series of memoranda concerning gifts of lands and churches, which seem to have been collected by Ferdomnach with the object of giving further support to the claims of the See of Armagh'.[55] The IS-text's location in the manuscript appears to have been carefully chosen; it is found nestled among the *Additamenta*, in the last third of the second column of fo. 16v. The precise choice of location appears have been informed by more than a simple desire to utilize the first available space in the manuscript. Had the later scribes only desired to place their text among the *Additamenta*, all they had to do was turn over one more leaf and they would have found ample room, as the second column of fo. 17v is empty. On the first column of fo. 17r, however, directly adjacent to the column containing the IS-text, is the record of an incident whereby Patrick was said to have prevented a split among his followers and that henceforth they were to be united *cum uno fidei ritu sub potestate unius heredis suae apostolicae cathedrae Alti Machœ* ('with the profession of one faith under the authority of the one heir of his apostolic cathedral of Armagh').[56] These claims for Armagh's apostolic authority in the *Additamenta* complement the *causae* to be brought to the apostolic city (*apostolicœ urbi*) in the IS-text. Therefore, it is possible that the text was placed on fo. 16v so that it could be read in conjunction with the earlier claim, which was recorded in the *Additamenta* on fo. 17r (and not *Liber Angeli*),[57] and thus provide a means of validating Armagh's earlier claims.[58]

As for Armagh's jurisdiction and the application of the claims, it is not stated where they were to be levied; were they to come from churches supposedly founded by Patrick or from non-Patrician churches too? Something of a consensus seems to have developed in support of Reeves's maximal view by which this record 'confirmed to Armagh the ecclesiastical supremacy of Ireland'.[59] Whatever about Armagh's long-standing claims to

55 *Book of Armagh: the Patrician documents*, ed. Gwynn, p. iii. Gwynn assigned the role of collector of this material to Ferdomnach (d. 846), seemingly on the basis of the theory that Ferdomnach was the sole scribe of the Book of Armagh. It appears that Ferdomnach did not write the *Additamenta*. For a discussion of the different hands in the manuscript, see Richard Sharpe, 'Palaeographical considerations in the study of the Patrician documents in the Book of Armagh', *Scriptorium: revue internationale des études relatives aux manuscrits*, 36 (1982), 3–28. **56** Bieler, *Patrician texts*, pp 172–3. **57** The two texts are almost exactly parallel, as shown by the reagent stain above the initial 's' of the IS-text, which has transferred over onto the ending of the third and fourth lines of the fo. 17r text. Both texts begin (coincidentally?) with the words *Sanctus Patricius*. **58** The choice of Latin over Irish may have been intended as a means of aiding the later text to conform linguistically to the earlier records. Fo. 16v appears to have had an existing blank space, and no text was erased to make room for the IS-text. I am grateful to Dr Bernard Meehan for allowing me permission to inspect the manuscript while working on the *Emperor of the Irish* exhibition at TCD (2013–14). **59** Reeves, 'Memoir of the Book of Armagh', 4.

broad and even Ireland-wide jurisdiction, this text is more interested in securing the 'entire fruit' of the claims mentioned, rather than establishing a sphere of jurisdiction, suggesting that the issue of jurisdiction was not at issue. Nonetheless, the IS-text should probably be read in a more restricted sense than Reeves would allow. If Brian was *imperator scotorum*, one might expect that he would make an agreement binding upon all of Ireland, and yet it is clear from the second section of the text that Brian did not make an agreement on behalf of all the Irish, or every Irish king, but specifically *pro omnibus regibus maceriæ* ('on behalf of all the kings of Cashel'); the claims were only to be enforced in Munster (reading Cashel metonymically for Munster). Armagh had been advancing its claims in Munster during the second half of the tenth century, as in 973 when Brian's elder brother, Mathgamain, appears to have favoured Armagh over Emly, the chief church of his Eóganachta rivals.[60] The IS-text should not be read as an Ireland-wide manifesto of a Brian–Armagh diarchy, but rather be read as one more piece of evidence for Armagh's long-standing attempts to strengthen its presence in Munster (an ongoing process witnessed by other texts from at least a century earlier, such as the Tripartite Life of Patrick and the second recension of *Senchas fagbála Caisil* ('The story of the finding of Cashel')).[61] Notable absentees from the IS-text are the clergy of Munster, who do not appear to have been present to give their assent to the agreement (except Máel Suthain, although he is not known to have held a clerical grade). It seems that Eugene O'Curry's interpretation of the text was both perceptive and somewhat wide of the mark, as was his wonted brilliant intellectual manner:

> The entry was in fact made as a solemn determination by the *Ard-Righ* (Chief-King, 'Imperator', Emperor) of the Gaedhil (Scots), of the supremacy of the Primatial seat of Armagh over the Archiepiscopal capital of Cashel, over which Brain, as King of Munster, was the immediate monarch.[62]

Anachronisms aside, O'Curry seems to have been correct in assigning a Munster focus to the IS-text. One further piece of evidence that points to a restricted and possibly Munster-only interpretation of the agreement is the record of a hosting by Brian to Mag Muirthemne (Co. Louth) in 1012, during which he granted the churches of Patrick complete immunity (*ogshoere*).[63] If

60 *AI* 973.3. **61** A short version of *Senchas fagbála Caisil* is also found at the beginning of the twelfth-century Dál Cais/Uí Briain text *Lebor na cert*. It appears to be based upon the second recension, as it focuses on Patrick: Myles Dillon (ed. and trans.), *Lebor na cert: the book of rights*, ITS 46 (Dublin, 1962), pp 2–5. The list of blessings supposedly uttered by Patrick, at the end of *Lebor na cert*, however, is based on the first recension of *Senchas fagbála Caisil*; ibid., pp 120–1 and Myles Dillon (ed. and trans.), 'The story of the finding of Cashel', *Ériu*, 16 (1952), 61–73, at 65 (edition) and 68–9 (translation) (§2). **62** O'Curry, *Lectures on the manuscript materials*, p. 654. **63** *AU* 1012.3.

Calvus Perennis, the scribe of the IS-text, was indeed Máel Suthain Ua Cerbaill who died in 1010, then presumably Patrick's churches in what is now north Co. Louth should have been immune from plunder/billeting/supplying provisions before 1012, unless the text was not a statement of general concord and/or it was only applicable in Munster.[64]

THE DATE OF THE IS-TEXT

As alluded to above, the IS-text may not have been written in one sitting. Scholars since at least the time of William Reeves in the middle of the nineteenth century have linked the text with Brian's gift of twenty ounces of gold to Armagh in 1005, an incident that is recorded in the Annals of Ulster and the Annals of the Four Masters.[65] In the Annals of Ulster:

> *Slogad la Brian co rigraidh Erenn ime co hArd Macha co farcaibh .xx. unga do ór for altoir Patraicc. Luidh fora culu co n-etire fer nErenn laiss.*
>
> Brian, accompanied by the royalty of Ireland, brought an army to Ard Macha, and left twenty ounces of gold on Patrick's altar. He went back, bringing the pledges of the men of Ireland.[66]

Likewise the Four Masters claim:

> *Slóigheadh lá Brian, mac Cindeidigh co fferaibh deisceirt Ereann imme co Cenel nEoghain 7 co hUltoiph, do chuinghidh giall. Aseadh lodar dar Mide co mbattar aidhche i tTailltin. Lotar iaromh co mbáttar sechtmhuin occ Ard Macha, co farcaibh Brian xx uncca dór for altóir Arda Macha.*

64 This interpretation is contingent upon seeing a formal relationship between Armagh and the Patrician churches of Mag Muirthemne. 65 Reeves claimed that it was most likely during Brian's 1004 (recte 1005) visit to Armagh that the entry was made, during which 'he presented a golden ring of twenty ounces as an offering': Reeves, 'Memoir of the Book of Armagh', 4. John Gwynn (seemingly drawing on Reeves) suggested 'He became King at the age of seventy-six, in 1002; and in 1004 he made a royal progress through Ireland, receiving the submission of the people as he went along. Having arrived in Armagh, he remained in that city for a week, and presented a golden ring of twenty ounces as an offering on St. Patrick's altar. Presumably it was on this occasion that he caused the entry to be made': *Liber Ardmachanus*, ed. Gwynn, p. ciii. The year 1004 is based on the Annals of the Four Masters and Hennessy's *Annals of Ulster*; *Liber Ardmachanus*, ed. Gwynn, p. ciii, n. 1. John V. Kelleher also linked the gift of 22oz of gold in 1005 to the IS-text (in claiming it was 22oz he was following a misprint in Hennessy's translation (though not edited text)): John V. Kelleher, 'Early Irish history and pseudo-history', *Studia Hibernica*, 3 (1963), 113–27, at 119. The suggestion that the gold was in the form of a ring seems to be based upon a claim made in the so-called Dublin Annals of Inisfallen: Gwynn, 'Brian in Armagh (1005)', 47, n. 1. 66 *AU* 1005.7.

> A hosting by Brian, son of Ceinneidigh, with the men of the south of Ireland, into Cinel-Eoghain and Ulidia, to demand hostages. They proceeded through Meath, where they remained a night at Tailltin. They afterwards marched northwards, and remained a week at Ard-Macha; and Brian left twenty ounces of gold [as an offering] upon the altar of Ard-Macha.[67]

However, there is no evidence to support the assumption that Brian's offering and the writing of the IS-text occurred at the same time or in the same place, and the IS-text has no internal dating criteria (except, by implication, the deaths of Brian and Máel Suthain). There is neither any mention of Brian's offering in the Book of Armagh nor any pledges or hostages that he may have taken, which might be expected if the two events were linked.[68] If the IS-text was written in Armagh, then it may just as easily have been penned during one of Brian's subsequent expeditions to the North.[69] For example, Brian made a successful royal progress through the North in 1006, and on that occasion, the Annals of Ulster claim that he granted the *ógríar* ('full demand') of the community of Armagh.[70] That *ógríar* could theoretically have been the recognition of Armagh's claims, as espoused in the first section of the IS-text.

Furthermore, just as it is an assumption that the text was written in 1005, so too is it an assumption that it was written in Armagh, whereas it is perfectly feasible that it was written in Munster. The final phrase of the text, *pro omnibus regibus maceriæ* ('on behalf of all the kings of Cashel'), may suggest that the text (or at least Máel Suthain's section) was written in Munster. If this statement simply indicates who was bound by the terms of the agreement, then it cannot be used to localize the place of writing. If, however, it is read as an indication of who was present, then it may suggest that the text was written in Munster. After all, if it was written in Armagh then it might be expected that more than just Munster kings would be alluded to, since Brian travelled to Armagh in 1005 *co rigraidh Erenn* ('accompanied by the royalty of Ireland') according to the Annals of Ulster, and the Annals of Inisfallen claim he was accompanied by *fer nErend eter Gullu 7 Goedelu* ('the men of Ireland, both Foreigners and Irish').[71] The Book of Armagh may have had the status of a relic (it may have been enshrined in the tenth century) and was possibly one of the insignia of the *comarbai Pátraic* ('heirs of St Patrick'), which makes it conceivable that it may have been carried about by Armagh clerics on official

67 *AFM* 1004. **68** Although Mac Airt and Mac Niocaill translate *etire* as 'pledges', the *aitire* of early Irish law was a 'hostage-surety'. For the *aitire*, see Kelly, *Guide to early Irish law*, pp 172–3. **69** Duffy, *Brian Boru*, p. 141. **70** *AU* 1006.4: *co tarait oighreir samhtha Patraicc 7 a comharbai, .i. Mael Muire mc. Eochadha* ('and the full demand of the community of Patrick and of his successor i.e., Mael Muire son of Eochaid, was granted'). This circuit is also reported in *AI* 1006.2, *CS* 1004 and *AFM* 1005. **71** *AU* 1005.7 and *AI* 1005.3.

business.[72] Furthermore, Armagh appears to have had a representative in Munster in the first decade of the eleventh century, in the person of Tuathail ua Maíl Macha, *comarba Patraic i mMumhain* ('successor of Patrick in Munster'), who died in 1007.[73] It is not impossible that he possessed the book temporarily, at some point either before or after 1005 and that the IS-text was entered into it during that period. The Annals of the Four Masters accord him the additional title of *saoi* (*suí*), and a scenario could be imagined in which the IS-text was an agreement negotiated by him and his fellow *suí*, Máel Suthain Ua Cerbaill. Regardless of the latter suggestion, if the text was written before 1005, then it may be possible to read Brian's gift of twenty ounces of gold as a partial fulfilment of the agreement.

Brian's title in the text also has relevance to its dating. John V. Kelleher (like John Ryan in discussion with Aubrey Gwynn) saw in *imperator scotorum* a translation of *árd-rí Érenn*,[74] but Gwynn himself suggested that it was inspired by the title adopted by the Holy Roman Emperor Otto III, who styled himself *imperator romanorum* ('emperor of the Romans').[75] Consequently, Gwynn implied a *terminus post quem* for the IS-text of 996 (the beginning of Otto III's reign).[76] Gwynn – by his own admission relying on a revised version of a textbook from the 1890s – claimed that Otto III had abandoned his father's and grandfather's title, *imperator romanus*, in favour of this new title.[77] However, Otto III was not actually that innovative, and his father Otto II had already styled himself *imperator romanorum Augustus* since 982, thus weakening Gwynn's dating argument.[78] There is also an alternative source for Brian's title, one much closer to home, namely the Book of Armagh itself. In Muirchú's *Vita Sancti Patricii* ('Life of St Patrick'), Lóegaire mac Néill, king of Tara, is described as

> *rex quidam magnus ferox gentilisque, imperator barbarorum regnans in Temoria, quae tunc erat caput regni Scotorum, Loiguire nomine filius Neill, origo stirpis regiae huius pene insolae.*

72 The Book of Armagh may have been the *Canóin Phátraic* ('Canon of Patrick'), which was enshrined in the 930s by Donnchad mac Flainn, grandfather of Brian's sometime enemy and ally, Máel Sechnaill mac Domnaill: *AFM* 937. 73 *CS* 1005; *AFM* 1006. His grandfather's name (Máel Macha, 'servant of [Ard?] Macha') and his own title suggests that he was Armagh's representative in Munster. Officials known as *maír Pátraic* ('Patrick's stewards') and *maír Muman* ('stewards of Munster'), presumably associated with Armagh, appear frequently in the eleventh- and twelfth-century annals. For a list of these stewards, see Ní Mhaonaigh, *Brian Boru*, p. 147, n. 180. 74 Kelleher, 'Early Irish history and pseudo-history', 119–20. 75 Gwynn, 'Brian in Armagh (1005)', 45. Marie Therese Flanagan has suggested that Brian's title may be comparable to the kind of titles used in contemporary England: M.T. Flanagan, *Irish society, Anglo-Norman settlers, Angevin kingship: interactions in Ireland in the late twelfth century*, Oxford Historical Monographs (Oxford, 1989), p. 179. 76 Gwynn, 'Brian in Armagh (1005)', 44. 77 Ibid. 78 Timothy Reuter, *Germany in the early Middle Ages*, c.*800–1056* (London and New York, 1991), p. 177.

> a great king, a fierce pagan, an emperor of non-Romans, with his royal seat at Tara, which was then the capital of the realm of the Irish, by name Loíguire son of Níall, a scion of the family that held the kingship of almost the entire island.[79]

Muirchú's *imperator barbarorum* ('emperor of the barbarians', tactfully translated by Bieler as 'emperor of non-Romans'), may have been the inspiration for *imperator scotorum*, and Máel Suthain – who claimed to have perused the 'libraries of the Scots' – may have wished to draw a partial comparison between Brian (a would-be ruler of all Ireland who had done a deal with Patrick's successors) and Lóegaire (a supposed ruler of almost all Ireland who had allegedly reached an accommodation with Patrick himself). If this is so, then the Ottonian imperial title cannot be used as a dating criterion.

CONCLUSION

The IS-text is but one indicator of Armagh's long-term interests in Munster, and indeed of their relationship with its new rulers, Dál Cais, which had been growing since at least the 970s. The provisions of the agreement, written in two hands (one of which was probably that of Máel Suthain Ua Cerbaill, and not Brian's *anmchara*), indicate a negotiated deal between Armagh's and Brian's representatives and the claims made may have been both restricted in scope and in geographical application, and should not be taken as evidence of an Ireland-wide Brian–Armagh agreement. Brian's death did not terminate this relationship and his burial in Armagh after the battle of Clontarf was inspired by more than just loyalty to the dead king, and was probably intended to bind his heirs to Patrick's church.[80] Indeed, there is ample evidence that Brian's Dál Cais successors enjoyed a close working relationship with Armagh over the following century and it is perhaps more than a coincidence that when his great-grandson Muirchertach Ua Briain visited Armagh almost a century later, he gave and pledged offerings that exactly equalled in value those given by Brian in 1005.[81] Nonetheless, Brian alone was acclaimed as *imperator scotorum*.[82]

79 Bieler, *Patrician texts*, pp 74–5 (Muirchú, §I.10). **80** See Denis Casey, 'Historical and literary representations of Brian Boru's burial in Armagh, 1014AD', *NMAJ*, 50 (2010), 29–44. **81** *AU* 1103.5. **82** Muirchertach received no acknowledgment in the Book of Armagh, and despite his glowing obit in the Annals of Ulster, he was not afforded an imperial style like Brian was in his obit (where he was referred to as an Augustus); for their obits see *AU* 1014.2 and *AU* 1119.2.

Clontarf 1014: military significance, external dimension and outcome

COLMÁN ETCHINGHAM

This paper makes three points. The first is that the battle of Clontarf, a pitched battle in which large numbers engaged and numerous casualties were inflicted, was unusual in early Irish military history. Second, Scandinavian royal politics, those of Norway as well as Denmark, may be a part of the context for the battle that has not been widely appreciated. The third point, perhaps the most controversial, is that the outcome of the battle was not as is generally imagined.

THE MILITARY SIGNIFICANCE

It has been shown that a record of events, spanning three weeks or so in the late summer of 917, and preceding the battle of Cenn Fúait, presents exceptional circumstantial detail of military manoeuvres involving Vikings and Irish.[1] The record, in the Annals of Ulster, is unprecedented in Irish annalistic chronicling and is also without sequel.[2] No such circumstantial detail of warfare is found again before the late eleventh century. The normal conventions of annalistic battle-reporting after 917 as well as before are formulaic, stereotyped and predictable. Typically, they comprise some variation on the following: 'Battle-defeat of L (location) upon X (leader/force) by Y (leader/force) in which were killed A, B, and C (on vanquished side)'. If casualties on the victorious side are noted, it is often in the form 'D and E were killed in the counter-slaughter of battle'. A large number or sometimes a specific estimate of casualties is occasionally recorded. This kind of reporting reveals nothing of the conduct of warfare. Unfortunately, the annalistic record of the fighting at Clontarf is of the formulaic, stereotyped and predictable kind, making an evaluation difficult. A comparatively succinct notice in *AI* 1014.2 apart (of which more below in the last part of this paper) *AU* 1014.2 may have best claim to be relatively, but not wholly, free of literary embellishment and contamination by later 'tradition'.[3] It is presented here to show the limitations of a mostly contemporary report of the battle:

1 Colmán Etchingham, 'The battle of Cenn Fúait: location and military significance', *Peritia*, 21 (2010), 208–32. 2 *AU* 917.3; a group of records in *AU* for the earlier tenth century is marked by distinctive vocabulary and a lively interest in military campaigns, as shown in the painstaking analysis of Nicholas Evans, *The present and the past in medieval Irish chronicles* (Woodbridge, 2010), pp 34–40. 3 A still valuable survey of the various

Slóghud la Brian mac Cennéitigh meic Lorcáin la rígh nÉrenn 7 la Máel Sechlainn mac Domnaill la rígh Temhrach co hÁth Clíath. Laighin uile do léir i tinól ar a cinn 7 Gaill Átha Clíath 7 a coimlín do Ghallaib Lochlainne leó .i. .x. cét lúirech. Gníthir cath cródha etorra doná fríth inntsamail. Maidhis íarum for Gallu 7 for Laighniu i tosaigh corus-díleghait uile do léir. In quo bello cecidit ex adhuersa caterua Gallorum Máel Mórdha mac Murchada rí Laigen 7 Domnall mac Fergaile rí na Fortúath: cecidit uero a Gallis Dubghall mac Amlaím, Siuchraidh mac Loduir íarla Innsi Orc 7 Gilla Cíaráin mac Glúin Iairnn rígdomna Gall 7 Oittir Dub 7 Suartgair 7 Donnchad húa Eruilb 7 Grisene 7 Luimne 7 Amlaím mac Laghmaind 7 Brótor .i. toísech na loingsi Lochlannaighi 7 .ui. míle iter marbad 7 báthad.

Do-rochuir immorro a fritguin ó Gaídhelaibh: .i. Brian m. Cennéitigh ardrí Gaídhel Érenn 7 Gall 7 Bretan, August íartair tuaiscirt Eorpa uile; 7 a mac .i. Murchad 7 a mac-sidhe .i. Toirrdelbach mac Murchada 7 Conaing mac Duinn Chuan meic Cennéitigh rígdomna Muman 7 Mothla mac Domnaill meic Fáeláin rí na nDéisi Muman; Eocho mac Dúnadhaigh 7 Níall húa Cuind 7 mac Cennétigh, trí coimthe Briain; da rígh Húa Maine, húa Ceallaig [*sic*]; 7 Máel Rúanaigh húa hEidhinn rí Aidhne 7 Géibhinnach húa Dubagáin rí Fernmaighi [read Fer Maighi] 7 Macc Beathadh mac Muiredaigh Cloín rí Cíaraidhe Lúachra 7 Domnall m. Díarmada rí Corco Baiscind 7 Scannlán mac Cathail rí Éoganachta Locha Léin 7 Domhnall mac Eimhin meic Cainnigh mormháer Marr i nAlbain 7 alii multi nobiles.

Luidh tra Máel Muire comarba Pátraicc co sruithibh 7 co minnaibh co nnice Sórd Coluim Cille co tuc as corp Briain rígh Érenn 7 corp Murchada a mac 7 cenn Conaing 7 cenn Mothlai coro adhnacht i nÁrd Macha i n-ailaidh nui. Dí aidhci dhéc immorro do samhadh Pátraicc ic are na corp propter honorem regis possiti.

A hosting by Brian mac Cennétig meic Lorcáin king of Ireland and by Máel Sechlainn mac Domnaill king of Tara to Dublin. All the Leinstermen assembled to meet them and the Foreigners of Dublin and a like number of the Foreigners of *Lochla(i)nn* with them, that is, a thousand mail-clad warriors. A valiant battle was fought between them, the like of which was not [previously] experienced. It [presumably the 'hosting'] defeated[4] the Foreigners and Leinstermen at first and they

'traditions' about Clontarf is A.J. Goedheer, *Irish and Norse traditions about the battle of Clontarf* (Haarlem, 1938). 4 For *maidis*, Middle Irish 3 sg. preterite of *maidid* ('breaks', hence 'defeats'), see *DIL*, M col. 28; for the reduplicated form *memaid* in Early Middle Irish, see Liam Breatnach, 'An Mheán-Ghaeilge' in Kim McCone et al. (eds), *Stair na Gaeilge* (Maynooth, 1994), pp 221–333, at p. 304.

were all destroyed. In this battle there fell of the hostile troop of the Foreigners Máel Mórdha mac Murchada king of Leinster and Domnall mac Fergaile king of the Forthúatha; there fell indeed of the Foreigners Dubgall mac Amlaíb, Siuchraid mac Loduir *jarl* of the Orkney Isles, Gilla Cíaráin mac Glúin Iairn, 'king material'[5] of the Foreigners, Oittir Dub, Suartgair, Donnchad úa Eruilb, Grisene, Luimne, Amlaíb mac Laghmaind, Brótor, that is, commander of the *Lochlannach* fleet, and six thousand either slain or drowned.

There fell of the Gaels, however, in the counter-slaughter, Brian mac Cennétig over-king of the Gaels of Ireland and of the Foreigners and Britons, Augustus of all northwestern Europe, his son Murchad, the latter's son Tairdelbach mac Murchada, Conaing mac Duinn Chuan meic Cennétig, 'king material' of Munster, Mothla mac Domnaill meic Fáeláin king of the Déisi of Munster, Eochu mac Dúnadaig and Níall úa Cuinn and mac Cennétig, Brian's three bodyguards, the two [joint-]kings of Uí Maine úa Cellaig [*sic*], Máel Rúanaig úa hEidin king of Aidne, Géibennach úa Dubagáin king of Fir Maige, Mac Bethad mac Muiredaig Cloín king of Cíarraige Lúachra, Domnall mac Díarmata king of Corcu Baiscinn, Scanlán mac Cathail king of Éoganacht Locha Léin, Domnall mac Eimin meic Cainnig 'supreme officer'[6] of Mar in Scotland, and many other nobles.

Máel Muire successor of Patrick came therefore to Swords of Colum Cille with venerable clerics and insignia and brought away the body of Brian king of Ireland, the body of Murchad his son, the head of Conaing

5 The editors' 'heir designate' for *rígdomna* is misleading; my literal translation signifies a person qualified by birth and otherwise to compete for succession to the kingship; also so qualified was Dubgall mac Amlaíb – although not termed *rígdamna* – Sitriuc's brother, who would arguably have been at least as well placed to succeed Sitriuc as Gilla Cíaráin, son of Sitriuc's half-brother and predecessor; this interpretation of *rígdomna* in the annals is essentially also that of Jaski, *Early Irish kingship*, especially pp 236–47; Viking and Irish royal succession procedures were apparently similar. 6 The editors' 'earl' for *mormháer* begs the question; my translation is deliberately vague and tentative because the meaning is unclear. *Máer* in Ireland has been seen as a 'steward' or revenue collector, but his primarily legal role apparently encompassed judicial functions and law enforcement, including collection of dues as 'profits of justice' arising under *cáin* or 'enacted law': see Colmán Etchingham, *Church organisation in Ireland, AD650–1000* (Maynooth, 1999), pp 211–14. In the title of the Scottish official, it is possible that the first element is from *muir* ('sea'): for recent discussion, see Alex Woolf, *From Pictland to Alba, 789–1170* (Edinburgh, 2007), pp 342–4, and James Fraser, *From Caledonia to Pictland: Scotland to 795* (Edinburgh, 2009), pp 356–8, who do not mention the Irish references, but it is more likely *mór* ('great, supreme'), as suggested by *Osli mac Dubcind … mórmáer dá máeraib* ('Osli mac Dubcinn … supreme officer of his [Brian's] officers') in *CGG*, §84; interestingly, he was grandson of Ímar king of Limerick (d. 977) and so probably in reality a subordinate official of Brian's in Limerick (cf. J.H. Todd in *CGG*, p. 275). 7 I follow Seán Mac Airt's and Gearóid Mac Niocaill's text,

and the head of Mothla, and buried them in Armagh in a new tomb. For twelve nights, moreover, the community of Patrick waked the bodies in honour of the king laid out for burial.[7]

This annal record is exceptionally long, but mostly because of an extended casualty-list including, among the Vikings, five persons without patronymics – Oittir Dub, Suartgair, Grisene, Luimne and Brótor – four of whom also lack any indication of office or function, while that of the fifth, Brótor, is given only in a gloss. To set aside these conventions of annalistic identification normally bepeaks familiarity, but a suspicion of accretion from later 'tradition' attaches to these five persons.[8] This serves to alert that, despite the well-deserved reputation of *AU* as a contemporary record not only in substance, but linguistically and stylistically, as exemplified by four Latin tags (underlined), characteristically scattered through the Middle Irish text, *AU* 1014.2 shows signs of later editing. The only circumstantial detail is of funerary arrangements made by Armagh for the leading casualties on Brian's side. The battle is cast as unprecedented – more likely a retrospective reflection than contemporary reporting – and a round and suspiciously large number (six thousand) of casualties on the side of Brian's adversaries is given. This may be compared with the arguably more plausible 600 claimed in *CS* to have fallen at Cenn Fuait in 917. The actual battle report of Clontarf is predictable and stereotyped, without insight into manoeuvres or tactics but, remarkably, lacks a formula clearly identifying the victor. Rather, it is reported that Vikings and Leinstermen suffered annihilation, but *i tosaigh* ('at first'). Is this adverbial clause a hint of the actual circumstances of battle? The question is explored in the last part of this paper.

A factual reference to military equipment is noteworthy: *.x. cét lúirech* ('a thousand mail-clad warriors'),[9] albeit only in a gloss on the 'Foreigners of *Lochla(i)nn*'.[10] If contemporary, it is the first annalistic mention of armour, a Viking military innovation alongside battle-axes, better swords, and bows and

but read *Lochlainne* (fem. gen. sg.); I add length-marks, extend *m.* and *mc.* and emend the translation where necessary. 8 See also Ní Mhaonaigh, *Brian Boru*, pp 55–6; Duffy, *Brian Boru*, p. 179; two of the names themselves are dubious: Grisene may be Old Norse Gríss with an Irish diminutive suffix (Carl Marstrander, *Bidrag til det Norske sprogs historie i Irland* (Kristiania, 1915), p. 51) while Luimne does not seem to be Norse. 9 A loan from Latin *lorica*, often rendered 'breastplate' (as it is by the editors of *AU*), but the Latin may denote a 'corselet'; coats of mail but not 'breastplates' are attested in the Viking age. The Welsh account of Clontarf in *Brut y Tywysogion* has Sitriuc recruiting ships full of mail-clad warriors (*yn gyflawn o wyr llurugawc*) (*Brut y Tywysogyon or the Chronicle of the Princes: Red Book of Hergest version*, ed. and trans. Thomas Jones [Cardiff, 1955], pp 20–1). Welsh *llurig / llurug* and *llurigog / llurugog* are also derived from *lorica* and mean 'coat of mail' and 'mail clad (warrior)' – *Geiriadur Prifysgol Cymru*, ii (Cardiff, 1987), pp 2229–30 – precisely the primary and extended connotations of Irish *lúirech*; cf. *CGG*, §100: *tánic Plait a cath na lúreach amach* ('Plait emerged out of the battalion of mail-clad warriors'). 10 For *Lochla(i)nn* – here either the 'Viking world' of literary imagination or, perhaps, as in later

arrows,[11] and the only one noticed in Irish annals, apart from sea-fleets, as discussed elsewhere.[12] The Irish 'wisdom text' known as the Triads shows that, already in the ninth century, a Viking's coat of mail was distinctive. Such armour is attested archaeologically for tenth-century Norway.[13]

What is not in doubt is that Clontarf was in reality a major battle in which large numbers were engaged, with elite casualties – including outsiders on both sides – and with numerous other casualties, notwithstanding the dubious specific figure given. This marks the battle of Clontarf out as exceptional in Viking-age warfare and, indeed, in early medieval Irish warfare generally, in which major pitched battles were rare.[14] Those involving Vikings occurred at crucial turning-points in their fortunes in Ireland. Vikings normally avoided such potential catastrophes, which is not surprising given their poor fighting prowess: ninth-century Vikings in Ireland were defeated between two and three times as often as they were victorious.[15] Their tenth-century battlefield record was even worse, as they were defeated at least three times as often as they enjoyed victory.[16] Vikings did win two crucial battles in the early tenth century – Cenn Fúait aforementioned in 917 and a follow-up at Dublin in 919 – that renewed and secured their control of Dublin, and with it intermittent control of York up to 952. On the other hand, Vikings suffered defeat in two major battles of the later tenth century, at Tara in 980 and Glenn Máma in 999. Clontarf in 1014 was the last in this later series of pitched battles.[17]

The circumstantial account of manoeuvres preceding Cenn Fúait in 917 is a unique insight into the doubtless more typical caution of kings, Viking and

annals, Norway specifically – see Colmán Etchingham, 'The location of historical *Laithlinn/Lochla(i)nn*: Scotland or Scandinavia?' in Mícheál Ó Flaithearta (ed.), *Proceedings of the Seventh Symposium of Societas Celtologica Nordica* (Uppsala, 2007), pp 11–31, at pp 17–23. 11 See Andrew Halpin, *Weapons and warfare in Viking and medieval Dublin* (Dublin, 2008), pp 17–21, 35–9, 150–57, 163–5. 12 See Colmán Etchingham, 'Skuldelev 2 and Viking-age ships and fleets in Ireland' in Emer Purcell et al. (eds), *Clerics, kings and Vikings: essays on medieval Ireland in honour of Donnchadh Ó Corráin* (Dublin, 2015), pp 79–90. 13 *The Triads of Ireland*, ed. and trans. Kuno Meyer (Dublin, 1906), §232: *Gall ina lúirig* ('a Foreigner in his coat of mail'); on the Triads, see Fergus Kelly, *A guide to early Irish law* (Dublin, 1988), pp 284–5; see the coat of mail from an elite tenth-century warrior burial at Gjermundbu, Ringerike, Buskerud, in the Kulturhistorisk Museum, Oslo. 14 A point made in relation to the later Middle Ages by Katharine Simms, 'Warfare in the medieval Gaelic lordships', *Irish Sword*, 12 (1975–6), 98–108, who attributed it to demography, geography and socio-political culture; for the rarity of pitched battles in the Viking age and discussion of why this was so, see Etchingham, 'Cenn Fúait', 223–9. 15 Etchingham, 'Cenn Fúait', 226; see Howard Clarke, 'The bloodied eagle: the Vikings and the development of Dublin, 841–1014', *Irish Sword*, 18 (1991), 91–119, at 97–8. 16 Clarke, 'Bloodied eagle', 105–6, gave a figure of 10 victories out of 25 for Dublin, 917–1014; I calculate that Irish-based Vikings in that period won at most 9 battlefield victories (*AU* 917.3, 919.3, 933.1, 935.6, 956.3, 970.4, 978.3; *CS* 970; *AT* 983.1) – a number of them with Irish allies – while suffering defeat 22 times (*AI* 917, 967, 977.3; *AU* 920.2, 926.2, 926.6, 933.3, 943.1, 947.1, 948.1, 950.5, 960.3, 980.1, 999.8; *CS* 930 [929], 941 [940], 943 [942], 988 [986]; *AT* 989.2; *AFM* 930 [928.13], 962 [960.14], 964 [962.14]) – some of those also with Irish allies. 17 See Etchingham, 'Cenn Fúait', 228–9.

Irish, about risking all in a full-blooded encounter, no matter what the bravado of both warrior cultures might suggest. An obvious question then arises: what induced Vikings – and Irish for that matter – to risk all-out battle such as that at Clontarf? This and the earlier battles at Tara and Glenn Máma appear to be points of resistance on Dublin's part to decline and subjugation. Dublin was faced with paying tribute to overkings of Ireland, first Máel Sechnaill of the Southern Uí Néill and then Brian Boru. The battle of Tara in 980 was a follow-up to what the annalist for 975, with an obvious touch of hindsight, terms the *cétna toisc* ('first campaign') by Máel Sechnaill against Dublin. In response to the threat he posed, the Dubliners recruited outside support, for Máel Sechnaill in 980 inflicted defeat at Tara *for Gallaibh Átho Clíath 7 na nIndsedh* ('upon the Foreigners of Dublin and the Isles') and then imposed tribute. Dublin's tributary position was evidently reinforced by Máel Sechnaill in 989 and 995. In the battle of Glenn Máma in 999, Dublin allied with Leinster in a bid to shake off their subjection since 997 to Brian, who displaced Máel Sechnaill as the leading Irish king. Defeat at Glenn Máma led to renewed subjugation of Dublin and its king Sitriuc (Sigtryggr).[18] In 1014, Dublin recruited both Islesmen (as in 980) and Leinstermen (as in 999) in a further attempt to escape tributary status.

Yet it remains unclear why precisely Vikings, Leinstermen and their adversaries risked pitched battle in 1014, with a disastrous outcome for all, as regards the eminence and numbers of the casualties. Why did Dublin not play a longer game? Why did it not engineer a stalemate or come to terms with Brian? Why did it not try to replicate the indecisive outcome of comparatively low-level hostilities in 1013? Although characterized by both Munster and midlands annalists as 'great warfare', action in 1013 included raiding of Leinster and the Dublin area both by Brian's son Murchad and by Brian's sometime ally Máel Sechnaill that was apparently indecisive, while Dublin raiding of south Munster by sea was not notably successful. Manifestly inconclusive was Brian's three-month-long encampment against Leinster, Osraige and Dublin, withdrawn at Christmas 1013 without pacifying his

18 *AT* 975.4, 980.3, 980.4, 989.2, 995.5, 998.1 (misplaced, for 999), 999.3, 1000.3; *AU* 980.1, 999.8, 1000.4; *AI* 997.2, 999.4, 1000.2; while the case must be made elsewhere, I do not agree that Amlaíb Cúarán had extensive sway in the midlands, or that the battle of Tara in 980 was his challenge for the 'kingship of Tara', as has been claimed: cf. Edel Bhreathnach, 'The documentary evidence for pre-Norman Skreen, Co. Meath', *Ríocht na Midhe*, 9 (1996), 37–45, at 40–43; eadem, 'Columban churches in Brega and Leinster: relations with the Norse and the Anglo-Normans', *JRSAI*, 129 (1999), 5–18, at 8–11; Charles Doherty, 'The Vikings in Ireland: a review' in Clarke et al. (eds), *Ireland and Scandinavia*, at pp 297–8, 305; Alex Woolf, 'Amlaíb Cuarán and the Gael, 941–81' in Seán Duffy (ed.), *Medieval Dublin III* (Dublin, 2002), pp 34–43, at pp 42–3; Clare Downham, 'The Vikings in Southern Uí Néill to 1014', *Peritia*, 17/18 (2003/4), 233–55, at 239–40; Clare Downham, *Viking kings of Britain and Ireland: the dynasty of Ívarr to AD1014* (Edinburgh, 2007), pp 50–53; Mary Valante, *The Vikings in Ireland* (Dublin, 2008) p. 112; Duffy, *Brian Boru*, pp 246–8.

enemies.[19] Was Clontarf a miscalculation, on Sitriuc's part and on that of his external Viking allies and of the Leinstermen, regarding Brian's advancing years – he was seventy-three in 1014 – and the impact of the evident draining away of his support-base.[20] Could other strategic factors have been at work? Perhaps accidents caused developments over which the leaders lost control. Did the muster of enhanced force on both sides simply create a momentum that was beyond the capacity of anyone involved to stop?

What distinguishes the protracted low-level skirmishing and inconclusive beleaguering of 1013 from the cataclysm at Clontarf in the spring of 1014 is, most obviously, external interests. The presence on Brian's side of a magnate of Mar in Aberdeenshire, Scotland, may surprise, but he was not the first Scottish *mórmáer* ('supreme officer') to be involved in Irish affairs.[21] It may indicate Brian's residual influence, albeit declining, even beyond Ireland, also perhaps implicit in his title *Imperator Scotorum* ('Emperor of the Gaels') in the Book of Armagh.[22] For present purposes most interest attaches to those casualties cast as external allies of Sitriuc's: Siuchraid mac Loduir (Sigurðr Hlǫðvisson), jarl of Orkney, and Brótor, commander of the Lochlannach fleet. The notion that Amlaíb mac Laghmaind was a third external ally of Dublin, an Islesman, the son or grandson of Gofraid mac Arailt (Guðfrøðr Haraldsson), king of Man and the Isles (d. 989), is ill founded. It depends on conflating *AU* 1014.2, and the corresponding Clontarf casualty list in *CGG*, with a different passage and conflicting identification in the latter text.[23] If Amlaíb mac

19 *AU* 1013.5, 1013.6, 1013.7, 1013.8, 1013.12; *AI* 1013.2; *CS* 1013 (1011). 20 Notice of Brian's birth at *AU* 941.2 is obviously retrospective but possibly accurate, reflecting contemporary interest of Armagh in Brian; for an Armagh strand in *AU* in the tenth and eleventh centuries, especially after *c.*980, see Evans, *Irish chronicles*, pp 20–44; Brian's loosening grip after 1011 vis-à-vis the Northern Uí Néill, Ulaid, Síl Muiredaig and Uí Ruairc of Connacht is indicated by the absence of any northerners and most of Connacht from his forces at Clontarf; see also *AU* 1011.2, 1011.6, 1012.2, 1013.2, 1013.3, 1013.9; *AI* 1011.2. 21 *AT* 976.7 reports a campaign in the midlands by the Cenél Conaill pretender to Uí Néill overkingship, Gilla Coluim Ua Canannáin, along with *trí mórmaír Alban* ('three supreme officers of Scotland'); for a later *mórmáer* of Mar see early twelfth-century records in the Book of Deer (A.O. Anderson, *Early sources of Scottish history* (2 vols, Edinburgh, 1922), ii, p. 178); Duffy, *Brian Boru*, pp 150–1, notices the *mórmáer* of 1014 but not those of 976. 22 Aubrey Gwynn, 'Brian in Armagh in 1005', *Seanchas Ardmhacha*, 9 (1978/79), 35–50; Duffy, *Brian Boru*, pp 150–1; on the inscription in the Book of Armagh, see Casey, above. 23 The casualty list in *CGG* §117 mentions *Amlaíbh mac Lagmain* but not a Gofraid, thus agreeing with *AU* 1014.2; only *CGG* §94, listing the leaders before the battle, refers to *Amlaíb Lagmaind mac Gophraid* among *cethri rígdamna Gall* ('four "king materials" of the Foreigners'), the understanding of *CGG* being that he was a Dublin royal: Dubgall mac Amlaíb and Gilla Ciaráin mac Glúin Iairn – the latter explicitly designated *rígdamna* in the *AU* 1014.2 casualty list, as we have seen – are two of the four. The speculation of Todd (*CGG*, pp 271–2) that *Amlaíb Lagmaind mac Gophraid* is the *mac Amhlaíph* of *AFM* 962 (960) neither explains how he could also be at Clontarf over 50 years later, nor resolves the conflicting testimony of *CGG*; cf. Clare Downham, 'England and the Irish-Sea zone in the eleventh century', *Anglo-Norman Studies* 26 (2003), 55–73, at 61; Downham, *Dynasty of Ívarr*, pp 59, 132–4, 193, 197–8; Benjamin Hudson, *Viking pirates and Christian princes* (Oxford,

Laghmaind is not merely an accretion from later 'tradition', he may just as well have been a Dublin royal.[24]

As regards Brótor, his lack of a patronymic and description only in a gloss as commander of the *Lochlannach* fleet arouse suspicion. Later Irish and Old Norse literary 'traditions' alike – *CGG* and the thirteenth-century Icelandic *Njáls saga* – portray him as Brian's killer, something reflected only in an interlinear gloss in *AU*.[25] If he is not merely a literary accretion, it is possible that *Lochla(i)nn* and its derivative Lochlannach in *AU* 1014.2 refer to Norway, specifically, as *Lochla(i)nn* certainly does in later annals of the mid-eleventh to mid-thirteenth centuries, rather than to the 'Viking world' of literary imagination.[26] However, the name Brótor – Bróðir in *Njáls saga* – suggests an Insular Viking: it is not Old Norse, but a borrowing of a Gaelic name that seems to have been fashioned, in turn, from a borrowing of the Old Welsh common noun *broder/brodyr* ('brother'). *Njáls saga* associates Bróðir with the Isle of Man.[27] Therefore, his presence, if historical, and that of Siuchraid of Orkney, certainly, hark back to the involvement at the battle of Tara in 980 of Islesmen, though whether these were Hebridean or Orcadian is not specified in that instance. Was there another external dimension to the battle of Clontarf?

THE EXTERNAL DIMENSION

Did late Viking-age Scandinavian politics and Scandinavian intervention in England in the late tenth and early eleventh centuries have any bearing on the conflict at Clontarf? Was there a connection, specifically, with the subjugation of England by the Danes at the end of 1013, which was interrupted by King Sveinn's death in February 1014, but resumed after an interlude by his son Knútr, who came eventually to reign in England, Denmark and Norway? Over twenty years ago, Benjamin Hudson drew attention to Dublin links with Knútr's England, and held that Dublin actually submitted to Knútr 'by the second quarter of the eleventh century'. He raised important issues, but the case as made is hardly compelling and the evidence may be otherwise explained.[28]

2005), pp 76–7, 98, 132, 162; Ní Mhaonaigh, *Brian Boru*, p. 56. **24** One Lagmann was a son of Godred Crovan/Gofraid Méránach, king of Man, the Isles and briefly Dublin (d. 1095); he was *mac maic Arailt* (*AT* 1091.5) and so a son or nephew of Ímar mac Arailt (Haraldr), king of Dublin 1038–46 (d. 1054) and Sitriuc's nephew; see Hudson, *Viking pirates*, 53–4, 154, 171, 188, who assumed Godred Crovan was a son of Ímar. **25** *CGG* §114; *Brennu-Njáls saga*, ed. Einar Ólafur Sveinsson (Reykjavík, 1954), pp 452–3 §157; *Njal's saga*, trans. Magnus Magnusson and Hermann Pálsson (Harmondsworth, 1960), p. 348 §157. **26** Etchingham, 'Historical *Laithlinn/Lochla(i)nn*', pp 17–23; see also the usage in *AU* 1263.6, *ALC* 1263.4 and *AC* 1263.5, referring to King Hákon IV Hákonarson of Norway. **27** Etchingham, 'Historical *Laithlinn/Lochla(i)nn*', p. 19; Benjamin Hudson, '"Brjáns saga"', *Medium Ævum*, 71 (2002), 241–68, at 253–4; see *Njáls saga*, ed. E.O. Sveinsson, p. 445 §155; *Njal's saga*, trans. M. Magnusson and H. Pálsson, p. 344 §155. **28** Hudson, 'Knútr and Viking Dublin',

Hudson, doubtless wisely, did not seek to link Dublin with the Danes in the period of the battle of Clontarf. More recent commentators have been less circumspect. It has been supposed that Brótor's fleet 'may have included Danish warships' and that 'the presence of a Scandinavian contingent at the battle could be explained by the employment of mariners who had participated in the conquest of England'.[29] On the strength of non-contemporary embellished literary references to stereotypical *Danair/Danmargaig* ('Danes'), involvement at Clontarf of 'large numbers of Danish warriors who had seen their conquest of England slip away before their eyes' has been postulated. With the stalled conquest of England 'surely some of them enlisted' with Siuchraid of Orkney. For such putative Danish adventurers, 'if England could be won and lost, Ireland surely seemed a sitting duck'.[30] Apart from the lack of positive evidence for Danish involvement at Clontarf – implied by 'surely' in two of these remarks – it is counter-intuitive. The death of the Danish King Sveinn in February 2014 ended abruptly the sweeping triumph achieved in England between August and December 2013. When the English magnates recalled Æthelred from his exile in Normandy, Sveinn's son Knútr, although acclaimed successor by the Danish forces, withdrew from England.[31] This meant Knútr was in no position to intervene in support of Sitriuc at Clontarf, if he were minded to, and the notion that his warriors did so independently, after their morale-sapping setback in England, is unsubstantiated and unlikely.

Yet late tenth-century Scandinavian intervention in the Irish Sea or, rather, in the more extensive 'Insular Viking zone', that may bear on the disposition of forces at Clontarf, is evidenced. This intervention by Danish Vikings was highlighted some years ago and it will be useful to reiterate and elaborate on the salient points. The *Anglo-Saxon Chronicles* (*ASC*) report sporadic Viking coastal raiding, beginning in 980, and evidently the precursor to major campaigns, primarily by Danes, against England in the 990s.[32] Irish and Welsh annals also reflect raiding activity in the period 986–90, by *Danair* ('Danes'), a novel usage of the Irish annalists, or by 'Black Heathens', according to the Welsh. In 987, they allied with (Gofraid) mac Arailt/Gothrith filius Haraldi (Guðfrøðr Haraldsson) in a battle at the Isle of Man and in a raid on Anglesey. Gofraid is one of the earliest kings of Man and the Isles known to the annals.

Scandinavian Studies, 66 (1994), 319–35 (quotation from 335); Colmán Etchingham, 'North Wales, Ireland and the Isles: the Insular Viking zone', *Peritia*, 15 (2001), 145–87, at 161–2. **29** Downham, *Dynasty of Ívarr*, pp 59–60 and n. 244. **30** Duffy, *Brian Boru*, pp 242–5 (quotation at pp 244–5), 248; the latter remark is loosely evocative of John Ryan, 'The battle of Clontarf', *JRSAI*, 68 (1938), 1–50, at 7. **31** For the course of events in England in 1013–14, see *The Anglo-Saxon Chronicles* (*ASC*), ed. and trans. Michael Swanton (rev. pbk ed., London, 2000), pp 143–5. **32** *ASC*, pp 124–5 for AD980, 981, 982, 987, 988; Etchingham, 'Insular Viking zone', 176; in view of the distinctions drawn by both Irish and Welsh chronicles, there are no real grounds for doubt that the raiders of England in and after 980 were, in fact, Danes; cf. Simon Keynes, 'The historical context of the battle of Maldon' in Donald Scragg (ed.), *The battle of Maldon AD991* (Oxford, 1991), pp 81–113, at p. 85.

There is reason to think that by 987, however, a limited sway in the Hebrides and an insecure grip even on Man prompted his resort to Danish Viking aid.[33] We will return to this matter below. For present purposes it suffices to note that one of the Danish raiders' Hebridean targets in 986 was Iona, suggesting it may not then have been within the sphere of influence of the Danes' ally of the following year, Gofraid mac Arailt.[34] Iona had been the place of death and burial of the retired Dublin king Amlaíb Cúarán six years previously, in 980.[35]

A frequently overlooked episode of the Danes' activity in the Insular Viking zone in the later 980s brought them to Ireland in 990. *AFM* records *Sluagh na nGall 7 na nDanar 7 Laighean i Midhe co ro inderseat co Loch Aindind* ('A muster of the Foreigners, the Danes and the Leinstermen into Mide and they plundered as far as Lough Ennell'). If not merely overlooked, this record may have been discounted by some because it is exclusive to *AFM*. However, the role of Leinster points to a probable origin in a southeastern annals recension reflected both in the *Fragmentary Annals of Ireland* and *AFM* from the mid-ninth century to the early tenth, but thereafter uniquely preserved in

33 Etchingham, 'Insular Viking zone', 175–9. **34** *AU* 986.3 (cf. 986.2); *AI* 986.4; *CS* 986 (984); *AR* §291; *AClon* 986 (980); *AFM* 986 (985.2) – the last four claiming that an Iona ecclesiastic was killed by the Danes at Dublin. **35** It is repeatedly stated that Amlaíb died in 981. The 'Clonmacnoise group' annals – *AT* 980.6; *CS* 980 (978); *AClon* 980 (974) – show that he died in his year of retirement, i.e., 980. Confusion may stem from *AFM*, which report events of 980 under both 978 and 979 (duplicating Amlaíb's retirement and death); John O'Donovan's chronological annotation is misleading. Failure to correct *AFM* – and unexplained willingness to accord priority to their uncorrected testimony – occasioned the error of F.J. Byrne and Doherty about Amlaíb's death-date – Byrne and Doherty, 'Chronology (B): 431–1169', *NHI*, viii (Oxford, 1982), pp 16–71, at p. 46. Others misdated Amlaíb's death: A.P. Smyth, *Scandinavian York and Dublin*, 2 vols (Oxford, 1979), ii, p. 108; Clarke, 'Bloodied eagle', 108: Seán Duffy, 'Irishmen and Islesmen in the kingdoms of Dublin and Man, 1052–1171', *Ériu*, 48 (1992), 93–133, at 95–6 and n. 10; Duffy, *Brian Boru*, pp 54, 246; Hudson, 'Knútr', 321; Hudson, *Viking pirates*, p. 52; Doherty, 'Vikings in Ireland', p. 299; Charles Doherty, 'The Viking impact upon Ireland' in Anne-Christine Larsen (ed.), *The Vikings in Ireland* (Roskilde, 2001), pp 29–35, at p. 35; Donnchadh Ó Corráin, 'Ireland, Wales, Man and the Hebrides' in P.H. Sawyer (ed.), *The Oxford illustrated history of the Vikings* (Oxford, 1997), pp 83–109, at p. 105; idem, 'Viking Ireland: afterthoughts' in Clarke et al. (eds), *Ireland and Scandinavia*, pp 421–52, at p. 451; idem, 'The Vikings in Scotland and Ireland in the ninth century', *Peritia*, 12 (1998), 296–339, at 307, 339; idem, 'The Vikings in Ireland' in Larsen (ed.), *Vikings*, pp 17–27, at pp 19, 24; Ailbhe Mac Shamhráin, *The Vikings: an illustrated history* (Dublin, 2002), p. 60; Woolf, 'Amlaíb Cuarán', passim, esp. p. 35. Amlaíb's death was dated correctly to 980, however, by Máire Herbert, *Iona, Kells and Derry* (Oxford, 1988), p. 83; Bart Jaski, 'The Vikings and the kingship of Tara', *Peritia*, 9 (1995), 310–51, at 348; E. Bhreathnach, 'Skreen', 40, 42; eadem, 'Columban churches', 5, 6, 9; Máire Ní Mhaonaigh, 'Friend and foe: Vikings in ninth- and tenth-century Irish literature' in Clarke et al. (eds), *Ireland and Scandinavia*, pp 381–402, at pp 398–9; Cormac Bourke, 'A view of the early Irish church' in Larsen (ed.), *Vikings*, pp 77–86, at p. 85; Downham, *Dynasty of Ívarr*, pp 29, 52, 190, 193, 242, 252–3, 267. **36** For the Leinster/southeastern annals, see *FAI*, pp xiii–xvii. **37** *AFM* 990 (989.6); cf. *AT* 989.2; *CS* 989 (987); Poul Holm, 'The naval power of Norse Dublin' in Purcell et al. (eds), *Clerics, kings and Vikings*, pp 67–78, at pp 76–7, doubted that *garðr* denotes a house-plot,

AFM.[36] The allies – of whom the 'Foreigners' denote the Dublin Vikings distinguished from the Danes – penetrated the heartland of Máel Sechnaill, the Uí Néill overking, in a raid that must have been a response to the latter's third subjugation of Dublin the previous year, following those of 975 and 980 aforementioned. In 989 Máel Sechnaill had followed up a battlefield victory at Dublin by besieging the town and imposing what seems a crushing annual tribute of an ounce of gold per *garda* (< Old Norse *garðr*) ('house-plot').[37] The allied raid of 990 seems readily explained, then, as Dublin's attempt to relieve pressure by resorting to Danish Viking aid, simply because it was available, as the Islesman Gofraid mac Arailt had done three years earlier. Closer scrutiny, however, reveals a more complex picture of Viking factionalism and more extensive rival networks of alliance.

We must return to Máel Sechnaill's previous subjugation of Dublin in 980 which, as noted above, followed upon the battle of Tara and defeat therein of Dublin and its Islesmen allies. Amlaíb Cúarán retired to die in Iona and was succeeded at Dublin by his son Glún Iairn (Jarnkné), also the uterine half-brother of Máel Sechnaill. Glún Iairn was ally or subordinate of Máel Sechnaill in 983, when together they defeated Leinster and the Waterford Vikings under their king Ímar (Ívarr), whose son Gilla Pátraic mac Ímair was killed. In 984 these rival alignments were augmented when the large fleet of the Haraldssons of Man and the Isles – Gofraid and his brother (joint-king?) Maccus – came to Waterford to form a pact with Brian Boru. They proceeded against Glún Iairn's Dublin and, it would seem, against his overlord Máel Sechnaill. The endeavour was unsuccessful, but Waterford again acted as Brian's subordinate in a campaign in Connacht in 988. In the 980s, then, Dublin and Waterford became appendages of Máel Sechnaill and Brian, respectively, the two great rivals for overkingship of Ireland, while the Haraldssons of Man and the Isles became involved, via Waterford, on the side of Brian.[38]

Given this alignment of forces, Máel Sechnaill's attack on Dublin in 989 and imposition of heavy tribute come as a surprise. The explanation is doubtless the death, earlier in 989 it seems, of Máel Sechnaill's loyal Dublin agent Glún Iairn mac Amlaíb. He was killed *dia moghaidh féin* ('by his own slave'), named Colbain (Kolbeinn) in some annals, *i meisce* ('when drunk'), according to others.[39] There is no hint of a political assassination or that this was other than an unpremeditated, sordid incident of barbarian court life. Yet

considering a levy of an ounce of gold on each improbable. However, in a precursor of later medieval burgage-plots, it may be that the *garðar* carried with them citizenship of some kind, but were held by persons who also had estates outside the town. 38 *AT* 980.3, 980.4, 980.6, 983.1; *AU* 980.1, 983.2; *AI* 984.2; *CS* 988 (986); see Etchingham, 'Insular Viking zone', 173–5; the mother of Máel Sechnaill and Glún Iairn was Dúnlaith daughter of Muirchertach mac Néill of Cenél nÉogain: Margaret Dobbs, 'The Banshenchas (suite)', *Revue Celtique*, 48 (1931), 163–234, at 188, 227. 39 *AU* 989.3; *AT* 989.1 (and cf. 989.2); *AI* 989.3; for Colbain, see Marstrander, *Bidrag*, p. 49.

Máel Sechnaill's immediate move to secure Dublin suggests that, if his adversaries did not cause Glún Iairn's demise, they sought to profit from it. That this was indeed the case becomes clear when it is realized that the invasion of Máel Sechnaill's heartland by Dubliners, Leinstermen and Danes in the following year, 990, apparently followed a coup that brought Ímar of Waterford to power in Dublin.

This remarkable development must be pieced together from laconic annalistic records. In the year of the joint invasion itself, *AI* has the cryptic report *macc Ímair do déruch Puirt Láirgge* ('the son of Ívarr vacating Waterford'). *Dérach* is a variant of *déirge*, verbal noun of *do-érig* ('leaves, vacates, forsakes'). *Déirge* occurs four times in *AU* and *AFM* in the earlier tenth century to report departure of the Dublin-based Viking leadership and its associates to make intermittent claim to the kingship of York and Northumbria.[40] In *AI* for 990, accordingly, the expression suggests that elements of the Waterford regime left to pursue ambitions elsewhere. Perhaps *macc Ímair* of *AI* denotes a brother of Gilla Pátraic – son of the Waterford king Ímar, who had been killed in 983 fighting against Dublin and Máel Sechnaill – or is a slip for Ímar himself.[41] That Ímar of Waterford (d. 1000) did indeed seize Dublin is retrospectively implied by the laconic contemporary record for 993 of his expulsion from Dublin, with *lucht teora long* ('the company of three ships'), by *macc Amlaíb* – evidently the first appearance on the scene of Sitriuc son of Amlaíb Cúarán. In 994 Sitiuc was in turn expelled from Dublin and replaced in that year or 995 by Ímar, who was in the latter year expelled for the second and last time. Sitriuc then finally restored the Dublin dynasty's control, while Dublin also in 995 submitted for the fourth and last recorded time to Máel Sechnaill.[42]

The upshot of all this is that, for the first time since Sitriuc úa hÍmair restored the rule at Dublin of the descendants of Ímar in 917, Dublin fell out of local hands, continuously from 989/990 to 993 and intermittently in 993–5. When Máel Sechnaill's heartland was invaded in 990 by Dubliners, Leinster and the Danes, rule at Dublin had apparently been seized by Waterford, long-term subordinate of Brian Boru. In the 980s, then, Danish Vikings sided with elements of this Haraldsson/Waterford/Brian Boru axis, by supporting Gofraid mac Arailt at Man in 987 and by allying with Waterford-controlled

40 *AI* 990.2; cf. *AU* 918.4, 920.5, 927.3; *AFM* 939 (937.16). 41 Ragnall mac Ímair, evidently a son of the Waterford royal intruder into Dublin, was killed in 994 or 995, precipitating expulsion of the Waterfordmen (*AU* 994.7; *AT* 995.2; cf. *AI* 995.3). 42 *AI* 993.6, 995.3; *AU* 994.6, 994.7; *AT* 995.1, 995.2, 995.5 (cf. 995.4); *AFM* 993 (992.21) (cf. 994 [993.9], 995 [994.7]), 995 (994.10); the sequence of these events in *AFM* for 995 suggests a raid on Donaghpatrick by Dublin and the resubjugation of Dublin by Máel Sechaill occurred before the final expulsion of Ímar of Waterford and his replacement once more by Sitriuc; this differs from the sequence in *AT*, which has the raid and subjugation preceded by this final regime change.

Dublin against Máel Sechnaill in 990. The Danish intervention in 990 seemingly won a breathing space for Dublin. It is noteworthy that Máel Sechnaill's heartland at Lough Ennell, target of the joint Dublin/Leinster/Danish invasion of 990, was also raided by Brian Boru himself in 992. The first raids by Dublin on churches in Máel Sechnaill's sphere of influence in the modern Co. Meath, since a raid on Kells in 970, also took place in the 990s. Ardbraccan, Donaghpatrick and Muine Brocáin were raided in 993. These, and a raid on Donaghpatrick in 995, may be attributed to the period of Waterford intrusion at Dublin. The sequence of events in 995 is uncertain, however, and so the raid of that year may have been prosecuted by Ímar of Waterford's regime, or by that of his successor Sitriuc mac Amlaíb.[43] The aggressive posture of Dublin towards Máel Sechnaill in and after 990 accompanied an intrusion by the Waterford dynasty, an alignment with the interests of Brian Boru, and an alliance with Danish Vikings.

Máel Sechnaill's renewed imposition of tribute on Dublin in 995 coincided with the final expulsion of the intrusive Waterford regime and Sitriuc's restoration. Sitriuc remained king of Dublin up to and beyond 1014. His half-brother and predecessor Glún Íairn, of course, had been Máel Sechnaill's agent until his killing in 989, and, as noted above, Glún Íairn was also Máel Sechnaill's uterine half-brother. There was no such relationship between Sitriuc and Máel Sechnaill, and raids on the Meath churches of Kells and Clonard in 997 clearly took place on Sitriuc's watch and imply antagonism towards Máel Sechnaill. A change of overlord from Máel Sechnaill to Brian, for Dublin and for the southern half of Ireland, in 997 or 998, was no more welcome. The Dubliners and Leinstermen revolted, but were decisively defeated by Brian at the battle of Glenn Máma in 999. Brian occupied Dublin, rendered it tributary and expelled Sitriuc, who was reinstated as king in 1000 only on giving hostages.[44] Thereafter up to 1013, the dominance of Brian was such that Sitriuc appears to have had no option but to acquiesce, and was perhaps rewarded for supplying warriors and ships for Brian's expeditions to secure the overkingship of Ireland.[45]

The circumstances that aligned Dublin with Danes, with Waterford and with Brian Boru had an additional dimension. Dublin's was not the only precarious position in the 980s: its sometime adversaries, the Haraldssons of

43 *AT* 992.1, which claim that Brian's raid on Mide, jointly with the Connachta, was less than successful, although this might reflect merely *AT*'s partiality towards Máel Sechnaill; the Munstermen and Connachta evidently took advantage of the absence from home of Máel Sechnaill, who was raiding Connacht, successfully according to *AU* 992.3 – *AFM* 993 (992.18); *AFM* 995 (994.7); *AU* 995.2; *AT* 995.4; *CS* 995 (993); cf. *AU* 970.1, *CS* 970 (968); for the sequence of events in 995, see n. 42 above. 44 *AU* 997.3, 998.1, 998.5, 999.8, 1000.4; *AI* 997.2, 999.4, 1000.2; *AT* 999 (998.1), 1000 (999.3); *CS* 998 (996), 999 (997), 1000 (998). 45 For a recent account of events in the years up to 1013, see Duffy, *Brian Boru*, pp 116–64.

the Isles, also faced difficulty. It was suggested above that reduced sway in the Hebrides and an insecure grip even on Man prompted Gofraid mac Arailt to resort to Danish Viking aid in 987. The Danes evidently proved useful allies against unidentifed enemies in a battle at Man in 987. Gofraid mac Arailt was killed in 989 in Dál Riata in circumstances that are unclear, but this was where his Danish allies had raided in 986.[46] Sveinn of Denmark raided Man in 995 and, given earlier Danish alliance with Gofraid mac Arailt, this would appear to imply that the Manx-Hebridean Haraldsson dynasty had lost control even of Man. Gofraid's son Ragnall is called *rí na nInnsi* ('king of the Isles') at his death in 1004 or 1005, with AI reporting that he died in Munster. This implies that the accord with Brian Boru, initiated by his father and uncle at Waterford twenty years earlier, was perpetuated by Ragnall. It might also be supposed – if the above interpretation of Sveinn's raid on Man is correct – that Ragnall died in exile.[47] As against this, whatever about the position in 995, there is evidence, as we will see, that in 1000 Man was in the sphere of influence of the Danes and, presumably, of their erstwhile allies the Manx–Hebridean Haraldsson dynasty. However, if the latter's grip on Man and the Isles was threatened in the late tenth and early eleventh centuries, we must ask what the source of this threat was. The most likely answer is the jarldom of Orkney.

Notwithstanding the misapprehensions of some, it is not ascertained fact that Orkney controlled Man from the 980s and that this was an achievement of Jarl Sigurðr's early career.[48] Nevertheless, hints that Gofraid mac Arailt's sway in the north Irish Sea and the Hebrides was not secure constitute circumstantial evidence for significant Orcadian influence in the Insular Viking zone from the 980s. Moreover, there is the positive if problematic evidence of *Njáls saga*, which has two variants of a defeat of a king Guðfrøðr by Kári Solmundarson and the Njálssons, agents of Sigurðr of Orkney:

> (1) Þeir bǫrðusk við Guðrøð konung í Mǫn ok sigruðu hann … ok hǫfðu fengit mikit fé … (2) heldu þeir til Manar. Þar mœttu þeir Guðrøði konungi ór Mǫn ok berjask þeir við hann; þeir hǫfðu sigr ok drápu Dungal son konungs; þar tóku þeir fé mikit
>
> (1) They fought with King Guðfrøðr in Man and defeated him … and had taken great booty … (2) they sailed to Man. There they met with King Guðfrøðr from Man and they fight with him; they had victory and killed Dúngal the king's son; there they took great booty.[49]

46 Gofraid mac Arailt's killing is said in *AU* 989.4 merely to have occurred 'in Dál Riata', while *AT* 989.3, *CS* 989 (987) and *AClon* 989 (982) make Dál Riata the perpetrators. 47 For Sveinn's raid on Man and Ragnall's death, see Etchingham, 'Insular Viking zone', 177–8, 180. 48 See Etchingham, 'Insular Viking zone', 178. 49 *Njáls saga*, ed. E.O. Sveinsson, pp 208, 224 (§§86, 89); *Njals saga*, trans. M. Magnusson and H. Pálsson, pp 184, 196, are very loose translations of these passages, including rendering imprecisely 'Gudrod,

Scepticism is in order as this is, on the face of it, thirteenth-century Icelandic literature. *Njáls saga*, of course, also incorporates the well-known account of the battle of Clontarf that is broadly consistent with contemporary Irish annals, albeit recast with a propagandist intent that points to an origin in the Insular Viking zone *c.*AD1100.[50] The account of Clontarf in *Njáls saga* has no egregious chronological or other blunders, such as often frustrate the seeker after historical fact in medieval Icelandic literature.

On the other hand, as pointed out elsewhere, one of the Manx/Hebridean episodes of *Njáls saga*, excerpted above, reveals confusion more typical of such literature, in this case geographical confusion about the Insular Viking zone. Moreover, the variant accounts of the fight with Guðfrøðr claim victory for the agents of Sigurðr of Orkney, whereas *AU* for 987 report the battle at Man as a victory for Gofraid mac Arailt and Danish allies over unidentified adversaries.[51] Yet a battle with a King Guðfrøðr connected with Man is consistent with the annals. The killing of Guðfrøðr's son, with a Gaelic name Dúngal, is a credible detail: Gofraid's grandson Echmarcach mac Ragnaill (d. 1064) bore a Gaelic name.[52] Accordingly, *Njáls saga* may supplement *AU* for 987 by plausibly identifying the adversaries of Guðfrøðr and his Danish allies as agents of Sigurðr of Orkney. The annals for 987 also report that Danes who had plundered Iona the previous year were slaughtered to the number of three hundred and sixty. The annals thus witness a setback in this year for an element of the Haraldsson-Danish alliance, alongside their victory at Man.[53] In a general sense, therefore, this *Njáls saga* episode may be loosely historical, a reflex of the apparent implication of the annals, namely, that Gofraid mac Arailt's Danish Viking alliance of the late 980s was directed against, among others, Orcadian influence in the Insular Viking zone. Such influence in the Hebrides and Man is also reflected in *Eyrbyggja saga* and *Orkneyinga saga*, as Hudson noticed.[54]

The raid by Sveinn of Denmark on Man in 995 is attested only in Welsh annals.[55] It is a most interesting development in the context of unfolding events on a bigger stage. There was a dramatic increase in Scandinavian pressure on England in 991, led at first it seems by Óláfr Tryggvason, later king of Norway, although Sveinn may also have been involved. Arriving in south-eastern England with a fleet of ninety-three ships, Óláfr defeated

the king of the Isle of Man' and 'King Gudrod of Man'; previously, I followed these translations: Etchingham, 'Insular Viking zone', 174. **50** Ó Corráin, 'Viking Ireland', pp 447–52, made key points, but the case requires elaboration and significant modification; a substantial reconsideration is part of a forthcoming publication. **51** Etchingham, 'Insular Viking zone', 174, 178. **52** Ibid., 181–3. **53** *AU* 987.3 (cf. 987.1). **54** Hudson, *Viking pirates*, p. 75; his view that the adversary of Sigurðr at Man in *Njáls saga* was in reality Gofraid's son Ragnall, and not Gofraid himself (cf. p. 78), seems to be based on an unsubstantiated assumption that the battle dates to the 990s and not 987. **55** *Annales Cambriae*, ed. John Williams ap Ithel (London, 1860), p. 21; *Brut y Tywysogyon*, pp 18, 19.

English levies at the battle of Maldon in Essex, resulting in payment of the tax or tribute known as Danegeld. Óláfr returned in 994, this time certainly accompanied by Sveinn, and with a fleet of ninety-four ships, but although further tribute was paid, Æthelred king of England crucially succeeded in recruiting Óláfr and thus splitting the alliance.[56] Óláfr subsequently operated as agent of Æthelred against Sveinn, from whom he sought to wrest Norway. Óláfr was eventually killed by Sveinn in 1000, but (St) Óláfr Haraldsson maintained the effort to keep Norway from the Danish grasp. Sveinn's son Knútr came to control Norway only in 1028, expelling Óláfr Haraldsson, who was killed at the battle of Stiklestad in 1030.[57]

Sveinn's Manx raid of 995 occurred just at the point when the Norwegian–Danish breach had opened. Sveinn, soon after the cooption in 994 of Óláfr Tryggvason by Æthelred, seems to have returned to Scandinavia and stayed there until he had overcome Óláfr. He returned to England only in the early years of the eleventh century, reappearing in *ASC* for 1003. Accordingly, it has even been doubted whether it was the same Sveinn who mounted the raid on Man in 995.[58] The identification of the assailant as *Sweyn filius Haraldi* ('Sveinn son of Harald' [Bluetooth]) by *Annales Cambriae* leaves little room for such doubt, however. In view of the Danes' earlier alignment with the Haraldssons, and of the Danes' taking sides with Brian Boru in Ireland, the raid of 995 is readily interpreted as a strike against the influence in the north Irish Sea of Sigurðr of Orkney, who was perhaps perceived as at least 'Norwegian-friendly'. By 1000, however, the balance seems to have shifted, at least in Man. A high level of Danish Viking activity in southern England and Wales is again reported in *ASC* from 997 and in 1000 Æthelred's Chester fleet raided the Isle of Man, reportedly in a context in which it was unable to link up with the English king's land army in Cumbria/Strathclyde.[59] This may imply that the north Irish Sea was again in the sphere of influence of the Danes and, presumably, their erstwhile allies the Manx-Hebridean Haraldsson dynasty.

In light of all of this, I would conjecture that Dublin's recruitment of the Orcadians, and perhaps of *Lochlannaig*, for the battle of Clontarf shows that Sitriuc's regime was much more in the 'Norwegian' sphere. This would be in keeping with the pattern of rival networks of alliance in the late tenth century. Three further points are worthy of mention, albeit that two rely exclusively on medieval Icelandic saga literature. First, *Óláfs Saga Tryggvasonar* and *Orkneyinga saga* claim that Óláfr Tryggvason married Gyda, said to be the aunt of Sitriuc of Dublin, but perhaps his sister, as Hudson proposed.[60] Second,

56 *ASC*, pp 126–9. **57** For the English background, see Keynes, 'Historical context', pp 88–95; for the Scandinvian background, see briefly Niels Lund, 'The Danish empire and the end of the Viking age' in Sawyer (ed.), *Oxford illustrated history*, pp 156–81, at pp 169, 171, 174–5. **58** See Keynes, 'Historical context', pp 92–3; *ASC*, pp 134–5. **59** *ASC*, pp 131, 133; see Keynes, 'Historical context', p. 93. **60** Hudson, 'Knútr', 323; Hudson, *Viking*

Icelandic saga also brings Óláfr into contact with Sigurðr of Orkney, forcing him to convert to Christianity at sword-point. However, *Orkneyinga saga* is quick to claim that Sigurðr paid no 'homage' to Óláfr Tryggvason.[61] Whatever of that, it is striking, third, that Óláfr Tryggvason was responsible for the first Norwegian coinage, modelled closely on Æthelred's *Crux* pennies and thus datable to between 995 and early 998 at the latest – which is, of course, just when Sitriuc of Dublin's coins, with the same model, first appeared.[62] Incidentally, bearing in mind Sitriuc's fortunes discussed above, the timing of his coinage doubtless had to do with bolstering his prestige as king of Dublin, a position he had just secured against Ímar of Waterford. In any event, in view of the rival networks of alliance here outlined, extending from Scandinavia into the Insular Viking zone in the late tenth century, I would conjecture further that, had Knútr been in a position to intervene at Clontarf in 1014 – which of course he was not – he would have supported Brian.

THE OUTCOME

My third and final point is that the outcome of the battle of Clontarf was not as is generally imagined. Those annalistic records of the event that have best claim to be relatively free of the embellishments of later 'tradition' are remarkably coy about the outcome. The extended account in *AU* 1014.2, quoted in full above, signally fails to identify unambiguously victor and vanquished with, for example, a time-honoured formula such as 'battle defeat upon X by Y'. This is despite the fact that the account of the battle is in essence 'formulaic, stereoptyped and predictable', as well as being exceptionally long mostly because it gives a long list of the dead, and offering circumstantial detail only of Armagh's funeral arrangements for Brian and other eminent casualties on his side.

One might suppose that victory for Brian's forces is implied, nevertheless, by claiming that their named dead fell – in the stock formulation – *i frithguin* ('in the counter-slaughter'). In other battle reports, as remarked at the outset, this formula merely distinguishes dead on the victorious side from dead on the vanquished. It does not necessarily indicate an actual counter-attack. However, the annihilation reportedly suffered by Foreigners and Leinstermen is qualified in *AU* 1014.2 by the adverbial clause *i tosaigh* ('at first'). After initial success, it seems, Brian's side suffered heavy casualties after a turning of the tide of battle, in what therefore seems in this instance to have been an actual counter-attack. It would appear that the entirety of the forces opposing Brian were by no means annihilated in the first encounter.

pirates, pp 53, 84, 124, 154. **61** *Orkneyinga saga*, ed. Finnbogi Guðmundsson (Reykjavík, 1965), p. 27 §12: *veitti Sigurðr jarl Óláfi konungi enga lýðskyldu.* **62** See Kolbjørn Skaare,

In the nature of this evidence, we cannot hope to discover further what actually happened. Yet it is tempting to speculate that leading survivors on each side of the battle were in fact the military victors of attack and counter-attack, respectively – as they most certainly were political beneficiaries of the outcome of the battle. Thus on Brian's side, perhaps Máel Sechnaill survived not because, as later partisan 'tradition' claimed, he deserted Brian at the eleventh hour – *AU* gives no hint of this – but because he was leader of the first devastating onslaught that cost Máelmórda of Leinster and Sigurðr of Orkney and their followers their lives. Similarly, could Sitriuc of Dublin's survival have been due, not to ignominious flight from the field (*Njáls saga*), or to his remaining on the sidelines behind Dublin's ramparts, the equally disreputable picture painted by *CGG*, but because he led the counter-attack that cost Brian and so many of his followers their lives? This can be no more than speculation, but in Sitriuc's case one literary account does cast his role positively, of which more shortly.

Returning for the present to the firmer ground of what the annals actually do report, it seems that, shorn of assumptions born of later 'tradition', *AU* 1014.2 reflects an inconclusive stalemate on the battlefield. If the testimony of *AU* is revealing, even more so is the failure of *AI*, a chronicle that is strongly partisan towards Brian, to hail Clontarf as a victory for Brian's side.[63] The text of the comparatively succinct notice at *AI* 1014.2 brings this out:

> Cocad mór eter Brian 7 Gullu Átha Clíath co ruc Brian íarum mórthinól fer nÉrend co Áth Clíath. Is íar sain doratsat Gaill Átha Clíath cath do Brian corro marbad Brian mac Cennétich 7 a macc Murchad rígdamna hÉrend 7 a mac-side .i. Tairdelbach 7 rígrad Muman im Chonaing mac Duind Chuan 7 im Domnall mac nDíarmata rí Corcu Bascind 7 im Macbethad mac Muirethaich rí Cíarraige Lúachra 7 im Thadg hÚa Cellaich rí hÚa Máne 7 alii multi. Ro marbad dano isin chath sein Moel Mórda mac Murchada rí Laigen co rígráid Laigen imbi; ocus ár Gall íarthair domain isin chath chétna.
>
> Great warfare between Brian and the Foreigners of Dublin and Brian afterwards brought a great muster of the men of Ireland to Dublin. Then the Foreigners of Dublin gave battle to Brian, and Brian mac Cennétig was slain, as was his son Murchad 'king material' of Ireland and his son, that is Tairdelbach, and the royals of Munster, including Conaing mac Duinn Chuain, Domnall mac Díarmata king of Corcu Baiscinn,

Coins and coinage in Viking-age Norway (Oslo, 1976), pp 58–60, a reference I owe to Clare Downham. 63 Duffy, *Brian Boru*, pp 176–7, noticed that *AI* is coy about the outcome of the battle, and might have made more of it; cf. p. 212: 'no account suggests that the victorious army followed up their triumph by marching on and taking the now defenceless town' – but then explained this by reference to *CGG*'s tale of Sitriuc remaining in Dublin.

> Macbethad mac Muiredaig king of Cíarraige Lúachra, Tadg Úa Cellaig king of Uí Maine and many others. Also slain in that battle were Máelmórda mac Murchada king of Leinster, along with the royals of Leinster; and a slaughter of the Foreigners of the western world in the same battle.

As in *AU*, there is no clear indication as to who was victor and who was vanquished and, indeed, given the conventions of 'formulaic, stereoptyped and predictable' battle-reporting, the precedence *AI* gives the dead on Brian's side, as well as their far greater number named, might be taken to indicate that they were on the losing side. Participation by Leinster is reflected only in the fact that Máelmórda of Leinster alone is a named casualty on the side of Brian's adversaries. Neither the presence of the Orkneymen nor the death of Sigurðr is explicitly mentioned and the 'slaughter of the Foreigners of the western world' reads like something tacked on, perhaps only in the light of later 'tradition'. The annalist of *AI* depicts Clontarf as part of a war, essentially between Brian and Dublin, in which 'the Foreigners of Dublin gave battle to Brian'. This is consistent with the conjecture above that it was Sitriuc and his Dubliners themselves who were responsible for the devastating slaughter of Brian and his retainers. As in *AU*, the Latin tag (underlined) inspires confidence that the core record in *AI* 1014.2 is contemporary. As such, it is a most downbeat reflection, on the part of the Munster chronicler, of what later 'tradition' would portray as Brian's victory in martyrdom.

If an inconclusive stalemate at best is what the most reliable contemporary annals appear to reflect of what happened on the battlefield itself, what ensued afterwards is powerful circumstantial evidence: Brian's supposedly victorious side was unable to press home an advantage by entering, occupying and plundering Dublin and obliging Sitriuc to give tokens of submission – all of which had happened after Brian's conclusive victory at Glenn Máma fifteen years earlier. Instead, the Munstermen retreated home and a far from triumphant outcome was compounded by conflict later in 1014 between Brian's two surviving sons Donnchad and Tadc.[64] On the other hand, Sitriuc remained king of Dublin for twenty-two years after Clontarf and, while by no means unmolested by Irish kings in that role, it seems that Dublin was more autonomous than it had been under the overlordships, consecutively, of Máel Sechnaill and Brian, from 975 to 1014. In terms of the matters at issue in 1013–14, then, despite the loss of allied leaders from far and near, the position of Sitriuc of Dublin was secured, whether by strategy or accident. Dublin enjoyed almost forty years free of any Gaelic overlordship, until Diarmait mac Maíl na mBó of Leinster imposed himself in 1052.[65] Meanwhile, Máel

64 *AU* 1014.6; *CS* 1014 (1012); cf. *AI* 1014.7. **65** See Duffy, 'Irishmen and Islesmen', 94–101.

Sechnaill, whether or not his military contribution at Clontarf was considerable, as conjectured above, was a short-term political beneficiary. He resumed his claim to overkingship of Ireland and made real efforts to give it effect until his death in 1022, during which period he raided or defeated Dublin in 1015, 1021 and 1022.[66]

That the most significant outcome of Clontarf was in fact qualified success for Sitriuc of Dublin is reflected in the remarkable skaldic poem *Darraðarljóð* that is incorporated in the final part of the Clontarf episode in *Njáls saga*. The poem describes twelve valkyries or norns weaving a piece of cloth from body-parts, this being an image of doom associated with the slaughter of battle.[67] Verse embedded in sagas is usually seen as earlier than the prose. In this case, Hudson declared that *Darraðarljóð* was 'probably composed in the first generation after the battle', although he gave no reason for this opinion.[68] John Hines too was minded to date the poem to the post-Clontarf reign of Sitriuc of Dublin.[69] Hudson made the further point that the author of *Njáls saga* apparently did not recognize *darraðr* as an archaic (or rather, a rare poetic) word denoting either a spear or a banner and took it to be the name of an observer of the twelve valkyries or norns at work.[70] Neither Hudson nor Hines was persuaded, it seems, by Russell Poole's suggestion that *Darraðarljóð* really refers to the battle of Dublin in 919, one of the most crushing defeats of Irish by Vikings in the ninth or tenth centuries, in which the Irish overking Níall Glúndub was killed.[71]

Poole's reluctance to accept that *Darraðarljóð* refers to the battle of Clontarf stems from its content. Although the language is relatively transparent and is 'free of the dense kennings and convoluted syntax characteristic of most skaldic poetry', it is, nonetheless, allusive rather than straightforward narrative.[72] Yet it is inescapable that the subject matter of the poem is a battle victory for a certain *ungr konungr* ('young king'). The Irish will suffer grief – *Ok munu Írar / angr um bíða* – and the Valkyries declare: *Vel kváðum vér / um konung ungan / sigrhljóða fjǫlð syngjum heilar* ('We spoke well about the young king; let us sing a multitude of victory-songs with good fortune').[73] Since Brian was anything but a young king, and since a different verse summary of the battle of Clontarf in *Njáls saga* is *Briánn fell ok helt velli* ('Brian fell and [yet] held the field'), it is easy to see why one might think that *Darraðarljóð* refers to a different battle.[74] But *Darraðarljóð* juxtaposes the death of a mighty king

66 *CS* 1015 (1013); *AFM* 1021, 1022; *AU* 1022.3 (cf. *AI* 1022.4). **67** *Njáls saga*, ed. E.O. Sveinsson, pp 454–8. **68** Hudson, '"Brjáns saga"', 246. **69** John Hines, *Old Norse sources for Gaelic history*, Quiggin Pamphlets 5 (Cambridge, 2002), pp 3–7, 24–5, at p. 5. **70** Hudson, '"Brjáns saga"', 246; Russell Poole, *Viking poems on war and peace* (Toronto, 1991), pp 128–31, argued that the word means 'banner' not 'spear'. **71** Hudson, '"Brjáns saga"', 246–7; Poole, *Viking poems*, pp 120–5. **72** Hines, *Old Norse sources*, p. 4. **73** *Njáls saga*, ed. E.O. Sveinsson, pp 456 v. 4, 457 v. 8, 458 v. 10; Hines, *Old Norse sources*, pp 24–5. **74** *Njáls saga*, ed. E.O. Sveinsson, p. 460 §157.

(*ríkum gram*) and that of a jarl *fyrir oddum* ('before spear-points'). This must refer to the spear with which the prose of *Njáls saga* says Sigurðr was killed, after he was obliged to take possession personally of the banner that brought victory to his forces but death to its actual bearer.[75] There seems no reason to doubt that these references are to the deaths in the battle of Clontarf of Brian and Sigurðr as recounted in the prose of *Njáls saga*. The perspective of *Darraðarljóð*, therefore, is that a young king was victorious. Brian was in his seventy-third year in 1014, and if agents of Sigurðr were active in the Irish Sea in 987, as proposed above, then he too was no youngster in 1014 and was in any event not a king and could not possibly be represented as victor – his death, like that of Brian, is acknowledged.

Sitriuc of Dublin, however, was comparatively young in this company: he survived as king of Dublin until 1036 and did not die until 1042. If he was born very late in his father Amlaíb Cuarán's long career, perhaps in or not long before its final year, 980, this will help explain various things. As already outlined, when Sitriuc's older half-brother Glún Iairn, king of Dublin and agent of Irish overking Máel Sechnaill, was killed by his slave in 989, Ímar of Waterford was able to intrude himself into the kingship of Dublin and contest that kingship until Sitriuc secured his position in 995. As we have seen, Sitriuc first asserted himself by temporarily expelling Ímar in 993. If he was born only in or not long before 980, he was but a teenager as he struggled to wrest power from Ímar. This in turn would allow Sitriuc's mother Gormlaith still to be of child-bearing age in 997, the earliest likely date for her becoming wife of Brian – because this is the point at which Máel Sechnaill conceded to Brian overkingship of southern Ireland (including Leinster, to the royal family of which Gormlaith belonged). This would explain Gormlaith's being the mother of Brian's son Donnchad, who in turn would have been only a teenager when he survived Clontarf, rendering more explicable his survival for another fifty years. Sitriuc would, accordingly, be a relatively *ungr konungr* of about thirty-five in 1014.

The most significant implication of *Darraðarljóð* is that the *ungr konungr* emerged successfully from the momentous battle. Hines evidently baulked at so radical a conclusion and instead interpreted the poem as merely 'careful to apologize for Sigtryggr's surviving the battle', because he was protected by the valkyries or norns.[76] A bolder verdict is possible. A.J. Goedheer, eighty years ago, showed no such reticence about relating *Darraðarljóð* to the contemporary realities of 1014 and after, although what he wrote seems to have been generally overlooked or perhaps discounted: 'The battle did not cause the fall of the Dublin kingdom; Sigtryggr remained king, while his great opponent was slain,

75 Ibid., p. 457 v.8; cf. p. 451 §157; Hines, *Old Norse sources*, p. 24; accordingly, perhaps the title of the poem deliberately invokes an ambiguity about the meaning of *darraðr*, 'spear' or 'banner', juxtaposed in the circumstances of Sigurðr's death. 76 Hines, *Old Norse sources*,

and among the Irish there arose new troubles in the contest for hegemony.'[77] Hudson made several important points about *Darraðarljóð*, among them that Sitriuc of Dublin is the subject of another (praise-)poem in Old Norse, mentioned in *Gunnlaugs saga Ormstungu*.[78] In recent comments on *Darraðarljóð*, Hudson recognized that the poem depicts Sitriuc of Dublin as victor at Clontarf and considered this to be a plausible evaluation of the outcome.[79]

It is clear that the idea that the battle of Clontarf was a qualified success for Sigtryggr is not so outrageous a proposition as might be imagined. Careful analysis of the contemporary record of the battle in Irish chronicles admits its interpretation as a stalemate, or worse, from the point of view of Brian's side. It is certainly not portrayed by contemporary annalists as the overwhelming defeat of the Foreigners and Leinstermen that later Irish 'tradition' and the prose of *Njáls saga* alike depict. Both Irish and Old Norse prose literary 'traditions' about the battle of Clontarf can be and have been shown to be tendentious. A forthcoming analysis of the prose account in *Njáls saga*, and of related Old Norse material, will shed new light on the place, time and motive of composition and the likely route by which it was available to a thirteenth-century Icelandic saga writer. In the meantime, in the light of what has been discussed, we should countenance that *Darraðarljóð* could prove to be among the most authentic contemporary or near-contemporary evaluations of the outcome of the battle of Clontarf, albeit that it too is couched as literary conceit. If so, it is intriguing that it was incorporated in *Njáls saga*, alongside a highly tendentious Old Norse prose account that originated seemingly about a hundred years after the battle and had an entirely different story to tell. It is a problem that is obviously worthy of investigation, but this cannot be undertaken here.

p. 5. 77 Goedheer, *Irish and Norse traditions*, p. 76. 78 Hudson, 'The Viking and the Irishman', *Medium Ævum*, 60 (1991), 257–67, at 262; Hudson, '"Brjáns saga"', 247. 79 Hudson, *Viking pirates*, pp 8, 103.

Brian Bóraime, the Insular Viking world and the battle of Clontarf[1]

PATRICK WADDEN

'The battle of Clontarf, fought outside Dublin on Good Friday, 23 April 1014, was the greatest battle of the early period of Irish history. Its lustre has not, over the intervening centuries, been dimmed; rather has its fame increased.'[2] In the aftermath of the recent millennial commemorations, it is fair to say that the fame of Clontarf has reached new heights. From a very early date, however, the battle became 'a remarkably elastic encounter', retellings of which were shaped to fit a variety of political and literary needs.[3] The most common image of the battle – that it was a great national struggle in which the Christian king of Ireland defeated and expelled the pagan vikings, thus bringing to an end the suffering Ireland had endured at their hands for over two hundred years – owes a lot to *Cogadh Gáedhel re Gallaibh*, a propagandist text written for the benefit of Brian Bóraime's descendants in the early twelfth century.[4] This image survived among academic historians until the second half of the twentieth century, and continues to influence popular perceptions of the battle. So, for G.A. Hayes-McCoy, Clontarf was 'a victory for the native side', that 'ended in the tumbling of the Norsemen into the sea', and after which 'Ireland experienced no more Viking raids'.[5] For Edmund Curtis, it brought to a close 'the Norse tyranny',[6] and for Máire and Liam de Paor, Clontarf represented 'a last rally of the Vikings, of Dublin, of Man and the Isles, and of Scandinavia itself'.[7]

The process of re-evaluating Clontarf began in the 1930s, and really picked up steam in the 1960s, as broader historiographical trends favoured the reassessment both of the role of Scandinavians in European history, and of the traditional, nationalist interpretation of Irish history.[8] In Ireland, the

1 Versions of this paper were presented at the annual conference of the Southeastern Medieval Association in Atlanta, 2014, and at the Harvard Celtic Colloquium, 2014. I am grateful to all those who offered comments on those occasions. 2 G.A. Hayes-McCoy, *Irish battles: a military history of Ireland* (Belfast, 2009, first published, 1969), p. 12. 3 Ní Mhaonaigh, *Brian Boru*, pp 53–99, at p. 67. See also A.J. Goedheer, *Irish and Norse traditions about the battle of Clontarf* (Haarlem, 1938); Clare Downham, 'The battle of Clontarf in Irish history and legend', *History Ireland*, 13.5 (Sept./Oct. 2005), 19–23; Clare O'Halloran, 'Brian Boru and his afterlife', *History Ireland*, 22:2 (Mar./Apr. 2014), 38–41. 4 *CGG*; Máire Ní Mhaonaigh, '*Cogad Gáedel re Gallaib*: some dating considerations', *Peritia*, 9 (1995), 354–77. 5 Hayes-McCoy, *Irish battles*, p. 12. 6 Edmund Curtis, *A history of Ireland* (London, 1932), pp 22–30. 7 Máire and Liam de Paor, *Early Christian Ireland* (London, 1958), p. 160.

contribution of Scandinavians to the development of urban centres, industry, and trade was recognized, and they were no longer seen simply as the destroyers of 'the old order' of the early Christian era.[9] Their cultural assimilation, including conversion to Christianity, and integration into the Irish political landscape, through intermarriage and other peaceful interaction, was also highlighted. It also became clear that the battle of Clontarf, whatever its causes, did not lead to the departure from Ireland of the resident Hiberno-Scandinavian population, nor the destruction of their coastal towns, which instead became prizes for control over which ambitious Irish kings fought during the rest of the eleventh and twelfth centuries.

As a result of these broader historiographical changes, the battle of Clontarf was thoroughly reassessed. If not a national struggle against foreign tyranny, then what was the battle all about? Fr John Ryan, in his seminal 1938 article, provided the following answer:

> Fundamentally, then, the issue at Clontarf was the age-old determination of the Leinstermen to maintain their independence against the High-King … One with them in policy were the Norse of Dublin, a small state, indeed, in extent and weak in manpower, but rich out of all proportion to its size and skilful in securing mercenary aid from willing kin.[10]

This interpretation found support among the most prominent Irish historians of the second half of the twentieth century. Donnchadh Ó Corráin, for example, reiterated the fundamental point of Ryan's argument in a series of influential publications:

> The battle of Clontarf was not a struggle between the Irish and the Vikings for the sovereignty of Ireland. Neither was it a great national victory which broke the power of the Vikings forever. Long before the Battle of Clontarf the Vikings had become a minor political force in Irish

8 Seán Duffy, 'Ireland, *c.*1000–*c.*1100' in Pauline Stafford (ed.), *A companion to the early Middle Ages: Britain and Ireland* c.*500*–c.*1100* (Oxford, 2009), pp 286–9. For changing attitudes towards the Vikings, see Peter Foote and David M. Wilson, *The Viking achievement: the society and culture of early medieval Scandinavia* (London, 1970). For a survey of some of the most important contributions to the debate on Irish history, see Ciaran Brady (ed.), *Interpreting Irish history: the debate on historical revisionism* (Dublin, 1994). 9 P.F. Wallace, 'The origins of Dublin' in Howard Clarke (ed.), *Medieval Dublin: the making of a metropolis* (Blackrock, 1990), pp 70–97; Mary A. Valante, *The Vikings in Ireland: settlement, trade and urbanization* (Dublin, 2008). The quotation is from Daniel A. Binchy, 'The passing of the old order' in Brian Ó Cuív (ed.), *The impact of the Scandinavian invasions on the Celtic-speaking peoples,* c.*AD800–1100: introductory papers read at plenary sessions of the International Congress of Celtic Studies held in Dublin, 6–10 July, 1959* (Dublin, 1983), pp 119–32. 10 John Ryan, 'The battle of Clontarf', *JRSAI*, 68 (1938), 1–50. See also, idem, 'Brian Boruma, king of Ireland' in Etienne Rynne (ed.), *North Munster studies: essays in commemoration of Monsignor Michael Moloney* (Limerick, 1967), pp 355–74.

> affairs. Traders and merchants in the cities of Dublin, Wexford, Waterford, Cork and Limerick, they were no longer of any military significance in the wars that were being conducted by the Irish kings. In point of fact, Clontarf was part of the internal struggle for sovereignty between the great Irish provincial rulers and it was in essence the revolt of the Leinstermen against dominance from Munster, a revolt in which their Viking allies played a very important but secondary role.[11]

Francis John Byrne characterized the battle as 'a revolt of the Leinstermen and Dublin aided by Sigurd of Orkney',[12] and Dáibhí Ó Cróinín stated that Irish historians 'are almost unanimous in the verdict that the encounter was of no real political significance'.[13] By the end of the twentieth century, and into the twenty-first, this 'internal struggle' interpretation of the battle of Clontarf had become almost universally accepted.[14] By the time of the battle's millennium, the impact of this new orthodoxy had begun to impact on popular opinion, as evident in historical fiction written about Brian and Clontarf.[15]

Recently, however, a challenge to the dominant perspective has begun to emerge. It was spearheaded by Seán Duffy, who first articulated his dissatisfaction with the orthodox view in an essay published in 2009. In place of the 'naïve certainty' of the traditional image of the battle, he wrote, the idea that it was part of 'a confused picture of petty provincial rivalries' left him with 'a vague curiosity as to what all the fuss was about'.[16] He pointed out what he

11 Donnchadh Ó Corráin, 'Brian Boru and the battle of Clontarf' in Liam de Paor (ed.), *Milestones in Irish history* (Dublin, 1986), p. 39. See also, idem, *Ireland before the Normans* (Dublin, 1972), p. 130, and idem, 'Prehistoric and early Christian Ireland' in R.F. Foster (ed.), *The Oxford history of Ireland* (Oxford, 1989), p. 38. **12** F.J. Byrne, 'Ireland and her neighbours, *c.*1014–*c.*1072' in *NHI*, i, pp 862–3. **13** Dáibhí Ó Cróinín, *Early medieval Ireland 400–1200* (London, 1995), p. 266. **14** Bart Jaski, 'The Vikings and the kingship of Tara', *Peritia*, 9 (1995), 310–53, at 349; Benjamin Hudson, *Viking pirates and Christian princes: dynasty, religion and empire in the North Atlantic* (Oxford, 2005), pp 96–100; Clare Downham, *Viking kings of Britain and Ireland: the dynasty of Ívarr to AD1014* (Edinburgh, 2007), pp 59–61. For dissenting voices, see Nora K. Chadwick, 'The Vikings and the Western World' in Ó Cuív (ed.), *Impact of the Scandinavian invasions*, p. 38; James Lydon, *The making of Ireland from ancient times to the present* (London, 1998), p. 36. **15** See, for example, the contrast between Morgan Llywelyn's *Lion of Ireland: the legend of Brian Boru* (Boston, 1980), in which the devout Brian fights pagan Vikings to save Ireland, and Eithne Massey's *Blood brother, swan sister: 1014 Clontarf, a battle begins* (Dublin, 2014), in which Clontarf is a fight to re-establish Brian's authority over the rebellious – though Christian – Hiberno-Scandinavians of Dublin and the Leinstermen. The marketing material for *Brian Boru Irish Style Red Ale*, produced by the Three Floyds Brewing Company in Munster, Indiana, blends elements of these two views of Brian's career and the battle of Clontarf. It borrows from Llywelyn the idea that Brian spent his career fighting the Vikings in retaliation for the murder of his mother, but states that he was 'killed at Clontarf on Good Friday 1014 putting down a rebellion by the king of the province of Leinster' (http://mybeerbuzz.blogspot.com/2013/03/3-floyds-brian-boru-irish-red-22oz.html, viewed on July 3, 2014). **16** Duffy, 'Ireland, *c.*1000–*c.*1100', p. 288.

perceived as a fundamental flaw of this theory, namely, that it failed to explain how the battle could be seen as a victory for Brian Bóraime. Brian's death in battle could not be considered victorious if his goal had been to reassert his authority over the Dublin and Leinster rebels; in order for his victory to have been worth the sacrifice of his life, he must have been confronting some potentially much more threatening enemy, or staving off a much more terrifying eventuality than the reduction of his own power. Duffy was careful to point out that he was not proposing a return to the traditional view of the battle, but warned of the danger 'that in "talking down" the significance of Clontarf – albeit in a laudable attempt to expose an illusion – we have thrown the baby out with the bathwater'. 'It is strange', he noted, 'how little attention is paid to the temporal context of the encounter', which he considered 'something of an indictment of the insularity of Irish historiography'.[17] Duffy's response was to set the battle firmly within the context of the Danish conquest of England in 1013, a line he pursued more fully in his book, *Brian Boru and the battle of Clontarf*, published in 2013. There, he showed that Dublin, rather than Leinster, was, according to the contemporary annals, the primary focus of Brian's army in 1014. The Annals of Inisfallen begin their account with the simple statement that there was 'great warfare between Brian and the Gaill of Dublin' before claiming that the casualties included 'the Gaill of the western world'.[18] And the Annals of Ulster state that Máelmórda, king of Leinster, was fighting in the army of the Gaill when he died at Clontarf.[19] Leinster, in other words, was the junior member rather than the leader of the alliance. Dublin, Duffy argued, had reluctantly tolerated Brian's domination of its military, naval and economic resources, for over a decade. The long-awaited opportunity to break free came in 1013

> amidst the upheaval of the Danish conquest of England, when carnage was in the air, when unparalleled numbers of Scandinavian and Insular troops and warships were at hand, battle-ready and confident of the new possibilities … There is no telling, at this remove, what they hoped to achieve, but if England could be won and lost Ireland surely seemed a sitting duck. And the question asked of Brian on that Good Friday was whether he would crumple as Æðelræd the Unready had done in the face of Sveinn Forkberard the previous summer. That he did not was his claim to fame.[20]

Since Duffy first aired his frustration with the 'internal struggle' theory in 2009, others have also recognized the importance of setting Clontarf within its international context. Another book published to mark the anniversary of the

17 Ibid., pp 288–9. 18 *AI* 1014. 19 *AU* 1014. 20 Duffy, *Brian Boru*, pp 242–8, at p. 248.

battle, Darren McGettigan's *The battle of Clontarf, Good Friday 1014*, draws attention to the 'Anglo-Saxon and Scandinavian backgrounds … important arenas that contributed to events in Ireland around the year 1014'.[21] Clare Downham's contribution to the special edition of *History Ireland* magazine published to coincide with the battle's millennium, entitled 'Clontarf in the wider world', offers further context. She believes that 'the conflict was much more than an internal squabble between an Irish over-king and some reluctant subjects', highlighting Brian's probable involvement in a struggle for political influence in the Irish Sea world and the likelihood that Hiberno-Scandinavians from that region participated in the almost incessant raiding in England that led to the Danish conquest of that kingdom.[22]

This article follows the path signposted by Duffy by setting Clontarf, and Brian's career in general, within the context of political developments in the Insular Viking zone during the late tenth and early eleventh centuries.[23] It begins by examining briefly the political scene in Ireland in the late 970s, at the beginning of Brian's career, and highlighting the power and international connections of the Uí Ímair kingdom of Dublin. It then discusses Brian's relationship with the Uí Ímair and how it changed over the course of his career as he manipulated the divisions that existed between different branches of that dynasty. Finally, the sudden, and short-lived, rapprochement between the rival branches of the Uí Ímair, when they united against Brian in 1014, will be discussed in comparison with similar, eleventh-century episodes, the result of which will be to shed further light on the significance of the international political context of the battle.

Brian spent the years after the death of his brother, Mathgamain (d. 976), establishing his authority in Munster.[24] At the same time, a political struggle on a larger scale was unfolding in the midlands, between Domnall ua Néill, the Cenél nEógain king of Tara, and Amlaíb Cuarán (Óláfr Kvaran), king of Dublin. Amlaíb is one of the great figures in the history of Britain and Ireland in the tenth century. He belonged to the Uí Ímair, the dynasty descended from Ímar (Ívarr, d. 871), that ruled many of the viking kingdoms of Britain and Ireland during the tenth and later centuries.[25] Amlaíb had enjoyed two spells as king of Viking Northumbria earlier in his career, during the first of which he had converted to Christianity and been baptized, with King Edmund of

21 Darren McGettigan, *The battle of Clontarf, Good Friday 1014* (Dublin, 2013), pp 16, 86, 88. 22 Clare Downham, 'Clontarf and the wider world', *History Ireland*, 22:2 (Mar./Apr. 2014), 22–6, quoted at 22–3. 23 Colmán Etchingham. ('North Wales, Ireland and the Isles: the Insular Viking zone', *Peritia* 15 (2001)) prefers the term 'Insular Viking zone', rather than 'Irish Sea world/zone' in recognition of the activities in the region of actors from beyond the Irish Sea littoral, including Scandinavians. I consider the Irish Sea world, including the east coast of Ireland, the west coast of England, Wales, Man and the Hebrides, a component part of the Insular Viking zone that included all of Britain, Ireland and the surrounding islands, as well as northern France and Scandinavia. 24 *AU* 976; *AI* 976; *AT* 976; *CS* 974 (=976); Duffy, *Brian Boru*, pp 92–124, esp. pp 103–6. 25 Downham, *Viking*

England standing as his godfather.[26] For over a decade after his second expulsion from Northumbria in 950 or 952, Amlaíb's whereabouts are uncertain, but in 964 he led an attack on Kildare at the head of a Dublin army.[27] Over the next sixteen years, Amlaíb set about making himself a dominant force in Irish politics. At first, he operated in alliance with Domnall mac Congalaig, king of Brega. This brought Amlaíb into conflict with Domnall ua Néill, who had succeeded Domnall mac Congalaig's father, Congalach mac Maíle Míthig, to the kingship of Tara in 956, and thereafter seemed intent on breaking the strength of the midland kingdoms of Brega and Mide. In 970 Amlaíb and his ally inflicted a serious defeat on Domnall ua Néill in the battle of Cell Móna. In response, ua Néill attacked several churches, some of which seem to have been under Amlaíb's protection.[28] Amlaíb was a great patron of Columban churches in particular, and in 976, Domnall targeted the Columban church at Skreen as part of another strike against him.[29] That same year, Domnall mac Congalaig died, but Amlaíb continued to take the fight to Domnall ua Néill by himself, capturing the king of Leinster, Úgaire mac Tuathail.[30] The following year, Amlaíb killed both the son of his long-time enemy, Domnall ua Néill, and the son of his former ally, Domnall mac Congalaig, thus asserting his power and independence.[31] In 978, his men killed the king of Leinster in battle and, in the following year, they captured his successor and took him as a hostage to Dublin.[32] As Thomas Charles-Edwards put it, 'in one decade Olaf Cuarán had reduced the Leinstermen to abject submission and had humiliated and defeated the Uí Néill, including the king of Tara, Domnall ua Néill'.[33] Domnall retired in 980, and, according to a centuries-old pattern of alternating succession, the kingship of Tara should then have passed to Máel Sechnaill mac Domnaill of Clann Cholmáin. Amlaíb, however, had other ideas, and, having shown himself more than a match for Domnall ua Néill, decided to challenge Máel Sechnaill for the greatest prize in Irish politics.[34] He dispatched an army, under his sons, to Tara, where they came face to face with Máel Sechnaill, possibly during his inauguration.[35]

Amlaíb's gambit was unsuccessful, and his army was routed by Máel Sechnaill's, with so great a loss of life that, according to the Annals of

kings. **26** *The Anglo-Saxon Chronicles*, trans. Michael Swanton, rev. ed. (London, 2000), (A, D) 943, (A, D, E) 944; Alex Woolf, 'Amlaíb Cuarán and the Gael' in Seán Duffy (ed.), *Medieval Dublin III* (Dublin, 2002), pp 36–7; A.P. Smyth, *Scandinavian York and Dublin: the history and archaeology of two related Viking kingdoms*, 2 vols (Dublin, 1975–9), ii, pp 107–90. **27** *AU* 964; *CS* 962 (=964); Woolf, 'Amlaíb Cuarán', p. 39. **28** *AU* 970; *CS* 968 (=970); Woolf, 'Amlaíb Cuarán', p. 42; T.M. Charles-Edwards, *Wales and the Britons 350–1064*, The History of Wales (Oxford, 2013), p. 542. **29** *AT* 976; *CS* 974 (=976); Woolf, 'Amlaíb Cuarán', 42; Edel Bhreathnach, 'The documentary evidence for pre-Norman Skreen, county Meath', *Ríocht na Midhe*, 9:2 (1996), 37–45; Hudson, *Viking pirates*, pp 46–7. **30** *AT* 976. **31** *AU* 977. **32** *AU* 978; *AT* 979; *CS* 977 (=979). **33** Charles-Edwards, *Wales and the Britons*, p. 543. **34** Woolf, 'Amlaíb Cuarán', 34–43; Duffy, *Brian Boru*, 246–7. **35** *AT* 980; *CS* 978 (=980).

Inisfallen, 'a measuring rod [was] required everywhere'.[36] Máel Sechnaill followed up his victory by sacking the town of Dublin, taking a great spoil of cattle and treasure. According to the Annals of Tigernach and Chronicum Scotorum, both of which draw on a source from Clonmacnoise favourable to Máel Sechnaill, he also liberated 'the hostages of Ireland', including Domnall Cláen, king of Leinster, and secured the release of 'the sureties of the Uí Néill' and 'freedom of the Uí Néill from the Shannon to the sea'.[37] With a flourish, the annalist added that Máel Sechnaill's attack 'was the harrying of the Babylon of Ireland', while the Annals of Ulster reported that 'foreign power was ejected from Ireland as a result'.[38] The hyperbole of the Clonmacnoise annalist aside, it is clear that what occurred at Tara in 980 was a battle on a grand scale and of considerable importance. Máel Sechnaill, the most powerful of the Irish kings, fought Amlaíb, a man of international renown and reputation, whose army was drawn not just from Dublin but also from the Irish Sea world. The prize for the victor was the kingship of Tara, and the result of the battle was to determine the place of Dublin in Irish affairs for the next generation. Despite all of this, the battle made no impact on the historical record outside Ireland; foreign chroniclers were not usually concerned to record the affairs of Irish kings, even when they were of such obvious significance. The fact that, thirty-four years later, the battle of Clontarf was deemed worthy of note in Wales and Aquitaine ought, therefore, to be read as a sign that its impact was perceived as extending beyond the internal politics of Ireland.

Máel Sechnaill had to win the freedom of the Southern Uí Néill in 980 because before that date they were, to some extent, unfree, subject to the authority of Amlaíb, who held their hostages. Likewise, by holding hostage the king of Leinster, Amlaíb was asserting his overlordship over that province. In other words, Dublin, during the reign of Amlaíb Cuarán, dominated of a large portion of Ireland, including the southeast and the midlands.[39] Amlaíb's power was based on more than his control of Dublin. The army he sent to Tara in 980 included contingents from the Isles – probably Man and/or the Hebrides – and in the aftermath of that crushing defeat, Amlaíb retired to the monastic island of Iona, where he soon afterwards died.[40] This supports the idea that Amlaíb ruled at least some portion of the Isles. His authority might have extended farther still. Colmán Etchingham and Thomas Clancy have drawn attention to the obituary, in the Annals of Roscrea, of Mugrón, abbot of Iona and bishop of *na Trí Rand*, 'the Three Parts', who died in 980.[41] Etchingham has suggested that the three parts of Mugrón's diocese were Ireland, Scotland and Man.[42] Clancy prefers to see them as 'distinct parts of Amlaíb Cuarán's

36 *AI* 980. 37 *AT* 980; *CS* 978 (=980). 38 *AT* 980; *AU* 980; Duffy, *Brian Boru*, pp 246–8. For the translation of *AT*, see Charles-Edwards, *Wales and the Britons*, p. 542, n. 29. 39 Charles-Edwards, *Wales and the Britons*, p. 542. 40 *AU*, *AT*, *AI* 980; *CS* 978 (=980). 41 *AR* 980; *AU* 980; *CS* 978 (=980). 42 Colmán Etchingham, *Church organisation in*

dominion: these would probably be *Fine Gall* (Dublin and its extensive hinterland, which extended as far as the Boyne valley during Amlaíb's reign); *na hInnsi*, 'the isles', including Man; and … *na Renna*, 'the Rhinns', corresponding to modern Wigtownshire', in Galloway.[43] Having the resources of these extensive territories at his disposal was part of what had made Amlaíb such a formidable force in Irish politics.

After the battle of Tara, for a period of nearly two decades, Dublin fell under the overlordship of Máel Sechnaill mac Domnaill, king of Tara. His first action was to install as the new king Amlaíb's son, his own uterine half-brother, Glún Iairn.[44] Máel Sechnaill also probably married Amlaíb's widow, Gormlaith, at this point, and possibly took her son, Sitriuc, into his household.[45] Máel Sechnaill's authority over Dublin was clear in 983, when Glún Iairn and the Dublin army accompanied him on campaign in Leinster.[46] When Glún Iairn died in 989, Máel Sechnaill attacked and pillaged Dublin to reassert his authority and to ensure that the succession did not alter his relationship with the town.[47] As Alex Woolf put it, 'Glúniairn's death might have spelled trouble for Máel Sechnaill, but luckily he had a spare son of Amlaíb Cuarán to hand: his own step-son Sitric, perhaps still a teenager, whom he placed on the throne of Dublin.'[48] Sitriuc faced serious challenges to his authority in the early 990s. In 993, he drove a rival, Ímar, out of the town, and although Ímar returned to expel him in either 994 or 995, by the end of 995 Sitriuc was again in control.[49] It is likely he secured his position with the assistance of Máel Sechnaill, who, in 995, again entered the town and took possession of its royal regalia, Tomar's ring and the sword of Carlus.[50] Having been in a position to dominate Leinster and the Southern Uí Néill during Amlaíb Cuarán's reign, for nearly two decades after the battle of Tara, Dublin was securely under Máel Sechnaill's thumb.

Brian Bóraime, no doubt, was an interested observer of the rise and fall of the fortunes of the Uí Néill and Dublin in the 970s and early 980s, during which period he secured his control over Munster and began to flex his muscles beyond its borders. As part of his campaign to unite Leth Moga, the southern half of Ireland, under his authority, in 984 Brian visited Waterford, where he made an alliance with 'the sons of Aralt' to attack Leinster and Dublin together.[51] The sons of Aralt (Haraldr) were the rising power in the

Ireland AD650 to 1000 (Maynooth, 1999), pp 185–6. **43** Thomas Owen Clancy, 'The Gall-Ghàidheil and Galloway', *Journal of Scottish Names Studies*, 2 (2008), 19–50, at 27–8. **44** *AU* 983; *AT* 983; 'The *Ban-shenchus*', ed. M.C. Dobbs, *Revue Celtique* 47 (1930), 282–339; 48 (1931), 163–234; 49 (1932), 437–89, at 47:314 and 48:188. **45** Alex Woolf, *From Pictland to Alba, 789–1070*, The New Edinburgh History of Scotland 2 (Edinburgh, 2007), pp 214–15. **46** *AU* 983; *AT* 983; *CS* 981 (=983); *AFM* 982 (=983). **47** *AU* 989; *AT* 989; *CS* 987 (=989). **48** Woolf, *From Pictland to Alba*, p. 219. **49** *AI* 993; *AU* 994; *AT* 995; *AI* 995. **50** *AT* 995; *CS* 983 (=985). **51** *AI* 984. **52** *AI* 940; *CS* 939 (=940); *AFM* 938 (=940); Etchingham, 'North Wales', 171–83; Woolf, *From Pictland to Alba*, 206–7;

Irish Sea. Maccus mac Arailt and his brother Gofriad (Guðrøðr) were almost certainly the sons of Aralt son of Sitriuc son of Ímar, the king of Limerick who died in 940.[52] Like the kings of Dublin, they belonged to the dynasty descended from Ívarr. In fact, their father, Aralt, was probably a brother of Amlaíb Cuarán, and he may have been imposed on Limerick from Dublin.[53] The sons of Aralt had made their first appearances in the historical record in 971 and 972, when they were reported to have attacked Anglesey, on the second occasion possibly completing a temporary conquest of the island.[54] It was perhaps because of these attacks on Wales, or possibly because of the rising fortunes of Amlaíb Cuarán in Ireland, that King Edgar of England convened a meeting of Insular kings in Chester the following year.[55] Contemporary records of this event claim that 'six kings came to meet him, and all pledged that they would be his allies on sea and on land'.[56] The Anglo-Saxon Chronicle does not name those kings, but twelfth-century sources do, and David Thornton has shown that there is reason to believe that those later records may be accurate.[57] According to those later accounts, one of those present was Maccus, 'king of very many islands'.[58]

After this meeting with Edgar, the sons of Aralt seem to have temporarily ceased their activities in Wales, and the following year Maccus led a fleet to Scattery Island, in the Shannon estuary. There he captured Ímar, who had previously been ruling Limerick and who might have been responsible for excluding the sons of Aralt from their inheritance in that town.[59] Ímar was resident on Scattery Island in 974 because he had been driven from Limerick by Mathgamain mac Cennétig, Brian Bóraime's brother, two years earlier.[60] Ímar survived Maccus's attack and, in 976, he was implicated in Mathgamain's death, as a result of which, in 977, Brian tracked him to Scattery Island and killed him and his two sons.[61] Their enmity towards Ímar and their association with Limerick makes it possible that the sons of Aralt were allies of Brian Bóraime's family in the 970s and that the alliance Brian forged with them in

Downham, *Viking kings*, pp 185–90; *pace* Ben Hudson, *Viking pirates*, 65–74. Hudson follows the Four Masters' mistake of representing the name 'Maccus' as 'Magnus'. For a discussion of the name Maccus in this and other contexts, see D.E. Thornton, 'Hey, Mac! The name *Maccus*, tenth to fifteenth centuries', *Nomina*, 20 (1997), 67–98. **53** Downham, *Viking kings*, p. 43; Etchingham, 'North Wales', 171–2. **54** *Brut y Tywysogion or the Chronicle of Princes: Peniarth MS. 20 Version*, trans. Thomas Jones, Board of Celtic Studies, University of Wales, History and Law Series 11 (Cardiff, 1952), 971, 972; *Brut y Tywysogion or the Chronicle of Princes: Red Book of Hergest Version*, ed. Thomas Jones, Board of Celtic Studies, University of Wales, History and Law Series 16 (Cardiff, 1955, 2nd ed. 1973), 971, 972; Woolf, *From Pictland to Alba*, p. 206; Downham, *Viking kings*, pp 192, 221–2; Charles-Edwards, *Wales and the Britons*, pp 539, 547. **55** Etchingham, 'North Wales', 171; Charles-Edwards, *Wales and the Britons*, pp 543–4. **56** *Anglo-Saxon Chronicles*, (E) 973. **57** David E. Thornton, 'Edgar and the eight kings, AD973: *textus et dramatis personae*', *Early Medieval Europe*, 10 (2001), 49–79. **58** Alan Orr Anderson, *Scottish annals from English chroniclers AD500 to 1286* (London, 1908), p. 76. **59** Downham, *Viking kings*, p. 190. **60** *AI* 972. **61** *AU* 976; *AI* 976; *AT* 976; *CS* 974 (=976); *AI* 977; *AT* 977; *CS* 975 (=977); *CGG*, pp 86–8.

984 was the renewal of an old relationship rather than a new departure.[62] After Maccus' attack on Scattery Island, the sons of Aralt next appear in the early 980s, back in their old stomping ground, Wales. Gofraid attacked Dyfed and the church of St Davids in South Wales in 982.[63] The base from which the sons of Aralt carried out these and their earlier attacks on Wales and Ireland was probably in the Isles. When Maccus attacked Scattery Island in 974 he was in the company of what the Annals of the Four Masters called the 'lawmen of the isles'.[64] This was the second reference to the lawmen in a little over a decade and suggests that some, at least, of the Isles were ruled by assemblies of freeholders who regularly elected lawmen to preside over their public affairs, as was the situation in Iceland and certain Scandinavian provinces.[65] The twelfth-century description of Maccus as 'king of very many islands' probably reflects the fact that, during the 970s and early 980s, those island communities were gradually losing their independence as the sons of Aralt built a power-base in the Isles.

If, as appears to have been the case, the sons of Aralt were operating from a base in the Isles, a question arises regarding their relationship with Amlaíb Cuarán. As noted above, Amlaíb seems to have ruled Iona and some of the other Isles in 980, so were the sons of Aralt his allies, perhaps subordinate rulers in his empire, or were they perhaps rivals? Downham believes that the sons of Arailt were Amlaíb's allies up to and including the battle of Tara.[66] However, political divisions within the Isles seem to have been the norm rather than the exception during much of the later medieval period.[67] Factionalism was a prominent characteristic in the history of Uí Ímair during the second half of the tenth century, and in the early 960s a disgruntled branch of the dynasty seems to have set itself up in the Isles and to have attacked Dublin's hinterland from there.[68] The same might have been the case in the 970s. In 975, the Annals of Ulster record the murder by heathens of Ferdal, head of the Columban church on Lambay Island, off the Dublin coast.[69] It is unlikely that the attack was carried out by Amlaíb Cuarán, who was a patron of Columban churches in Dublin's hinterland, and much more likely that it was an attack on a church associated with the Dublin king by his enemies, possibly the sons of Aralt.[70] The following year, as noted above, Domnall ua Néill adopted a similar

62 Duffy, *Brian Boru*, 149–50. 63 *Brut y Tywysogion (Pen. 20)*, 981 (=982); *Brut y Tywysogion (RBH)*, 980 (=982); Downham, *Viking kings*, pp 223–4. 64 *AFM* 972 (=974). 65 *AFM* 960 (=962); Woolf, *From Pictland to Alba*, pp 213, 298–300; Downham, *Viking kings*, pp 184–5. 66 Downham, *Viking kings*, pp 190–1. 67 Hudson, *Viking pirates*, pp 57–8; R. Andrew McDonald, *The kingdom of the Isles: Scotland's western seaboard, c.1100–c.1336*, Scottish Historical Review Monograph Series 4 (East Linton, 1997). 68 *AFM* 960 (=962); Downham, *Viking kings*, pp 48–9, 185; Hudson, *Viking pirates*, pp 40–1; Etchingham, 'North Wales', 169–71; Charles-Edwards, *Wales and the Britons*, pp 539–40. 69 *AU* 975. 70 Edel Bhreathnach, 'Columban churches in Brega and Leinster: relations with the Norse and the Anglo-Normans', *JRSAI*, 129 (1999), 8–9; eadem, 'The documentary evidence for pre-Norman Skreen', 7–45.

tactic, attacking churches in the midlands associated with Amlaíb and, as will be discussed below, this was a strategy adopted by Gofraid mac Arailt again a few years later. It is unclear, then, whether the sons of Aralt were allies of Amlaíb Cuarán in the 970s, or rivals based in a portion of the Isles beyond the reach of his authority. In the aftermath of Amlaíb's death, however, and the succession of Glún Iairn as a puppet-king of Máel Sechnaill mac Domnall, the enmity of the sons of Aralt toward Dublin became clear, and brought them, in 984, into an alliance with Brian Bóraime. There is no evidence that the planned expedition that year ever made it as far as Dublin, but in the following years the sons of Aralt found other ways to extend the boundaries of their kingdom at Glún Iairn's expense.

Maccus having either died or left the region, Gofraid mac Arailt seems to have taken sole charge in the late 980s, when he is found associated with a group described in the annals as *Danair*. This is the first mention of *Danair* in the Irish annals, and their identity has been a matter of some debate. The most likely explanation for their appearance in the record at this stage is that the author of the annals used the term to identify a group of vikings who had come directly from Scandinavia and who were, therefore, distinct culturally from the Hiberno-Scandinavians with whom he was more familiar and whom he described as Gaill.[71] That does not necessarily mean that they were Danes rather than Norwegians or other Scandinavians: 'Insular words which might appear to be translatable as "Danes" or "Danish" could simply mean "Scandinavian", in line with Old-Norse usage.'[72] On the other hand, the reference in *Saltair na Rann*, 'The Metrical Psalter', to the presence in the Irish Sea of '*Danair* from the lands of Denmark' during this period suggests that perhaps some in Ireland were familiar with the political geography of Scandinavia.[73]

These *Danair* first turn up in 986, when they attacked Iona and suffered a defeat in Dál Riata.[74] The following year, they won a battle on the Isle of Man alongside Gofraid mac Arailt but also suffered a serious defeat at the hands of unnamed enemies.[75] Welsh sources report a large-scale attack on Angelsey in the same year that almost certainly involved the same group.[76] These actions can be understood as part of Gofraid's campaign to wrest territory from the control of Dublin.[77] In 980, Iona had been part of Amlaíb Cuarán's kingdom,

71 Woolf, 'Amlaíb Cuarán', pp 34–5; Clare Downham, 'England and the Irish-Sea zone in the eleventh century', *Anglo-Norman Studies*, 26 (2004), 55–73, at 59; Downham, 'Viking identities in Ireland: it's not all black and white' in Seán Duffy (ed.), *Medieval Dublin XI* (Dublin, 2011), pp 185–201, at pp 198–9; Etchingham, 'North Wales', 177. 72 David N. Dumville, 'Old Dubliners and New Dubliners in Ireland and Britain: a Viking-Age story' in Seán Duffy (ed.), *Medieval Dublin VI* (Dublin, 2005), pp 81, 91. 73 *Saltair na Rann*, ed. Whitley Stokes, *Anecdota Oxoniensia*, Mediæval and Modern Series, vol. 1, Part 3 (Oxford, 1883), p. 34; Hudson, *Viking pirates*, p. 69. 74 *AU* 986; *AI* 986; *CS* 984 (=986); *AR* 986. 75 *AU* 987. 76 *Brut y Tywysogion (Pen. 20)*, 987; *Brut y Tywysogion (RBH)*, 987. 77 Etchingham, 'North Wales', 157–8, 175–7; Seán Duffy 'Ostmen, Irish and Welsh in the

and the 986 attack should be seen as an act of conquest rather than a simple raid.[78] The same is probably true of the attack on Man in 987. That Gofraid was successful in establishing his authority and that these were defining moments in the history of the Isles is suggested by the fact that, when he died in 989, Gofraid was the first person given the title 'king of *Innsi Gall*' in the Irish annals.[79] The sons of Aralt had been based in some portion of the Isles since the 970s, but it was evidently the conquest of Man and Iona that made Gofraid king of the Isles. It is impossible to know the full extent of Gofraid's kingdom, whether it included some or all of the Northern Isles as well as the Hebrides. As Alex Woolf has noted, the Old Norse *Suðreyjar* and Gaelic *Innsi Gall* 'both seem to refer to the Western Isles, but whether either was at any time used in a more restrictive or indeed a more general sense is unclear. Did Innse Gall, for example, at any time refer to Orkney and Shetland as well as the Hebrides?'[80] 989 also witnessed the death of Glún Iairn mac Amlaíb. In his obituary, the annals give Glún Iairn the title 'king of the Gaill', the same title his father had borne in 980, though in reality he probably only ruled over Dublin and its hinterland, the town having been stripped of its overseas territories, including the Isles and, possibly, the Rhinns of Galloway.[81]

Gofraid's ambitions extended beyond just those territories formerly ruled by Dublin. His obit in the annals records that he died in Dál Riata.[82] That report and the notice of the defeat suffered there by the *Danair* three years earlier are the first references to Dál Riata in the annals for over two centuries. The kingdom of Dál Riata had formerly spanned the North Channel, incorporating territory in Ireland, the Hebrides and the Scottish mainland. Gofraid's obituary has been taken by some to mean that he died in Ireland, but it seems more likely, given his interests in Iona, that the Dál Riata in question was territory in Britain.[83] Alex Woolf has suggested that the arrival of the vikings might have precipitated 'a formal division of Dál Riata between Norse kings and natives' comparable to what happened in the Anglo-Saxon kingdoms of Mercia and Northumbria. The islands of Dál Riata, the southern Hebrides, became part of the Scandinavian world, *Innsi Gall*, 'Islands of the Gaill', while the mainland portion of Dál Riata survived as *Airer Gaedel* (Argyll), 'Coastline of the Gaels', which probably passed under the control of the kings of the Picts, and later the kings of Alba.[84] Gofraid's death in this territory, and the fact that his allies, the *Danair*, had been active there just a few years earlier,

eleventh century', *Peritia*, 9 (1995), 381–2. **78** Thomas Owen Clancy, 'The Christmas Eve Massacre, Iona, AD986', *The Innes Review*, 64:1 (2013), 66–71, at 69 and 71. **79** *AU* 989; *AT* 989. **80** Woolf, *From Pictland to Alba*, p. 298. **81** *AU* 989; *AI* 989; *AT* 989; *CS* 987 (=989); Woolf, *From Pictland to Alba*, p. 219. **82** *AU* 989; *AT* 989; *CS* 987 (=989). **83** Hudson, *Viking pirates*, p. 62; Woolf, *From Pictland to Alba*, p. 298; Charles-Edwards, *Wales and the Britons*, p. 550; *pace* Downham, *Viking kings*, pp 129, 196. **84** Alex Woolf, 'The age of the sea kings: 900–1300' in Donald Omand (ed.), *The Argyll Book* (Edinburgh, 2004), pp 94–109, at pp 94–5; Woolf, *From Pictland to Alba*, p. 298.

should be seen as evidence that he was attempting to add Dál Riata/Argyll to his kingdom.[85]

Gofraid's activities brought him into contact with some of the greatest figures in Europe. The Anglo-Saxon Chronicle records a series of raids on England's west coast in the 980s by unnamed assailants.[86] These attacks occurred in the same years as incursions into neighbouring parts of Wales led by Gofraid mac Arailt.[87] For instance, the raid on Cheshire in 980 coincided with Gofraid's attack on North Wales in the same year reported in Welsh sources.[88] Likewise, in 982 and 988 Welsh chronicles recorded attacks on South Wales in the same years that the Anglo-Saxon Chronicle reported viking activity in neighbouring Devon and Somerset.[89] The English seem to have believed that Duke Richard I of Normandy was in some way connected with the perpetrator of these attacks. This much is apparent from the fact that the English king, Æðelræd, initiated a diplomatic effort to persuade the duke to stop supporting England's enemies.[90] In response to a request from King Æðelræd, in 991 Pope John XV wrote to Duke Richard asking him 'to receive none of the king [of England]'s men, or of his enemies ... without his seal'.[91] If there is any foundation to Æðelræd's suspicions, then it suggests that a relationship existed at this stage between the ruler of the Isles and the dukes of Normandy.

The alliance of 984 linked Brian Bóraime with the rulers of this expansionary kingdom of the Isles, and, through them, into a political network that extended across the Insular Viking zone. It also showed that Brian was informed about the divisions that existed between the two rival branches of the Uí Ímair, and that he was willing and capable of manipulating them to his own benefit. Ailbhe Mac Shamhráin has suggested that Brian might have had aspirations in the Irish Sea world as early as 984, and that his alliance with the sons of Aralt was potentially a first venture into the politics of the region.[92]

85 Charles-Edwards, *Wales and the Britons*, p. 550. **86** Simon Keynes, 'The historical context of the battle of Maldon' in Donald Scragg (ed.), *The battle of Maldon AD991* (Oxford, 1991), pp 81–113, at p. 85. **87** Downham, 'England and the Irish-Sea zone', 59; eadem, *Viking kings*, pp 128–9, 223–4; Hudson, *Viking pirates*, pp 60–3; Woolf, *From Pictland to Alba*, p. 217. **88** *Brut y Tywysogion (Pen. 20)*, 979 (=980); *Brut y Tywysogion (RBH)*, (980); *Anglo-Saxon Chronicles*, (C) 980. **89** *Brut y Tywysogion (Pen. 20)*, 981 (=982), 987 (=988); *Brut y Tywysogion (RBH)*, (988); *Anglo-Saxon Chronicles*, (C) 982, (C, E) 988; Downham, 'England and the Irish-Sea zone', 59; eadem, *Viking kings*, pp 223–5. **90** F.M. Stenton, *Anglo-Saxon England*, 3rd ed. (Oxford, 1971), pp 375–6. **91** 'Letter of Pope John XV (991), concerning the reconciliation of Ethelred, king of England, and Richard, duke of Normandy', trans. Dorothy Whitelock, *English historical documents I: 500–1042*, 2nd ed. (London, 1979), no. 230, pp 894–5; Patrick Wadden, 'The Normans and the Irish Sea world in the era of the battle of Clontarf' in Vicky McAlister et al. (eds), *Space and settlement in medieval Ireland* (Dublin, 2015), pp 15–33. **92** Ailbhe MacShamhráin, 'Brian Bóruma, Armagh and the high kingship', *Seanchas Ard Mhacha*, 20:2 (2005), 1–21, at 6; idem, 'The battle of Glen Máma, Dublin and the high-kingship of Ireland: a millennial commemoration' in Seán Duffy (ed.), *Medieval Dublin II* (Dublin, 2000), pp 53–64, at p. 57.

While this is certainly possible, care must be taken not to exaggerate Brian's power at this early stage in his career. Brian's goal in the early 980s seems to have been to make himself the master of the southern half of Ireland. Máel Sechnaill had asserted his dominance over Leinster in 983 with the help of the Dublin army and Brian must have felt that his chances of wresting control of Leinster from the king of Tara would have been much improved if the Dubliners were removed from the equation.[93] The attack on Dublin planned for 984 never took place but, if it had, it is not clear that Brian would have taken control of the town. His home base was much farther from Dublin than Máel Sechnaill's, and he was not yet in a position to campaign regularly to Dublin to enforce his authority, as Máel Sechnaill had to do repeatedly. The report of the 984 meeting between Brian and the sons of Aralt in the Annals of Inisfallen makes it clear that the alliance was one between equals, as each side handed over hostages to the other.[94] Waterford, a Hiberno-Scandinavian port with its own king, might be thought of as neutral ground for a meeting between peers. The benefit to Brian of such a deal was surely to make his conquest of Leinster easier, and perhaps the *quid pro quo* was that the sons of Aralt would take control of Dublin. Brian would then have had an ally in Dublin, though it is difficult to imagine that the town would have been subject to him in the same way that it was to Máel Sechlainn under Glún Iairn.

As it turned out, Brian had to wait another thirteen years to secure his authority over Leinster and Dublin. After years of fighting, in 997 Mael Sechnaill was forced to recognize Brian's power and to acknowledge his status as king of Leth Moga. As part of the deal, Máel Sechnaill handed over to Brian the hostages of Dublin and Leinster, and with them his claim to overlordship.[95] Máel Sechnaill was to retain the title of king of Tara, but his authority was to be limited to Leth Cuinn, the northern half of Ireland. In the following year, the two kings cooperated to solidify their new positions in accordance with the treaty, campaigning together in Connacht to consolidate Máel Sechnaill's authority there, and doing the same in Dublin for Brian's benefit.[96] The Dubliners, however, seem to have been dissatisfied with the new situation in which they found themselves, and in late 999 Brian was forced to bring his army to confront the armies of Dublin and Leinster at Glenn Máma, about a day's march from the town.[97] Brian won a great victory, and followed it up, as Máel Sechnaill had in 980, by attacking, plundering and burning the town, taking hostages from its inhabitants, and forcing its king, Sitriuc, to flee in exile.[98] The following year, Sitriuc returned to Dublin and handed over hostages to Brian, in return for which he was reinstated as king under Brian's overlordship.[99]

93 Etchingham, 'North Wales', 175. **94** *AI* 984. **95** *AI* 997. **96** *AU* 998; *AT* 998; *AI* 998; *CS* 996 (=998). **97** *AU* 999; *AT* 999; *AI* 999; *CS* 997 (=999); *AI* 1000; MacShamráin, 'The battle of Glen Máma', 53–64. **98** *AU* 999; *AT* 999; *AI* 1000; *AT* 1000; *CS* 997 (=999), 998 (=1000). **99** *AU* 1000; *AT* 1000; *CS* 998 (=1000).

Gaining control of Dublin proved to be crucial in Brian's elevation to the kingship of Ireland, as it provided him with the additional economic and military resources required to attack Máel Sechnaill on his own patch and to campaign into the far north of Ireland. Before the end of 1000, Brian had broken his treaty with Máel Sechnaill by invading Brega with an army that included the Gaill of Dublin.[100] They were present again in Brian's campaigns against Máel Sechnaill two years later, the result of which was that the king of Tara handed over to Brian the hostages of Connacht and Mide, effectively submitting to him and recognizing his status as the most powerful king in Ireland.[101] Brian's new position with regard to Dublin in 1000 raises questions about his relationship with the rulers of the Isles. In 1005, the annals report the death in Munster of Ragnall mac Gofraid, 'king of the Isles'.[102] The exact context for Ragnall's presence in Munster is unknown, but it is tempting to view it in light of Brian's other activities that year. On his northern campaign of 1005, Brian made his famous visit to Armagh where he left an offering of twenty ounces of gold on the altar. He did so, according to the Annals of Ulster, 'accompanied by the royalty of Ireland'.[103] Perhaps Ragnall was in Munster in 1005 to participate in Brian's campaign as one of the subordinate kings in his retinue.

Since Brian had made the treaty of 984 with Ragnall's father and uncle, his status had changed dramatically. No longer the ambitious provincial king he had been back then, Brian, in 1005, was the dominant force in Irish politics and recognized overlord of almost the entire country, including all the Hiberno-Scandinavian towns. While Brian's star had continued to rise between 984 and 1005, it is possible that Ragnall was in a weaker position than his father had been before his death in 989. The *Danair* had assisted Gofraid in his conquest of Man and Iona in the 980s, but the appearance of more Scandinavians in the region in the following decade might have weakened Ragnall's grip on some or all of the territories Gofraid had ruled.[104] In 995, Man was attacked by Sveinn Forkbeard, who seems to have used the island as a base for raids on England over the following years.[105] That would explain why, in 1000, Æðelræd's navy attacked Man, an event associated in the Anglo-Saxon Chronicle with the departure of Sveinn's fleet to Normandy.[106] It is unclear whether, between 995 and 1000, Sveinn was Ragnall's overlord or whether Ragnall was driven from the kingdom, perhaps temporarily, while Sveinn was in the region. The Irish annals call Ragnall 'king of the Isles' in 1005, but it seems that he was not as formidable a figure as his father had been in the 980s.

100 *AU* 1000; *AT* 1000; *CS* 1000. **101** *AU* 1002; *AI* 1002; for Brian's career between 1000 and 1011, see Duffy, *Brian Boru*, chap. 3, 'Emperor of the Gael', pp 125–64. **102** *AU* 1005; *CS* 1003 (=1005); *AI* 1004. **103** *AU* 1005; see also *AI* 1005, *CS* 1003 (=1005); for discussion, see Casey above. **104** Etchingham, 'North Wales', 173–4, 178–9. **105** *Brut y Tywysogion (Pen. 20)*, 995; *Brut y Tywysogion (RBH)*, 995; Downham, *Viking kings*, pp 196–7. **106** *Anglo-Saxon Chronicles*, (E) 1000; Hudson, *Viking pirates*, pp 75–7.

There is no reason to believe, therefore, that Ragnall and Brian were equal partners in 1005, as Brian and the sons of Aralt had been in 984, and Ragnall's presence in Munster is best understood as a sign of his subordination to Brian.

Ragnall has not left much of a mark on the historical record, but it appears that, in the years prior to his appearance in Munster, there still existed a degree of animosity between Dublin and the Isles. When Brian attacked Dublin after the battle of Glenn Máma, Sitriuc fled, the annals report, to the Ulaid in east Ulster.[107] This suggests that relations with the rulers of the Isles were not on a friendly footing because, as Duffy suggested, 'if Man had been in friendly hands he would surely have disembarked there'.[108] In light of the fact that Brian had a friendly relationship of long standing with the rulers of the Isles, it is interesting that, in 1000, he allowed Sitriuc to return to Dublin rather than presenting the town to Ragnall. No doubt Brian remembered the great military power commanded by Amlaíb Cuarán when he had ruled both Dublin and the Isles and, recognizing that reuniting those territories under a single ruler might create a serious threat to his own position, he evidently decided to maintain the divisions between the rival branches of the Uí Ímairr that had emerged after Amlaíb's death. Rather than facing a challenge from a rejuvenated, unified kingdom of the Gaill, Brian was in a position to dominate both Dublin and the Isles, so that both contributed to his campaigns against the reticent kings of the North.[109]

It was probably on his 1005 visit to Armagh that Brian's secretary entered a note in the Book of Armagh in which he described Brian as *imperator Scotorum*.[110] This inscription was not the only instance of imperial language being used to describe Brian; in his obituary, he was described as 'high-king of the Gaels of Ireland and the Gaill, and the Britons, the Augustus of the whole of north-west Europe', and *Cogadh Gáedhel re Gallaibh* compares him with Octavian.[111] The inspiration for the adoption of the imperial title at Armagh might have come from Germany or from Anglo-Saxon England, and its exact implications are difficult to apprehend, but at the least it implied that Brian was more than just a high-king of Ireland.[112] These claims were probably more than empty rhetoric. Máire Herbert has argued that, in the late tenth and early eleventh centuries, Armagh saw Scotland as within its sphere of influence and that 'Alba was part of the *imperium* being claimed both for Armagh and for Brian' in 1005.[113] In relation to this point, it is, of course, interesting that

107 *AI* 1000. **108** Seán Duffy, 'The royal dynasties of Dublin and the Isles in the eleventh century' in idem (ed.), *Medieval Dublin VII* (Dublin, 2006), pp 51–65, at p. 54. **109** For Dubliners' service in Brian's army, see *AI* 1005, 1006, 1007. **110** Aubrey Gwynn, 'Brian in Armagh (1005)', *Seanchas Ard Mhacha*, 9:1 (1978), 35–51; cf. Casey above. **111** *AU* 1014; *CGG*, p. 204; Duffy, *Brian Boru*, pp 142–4. **112** Gwynn, 'Brian in Armagh (1005)', 42; Marie Therese Flanagan, *Irish society, Anglo-Norman settlers, Angevin kingship: interactions in Ireland in the late twelfth century* (Oxford, 1989), p. 179. **113** Máire Herbert, 'Sea-divided

Domnall mac Eimin, the *mormaer* of Mar in northeast Scotland, died fighting with Brian at Clontarf.[114] The title also likely refers to Brian's lordship over Ragnall's kingdom of the Isles, which may sometimes have included parts of Wales and Gaelic Scotland.[115]

According to *Cogadh*, as part of his northern campaign of 1006, Brian assembled a fleet on the Irish Sea, 'and they levied royal tribute from the English and the Britons and the men of Lennox and Alba and all of Argyll, and their pledges and hostages along with the chief tribute'.[116] As mentioned above, *Cogadh* was written about a century after the battle of Clontarf with specific political and propagandist goals in mind, and so cannot always be considered an accurate account of Brian's career. It is also true, though, that the early portion of the text is based on a lost set of annals.[117] Duffy has suggested that the report of this episode might derive from those annals, and that the event could well have happened. There is, at the very least, nothing implausible about the idea that Brian would put a fleet on the Irish Sea.[118] In 1002, Brian led a force against the Ulaid that included the Gaill of Dublin. The Annals of Tigernach report that, in the same year, Sitriuc of Dublin led a fleet to Ulaid and took a great spoil, including captives, from two major churches.[119] We should perhaps read these as two records of a single episode, in which Brian's land forces were supported by a naval contingent from Dublin. Brian campaigned in Ulaid again in 1006, and again the annals report the participation of the Gaill in his army.[120] If Brian had a fleet off the Ulster coast, in the North Channel, it would have been within easy striking distance of all the peoples mentioned by *Cogadh*. The English of Lothian, including, perhaps, parts of modern Galloway, the Britons of Cumbria/Strathclyde, Lennox around Loch Lomond, and Argyll were all close enough to have been targeted on a single expedition into the Firth of Clyde.[121] A raid by some of Sitriuc's ancestors on the same area in 870–1 resulted in the taking of English, British and Pictish captives.[122] Allowing for some exaggeration on the part of the author of *Cogadh*, this episode very possibly reflects an expedition launched by Brian into the territory of the kings of the Isles. The reason for such an attack in 1006 can be found in the death of Ragnall the previous year. When Glún Iairn of Dublin died in 989, Máel Sechnaill had immediately plundered the

Gaels? Constructing relationships between Irish and Scots *c*.800–1169' in Brendan Smith (ed.), *Britain and Ireland 900–1300: Insular responses to medieval European change* (Cambridge, 1999), p. 91; see also, Seán Duffy, 'Ireland and Scotland, 1014–1169: contacts and caveats' in Alfred P. Smyth (ed.), *Seanchas: studies in early and medieval Irish archaeology, history and literature in honour of Francis J. Byrne* (Dublin, 2000), pp 348–56, at pp 348–50; idem, *Brian Boru*, pp 145–6. **114** *AU* 1014. **115** Downham, 'Clontarf and the wider world', 23; Etchingham, 'North Wales', 180. **116** *CGG*, p. 136. I have altered Todd's translation. **117** Máire Ní Mhaonaigh, '*Cogad Gaedel re Gallaib* and the annals: a comparison', *Ériu*, 47 (1996), 101–26. **118** Duffy, *Brian Boru*, pp 148–9. **119** *AI* 1002; *AU* 1002; *AT* 1002; *CS* 1000 (=1002). **120** *AI* 1006; *AU* 1006; *CS* 1004 (=1006). **121** Duffy, *Brian Boru*, pp 148–9. **122** *AU* 871; *CS* 871.

town in order to guarantee its submission to his authority under its new king. He did the same in 995 when Sitriuc secured the kingship. If Brian ordered an attack on the kingdom of the Isles in 1006, it was likely intended to ensure that Ragnall's successor continued to recognize his overlordship.

Other than the participation of the Dubliners in Brian's annual campaigns, and the death of Ragnall in 1005, there is a marked decrease in reports of viking activity in Ireland between 1001 and 1013, a period that coincided with some of the most intense raiding on England. This was likely the result of several factors: Brian's strength no doubt meant that there were fewer opportunities for raiding in Ireland; Downham has also suggested that the Scandinavian forces active in England might have made an agreement not to interfere in the sphere of the Uí Ímair;[123] and it also seems to have been the case that the Hiberno-Scandinavians of the Irish Sea world were cooperating with the leaders of the attacks on England to avail themselves of opportunities for plunder and extortion.[124] As mentioned above, there is evidence to suggest that the Isle of Man was being used as a base for attacks on England in the late 990s. Sveinn was back in the Irish Sea in 1011, when he was shipwrecked off the Welsh coast, and his presence in the region might have been the reason why the English attacked South Wales that year.[125] Further cooperation between a ruler of the Isles, the Danish king, and Normandy during this period is recorded a Norman source.[126] William of Jumièges, writing forty or fifty years after the events in question, reported that, after the death of King Sveinn in 1014, Knútr sent messengers to two kings asking for support, Óláfr of the Northmen and Lacman of the Swedes.[127] The first of these has been identified as Óláfr Haraldsson, future king and patron saint of Norway. There was, however, no known king of the Swedes at this time, and certainly none of that name. Jean Adigard des Gautries suggested that William was mistaken, and that the Latin text should be emended from *Suauorum*, 'of the Swedes', to *Sudrorum*, derived from Old Norse *Suðreyjar*, 'the Southern Islands'/'the Hebrides'.[128] In other words, he suggested seeing Lacman as a king of the Isles. In support of this idea is the fact that the name Lagmann was associated with the Hiberno-Scandinavian world rather than with Scandinavia.[129] Furthermore, the Irish annals record the death at Clontarf of Amlaíb son of Lagmann, and *Cogadh Gáedhel re Gallaibh* describes this Lagmann as the son

123 Downham, 'England and the Irish-Sea zone', p. 60. **124** Downham, *Viking kings*, pp 132; see also Charles-Edwards's comments that the same factors were responsible for the absence of viking attacks on Wales: *Wales and the Britons*, pp 550–1. **125** *Annales Cambriae*, ed. John Williams ab Ithel, RS (London, 1860), 1011; Downham, 'England and the Irish-Sea zone', 60. **126** Downham, *Viking kings*, pp 132–3; Wadden, 'Normans and the Irish Sea world'. **127** William of Jumièges, *Gesta Normannorum Ducum*, ed. E.M.C. van Houts (Oxford, 1995), ii, pp 18–21. **128** J. Adigard des Gautries, *Les noms de personnes scandinaves en Normandie de 911 à 1066* (Lund, 1954), p. 69; *Gesta Normannorum Ducum*, ii, p. 20, n. 1; Downham, *Viking kings*, p. 133; Downham, 'England and the Irish-Sea zone', 60–1. **129** Diarmuid Ó Murchada, 'Lagmainn, Lögmenn', *Ainm*, 2 (1987), 136–40.

of Gofraid.[130] In other words, this Lacman/Lagmann, whom Knútr sought out for assistance, appears to have been the brother, and probably the successor, of Ragnall mac Gofraid who died as king of the Isles in 1005. William of Jumièges also reported that, after Lagmann and Óláfr had assisted Knútr, they were sought out by Duke Richard II of Normandy, to support him in his struggle against Odo, count of Chartres. For Lagmann, this possibly represented the continuation of his father's relationship with the rulers of Normandy discussed above. After the duke made peace with Odo, 'he returned joyfully to his kings. He rewarded them with gifts fitting for kings and allowed them permission to return home in triumph after they had promised to return to him whenever he was in need of their support'.[131] As Downham noted, 'Lagmann was rubbing shoulders with the leading powers of north-western Europe in his day', including the future kings of Norway and Denmark.[132]

Hiberno-Scandinavians from the Isles or elsewhere in the Irish Sea world also cooperated with Scandinavian forces in an attack on Aquitaine.[133] The chronicler Adémar de Chabannes reported an attack on the port of Saint-Michel-en-l'Herm shortly before the battle of Clontarf by 'an infinite multitude of Northmen (*Normanni*) from Denmark and the Irish region with an immense fleet'.[134] Adémar is not always considered trustworthy,[135] but, in addition to the evidence previously discussed, this report supports the belief that certain Hiberno-Scandinavians, especially perhaps the rulers of the Isles, were cooperating with those Scandinavian raiders who were active in England and elsewhere in the years before the battle of Clontarf. Adémar went on to report that this same group of Northmen invaded Ireland intent on conquest, but was defeated and slaughtered in a battle that is usually identified with Clontarf.[136] Adémar's statement that there were forces from Scandinavia as well as Hiberno-Scandinavians from the Irish Sea world at the battle of Clontarf is supported by the evidence from the Irish annals. Among those whose deaths at Clontarf are reported in the Annals of Ulster is Brotor (Broðir), who is said in this and later accounts to have slain Brian. Broðir is variously described in the sources as the leader of a fleet from Lochlann or chief of the *Danair*.[137] As discussed above, the annals used the term *Danair* in the 980s to refer to vikings from Scandinavia rather than the Irish Sea world, and, as Etchingham pointed out, they use the term Lochlann accurately for Norway in 1058, and use

130 *CGG*, pp 164 (where the absence of 'mac' between 'Amlaib' and 'Lagmaind' is evident from the fact that the latter is in the genitive case), 206. Todd (*CGG*, pp clxxiv, 271–2) made this connection, although he repeated an error in the text by conflating Olaf and Lagmann as a single person; see also, Downham, *Viking kings*, pp 132–4, 193. **131** *Gesta Normannorum Ducum*, ii, pp 25–7; Hudson, *Viking pirates*, pp 70–1. **132** Downham, *Viking kings*, p. 134; Downham, 'England and the Irish-Sea zone', 60–1. **133** Downham, 'England and the Irish-Sea zone', 61–2. **134** Adémar de Chabannes, *Chronicon*, ed. J. Chavanon (Paris, 1897), p. 177. The translation is my own. **135** Ní Mhaonaigh, *Brian Boru*, pp 57–8. **136** Adémar de Chabannes, *Chronicon*, p. 177. **137** *AU* 1014; *CS* 1012

Danmarg for Denmark in 1035.[138] It seems likely, therefore, that the Irish records of the battle of Clontarf accurately reported the presence of troops from Scandinavia. These Scandinavians were more than likely individuals who had originally come to participate in the Danish conquest of England but who were, after Sveinn's death and Knút's departure, looking for alternative sources of revenue and adventure.[139]

Finally, after years of campaigning, Brian Bóraime forced the last of the northern kings into submission in 1011, thus completing the task of uniting the whole of Ireland under his authority.[140] Within three years, however, he was dead, and the unity he had created crumbled. The immediate build-up to the battle of Clontarf began in 1013, when the Dubliners inflicted a defeat on the army of Máel Sechnaill mac Domnaill and sent a fleet to pillage along the Munster coast.[141] Brian's initial response was cut short by the coming of winter, but in the spring of 1014 he gathered his army and marched to Clontarf. Brian's army, which in previous years had included Gaill drawn from Dublin and elsewhere, in 1014 consisted primarily of contingents from Munster and south Connacht, from which Hiberno-Scandinavians were conspicuously absent.[142] Whereas, over the course of the previous thirty years, the rulers of the Isles and of Dublin had been rivals, allowing Brian to dominate both, the army he faced at Clontarf included all the major groups of Hiberno-Scandinavians in the Irish Sea world, including Dublin, the Isles and the earldom of Orkney. The casualties at Clontarf included Earl Sigurðr of Orkney and Amlaíb mac Lagmainn, apparently son of the king of the Isles whose activities in England and Normandy were reported by William of Jumièges.[143] The descendants of Aralt of Limerick and those of Amlaíb Cuarán of Dublin had been rivals since, at the latest, the early 980s and, as will be discussed below, they would be again shortly after the battle of Clontarf, but in 1014 they stood side by side to fight Brian Bóraime.[144] The temporary rapprochement between these two warring factions of the Uí Ímair was fundamental to Brian's downfall; it reunited the territories that had previously been ruled by Amlaíb Cuarán, and likely, therefore, gave its leaders access to the same kind of military power that he had possessed in the build-up to the battle of Tara. With the additional forces of Sigurðr of Orkney and others, the army that confronted Brian at Clontarf must have been considerably larger than that Máel Sechnaill had defeated in 980. Why, after more than thirty years of rivalry, were the rulers of the Isles willing to fight and die alongside the king of Dublin? To answer this question, it will be instructive to look at another eleventh-century instance when the different factions in the Irish Sea world were brought together for a common purpose.

(=1014). **138** *AT*, 1031 (=1035), 1058; Etchingham, 'North Wales', 153. **139** Downham, 'Clontarf and the wider world', 23; Duffy, *Brian Boru*, p. 244. **140** *AU* 1011; *AI* 1011; *CS* 1009 (=1011). **141** *AU* 1013; *AI* 1013; *CS* 1011 (=1013). **142** *AU* 1014; *AI* 1014. **143** *AU* 1014. **144** Hudson, *Viking pirates*, pp 5, 98; Downham, 'Clontarf and the wider

In 1058, Magnús Haraldsson, son of the reigning king of Norway, Haraldr *harðráði* ('hard-ruler') Sigurðarson, arrived in the Irish Sea at the head of a large Norwegian fleet. The intended purpose of his expedition is uncertain, but the actual outcome was that Magnús united with Gruffudd ap Llywelyn, king of Gwynedd, in assisting the exiled Ælfgar of Mercia to reclaim his English earldom.[145] The Annals of Tigernach, perhaps believing that this was the opening gambit in a planned invasion and conquest of England, reported that 'a fleet [was] led by the son of the king of Norway, with the Gaill of the Orkneys and the Hebrides and Dublin, to seize the kingdom of England, but to this God did not consent'.[146] In 1058, Dublin, the Orkneys and the Isles were under the control of different, and, in the case of Dublin and the Isles, rival rulers. The exact date of the death of Thorfinr Sigurðsson, earl of Orkney, is unknown, but Woolf has suggested that Magnús's expedition might initially have been intended to deal with the disputed succession between his two sons, Paul and Erlend.[147] Dublin had been conquered by Diarmait mac Maíl na mBó, king of Leinster, in 1052. This was a momentous occasion in Dublin's history because, as the annals report, Diarmait assumed the kingship of the town himself rather than appointing a member of the local royal dynasty to rule under his authority as, for example, Máel Sechnaill mac Domnaill and Brian Bóraime had done.[148] The Dubliners, whom the Annals of Inisfallen call 'the Gaill of mac Maíl na mBó', fought on the Leinster king's campaigns of 1054, 1057 and 1058.[149] Diarmait had won Dublin from Echmarcach mac Ragnaill, the son of the king of Isles who had died in Munster in 1005. In 1036, Echmarcach had achieved what his predecessors had long desired when he drove Sitriuc mac Amlaíb overseas and united Dublin with the territories he already controlled, probably the Isles and the Rhinns of Galloway.[150] He was temporarily deposed between 1038 and 1046 by Ímar mac Arailt, almost certainly a representative of the dynasty of Amlaíb Cuarán, but regained the kingship after Ímar's death in 1046.[151] When Diarmait conquered Dublin in 1052, Echmarcach 'went overseas' and when he next appeared, in 1061, he was being driven from Man by Diarmait's son, Murchad.[152] In the years between 1052 and 1061, the evidence suggests that Dublin was ruled by Diarmait mac Máil na mBó while Man and, presumably, the Isles, were ruled by his rival, Echmarcach mac Ragnaill.

It is highly unlikely that Diarmait supported Magnús Haraldsson's campaign of 1058. It is difficult to envisage why he would have allowed his men to participate in an expedition to reinstate Ælfgar of Mercia, for he was a

world', 23. **145** Etchingham, 'North Wales', pp 52–3. For the Welsh context, see Charles-Edwards, *Wales and the Britons*, pp 565–6. **146** *AT* 1058. **147** Woolf, *From Pictland to Alba*, pp 267–8. **148** *AU* 1052; *AT* 1052; *CS* 1050 (=1052); Seán Duffy, 'Irishmen and Islesmen in the kingdoms of Dublin and Man, 1052–1171', *Ériu*, 43 (1992), 94–101. **149** *AI* 1057, 1058. **150** *AT* 1036. **151** *AT* 1038, 1046. **152** *AT* 1061.

close ally of the family of Earl Godwin of Wessex, Ælfgar's arch-rival.[153] Furthermore, he would hardly have participated, or allowed his men to have participated, in a campaign alongside the followers of his rival, Echmarcach. 'An alternative explanation for the events of 1058 might be that, in the course of that year, Norwegian royal influence at Dublin came to outweigh temporarily that of Diarmait mac Mael na mBó.'[154] Magnús did not remain very long in the Irish Sea world, and after his departure Diarmait's control over Dublin was again secure and his rivalry with Echmarcach resumed. For a brief period in 1058, however, Magnús was able to unite the Hiberno-Scandinavians of Dublin, Orkney and the Isles in what has been interpreted as an assertion of Norwegian royal authority in the region.[155]

Forty years after Magnús Haraldsson's campaign, his nephew and namesake, Magnús Óláfsson, better known as Magnús *berfœttr*, 'barefoot', king of Norway, made the first of his two expeditions to the West.[156] One of his goals on these expeditions seems to have been, as it was for his uncle, to assert his authority over the Hiberno-Scandinavian settlements of the Irish Sea world. On his first expedition, in 1097–8, he succeeded in establishing his claim to Orkneys, that portion of the Scottish mainland controlled by the earls of Orkney, the Western Isles, Man, and possibly Galloway.[157] This brought him into conflict with Muirchertach Ua Briain, Brian Bóraime's great-grandson, who, as ruler of Dublin and the most powerful king in Ireland, was intent on expanding his authority into the Irish Sea world.[158] Muirchertach had, at the request of the noblemen of the Isles, sent a relative to rule Man in 1095, which was possibly what motivated Magnús to intervene in the region.[159] When Magnús returned to the Irish Sea world in 1102, his attention was focused firmly on Ireland. Both Irish and Manx sources claim that he was intent on invading and conquering Ireland, although it is perhaps more realistic to think that Dublin was his real target, and his goal, at least initially, was to unite it with the rest of the territories he controlled around the Irish Sea.[160] An attack on Dublin either occurred or was anticipated, for in 1102 the Annals of the Four Masters report 'a hosting of the men of Ireland to Dublin, to oppose Magnus and the Gaill of Lochlann, who had come to plunder Ireland'.[161] The 'men of Ireland' were almost certainly led in this instance, as on other occasions in the 1100s, by Muirchertach Ua Briain.[162] In Duffy's opinion, 'the

153 Benjamin Hudson, 'The family of Harold Godwinsson and the Irish Sea province' in Benjamin Hudson, *Irish Sea studies 900–1200* (Dublin, 2006), pp 100–7 (originally published in *JRSAI*, 109 (1981), 92–100). **154** Etchingham, 'North Wales', 153–5, at 155. **155** Ibid. **156** Rosemary Power, 'Magnus Barelegs' expeditions to the West', *SHR*, 65:2 (1986), 107–32. **157** Duffy, 'Irishmen and Islesmen', 110; Hudson, *Viking pirates*, pp 198–9. **158** Duffy, 'Irishmen and Islesmen', 111–13; Etchingham, 'North Wales', 148–50. **159** Duffy, 'Irishmen and Islesmen', 108–10. **160** *AU* 1102; *AI* 1102; *AT* 1102, 1103; *CS* 1099 (=1103); Duffy, 'Irishmen and Islesmen', 110–11. **161** *AFM* 1102; Duffy, 'Irishmen and Islesmen', 110–11; Hudson, *Viking pirates*, pp 194–5; Etchingham, 'North Wales', 150–1. **162** *AT* 1101; *AU* 1102; *AI* 1103.

effect, and presumably the original intention, of Magnus's assertion of overlordship in the Irish Sea was to circumscribe Munster's sphere of influence. From the latter's point of view, the threat which the Norse king posed to Dublin was more worrying still'.[163] Warfare between the two kings was avoided at the last minute, when they forged an alliance that included the betrothal of Magnús' son to Muirchertach's daughter.[164] Magnús Barefoot's Saga claims that 'King Magnús set up his son as chief over all the dominions that he had subdued to himself in the west over the sea [that is, in the territories he had conquered in the Irish Sea world]. And he gave him the title of king.'[165] This settlement seems to have appeased both parties. Muirchertach now had an ally in the king of Norway, and a close family link with the new royal dynasty that was to rule a kingdom consisting of the Orkneys, the Isles and, possibly, Dublin; Magnús had provided for his son, and left him in the relatively secure position of having a powerful ally nearby. In 1103, however, Magnús was killed in Ulster, possibly while assisting Muirchertach campaign against the Northern Uí Néill.[166] Hearing the news, his son returned to Norway, leaving his Irish bride behind, and shortly thereafter members of Muirchertach's family attempted to establish themselves in the kingship of the Isles again.[167]

In the 1050s and the 1090s, the expansion of the power of, respectively, Diarmait mac Maíl na mBó and Muirchertach Ua Briain into the Irish Sea world, initially through the conquest of Dublin but later also as they attempted to extend their authority over the Isle of Man, brought them into competition with members of the Norwegian royal dynasty who asserted a claim over those and the other Hiberno-Scandinavian territories in the region. Brian Bóraime's ambitions in the Irish Sea world, apparent in his relationship with Dublin and with the rulers of the Isles, likewise brought him into competition with a powerful Scandinavian king. That Sveinn of Denmark had an interest in the region can be seen from the fact that he had attacked Man, and possibly driven its king into exile at Brian's court, in 995. And while Sveinn died in 1014, Danish interest in the region survived him. As noted above, in the aftermath of Sveinn's death, Knútr called on Lagmann, king of the Isles, for support before deciding to return to Denmark. Two years later, Knútr conquered England, and during his reign he exercised influence over both Dublin and the Isles. Sitriuc mac Amlaíb, of course, not only survived the battle of Clontarf, but continued to rule Dublin for another twenty-two years. Ben Hudson has accumulated abundant evidence to support the idea that, during this period, Sitriuc was a close ally of Knútr, even if it is not certain that Knútr was Sitriuc's overlord, as Hudson argues.[168] In 1030, for example, the Dublin fleet

163 Duffy, 'Irishmen and Islesmen', 111. **164** *AI* 1102. **165** A.O. Anderson, *Early sources of Scottish history AD500 to 1286*, 2 vols (Edinburgh, 1922), ii, pp 116–17. **166** *AU* 1102; *AI* 1102; *AT* 1102, 1103; *CS* 1099 (=1103). **167** Duffy, 'Irishmen and Islesmen', 112–16. **168** Benjamin Hudson, 'Cnut and Viking Dublin' in Hudson (ed.), *Irish Sea studies, 900–*

campaigned alongside the English in Wales, as it had campaigned previously alongside the armies of Brian and Máel Sechnaill.[169] It is not known who ruled the Isles in the immediate aftermath of Clontarf, but by the early 1030s the kingship was in the hands of Echmarach mac Ragnaill. Echmarcach's first appearance in the historical record was in the Anglo-Saxon Chronicle's report of events in 1031. That year, Knútr travelled to Scotland, where three kings submitted to him.[170] These three were Máel Coluim of Scotland, Macbethad of Moray, and Echmarcach, who was probably the king of the Isles and the Rhinns of Galloway at this date.[171] Knút's precise motivation for extracting submission from Echmarcach is uncertain, but one result might have been to check Echmarcach's ambitions with regard to Dublin. It is, perhaps, more than a coincidence that, within a year of Knút's death, Echmarcach had invaded and conquered Dublin and driven Sitriuc into exile.[172]

Knút's involvement in the politics of the Irish Sea world was a continuation of both Danish and Anglo-Saxon policy in the region. His meeting with the Scottish kings in 1031 is reminiscent of Edgar's royal convention in 975, at which Echmarcach's grand-uncle, Maccus, had been present. Sveinn and Æthelred had fought for influence in Man in the late 990s, and Sveinn had been in the region again as late as 1011. Is it possible that, having completed the conquest of England late in 1013, Danish ambitions shifted in early 1014 to the Irish Sea world? Whether Sveinn had designs on Ireland is impossible to know, but it is certainly plausible that he would have asserted authority over the Hiberno-Scandinavian kingdoms of Dublin and the Isles as kings of Norway did later in the eleventh century. The military might of the Danish king would have been sufficient to impose a sense of unity on the Dubliners and the Islesmen, and the opportunity to throw off Brian's overlordship – even in the knowledge that it would be replaced by that of the Danish king – was, no doubt, very attractive.

The problem with such a theory, of course, is that neither Sveinn nor Knútr was present at Clontarf, nor even in England at the time the battle was fought, Sveinn having died and Knútr returned to Denmark. But perhaps Danish royal interests were represented by someone else who was there. The record of the death of Sigurðr Hlödvisson at Clontarf is the first reference to the existence of the earldom of Orkney in a contemporary source. Grand claims have been put forth regarding the history of the earldom and the extent of the earl's authority since its supposed foundation in the late ninth century.[173]

1200, pp 47–59 (originally published as 'Knútr and Viking Dublin', *Scandinavian Studies*, 66 (1994), 319–35); Hudson, *Viking pirates*, 119–23; Downham, 'England and the Irish-Sea zone', 62–3; Etchingham, 'North Wales', 161–2. **169** *AT* 1030; discussed by Downham, 'England and the Irish-Sea zone', 64. **170** *Anglo-Saxon Chronicles*, (D, E) 1031. **171** Benjamin Hudson, 'Cnut and the Scottish kings' in Hudson (ed.), *Irish Sea studies*, pp 60–70, at 65–6 (originally published as 'Cnut and the Scottish kings', *EHR*, 107 (1992), 350–60). **172** *AT* 1036; Downham, 'England and the Irish-Sea zone', 65. **173** Barbara

These claims, however, are entirely dependent on the evidence of the later saga tradition, especially Orkneyinga saga. According to Orkneyinga saga, the earldom was created during the reign of King Haraldr *hárfagri*, 'fairhair', of Norway, who set up a certain Sigurðr as the first earl about 880.[174] The sagas are not reliable historical sources, however, as they were written centuries after the period they describe and were influenced by both hindsight and contemporary political and literary requirements. Alex Woolf has discussed the difficulties involved in using sagas as a source for the history of this period, both generally and with specific reference to Orkney. Attempts to make the sagas fit with contemporary evidence, he argues, are misguided.[175] Woolf has suggested that the tradition represented in Orkneyinga saga was created at a later date, after the Orkneys had come under Norwegian suzerainty, by projecting the real story of the origins of the earldom back into a period when a Norwegian foundation would have been more plausible. Woolf has offered an alternative interpretation of the origins of the earldom, according to which,

> as in *Orkneyinga saga*, the first earl was named Sigurðr and received his earldom from a king named Haraldr, but the event took place *c*.980 rather than *c*.880 and Haraldr was a Dane not a Norwegian. Before this there may have been no central authority on Orkney … Orkney, as I have suggested for the Western Isles, may, like Iceland and the forest provinces of Sweden, have been a land where small-scale chieftains competed for influence among farmer clients.

In other words, 'the earldom of Orkney … was a creation of the Danish empire' established by King Haraldr *blátǫnn* ('bluetooth') Gormsson, Sveinn's father.[176] If Woolf is correct, it would explain why the earls of Orkney, men of significant power in the eleventh and twelfth centuries, made no impression on the historical record prior to 1014 and why, although they ruled over territories much larger than the kingdom of the Isles, the earls never bore the royal title. Earl Sigurðr of Orkney was no hired hand at Clontarf, but a powerful ruler in his own right. He might have been the instigator of the battle himself, attempting to bring the Hiberno-Scandinavian kingdoms of the Irish Sea world under his sway as he expanded the borders of his new earldom. Alternatively, he might have been acting on behalf of his putative overlord, the Danish king, who, like other eleventh-century Scandinavian kings, was intent on expanding his authority over the same region.

Crawford, *Scandinavian Scotland: Scotland in the early Middle Ages 2*, Studies in the Early History of Britain (Leicester, 1987), pp 66–7. **174** *Orkneyinga saga: the history of the earls of Orkney*, ed. Paul Edwards and Hermann Palsson (London, 1978), pp 26–7. **175** Woolf, *From Pictland to Alba*, pp 242–4, 277–85. **176** Ibid., pp 300–8, at p. 308.

Internal Irish politics no doubt played an important part in bringing about the battle of Clontarf. The desire of the king of Leinster to be free of Brian Bóraime's overlordship explains his willingness to fight in the army of the Gaill. But Clontarf was more than an internal struggle. According to the interpretation offered here, the battle must be viewed in light the context of both Brian's ambitions in the Irish Sea world and the Danish conquest of England. For decades before the battle, Brian had manipulated the rivalry between the rulers of Dublin and of the Isles for his own benefit, while, beginning in the 990s, Danish and English rulers also occasionally competed for influence in the region. Then, in 1014, the Dubliners and the Islesmen united, albeit briefly, to fight against Brian. A comparison between the events of 1014 and those of 1058 and 1097–1103 suggests that Danish influence in the region might have been crucial in bringing about this course of events. Danish kings certainly sought to throw their political weight around in the Irish Sea world in the years before and after Clontarf, and it is possible that one of the key players in the battle was a Danish royal agent. According to Adémar de Chabannes, the army that fought Brian at Clontarf sought 'to exterminate the Irish and occupy their very rich land'.[177] The attack may have been a full-scale invasion of Ireland, an effort to conquer it for the Danish crown, or, perhaps more likely, was part of a struggle for control over the Hiberno-Scandinavian kingdoms of the Irish Sea world.[178] As a final comparison, it may be instructive to think that, had Muirchertach Ua Briain and Magnús Óláfsson not been able to forge a peace agreement in 1102, then the king of Ireland and the king of Norway might have fought a battle outside Dublin over the fate of the town, the Isles, and maybe even Ireland itself. It was a battle of this kind, fought on Irish soil but part of a broader struggle for power and influence in the Irish Sea world, that took place at Clontarf in 1014.

177 Adémar de Chabannes, *Chronicon*, p. 177; Duffy, *Brian Boru*, p. 226. 178 Hudson, *Viking pirates*, pp 97–8; Downham, 'Clontarf and the wider world', 25.

Glorious by association: the obituary of Brian Boru

MÁIRE NÍ MHAONAIGH

More than a thousand years after the battle of Clontarf, the principal source concerning the battle, a twelfth-century literary account, *Cogadh Gáedhel re Gallaibh* (The War of the Irish against Foreigners) has lost none of its appeal.[1] Presenting a detailed description of the encounter as the noble end-point in what is set out as the glorious career of Brian Boru (Brian Bórama), its skilful creator composed what is in effect an heroic biography of his main subject, a Munster king whose power extended throughout much of Ireland during the latter part of his long period of rule.[2] Written at the behest of Brian's great-grandson, Muirchertach, in the early years of the twelfth century, it was designed, in part at least, to bolster the younger man's ambitions.[3] The first of his dynasty to bear the surname of Ua Briain (O'Brien), this successful ruler consciously cultivated his ancestor's image, in whose reflected glory he sought profitably to bask. It is in this narrative text that Brian's persona was primarily cultivated, Clontarf being cast as a quasi-national conflict and one in which the aged, holy king was well-nigh martyred. This much has long been recognized and the literary nature of the *Cogadh* is clearly signalled in recent discussions of the events of a millennium ago.[4] Such is the dramatic power and pervasive influence of this sophisticated composition, however, that many contemporary commentators remain in its thrall and our perception of the battle fought at Clontarf in April 1014 continues to owe much to its author's pen.[5]

It was ever thus, and the *Cogadh*'s effects can be detected not long after it came into being. In form, content, as well as style, it provided a model for the story of Brian's Mac Carthaig counterpart, Cellachán mac Buadacháin (d. 954), *Caithréim Cellacháin Chaisil* ('The Martial Career of Cellachán of

1 *CGG*. 2 An excellent introduction to his career is provided in Ó Corráin, *Normans*, pp 120–31; I discuss the medieval sources concerning him in Ní Mhaonaigh, *Brian Boru*. 3 Anthony Candon, 'Muirchertach Ua Briain, politics and naval activity in the Irish Sea, 1075–1119' in Gearóid Mac Niocaill and Patrick F. Wallace (eds), *Keimelia: studies in medieval archaeology and history in memory of Tom Delaney* (Galway, 1988), pp 397–415; Máire Ní Mhaonaigh, '*Cogad Gáedel re Gallaib*: some dating considerations', *Peritia*, 9 (1995), 354–77. 4 See, for example, Duffy, *Brian Boru*, who suggests that the *Cogadh* 'must be taken with a pinch of salt' (p. 198), drawing attention to the text's 'good deal of embroidery' (p. 199). Similarly, Darren McGettigan, *The Battle of Clontarf: Good Friday 1014* (Dublin, 2013), claims 'that it is a mistake to try to find a historical basis for much of what appears in the Irish and Icelandic sagas' (p. 130, n. 1), among which the *Cogadh* is paramount. 5 See, for example, Máire Ní Mhaonaigh, 'The life and after life of Brian Boru', *Irish Literary Supplement: A Review of Irish Books*, 35:2 (Spring 2016), 14–15.

Cashel') probably composed in the second or third decade of the twelfth century, as argued by Donnchadh Ó Corráin.[6] There may indeed have been two versions of the *Cogadh* circulating at that point, if the ending highlighting the heroic endeavours of Brian's son and successor, Donnchad mac Briain, represents a reworking on the part of the latter's grandson, Brian, son of Murchad in Sgéith Girr mac Donnchada, known as Brian Gleanna Maidhir (d. 1118), as Denis Casey has suggested.[7] The original form of the narrative remains a matter of uncertainty, as the only complete surviving copy is that written by Míchéal Ó Cléirigh in Multyfarnham, Co. Westmeath, in 1635 based on a transcript he had made seven years previously of the now lost manuscript *Leabhar Con Chonacht Uí Dhálaigh* ('The Book of Cú Chonnacht Ó Dálaigh').[8] Emphasis on Muirchertach's line through his grandfather, Brian's son Tadc, whom his brother, Donnchad, had killed in 1023 is a prominent feature of *Brjáns saga*, the name given to a postulated Old Norse account of the battle which is preserved in the thirteenth-century text *Brennu-Njáls saga*.[9] This too was likely to have been written during Muirchertach's reign.[10] The popular composition was revised again in the middle of the twelfth century and interpolations were incorporated reflecting relations between Uí Briain and the influential king of Bréifne, Tigernán Ua Ruairc (d. 1172), at the time.[11] This version also lies behind a list of Clontarf battalions surviving in fragmentary fourteenth-century form.[12]

Cogadh Gáedhel re Gallaibh thus found immediate resonance and its composition was a significant event.[13] It was accorded space in a late twelfth-century codex, the Book of Leinster, though a lacuna in the manuscript means

6 '*Caithréim Chellacháin Chaisil*: history or propaganda?', *Ériu*, 25 (1974), 1–69 at 5, 61, 63–4. 7 Denis Casey, 'A reconsideration of the authorship and transmission of *Cogadh Gáedhel re Gallaibh*', *PRIA*, 113C, 1–23, at 20–1. Casey considers the possibility that the text may have been written at one of two points in the eleventh century, but ultimately rejects this view (18–20); Seán Duffy's claim that Casey's work points to this earlier date is therefore misleading: *Brian Boru*, p. 198 and n. 9. 8 Brussels, Bibliothèque Nationale, Manuscript 2569–2572, fos 103–35; for the significance of the manuscript evidence for his argument, see Casey, 'Reconsideration', 6–7. 9 Einar Ólafur Sveinsson (ed.), *Brennu-Njáls saga*, Íslenzk fornrit 12 (Reykjavík, 1954), pp 44–60 (§§154–5); see also Donnchadh Ó Corráin, 'Viking Ireland – afterthoughts' in Clarke et al. (eds), *Ireland and Scandinavia*, pp 421–52, at pp 450–2. Donnchad's treachery towards Tadc is recorded *AT*, pp 254–5; *AI* 1023.3 and *AU* 1023.5 do not specifically implicate Donnchad in his murder. 10 Ó Corráin, 'Viking Ireland', p. 450; see also Benjamin Hudson, 'Brjáns saga', *Medium Ævum*, 71 (2002), 141–68, reprinted in his *Irish Sea studies, 900–1200* (Dublin, 2006), pp 143–71. In a forthcoming collaborative volume, Colmán Etchingham, Máire Ní Mhaonaigh, Elizabeth Ashman Rowe and Jón Viðar Sigurðsson set out a time-period and location for the composition of this Old Norse text, as well as a context for its transmission to Iceland. 11 This version is preserved in Dublin, Trinity College, Manuscript 1319 (H.2.17), which is acephalous as well as lacking an ending; see Máire Ní Mhaonaigh, 'Bréifne bias in *Cogad Gáedel re Gallaib*', *Ériu*, 43 (1992), 135–58. 12 Máire Ní Mhaonaigh, 'A neglected account of the battle of Clontarf', *ZCP*, 59 (2012), 143–67, at 151–2. 13 There is evidence for repeated copying of other pseudo-historical texts also in this period. Different versions of

that only the first one-seventh or so of the composition now survives therein.[14] Its immediate context, surrounded as it is by texts concerned with both the theory and practice of kingship, suggests that this aspect of Brian's life is, not surprisingly, to the fore.[15] This is reinforced by the consequences allegedly brought about by his killing at Clontarf, heroes, clerics and women being robbed of their essential characteristics, namely 'valour and honour', 'piety and devotion', 'modesty and chastity' (respectively).[16] Employing a common literary motif, the author makes clear that the rightful king has been slain and the world is in disarray as a result. In Brian's case, his place in the next life is ensured and the language of resurrection is implied: death on Good Friday is followed by proper burial at Armagh on Easter Sunday, as well as generous payment of church dues.[17] Revival of Brian's power through control by his descendants is thus legitimized. As his heirs, they too have an innate and quasi-divine right to rule.

MEDIEVAL HISTORIOGRAPHY

In emphasizing Brian's authority and regal qualities, the *Cogadh* presents a story of his adult, active life. It constitutes his *res gestae*, the deeds specifically chosen to commend him to posterity. The narration of those selected actions

Táin Bó Cúailnge ('The Cattle Raid of Cúailnge') and *Mesca Ulad* ('The Intoxication of the Ulstermen') are preserved in two early vernacular manuscripts, *Lebor na hUidre* ('The Book of the Dun Cow') and the Book of Leinster (respectively, LU, pp 142–206; LL, ii, pp 261–399; and LU, 50–3; LL, v, pp 1171–87r). *Cath Ruis na Ríg* ('The Battle of Ross na Ríg') is also found in the latter codex (LL, iv, pp 761–79); Uáitéar Mac Gearailt has argued that an Early Modern Irish version of the latter text is derived from a copy earlier than and different from the copy in the Book of Leinster ('*Cath Ruis na Ríg* and twelfth-century literary and oral tradition', *ZCP*, 44 (1991), 128–53, at 141–6). We may also note that *Lebor Gabála Érenn* ('The Book of the Taking(s) of Ireland') circulated in various forms in the eleventh and twelfth centuries (John Carey, *A new introduction to* Lebor Gabála Érenn, ITS Subsidiary Series (London and Dublin, 1993), p. 6). The situation postulated for the *Cogadh*, therefore, was far from unique. **14** Dublin, Trinity College, Manuscript 1339 (H.2.18); LL v, pp 1319–25. **15** See Máire Ní Mhaonaigh, 'Celtic and Anglo-Saxon kingship revisited: Alfred, Æthelred and Brian Bórama compared' in John Bradley, Alan J. Fletcher and Anngret Simms (eds), *Dublin in the medieval world: studies in honour of Howard B. Clarke* (Dublin, 2009), pp 83–97, at pp 92–7. **16** *Ro sceind da ttrian einigh ocus engnama o laochaibh na hErenn le cloistecht an sceoil sin. Ro sceind da ttrian connla ocus crabhadh o cleirchibh Erenn don scel sin. Do cuaidh a náire ocus a ngeinmnaigecht ó mnaibh Erenn don scel cedna … Do cuaidh da ttrian lachta o ceitraibh fos don scel sin* ('Two-thirds of the valour and honour of Ireland's heroes vanished on hearing that news [of Brian's death]. Two-thirds of the piety and devotion of Ireland's clerics vanished because of that news. The modesty and chastity of Ireland's women disappeared because of that same news … In addition, two-thirds of cattle's milk disappeared because of that news'): *CGG*, pp 204–6 (§116). **17** *CGG*, pp 210–11 (§118); these arrangements are directed by Brian's son Donnchad; this portion of the text only survives in Ó Cléirigh's seventeenth-century copy.

casts him in a carefully constructed mould; through *narratio rerum gestarum*, Brian's *historia* was formed.[18] In representing Brian's past in this way, the author was working within well-established, intellectual parameters. Medieval chroniclers were concerned with *dramatis personae*, but also with the location (*locus*) of a given action, as well as its time (*tempus*).[19] By means of a chronological framework events were anchored in a linear history beginning with Creation and moving towards salvation itself. The idea of universal history and of the specific place of *res gestarum* within it, was the defining principle for much medieval discourse with the past.[20]

Within this overarching concept, memorialization and remembrance were achieved by various means and in many different, often interconnected forms, among them annals, sagas and hagiography. Chronicles set out happenings in sequence, synchronization orientating an audience by reference to what were perceived as defining world events, including the siege of Troy and the foundation of Rome.[21] For Marianus Scotus, alias Máel Brigte, a monk who received his early education in Moville, Co. Donegal, before moving in 1056 when he was in his late twenties to continental centres such as Cologne, Fulda and Mainz, the ordering of deeds was key. To accommodate historical happenings to his satisfaction within a temporal scheme, he adjusted the received Christian chronology, justifying his complex calculations.[22] Affairs in Ireland are recorded in his Chronicle (*Chronicon*), alongside biblical and imperial events. Brian's killing is noted by him, although not the actual encounter at Clontarf: according to Marianus, the Munster king was killed during the preparations for Easter 'with his hands and minds directed towards God' (*manibus et mente ad Deum intentus*).[23] The author of the Cogadh draws

18 Isidore of Seville specifically equated *historia* with *narratio rerum gestarum*; see Hans-Werner Goetz, 'The concept of time in the historiography of the eleventh and twelfth centuries' in Gerd Althoff, Johannes Fried and Patrick J. Geary (eds), *Medieval concepts of the past: ritual, memory, historiography* (Cambridge, 2002), pp 139–65, especially pp 143–5. **19** Goetz, 'The concept of time' provides a useful introduction, as do the essays in Jean-Philippe Genet (ed.), *L'historiographie médiévale en Europe: actes du colloque organisé par la Foundation Européenne de la Science au Centre de Recherches Historiques et Juridiques de l'Université Paris I du 29 mars au 1er avril 1989* (Paris, 1991). See also Franz-Josef Schmale, *Funktion und Formen mittelalterlicher Geschichtsschreibung: eine Einführung* (Darmstadt, 1985) and R.W. Southern, 'Aspects of the European tradition of historical writing: 1. the classical tradition from Einhard to Geoffrey of Monmouth', *TRHS*, 20 (1970), 173–96. **20** See, for example, Hans-Werner Goetz, 'On the universality of universal history' in Genet (ed.), *L'historiographie médiévale en Europe*, pp 247–61, and R.W. Southern, 'Aspects of the European tradition of historical writing: 2. Hugo of St Victor and the idea of historical development', *TRHS*, 21 (1971), 159–79. **21** In an Irish context, what was considered to be the foundation battle of Mag Tuired (*Cath Maige Tuired*), for example, is synchronized with the Trojan war: Elizabeth A. Gray (ed. and trans.), *Cath Maige Tuired: the Second Battle of Mag Tuired*, ITS 52 (London and Dublin, 1982), pp 40–1 (§69). **22** See, for example, Peter Verbist, *Duelling with the past: medieval authors and the problem of the Christian era (c.990–1135)*, Studies in the Early Middle Ages 21 (Turnhout, 2010), pp 85–146. **23** Bartholemew MacCarthy (ed. and trans.), *Codex Palatino-Vaticanus, no. 830:*

on chronicle entries, placing Brian's achievements in the context of a selective reading of earlier events.[24] The emphasis on successive waves of plundering Vikings signalled by the formula *tánic longes ele i* ('another fleet came to [a specific place]') sets the scene for Brian's ultimate triumph against ferocious foreign foes.[25] Behind this hovers a further structuring feature of medieval historiography, that of 'translation of imperial power (*translatio imperii*)' to accommodate change.

Translationes imperii provided a model whereby change could be accommodated, while continuity was also maintained. Within fixed points along a timeline, history could be viewed as cyclical, one great kingdom succeeding another in an ordered transfer of control.[26] Thus, the Assyrians, Persians and Macedonians were believed to have held power in turn before it moved westwards through Alexander the Great from Babylon to Rome.[27] The Roman Empire was deemed similarly flexible to allow translation of authority from one dynasty to another: as successors of Augustus Caesar, later rulers were accorded the mantle of rule.[28] Brian claimed the same imperial sanction, his spiritual advisor, Máel Suthain, describing him as *imperator Scotorum* (Emperor of the Irish) in the Book of Armagh.[29] The parallel with the designation, *imperator Romanorum*, accorded to his German contemporary, Otto III, has long been noted. The latter's predecessor, Otto II, was linked directly with Augustus, being known as *Romanorum imperator Augustus* from the 980s.[30] Brian too is styled *August iartair tuaiscirt Eorpa uile* ('the Augustus of the whole of northwest Europe'), in what is an augmented later record of the battle of Clontarf in the Annals of Ulster.[31] Prestige and precedence were expressed through identification with the first Roman emperor Augustus, or Octavianus, as he was originally known.[32] The decline of that empire led

texts, translations and indices, RIA, Todd Lecture Series 3 (Dublin, 1892), p. 8; Ní Mhaonaigh, *Brian Boru*, pp 58–9. **24** I have attempted to identify his sources in '*Cogad Gáedel re Gallaib* and the annals: a comparison', *Ériu*, 47 (1996), 101–26. **25** Ní Mhaonaigh, '*Cogad Gáedel re Gallaib* and the annals', 118–20; see most recently, Clare Downham, 'The "annalistic section" of *Cogad Gáedel re Gallaib*', *Peritia*, 24–5 (2013–14), 141–72. **26** See, for example, Goetz, 'The concept of time', 154. **27** See, for example, Emily Reiner, 'Meanings of nationality in the medieval Alexander tradition' in Markus Stock (ed.), *Alexander the Great in the Middle Ages: transcultural perspectives* (Toronto, 2016), pp 30–50, at pp 33–5. **28** For vivid visual representation of this, see Goetz, 'The concept of time', pp 155–7. **29** John Gwynn (ed.), *The Book of Armagh: Liber Ardmachanus* (Dublin, 1913), fol. 16v; for discussion, see Duffy, *Brian Boru*, pp 140–4; Denis Casey and Bernard Meehan, 'Brian Boru and the Book of Armagh', *History Ireland*, 22:2 (Mar./Apr. 2014), 28–9; and see also Casey in this volume, above. **30** Aubrey Gwynn, 'Brian in Armagh (1005)', *Seanchas Ard Mhacha*, 9 (1978), 38–51; Odilo Engels, 'Theophano, the western empress from the east' in Adelbert Davids (ed.), *The empress Theophano: Byzantium and the West at the turn of the first millennium* (Cambridge, 1995), pp 28–48, at p. 35; for context see the article by Karl Leyser in the same volume, '*Theophanu divina gratia imperatrix Augusta*: western and eastern emperorship in the later tenth century', pp 1–48. **31** *AU* 1014.2; on the nature of this record, see Duffy, *Brian Boru*, pp 177–86; Ní Mhaonaigh, *Brian Boru*, pp 55–6. **32** Tenth-century Anglo-Saxon kings were

seamlessly to the triumph of Christianity, and it was as part of that historical tradition that these global Christian rulers were portrayed.[33]

BRIAN'S DEATH-NOTICE

That Brian Boru should be placed in such company is entirely to be expected: Ireland was part of this wider learned Latinate world. Its history was Christian history; a biblically inspired origin-legend, *Lebor Gabála Érenn* (The Book of the Taking(s) of Ireland), situated Ireland among divine nations, equating the Irish (Gaídil) with God's chosen people, the Israelites, *tuatha Dé*.[34] That Brian saw himself in these terms can be deduced from the fact that Máel Suthain accorded him the title 'Emperor' in the king's own presence (*in conspectu Briani*).[35] The *Cogadh* followed its subject's lead but went further, particularly in one passage which functions as the death-notice of the king (see appendix 8.1 below).[36] In a eulogistic obituary occurring at a point in the text immediately after the account of Brian's slaying at Clontarf, he is proclaimed as *an tOchtauin aobhdha ilbhuadhach im shochar ocus im saordhacht a atharrdha ocus a chineoil* ('the beautiful, ever-victorious Octavian, as far as the benefit and nobility of his patrimony and kin is concerned').[37] There are echoes in this passage of the Aeneid, specifically of Virgil's portrayal of Augustus Caesar therein, encompassed in the prophecy attributed to Anchises in Book 6 of that work: *hic vir, hic est tibi quem promitti saepius audis / Augustus Caesar, divi genus* ('this is the man, this is he who you are frequently told is promised to you, Augustus Caesar, offspring of a god)'.[38] The detail is not reproduced in the vernacular Irish prose version of the poem, *Imtheachta Aeniasa* ('The Wanderings of Aeneas'), which was adapted about the same time as the *Cogadh*

also styled emperor, though not specifically of Rome. Edgar, for example, was deemed *basileus et imperator omnium regnum Anglorum*; see Marie Therese Flanagan, *Irish society, Anglo-Norman settlers, Angevin kingship: interactions in Ireland in the late twelfth century* (Oxford, 1989), p. 179. 33 The link between these two major powers, Roman and Christian, was the dominant theme of an influential fourth-century history by a student of St Augustine, Orosius, *Historiarum adversum paganos libri VII* ('History against the pagans in seven books'): Carolus Zangemeister (ed.), *Pauli Orosii Historiarum adversum paganos libri VII*, Corpus Scriptorum Ecclesiasticorum Latinorum 5 (Heidelberg, 1882; reprinted Hildesheim, 1967). 34 See Carey, *New introduction to* Lebor Gabála Érenn and his '*Lebor Gabála* and the legendary history of Ireland' in Helen Fulton (ed.), *Medieval Celtic literature and society* (Dublin, 2005), pp 32–48. 35 Gwynn, *Book of Armagh*, fol. 16v; the assumption that the inscription was written in Armagh during Brian's well known visit there in 1005 has been challenged by Casey and Meehan, 'Brian Boru and the Book of Armagh', 29, and in Casey, above. 36 *CGG*, pp 202–5 (115). I refer throughout to my transcription and translation of the death-notice in Appendix 8.1 below, while also providing references to Todd's edition of the paragraph in question. This passage is only preserved in the seventeenth-century copy of the text written by Míchéal Ó Cléirigh. 37 *CGG*, p. 204 (§115). 38 J.W. Mackail (ed.), *The Aeneid* (Oxford, 1930), 6.791–5.

was composed.[39] Nonetheless, the essence of Virgil's text remains in the Irish work, *Iuil Cesair 7 Octafin airdri in domain co fine na Sesarda* ('Julius Caesar and Octavian, emperor of the world, with the family of the Caesars') being included among the kings and nobles numbered among Aeneas's illustrious descendants.[40] In the case of the original Latin text, the exact tenor of the depiction of the Emperor and the poet's view of his contemporary has been intensely debated.[41] Notwithstanding the perceived ambiguities in Virgil's own text, later commentators predominantly favour a pro-Augustan stance, including Servius, a fourth-century critic, whose work formed part of a wider compendium (known as Servius Danielis) which was highly influential in the Middle Ages.[42] As the successor of Rome's founder, Aeneas, Augustus represents a crucial stage in the continuation of power and thus its ultimate transfer into a Christian era.

This is the perspective reflected in Irish material and the *Cogadh* is no exception in this regard. In the narrative, Brian is praised as Augustus for his beauty and military victories, as well as the benefit he brought to his kin. The emphasis on the quasi-legal terms *sochar* ('valid contract', as well as more generally 'privileges, profit') and *sáerdacht* (the concept of being *sáer*, 'free, possessing legal status') could have recalled the *pax Romana* with which Rome's first emperor was associated. As Augustus brought law, order and stability to his kingdom, so too was Ireland in Brian's time peaceful and secure.[43] The point is reinforced in more familiar rhetoric in the paragraph following the equation of the Roman emperor and the Munster king, with reference to the calamitous effects experienced as a result of Brian's death. In addition to the loss of valour, devotion and chastity on the part of heroes, clerics and women in turn (noted above), two-thirds of cows' milk will be dissipated in a dramatic depiction of the reduction in fertility that Brian's

39 George Calder (ed. and trans.), *Imtheachta Aeniasa: the Irish Aeneid being a translation made before AD1400 of the XII books of Vergil's Aeneid into Gaelic*, ITS 6 (London, 1907); see also Erich Poppe, *A new introduction to* Imtheachta Aeniasa *The Irish Aeneid: the classical epic from an Irish perspective*, ITS Subsidiary Society 3 (London and Dublin, 1995), and his, 'A Virgilian model for *lúirech thredúalach*', *Ériu*, 54 (2004), 171–7, at 176. **40** Calder, *Imtheachta Aeniasa*, pp 90–1 (line 1447). A further specific reference to Augustus in Book VII of the Aeneid concerning his entry into Rome as depicted prophetically on Aeneas's shield is not reproduced in the Irish text: Mackail, *The Aeneid*, Book 7; Calder, *Imtheachta Aeniasa*, pp 124–5 (lines 1960–67). **41** For a summary of the debate, see Richard F. Thomas, *Virgil and the Augustan reception* (Cambridge, 2001), pp 2–14. Thomas himself reads Virgil as critical of Augustus; for a more positive interpretation, see James E.G. Zeitzel, 'Rome and its traditions' in Charles Martindale (ed.), *The Cambridge companion to Virgil* (Cambridge, 1997), pp 188–203, at pp 197–9. **42** On Servius's view of Virgil and Augustine, see Thomas, *Virgil and the Augustan reception*, pp 92–121; use of Servian commentary in Ireland is discussed by Brent Miles, *Heroic saga and classical epic in medieval Ireland*, Studies in Celtic History 30 (Woodbridge, 2011), pp 23–33. **43** This is stated clearly in an earlier panegyric of Brian's reign: *CGG*, pp 100–1 (§63), pp 138–41 (§80); see Ní Mhaonaigh, 'Celtic and Anglo-Saxon kingship revisited', 93–4.

killing will cause.[44] Warfare will become prevalent, in fulfilment of the prophecy of Berchán: 'blood-red' (*fordercc*) will be the conflicts of Foreigners and Irish – *Gaill* and *Gaídil*.[45] In combination with this well-known imagery, the equivalence of Brian and Augustus becomes focussed on their mutual role as successful leaders and dynastic founders. And as Roman power is translated to a Christian successor, the underlying implication is that Brian's descendants can (and will) triumph in time.

The reference to Augustus may also have recalled another great leader, Conchobar mac Nessa, king of the Ulaid. As Ireland's history was aligned with global events in annalistic and other sources, it is with Augustus's period as emperor that Conchobar's rule was synchronized. Thus, both leaders are said to have come to power at the same time; the beginning of the reign of Conchobar is recorded immediately after the defeat by his Roman counterpart of Mark Anthony and Cleopatra, marking the end of the Roman Republic and the commencement of Empire: *Marcus Antonius Niger uictus ab Augusto … Hoc anno cepit regnare in Emain Conchobor mac Nessa ….*[46] This equation forms part of material from the so-called Irish World Chronicle, the source from which non-contemporary annals concerned with the period before the time of St Patrick are likely to have been derived.[47] Augustus predeceased Conchobar according to this scheme.[48] However, one version of Conchobar's death-tale (*Aided Chonchobair*), claims that Octavian (alias Augustus) sent a tax official, Altus, to the Ulster king, who also brought news of Christ's crucifixion to him.[49] Conchobar died of anger and grief as a result, one of only two men in Ireland who believed in God 'before the coming of Christianity (*rīa tiachtain creitmi*)'.[50] Octavian's son, Tiberius, is ruling when Jesus was crucified, in other versions of the story, in line with biblical chronology.[51]

Through Conchobar's precocious conversion in this and other sources, Ireland's pre-Christian heroes are associated with Christ and placed at the beginning of what was known as the Sixth Age which began with the Incarnation and would lead on to eternity in the Seventh. In the universal chronology within which medieval historiography was structured, therefore, the Ulster king was something of a lynchpin. Any association between him and Brian in the *Cogadh* is at best indirect: if **A**[ugustus] = **B**[rian], then **B** must

44 *CGG*, p. 205 (§115). 45 *CGG*, pp 204–5 (§116). 46 *AT*, p. 35. 47 Thomas Charles-Edwards (trans.), *The chronicle of Ireland*, Translated Texts for Historians 44, 2 vols (Liverpool, 2006), i, p. 3. 48 *AT*, p. 38. 49 *Nō dano co mbad é Altus in consul dodechaid ō Ochtauīn do chungid in chīsa co Gǣdelaib no-innised do Chonchobur Crīst do chrochad* ('Or, again it may have been Altus, the consul who had come to the Gaels from Octavian to seek the tribute, who told Conchobar that Christ was crucified'): Kuno Meyer (ed. and trans.), *The death-tales of the Ulster heroes*, RIA, Todd Lecture Series 14 (Dublin, 1906), pp 10–11 (§14). 50 Meyer, *Death-tales*, pp 9–10 (§12). 51 Meyer, *Death-tales*, pp 12–13 (§1) in which Tiberius is *mac Auguist rī[g] Rōmān* ('the son of Augustus, king of the Romans'); pp 14–15 (§2): *Tibir Sesair Aughiust rīgh Rōmān* ('Tiberius Caesar Augustus, king of the Romans').

equal C[onchobar]. By contrast, a comparison between Brian and other Irish heroes is made explicit in the elegy of Brian with which we are concerned: together with Lug Lámfhata and Finn mac Cumaill, he forms the triad of Ireland's best births (*an treas gein as fearr rugadh a nÉrinn riamh*).[52] Significantly, Lug Lámfhata is accorded a key position in a sophisticated chronology of heroes into which Brian's son and chief commander, Murchad, is placed at an earlier point in the text.[53] Subservient only to Hector in strength, Lug also functions as a key anchor since the foundational battle with which he is associated, *Cath Maige Tuired* ('The Battle of Mag Tuired') was coeval with the conflict in which Hector lost his life, the destruction of Troy.[54] Immediately above Murchad in this heroic hierarchy in the earlier passage is Mac Samáin who is associated with Finn mac Cumaill elsewhere. In this panegyric of Brian, therefore, placed after the narrative of his killing, it is likely that the powerful eulogy of his valorous son, Murchad, is being deliberately recalled.

As Murchad is stated specifically to be *int Ectoir intamlaigtech* ('the metaphorical Hector'), in the earlier passage in the *Cogadh*, does this make Brian the equivalent of Hector's father, Priam?[55] This is nowhere clearly expressed in the text and, indeed, Brian is equated with Alexander in his death-notice. Following on from his identification as 'the beautiful, ever-victorious Octavian', he is described as *an tAlaxandar tailc, talcar tánaiste ar treoir ocus ar oirbert, ocus ar innsaighidh, ar chathaibh, ocus ar chosccraibh* ('the second strong, resolute Alexander for effort, exploit and attack, for battles and for triumphs').[56] In this way is Brian's military prowess hailed, by comparison with the heroism of the most celebrated of war commanders, Alexander the Great. As Macedonian king, the latter's triumphant campaign secured the successful transfer of power from east to west, for which he is celebrated in medieval sources.[57] It is with this significant legacy that Brian's success is thus placed on a par.

By contrast, Priam is less exalted, overshadowed by his heroic sons, Hector and Troilus, as well as by his more distant relative, Aeneas, who went on to

52 *CGG*, pp 202–3 (§115). 53 *CGG*, pp 186–7 (§107). I discussed this passage in my lecture at the millennial conference commemorating Clontarf; my assessment of it has since been published: '"The metaphorical Hector": the literary portrayal of Murchad mac Bríain' in Ralph O'Conor (ed.), *Classical literature and learning in medieval Irish narrative*, Studies in Celtic History 34 (Woodbridge, 2014), pp 140–61, especially pp 145–55. 54 Gray, *Cath Maige Tuired*, pp 40–1 (§69), as noted above; see also Peter Smith (ed. and trans.), *Three historical poems ascribed to Gilla Cóemáin*, Studien und Texte zur Keltologie 8 (Münster, 2007), pp 186–7 (stanza 17) and Leslie Diane Myrick, *From the* De excidio Troiae historia *to the* Togail Troí*: literary-cultural synthesis in a medieval Irish adaptation of Dares' Troy tale*, Anglistische Forschungen 223 (Heidelberg, 1993), p. 84. 55 Alex Wolf asked precisely this question at the end of the lecture I gave at the conference in April 2014, with apologies to him for the delayed fuller response presented here. I am also grateful to Denis Casey for discussion on this point. 56 *CGG*, pp 204–5 (§115). 57 See, for example, George Cary,

found Rome. His story was well-known to Irish audiences, since *De excidio Troiae historia*, a fourth- or fifth-century Latin account of the Trojan war, purported to be derived from the report of an eye-witness, Dares Phrygius, was translated into Irish in a number of different versions between the tenth or eleventh century and the twelfth.[58] The Irish adaptation, *Togail Troí* ('The Destruction of Troy'), was a seminal text in the medieval Irish literary corpus the influence of which was pervasive; it is preserved along with the *Cogadh*, *Táin Bó Cúailnge* and other narratives in the Book of Leinster.[59] The ruling Trojan king at the time of Troy's destruction, Priam is, not surprisingly, matched with Ulster's ruler and Augustan counterpart, Conchobar mac Nessa, in a sustained comparison between the warriors of Troy and the Ulaid (*Tro-fhian fhir na hÉireann*, 'the true Trojan band of Ireland') in a well-known twelfth-century poem, *Clann Ollaman úaisle Emna* ('The children of Ollam are the nobles of Emain').[60] A eulogy of a contemporary ruler of the Ulaid, Eochaid mac Duinnshléibe, to whom the poet turns after cataloguing the latter's sixty-six predecessors, the poem casts the twelfth-century king, however, as Hector rather than Priam. The heroism of the younger Trojan warrior would have served Eochaid well in literary terms at many points in what was often a chequered career. In addition, the specific association with Hector may also have highlighted a subtle link with an earlier northern leader, Muirchertach mac Néill, who is termed *Echtair iarthair beatha* ('Hector of the western world') in his annalistic obit of 983, as I have argued elsewhere.[61] Nevertheless, in general Hector appears to have been considered a more appropriate heroic comparison than his father Priam.

Notwithstanding this, an association between Brian and Priam could have naturally presented itself to the author of the *Cogadh*, and there are specific points of comparison between the two men. In their respective final battles in which neither plays an active part, both are apprised of events by an observer in variations of the literary technique known as the 'watchman device'. In

The medieval Alexander, ed. D.J.A. Ross (Cambridge, 1956) and Z. David Zuwiyya (ed.), *A companion to Alexander material in the Middle Ages*, Brill's Companions to the Christian Traditions 19 (Leiden and Boston, 2011), pp 255–90. **58** Ralph O'Connor provides a convenient summary of the editions and scholarship concerning the date of the text: 'Irish narrative literature and the classical tradition 900–1300' in his edited volume, *Classical literature*, pp 1–22, at pp 13–14 (with earlier references). To his list we can add the twelfth-century poetic version of the Troy tale: Gearóid Mac Eoin, 'Dán ar chogadh na Traoi', *Studia Hibernica*, 1 (1961), 19–55. The relationships between the manuscript witnesses to the text's recensions, including the unpublished Recension II, are set out clearly in Michael Clarke, 'The extended prologue of *Togail Troí*: from Adam to the wars of Troy', *Ériu*, 64 (2014), 23–106, at 27–8. **59** LL, iv, pp 1063–117; Whitley Stokes (ed. and trans.), *Togail Troi: the Destruction of Troy from the facsimile of the Book of Leinster* (Calcutta, 1881). **60** Francis John Byrne (ed. and trans.), 'Clann Ollaman uaisle Emna', *Studia Hibernica*, 4 (1964), 54–94, at 61 and 76 (stanza 3): *Priam ainm Conchobair Codail / borrfadaig im Thoraig thuaid* ('Priam is the name of Conchobar of Codal who rages around northern Troy'). **61** 'The Hectors of Ireland and the western world' in John Carey, Kevin Murray and

Brian's case, his attendant, Latean, reports to him the progress of the battle, punctuating the king's psalm recital at regular intervals. It is from him that the king learns of the fall of Murchad's standard, as a result of which Brian realizes that all is lost.[62] A more conventional watchman device, with typical riddling treatment,[63] is employed in *Togail Troí* at a point in the two main versions of the text (recensions I and II) in which Dares presents what is termed the 'Portrait Catalogue', a descriptive list of warriors involved in the encounter.[64] This addition to Dares's text is thus the work of an Irish author, though whether his inspiration is classical or Irish is a matter of some debate.[65] The two recensions differ in the role accorded to Priam in the sequence. In the more elaborate version in the Book of Leinster, in contrast to Brian in the *Cogadh*, Priam is the expert witness, explaining to a Trojan messenger the true meaning of what the latter has erroneously interpreted as mighty mountains, a roar of wind and the like.[66] In the earlier Recension I, the role of the king of Troy is more of a bystander, his questions prompting a messenger to reveal what he has described in terms of natural features (similar to those in Recension II) really are.[67] In this narrative scenario, therefore, observer and expert are one. Notwithstanding this (and other) differences, in both versions of *Togail Troí* the interchange functions very much as a set piece. In the *Cogadh*, on the other hand, the conversation between a royal leader anxiously praying while he awaits battle-developments, and his observant retainer has a much more realistic feel.

Brian's study of the psalter during the battle, as depicted in the *Cogadh*, ensures that his slayer, Brodar, initially mistakes him for a priest. His real identity is betrayed by a Judas-figure who had been a warrior of the Munster king (*robh ócclach do Brian féin e*).[68] Priam was slain at Minerva's altar by Pyrrhus for whom there was no uncertainty concerning his victim. The contrast between Brodar happening upon Brian and the violent means by which Achilles's son reached Priam could not be more stark.[69] Priam's attempt to defend himself with a spear-cast is presented as ineffectual *fo bíth robo senoir*

Caitríona Ó Dochartaigh (eds), *Sacred histories: a Festschrift for Máire Herbert* (Dublin, 2015), pp 258–68, at pp 264–6. **62** *CGG*, pp 196–201 (§113); most of this passage is preserved only in the seventeenth-century copy of the text by Ó Cléirigh, the earlier manuscript breaking off *CGG*, p. 198. **63** The typical feature is that the observer mistakes what he sees for something else, usually natural features: see Patrick Sims-Williams, 'Riddling treatment of the "watchman device" in *Branwen* and *Togail Bruidne Da Derga*', *Studia Celtica*, 12/13 (1977–8), 83–117, republished in revised form in his *Irish influence on medieval Welsh literature* (Oxford, 2011), pp 95–133. **64** Myrick, *From the* De excidio, p. 136. **65** The matter has been reassessed by Ralph O'Connor, 'Was classical imitation necessary for the writing of large-scale Irish sagas? Reflections on *Táin Bó Cúailnge* and the "watchman device"' in his edited volume *Classical literature*, pp 165–95. **66** LL, iv, pp 1098–101 (lines 32169–263). **67** Whitley Stokes (ed. and trans.), 'The Destruction of Troy' in Whitley Stokes and Ernst Windisch (eds), *Irische Texte mit Übersetzungen und Wörterbuch*, Series II, part 1 (Leipzig, 1884), pp 1–142, at pp 28–30, 93–5 (lines 847–904). **68** *CGG*, pp 202–3 (§114). **69** Stokes, 'Destruction of Troy', p. 58 and p. 130.

díblide hé ann ('because he was then a feeble old man').[70] Notwithstanding Brian's similarly advanced age, he slew both Brodar and one of his companions in the attack in which he lost his life.[71] We may also note the very different reactions to the two elder statesmen after the deaths of their fighting sons. Priam is advised to surrender Helen and enter into an agreement with his enemies. Instead he advocates war and plans to betray his advisers who have counselled peace with disastrous results.[72] While he does not advise retreat (*ní maisi an teiched*), Brian's tone is above all grief-stricken in the *Cogadh* and accepting of his prophesized fate.[73] He arranges his affairs, concerned for his dynasty's continued prosperity before encountering Brodar's battle-axe (*tuag*).[74]

As the father of a Hector-figure, Brian's likeness to Priam may have occurred to some of those experiencing the text. Yet the *Cogadh* does not advocate the connection, despite apparent similarities between the two men. Clontarf's resonance with Troy highlighted by means of the equivalence between Murchad and Hector, may also extend to the parallel triumph of both fallen Trojans and Munster men through the supremacy of their descendants.[75] In this regard, it was Aeneas's subsequent foundation of Rome which was significant and that key moment in history is alluded to through Brian's identification with Augustus, as well as with Alexander who facilitated the move westwards of imperial power, as we have seen. The comparative strand in the *Cogadh* continues throughout the remainder of Brian's death-notice and the Munster king is identified with three biblical greats, Solomon, David and Moses in turn. As *Solamh … na nGaoidel* ('Solomon of the Gaídil'), his 'prosperous, powerful, peaceful (*sona, saidbhir, siodhamail*)' attributes are brought to the fore. Embodying Solomon's father as 'the David of Ireland (*Dauit … na hÉrenn*)', his 'ingegrity (*fírinne*)', 'honour (*inracas*)' and 'guarding of sovereignty (*coimhétt flaithemhnais*)' is extolled. In Moses the parallel is deemed to be their mutual 'piety (*cundla*)' and 'devout holiness (*cáidhe cráibthighe*)'.[76]

David and Solomon, together with Samuel and Saul, are the defining figures of early medieval kingship.[77] As outstanding kings of Israel, they formed an important part of the depiction of particular peoples, including the Irish, as the Israelites, God's chosen people.[78] The enduring significance of

70 Ibid., lines 18887–8. **71** *CGG*, pp 202–3 (§114). **72** Stokes, 'Destruction of Troy', pp 54–5, 125–6. **73** *CGG*, pp 200–1 (§113). **74** *CGG*, pp 202–3 (§114). **75** Ní Mhaonaigh, '"The metaphorical Hector"', p. 161. **76** *CGG*, pp 204–5 (§115). **77** The extensive literature on this topic includes Yitzhak Hen, 'The uses of the Bible and the perception of kingship in Merovingian Gaul', *Early Medieval Europe*, 7 (1998), 277–90; Janet L. Nelson, 'Kingship and royal government' in Rosamond McKitterick (ed.), *The new Cambridge medieval history, III,* c.*700*–c.*900* (Cambridge, 1995), pp 383–430; Walter Ullman, *The Carolingian Renaissance and the idea of kingship* (London, 1969); Hans Hubert Anton, *Fürstenspiegel und Herrscherethos in der Karolingerzeit* (Bonn, 1968). **78** See, for example,

biblical rulers in this regard is evident in medieval illustrations pertaining to Ottonian emperors, including the late tenth-century portrait of Otto III in the Reichenau Gospel-book,[79] and a late twelfth-century wax seal belonging to Otto IV, both of whom are adorned with insignia (sceptre and orb) associated with biblical kings.[80] Moreover, David and Solomon are represented on the eleventh- or twelfth-century German imperial crown.[81]

The importance of this ideology in Irish terms can be seen in the deliberate and extended comparison between Solomon and Cormac mac Airt, who is portrayed as an ideal ruler in medieval Irish narratives.[82] In Cormac's case, the typology centred on the comparable wisdom of both kings, while this is only indirectly alluded to in the *Cogadh* with reference to the peaceful nature of Solomon-Brian.[83] The biblical ruler's famed wealth informs the depiction of the composite character in our text as *saidbir*, 'rich, prosperous, powerful'. Such was the prevalence of the specific association between Cormac and Solomon in the Middle Irish literary corpus, including texts sharing with the *Cogadh* the Book of Leinster's pages,[84] that it may have resonated with an audience encountering a correlation between the biblical ruler and Brian. Moreover, like Brian, Cormac too 'was comparable to Octavian Augustus', specifically in his collection of *in cís rígda* ('the royal rent'), though 'Cormac never deprived any one of that which was his own'.[85] Solomon is also adduced by Asser in his 'Life of King Alfred' to highlight his subject's wisdom and learning in a passage in which the biblical ruler's great wealth is also noted: 'In

Mary Garrison, 'The Franks as the new Israel? Education for an identity from Pippin to Charlemagne' in Yitzhak Hen and Matthew Innes (eds), *The uses of the past in the early Middle Ages* (Cambridge, 2000), pp 114–61 and Samantha Zacher, *Rewriting the Old Testament in Anglo-Saxon verse: becoming the chosen people*, New Directions in Religion and Literature (London and New York, 2013); for an Irish context, see Ralph O'Connor, *The Destruction of Da Derga's Hostel: kingship and artistry in a mediaeval Irish saga* (Oxford, 2013), pp 272–5. **79** Munich, Bayerische Staatsbibliothek, Clm. 4453, fol. 24, reproduced in Henry Mayr-Harting, *Ottonian book illumination: an historical study, part I: themes* (London, 1991), illustration XXI; for general discussion, see pp 157–78. **80** Aliza Cohen-Mushlin, *Scriptoria in medieval Saxony: St Pancras in Hamersleben* (Wiesbaden, 2004), p. 122 (and references n. 56); parallel contemporary biblical illustrations are presented by her pp 120–1. **81** Reinhart Staats, *Theologie der Reichskrone: Ottonische 'renovatio imperii' im Spiegel einer Insignie*, Monographien zur Geschichte des Mittelalters 13 (Stuttgart, 1976), pp 36–43 and more generally his *Die Reichskrone: Geschichte und Bedeutung eines europäischen Symbols* (Göttingen, 1991). **82** Tomás Ó Cathasaigh, *The heroic biography of Cormac mac Airt* (Dublin, 1978), pp 85–6; Edward Gwynn (ed. and trans.), *The Metrical Dindshenchas, part I: text, translation and commentary*, RIA, Todd Lecture Series 8 (Dublin, 1903), pp 70–4. **83** On Cormac's Solomonic wisdom, see, for example, Máirín O Daly (ed. and trans.), *Cath Maige Mucram: the battle of Mag Mucrama*, ITS 50 (London and Dublin, 1975), pp 58–9 (§§ 63–4); and Standish Hayes O'Grady (ed. and trans.), *Silva Gadelica: a collection of tales in Irish with extracts illustrating persons and places*, 2 vols (London, 1892), ii, pp 96–9 ('The Panegyric of King Cormac'), at p. 96 (§2). **84** See Dagmar Schlüter, *History or fable? The* Book of Leinster *as a document of cultural memory in twelfth-century Ireland*, Studien und Texte zur Keltologie 9 (Münster, 2010), p. 118. **85** O'Grady, *Silva Gaedlica*, ii, p. 97 (§3).

this respect he resembled the holy, highly esteemed and exceedingly wealthy Solomon …'.[86] This Latin *vita* has been posited as a possible model for Brian's biography in the *Cogadh*, although it is more likely that both were drawing either directly or indirectly on the same source, Einhard's *Vita Caroli magni*.[87] The common reference to Solomon is not sufficient to allow a connection between the two texts to be drawn, in particular since the Welsh author emphasizes the biblical ruler's wisdom, unlike his Irish counterpart, as we have seen.[88]

The Davidic reference in the *Cogadh* is longer and somewhat more specific than the allusion to Solomon which immediately precedes it. It draws attention to the universal regal trait of *fírinne*, the quality of justice which marks out the legitimate king. The imperial crown (*Reichskrone*) presents the Old Testament ruler in similar terms, since he holds a scroll citing Psalm 99:4: 'The renowned king delights in doing justice'.[89] King David's role as author of the psalms assured his place in intellectual circles in Ireland, as elsewhere.[90] In the *Cogadh*, however, it is his association with retention of rule (*coimét flaithemnais*) that is most striking. This may be an allusion to David's extensive struggles to retain his kingship in 2 Samuel; having triumphed against a range of adversaries, he also ensured the succession of his chosen son, Solomon. References to David elsewhere in medieval Irish literature draw more frequently on 1 Samuel, Ralph O'Connor having noted that a prime focus of interest is the interplay between David and Saul.[91] Notwithstanding this, the king's depiction is varied in Irish narrative sources;[92] he is seen as the source of Solomon's wisdom in one anecdote concerning him,[93] but his lack of charity in another may reflect anti-clerical feeling in the twelfth century, as Elizabeth Boyle has proposed.[94] In its allusion to David's success in maintaining his

86 William Henry Stevenson (ed.), *Asser's life of King Alfred, together with the annals of Saint Neots erroneously ascribed to Asser* (Oxford, 1904), pp 60–1; Simon Keynes and Michael Lapidge (trans.), *Alfred the Great: Asser's life of King Alfred and other contemporary sources* (Harmondsworth, 1983), p. 92. 87 See Ní Mhaonaigh, 'Celtic and Anglo-Saxon kingship revisited', pp 90–1. 88 For discussion of the passage in Asser and its dependence on Matthew, see Zacher, *Rewriting the Old Testament in Anglo-Saxon verse*, p. 46 n. 142 and the more detailed analysis in David Pratt, *The political thought of King Alfred the Great*, Cambridge Studies in Medieval Life and Thought, 4th ser., 67 (Cambridge, 2007), pp 152–3. 89 Staats, *Die Reichskrone*, p. 55. 90 See Martin McNamara, *The psalms in the early Irish church* (Sheffield, 2000). 91 O'Connor, *Destruction*, pp 264–5. 92 Kuno Meyer, 'Nachlass Kuno Meyer: Mitteilungen aus irischen Handschriften', *ZCP*, 13 (1920), 166–94, at 175–9; one of the David stories (177) is translated in Máire Herbert and Martin McNamara (trans.), *Irish biblical apocrypha: selected texts in translation* (Edinburgh, 1989), p. 22. 93 See Meyer, 'Nachlass Kuno Meyer', *ZCP*, 13 (1920), p. 179; the text has been translated by Elizabeth Boyle, 'David and Solomon', https://blogafragments.wordpress.com/page/4/ (accessed July 2016). 94 Paul Grosjean (ed. and trans.), 'King David and the beggar' in John Fraser, Paul Grosjean and J.G. O'Keefe (eds), *Irish texts*, part 4 (London, 1934), pp 113–18; Elizabeth Boyle discussed the text and other David narratives in a lecture at the Department of Anglo-Saxon, Norse, and Celtic, Cambridge, 23 Jan. 2015:

kingship in the struggle against foes, the *Cogadh* may have made the Brian-David parallel particularly apposite. In associating the Munster king with the biblical father-son royal duo, a general message concerning the excellence of Brian's kingship throughout the narrative was reinforced.

In casting Brian as the equivalent of 'great, graciously illustrious' Moses (*mórdha mínéttrocht*), it is the latter's piety that is to the fore. It is as lawgiver that the biblical prophet is primarily renowned in Irish sources, as elsewhere in the medieval world. *Liber ex lege Moysi* was an influential Irish compendium of Old Testament law which may date from the seventh century.[95] It has been suggested that King Alfred drew on the text in his compilation of his lawbook, *Domboc*.[96] *Recht Moisi* ('the law of Moses') is frequently referred to in Irish texts, and was brought to Ireland by St Finnian of Moville, Co. Donegal, according to some sources.[97] The tablets on which this law was written are also prevalent throughout the literature.[98] Moreover, his fame as a poet is reflected in the attribution to him of a cosmological poem in Irish.[99] Nevertheless, this is not the Mosaic aspect highlighted in the *Cogadh* at least overtly; as a religious leader, Moses recalls the holy Brian beseeching God through the psalms as the Clontarf battle raged. The image of a Christian leader seeking God's assistance in a conflict presented as one against a heathen enemy had very particular resonances against a contemporary background of crusading.[100] The implication is that as the equivalent of Moses, Brian's actions and approach are justified by God.[101]

Cumulatively, the identification of Brian with a trio of biblical leaders in turn – David, Solomon and Moses – serves to justify his life's work in divine terms. As a result, his legacy should continue, an implication reinforced by the preceding depiction of him as Augustus Caesar and Alexander the Great who are both associated with imperial continuity in medieval historiography. It was in this context, therefore, that the *Cogadh* was read. As part of that reading, a

'Absalom, Absalom! Translating the story of King David in medieval Ireland'. **95** Sven Meeder, 'The Liber ex lege Moysi: notes and text', *Journal of Medieval Latin*, 19 (2009), 173–219; on the difficulties of dating the text, see 181–2; for a general introduction, see Raymond Kottje, 'Der Liber ex lege Moysis' in Próinséas Ní Chatháin and Michael Richter (eds), *Irland und die Christenheit: Bibelstudien und Mission, Ireland and Christendom: the Bible and the missions* (Stuttgart, 1987), pp 59–69. **96** Pratt, *Political thought of King Alfred the Great*, p. 230; also Patrick Wormald, *Legal culture in the early medieval west: law as text, image and experience* (London, 1999), p. 34, n. 153. **97** See John Carey, 'Scél Tuáin meic Chairill', *Ériu*, 35 (1984), 93–111, at 107. **98** See, for example, R.I. Best (ed. and trans.), 'The settling of the manor of Tara', *Ériu*, 4 (1910), 121–72. **99** John Carey, 'A cosmological poem attributed to Moses' in Seán Duffy (ed.), *Princes, prelates and poets in medieval Ireland: essays in honour of Katharine Simms* (Dublin, 2013), pp 412–43. **100** See Máire Ní Mhaonaigh, 'Pagans and holy men: literary manifestations of twelfth-century reform' in Damian Bracken and Dagmar Ó Riain-Raedel (eds), *Reform and renewal: Ireland and twelfth-century reform* (Dublin, 2006), pp 143–61, at pp 149–51. **101** O'Connor has suggested that the comparisons with David, Solomon and Moses in the text 'help to justify and even glorify the harsh treatment of infidels ascribed to Brian': *Destruction*, p. 298.

pair of Irish heroic kings, Conchobar mac Nessa and Cormac mac Airt, may have been compared with Brian by association, since they were firmly identified with Augustus and Solomon respectively in texts contemporary with the *Cogadh*. It is with Lug Lámfhata and Finn mac Cumaill, the Munster leader is linked, however (though not specifically equated), as the eulogy opens, echoing the earlier panegyric on his military leader and son, Murchad. Though his offspring may be Hector, the author of the *Cogadh* does not develop a parallel portrait of Brian as Priam, though he would have been well equipped intellectually to do so. This may have been deliberate; shadows surrounding the Trojan king's depiction should not be allowed to diminish the light of Brian.

Curiously perhaps, this litany of seven historical giants on whom Brian is set on an equal footing (two Irish heroes, an emperor and classical war leader, as well as three biblical kings), is preceded by an introductory observation concerning an earlier Munster ruler, the king-bishop of Cashel, Cormac mac Cuilennáin (d. 908). While the Ua Briain ancestor is said to stand shoulder to shoulder with illustrious past figures, the beheading of a royal predecessor (*oirlech chinn Corbmaic maic Cuilennáin*), may be the sole deed greater than the killing of Brian (*aongníomh badh mó iná sin*).[102] Cormac's role at an earlier point in the narrative is pivotal, as he is cited as the expert (*in rigfilid ocus in sai senchais*, 'the royal poet and sage in *senchas*') concerning the legal privileges of Brian's dynasty, Dál Cais.[103] Elsewhere his famed wisdom in the matter of royal behaviour and procedure is also to the fore, specifically in *Tecosca Cormaic* ('The Teachings of Cormac'), a *speculum principum*-type text associated with him.[104] As an authority on matters of succession, with which Brian's descendants and the *Cogadh*'s audience would have been particularly concerned, Cormac's status was of a special kind. This may explain the exalted position he is given in the text in general and specifically introducing this eulogistic obituary of Brian.

As an ideal king himself and acknowledged expert on royal behaviour and *historia* more generally, Cormac mac Cuilennáin's paramount position underlines the importance of kingship in the text. A narrative *of* kings and *for* kings, the *Cogadh* told the story of royal leaders, at the apex of which was Brian, for his own and other's ruling descendants. It was as medieval historiography, therefore, that the narrative was read. It is in this context that Brian's elaborate obituary and its carefully chosen litany of prominent personages with whom the Munster king is equated should be understood. Whether Irish, imperial, classical or biblical, each specific correspondence was designed to evoke particular resonances embedding the preeminent Ua Briain royal ancestor and 'emperor of the Irish' in a universally recognizable, elevated

102 *CGG*, pp 202–3 (§115). **103** *CGG*, pp 54–5 (§51). **104** Kuno Meyer (ed. and trans.), *The instructions of King Cormac mac Airt*, RIA, Todd Lecture Series 15 (Dublin, 1909).

world. While Brian's heroic deeds were recounted in the body of the *Cogadh*, his glory was reinforced by association with the world's outstanding figures in the skilful death-notice with which the account of the king's killing ends. Embodying the collective traits of seven such influential characters, Brian could tower over them individually; in a familiar medieval rollcall of world leaders, he has been accorded the perfect place.

APPENDIX 8.1

Brian's obituary: text and translation[1]

Nocha dern*adh* i*ar* ccreidem*h* i nÉr*inn* *acht* oirlec*h* chin*n* Corbm*aic* m*aic* Cuilen*n*áin aongníom*h* b*adh* mó iná sin. Rob é sin iar*amh* an treas gein as fearr rug*adh* a nĒr*inn* riam*h*, ocus an treas fer soc*hair* Ér*enn* .i. Lug*h* Lámfada ocus Fiond m*ac* *Cu*m*aill* ocus B*r*ian m*ac* Cein*n*éitt*igh*. Dóig*h* is ē ro fuaslaic fir Ér*enn* ocus a mnā a daeire ocus ó doc*har* gall ocus allm*ur*ach; is ē ro b*r*is cūicc c[h]atha fic*hi*t f*or* gall*aibh*, ocus ros m*ar*b*h* ocus ros ind*ar*b am*al* ro rāidsem*ar* rom*h*ain*n*. Rob ē sin an tOchtauin aob*hdha*, ilb*h*uad*h*ac*h*, im s*h*oc*har* ocus im saordac*h*t a at*h*arr*dha* ocus a c*h*ineoil. Rob é an tAlaxand*ar* tailc, talc*ar* tánaiste *ar* treoir ocus *ar* oirbert ocus *ar* in*n*saigh*idh*, *ar* c*h*ath*aibh* ocus *ar* c*h*osccr*aibh*. Ocus rob ē an Solam*h* sona, saidb*h*ir síod*h*am*ail* na nGaoidel. Rob ē an Dauit dil, díochra, deg*h*menm*nach*, deg*h*gníom*ach* na hÉr*enn* *ar* fīrin*n*e ocus *ar* inracas ocus *ar* coim*h*éitt flait[h]em*h*nais. Rob ē an Maoisi mōr*dha*, mīnétt*r*oc*h*t *ar* c*h*undla ocus *ar* c*h*āid*h*e cr*á*ibt[h]ig*h*e.

'Apart from the beheading of Cormac mac Cuilennáin, there was not committed in Ireland since the coming of Christianity a more significant deed than that [Brian's killing]. Moreover, he was one of the three best people ever born in Ireland, and one of the three men of true benefit for Ireland, i.e., Lug Lámfhata, Finn mac Cumaill and Brian mac Cennétig. For it was he who released the men of Ireland, along with her women, from bondage, and from the oppression of Vikings and foreigners; it was he who won twenty-five battles against Vikings, and he killed and banished them, as we have already related. It was he who was the beautiful, ever-victorious Octavian, as far as the benefit and nobility of his patrimony and kin is concerned. He was the second strong, resolute Alexander for effort, exploit and attack, for battles and for triumphs. And he was the prosperous, powerful, peaceful Solomon of the Irish. He was the faithful, fervent David of Ireland, noble in mind and deed, in terms of integrity and honour, as well as guarding of sovereignty. He was the great, graciously illustrious Moses in the matter of piety and devout holiness.'

1 The text here is reproduced from Brussels, Bibliothèque Nationale, MS 2569–2572, fol. 132, written by Míchéal Ó Cléirigh; the translation is my own. All expansions are italicized; 7 has been silently expanded to *ocus*. Punctuation is editorial, as are accents indicating length; macrons are used when the length mark is scribal. Square brackets mark letters omitted by the scribe.

The battle of Clontarf: the archaeological evidence

ANDREW HALPIN

INTRODUCTION

An essay on the archaeological evidence for the battle of Clontarf could prove to be a very thin affair because, if the truth be told, there is in fact no direct archaeological evidence for the battle. Not a single weapon or any other item of militaria is known that can definitely be associated with this great event. The only known eleventh-century object from Clontarf is a fine ringed pin (fig. 9.1), decorated with inlaid silver and niello ornament in Ringerike style.[1] It could, perhaps, have been worn by somebody who fought at Clontarf – although even that is far from certain – but it cannot be considered as archaeological evidence of the battle in any meaningful sense. The best candidate for a weapon that might actually have been used at the battle is a fragmentary sword (fig. 9.2) probably discovered in the late nineteenth century at Dollymount, on the shore of Dublin Bay directly east of Clontarf. This is at least 1km from Clontarf, although it could be suggested with some plausibility that the presence of a sword at Dollymount might reflect an attempt by at least one defeated warrior to get back to his ship in the bay. A more substantial difficulty in linking this sword with Clontarf is chronology, as the sword is of Petersen Type H, which is dated (in Norway) from *c*.800 to *c*.950.[2] Thus it could have been over two hundred years old at the time of the battle, although there is a suggestion that this sword can be dated later, rather than earlier, within this range.[3] It is not impossible that swords of considerable vintage were used at Clontarf but the alternative explanation by Harrison and Ó Floinn, that the sword reflects the presence of an otherwise unrecorded Viking burial at Dollymount, is probably more likely to be true.[4] One other sword might, even more speculatively, be linked with Clontarf. This sword (fig. 9.3) was excavated from a later eleventh-century context at Christchurch Place in Dublin but probably dates to the late tenth or early eleventh centuries.[5] Thus it may well

1 Thomas Fanning, *Viking Age ringed pins from Dublin*, National Museum of Ireland, Medieval Dublin Excavations 1962–81, Ser. B, vol. 4 (Dublin, 1994), p. 109: DRP252. 2 Jan Petersen, *De Norske vikingesverd: En typologisk-kronologisk studie over vikingetidens vaaben* (Christiania/Oslo, 1919), pp 89–101. 3 Stephen J. Harrison and Raghnall Ó Floinn, *Viking graves and grave-goods in Ireland*, National Museum of Ireland Medieval Dublin Excavations 1962–81, Ser. B, vol. 11 (Dublin, 2015), pp 83, 524. 4 Ibid., pp 523–4. 5 Andrew Halpin, *Weapons and warfare in Viking and medieval Dublin*, National Museum of Ireland Medieval Dublin Excavations 1962–81, Ser. B, vol. 9 (Dublin, 2008), pp 153–5, 249–50: DWP609.

9.1 Copper alloy ringed pin, decorated with inlaid silver and niello Ringerike-style interlace, found at Clontarf *c.*1905 (National Museum of Ireland acq. no. 1907:116; photograph courtesy of National Museum of Ireland).

have been in Dublin in 1014 and could, conceivably, have actually been used at Clontarf – in which case it must have belonged to one of those fortunate Dublin warriors who returned alive from the battle. This is, however, pure speculation and should not be taken too seriously.

BATTLEFIELD ARCHAEOLOGY AND THE NATURE OF EVIDENCE

Before proceeding to discuss any other matters, therefore, it is necessary to consider why there is no direct archaeological evidence for this famous battle. Needless to say, any doubts about the historicity of the battle can be dismissed; it definitely took place in 1014, quite possibly on Good Friday.[6] But where did it take place? Has the site of the battle been definitively established, or is it possible that we are simply looking in the wrong place for archaeological evidence? Perhaps the earliest and most reliable documentary sources for the battle, the Annals of Ulster and the Annals of Inisfallen, do not actually mention Clontarf at all, merely referring to the battle as taking place at or near Dublin.[7] Clontarf is first mentioned two or three generations later, in *Cogadh Gáedhel re Gallaibh*.[8] In this context it is, however, the kind of relatively minor

6 Duffy, *Brian Boru*, pp 220–1. 7 *AU*, *AI*; see Duffy, *Brian Boru*, pp 174–89 for an assessment of the value of these sources. 8 For differing views on the dating of *Cogadh*

9.2 Iron sword of ninth- or tenth-century date 'found in the sand near Dollymount Co. Dublin' in or before 1872 (National Museum of Ireland acq. no. 1872:36; photograph courtesy of National Museum of Ireland).

incidental detail that is not easily explained except as a genuine memory of the event. There can, therefore, be no reasonable grounds for doubting that something happened that day at Cluain Tarbh. But this begs further questions: what exactly was that 'something' and why did it happen at Cluain Tarbh? What, moreover, *was* Cluain Tarbh in 1014 and where, precisely, was it?

Irish place-names like Clontarf that contain the element *cluain* (meaning a meadow, often one reclaimed from water, forest or bog) are frequently associated with early medieval church sites.[9] There is a medieval church site at Clontarf but there is no definite evidence that it existed before the late twelfth century. In the most recent discussion of this issue, Colm Lennon appears not to rule out the church site 'possibly stretching back to the early Christian period' but acknowledges that the late twelfth-century Templar church is 'the first certain ecclesiastical structure' and that 'modern authorities do not attribute greater antiquity to the church and parish of Clontarf than the time of the Anglo-Norman settlement'.[10] Although the matter is not finally settled, it is fair to say that the burden of evidence and of scholarly opinion points to there being no church here in 1014. It can also be said, with considerable confidence, that there is no evidence at all for any other – non-ecclesiastical – settlement at Clontarf in the early eleventh century. Lennon suggests that the 'vill of Clumtorf' recorded in 1199 may have originated as a 'coastal station' or 'outpost' of Hiberno-Norse Dublin but even this is dated after 1014.[11] In 1014, therefore, Cluain Tarbh may have referred to nothing more than an area of low-lying land on the north shore of Dublin Bay, without any permanent settlement and whose only significance was that it lay on the coastal route from Dublin towards Howth. *Cogadh Gáedhel re Gallaibh*

Gáedhel re Gallaibh, see Máire Ní Mhaonaigh, 'Cogad Gáedel re Gallaib: some dating considerations', *Peritia*, 9 (1995), 354–77; Denis Casey, 'A reconsideration of the authorship and transmission of *Cogadh Gáedhel re Gallaibh*', *PRIA*, 113C (2013), 139–61. **9** Patrick J. O'Connor, *Atlas of Irish place-names* (Newcastle West, Co. Limerick, 2001), p. 53. **10** Colm Lennon, 'The medieval manor of Clontarf, 1171–1540' in Seán Duffy (ed.), *Medieval Dublin XII* (Dublin, 2012), pp 190–2; see also idem, *That field of glory: the story of Clontarf, from battleground to garden suburb* (Dublin, 2014), pp 9, 81, n.2. **11** Lennon, 'The medieval manor of Clontarf', p. 190; Lennon, *That field of glory*, p. 10.

9.3 Iron sword, probably of late tenth- or early eleventh-century date, excavated from a later eleventh-century context at Christchurch Place, Dublin (National Museum of Ireland acq. no. E122:94; photograph courtesy of National Museum of Ireland).

seems to suggest that the battle began when Sitriuc's forces and their allies marched out, presumably from Dublin, in response to Brian's army raiding Fine Gall and specifically Howth.[12] It is quite conceivable that Brian pillaged these important lands around Dublin specifically to draw Sitriuc out of the town and provoke a battle, bearing in mind Brian's experience of unsuccessfully besieging Dublin for several months at the end of 1013. If we imagine Sitriuc's forces marching out from Dublin to engage Brian's army in the

12 *CGG*, p. 155.

vicinity of Howth, an initial encounter at Cluain Tarbh makes a good deal of sense.

Even granting that the action began at Cluain Tarbh, however, it could well have extended over a much larger area, particularly if reports of the battle lasting from early morning until late evening are accurate. It is quite clear from all the historical sources that Brian's objective – and the true focus of the battle – was Dublin itself. The battle, therefore, could potentially have extended over much of the area between Clontarf and Dublin. Centuries of urban development and reclamation of the bay have radically changed this landscape, adding to the difficulty of discussing the site of the battle. The early eleventh-century town of Dublin was vastly smaller than today and the bay extended much further inland, meaning that Clontarf in 1014 was located over 4km away from Dublin across the bay (see fig. 9.4). The annals known as Chronicon Scotorum claim that the battle was fought 'from the Tolcha to Áth Cliath', although this is perhaps qualified by a statement in the Annals of the Four Masters that the defeated forces were 'routed … from Tulcainn to Áth-cliath'. While neither of these sources would generally be regarded as the most reliable accounts of Clontarf, this particular detail of a rout of the defeated army back towards Dublin is entirely credible. In the 1760s, while what is now Parnell Square was being laid out, it was reported that large deposits of human remains, apparently with associated weapons, were discovered.[13] These were considered, at the time, to be remains from the battle of Clontarf, which seems a bit far-fetched until one looks at the location in relation to the original topography of the area. Parnell Square is, in fact, right on what would have been the main route from Clontarf and the mouth of the river Tolka to medieval Dublin. Unfortunately, none of the material reported in the 1760s survives and a connection with Clontarf can neither be proved nor disproved. Nevertheless, this very uncertainty points to one possible explanation for the lack of archaeological evidence for the battle – it may simply be that we have not identified the right location.

A more convincing explanation for the lack of archaeological evidence, however, is rooted in the nature of battlefield archaeology. A recent episode of the popular television series 'Time Team', first broadcast in December 2013, explored another famous eleventh-century battle, at Hastings in 1066, whose status in English history is comparable to that of Clontarf in Irish history. Both the traditionally accepted site of the battle and the leading alternative location were investigated by 'Time Team' and ultimately rejected in favour of a third – so far entirely unproven – location. This is in spite of the fact that the battle of

13 Patrick Traynor, 'Where was the battle of Clontarf fought', *The Irish Builder*, 39 (1897), 106, quoting an account in the *Dublin Magazine* for June 1763, attributed to Edward Ledwich; see also Raghnall Ó Floinn, 'The archaeology of the early Viking Age in Ireland' in Clarke et al. (eds), *Ireland and Scandinavia*, p. 134.

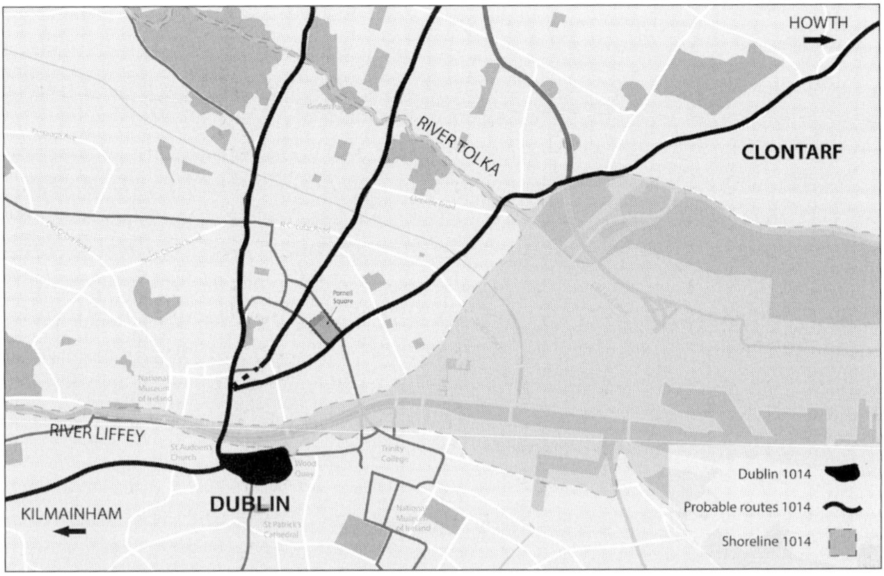

9.4 Conjectural map of the Dublin Bay area as it might have been in 1014.

Hastings undoubtedly has far better documentation than Clontarf, including the not inconsiderable fact of the Benedictine abbey of Battle, founded by William the Conqueror himself within a few years of 1066. The location of the abbey's high altar traditionally marks the very spot where the English King Harold died at the height of the battle – a tradition that has nearly contemporary attestation and which essentially represents the *raison d'être* of the abbey.[14] Notwithstanding this apparently clear evidence, 'Time Team' rejected the traditional battle site, largely because extensive excavation and metal detector survey failed to produce any tangible evidence for the battle.[15] There were, to be sure, other considerations in this rejection and it is not the purpose of this essay to assess the merits of the various contenders for the site of the battle of Hastings. However, the implicit assumption that the correct location should be identifiable by physical evidence – presumably in the form of weaponry or other artefacts, or perhaps human remains – is open to serious question. There are good reasons for suggesting that this is not necessarily the case.

Hastings is not alone among major medieval battlefields in Britain to have produced little or nothing in the way of archaeological evidence. At the site of Scotland's iconic battle of Bannockburn (1314) intensive archaeological

14 *The Anglo-Saxon chronicle*, ed. and trans. M.J. Swanton (London, 1996), p. 219; William of Malmesbury, *Gesta regum Anglorum. The history of the English kings*, ed. and trans. R.A.B. Mynors, R.M. Thomson and M. Winterbottom (Oxford, 1998), iii, 267.3, p. 493. 15 'Renewed debate over battle of Hastings location', http://www.historyextra.com/feature/renewed-debate-over-battle-hastings-location, accessed 3 Apr. 2016.

fieldwork has undoubtedly enhanced our understanding of the probable course of the battle. Nevertheless, in terms of hard archaeological evidence it has produced only three equestrian artefacts – a spur fragment, a stirrup and a harness pendant – none of which can definitively be associated with the battle.[16] These results from Hastings and Bannockburn should come as no surprise, as there is considerable evidence to suggest that medieval battlefields were typically picked clean shortly after the fighting ended. Weapons and armour were far too valuable to be left lying around and would have been gathered up in the immediate aftermath of the battle, mainly by the victorious side as part of the spoils of victory. Once the victors had moved on, anything they left behind – including the clothing and other equipment of the dead – was likely to be picked up by local inhabitants. Indeed, if one looks at the very scene in the Bayeux Tapestry where Harold is killed at Hastings, one can see precisely this process illustrated in the lower margin, where the bodies of the slain are already being stripped of their armour and weapons, apparently by civilians.[17] Pollard notes that 'the scavenging of battle sites was almost an industry' in the medieval period.[18] Even on a battlefield as recent and as well recorded as Little Bighorn (1876) in the United States, modern archaeological research uncovered relatively little evidence for the equipment or clothing of the combatants and this was explained largely in terms of the scavenging of the battlefield in the wake of the action.[19]

Once stripped, the corpses of the slain would not have been left lying on the battlefield but would normally have been removed, either for formal burial elsewhere, or to be interred in mass graves such as those discovered at the site of the battle of Towton in Yorkshire, fought in 1461 during the Wars of the Roses.[20] *Cogadh Gáedhel re Gallaibh* explicitly describes both processes taking place in the aftermath of Clontarf, when the remnants of Brian's army returned to the battlefield three days later and 'buried every one of their people that they were able to recognize' and 'carried thirty of the nobles who were killed there to their territorial churches, wherever they were situated all over Erinn'. This account, while it cannot be verified, again carries the ring of truth. Such mass graves could often be located some distance from the actual battlefield and even when discovered they generally – as at Towton – contain

16 'Finding the Battle of Bannockburn', http://www.medievalists.net/2015/09/02/finding-the-battle-of-bannockburn/, accessed 3 Apr. 2016. **17** David M. Wilson and Jean Le Carpentier, *The Bayeux Tapestry* (London, 2004 ed.), Plates 71–2. **18** Tony Pollard, 'Battlefield Archaeology' in C.J. Rogers et al. (eds), *The Oxford encyclopaedia of medieval warfare and military technology*, 3 vols (Oxford, 2010), i, p. 132. **19** Douglas D. Scott, Richard A. Fox, Melissa A. Connor and Dick Harmon, *Archaeological perspectives on the battle of the Little Bighorn* (Norman, OK, USA, 1989), p. 90. **20** See Veronica Fiorato, Anthea Boylston and Christopher Knüsel (eds), *Blood red roses: the archaeology of a mass grave from the battle of Towton AD1461* (Oxford, 2000). **21** The only potentially military object recovered from the main mass grave at Towton was a possible armour attachment; Fiorato et al. (eds), *Blood red roses*, pp 30–2, Figure 3.4.

no weapons or armour, because the bodies had been stripped prior to burial.[21] In many ways the exception that proves the rule is the series of mass graves discovered outside the Swedish town of Visby, linked to a battle fought in 1361. Unusually, the corpses of the slain seem to have been left lying on the battlefield for a number of days, in hot weather, before burial began – by which time stripping the bodies was apparently either impossible or unacceptably unpleasant. Almost uniquely, on this occasion, the corpses were buried in their armour and, as a result, the Visby mass graves have become a treasure trove for students of medieval armour.[22] Nevertheless, Visby is very much an exceptional case and it is far more normal for medieval battlefields to produce little or nothing in terms of physical archaeological evidence.

A final and rather obvious issue is the fact that, whatever the location and extent of the area in which the battle of Clontarf was fought, it has – unlike Hastings or Bannockburn – been subjected to intensive urban development, particularly over the past two centuries, which is likely to have destroyed much, if not all, of whatever archaeological evidence may once have existed. It may not, therefore, be reasonable to expect any direct archaeological evidence of the battle of Clontarf to survive. It might in fact be far more surprising if, at some point in the future, any such evidence is discovered.

WEAPONS, ARMOUR AND TACTICS

Be that as it may, while we may not have any evidence directly from the battle itself, we have a wealth of archaeological evidence for the types of weapons and armour that would have been used at Clontarf. Combined with information from historical sources about the tactics of warfare and how these weapons were used, this allows us to recreate the likely outline of the battle. The *Cogadh* lists the weapons used by the 'Viking' side (i.e., Sitriuc's Dublin forces and their Scandinavian allies) as 'murderous, poisoned arrows … polished, yellow-shining bows … sharp, rough, dark spears … [and] strong, powerful, stout swords'; there is also a later reference to 'the stout bright axes of the stern, murderous Danars'.[23] The weapons used by Brian's forces are listed as 'spears glittering, well riveted, empoisoned … terrible sharp darts (*biraithi*) … to be violently cast at the heroes of valour and bravery … great warlike, bright, beautiful, variegated shields, with bosses of brass, and elegant chains of bronze … powerful, strong … broad, well-set Lochlann axes … for cutting and maiming the close well-fastened coats of mail … well-tempered, quick, sharp swords … for hewing and for hacking'.[24] From this account it will be seen that spears, axes and swords are common to both sides whereas bows and

22 See Bengt Thordemann, *Armour from the battle of Wisby, 1361*, 2 vols (Stockholm, 1939).
23 *CGG*, pp 159–61, 181. 24 *CGG*, pp 161–3.

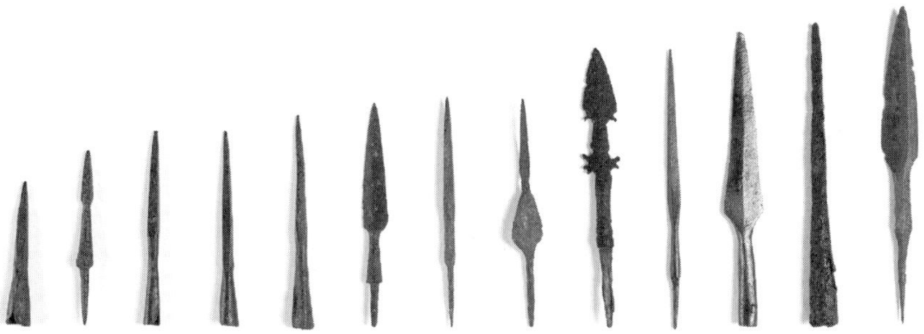

9.5 Selection of iron arrowheads excavated in Dublin, typical of the range of arrowheads that would have been used at Clontarf (photograph courtesy of National Museum of Ireland).

9.6 Wooden bow excavated at Ballinderry crannog, Co. Westmeath (National Museum of Ireland acq. no. 1932:7252; photograph courtesy of National Museum of Ireland).

9.7 Selection of very small iron spearheads of tenth- or eleventh-century date, excavated in Dublin (photograph courtesy of National Museum of Ireland).

arrows are apparently unique to the 'Viking' side and darts are unique to the 'Irish' side. All of this is fully supported by the broad pattern of archaeological and historical evidence.[25]

We can imagine that the fighting at Clontarf would probably have begun with an exchange of volleys of light missiles – arrows (fig. 9.5), small spears or darts and probably sling-stones – from distance. Abundant evidence for the widespread use of archery by Viking and Hiberno-Norse warriors contrasts with remarkably little evidence for the use of the bow by the Irish at this period.[26] This is despite the fact that the finest medieval bow known from Ireland came from a tenth-century context at Ballinderry crannog, Co. Westmeath (fig. 9.6).[27] However it is explained, it seems that this powerful bow

25 See Halpin, *Weapons and warfare*. **26** Ibid., pp 35–8, 50–62, 75–129. **27** Andy Halpin, 'The Ballinderry bow: an under-appreciated Viking weapon?' in Howard B. Clarke and Ruth Johnson (eds), *The Vikings in Ireland and beyond: before and after the battle of Clontarf* (Dublin, 2015), pp 151–60.

9.8 A selection of large iron spearheads from the period of Clontarf, one of which (1185:Wk046) produced a radiocarbon determination at 95% probability of AD898–1024 (National Museum of Ireland acq. nos, left to right, 1995:1580, 1995:1583, P0920, 1185:Wk046 and 1995:1581; photograph courtesy of National Museum of Ireland).

must ultimately be regarded as a Viking, rather than an Irish weapon and may be typical of the types of bows used at Clontarf. All the indications are that the Vikings and their Hiberno-Norse descendants used archery mainly in preliminary missile exchanges, to 'soften up' the enemy at the beginning of a battle. The corresponding weapon on the Irish side, used in the initial exchanges,

9.9 Iron sword with hilt fittings decorated with interlace in silver and niello, probably late eleventh century in date, from Lough Derg on the river Shannon near Curraghmore, Co. Tipperary (National Museum of Ireland acq. no. 1988:226; photograph courtesy of National Museum of Ireland).

was the 'dart', or short throwing spear, for which there are abundant historical references. Ironically, the best archaeological evidence for this weapon may come from Dublin, where a striking preponderance of very small spearheads is best explained as evidence that Hiberno-Norse warriors were borrowing the use of very small throwing spears from the Irish (fig. 9.7).[28]

After such exchanges from distance, the armies would have come together in hand-to-hand fighting where spears, swords and axes were the main weapons used. Both sides would have used round wooden shields for defence.[29] Larger spears with long, well-made iron heads would have been used on both sides, by warriors of all social grades, for boring and thrusting in hand-to-hand combat (fig. 9.8).[30] The sword was, of course, the most prestigious weapon – though not necessarily the most important in military reality. The sword referred to earlier, found in a later eleventh-century context at Christchurch Place in Dublin but probably dating to the late tenth/early eleventh centuries (fig. 9.3), could conceivably have actually been used at Clontarf. Whether it was or not, it is an example of the type of very well-made swords available to the wealthier warriors at Clontarf. Lest one is tempted to think of such swords being used only on the 'Viking' side, one should recall the very fine sword that was recovered in the 1980s from Lough Derg on the Shannon – the very heart of Brian's kingdom. Although this sword (fig. 9.9) is probably a generation or two later than Clontarf, it should remind us that by the eleventh century good-quality swords were available to Irish warriors of means. Another fine sword, probably dating to the later tenth century, was recently recovered from the Shannon at Banagher, Co. Offaly (fig. 9.10). Given how frequently Brian Boru sent fleets of ships up the Shannon in the late tenth century,[31] it is entirely possible that this sword could have belonged to one of Brian's warriors.

For those who could not afford such swords, the axe was a cheaper but very effective substitute. The use of axes as weapons seems to have been introduced by the Vikings to Ireland, where it was previously unknown.[32] Finds from Viking graves indicate that during the ninth century the axes used by Viking warriors were essentially similar to those used as woodworking tools.[33] During the tenth century, however, specialized forms of axes, lighter in weight but with broader cutting edges, were developed – presumably within Scandinavia – for use in warfare. These axes – referred to as Type M in the typology developed by the Norwegian archaeologist Petersen – were widely adopted by Irish warriors during the eleventh and twelfth centuries and it is interesting that the author of the *Cogadh* still refers to them as *Lochlann* (or 'Viking') axes.[34] Three such

28 Halpin, *Weapons and warfare*, pp 131–2, 147. **29** See Harrison and Ó Floinn, *Viking graves*, pp 116–28. **30** Halpin, *Weapons and warfare*, pp 131–47; Harrison and Ó Floinn, *Viking graves*, pp 93–114. **31** Halpin, *Weapons and warfare*, pp 14–15. **32** Ibid., p. 163. **33** Harrison and Ó Floinn, *Viking graves*, pp 114–16. **34** Halpin, *Weapons and warfare*, pp 163–5; *CGG*, p. 163.

9.10 Iron sword, probably dating to the later tenth century, from the river Shannon at Banagher or Kylebeg, Co. Offaly (National Museum of Ireland acq. no. 2012:227; photograph courtesy of National Museum of Ireland).

9.11 Three battle axes recovered from a boat sunk in Lough Corrib at Carrowmoreknock, Co. Galway; both the boat and one of the axe shafts have returned radiocarbon dates (UBA-24468–9) calibrated, at 95% probability, to 1018–1155 (National Museum of Ireland acq. nos 13E0213:001–3; photograph courtesy of National Museum of Ireland).

axes were discovered in 2013 in a boat that sank in Lough Corrib at Carrowmoreknock, near Oughterard, Co. Galway, sometime between 1020 and 1150 (fig. 9.11). These give us a good idea of the type of axes that would have been used – on both sides – at Clontarf. They are specialized battle-axes with broad cutting edges of welded steel and occur in a range of sizes. The smaller axes were probably mounted on relatively short shafts and used one-handed but the largest axes seem, in some cases at least, to have been mounted on longer shafts for two-handed use, a thoroughly fearsome prospect. A scene from the battle of Hastings on the Bayeux Tapestry shows both one-handed and two-handed axes being used by Anglo-Saxon – or Anglo-Danish – warriors,[35] and it seems reasonable to assume the same for Clontarf. Interestingly, the Bayeux Tapestry depicts the English King Harold holding a long, two-handed axe on at least two occasions – once, apparently, on the occasion where he is offered the English crown and again in the famous scene where he is killed at Hastings.[36] This might warn us against an automatic assumption that such axes were used only by warriors of lower social and economic status.

35 Wilson and Le Carpentier, *The Bayeux Tapestry*, Plate 62. **36** Ibid., Plates 31, 71.

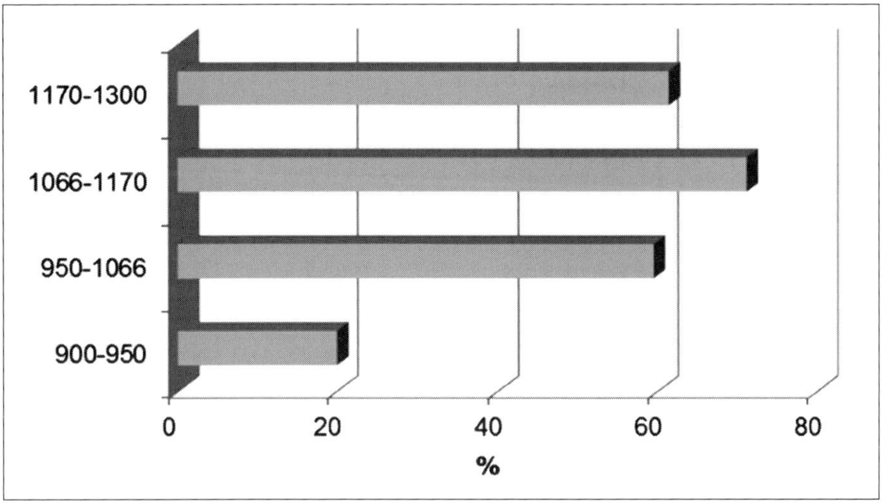

9.12 Relative popularity of armour-piercing arrowheads (as a percentage of total arrowhead assemblage) in Dublin, *c.*950–1300, by chronological sub-periods (after Halpin 2008, Chart 43).

Cogadh Gáedhel re Gallaibh also describes what the different sides wore at the battle and here an important distinction is visible. As in other Irish sources of this period, the text suggests that the clothing worn in the battle by Brian's forces, even by the nobility, did not differ significantly from normal civilian dress. We are told that the Dál Cais fought in tunics or shirts known as a *léine* or *scuird* (a loanword from Old Norse *skyrta*), both probably of linen and both common in civilian as well as military contexts. Over these was worn another garment, the *inar*, which could also be a civilian's tunic although there are suggestions that it could be made of leather when worn in battle.[37] On the 'Viking' side, however, significant numbers were apparently wearing armour referred to by the term *lúirech*, from the Latin *lorica*, which by the ninth century was regularly used to refer to the hauberk of mail.[38] There is nothing revolutionary in suggesting that Scandinavian and Hiberno-Norse warriors wore mail armour in the eleventh century; this would be readily accepted in other parts of the Viking world.[39] The wearing of mail hauberks was standard among the European warrior elite by the eleventh century at the latest and for Anglo-Saxon England Nicholas Brooks suggests that the widespread use of armour can be traced to the late tenth century in response to the renewed Viking attacks of that period.[40] The common use of armour is also indicated by

37 *CGG*, pp 160–3; Halpin, *Weapons and warfare*, pp 18–20; Mairéad Dunlevy, *Dress in Ireland* (London, 1989), p. 21. 38 Philippe Contamine, *War in the Middle Ages*, trans. Michael Jones (pbk ed., Oxford, 1986), p. 187. 39 See, for instance, Else Roesdahl, *The Vikings*, trans. S.M. Margeson and Kirsten Williams (London, 1992), pp 143–4. 40 Nicholas P. Brooks, 'Arms, status and warfare in Late-Saxon England' in David Hill

archaeological evidence, particularly the predominance of specialized armour-piercing arrowheads which are consistently the most common arrowhead form found in Hiberno-Norse contexts in Dublin from the later tenth century onwards (fig. 9.12).[41] Such evidence suggests that the warriors of Dublin, at the time of Clontarf, were well in touch with the latest military standards of the emerging feudal European nobility and tends to give credence to the literary accounts of widespread use of armour.

It does not seem unreasonable, on the basis of this evidence, to suggest that Dublin, like Anglo-Saxon England, witnessed a major increase in the use of armour from the late tenth century. Little or no direct evidence survives for the forms of armour worn in the early eleventh century, in Ireland or elsewhere,[42] and discussion has, therefore, been largely based on representational evidence, especially the Bayeux Tapestry.[43] The main form of body armour was the hauberk, a mail shirt reaching usually to the knees, under which a long padded undergarment, the aketon or gambeson, was probably worn. Legs could be protected by stocking-like chausses of mail, but these were probably rare at this date.[44] Over the head, throat and neck was worn a mail coif with padded leather cap or hood underneath and over which a helmet was worn in combat. The *Cogadh* repeatedly describes the hauberks (*lúirig*) of the 'Vikings' at Clontarf as *trénduailaig* or *trédualach*, variously translated by Todd as 'treble', 'triple-plated' and 'thrice-riveted'.[45] Whatever its precise meaning, this term *trédualach* echoes the reference to 'triple armour (*lorica trilicem*)' in an Anglo-Saxon source describing a group of Danish huscarles in 1040.[46] Typical helmets of this period were of simple, conical form; these could be of single-piece construction or formed of triangular plates of iron riveted to a framework of iron bands – the *Spangenhelm*.[47] In the latter case an arrangement of four vertical bands, rising from a circular basal band, and meeting at the apex, was typical and this type of construction may possibly be intended in a reference to 'four-cornered (*cetharchoir*)' helmets in *Táin Bó Cúailgne*.[48]

(ed.), *Ethelred the Unready: papers from the millenary conference*, British Archaeological Reports, British Series 59 (Oxford, 1978), pp 81–103. **41** Halpin, *Weapons and warfare*, pp 168–9, 176–80. **42** See Halpin, *Weapons and warfare*, p. 178 and Pl. XXIX for a small fragment of mail armour found at Christchurch Place in Dublin in a possibly eleventh-century context. **43** For example, Claude Blair, *European armour* circa *1066 to* circa *1700* (London, 1958), pp 19–27; Ian Peirce, 'Arms, armour and warfare in the eleventh century' in R. Allen Brown (ed.), *Anglo-Norman studies X: proceedings of the Battle Conference 1987* (Woodbridge, 1988), pp 237–57; Brooks, 'Arms, status and warfare', pp 94–7. **44** Blair, *European armour*, pp 23–4; Ian Peirce, 'The knight, his arms and armour *c*.1150–1250' in Marjorie Chibnall (ed.), *Anglo-Norman studies XV: proceedings of the XV Battle Conference and of the XI Colloquio Medievale of the Officina di Studi Medievali 1992* (Woodbridge, 1993), p. 251. **45** *CGG*, pp 53, 153, 159, 181. **46** Nicholas Hooper, 'Anglo-Saxon warfare on the eve of the conquest: a brief survey' in R. Allen Brown (ed.), *Proceedings of the Battle conference on Anglo-Norman studies I 1978* (Ipswich, 1979), p. 85. **47** Blair, *European armour*, pp 25–7; Peirce, 'Arms, armour and warfare in the eleventh century', pp 240–3. **48** *TBC LL* l. 2212.

Downward-projecting nasal guards appear to have been common on both types of helmet.

There are, however, a number of references to armour being worn by Irish warriors at this date. On two occasions in the twelfth-century version of *Táin Bó Cúailgne* in the Book of Leinster, descriptions of the noise of approaching warriors include references to the sounds of helmets (*cathbarr*) and armour (*lúrech*).[49] The eleventh-/twelfth-century *Lebor na Cert* contains frequent references to *lúirecha* – presumably mail hauberks – as stipends given by overkings to subordinates, to be used in reciprocal military service.[50] Such evidence has sometimes been viewed with suspicion by historians. In his edition of *Lebor na Cert* Dillon expressed uncertainty about the reliability of these references, while Kathleen Hughes had no doubts, seeing them as evidence for the unreliability of *Lebor na Cert* itself and remarking disdainfully that 'it is little use for archaeologists to look for all these hundreds of coats of mail'.[51] An open mind might, however, be a more appropriate response. The early twelfth-century text *Caithréim Cellacháin Chaisil* contains a possible reference to armour being worn by Irish warriors, in its description of the armies of a number of Leinster kings as equipped with armour (*lúirech*), aketons (*cotún*) and helmets (*cathbarr*), although it is possible that the reference may alternatively be to Hiberno-Norse allies of the Leinster kings.[52] The text also refers to a thousand men of the Delbna, Gailenga and Luigne as being composed of equal numbers with armour and without armour;[53] the terms used are *eidedac* and *gan eided* and the root term *eided*, denoting armour in a generic sense, also begins to occur in annalistic sources of the twelfth century.[54] But what form of armour is being referred to? In view of the overall thrust of the sources that Irish warriors did not wear armour, it may be that *eided* – at least in a twelfth-century context – refers to protective clothing of organic materials, rather than mail or other metallic armour. Harbison has discussed references to such clothing in later medieval sources,[55] but important information also exists in pre-Anglo-Norman sources. In *Caithréim Cellacháin Chaisil* the account of a battle between the armies of Munster and the Norse of Limerick tells us that the Munster men wore *inair* – similar to the Dál Cais at Clontarf in *Cogadh Gáedhel re Gallaibh* – but also wore garments called *cotúin*

49 *TBC LL*, ll. 2852ff, 4213ff. 50 Myles Dillon (ed.), *Lebor na Cert: The Book of Rights*, ITS 46 (Dublin, 1962), pp 5, 8–11, 30–43, 56–61, 66–71, 78–91, 95–99, 104–09, etc.; see also Marie Therese Flanagan, 'Irish and Anglo-Norman warfare in twelfth-century Ireland' in Thomas Bartlett and Keith Jeffery (eds), *A military history of Ireland* (Cambridge, 1996), p. 55. 51 Dillon (ed.), *Lebor na Cert*, p. xix; Kathleen Hughes, *Early Christian Ireland: introduction to the sources* (London, 1972), p. 287. 52 Alexander Bugge (ed.), *Caithréim Cellacháin Caisil: the victorious career of Cellachan of Cashel, or the wars between the Irishmen and the Norsemen in the middle of the 10th century* (Christiania/Oslo, 1905), p. 114. 53 Ibid., p. 89. 54 Peter Harbison, 'Native arms and armour in medieval Gaelic literature, 1170–1600', *The Irish Sword*, 12 (1975–6), 180–1; *AT* 1116, 1131. 55 Ibid.

and collars or neck protection called *muincedha*.[56] The *cotún* is clearly a loanword, either from the Middle English *aketoun* or Old French *haqueton*, both of which refer to the long, padded garment of leather or cloth normally worn under a mail hauberk but which, in this case, seems to have been the first line of defence. Regardless of whether the *inar* can be seen specifically as a form of armour, the *cotún* and *muince* can hardly be anything else and are further evidence that armour, if only of a non-metallic character, was worn by the Irish, at least in the twelfth century.

In reality we know very little about the actual course of the battle of Clontarf. Annalistic references tell us little or nothing and even if one accepts the reliability of the account in the *Cogadh*, it actually gives relatively little detail, devoting most of its attention instead to a stylized series of snapshots of the exploits of prominent individuals. There are, however, a number of significant details that one would dearly love to be able to verify. These include the claim that the battle lasted 'from sunrise to evening' and that 'it was at the full tide the Foreigners came out to fight the battle in the morning and the tide had come to the same place again at the close of the day, when the Foreigners were defeated'.[57] This particular detail was famously 'confirmed' for the translator of the *Cogadh*, James Henthorn Todd, by the mathematician Samuel Haughton, who calculated that on Good Friday (April 23rd) 1014 sunrise would have occurred in Dublin Bay at approximately 5.30a.m. and sunset at 5.55p.m.[58] On other points, however, no confirmation is currently available, such as the claim that some, at least, of the fighting could be seen from the ramparts of Dublin,[59] and extended as far as 'Dubhgall's Bridge' (presumably, therefore, a bridge over the Liffey, rather than the Tolka).[60] The text also claims that Brian's army adopted a relatively complex arrangement at the outset of the battle. At its core were three main divisions – which is fairly standard for the period – consisting of the men of Dál Cais (or Tuadmuman), the rest of Munster (or Desmuman) and Connacht, respectively, although the author notes conflicting traditions as to whether the Munster men were drawn up behind the Dál Cais or whether the two divisions fought side by side.[61] In either case the three main divisions were flanked by 'the ten great stewards (*mórmair*) of Brian … with their Foreign auxiliaries (*gall socraitib*)' on the right wing and by the Uí Briúin and Conmaicne on the left. On the opposing side there were also three main divisions. At the front were the overseas forces that Sitriuc of Dublin had recruited from Orkney, Man and elsewhere; next came

56 Bugge, *Caithréim Cellacháin Caisil*, pp 64–6. **57** *CGG*, p. 191. **58** Samuel Haughton, 'On the time of High Water in Dublin Bay, on Good Friday, the 23rd April, 1014, the day of the battle of Clontarf', *PRIA*, 7 (1857–61), 495–8; James Henthorn Todd, 'Some remarks on the history of the battle of Clontarf, in connexion with Mr Haughton's determination of the time of High Water in Dublin Bay on Good Friday, April 23, 1014', *PRIA*, 7 (1857–61), 498–511. **59** *CGG*, pp 181, 191. **60** *CGG*, p. 185. **61** *CGG*, pp 167–9.

the men of Dublin; to the rear (apparently) were the men of Leinster, under Máelmórda mac Murchada, king of Leinster.

Whatever the truth of this disposition of forces, *Cogadh Gáedhel re Gallaibh*'s description of the actual fighting – other than the formulaic single combats – rings true. Like most battles of the period Clontarf was probably, in the main, a trial of strength between the two armies in which the solidity, rigidity and strength of the formation as a whole was decisive. The *Cogadh* tells us that at Clontarf the armies were drawn up in such a way that 'a four-horsed chariot could run from one end to the other of the line, on both sides'.[62] The meaning of this statement is somewhat obscure but it is clarified by a slightly fuller version given in the roughly contemporary Book of Leinster recension of *Táin Bó Cúailgne*, where at the final battle between Ulster and the rest of Ireland Cú Chulainn's charioteer, Laeg, notes that 'if we were to go in two chariots from one wing of the army to the other along the tips of their weapons, not a hoof nor a wheel nor an axle nor a shaft of those chariots would touch the ground, so densely, so firmly and so strongly are their weapons held in the hands of the soldiers'.[63] This emphasis on the denseness of formations reflects the fact that the principal aim of most fighting in pitched battle at this date was to force the opposing army first to give ground, then to break ranks and finally to flee the field. At the level of the individual warrior the aim was, ideally, to force a breach or opening in the opposing line. Thus the *Cogadh* describes how Brian's son Murchad 'made a hero's breach … through the battalion of the Danmarkians', while on the other side 'the son of Ebric, son of the king of Lochlann [went] into the bosom and centre of the Dál Cais … and the breach of a hero was opened for him wherever he went'.[64] Translated over an entire battle line, a sufficient number of such breaches would result in the opposing formation being forced to break up and, probably, to flee – which, apparently, is what eventually happened at Clontarf.[65]

CONCLUDING REMARKS

Two final points need to be made about the battle. The first is that Clontarf is quite unusual in being, apparently, a genuine pitched battle, something that was quite rare in medieval warfare and especially in Ireland, where most warfare took other forms such as cattle-raids and ambushes.[66] Moreover, it appears to have been a large-scale battle, to judge from the figure in the Annals of Ulster of six thousand dead on Sitriuc's side alone. While this figure cannot be taken literally, it may well be a credible indication of unusually high casualty figures – especially when taken in conjunction with the relatively long list of

62 *CGG*, p. 173 and n. 5. **63** *TBC LL*, ll. 4673ff. **64** *CGG*, pp 189, 195. **65** Halpin, *Weapons and warfare*, pp 21–5. **66** Ibid., pp 21–2.

9.13 Fragment of an antler crossbow nut, from an early eleventh-century context in Fishamble Street, Dublin (National Museum of Ireland acq. no. E190:4321; photograph courtesy of National Museum of Ireland).

named nobles and other prominent figures that died. Duffy may well be justified in referring to 'the sheer unprecedented extent of the slaughter'.[67] While the political and nationalistic dimensions of Clontarf have all too frequently been misinterpreted, its reputation as an unusually important and momentous battle would appear to be fully deserved.

The second point to be noted is that in this context of a major, all-out pitched battle, Brian's army was victorious, albeit with heavy losses. This may seem like stating the obvious but in fact it is extremely significant in view of the quality of the opposition they faced. Several writers have highlighted the superiority of Viking military technology and organization and their more ruthless attitudes to warfare, in the early encounters between Vikings and Irish.[68] One important feature of the archaeological material recovered during excavations in Dublin is the clear evidence that the Hiberno-Norse town, from the later tenth century, was in the vanguard of European military technological development. This is seen in the general quality of the weaponry discovered there, in the evidence for the use of armour and the fact that two-thirds of all arrowheads from Hiberno-Norse Dublin are armour-piercing types, a higher proportion than that recorded in most contemporary excavated sites elsewhere

67 *AU*; Duffy, *Brian Boru*, pp 177–89. 68 Most famously, Daniel Binchy, 'The passing of the old order' in Brian Ó Cuív (ed.), *Proceedings of the International Congress of Celtic Studies* (Dublin, 1962), p. 128 and Etienne Rynne, 'The impact of the Vikings on Irish weapons', *Atti del VI Congresso Internazionale delle Scienze Preistoriche e Protostoriche*, III (Rome, 1966), pp 181–5; see also Francis John Byrne, 'The trembling sod: Ireland in 1169' in *NHI*, ii, p. 10.

in Europe (and the numbers involved are sufficiently large to be statistically meaningful).[69] It is also seen in the presence, in early eleventh-century Dublin, of probably the most advanced weapon then known in northern Europe – the crossbow. In England, debate still continues over whether there is any evidence for the presence of the crossbow prior to the Norman conquest of 1066.[70] In Ireland – or at least in Dublin – that debate is over. A fragment of the antler nut, part of the trigger mechanism of an early crossbow, recovered from an early eleventh-century context in Dublin, raises the distinct prospect that crossbows may have been in use on the Dublin side at Clontarf (fig. 9.13).[71]

Not only did Brian have to face such well-equipped warriors from Dublin but also, as the Annals of Ulster describe them, 'a like number of the Foreigners of Lochlainn along with them, i.e. a thousand breastplates (*lúirech*)'. Regardless of whether these are seen as mercenaries from the Scandinavian settlements of Orkney and Man or, as Duffy has recently suggested, as also including detachments from the Danish forces that had conquered England in 1013,[72] there is no reason to think they were less well equipped than the Dubliners. The fact that a Gaelic Irish army could hold its own and actually emerge victorious against such formidable opposition is surely one of the most outstanding features of this memorable battle. Was this due in part to good fortune, to inspired tactics or to simple superiority of numbers? The surviving sources do not give us the evidence to answer these questions but one conclusion, at least, seems inescapable – that in terms of its equipment and organization, Brian's army must have come close to matching its opponents. Brian's victory at Clontarf is surely evidence for the increasing militarization – among other profound changes – taking place in Ireland, largely as a result of the various impacts (economic, as well as military) of Viking activity. These changes are most clearly visible in the later eleventh and twelfth centuries,[73] but Clontarf is evidence of how far they had progressed by 1014.

69 Halpin, *Weapons and warfare*, especially pp 176–80. **70** Arthur MacGregor, 'Two antler crossbow nuts and some notes on the early development of the crossbow', *Proceedings of the Society of Antiquaries of Scotland*, 107 (1975–6), 317–21; Jim Bradbury, *The medieval archer* (Woodbridge, 1985), pp 25–7; Martin Biddle, *Object and economy in medieval Winchester* (Oxford, 1990), ii, pp 1078–9; Matthew Strickland and Robert Hardy, *The great warbow: from Hastings to the Mary Rose* (Stroud, 2005), pp 65–8. **71** Halpin, *Weapons and warfare*, pp 62–6. **72** Duffy, *Brian Boru*, pp 242–8. **73** Halpin, *Weapons and warfare*, pp 10–15.

Dál Cais after Clontarf

PAUL MacCOTTER

INTRODUCTION

This contribution attempts a brief sketch of the fortunes of the Uí Bhriain descendants of King Brian Bóraime in the secular and ecclesiastical worlds between the time of the battle of Clontarf and the arrival of the Anglo-Normans.

THE UÍ BHRIAIN KINGS AFTER THE DEATH OF BRIAN

Following Brian's death, the rulership of the kingdom of Dál Cais, as we may continue to call it at this time, was disputed between two of his sons, Donnchad and Tadc.[1] This was against the background of the losses suffered by Dál Cais at Clontarf, and which immediately saw an unsuccessful challenge for the kingship of Munster by Eóganacht Raithlind and their king, Domnall son of Dub dá Bairenn. Their territory lay to the west of Cork. Initially Donnchad obtained the kingship with opposition from Tadc, and narrowly escaped an assassination attempt, apparently by a follower of Tadc, in 1019, in which he, Donnchad, had a thumb severed.[2] During this period Dál Cais was plundered by a Connacht army, and lay firmly under the overlordship of Brian's successor as high-king, Máel Sechnaill of Mide. Things improved for Donnchad with the assassination of Tadc in 1023, which he had instigated, and this was followed up by invasions of Connacht, Mide and Laigin to take their hostages, but this effort to expand Dalcassian overlordship was stymied by the opposition of the Uí Néill king of Cenél nEógain and came to nothing.

These efforts marked one of the few highlights of the rather unimpressive career of Donnchad mac Briain. His main problems lay to his east, in the alliance formed between Eóganacht Chaisil and Osraige during the mid-1020s. At this time Eóganacht Chaisil, erstwhile kings of Munster, were experiencing something of a renaissance, having been totally eclipsed by Dál Cais from the mid-960s. There is evidence to suggest that the Eóganacht Chaisil king, Dúngal ua Donnchada, had also challenged for the kingship of Munster after Clontarf.[3]

1 Much of the historical account of the various royal descendants of the line of Brian given here is taken from the excellent synthesis of the sources in Ó Corráin, *Normans*, esp. pp 131–62; see also, John Ryan, 'The O'Briens in Munster after Clontarf', *NMAJ*, 2 (1941), 141–52; 3 (1942–3), 1–52; 189–202. 2 *AI* 1019.6. 3 For a detailed account of east Munster during the eleventh century, and in particular the struggles between the rival

After his death on pilgrimage, in 1025, he was succeeded by MacRaith ua Donnchada, who immediately formed an alliance with Mac Gilla Pátraic, king of neighbouring Osraige to the east. This alliance would endure at least until 1057, in the face of significant Dalcassian pressure, and would accrue significant advantage to both adjacent polities in their respective spheres of Aurmumu and Laigin. The combined territory of both approximated to South Tipperary and Kilkenny, and the evidence would suggest that a constant state of territorial flux existed between these allies and King Donnchad. In 1031, the latter possessed a fortress at Donaskeagh, well within the borders of Eóganacht Chaisil, and yet the king of Arad in northwest Tipperary, a territory on the very borders of Dál Cais itself, was among the followers of the Eóganacht/Osraige alliance in 1043. It may also be significant that the only polities named in the annals as following Donnchad in Munster lay in Clare, north Tipperary and Limerick, the very area that half a century later would come to constitute and delineate the Uí Bhriain kingdom of Tuadmumu or Thomond.[4]

Yet further evidence of the weakness of Donnchad's rule is found in a study of a segment of Eóganacht Chaisil, Clann Donngaile, descendants of Cellachán, the last significant Eóganacht king of Munster (d. 954).[5] His grandson, Sáerbretach (d. 1025) had obtained the temporal lordship of the great Eóganacht monastery of Emly during the early 1000s, using its wealth as a powerbase to reconstruct his family's fortunes. His son in turn, Carthach (a quo MacCarthy), appears to have extended his rule over the western part of Eóganacht Chaisil in opposition to the Uí Donnchada rulers of the east, and had possession of Donaskeagh by 1043, when described as king of Eóganacht. Though slain by Dál Cais in 1045, they were not able to extinguish his line, and his son, Muiredach, seized the headship of Emly by force in 1052, expelling its Dalcassian abbot in the process. During his long life Muiredach appears to have been victorious over the Uí Donnchada, becoming sole king of Eóganacht Chaisil before his death, in 1092. The main point here is that the Clann Donngaile, soon to become Clann Charthaig, were able to resist Donnchad mac Briain to the west and the Uí Donnchada and their Osraige allies to the east for most of the eleventh century. The implications for Donnchad's power in this situation are obvious. However, even though apparently ruling securely only parts of north Munster, we should also note the laws promulgated by Donnchad, which may suggest that, as son of the great 'emperor' Brian Bóraime, Donnchad retained at least some honorary status beyond his actual territorial rule.[6] (His successor Tairdelbach ua Briain would later promulgate an agricultural law in Munster, in 1068.)[7]

claimants to the kingdom of Eóganacht Chaisil, see Paul MacCotter, 'The rise of Meic Carthaig and the political geography of Desmumu', *JCHAS*, 111 (2006), 59–76, at 60–3.
4 *AI* 1031.6, 7; 1043.4; 1058.4. 5 See n. 3 above. 6 *AI* 1040.6, 1050.2. 7 *AI* 1068.4.

The end for Donnchad's rule was engineered by his nephew Tairdelbach, son of Tadc. Tairdelbach had actively opposed his uncle since at least 1031, although this had little effect until twenty years later, when Tairdelbach formed a subservient alliance with the king of Laigin, Diarmait mac Maíl na mBó. The following decade saw extensive warfare targeting Donnchad and led by the Leinster king and his allies. Eventually, in 1063, following several burnings of his capital, Limerick, Donnchad abdicated and went on pilgrimage to Rome where he died.

Tairdelbach's career was much more impressive than that of Donnchad. Initially placed upon the throne of Munster by his overlord, Diarmait mac Maíl na mBó, and facing the opposition of his cousin, Murchad son of Donnchad, he would win out. With Murchad's death, in 1068, Tairdelbach ruled in Munster unopposed. With the death of mac Maíl na mBó in 1072 Tairdelbach immediately went on the offensive, consolidating his position in Munster and, by the following year, had established his authority over Laigin, Mide, Dublin and Connacht. Over the following years he would maintain this dominance and even extend it to include parts of Ulster. The annalists record him as high-king upon his death in 1086, the first Dalcassian to merit this title since his grandfather, Brian.[8]

Tairdelbach was succeeded by his sons Diarmait and Muirchertach, the latter triumphing in the contest to succeed his father. Muirchertach's career began with a six-year war in which he attempted, initially unsuccessfully, to establish his authority in the south. At some stage between 1092 and 1101 he expelled the ruling lines of the Éóganacht Chaisil from their native territory and drove them southwards to Cork.[9] At this time Laigin came under his authority. The tide began to turn in his favour on the national front in 1092 when he established temporary authority over Connacht and Mide. Over the following years this was consolidated, and Muirchertach would then spend the last years of his rule in vain attempts to conquer Ulster. While given the title of high-king, Muirchertach's authority died with him and his successors would never again hold this honour.[10]

The years after 1119 in Munster were largely marked by the division of Munster into northern and southern sections, Tuadmumu and Desmumu, respectively marking the kingdoms of the Uí Bhriain (O'Briens) and Clann Charthaig (MacCarthys). This division was imposed at Glanmire near Cork by the power of Tairdelbach Ua Conchobair, the new high-king.[11] This division tended to hamstring Munster in terms of its relationships with the Uí Chonchobair high-kings and other powers, and was so valuable to its instigators that it was repeated in 1151. The period from 1118 to 1138 was largely one of Clann Charthaig dominance, including the period 1127 to 1138

8 *AU* 1086.4; *AI* 1086.4. **9** MacCotter, 'Rise of Meic Carthaig', 63–4. **10** *AI* 1119.2; *AU* 1119.2. **11** *AI* 1118.8.

when Cormac Mac Carthaig held the kingship of Munster, a rule ended in 1138 with his assassination at the hands of the Uí Bhriain. During this period the Meic Carthaig appear to have regained some foothold in Aurmumu, if indeed they had ever been entirely expelled, and renewed the old alliance with the Osraige. During the period 1118x1121 Cormac Mac Carthaig, then *rigdamna* of Desmumu, dwelt in Rathanny a few miles west of Emly while there are references to other Clann Charthaig connections to Cashel itself during the 1120s and 1130s.[12] The period 1139 to 1151 saw another Tairdelbach Ua Briain secure as king of Munster, only for his rule to collapse in 1151 at the battle of Móin Mór at the hands of the Uí Chonchobair, Meic Carthaig and their allies, re-establishing the Meic Carthaig as kings of Desmumu. Remarkably this conflict remained active even in the face of the Anglo-Norman invasion: as late as 1193 Domnall Mac Carthaig briefly captured Limerick city, not yet invested by the Anglo-Normans. I have elsewhere plotted in some detail the actual boundary changes and border disputes between Tuadmumu and Desmumu during this period, and suffice it to note that the Uí Bhriain were limited to rule of Tuadmumu during the period 1151 to the early 1190s.[13]

DALCASSIAN EXPANSION

One remarkable feature of the reign of both Tairdelbach (d. 1086) mac Taidc and his son Muirchertach (d. 1119) was the number of Uí Bhriain who became kings of territories outside of the Dalcassian homelands. Sometimes these were instituted by these kings themselves as a new development in governance policy but in other cases they were rivals to the main Ua Briain king and were appointed to territories by the latter's enemies. Tairdelbach had made his son and eventual successor Muirchertach king of Dublin in 1075, an appointment repeated by Muirchertach in 1094 in the case of his son, Domnall. In 1079, Art Ua Ruairc, an Ua Briain enemy, made Cennétig Ua Briain king of the Meath petty state of Gailenga while the kingdom of Cenél nEógain itself appointed another Ua Briain renegade, Conchobar, as its king in the 1070s. Perhaps the strangest appointment was that of Domnall mac Taidc as king of the Isles, in 1111, apparently by petition of the native aristocracy.[14]

Nearer to home we note the replacement of non-Dalcassian ruling lines by Uí Bhriain relatives. In the middle of the eleventh century the kingship of the neighbouring territory of Múscraige Tíre (north Tipperary) appears to have been the target of Cú Chaille son of Brian's nephew Cennétig (a quo O'Kennedy), and Cú Chaille's Uí Chennétig descendants had certainly

12 MacCotter, 'Rise of Meic Carthaig', 66–7. 13 Ibid., 70–74. 14 *AI* 1075.4; Byrne, *Irish kings*, 297; Jaski, *Early Irish kingship*, p. 311; Donald Gregory, *History of the Western Highlands and Isles of Scotland* (Edinburgh, 1837), p. 7.

triumphed by the 1150s.[15] Mathgaman, son of King Muirchertach, who died in 1129, appears to have established himself as king of Corcu Baiscinn in west Clare.[16] While such expansion could take the form of replacing kings of existing kingdoms or minimal polities, there is surprisingly little evidence for such expansion. Rather it seems that political power in this period was exercised by imposing taxation and military levy on existing kingdoms and generally not removing their regnal lines. Other expansions at this period were at a lower political level. The expulsion of the Eóganacht from the Cashel area *c*.1100 was not followed by any major resettlement of Dalcassian septs there, but then again not all Eóganacht septs were expelled, while some evidence exists for the reappearance of those expelled. However, there is some evidence of strategic expansions, such as that of the Meic Briain into Aherlow probably during the 1120s.[17]

Another element of Dál Cais power in Munster was fortress-building at strategic locations. A list of these is credited to Brian in *Cogadh Gáedhel re Gallaibh* and this may well have been the case, although some may have been erected later. While some of these appear to have been the result of military occupation of conquered territories, others were clearly aimed at protecting strategic routs leading to Cenn Corad (Kincora), such as Limerick to Cork and the spurs branching off to Aurmumu and Uí Fhidgente, thus controlling all the main routes in central Munster. Others were clearly built along the border with Desmond. The sources name these fortresses as follows:

- Cashel, Co. Tipperary
- Cenn Abrat (Glenosheen near the Red Chair Gap or Bearna Dearg, Co. Limerick)[18]
- Inis Locha Cend (Lough Kent, Newinn, Co. Tipperary)[19]
- Inis Locha Gair (Lough Gur, Co. Limerick)
- Dún Eochair Maige (near Kilmallock, Co. Limerick)[20]
- Dún Trí Liag (Duntryleague, Co. Limerick)
- Dún Crot (Dungrud, near Aherlow, Limerick/Tipperary border)[21]
- Rosach na Riogh (Rossagh near Doneraile, Co. Cork)[22]
- Dún na Sciath (Doneskeagh, northeast of Tipperary town)
- Inis Locha Saiglend (Singland, Limerick city).

15 *AI* 1033.14; 1037.3; 1068.2; 1078.6. **16** *AI* 1129.14. **17** Descended from King Brian mac Murchaid slain at Glanmire in 1118, the branch of Uí Bhriain known as the Meic Briain Eatharlach (MacBriens of Aherlow) had held this territory since pre-Invasion times (MacCotter, 'Rise of Meic Carthaig', 70). **18** Diarmuid Ó Murchadha, 'Cenn Ebrat, Sliab Caín, Belach Ebrat, Belach Legtha/Lechta', *Éigse*, 29 (1996), 153–71, passim. **19** Edmund Hogan, *Onomasticon goedelicum locorum et tribuum Hiberniae et Scotiae: an index, with identifications, to the Gaelic names of places and tribes* (Dublin, 1910; repr. Dublin, 1993, 2000), s. v. Loch Cenn. **20** Paul MacCotter, 'Túath, manor and parish: kingdom of Fir Maige, Cantred of Fermoy', *Peritia*, 22–3 (2011–12), 224–74, at 253. **21** Hogan, *Onomasticon*, s.v. Dún Crot. **22** Patrick Power, *Críchad an chaoilli, being the topography of*

While this list is attributed to the efforts of Brian Bóraime, contemporary annals do not include all of these fortresses in their lists of his works, and some, in particular those located in the Limerick–Tipperary border area, are much more likely to have been later constructions, bearing in mind the date of composition of the *Cogadh*, which may have been during the reign of Muirchertach Ua Briain (1086–1114), or perhaps somewhat earlier.[23] Independent confirmation of the existence of some of these forts can be found in the annals, such as for Inis Locha Gair (995) and Dún Trí Liag (1054). Another such fortress was Dún na Sciath (Donaskeagh northeast of Tipperary) which appears to have belonged to Carthach mac Sáerbrethaig in 1043 but had passed to Uí Bhriain by 1090.[24]

Of particular interest here are the fortifications in Eóganacht Áine and in Fonn Timchill. The first polity and its ecclesiastical town of Emly were both prominent in opposing the rise of Dál Cais in the tenth century and we have noted the role of Emly in the rise of Clann Charthaig.[25] I suspect that, from about 1050 onwards, the resurrection of Dalcassian power saw the erection of these fortresses in an effort to subdue this antipathetic region. In the case of Eóganacht Áine the support of the local kings for Clann Charthaig after 1118 must have helped eliminate this Uí Bhriain occupation but a different picture emerges in Fonn Timchill. This term relates to the entire area or polity north of Fir Maige as indicated by the twelfth-century (?) topographical tract *Críchad an Chaoilli*. The Anglo-Normans retained the name and territory in the guise of their cantred of Fontymkill. The western half of Fonn Timchill contained the polity of Déis Becc which had been an enthusiastic supporter of the rise of its Dál Cais 'cousins' and maintained this policy under its Uí Gebennaig kings throughout the eleventh century.[26] It is likely that the Uí Bhriain fortifications of Cenn Abrat and Rosach na Riogh on the southern borders of this territory were supported by the kings of Déis Becc as a defence against the men of Desmumu and in particular against Eóganacht Glennamnach.

DÁL CAIS EXPANSION POST-BRIAN IN THE ECCLESIASTICAL WORLD

The ancient churches of Dál Cais (Déis Tuascirt) were those of St Mainchín (or Munchin) in Limerick and nearby Singland.[27] By the tenth century the dynasty had gained control of Killaloe which became their chief church. Most

ancient Fermoy (Cork, 1932), pp 49, 122. **23** Denis Casey, 'A reconsideration of the authorship and transmission of Cogadh Gáedhel re Galliabh', *PRIA*, 113 (2013), 139–61. **24** *AI* 995.6; 1012.5; *AT* 1043.5, 1054.8; *AFM* 1043.13, 1054.14, 1090.13. **25** *CGG*, p. 83; *AI* 968, 973.6. **26** *CGG*, p. 93; *AI* 1021.2, 1058.4; MacCotter, 'Túath, manor and parish', 255–6. **27** Paul MacCotter, 'The church lands of the diocese of Limerick', *NMAJ*, 53 (2013), 99–122, at 120–1.

of the major churches in Thomond remained non-Dalcassian throughout our period. The exception was Terryglass, where from the 970s the abbacy was dominated by Uí Lonngargáin (O'Lonergans) and Uí Chennétig (O'Kennedys) descended from Brian's brother Donncuan. This suggests a deliberate policy of toleration of the old native clerical dynasties by the Uí Bhriain.[28] Evidence for a deliberate policy of interference and aggression by Uí Bhriain against major churches is clearly based on political enmity, and was reserved for 'enemy territory'. As early as the 980s, Brian had taken hostages of the churches of Emly, Cork and Lismore. Emly was a particular target as the chief church of the Eóganacht confederation.[29] First plundered by Brian's brother Mathgamain in 968, we find Emly in Dál Cais possession between 989 and 1014 (Marcán, another of Brian's brothers). After this its abbacy comes into possession of the Eóganacht Chaisil dynasts Saerbretach (d. 1025) and later his grandson Muiredach (d. 1092), with one Dalcassian in between.[30] Emly remained in the Clann Charthaig sphere of influence through to the 1130s and even later, as illustrated by Uí Bhriain-sponsored Killaloe hagiography of the 1160s, in which hatred of Emly is manifest.[31] We may also note the Mac Carthaig residence at Rathanny near Emly, around 1120.

Therefore, such Dalcassian efforts at control were not particularly successful. This changed however with the reign of Muircertach son of Tairdelbach, who successfully exercised a ruthless control over churches with 'enemy' associations. Cork was ruled by four Dalcassian clerics between 1088 and 1137, intermixed with native clerics, an occupation apparently initiated by the plunder of Cork by Diarmait brother of Muircertach, in 1088.[32] Nearby Cloyne was plundered by Diarmait during the same campaign in 1088. Then we have the donation of Cashel to the church by Muircertach in 1101 in what must be seen as his major anti-Eóganacht clerical manoeuvre. This seems to have occurred in tandem with an expulsion of the main Eóganacht families from the area southwards to Cork. Yet note the recovery of at least part of the lands of Cashel, even to a portion of the Rock itself (location of a Mac Carthaig palace), by the Meic Carthaig in the period 1118 to 1138. Note also the presence of the Dalcassian Uí Lonngargáin as archbishops of Cashel from 1131 onwards. One of this family had been the assassin who had slain Carthach

28 Donnchadh Ó Corráin, 'Dál Cais – church and dynasty', *Ériu* 24 (1973), 51–63. The Leix church of Killeshin appears to be a singular exception, see Edel Bhreathnach, 'Killeshin: an Irish monastery surveyed', *CMCS*, 27 (1994), 33–47, at 36–7 (where the author's assessment of Dalcassian ecclesiastical influence is exaggerated). **29** For a discussion see Paul MacCotter, *Colmán of Cloyne: a study* (Dublin, 2004), pp 91–3. **30** MacCotter, 'Rise of Meic Carthaig', 61–3. **31** Donnchadh Ó Corráin, 'Foreign connections and domestic politics: Killaloe and the Uí Bhriain in twelfth-century hagiography' in Dorothy Whitelock et al. (eds), *Ireland and early medieval Europe: studies in memory of Kathleen Hughes* (Cambridge, 1981), pp 213–31, at pp 229–30. **32** *AI* 1095.8; *AFM* 1106.2; 1152.1; Ó Corráin, 'Dál Cais: church and dyasty', 58.

in Cashel in 1045. We should note further Muirchertach's sponsorship of the synods of Cashel in 1101 and Ráith Bressail in 1111.

In summary, the main obstacle to the Uí Bhriain from the death of Brian to the arrival of the English was the polity of Eóganacht Chaisil. In dealing with this the Uí Bhriain may have been responsible for the obliteration of Uí Donnchada after 1078, thus removing the main obstacle to a Mac Carthaig rise to power in Eóganacht Chaisil. After this it is the Clann Charthaig who become the main obstacle to the restoration of Uí Bhriain rule in Munster, as can be seen in particular by the donation of Cashel to the Church and the driving out of the various Eóganacht septs from the Cashel area during the last years of the eleventh century, including Mac Carthaig, Ua Súillebáin (O'Sullivan), Ua Cellacháin (O'Callaghan), Ua Rígbarddáin (O'Riordan), Ua hÉcertaig (O'Hegerty), etc. Despite this, Clann Charthaig re-established a presence in Cashel between 1118 and 1138, and again rose to power in south Munster from 1151 onwards.

After Brian Bóraime: the high-kingship and the kings of Connacht

MARIE THERESE FLANAGAN

In 1118, Tairdelbach Ua Conchobair, king of Connacht since 1106, successfully challenged Muirchertach Ua Briain, great-grandson of Brian Bóraime, for the title of high-king. Tairdelbach was to die peacefully aged 68 in 1156, not on the battlefield, in itself an achievement for a provincial king in twelfth-century Ireland, and having made an elaborate will testifying to his self-perception as a Christian ruler, details of its benefactions to various churches being recorded in the annals.[1] He was immediately succeeded as king of Connacht by his son, Ruaidrí, one measure of Tairdelbach's secure control of the province of Connacht; by 1166 Ruaidrí was in a position to make a bid for the high-kingship and was the acknowledged high-king when English intrusion into Ireland commenced in the autumn of 1167.[2]

The high-kingships of Tairdelbach and of Ruaidrí Ua Conchobair, described as 'one of the greatest surprises in Irish history',[3] were a direct consequence of Brian Bóraime's breaking of the Uí Néill monopoly of the title in 1002, which had endured in near unbroken succession from the late seventh century. One might have expected the eighteenth-century antiquarian, Charles O'Conor of Ballinagare, as a descendant of Ruaidrí Ua Conchobair, to have welcomed the developments that ensued following the death of Brian since his own ancestors had benefitted directly from Brian's displacement of the Uí Néill dynasty. Yet the opposite was the case. In his *Dissertations on the antient history of Ireland*, O'Conor depicted Brian as having 'produced a fatal Change in the Constitution', a 'fatal Revolution' that had 'set aside the Niallian Succession, which governed Ireland for 600 Years before, and thrust himself into the Throne, although *incapacitated by Law*'.[4] Brian's assumption of the

1 *AT* 1156.4; cf. *AFM*. See also below, n. 96. For Tairdelbach's career, see John Ryan, *Toirdelbach Ó Conchubair (1088–1156), king of Connacht, king of Ireland 'co fresabra'*, O'Donnell Lecture 10 (Dublin, 1966); Ó Corráin, *Normans*, pp 150–62; Katharine Simms, 'Ua Conchobair, Toirdelbach Mór' in *ODNB*, lv, pp 839–41; Daibhí Ó Cróinín, 'Ua Conchobair, Tairdelbach (O'Conor, Turlough)' in *DIB*, ix, pp 577–9. 2 See Ailbhe Mac Shamhráin, 'Ua Conchobair, Ruaidrí' in *DIB*, ii, 2–6, 9, pp 572–6; M.T. Flanagan, 'Ua Conchobair, Ruaidrí [Rory O'Connor] (*c.*1116–1198)' in *ODNB*, lv, pp 836–9. 3 F.J. Byrne, 'The trembling sod: Ireland in 1169', *NHI*, ii, p. 35. 4 Charles O'Conor, *Dissertations on the antient history of Ireland wherein an account is given of the origine, government, letters, sciences, religion, manners and customs, of the antient inhabitants* (Dublin, 1753), pp 83–4. For O'Conor's life and writings, see Luke Gibbons and Kieran O'Conor (eds), *Charles O'Conor of Ballinagare: life and works* (Dublin, 2015).

high-kingship was interpreted as a usurpatory act. O'Conor's use of the term *constitution* reflected eighteenth-century political discourse and the political preoccupations of his own time, but what he sought to emphasize was that Brian had had a negative impact on subsequent political developments. 'The several Provincial Sovereigns of *Ireland* easily entered the Gap, made by *Brian Borovy*. Following his Example they set themselves up for Candidates to the Throne of *Ireland*; each courting a separate and private Interest … and for more than a hundred Years, while every such petty Prince contended to be King, none was admitted to be one'.[5] 'The *Irish* Constitution was in its Agony, for a considerable Time before the Invasion of this Country by the *English*, under their King *Henry Fitz-Empress*'.[6] In relation to Brian's career, O'Conor made no mention whatsoever of Vikings, nor the battle of Clontarf.

In a much expanded second edition of his *Dissertations*, published in 1766, O'Conor amplified his portrayal of Brian, and in a more positive way, acknowledging, for example, Brian's military capabilities, but he offset his more expansive presentation of Brian by his yet more favourable assessment of the Southern Uí Néill king, Máel Sechnaill (d. 1022), from whom Brian had secured hostages in 1002, thereby fatally compromising Máel Sechnaill's high-kingship.[7] Máel Sechnaill is described as beginning 'his Reign as he ended it by giving the strongest Proof that the public Good was the principal Object of his Administration'.[8] Brian, by contrast, was portrayed as a self-interested opportunist who pursued his own ambitions at the expense of the greater benefit of the country. Máel Sechnaill was obliged by the disloyalty of the Northern Uí Néill lineage to yield the title of high-king to Brian because 'the Expedient was necessary, though not constitutional'.[9] O'Conor regarded Brian as having overturned what he termed 'the Prescription of alternate Succession',[10] whereby the high-kingship had alternated between the Northern and Southern Uí Néill lineages.

> The Revolution before us deserves Notice: On the one Hand, a Prince, of the Age of seventy-six, mounting the Throne, from which his Family had been excluded for six hundred and twenty Years; and, on the other, a Prince in the Prime of Life resigning, for the public Good, a Monarchy, continued in his own Family for five hundred and twenty Years before. Such a Sacrifice is extremely uncommon. No Necessity of his Affairs could oblige *Malachy* [i.e., Máel Sechnaill] to make it, although that of

5 *Dissertations* (1753), p. 84. 6 Ibid., pp 58–9. 7 *AI* 1002.2; *AU* 1002.1, 8; *AT* 1001.7; *CS* 99=1001, 1000=1002; *AFM* 1001=1002, 1002=1003. It is surprising how little the annalists made of this event which has been interpreted as so significant by subsequent historians; the non-contemporary pseudo-historical biography of Brian, *Cogadh Gáedhel re Gallaibh*, accords it much greater significance (*CGG*, pp 118–33). 8 *Dissertations on the history of Ireland to which is subjoined a dissertation on the Irish colonies established in Britain* (Dublin, 1766), p. 255. 9 Ibid., p. 256. 10 Ibid., p. 255; cf. pp 188, 221–2, 230, 234, 238, 239, 252,

> the Public did. He gave the Title of *Brian* the best Colour it could bear, that of conferring his own upon him. He hereby preserved an able and virtuous Prince from the Odium of open Usurpation; and he supported him afterwards as he engaged to do, by his whole Interest which was still very considerable. – The World was amazed at such a Conduct, and may be so still; because Mankind, unworthy of so exalted a Character, seldom frame a proper Judgment of it'.[11]

In other words, Máel Sechnaill put the good of the country before his own personal ambitions.

O'Conor's very favourable assessment of Máel Sechnaill contrasts sharply with that of the seventeenth-century historian, Geoffrey Keating, whose work O'Conor knew well. Keating, in his *Foras feasa ar Éirinn*, had depicted Máel Sechnaill as no longer worthy of occupying the high-kingship, as devious, and corrupted by luxury, 'a line of action that was useless for the defence of Ireland at that juncture', whereupon Brian and his associates 'resolved to send envoys to Máel Sechnaill, king of Ireland, to inform him that it was not right that anyone should hold the sovereignty of Ireland, except one who should devote his energies to banishing the Foreigners from the country'.[12] This portrayal of Máel Sechnaill was not derived from *Cogadh Gáedhel re Gallaibh*, the heroic biography of Brian which, although it presented Máel Sechnaill as subservient to Brian, did not emphasize his incompetence in the same way.[13] By depicting Máel Sechnaill as ineffectual, Keating sought to circumvent a charge against Brian of usurpation. It was a justification not dissimilar to that which had been deployed to legitimate the displacement of the Merovingians by the Carolingian dynasty in Francia in 751: Máel Sechnaill was a *roi fainéant*, not fit to rule, and so it was no usurpation to displace him.

Although O'Conor acknowledged in the revised edition of his *Dissertations* that Brian was skilled in arms, brave, pious even, and 'superior to every Prince of his Time', yet he described him as

> inferior to *Malachy* in one Instance only, that of sacrificing a Crown to the Good of his Country. Malachy II well deserved the Crown he resigned and *Brian* departed from his Magnanimity in accepting it. By leaving it where it was, he might have the Merit of establishing a more orderly Form of Government in the royal Hy-Niall Family, and of laying

252, 267. 11 Ibid., p. 259. O'Conor derived Brian's reputed age of 76 from *AFM* 1002; cf. the retrospective entry for Brian's birth in 925: *AFM* 925. For O'Conor's ownership of a copy of *AFM*, see below, n. 26. 12 Keating, *Foras feasa*, iii, pp 248–9. 13 For analysis of the portrayal of Máel Sechnaill's career in Middle Irish sources, see Máire Ní Mhaonaigh, 'A man of two faces: Máel Sechnaill mac Domnaill in Middle Irish sources' in H.B. Clarke and Ruth Johnson (eds), *The Vikings in Ireland and beyond: before and after the battle of Clontarf* (Dublin, 2015), pp 233–52. It serves to highlight how independent O'Conor was in

> the Foundations of a new Monarchy, which might have preserved the Nation from its approaching Destruction … nor doth it appear that the King's Extent of legislative Knowledge, any more than his great Age, qualified him for new-modelling the Manners and Feelings of Mankind … he was rather to be pitied than envied. Without the Co-operation of the Prince who resigned to him, he would probably be obliged himself to resign in Favour of some other powerful Oligarch, or reign with his faction in the Places subservient to his Government. With *Malachy*'s Assistance, he actually governed over most of the Provinces.[14]

There is a smack of ageism in the way in which O'Conor contrasted Máel Sechnaill in his prime with the older Brian. The battle of Clontarf gets a mention, but not in relation to Vikings. O'Conor's assessment was that it was fought because of a revolt by the men of Leinster and that 'Brian ended it gloriously, although little to the advantage of the Nation … and Domestic Contention proved the Fruit of it'.[15] The 'Chieftains, particularly such as were at the Head of great Provinces, became every day more and more independent of the supreme Authority, lodged by the original Constitution in the legislative Power of the monarch and the States assembled'.[16] Máel Sechnaill's 'Resignation proved fatal … to the Nation … And we may justly date its Destruction from that Revolution which opened to the several provincial Kings Pretensions and which … ought to be suppressed for ever'.[17] The end result of Brian's reign, in the assessment of Charles O'Conor, was to be English rule in Ireland.

O'Conor's ancestors, Tairdelbach and Ruaidrí Ua Conchobair (although O'Conor did not admit the relationship), were among those 'several provincial Kings whose Pretensions ought to have been suppressed', and who emerged as contenders for the high-kingship in the twelfth century in consequence of Brian having broken the Uí Néill monopoly of the title. O'Conor depicted Ireland at the beginning of the twelfth century as divided between the Northern Uí Néill king, Domnall Mac Lochlainn, king of Cenél nEógain, and Muirchertach Ua Briain, Brian's great-grandson, the one 'claiming a prescriptive Right of Succession, from his Family; the other claiming that of the new Constitution, which admitted the provincial Kings so long, and, as was pretended, so illegally excluded'.[18] In other words, O'Conor was still presenting Domnall Mac Lochlainn as the legitimist Uí Néill candidate for the high-kingship. 'These two Princes … contended for more than twenty Years and the People were ground between them'.[19] As for Tairdelbach Ua Conchobair who began a bid for the high-kingship in 1114, 'The young King

his stance. **14** *Dissertations* (1766), pp 261–2. **15** Ibid., pp 264–5. **16** Ibid., p. 268. **17** Ibid., p. 269. **18** *Dissertations* (1753), p. xxxii; cf. *Dissertations* (1766), p. 270, where 'illegally' has been replaced by 'unjustly'. **19** Ibid., p. 271.

of *Conaught*, Turloch the Great, following the example of *Brian Boromey*, set himself in Opposition to those Princes, towards the end of their motley Administration'.[20] Tairdelbach's son, Ruaidrí (the Roderic of O'Conor's account), is termed 'the last and most unfortunate of all the *Irish* Monarchs':[21]

> Since the Death of *Malachy* II (1022), this Nation was falling into a State of political Reprobation. Each Province set up for itself; and the Monarchy grew indifferent, the Monarch hateful, to the Majority of the Chieftains. When *Roderic* mounted the Throne, their Measure of Iniquity was full. He laboured to unite all Parties for common Defence, against a desperate provincial Tyrant and his foreign Allies; but the Oligarchs of the Time, were rather unanimous in rejecting their King, than the common Enemy: They loved their Country only in the second place: Domestic Animosities, personal Revenge, were uppermost; and to the Gratification of these Passions, they sacrificed every consideration favourable to their native Country, or useful to their own common Safety ... The Majority of these Chieftains, delivered up the Nation, as a Prey, to a Handful of foreign Free-booters. They deserted the reigning Prince, under whose Standard they could easily preserve their Liberties; and they certainly well deserved the Treatment they received from the new Masters they set over themselves.[22]

The new masters were, of course, the English.

It is noteworthy that O'Conor interpreted the significance of Brian's high-kingship almost exclusively in terms of its aftermath and its consequences for the high-kingship. The unremitting negativity of O'Conor's assessment of the destructive outcome of Brian's high-kingship is the more striking considered alongside prevailing views of O'Conor's contemporaries and immediate predecessors who placed their emphasis on Viking oppression of the Irish population and on Brian's victorious military campaigns which brought that threat to an end at the battle of Clontarf and drove the Foreigners out of

20 Ibid. **21** Ibid., p. 275. An early indication of O'Conor's assessment of his own ancestors as having contributed to political instability is evident from his comment in 1728 at the age of eighteen on the death of Tadhg Ó Conchobhair in 1464: 'There was no king of Connacht after him – they afterwards obtained the title of O'Conor, and because they were not themselves steady to each other, they were crushed by lawless power and the usurpations of foreigners. May God forgive them their sins. Domine ne status nobis hoc peccatum. This extract is taken from the book of Kilronan [Annals of Connacht], which has the approbation of the Four Masters annexed to it, by me *Cathal* O'Conor (of Belengare), 2 August 1728'. The original Irish version and an English translation are given in Eugene O'Curry, *Lectures on the manuscript materials of ancient Irish history* (Dublin, 1873), pp 114, 541, citing 'MS in Stowe Collect. No. 3, fol. 27b'; cf. Charles O'Conor, *Bibliotheca MS Stowensis: A descriptive catalogue of the manuscripts in the Stowe library*, 2 vols (Buckingham, 1819), i, p. 76. **22** *Dissertations* (1766), pp 276–7.

Ireland. Aodh Buidhe Mac Cruitín (otherwise Hugh MacCurtin)[23] who published *A brief discourse in vindication of the antiquity of Ireland* (Dublin, 1717), and Dermod O'Connor, who in 1723 produced an English translation of Geoffrey Keating's *Foras feasa ar Éirinn*, each extolled the reputation of Brian and of his successors, placing emphasis on Brian's victorious military campaigns and expulsion of the Foreigners from Ireland. Charles O'Conor's assessment was diametrically opposed to such portrayals. Of Dermod O'Connor's translation of Keating, published under the title, *A general history of Ireland*,[24] Charles O'Conor averred that 'the History given in *English*, under *Keating*'s Name, is the grossest Imposition that has been ever yet obtruded on a learned Age'.[25] He also eschewed the presentation of Brian's career in the seventeenth-century Annals of the Four Masters of which O'Conor had his own personal copy: Brian's death notice in the Annals of the Four Masters had described him as 'the Augustus of all the west of Europe'.[26]

O'Conor's jaundiced assessment may, in part, have been coloured by the fact that Brian Bóraime's posthumous reputation benefitted from the circumstance that his descendants, the O'Briens, under the policy of 'Surrender and Re-grant', and by converting to Protestantism and supporting the Protestant succession, had survived as one of the few families of Gaelic origin to become integrated into the eighteenth-century landed elite in a way in which the Catholic O'Conors had not been able to do.[27] Both Hugh MacCurtin's *Brief discourse* and Dermod O'Connor's translation of Keating's *Foras feasa* were dedicated to William O'Brien, earl of Inchiquin, a descendant of Brian Bóraime. Members of MacCurtin's family had served the O'Briens of Thomond as *seanchaithe* from the fourteenth century onwards. Dermod O'Connor's intended readership among the nobility was evidenced by the sumptuous binding with a frontispiece illustration of Brian Bóraime,[28] while the text was

23 See Vincent Morley, 'Mac Cruitín, Aodh "Buí" (MacCurtin, Hugh)' in *DIB*, v, pp 887–8; idem, *An Crann os Coill: Aodh Buí Mac Cruitín, c.1680–1755* (Dublin, 1995). 24 *The general history of Ireland, collected by the learned Jeoffrey Keating, D.D. Faithfully translated from the original Irish language, with many curious amendments taken from the psalters of Tara and Cashel, and other authentick records* (Dublin, 1723). 25 *Dissertations* (1766), p. x. Cf. in relation to Máel Sechnaill, 'Some Writers, who drew most of their Materials from modern Romances, accuse him of a malicious Desertion at the Battle of Clontarfe: But this Account being irreconcilable with the whole Tenour of his Life and Conduct, and not in the least supported by Tigernach, or any other Writer who lived near the Period in Question, must be deservedly rejected': ibid., pp 264–5. 26 *AFM*. In his *Dissertations* (1766), p. xx, O'Conor stated that most of his material for the Christian period 'had been extracted principally from the *Annals of the Four Masters*'. Cf. above, n. 11. See further Nollaig Ó Muraíle, 'Keeping the embers alive: Charles O'Conor and Irish manuscripts – his own and others' in Gibbons and O'Conor (eds), *Charles O'Conor*, pp 186–210 at pp 192–6; Maura O'Gara-Riordan, 'Charles O'Conor and the Annals of the Four Masters' in idem, pp 227–43. 27 O'Conor had a section on 'the chief *Milesian* families, who survived the Dissolution of the *Irish* Monarchy, 1175' in the 1753 edition of his *Dissertations*, pp 228–48, which mentioned both the O'Conors and O'Briens. It was omitted in the 1766 edition. 28 Described as 'perhaps

prefaced by the pedigree of the earl of Inchiquin tracing his ancestry back to King Milesius of Spain; and many of the subscribers were drawn from noble and gentry families who had converted to Protestantism but retained a pride in their native Irish ancestry.

It is worth noting that Charles O'Conor's individualistic viewpoint, grounded in his knowledge of primary sources,[29] did not disrupt or impact on the ever-more romanticized portrayals of Brian that were gathering pace during O'Conor's lifetime and thereafter.[30] In modern historiography, allusions to Brian's usurpation are thin on the ground, although the legal scholar, D.A. Binchy, did refer to Brian as a 'usurper'.[31] Political developments in the post-Brian era have also generally been interpreted in a more positive light than O'Conor's teleological foreshadowing of English intervention in Ireland in the late twelfth century.[32] There has been a near consensus view that the pace of political change in Ireland quickened as a result of Brian's reign and mostly in ways that have been given a dynamic and positive spin with a particular emphasis on feudalization. Edmund Curtis inaugurated the notion by briefly adverting to 'patriarchal institutions passing into feudalism',[33] an idea that was endorsed by Eoin MacNeill who suggested that Ireland 'was subject to a strong influx of feudal ideas from the Continent'.[34] Similar views have since been reiterated by a series of scholars: 'Irish society … moving rapidly in the direction of feudalism in the matter of landholding',[35] the emergence of 'a

the earliest surviving depiction of Brian' in Duffy, *Brian Boru*, plate 20 (see also the cover of the present volume). **29** O'Conor relied heavily on the Clonmacnoise series of annals. Cf. above, n. 25; below, n. 121. **30** See Clare O'Halloran, 'The triumph of "virtuous liberty": representations of the Vikings and Brian Boru in eighteenth-century histories', *Eighteenth-Century Ireland*, 22 (2007), 151–63. **31** D.A. Binchy, *Celtic and Anglo-Saxon kingship* (Oxford, 1970), p. 44. Contrast Seán Duffy, *Ireland in the Middle Ages* (London, 1997), p. 34: 'There was nothing illegal about this'. **32** For a modern historian who argued that Brian's high-kingship created the political conditions that resulted in Henry II's intervention in Ireland, see James Lydon, *The lordship of Ireland in the Middle Ages*, 2nd ed. (Dublin, 2003), p. 11. **33** Edmund Curtis, *A history of medieval Ireland from 1086 to 1513* (London, 1923), p. 9 and cf. p. 20. The idea was expanded on in the 2nd ed. (London, 1938), pp xxx–xxxi. Cf. also 'incipient feudalism': ibid. **34** Eoin MacNeill, *Early Irish laws and institutions* (Dublin, 1934), p. 24. He described Tairdelbach Ua Conchobair as 'probably inspired by Feudal influences' pursuing 'a centralising policy': ibid., p. 30; cf. also p. 129: 'there are signs of the influence of feudalism in Ireland before the feudal invasion'. In his earlier *Phases of Irish history* (Dublin, 1919), MacNeill had drawn a stronger contrast between pre-Invasion and post-Invasion Ireland with numerous references to 'feudal regime', 'feudal newcomers', 'Feudal conquests', 'feudal law of primogeniture', 'feudal invasion', 'Feudal settlement', 'feudal conquest', 'Feudal occupation', 'Feudal castles', 'Feudal colonists', 'Feudal settlers', 'Feudal dominion': ibid., pp 278, 288, 295, 310, 311, 320, 324, 326, 334, 338, 339, 340, 341, 342. **35** Ó Corráin, *Normans*, p. 171; idem, 'The type of society that was emerging in Ireland in the eleventh and twelfth centuries was one that was moving rapidly in the direction of feudalism' in his 'Nationality and kingship in pre-Norman Ireland' in T.W. Moody (ed.), *Historical Studies XI: nationality and the pursuit of national independence, papers read before the Conference held at Trinity College, Dublin, 26–31 May 1975* (Belfast, 1978), pp 1–35 at p. 32; 'Kings granted land in return for homage

native feudal society',[36] 'the birth-pangs of a new feudalism',[37] 'the feudalisation of Irish society', 'feudalizing lords of pre-Anglo-Norman Ireland',[38] 'feudalism in Gaelic Ireland', 'the rise of feudalism', 'the feudalisation of pre-colonial Irish society', 'pre-colonial feudalism',[39] all these descriptions have been applied to the post-Brian era.[40] They are intended in a general way to convey the strengthening of controls over political subordinates and enhancement of regnal infrastructures. To argue such a case in detail would require sustained analyses in the first instance of the individual careers of the various contenders for the high-kingship who challenged Brian's direct descendants, and who emerged in Leinster, Connacht, and Tír Eógain in the course of the eleventh and twelfth centuries,[41] an undertaking which is beyond the scope of this contribution. An attempt will be made instead to explore more generally how far novel developments in the post-Brian era may have resulted specifically from his reign, how geographically widespread they were manifest, and to what extent regional variations can be discerned. Some salient features must serve for more comprehensive coverage.

and military service, very much like the feudal kings of contemporary Europe, and those who were once minor kings in their own right were now becoming a feudal aristocracy' in his 'Prehistoric and early Christian Ireland' in Roy Foster (ed.), *Oxford illustrated history of Ireland* (Oxford, 1989), p. 50. But Ó Corráin also perceptively noted: 'However, feudal influence must not be overstressed … The Irish political development of the twelfth century is a parallel to feudalism rather than a derivative of it': *Normans*, p. 150. **36** Byrne, *Irish kings*, p. 269. **37** Byrne, 'Trembling sod', p. 10. **38** Ibid., p. 12; also Charles Doherty, 'The Vikings in Ireland: a review' in Clarke et al. (eds), *Ireland and Scandinavia*, pp 288–30, at pp 322–4 in an otherwise valuable discussion. **39** Tadhg O'Keeffe, *Medieval Ireland: an archaeology* (Stroud, 2000), pp 26–9. A section on 'Romanesque and feudalism' is included in his *Romanesque Ireland: architecture and ideology in the twelfth century* (Dublin, 2003), pp 285–8. See also 'incipient feudalism' and 'pre-Norman feudalisation' in his 'The fortifications of western Ireland, AD1100–1300, and their interpretation', *JGAHS*, 50 (1998), 184–200, at 187. Cf. Terry Barry, 'If we associate castles generally with the existence of some form of feudal structure in medieval Europe, then Turlough O'Conor comes closest of all the Irish kings to being a medieval feudal monarch': idem, 'The origins of Irish castles: a contribution to the debate' in Conleth Manning (ed.), *From ringforts to fortified houses: studies on castles and other monuments in honour of David Sweetman* (Bray, 2007), pp 33–40, at p. 36. A different emphasis, 'Irish society was moving rapidly towards a hierarchical structure, generally referred to as feudalism', is given by Billy Colfer, *Arrogant trespass: Anglo-Norman Wexford, 1169–1400* (Enniscorthy, 2002), p. 23. **40** Cf. the section titled 'Feudalisation in Ireland, *c.*1000' and references to a 'feudal system' and 'feudal administration' in Dáibhí Ó Cróinín, *Early medieval Ireland, 400–1200* (London, 1995), pp 291–2. There has been little attempt to follow Orpen and MacNeill in testing the hypothesis of pre-Invasion 'feudal' institutions against post-Invasion society in Ireland. For reservations relating to such descriptions and a preliminary exploration in relation to Leinster, see M.T. Flanagan, 'Strategies of lordship in pre-Norman and post-Norman Leinster', *Anglo-Norman Studies*, 10 (1998), 107–26. Note also the general comments of H.B. Clarke, '1066, 1169 and all that' in Judith Devlin and H.B. Clarke (eds), *European encounters: essays in memory of Albert Lovett* (Dublin, 2003), pp 11–36. While Lydon in the first edition of his *Lordship of Ireland*, p. 16, doubted whether there was much evidence for 'incipient feudalism' in Ireland, this was omitted from the revised edition, which placed more emphasis on changes in twelfth-century Irish society. **41** List in *NHI*, ix, pp 205–6;

First, warfare, since it was such a large facet of Brian's own career: there is no doubt that warfare in Ireland intensified in consequence of Brian's bid for the high-kingship. No king before him had placed such large armies in the field, and with such a significant naval component; nor had any expended as much economic resources and manpower on war and campaigned over such a wide geographical area of Ireland. Inevitably, this raised the stakes for those who sought to bid for the high-kingship after him: strong currents of competition and emulation are very evident in the post-Brian era. The chief body of evidence for warfare is the annals, although the terse and frequently formulaic notices of events, devoid of sustained description or connected narrative, make it difficult to reconstruct details of military organization, strategy and tactics; added to which there are major gaps in the twelfth-century annals and notably in relation to Leinster.[42] While the annals may be laconic in details, the dynastic propaganda texts, by contrast, are inflationary with the truth. The early twelfth-century heroic biography of Brian Bóraime, *Cogadh Gáedhel re Gallaibh*, although doubtless exaggerated and more reflective of tactics that had developed by the late eleventh/early twelfth century, when it was written, is nonetheless a useful source for gauging military capabilities by the early twelfth century. So too is *Caithréim Cellacháin Chaisil* ('The battle-career of Cellachán, king of Cashel'), which was intended as a counter-propagandist riposte to the *Cogadh* in support of the Meic Carthaig kings of south Munster. It likewise contains quite detailed descriptions of military tactics.[43] Imaginative reconstructions of warfare these texts may contain, but they cannot have been too far removed from reality if they were to work effectively as propaganda for the aristocratic audiences for whom they were written and intended to influence. The very titles of these works – *Cogadh and Caithréim* – highlight the importance by the early twelfth century of military capacity for aspirants to the high-kingship and the contemporary perception that military success was a key component of the career of an aspiring high-king. And when in 1166 Diarmait Mac Murchada, king of Leinster, sought to challenge Ruaidrí Ua Conchobair for the high-kingship his immediate need was for military forces and his response was to recruit elite mercenary troops abroad.

The early twelfth-century dynastic propaganda texts depict largescale armies that combined naval and land forces. The Shannon had provided Brian with ready access from Munster into Connacht and Southern Uí Néill territory, transporting troops via ships.[44] Viking raiding parties, attested on the

broad narrative in M.T. Flanagan, 'High-kings with opposition, 1072–1166' in *NHI*, i, pp 899–933. 42 Cf. otherwise unrecorded battles in *CS* from 1123=1127 onwards. 43 Donnchadh Ó Corráin, '*Caithréim Chellacháin Chaisil*: history or propaganda?', *Ériu*, 25 (1974), 1–69; M.T. Flanagan, 'Warfare in Ireland, 1000–1200' in Thomas Bartlett and Keith Jeffery (eds), *A military history of Ireland* (Cambridge, 1996), pp 52–75. 44 In 983, Brian had a 'great fleet' on the Shannon and in 988, Brian's fleet on the Shannon was

river as early as 837, had highlighted the strategic importance of the Shannon as a rapid access route between the northern and southern halves of Ireland.[45] The threat posed by Brian's deployment of the Shannon as a transit waterway is evidenced by the 'great obstruction' placed across the river in 1001 at the strategic location of Athlone by the men of Connacht and Mide (Meath) so as to deny passage to the Munster army onto Lough Ree.[46] The Shannon was to remain a vital access route for control of which Brian's successors competed with the kings of Connacht, Bréifne and Mide. At least five successive bridges at Athlone were built in the twelfth century by Tairdelbach and Ruaidrí Ua Conchobair to afford a ready approach into midland Ireland; and they were destroyed just as quickly by kings of Mide aiming to prevent such passage. Tairdelbach is recorded as having erected bridges at Athlone in 1120, 1129, 1140, and 1155.[47] As helpfully explained in relation to the bridge built at Athlone in 1155, it 'was made for him for the purpose of making incursions into Mide'.[48] Tairdelbach's son, Ruaidrí, constructed yet another bridge in 1159.[49] In 1071 a bridge had been built at Killaloe by Brian's grandson, Tairdelbach ua Briain, in the space of a fortnight.[50] Such public royal works demonstrated the capacity of kings to exact labour services from their subjects. It can be problematic to distinguish between what might be termed routine, or regular, exactions made by individual kings on their subjects – demands from those non-noble subjects within their patrimonial kingdoms, or home territories or heartlands – and the exceptional expansion or intensification of royal powers that may have developed, especially in relation to the waging of war and accelerating demands made on those of noble status.

Brian Bóraime's extensive use of fleets as a component of his military campaigns was to be maintained not only by his immediate Ua Briain successors but emulated by subsequent contenders for the high-kingship: Tairdelbach Ua Conchobair from 1115 onwards deployed fleets not merely on the Shannon but also seagoing vessels along the entire western seaboard northwards as far as Tory island and southwards as far as Cork and along the

numbered at 300 vessels: *AI* 983.2, 988.2. In 983 his 'naval raid' up the Shannon reached as far as Bréifne. In 993, he made a *crechlong*, 'naval raid', on Bréifne via Lough Ree: *AI* 993.2. In 1011, he took a great hosting to Cenél Conaill 'by land and sea': *AI* 1011.5. **45** *AU* 837.5, 6; *CS*. **46** *AI* 1001.5. The term used is *Mórimme*; cf. *AU* 1001.6; *AT* 1000.4; *AClon* p. 165; *CS* 999=1001 which record that a *tóchar*, 'causeway', was made at Athlone in the same year by Máel Sechnaill, king of Mide, and Cathal mac Conchobair, king of Connacht. Máel Sechnaill made another bridge at Áth Liag at the same time: *A Clon*, p. 165. **47** *CS* 1116=1120; *AMisc* 1120.5; *ALC* 1120; *AT* 1120.3, 1120.4, 1140.4, 5; *AFM*, 1120, 1129, 1133, 1144, 1153, 1155; *ACott* 1120, 1146; *AClon*, p. 191. In 1146 the bridge collapsed while the rear of Tairdelbach Ua Conchobair's army was crossing back into Connacht having plundered cattle from Muintir Máel Finna: *AT* 1146.1; *ACott*; *CS*; *AFM*. For bridges at Áth Crocha and Dún Leóda on the Suck in 1120 and at Áth Liag in 1140 and 1153, see *AT* 1120.4; *CS* 1114=1120; *AFM* 1120, 1140, 1153; *AClon* p. 191. **48** *AFM* 1155. **49** *AFM* with the same explanation given as for the building of the bridge in 1155. Cf. *AT* 1159.14; *AClon*, pp 204 ('that he might have passage to take the spoyles of Meath'), 205. **50** *AI* 1071.7.

Leinster coast up to Dublin.[51] To single out just one instance, in 1127, Tairdelbach had 190 ships on lower Lough Derg on the Shannon with which he devastated the adjoining districts of Munster;[52] it was a fleet possibly capable of transporting a force of upwards of 7000 fighters, allowing for around forty men per ship.[53] The entry relating to this fleet in the Annals of the Four Masters is immediately followed by an account of a fight (*comhrac*) of two fleets (*comlach*) at sea (*for fairrge*), in which the men of Connacht gained a victory over the men of Munster.[54] In 1132, in a naval engagement at Galway between the ships of Connacht and Munster, the names of the leaders of the Connacht and Munster fleets were recorded. Flaithbertach Ua Flaithbertaig was *toísech* of the Connacht fleet, while Lochlann, son of Amlaíb Ua Lochlainn, king of Corco Mruad, led the Munster, fleet and lost his life in the engagement.[55] What the 1132 and 1133 entries demonstrate is that by the early twelfth century, specialized military duties, including expertise in naval warfare, were becoming associated with specified political subordinates of provincial kings. Such specialization associated with particular families, as, for example, the Uí Fhlaithbertaig and the Uí Dubda[56] in Connacht, is attested also in the case of the kings of Munster, both the Uí Briain and Meic Carthaig.[57] The naval capacity of the kings of Leinster, however, is less apparent; they appear to have relied on availing of the fleets of Dublin, Wexford and Waterford, which would have been led by Hiberno-Scandinavian commanders.[58] Similarly, a weakness of the challenge for the high-kingship

51 In 1115, Tairdelbach Ua Conchobair may be said to have launched his bid for the high-kingship by placing a fleet on the Shannon, by fortifying Buinne in Beithe, an island on the Shannon, against the Munstermen and by donating a drinking horn, chalice and paten to the church of Clonmacnoise: *CS* 1111=1115; *AT* 1115.7; *AMisc* 1115.5; cf. *AFM*. For Cork, see *CS* 1119=1123 ('on land and sea') and cf. *AT* 1123.7, 1127.1; *AI* 1127.3; *AMisc* 1126.6 (*recte* 1127); *AU* 1127.1; *AFM*. For Dublin, see *AT* 11211.1. For Tory, see *AT* 1130.1; *AFM*. For additional examples and discussion, see Colmán Etchingham, 'Skuldelev 2 and Viking-age ships and fleets in Ireland' in Emer Purcell et al. (eds), *Clerics, kings and Vikings: essays on medieval Ireland in honour of Donnchadh Ó Corráin* (Dublin, 2015), pp 79–90. 52 *AT* 1127.3; *AFM* 1127. 53 When a ship (*long*) in the fleet (*coblach*) of Cathal Crobderg sank in 1190 on the Shannon, thirty-six men were drowned: *ALC*; *ACott*; *AFM* 1190 (where the vessel is termed *ethar*) and records that all the crew were drowned except Cathal Crobderg and six others, giving a total of forty-three in the ship. Cf. appendix 11.1 below, nos 2, 3, 9. 54 For earlier incidences of naval engagements between Munster and Connacht fleets, see *AT* 10811.1, 1089.1; *CS* 1085=1089; *AFM* 1088, 1089. For the seizing of ships on the Shannon by Áed Ua Conchobair in 1065, see *AT* 1065.1; *AFM*; cf. *AI* 1065.4. For a discussion of evidence relating to Munster and Connacht fleets in *Lebor na cert*, see Catherine Swift, 'Royal fleets in Viking Ireland: the evidence of *Lebor na cert*, AD1050–1150' in John Hines, Alan Lane and Mark Redknap (eds), *Land, sea and home*, Society for Medieval Archaeology, Monograph Series, 20 (Leeds, 2004), pp 189–206. 55 Appendix 11.1 below, no. 1. 56 Appendix 11.1 below, nos 1, 10. 57 Cf. *AT* 1124.2; *AFM* 1124; *AI* 1127.15; *AMisc* 1128.2, 1131.4, 1132.1, 1134.5 for Mac Carthaig fleets. 58 By the early eleventh century, the Dublin fleet could suffer defeat at sea at the hands of an Irish king, as was the case by the king of Ulaid in 1022: *AT* 1022.6; *AU* 1022.4; *AFM*. Cf. *AU* 1098.2,

launched from the 1140s onwards by Muirchertach Mac Lochlainn, king of Cenél nEógain, against Tairdelbach Ua Conchobair may have been his inability to sustain sufficient naval resources of his own, notwithstanding that a tenth-century predecessor, Domnall (d. 980), had carried out a series of precocious manoeuvres in 955, moving ships from Lough Neagh to Lough Erne and onto Lough Oughter.[59] In 1154, Muirchertach Mac Lochlainn was obliged to assemble a fleet from Galloway, Kintrye and the Isle of Man in order to take on the Connacht fleet off the Inishowen coast, the outcome nonetheless proving inconclusive.[60]

Another strategy deployed by Brian that was to be further developed by successive contenders for the high-kingship, was the use of fortifications. In 995, the building by Brian of a series of strongholds is recorded,[61] and again in 1012, when the first reference occurs to the *cathair* of Cenn Corad (Kincora).[62] These strongholds remained strategically important thereafter. Brian's capital at Kincora, was attacked by successive kings of Connacht between 1016 and 1118. In 1016, Kincora was broken down by the men of Connacht.[63] In 1061, Áed in Gaí Bernaig Ua Conchobair, king of Connacht, demolished Kincora and filled up the well and, according to Conell McGeoghegan's seventeenth-century translation in the Annals of Clonmacnoise, he 'broke down the mannorhouse of King Brian Boromwo in Kincoro',[64] 'mannorhouse' possibly translating *telach* in the sense of hearth or demesne. Although by 1061 Kincora was in the hands of Donnchad mac Briain, the annalist still referred to it as Brian's. In 1088 Ruaidrí na Saide Buide Ua Conchobair, king of Connacht, attacked Kincora against Tairdelbach ua Briain, where he found 160 soldiers, including Gaill and Gael.[65] In 1096, Brian's great-grandson, Muirchertach Ua Briain, rebuilt Kincora, after it had been destroyed by an attack from Leth

1100.5; *ALC* 1098, 1100; *AFM* 1045, 1098, 1100. The earliest reference to an Ulaid fleet (*nocoblach*, 'new fleet') occurs in 913: *AU* 913.5. **59** *AU* 955.3; cf. 963.1. The earliest reference to a Cenél nEógain fleet (*murcablach*) is in 941 when Muirchertach mac Néill carried off plunder and booty from Inse Gall: *AFM* 939=941; *CS* 940=941. **60** *AFM*. According to *AT* 1154.6 victory went to the Connacht fleet. Victory is also attributed to Connacht in *AFM*, but it is noted that a great number of Connacht men were killed, including An Cosnamach Ua Dubda. For the Uí Dubda, see appendix 11.1 below, no. 10. **61** 'The construction of Cashel, Inis Locha Gair, and Inis Locha Saingleand and many structures besides': *AI* 995.6; see also, MacCotter, above. **62** 'Many fortifications (*daingne*) were built by Brian', and reference was made to the *cathracha* of Kincora, Inis Gaill Duib, Inis Locha Saingean and Cnoc Fochuir: *AI* 995.6, 1012.5. Cf. the list of strongholds of the king of Cashel in *Lebor na cert*, pp 42–7. Brian is depicted in *CGG* erecting a series of *dúin 7 daingne* after this triumphal circuit of Ireland in 1005: *CGG*, pp 140–1. This is not to imply that Brian was the first to do so. In 971 Domnall ua Néill, king of Cenél nEógain (943–80), is recorded to have placed a *longphort* in every *tuath* in Mide: *AFM* 969=971. For comment on these garrisoned strongholds, see Doherty, 'Vikings in Ireland', pp 326–7; Byrne, 'Trembling sod', p. 8. **63** *AFM*; *AClon*, p. 169 ('Connaught men broke down Killaloe and Kynkorey (King Bryan his mannor house) and took away all the goodes therein'). **64** *ALC* 1061; *AT* 1061.1; *CS* 1059=1061; *AClon*, p. 178; *AFM* 1061. **65** *CS* 1084=1088; *AI* 1088.4; *ALC*; *AFM* 1088.

Cuinn (the northern half of Ireland) some time previously.[66] Tairdelbach Ua Conchobair was to attack Kincora in 1116, and again in 1118, against Muirchertach Ua Briain when both its 'stone and timber' were dismantled and thrown into the Shannon.[67]

As Brian Bóraime had penetrated northwards via the Shannon, so successive kings of Connacht used the Shannon as a route by which to attack Munster; and, as Brian had done in Munster, so kings of Connacht also built their own strongholds. As first highlighted by Donnchadh Ó Corráin, Tairdelbach Ua Conchobair was to make extensive use of fortifications, and, significantly, a number of these were described as *caisdeoil, caistél, caislén* in the annals, new loanwords borrowed into Irish.[68] In 1124, he built *trí caisdeoil* at Dunlo near Ballinasloe, at Galway and at Collooney in Sligo.[69] The manner of their construction is not known, but the adoption of a new term suggests that contemporaries perceived them as distinctive in some way. The annalists were to use the same term for the earliest fortifications erected by Anglo-Normans, including earthen mottes.[70] It is pre-eminently in Connacht that the notice of 'castle' strongholds is evidenced in the annalistic record.[71] Frustratingly, mostly, when there is written evidence there is no extant physical evidence. In east Ulster where there has been more archaeological excavation of medieval sites, physical evidence for pre-Invasion raths, dubbed 'raised raths', or 'platform raths', or 'recycled ringforts' has been identified archaeologically

66 *AFM*. **67** *AT* 1116.1, 1118.8; *CS* 1112=1116; *AFM* 1116, 1118. *ALC* place the destruction of Kincora at the beginning of 1119. For another Connacht fleet sailed to Killaloe in 1119, see below, p. 234. **68** Donncha[dh] Ó Corráin, 'Royal fortresses and military fortifications' in B.G. Scott (ed.), *Perspectives in Irish archaeology* (Belfast, 1974), pp 68–71; idem, *Normans*, p. 156; most recently, M.A. Valante, 'Fleets, forts and the geography of Toirdelbach Ua Conchobair's bid for the high-kingship' in Vicky McAlister and Terry Barry (eds), *Space and settlement in medieval Ireland* (Dublin, 2015), pp 48–63. It is suggested by Helen Perros-Walton, 'Church reform in Connacht' in Seán Duffy (ed.), *Princes, prelates and poets in medieval Ireland: essays in honour of Katharine Simms* (Dublin, 2013), pp 279–308 at p. 294, that Muiredach Ua Dubhtaig as 'bishop of Connacht' had attended the Lateran council in 1123 and that he had returned to Ireland with a relic of the True Cross and 'eyewitness accounts of the castles of Europe, including the tower of London'. Whatever about the possibility of the relic that was enshrined in the cross of Cong having come from the Continent with Muiredach, it is more difficult to credit that an ecclesiastic's description of strongholds seen abroad provided inspiration for castle-building in Connacht. For Tairdelbach's fortifying (*daingned*) in 1115 of Buinne in Beithe, an island on the Shannon, which had been occupied by a Munster fleet in 1089, see *AT* 1089.1; 1115.7; above, n. 51. The Connacht fleet inflicted a defeat on the Munster fleet and the Foreigners of Limerick at Buinne in Beithe in 1145: *AT* 1145.8. **69** *AT* 1124.3; *AFM*. In 1136, the *caislén* of Loch Cairrcín (Ardakillin Lake in par. Killukin, bar./Co. Roscommon) was burnt by the men of Tethba: *AT* 1136.9. **70** In 1173 the *caislen* of Cill Caindig (Kilkenny) and the foreigners (*Gaill*) who dwelt in it was attacked by the Munster king, Domnall Ua Briain: *AT* 1173.10. Cf. *Caislen Shláine* (Slane) attacked and destroyed by Máel Sechnaill Mac Lochlainn, king of Cenél nEógain, in 1176: *AT* 1176.21; the '*caislen*' of Kells built by the foreigners in 1178: *AT* 1178.6. Cf. *AMisc* 1176.10, 15, 17. **71** This may in part be because there is no twelfth-century lacuna in *AT*, as in *AU*, *AI*, *ALC*.

which, without excavation, can look very similar to an Anglo-Norman motte and have sometimes been assumed to be such.[72] One location for which there is both physical and written evidence is the impressive site of Dún Echdach (Duneight, Co. Down), mentioned in annals in 1004, that is, broadly contemporaneous with Brian's building initiatives. The context of the annalistic entries is the battle of Cráeb Tulcha (Crew Hill near Glenavy, Co. Antrim), the inauguration site of the Dál Fiatach kings of Ulaid. The battle was fought on 14 September 1004 between Eochaid mac Ardgaill, king of Ulaid, and Áed Ua Néill, king of Cenél nEógain, and described as stretching from Cráeb Tulcha as far as Dún Echdach and Drumbo, a distance of about fifteen kilometres, suggesting that the battle ranged widely.[73] The names of ten high-status individuals who died there are recorded, a reflection of the battle's significance, along with a slaughter of the army, 'both noble and non-noble'. Dún Echdach is mentioned again in 1011 when Flaithbertach Ua Néill, king of Cenél nEógain, led an army against the king of Ulaid to Dún Echdach, where he burnt the *dún* and demolished its *baile*.[74] Dún Echdach's large inner ditch and reinforced bank, dated by excavation to the tenth or eleventh century, was to be reused as a motte in the early decades of John de Courcy's conquest of Ulaid and is named in his dower charter for his wife, Affraic, on the occasion of their marriage, probably because it was part of the pre-Invasion *tellach*, or mensal land, of the king of Ulaid.[75] The term 'demesne' is used by historians of so-called feudal societies for those lands that were directly exploited by a lord. Irish kings also had what are usually referred to as mensal lands which they farmed directly: the term *dominicum* occurs in a Latin charter of Diarmait Mac Murchada in favour of St Mary's abbey, Ferns, 1160×1162, formulated in the European tradition, where Diarmait states that he grants to

72 Cóilín Ó Drisceoil, 'Recycled ringforts: the evidence from archaeological excavation for the conversion of pre-existing monuments to motte castles in medieval Ireland', *JLAHS*, 25 (2002), 189–201. The most recent discussion of pre-Anglo-Norman fortifications is Kieran O'Conor, Niall Brady, Anne Connon and Carlos Fidalgo-Romo, 'The rock of Lough Cé, Co. Roscommon' in Thomas Finan (ed.), *Medieval Lough Cé: history, archaeology and landscape* (Dublin, 2010), pp 15–40. 73 *AU* 1004.5; *CS* 1002=1004; *AFM*. Cf. the encounter at Cráeb Tulcha in 1099 between the king of Cenél nEógain and the king of Ulaid, when Cráeb Tulcha was burnt and its tree cut down: *AU* 1099.8; *ALC* 1099. Brian, on his circuit of Ireland in 1005, is depicted as halting at Cráeb Tulcha in *CGG*, pp 136–7. In the twelfth-century poem on the circuit of the ninth-century king, Muirchertach mac Néill, Muirchertach is described as taking the king of Ulaid prisoner at Dún Echdach: Edmund Hogan, *Móirthimchell Éirenn uile do rigne Muirchertach mac Néill* (Dublin, 1901), pp 18–19. For the date of this text, see Donnchadh Ó Corráin, 'Muirchertach Mac Lochlainn and the *Circuit of Ireland*' in A.P. Smyth (ed.), *Seanchas: studies in early and medieval Irish archaeology, history and literature in honour of Francis J. Byrne* (Dublin, 2000), pp 238–50. 74 *AU* 1011.6; *AFM*. 75 It occurs as Dunechti/Dunechthi: Edmund Curtis, 'Two unpublished charters of John de Courcy, *princeps Ulidiae*', *Proceedings of the Belfast Natural History Society*, session 1928–9 (1930), 1–9 at 1; A.J. Otway-Ruthven, 'Dower charter of John de Courcy's wife', *UJA*, 3rd ser., 12 (1949), 77–81, at 79.

St Mary's 'all tithes and first fruits of his *dominicum* in Uí Chennselaig'.[76] The abbey was situated close by Diarmait's residence at Ferns. The destruction of Diarmait Mac Murchada's *tech cloiche* ('stone house') at Ferns and the burning of its *longphort* by Tigernán Ua Ruairc, king of Bréifne, is noted in the Annals of Tigernach in 1166.[77] In the Annals of the Four Masters the description is 'Ferns was burnt by Mac Murchada from fear that the Connacht men would burn his *caisteóil* and his *tech*'; and the same annals recount that when Diarmait was banished overseas his *caistiall* at Ferns was demolished.

Fortified sites, on the basis of physical and documentary evidence, became an important feature of warfare in the post-Brian era among the provincial kings of Munster, Connacht, Ulster, Leinster, and Mide.[78] There has been scepticism on the part of some post-Invasion historians to accept that an Irish *caistél/caislén/caisdeol* could have been similar to an Anglo-Norman motte, and no one has been prepared to follow F.J. Byrne's suggestion that the term 'bailey' for the outer court of an Anglo-Norman castle could actually have derived from Irish *baile*.[79] What is not in doubt, however, is that even if the physical characteristics of the various *castéil, caisléin, caisdeoil, dúin, daingne,* and *longphoirt* mentioned in the annals remain obscure, and, setting aside the problematic question of what constitutes a 'castle', it is certain that garrisoned strongholds and more fortified dwellings became a strategic component of warfare and territorial control in the post-Brian era.

Brian had greatly extended the scale of warfare in Ireland. A precondition for the waging of largescale warfare was the acquisition of regular renewable sources of movable wealth or taxation. This could be most efficiently amassed by the exploitation of the Hiberno-Scandinavian settlements whose manufacturing and trading bases were expanding dramatically by the late tenth century. One of Brian's strategies had been utilization of those settlements, their deployment as royal residences or garrisoned strongholds, and the tapping of their military and economic resources. When, after 1052, Diarmait mac Maíl na mBó, king of Leinster, secured exploitative control over the Dublin settlement, there was a notably dramatic increase in his military and naval capacity.[80] Just how much economic dividend was generated by the

76 M.T. Flanagan, *Irish royal charters: texts and contexts* (Oxford, 2005), pp 284–5. Demesne lands may be distinguished from *mruig rí,* 'king's land', set aside specifically for the use of a king during his reign. See Fergus Kelly, *Early Irish farming* (Dublin, 1997), p. 403. 77 *AT* 1166.13; *AFM*; cf. *teach cloithi* in *AMisc* 1165.4 (*recte* 1166). 78 Cf. the reference to the *caislén* of Cuilenntrach destroyed by Tairdelbach Ua Conchobair in 1155: *AT* 1155.8; *AFM* (identified ibid., by John O'Donovan as Cullentragh, Co. Meath, while Diarmuid Ó Murchadha, suggested Cullentragh in par./bar. Rathcline, Co. Longford). This may have been an Ua Máel Sechnaill stronghold. 79 F.J. Byrne, 'Ireland and her neighbours' in *NHI*, i, p. 859. Cf. Doherty, 'Vikings in Ireland', p. 327: 'Is there any reason why *dún* and *baile* should not be translated as "motte" and "bailey"'? 80 Seán Duffy, 'Irishmen and Islesmen in the kingdoms of Dublin and Man', *Ériu*, 43 (1992), 93–133.

Hiberno-Scandinavian settlements and, more importantly, how far geographically it circulated beyond those settlements, is more difficult to quantify. Catherine Swift has highlighted how the late eleventh-/early twelfth-century text, *Lebor na cert* (Book of Rights), an Ua Briain propagandist production, affords evidence for the economic transfer of goods from the Hiberno-Scandinavian settlements into the Irish hinterland.[81] *Lebor na cert* details the chiefly agricultural renders or dues that are to be paid by subordinate kings to provincial kings and the reciprocal bestowal of a range of ceremonial gifts or *tuarastla* by overkings on their subordinates A proportion of those ceremonial gifts listed in *Lebor na cert* are goods identified as from abroad, items that were commodities of international trade in the Insular Viking zone, such as imported horses and slaves. Goods of foreign origin are bestowed as *tuarastal* by kings of all the provinces detailed in *Lebor na cert* with the exception only of Connacht.

One of the remarkable features of the emergence of Tairdelbach and Ruaidrí Ua Conchobair as contenders for the high-kingship in the twelfth century is that they did not have ready access to the economic or military resources of the Hiberno-Scandinavian coastal settlements that were so significant a factor for Brian Bóraime and his Dál Cais successors; as well as for their rivals in Munster, the Meic Carthaig, in the early twelfth century who gained control of the Hiberno-Scandinavian settlement of Cork; and for the provincial kings of Leinster, Diarmait mac Maíl na mBó in the eleventh century and Diarmait Mac Murchada in the twelfth century, with the Leinster kings having the added advantage of closest proximity to the monetized economy of Dublin. These kings were able to draw on the growing wealth of the Hiberno-Scandinavian settlements and thereby to project themselves beyond their heartlands and even at times to become players in the wider politics of the Irish Sea province, as was the case with Diarmait mac Maíl na mBó, Tairdelbach ua Briain, and Muirchertach Ua Briain.[82] The strategies, however, by which the Ua Conchobair kings of Connacht in the twelfth century marshalled the economic resources to wage largescale warfare, including naval capacity, without sustained direct exploitation of the geographically more distant Hiberno-Scandinavian settlements, remain obscure.[83] Not that Tairdelbach Ua Conchobair did not try to take control of Dublin: in challenging Muirchertach

81 Catherine Swift, 'Taxes, trade and trespass: the Hiberno-Norse context of the Dál Cais empire in *Lebor na Cert*' in Kevin Murray (ed.), *Lebor na cert: reassessments*, ITS, Subsidiary Series 25 (London, 2013), pp 34–61. 82 Duffy, 'Irishmen and Islesmen'. 83 For a pioneering attempt to assess the economic resources of Diarmait Mac Murchada, see Catherine Swift, 'Follow the money: the financial resources of Diarmait Mac Murchada' in Purcell et al. (eds), *Clerics, kings and Vikings*, pp 91–102. With its emphasis on the value of the Hiberno-Norse settlements of Dublin and Wexford as vital advantages for the conversion of agricultural renders into bullion, it serves indirectly to highlight the achievements of the Ua Conchobair kings in marshalling their material resources.

Ua Briain for the high-kingship, Tairdelbach had laid siege to Dublin in 1118, expelled Domnall Gerrlámach, son of Muirchertach, and, according to the admittedly partisan Connacht-based Annals of Tigernach, 'assumed the kingship of the Foreigners',[84] though in Mac Carthaigh's Book he is stated to have installed Énna Mac Murchada as king of Leinster and of Dublin.[85] That substance can be attributed to this claim is suggested by the fact that in 1119 Tairdelbach was accompanied by the *maithe* of the Foreigners of Dublin (along with the kings of Leinster and Osraige) when he sailed a great fleet on the Shannon as far as the Ua Briain stronghold at Killaloe.[86] In 1121 Tairdelbach sought, albeit unsuccessfully, to influence the episcopal election in the city of Dublin.[87] His limited control over Dublin is well illustrated by an annalistic entry for 1125, which records that, having spent a night in the city, he (re-) installed the king of Leinster as king of Dublin.[88] In 1126, following the death of Énna Mac Murchada, king of Leinster, Tairdelbach attempted to place his own son, Conchobar, in the kingship of Dublin, but he was deposed a year later.[89] In endeavouring to exploit Dublin, Tairdelbach Ua Conchobair failed to assert continuous control over the city and had to give way, on the one hand, to Diarmait Mac Murchada, king of Leinster, sometimes with the face-saving expedient of allowing Diarmait to hold the town under his nominal overlordship, and, on the other, to Muirchertach Mac Lochlainn, king of Cenél nEógain, who from the 1140s onwards emerged as a serious contender for the high-kingship.[90]

Charles O'Conor, who otherwise chose to say so little about his royal ancestors, remarked of Tairdelbach that 'as much as the Times would permit, he reformed the civil Government, and erected a Mint at *Clonmacnoise* for the coinage of Silver'.[91] The establishment of a mint at Clonmancois was the one achievement that O'Conor selected in relation to Tairdelbach's career, doubtless because he interpreted coinage as a sign of economic progress that would resonate with his eighteenth-century readers for whom he was anxious to correct the negative views of early Irish society as backward, and in line with

84 *AT* 1118.5. Emphasis is placed on his taking of hostages from the Dubliners, as well as those of Osraige and Leinster, and his forcible removal of Murchad son of Domnall Ua Máel Sechnaill, king of Mide: *AU* 1118.6; *CS* 1114=1118; *ALC*; *AFM*. Domnall Gerrlámach was to die *in clericatu* in 1135: *AT* 1135.11; *AFM*; *CS* 1131=1135. **85** *AMisc* 1119.2, where it is also stated that he took 'all the other hostages of Leth Cuinn who were with him' alongside Murchad; cf. above, n. 67. **86** *AT* 1119.5; *AFM*; *AMisc* 1119.3. **87** M.T. Flanagan, *Irish society, Anglo-Norman settlers, Angevin kingship: interactions in Ireland in the late twelfth century* (Oxford, 1989), pp 29–31; Colmán Etchingham, 'Episcopal hierarchy in Connacht and Tairdelbach Ua Conchobair', *JGAHS*, 52 (2000), 13–29, at 25–6. **88** *AT* 1125.5. The version in Mac Carthaigh's Book has Tairdelbach hosting to Dublin 'and he took the kingship of Leinster': *AMisc* 1125.2. **89** *AU* 1126.7; *AT* 1126.3; *ALC*; *AFM*; *CS* 1122=1126; *AMisc* 1126.7; *AU* 1127.5; *ALC*; *AMisc* 1126.12 (*recte* 1127). **90** Duffy, 'Irishmen and Islesmen', 116–28. **91** *Dissertations* (1766), p. 273. Neither Tairdelbach nor Ruaidrí Ua Conchobair were mentioned in the 1753 edition of his

his conviction that what was required for contemporaries was 'a philosophical history of Ireland', by which he meant a non-partisan history.[92] What O'Conor's source was for the claim that Tairdelbach Ua Conchobair had established a mint at Clonmacnoise is not clear. John Lynch, in his *Cambrensis eversus* (a refutation of the twelfth-century polemicist, Gerald de Barri otherwise known as Giraldus Cambrensis, who wrote in justification of English intervention in Ireland), published in 1662, in a sustained eulogy of Tairdelbach Ua Conchobair, included the laconic sentence 'and he ordered silver to be struck at Clonmacnoise'.[93] Charles O'Conor is likely to have derived his information from Lynch's work.[94] The Continentally-educated Lynch held the benefice of the archdeaconry of Tuam for almost forty years from around 1632, even though he left Ireland for the Continent in the 1650s, and was to die there in 1677. Lynch did have access to now-lost sources, including a parchment manuscript in his possession of a set of annals covering the period 1141 to 1200.[95] If there is substance in his account of the introduction by Tairdelbach Ua Conchobair of the coining of silver at Clonmacnoise,[96] one would also wish to consider how far goods traded through the Hiberno-Norse ports could have penetrated the Connacht hinterland, and to what extent effective marshalling of movable wealth and its conversion into

Dissertations. **92** W.D. Love, 'Charles O'Conor of Belanagare and Thomas Leland's "Philosophical" history of Ireland', *IHS*, 13 (1962), 1–25; Hilary Larkin, 'Writing in an enlightened age?: Charles O'Conor and the philosophes' in Gibbons and O'Conor (eds), *Charles O'Conor*, pp 97–115; John Wrynn, 'Charles O'Conor as a "philosophical historian"' in idem, pp 72–80. **93** 'Argentum que postea Clonmacnoisiae signari jussit': John Lynch, *Cambrensis eversus*; ed. Matthew Kelly, 3 vols (Dublin, 1850), ii, pp 60–1. Tairdelbach Ua Conchobair is also described as having erected a mint and coined silver at Clonmacnoise, citing Lynch's *Cambrensus eversus*, in *The whole works of Sir James Ware concerning Ireland* (Dublin, 1745), ii, p. 205. This is not mentioned in earlier versions of Ware's historical works and was likely added from *Cambrensis eversus* by Walter Harris who married a granddaughter of Ware, pursued similar scholarly interests, and produced English translations and augmented versions of Ware's writings. **94** O'Conor alluded directly to Lynch's *Cambrensis eversus* in his *Dissertations* (1766), pp x, 140. **95** 'Annales pergamenei ab anno 1141 usque ad annum 1200 penes me': John Lynch, *De praesulibus Hiberniae*; ed. J.F. O'Doherty, 2 vols (Dublin, 1944), ii, p. 310. For his career, see René D' Ambrières and Éamon Ó Ciosáin, 'John Lynch of Galway (*c.*1599–1677): his career, exile and writing', *JGAHS*, 55 (2003), 50–63; Éamon Ó Cíosáin, 'Lynch, John' in *DIB*, v, pp 627–9. **96** See the comments by Michael Dolley who was prepared to consider the possibility in his *Sylloge of coins of the British Isles: the Hiberno-Norse coins in the British Museum* (London, 1966), pp 142–5. Tairdelbach is recorded to have given 160 ounces of gold and sixty marks (*marg*) of refined silver by way of bequest to the churches of Ireland: *AT* 1156.4; cf. *RIA contributions*, fasc. M., col. 63. This appears to be the first occurrence of *marc/marg* in the annals. A mark was not a coin but a denomination of weight usually equivalent to eight ounces of silver and was in general use throughout medieval Europe. See Charles Du Fresne Du Cange et al., *Glossarium mediae et infimae Latinitatis* (Niort, 1883–1887) s.n. *marca* at http://ducange.enc.sorbonne.fr/marca. There have been no coin hoards recovered from Connacht and the numbers of single finds are also very low. See the distribution map in Andrew Woods, 'The coinage and economy of Hiberno-Scandinavian Dublin' in Séan Duffy (ed.), *Medieval*

bullion was a significant feature of Tairdelbach Ua Conchobair's high-kingship. Conall MacGeoghegan's seventeenth-century translation of the Annals of Clonmacnoise under the year 1170 recorded that 'there was money coined in Clonvickenos this year'.[97] This would appear to be independent of John Lynch's reference to Tairdelbach Ua Conchobair's mint since the mint would have to have been established before Tairdelbach's death in 1156. Given the substantial evidence for contemporary very fine ecclesiastical metalworking at Clonmacnoise, the technological expertise for the minting of coins would have been readily available.[98]

Equipping an army was a considerable expense, even allowing for the fact that the cost might be offset by the taking of spoils and captives.[99] Although there is no reference to specifically *overseas* horses in the Connacht *tuarastla in Lebor na cert*, horses are nonetheless the most numerous commodity bestowed by the king of Connacht on his sub-kings. By the early twelfth century, annalistic references to a cavalry element in Munster armies occur with increasing frequency. The first incidence of the term *marcshluag* occurs in 1095 when on a hosting by Muirchertach Ua Briain into Connacht his *marcshluag* inflicted a defeat on the Connacht army.[100] When in 1114 Tairdelbach Ua Conchobair launched his bid for the high-kingship against Muirchertach Ua Briain, the decisive engagement was between the *marcshluag* of Ua Conchobair and the men of Munster.[101] *Marcshluag* can be distinguished in the annals from *crech marcach*, 'a raiding party on horseback'.[102] There are no references to

Dublin XIII (Dublin, 2013), pp 43–69, at p. 62. **97** *AClon*, p. 214. Since the entry is immediately preceded by an account of the synod presided over by Lorcán Ua Tuathail, archbishop of Dublin and papal legate, at Clonfert in 1179, the implied date is actually that year. The next entry, also purported to be under the year 1170, records the death of Lorcán, which, as is well known, occurred on 14 Nov. 1180. The Annals of Clonmacnoise were written (or translated) a generation earlier than the publication of Lynch's work, that is, 1627 compared to 1662, as pointed out to me by Dr Nollaig Ó Muraíle. **98** See most recently, Griffin Murray, *The Cross of Cong: a masterpiece of medieval Irish art* (Dublin, 2014), esp. p. 119; idem, 'The art of politics: the Cross of Cong and the Hiberno-Urnes style' in Clarke and Johnson (eds), *The Vikings in Ireland and beyond*, pp 416–37, where it is argued that Scandinavian influence in the Urnes-style decoration of the Cross should be linked to Tairdelbach Ua Conchobair's 'political manoeuvrings, particularly his relationship with Dublin as well as his engagement with the church reform movement' (p. 416) and that Dublin 'provided the conduit by which elements of the Scandinavian Urnes style reached Connacht' (p. 433). **99** For specific references to plunder, consumption and destruction of enemy provisions, cattle, and captives and hostages being taken by Tairdelbach and Ruaidrí Ua Conchobair, drawing only on the Connacht-based Annals of Tigernach, see *AT* 1114.10, 1116.1, 1119.5, 1121.6, 7, 1122.2,6, 1123.7, 1124.2, 4, 5,1126.3, 1127.1, 3, 1130.1, 1132.1, 2, 1140.4, 5, 1145.3, 1146.1, 7, 1148.2, 1149.3, 1151.2, 1158.7, 1160.3, 12, 1161.3, 1165.11, 1166.1, 1167.4, 1169.2, 1170.19, 1171.1,4. **100** *AI* 1095.9. There are at least two references to *marcsluag* in *Lebor na Cert*, l. 994 (bestowal of *sé eochu marc-shluaig* on the king of Cenél mBogaine) and l. 1044 (*trí gabra mera marc-shluaig* to the king of Uí Thuirtre). In 1120 Tadc Mac Carthaig, king of Desmond, bestowed 'gold and horses' as stipend when Ua Gilla Pátraic, king of Osraige, submitted to him: *AI* 1120.4. **101** *AT* 1114.5. **102** Cf. *AU*

fighting on horseback in *Cogadh Gáedhel re Gallaibh* although it mirrors *Lebor na cert* in depicting horses as important items bestowed as *tuarastal*. Máel Sechnaill is presented in the *Cogadh* as meeting Brian at Tara in 1002 accompanied by 240 horsemen, and although Brian sought to bestow 240 horses on him as *tuarastal*, Máel Sechnaill's men refused to lead the horses away; whereupon they were given by Máel Sechnaill to Brian's son, Murchad, as an honourable compromise.[103] Again, according to the *Cogadh*, when in 1006 Brian visited Cráeb Tulcha, the inauguration site of the king of Ulaid, Brian is described as having bestowed 1200 horses on the men of Ulaid.[104] These notices suggest that it was in the course of the twelfth century that a horsed element became a significant component in mobilized armies. References in the annals to cavalry units become more frequent during the twelfth century in relation also to the kings of Ulaid,[105] Tír Eógain,[106] Bréifne,[107] Leinster[108] and Airgialla.[109] It is noteworthy that the term occurs relatively late in relation to Leinster. While allowing for gaps and uneven coverage in the annalistic record which makes extrapolation potentially misleading, this may nonetheless reflect less developed military capacity on the part of Diarmait Mac Murchada, possibly because he had been able to rely more readily on Hiberno-Scandinavian forces, which, in turn, once the Dubliners had deserted him, may have contributed to his pressing need to recruit overseas mercenaries in 1166. There is actually surprisingly little information in the annals pertaining to Diarmait Mac Murchada's military capabilities or engagements throughout his long career and leading up to his defeat and consequent exile by Ruaidrí Ua Conchobair in 1166. Not, of course, that there isn't evidence for belligerent and violent acts by Mac Murchada, but it could be argued that they are manifested in more outmoded strategies – such as the vicarious rape of the abbess of Kildare in 1132,[110] the blinding of seventeen north Leinster dissidents in 1141,[111] or the abduction in 1152 of Derbforgaill, wife of Tigernán Ua Ruairc, king of Bréifne,[112] a fact that can be obscured by Mac Murchada's perceived modernity in other areas, such as his issue of Latin charters in the European tradition, patronage of newly introduced Continental monastic orders, and his recourse in 1166 to the court of King Henry II in Aquitaine.[113]

1000.7; *CS* 998=1000. **103** *CCG*, pp 132–3. **104** Along with gold and silver and clothing: *CGG*, p. 137; above, n. 73. **105** First reference in 1099: *AU* 1099.8; *ALC*; *AFM*. **106** First reference in 1099: *AU* 1099.8; *ALC*; *AFM*. **107** First reference in 1128: *AU* 1128.3; *ALC*; *AFM*. **108** First reference in *AT* 1153.6; *AFM* (and to the cavalry of Uí Chennselaig in 1167: *AFM*). After cows, horses are the most numerous commodity bestowed as stipend by the king of Leinster on his client kings in *Lebor na cert* with the king of Uí Chennselaig receiving one hundred horses and ten saddles and bridles: *Lebor na cert*, p. 186. **109** First reference in *AT* 1171.2; *AFM*. **110** *ALC*; *CS* 1129=1132; *AClon*, p. 193. **111** *AT* 1141.5; *AClon*, p. 192; *AFM*. **112** *AT* 1152.6; *AFM*; *AClon*, pp 199–200. **113** Cf. 'Diarmait was far in advance of most of the Irishmen of his day': F.X. Martin, *No hero in the house: Diarmait Mac Murchada and the coming of the Normans to Ireland* (Dublin,

The intensity of warfare can be gauged by the long-term impact of certain battles. The battle of Clontarf had greatly depleted the resources of Brian's immediate successors. The battle of Sliab gCrot in the Galtee mountains in 1058 marked a downturn in the career of Brian's son Donnchad, leading to his eventual deposition and exile in 1063.[114] Ua Briain resources took another major hit in 1151 at the battle of Móin Mór, where Tairdelbach Ua Briain suffered a decisive defeat at the hands of Tairdelbach Ua Conchobair, king of Connacht.[115] The Uí Briain had barely recovered from Móin Mór by the time of the accession of Domnall Mór Ua Briain in 1168 who then had to face warfare with Anglo-Norman intruders into Munster. The defeat at Dublin in 1170 of Ruaidrí Ua Conchobair by Diarmait Mac Murchada and his overseas mercenaries had devastating consequences for Ruaidrí's high-kingship, such that it has been described as Ireland's battle of Hastings.[116]

Although the focus of the annals in the post-Brian era is overwhelmingly on violence and warfare, evidence, albeit to a lesser extent, is also afforded for relations between kings and individual churches. Strategic alliances with churches had been a notable feature of Brian Bóraime's pursuit of the high-kingship.[117] Such alliances were, of course, a long-established strategy, discernible already when the earliest documentation for individual churches becomes available in the early seventh century, as, for example, in Cogitosus's Life of Brigit with its reference to the treasures of kings kept at Kildare. Brian's novel achievement in the sphere of church–state relations was to undermine the Uí Néill monopoly of Armagh support for that dynasty's claims to high-kingship which had been acknowledged by Armagh from the late seventh century onwards and promoted in conjunction with its own claims to primacy, that is, over a three-hundred year period.[118] Brian's wish to be buried at Armagh was determined by the fact that the Uí Néill dynasty had a royal mausoleum at Armagh from no later than 935 and that successive Northern Uí Néill kings were buried there.[119]

In the volatile political circumstances that ensued following the battle of Clontarf and the death of Brian Bóraime, a critical issue for the church of Armagh was whom should it endorse as high-king; and would its choice be

1975), p. 21; Byrne, *Irish kings*, pp 273–4, arguing that Diarmait 'was aiming at total innovation' and sought to set himself up as a 'feudal king'. **114** *AU* 1058.3; *AT* 1058.3; *AI* 1058.4; *CS* 1056=1058; *AFM*. **115** See J.V. Kelleher, 'The battle of Móin Mhór, 1151', *Celtica*, 20 (1988), 11–27. **116** Seán Duffy, 'Ireland's Hastings: the Anglo-Norman conquest of Dublin', *Anglo-Norman Studies*, 20 (1998), 69–86. **117** See Donnchadh Ó Corráin, 'Dál Cais: church and dynasty', *Ériu*, 24 (1973), 52–63; idem, 'Foreign connections and domestic politics: Killaloe and the Uí Briain in twelfth-century hagiography' in Dorothy Whitelock, Rosamund McKitterick and David Dumville (eds), *Ireland in early mediaeval Europe: essays in memory of Kathleen Hughes* (Cambridge, 1982), pp 212–31. **118** See Ailbhe MacShamhráin, 'Brian Bóruma, Armagh and high-kingship', *Seanchas Ard Mhacha*, 20 (2005), 1–21. **119** *In cimeterio regum*: *AU* 935.7 (secondary entry). Cf. the burial at Armagh of Ardgal Mac Lochlainn, king of Ailech, *in mausolio regum*; *AU* 1064.7;

accepted by other churchmen? The so-called period of 'high-kings with opposition' reflected a failure of consensus less on the part of the secular polity, which had always mounted opposition to individual high-kings even before Brian's high-kingship, than a breakdown of consensus on the part of ecclesiastics and the learned elite. In the wake of Brian's death, the church of Armagh can be assumed to have reverted to endorsing the high-kingship of the Southern Uí Néill king, Máel Sechnaill: he died in 1022 at his residence in Cró-Inis in the presence 'close by him' of the heads of the churches of Armagh, Kells, and Clonmacnoise (*sibi artantibus venerabilium sanctorum Patricii scilicet et Columbae ac Ciaraini heredibus*), as recorded in *Chronicon Scotorum*, and having been anointed by Amalgaid, *comarba Pátraic* (the heir of St Patrick at Armagh), and with 'masses, hymns, psalms, and canticles being sung for his soul'.[120] In annalistic death-notices, Máel Sechnaill is described as 'king of Ireland', with the exception only of the partisan Dál Cais Annals of Inisfallen, where he is accorded the more localized title of 'king of Tara'. The northern and Clonmacnoise annalistic traditions were prepared to concede the resumption of the high-kingship to Máel Sechnaill after the death of Brian Bóraime.[121]

Following Máel Sechnaill's death in 1022, Armagh appears to have been prepared for a time to acknowledge the candidacy of Brian's son Donnchad, as suggested when Amalgaid of Armagh, celebrated Easter in 1026 with Donnchad at his royal residence at Kincora, a circumstance recorded only in the Annals of Inisfallen.[122] There is insufficient annalistic data to gauge how far, and for how long, the church of Armagh continued to support Donnchad, and, following his deposition and exile in 1063, how it responded to the accession of his nephew, Tairdelbach ua Briain. A *comarba Pátraic* is not attested again in Munster until 1068 when Máel Ísu, who had succeeded to the office in 1064, 'brought away his full visitation, both in tribute and offerings'.[123] That visit was likely determined primarily by the fiscal interests of the church of Armagh in Munster, which could be pursued routinely and independently of secular political circumstances, and yet the timing may nonetheless have been undertaken with a view to endorsing Tairdelbach's accession as king of Munster, and possibly even a bid for the high-kingship. Nevertheless, in 1073

ALC; in *AFM* it is given as *i ttumba rioghraide*: *AFM* 1064. In 870, there is reference to the 'door of the house of [the Northern Uí Néill king], Áed [Findliath], king of Temair ['Tara]', at Armagh: *AU* 870.4. **120** *CS* 1020=1022; *AFM* 1022; *AU* 1022.3; *AT* 1022.4; *ALC*; *AClon*, p. 171; Gearóid Mac Niocaill, 'Annála gearra as proibhinse Ard Macha', *Seanchas Ard Mhacha*, 3 (1959), 337–40, at 339. Contrast *AI* 1022.4. **121** *AU* present Máel Sechnaill in his death-notice as having had an uninterrupted reign of forty-three years as high-king, even though Brian had been described as 'king of Ireland' in his death-notice: *AU* 1014.2. Cf. *CS* 998=1000, 'the first revolt of Brian and the men of Connacht against Máel Sechnaill'. Cf. above, n. 29. **122** *AI* 1026.3. **123** *AU* 1068.2; *AFM*. For 'stewards of Patrick' in Munster, attested from 1007 onwards, see Aubrey Gwynn and D.F. Gleeson, *A history of the diocese of Killaloe* (Dublin, 1962), pp 91–3, and Casey in this volume, above.

the head of the church of Armagh is found extending his protection to the Southern Uí Néill king of Tara, Conchobar, grandson of Máel Sechnaill (d. 1022), albeit not very successfully since Conchobar was to be treacherously slain by his nephew, despite, as the annalist noted, being under 'the protection of the *Bachall Ísu* and in the presence of the *Bachall*'.[124] The *Bachall Ísu*, 'staff of Jesus', had become the principal symbol of office of the head of the church of Armagh and implies the latter's presence, although one could perhaps allow for the possibility that it may have been in the custody of a relic-bearing Armagh official on that occasion.[125] Conchobar's head was removed from his grave at Clonmacnoise in 1073 and conveyed to Tairdelbach ua Briain at Kincora, which suggests the latter's involvement in his killing.[126] The point of this gruesome act, apart from public humiliation of the Southern Uí Néill dynasty, was to deprive Conchobar of his place of resurrection at Clonmacnoise, in line with an Irish understanding that the soul resided in the head. In 1073, the *comarba Pátraic* was exercising a role which becomes ever more frequent in the twelfth century of acting as a protector of individual kings and mediator between warring kings, with his authority publicly manifested by the presence of the *Bachall Ísu*. In 1079, the *comarba Pátraic* with the *Bachall Ísu* was present at the submission made by Máel Sechnaill mac Conchobair, king of Mide, to Tairdelbach ua Briain at Dublin, acting, as the annalistic entries make plain, as guarantor for Máel Sechnaill's safety, and rather more successfully so than had been the case for Conchobar in 1073.[127] In 1093, Domnall Mac Lochlainn, king of Cenél nEógain, and Donnchad Ua hEochada, king of Ulaid, made a covenant *tre chombaig*, 'in common hostility', against Muirchertach Ua Briain with many relics including the *Bachall Ísu*.[128] Later in the same year, an agreement between Muirchertach Ua Briain and his brother, Diarmait, was negotiated at Cashel and Lismore 'with the relics of Ireland', including the *Bachall Ísu*, as pledges, though this need not necessarily prove the presence of the *comarba Pátraic*.[129] That Tairdelbach ua Briain could

124 *AU* 1073.2; *AI* 1073.2; *ALC* 1073; cf. *CS* 1070=1073; *AFM*. **125** The earliest annalistic reference to the *Bachall Ísu* occurs in 789 when the relic was 'dishonoured' by the Southern Uí Néill king, Donnchad mac Domnaill, in an assembly at Ráith Airthir: *AU* 789.17. The first allusion to the protection of the *Bachall Ísu* occurs in 1015, afforded to Áed Ua Ruairc, king of Bréifne, against Tadc in Eich Gil, king of Connacht: *AU*, 1015; *ALC*. In 1013 there is a reference to the 'breaking' of the *Bachall Patraic*: *AU* 1013.1; *AFM*. Thereafter, references are to the *Bachall Ísu* as the principal insignum of the head of the church of Armagh. **126** Recorded only in the Clonmacnoise group of annals, *CS* 1070=1073; *AClon*, p. 181. In 1084, the severed head of Donnchad Ua Ruairc was brought back to Limerick following his defeat by Muirchertach Ua Briain at the battle of Móin Chruinneóice: *AT* 1084.3; *AFM*; cf. *AU* 1084.6. In 1088, a combined force of Domnall Mac Lochlainn and Ruaidrí na Saide Buide Ua Conchobair invaded Munster and retrieved the head and brought it back to Connacht: *AT* 1088.3; *AI* 1088.3; *AU* 1088.2; *ALC*; *CS* 1084=1088; *AFM*. **127** *AT* 1079.4; *CS* 1076=1080; *AFM* 1080. **128** *AI* 1093.4. **129** *AI* 1093.11. In 1095, Domnall, *comarba* since 1091, is recorded to have 'made a visitation of Munster for the first time': *AFM*.

not rely on the exclusive endorsement of Armagh for his high-kingship may have been a factor contributing to his assent to recourse to the archbishop of Canterbury in 1074 and 1085 for the consecrations of Gilla Pátraic and Donngus, bishops-elect of Dublin.[130] By 1101, when Tairdelbach's son, Muirchertach, convened a council at Cashel at which he donated the royal site of Cashel 'as an offering to Patrick and to God', a rapprochement with Armagh can be assumed to be in train.[131] Nevertheless, on a series of campaigns against Domnall Mac Lochlainn in the north, Muirchertach Ua Briain's potential military advantage was neutralized by the peace-keeping interventions of successive heads of the church of Armagh. The *comarba Pátraic* negotiated a truce between Ua Briain and Mac Lochlainn, in 1097, 1099, 1102, 1105, 1107, 1109, and 1113 that worked to the advantage of Mac Lochlainn.[132] On five of those seven occasions, when the location is named, Muirchertach Ua Briain was in the north with his army but was prevented from deploying it by the interposition of the head of the church of Armagh. Peace-brokering activities proceeded alongside Armagh's reformulation of its primatial claims as metropolitan archbishop and primate in the context of the regularization of an island-wide hierarchical diocesan constitution with Armagh at its head as metropolitan primate, a redefinition of its role that arguably also called for a more non-aligned stance.

As in the political, so in the ecclesiastical sphere, Brian Bóraime had broken an Uí Néill monopoly and fractured the support link between the Uí Néill dynasty and the church of Armagh; his successors, however, did not succeed in retaining exclusive Armagh support. Nonetheless, contenders for the high-kingship, including the kings of Connacht, deemed it incumbent to try and secure Armagh support. The head of the church of Armagh undertook a visitation of Connacht in 1108 and again in 1116.[133] In 1140, the *comarba Pátraic*, that is, Gilla Meic Liac, who had become archbishop of Armagh in 1134, undertook a visitation of Connacht 'for the first time' and obtained his full tribute; and rather cryptically it is recorded uniquely in the Annals of the

130 Flanagan, *Irish society*, pp 12–21. Muirchertach Ua Briain also approved the consecration of Malchus, bishop-elect of Waterford, in 1096. Between 1097 and 1107 when Archbishop Anselm of Canterbury was either in exile or in dispute with King Henry I, it was no longer feasible for requests from Ireland for consecration to be made. See Martin Brett, 'Canterbury's perspective on church reform and Ireland, 1070–1115' in Damian Bracken and Dagmar Ó Riain-Raedel (eds), *Ireland and Europe in the twelfth century: reform and renewal* (Dublin, 2006), pp 13–35. **131** *CS* 1097=1101; *AT* 1101.8; *AFM*. There is no mention of this synod in *AI* or *AU*. **132** *AU* 1097.6, 1099.7, 1102.8, 1105.3, 1107.8, 1109.5, 1113.7; *AFM* 1097, 1099, 1103, 1106, 1109, 1113; *ALC* 1097, 1099, 1102, 1105, 1107, 1109, 1113; *AI* 1113.8; *AT* 1113.2. Cf. *AU* 1101.8; *AFM*, where the head of the church of Armagh negotiated between the king of Cenél nEógain and the king of Ulaid. By 1128, the head of the church of Armagh was negotiating peace between Connacht and Munster: *AU* 1128.9; *ALC*; *AFM*. **133** *AU* 1108.3, 1116.1; *ALC* 1108, 1116; *AFM* 1108, 1116 (not noticed in the Connacht-based *AT*).

Four Masters that the churches of Connacht 'were put under his jurisdiction by Tairdelbach Ua Conchobair and the nobles of Connacht, and the successor of Patrick and his clergy left a blessing on the king and the nobles of Connacht'.[134] This may allude to ongoing negotiations with Armagh that were to result in the recognition of an archiepiscopal province of Tuam at the synod of Kells in 1152 which was carved out of the archiepiscopal province of Armagh. In 1151, Gilla Meic Liac, *comarba Pátraic*, made a visitation of Connacht 'for the second time', obtained 'his full tribute' and received a gold ring weighing twenty ounces from Tairdelbach Ua Conchobair on that occasion.[135]

Strategic alliances with churchmen and effective exploitation of ecclesiastical patronage remained vital for aspirants to the high-kingship and for provincial kings in the post-Brian era, while from the late eleventh century onwards they developed in a more territorially defined direction. The diocesan boundaries demarcated at the synod of Ráith Bressail in 1111 with subsequent modifications, mapped onto, and served to reinforce, regnal units. The papal ratification of the archiepiscopal province of Tuam at the synod of Kells in 1152 as coterminous with the provincial kingship of Connacht is a notable instance: carved out of the archiepiscopal province of Armagh, the province of Tuam's obtaining of papal confirmation in 1152 was a significant achievement for Tairdelbach Ua Conchobair. New monastic foundations consequent upon the introduction of the monastic rules of Augustine and Benedict and of Continental Arroasian and Cistercian observances also had important implications for both the enhanced reputation and territorial grip of royal

134 'Ro dilsighíd a ccealla for a c[h]omus ó Thoirrdhealbhach Ó Conchobhair and ó mhaithibh Connacht': *AFM* (not in *AT*). *AU* and *CS* are lacunose. *DIL* translates *dilsighíd* in this instance as 'places under jurisdiction of' (see *eDIL*, s.v. *dílsigid*, *dísligid*). I am grateful to Professor Micheál Ó Mainnín for comments on this entry. In 1143 an unidentified *comarba Pátraic* with the *Bachall Ísu*, therefore presumably Gilla Meic Liac, was among the guarantors for the safety of Murchad Ua Máel Sechnaill, king of Mide, who had been taken prisoner by Tairdelbach Ua Conchobair: *AFM*; cf. *CS*; *AClon*, p. 197. However, among the guarantors for the safety of Tadc Ua Briain in 1147 the *comarba Pátraic* is identified in *AFM* as Máel Máedóc Ua Morgair (St Malachy). That this was not an error on the part of the Four Masters is suggested by the fact that at the synod of Inis Pátraic in 1148 Máel Máedóc is described as *comarba Pátraic* in *CS* and *AFM*. This was an office that technically he had relinquished to Gilla Meic Liac in 1137, although his status as papal legate from 1140 would have accorded Maél Máedóc precedence over Gilla Meic Liac. 135 *AFM*. In 1172, he is recorded on visitation in Connacht for the fourth time: *AFM*. A concern for good relations with the church of Armagh is evidenced also in the annual grant made in 1169 by Ruaidrí Ua Conchobair to the lector of Armagh in support of lectures for students of Ireland and Scotland: *AU* 1169; *AFM*. In 1180 Ruaidrí Ua Conchobair was to secure the translation of his nephew Tomaltach (Thomas) from the see of Elphin to the primatial see of Armagh. This could be said to reflect an acknowledged link between the church of Armagh and the high-kingship, though it may equally have been a reaction on Ruaidrí's part to a right of assent to episcopal appointments claimed by King Henry II. See Aubrey Gwynn, 'Tomaltach Ua Conchobair, coarb of Patrick (1181–1201): his life and times', *Seanchas Ard Mhacha*, 9 (1977), 231–74.

patrons. These new foundations, alongside reconfiguration of existing monastic sites, advanced royal as well as ecclesiastical agendas, and were used as a means of consolidating and extending royal authority.[136]

Returning to those generalized assessments that historians have offered for developments in the post-Brian period which posit that Irish society was moving in the direction of feudalism, it must be emphasized that no sustained definition of what these scholars understand by 'feudal' has been offered. This is the more regrettable in light of the fact that historians of so-called feudal societies for some time now have questioned the utility of 'feudalism' as a meaningful analytical tool.[137] The lack of consensus as to what constitutes 'feudalism', in effect, nullifies its use without very precise definition. There is a certain irony in the fact that feudalism has so often been associated with the breakdown of political power, the weakness or decline of public, or central, authority, and yet it has been used by historians of twelfth-century Ireland to argue for the intensification of royal control. Concrete analyses need to be privileged over general claims. Developments in eleventh- and twelfth-century Ireland still need to be explored in greater detail, and comparatively by region, before meaningful comparisons can be drawn with other so-called feudal societies.

That the pace of political change quickened in the post-Brian era is undeniable. The challenge is to find apposite ways of evaluating them and of assessing how far they were a direct result of his reign. It would be more appropriate, at least in the first instance, to focus on an intensification of kingship, or lordship, rather than to posit an ill-defined process of feudalization. Kingship was a superior form of lordship and it can be problematic to distinguish between prerogatives and strategies that are unique to the office of king as distinct from dominical, or non-royal lordship. Lordship was an institution common alike to so-called feudal and non-feudal societies. The term 'lordship' has the merit of encompassing the range of leadership terms which are attested in the annals in the post-Brian era, *rí*, *air-rí*, *toísech*, *tigerna*, *maor*, *muire*.[138] And unlike the eighteenth-century neologism, 'feudalism', lordship was a contemporary term: as noted above, Diarmait Mac Murchada referred to his *dominium* in the charter that he issued 1160×1162 in favour of St Mary's abbey, Ferns: he claimed a prerogative *causa dominii*, 'by reason of

136 Flanagan, *Irish royal charters*, pp 240–52; Perros-Walton, 'Church reform in Connacht', an important wide-ranging discussion of the ecclesiastical patronage of the kings of Connacht. 137 Among a substantial revisionist literature, the most sustained case is made by Susan Reynolds, *Fiefs and vassals: the medieval evidence reinterpreted* (Oxford, 1994). The most recent contribution is that of Charles West, *Reframing the feudal revolution: political and social transformation between the Marne and the Mosel, c.800–c.1100* (Cambridge, 2013). For a brief historiographical survey, see the entry by E.A.R. Brown in R.E. Bjork (ed.), *Oxford dictionary of the Middle Ages*, 4 vols (Oxford, 2010), ii, pp 620–2. 138 Cf. Ó Corráin, 'Nationality and kingship', p. 10.

lordship', to assent to the election of an abbot of Ferns.[139] The issuing of Latin charters by Irish kings in the twelfth century has been interpreted as a signifier of feudalization,[140] although this is unwarranted since charters were a ubiquitous form of recording land-grants in medieval societies that have not been categorized as 'feudal', such as, for example, Anglo-Saxon England. The adoption by a number of Irish kings of the Latin charter formulated in the European tradition, written in Continental minuscule rather than Insular script, and authenticated by the attachment of a seal impression, can be regarded as evidence of Europeanization but not necessarily of feudalization, certainly without more detailed analyses of lordship structures in twelfth-century Ireland.[141] Similarity of documentary form cannot automatically be assumed to signify comparable socio-legal structures.

The eleventh- and twelfth-century annals are an intractable source for exploring non-military strategies of regnal lordship or royal governance in Ireland, and yet with more resourceful strategies, there is much that is yet to be extracted from them. I wish to make a case here for more prosopographical analysis, an approach that would also have the merit of enabling more meaningful comparisons with so-called feudal societies.[142] It is first necessary to identify a king's associates before it is possible to explore and characterize the nexus of the relationship between them. One indicator of intensified control of political subordinates is the evidence that can be gathered for an inner core of associates that were found regularly in association with particular kings, or an affinity,[143] alongside evidence for the elaboration of royal administrative households. Of course, Irish kings had functionaries in their personal households or courts, as the evidence of early Irish literature readily attests, with a wide range of vernacular terms for those specialist functionaries, such as *rechtaire* and *techtaire, gilla cupáin* and *deogbaire*.[144] The growing importance, however, of administrative officials and the complexities of royal courts is reflected in the fact that death-notices for such royal officials begin to be recorded in the annals in the eleventh century. The first notice of a *rechtaire*

139 Flanagan, *Irish royal charters*, pp 284–5. 140 Curtis was the first to do so in relation to charters in his *History of medieval Ireland* (London, 1923), p. 20. In 1919 MacNeill, *Phases of Irish history*, p. 298, had alluded to these charters as indicators that Irish kings could grant 'ownership in land over the heads of all occupiers' in refutation of what he believed to be G.H. Orpen's inaccurate view of communal landholding in pre-twelfth-century Ireland. 141 On the 'Europeanization of Europe', see Robert Bartlett, *The making of Europe: conquest, colonization and cultural change, 950–1350* (London, 1992), pp 1–3, 269–91. 142 A notable example of genealogical sources used to great prosopographical effect to explore links between particular dynasties and local churches is Ó Corráin, 'Dál Cais'. 143 A term used by historians of Anglo-Norman societies, though it should be stressed that it has no necessary connotations of feudalism; cf. the prosopographical data assembled on William Marshal's 'affinity' by David Crouch, *William Marshal: knighthood, war and chivalry*, 2nd ed. (London, 2002), pp 144–5, 217–25. 144 Edel Bhreatnach, *Ireland in the medieval world, AD400–1000: landscape, kingship and religion* (Dublin, 2014), pp 108–15; F.J. Byrne, 'Ireland and her neighbours' in *NHI*, i, pp 873–89.

occurs in 1018 when the *rechtaire* of the Southern Uí Néill king, Máel Sechnaill, is named alongside three kings as having been killed on a raid into Éle across the Munster border.[145] In 1133, the death of Gilla na Náem Ua Birn, *toísech* of Tír Briúin and *rí rechtaire Érenn*, 'royal steward of Ireland', that is, steward of Tairdelbach Ua Conchobair, and Gilla na Náem's burial in the church of Roscommon are recorded in the Annals of Tigernach, the more noteworthy an entry because it was a non-violent death.[146] On the evidence of Diarmait Mac Murchada's Latin charters, Diarmait had a *notarius*, Florentius, who also occurs as his *cancellarius*, and a *senescallus*, and a *capellanus* and *capellania*.[147] The Latin *senescallus* can be equated with Irish *rechtaire*, as evidenced by a Latin charter issued in 1224 by Áed Ua Conchobair, king of Connacht: among the witnesses to Áed's charter was Torbertus, described as the king's *senescallus*.[148] Torbertus had already served Áed's father Cathal Crobderg in that capacity since, in an annalistic entry in 1210, which recorded that Toirbert, son of a Gall-Gaedel, had been taken as a hostage for Cathal Crobderg by King John, he is described as *rechtaire do reachtairibh*.[149] His status within the royal household is clearly indicated by his acting as a hostage on behalf of the king of Connacht. Arguably more novel than the office of *rechtaire/senescallus* was that of *notarius/cancellarius* mentioned in Diarmait Mac Murchada's charters.[150] This individual would have had oversight of the drafting of documents issued in the king's name and custody of his seal. When the treaty of Windsor was negotiated between Ruaidrí Ua Conchobair and King Henry II, in 1174, Ruaidrí was vicariously represented by his *cancellarius, Magister Laurentius*, a description implying that Laurentius had had a university education, which would undoubtedly have facilitated his input into the Latin draft of the text of the treaty.[151]

The witnesses to Diarmait Mac Murchada's charters, considered alongside annalistic entries, enable us to identify his affinity, those individuals who were

145 *AT* 1017.2; *AU* 1018.6; *ALC*; *AFM* 1017=1018. In 1021 the death of Mac Congaillig, *prímh-rechtaire* of Máel Sechnaill, occurred after he had plundered the shrine of Ciarán of Clonmacnoise: *AFM*. Cf. the killing in 1101 of Ua hIndredáin, *taoiseach teaghlaigh Uí Mhaoileachlainn*, along with two hundred others in a military engagement between Donnchad Ua Máel Sechnaill, king of Mide, and Cú Caisil Ua Cerbaill, king of Airgialla: *AFM*; the killing of Ragnall Ua hÓcáin, *rechtaire* of Tullahogue, in 1103, and the death of Donnsléibe Ua hÓcáin, *rechtaire* of Tullahogue, in 1122: *AU* 1103.4; *AFM* 1103, 1122. **146** *AT* 1133.3; *AFM*. Domnall Ua Birn was a casualty among the forces of Tairdelbach Ua Conchobair in 1154 when they suffered defeat by Muirchertach Mac Lochlainn: *AFM* 1154. **147** Flanagan, *Irish royal charters*, pp 265–6, 284–5. *Capellania* is a relatively unusual word perhaps better translated as 'chaplaincy' than 'chapel'. **148** Ibid., pp 350–1. **149** *ALC* 1210, 1211; *AFM* 1209=1210, 1210=1211; *AClon*, p. 223. Toirbert (Toirbheand in *AFM*) suggests Hiberno-Scandinavians in long-established service in Connacht. In 1153, Sitriuc mac Dubgaill was named among Connacht men slain by Muirchertach Mac Lochlainn, king of Cenél nEógain, at the battle of Fordruim: *AT* 1153.7; *AFM*. Cf. appendix 11.1 below, no. 10. **150** Flanagan, *Irish royal charters*, pp 63–4, 265–6, 284–5. **151** Flanagan, *Irish society*, pp 230, 253–4, 312.

most closely associated with him, and regularly in his company. No attempt has yet been made to collate evidence for the regular associates of Tairdelbach and Ruaidrí Ua Conchobair, a necessary component in evaluating their bid for the high-kingship and for drawing comparisons between pre-Invasion and post-Invasion Ireland. A small-scale example of the potential of prosopographical investigation is provided here (appendix 11.1, below). In the Norman French text composed around 1190, variously referred to as the 'Song of Dermot and the earl', 'Deeds of the Normans in Ireland' and 'La geste des Engleis en Yrlande', there is a list of individuals from Connacht who accompanied Ruaidrí Ua Conchobair in 1174 on an expedition to Trim against Anglo-Normans. It is remarkable that the non-native author had such detailed information about Ruaidrí's associates whom he listed as Ua Flaithbertaig, Mac Diarmata, Mac Airechtaig, Ua Cellaig of Uí Maine, Ua hEgra (?), Ua Fínnachta, Ua Cairbre (?), Ua Flannacáin, Ua Mannacháin, and Ua Sechnessaig of Poltilethan. Most of these individuals can be shown via twelfth-century annals to have been associated with the Ua Conchobair kings of Connacht.[152] More painstaking prosopographical analysis of those individuals named as casualties at the many battles that occurred in the post-Brian era also yields valuable information on the affinities of individual kings and enables historians to build up a clearer picture of a king's clients and their connections over several generations to his dynasty.[153] Named casualties who fell on the side of particular kings are one good indication that they were recognized as members of the king's influential circle. The marshalling of this data is a necessary component for analyzing political structures in twelfth-century Ireland. Fosterage and marriage links also need to be included, not least when dealing with a king like Tairdelbach Ua Conchobair who had twenty-two known sons by at least six different women.[154]

The endeavour to consolidate stable kingships in twelfth-century Ireland was based on a number of factors. One essential was territorial definition and control. The construction of fortifications, and even the diversion of the river Suck in 1139 by Tairdelbach Ua Conchobair, played a role in such territorial definition,[155] as did the drawing of diocesan boundaries and the foundation of new monastic houses which both enhanced the reputation of their royal patrons and strengthened their territorial grip, especially in contested areas that could be neutralized by generous grants to ecclesiastical institutions, thereby cutting out political rivals. Twelfth-century Ireland witnessed a smaller

152 See appendix 11.1, below. 153 Cf. the list of those who died at the battle of Downpatrick, 1177: *AMisc* 1177.2; also 1179.8. 154 Muireann Ní Bhrolcháin, 'The *Banshenchas* revisited' in Mary O'Dowd and Sabine Wichert (eds), *Chattel, servant or citizen: women's status in church and society* (Belfast, 1995), pp 70–81 at pp 75–6. 155 *AT* 1139.4; Anne Connon and Brian Shanahan, 'Creating borders in twelfth-century Ireland? Toirrdelbach Ua Conchobair's diversion of the River Suck' in Jenifer Ní Ghrádaigh and Emmett O'Byrne (eds), *The march in the islands of the medieval west* (Leiden, 2012), pp 139–70.

number of more powerful kings gain firmer control over territory and political subordinates. As competition increased and access to power became confined to fewer dynasties, exploitation of internal rivalry was intensified as a means of manipulation for powerful kings to influence affairs in rival kingdoms. Capitalization on tensions both within patrimonial kingdoms, and beyond, was a recurrent feature which impeded consolidation. Although there is a shift to narrower powerholding lineages, crucially, however, a universally accepted orderly regnal or lineal succession had not been achieved. The tendency to filial succession, while it could be a sign of strength, could also generate its own instabilities. There is a discernible move to filial succession in the kingship of Connacht coupled with advance designation to kingship,[156] and yet Tairdelbach and Ruaidrí Ua Conchobair each faced disaffection and opposition from their own sons. Not, of course, that this was unique to Ireland: Henry II as king of England faced comparable rebellions from his sons, but the principle of primogeniture, even if not yet fully adhered to, was becoming accepted as beneficial by the Anglo-Norman aristocracy with the eager urging of ecclesiastics.

Following English intrusion into Ireland, not only the high-kingship, but also provincial kingships underwent retraction. A reverse process of levelling up of once subordinated dynasties was set in train. Provincial lineages were obliged to share the political stage with those whom they had sought to depress in status and to convert into dependent clients, and these now began to acquire, or recover, equal or near-equal status. Qualitative disparities in lordship, so evident in the twelfth century, were unravelling. This had implications not only within the native Irish polity but critically also for its engagement with the colonists. Aristocratic concourse between native and newcomer was impeded by the absence of a recognized political centre to serve as a focus where the uppermost ranks of native and colonial society might have mingled. Geographical shifts in the high-kingship had prevented Brian Bóraime's court at Kincora/Killaloe, or Tairdelbach or Ruaidrí Ua Conchobair's at Tuam, or Diarmait Mac Murchada's at Ferns from emerging as capitals around which the political aristocracy could cohere. Dublin had materialized as the undoubted economic capital by the twelfth century, but it was a political capital in the sense only that control of Dublin's resources determined successful pursuit of the high-kingship. The battle of Dublin in 1170, whereby Ruaidrí Ua Conchobair lost control of the city, was, as argued by Seán Duffy, a crucial turning point in the English advance into Ireland, but Dublin had not yet become the centre of an island-wide political culture.

As is the case of the eighteenth-century scholar, Charles O'Conor, it is difficult to consider developments in the high-kingship after Brian Bóraime without foreknowledge of English intrusion into Ireland in the late twelfth

156 Cf. Byrne, *Irish kings*, pp 253, 300–1; appendix 11.1 below, no. 4.

century, a development which had such momentous consequences for the high-kingship, effectively spelling its end as an institution, but also impacting dramatically on the provincial kingships. Ruaidrí Ua Conchobair was indeed 'the last king of Ireland',[157] and subsequent attempts to revive the office proved unsuccessful. He was also the last provincial king of Connacht whose ambit was effectively coterminous with the archiepiscopal province of Tuam. In 1992, Seán Duffy argued that the time between the battle of Clontarf and the Anglo-Norman invasion 'remains one of the most neglected in Ireland's history'.[158] This still holds true: the period awaits more detailed attention than it has received, but it would be more appropriate to explore developments in post-Brian Ireland in the first instance within their own trajectory, to consider indigenous developments in kingship and lordship without recourse to generalized analogies with feudal society. Implicitly, such analogies may be driven by a concern to assess the relative degree of similarity or dissimilarity, continuity or discontinuity, between pre-Invasion and post-Invasion society in Ireland, to set a context, or prologue, for events after 1169, which, as so evident in the stance of Charles O'Conor, is hard to resist. Yet, the data in the annals has not been fully marshalled, as indicated by the limited prosopographical research in relation to the provincial kings of Connacht which would help to shed light on their very successful challenge to the descendants of Brian Bóraime and their remarkable emergence as contenders for the high-kingship in the twelfth century.

157 *AClon*, p. 206. 158 Duffy, 'Irishmen and Islesmen', 93.

Associates of Ruaidrí Ua Conchobair, king of Connacht and high-king, on campaign in Mide in 1174, as listed in the so-called 'Song of Dermot and the earl'[1]

1 'Oflaverti' > Ua Flaithbertaig (Uí Briúin Seola)

The Uí Fhlaithbertaig were the ruling family of Uí Briúin Seola, the linkage of the latter to Uí Briúin Aí being certainly remote and possibly fictitious. The Uí Fhlaithbertaig were serious contenders for the provincial kingship of Connacht during the tenth and eleventh centuries, but in the course of the eleventh century were displaced westwards from the plain of Mag Seóla around Tuam by the Uí Briúin Aí, more specifically, their dominant Síl Muiredaig lineage to which Tairdelbach Ua Conchobair and his son Ruaidrí belonged.[2] In 1061, Ruaidrí Ua Flaithbertaig, king of West Connacht, was killed in battle by Áed Ua Conchobair, king of Connacht.[3] In 1065, Flaithbertach Ua Flaithbertaig, king of West Connacht, was also killed by Áed Ua Conchobair.[4] In 1079, Áed Ua Flaithbertaig, king of West Connacht, was slain by Ruaidrí na Saide Buide Ua Conchobair, king of Connacht.[5] In 1092, Ruaidrí was blinded by Flaithbertach Ua Flaithbertaig even though Ruaidrí was his fosterer and his godfather and his *tigerna*.[6] At the battle of Fidnacha (i.e., Fenagh, Co. Leitrim) in 1094, Tadc mac Ruaidrí, king of Connacht, 'and the Síl Muiredaig' defeated 'the Uí Flaithbertaig'.[7] In 1098, Flaithbertach Ua Flaithbertaig, 'king of Connacht', was slain by Síl Muiredaig in revenge for the blinding of Ruaidrí, 'his lord'.[8] Flaithbertach was the last serious Uí Briúin Seola contender for the kingship of Connacht. In 1117, Brian

1 G.H. Orpen (ed.), *The song of Dermot and the earl* (Oxford, 1892), ll. 3238–3247; Evelyn Mullally (ed.), *The deeds of the Normans in Ireland: la geste des Engleis en Yrlande* (Dublin, 2002), ll. 3236–3245. The annalistic data assembled here for the period up to the death of Cathal Crobderg Ua Conchobair, king of Connacht (d. 1224), is by no means comprehensive and is intended primarily to demonstrate links with the Ua Conchobair kings in the twelfth century and to highlight the prosopographical potential of annals for identifying affinities and associations. There are substantial numbers of annalistic entries from the thirteenth century onwards relating to nos 1–5, 8, 10, 11 in this appendix. 2 The Síl Muiredaig eponym was Muiredach Muillethan, king of Connacht (d. 702). On the province of Connacht, see Byrne, *Irish kings*, pp 230–53; Paul Walsh, 'The Christian kings of Connacht', *JGAHS*, 17 (1937), 124–43; reprinted in Nollaig Ó Muraíle (ed.), *Irish leaders and learning through the ages, Paul Walsh essays collected* (Dublin, 2003), pp 177–94. 3 *AT* 1061.11; *CS* 1059=1061; *AI* 1061.8; *AClon*, pp 178–9; *AFM*; *AU* 1062.1. 4 *ALC*; *AU* 1065.6; *AT* 1065.1; *AFM*. 5 *AT* 1079.2; *CS* 1076=1079; cf. *AI* 1079.5. 6 *AT* 1092.1; *CS* 1088=1092; *ACott*; *AFM* ('ba cáirdes Criost fo shecht Ruaidhri dUa Flaithbhertaigh'); *AU* 1092.3; *AI* 1092.3; *AMisc* 1118.5. 7 *AT* 1094.2; *CS* 1090=1094; *AI* 1094.3; *AFM*. Cf. *ACott*; *ALC* 1095. 8 *ACott*; *CS* 1094=1098; *AI* 1098.2; *AU* 10911.1; *AFM*; *AClon*, p. 187. *ACott* and *AFM* name the slayer on behalf of the Síl Muiredaig as Matudán Ua Cuannu. Contrast *AT* 1098.3 (which states that Flaithbertach was blinded). Flaithbertach had taken the kingship of Connacht in 1097 according to *AT* 1097.3.

son of Murchad Ua Flaithbertaig fought alongside the sons of Cathal Ua Conchobair and the men of Connacht when they inflicted a defeat on the Dál Cais at the battle of Lacken (Co. Clare).[9] In 1121, on a predatory hosting by Tairdelbach Ua Conchobair, king of Connacht, into Munster, Muiredach Ua Flaithbertaig, king of West Connacht, was slain.[10] Flaithbertach Ua Flaithbertaig was leader of Ua Conchobair's fleet in 1132, when it was attacked by Lochlann Ua Lochlainn, king of Corco Mruad, leading the Munster fleet, who was killed in the encounter.[11] In the following year Flaithbertach was killed by the son of Lochlann Ua Lochlainn in revenge for his father's death.[12] In 1144, Tairdelbach Ua Conchobair was obliged by pressure from senior clergy to release his own son, Ruaidrí, and Domnall Ua Flaithbertaig.[13] In 1145, Ruaidrí Ua Flaithbertaig was killed during an attack by Munster men on Connacht.[14] In 1158, the son of Ua Flaithbertaig was taken prisoner during a raid by Ruaidrí Ua Conchobair, king of Connacht, into Tethba.[15] In 1159, Murchad, son of Domnall Ua Flaithbertaig, king of West Connacht, was among those slain at Ardee fighting in the army of Ruaidrí Ua Conchobair against Muirchertach Mac Lochlainn, king of Cenél nEógain, in contention for the high-kingship.[16]

The twelfth-century annalistic entries make it plain that Ua Flaithbertaig had been drawn into the orbit of Ua Conchobair no later than 1117, as is evident also from a prose tract describing the inauguration of the king of Connacht where the role of leader of the fleet at sea is assigned to Ua Flaithbertaig.[17] The prose tract is accompanied by a poem of forty-seven stanzas addressed to Fedlimid Ó Conchobair. Although it was suggested by Myles Dillon that it was written for Fedlimid, who was inaugurated as king of Connacht in 1310, Katharine Simms has argued persuasively that it more likely refers to Fedlimid Fionn (d. 1490) son of Ó Conchobair Ruaid and dates from *c.*1464–6. Notwithstanding the fifteenth-century date for the poem, the prose tract is based on an earlier source originating in the twelfth or early thirteenth century.[18] In 1178, Áed Ua Flaithbertaig, king of West Connacht, died at Annaghdown.[19] It was likely he who accompanied Ruaidrí Ua Conchobair into Mide in 1174. In 1181, Áed, grandson of Áed son of Ruaidrí Ua Flaithbertaig, king of West Connacht, was killed in battle between Flaithbertach Ua Máel Doraid, king of Cenél Conaill, and the sons of Tairdelbach Ua Conchobair.[20] In 1196, Ruaidrí Ua Flaithbertaig escaped by sea from the custody of Cathal Crobderg Ua Conchobair and took refuge with Ua Briain, who, however, was forced by Cathal Crobderg to give him up whereupon he took refuge in Tír Conaill. He returned from there in the company of the *comarba Pátraic*, that is, Tomaltach Ua Conchobair, archbishop of Armagh; peace was negotiated and his

9 *ALC*; *AFM*. Cf. *AI* 1117.6; *CS* 1113=1117. **10** *AU* 1121.5; *AI* 1121.7; *CS* 1117=1121; *ALC*; *AT* 1121.7; *ACott*; *AMisc* 1121.2; *AFM*. **11** *AT* 1132.6; *AFM*. Cf. *CS* 1128–1132. Conchobar Ua Flaithbertaig, king of West Connacht, is recorded as having been killed with slaughter of his people by the Munster fleet: *AMisc* 1132.1. **12** *AT* 1133.1; *AFM*; cf. *CS* 1129=1133. **13** *AT* 1144.7. **14** *CS*; *AT* 1145.7; *AFM*. **15** *AT* 1158.7; *AFM*. **16** *AU*; *AFM*. Cf. *AT* 1159.6. See also nos 2, 4, 9, 11 in this appendix. **17** Myles Dillon, 'The inauguration of O'Conor' in J.A. Watt, J.B. Morrall and F.X. Martin (eds), *Medieval studies presented to Aubrey Gwynn SJ* (Dublin, 1961), pp 186–202 at pp 190, 198. **18** Katharine Simms, 'Gabh umad a Fheidhlimidh: a fifteenth-century inauguration ode?', *Ériu*, 31 (1980), 132–45, at 141–3. It has been further suggested that a portion of the poem was also based on a tract dating from the reign of Fedlimid (d. 1265): Jaski, *Early Irish kingship*, pp 135–6, n. 81. **19** *AT* 1178.4; *ACott*; *AFM*. **20** *ALC*. Cf. *AI* 1181.4; *ALC*; *AFM*.

territory was restored to him.[21] Ruaidrí was once again taken prisoner by Cathal Crobderg in 1197 but released in 1199.[22] In 1200, Ruaidrí Ua Flaithbertaig, king of West Connacht, was killed fighting alongside Cathal Crobderg Ua Conchobair.[23] Later in the same year, Máel Culaird Ua Flaithbertaig, king of West Connacht, died fighting on the side of Cathal Crobderg against his dynastic rival, his great-nephew, Cathal Carrach.[24] In 1201, the sons of Ruaidrí Ua Flaithbertaig conspired against Cathal Crobderg.[25] In 1207, Áed Ua Flaithbertaig was expelled by Cathal Crobderg and his lands given to Cathal's own son, Áed.[26] In 1210, the son of Ua Flaithbertaig was in the army of Donnchad Cairprech Ua Briain, king of Thomond, and Geoffrey de Marisco when they invaded Connacht against Cathal Crobderg Ua Conchobair, king of Connacht.[27] In 1225, following the death of Cathal Crobderg there was a major rebellion against the accession of his son, Áed, and Áed Ua Flaithbertaig, king of West Connacht, was among the rebels though eventually a settlement was reached whereby Ua Flaithbertaig gave pledges and hostages to Áed Ua Conchobair.[28]

2 **'Macdermot' > Mac Diarmata** (Síl Muiredaig of Uí Briuin Aí)

The Mac Diarmata kings of Mag Luirg were descended from Máel Ruanaid, brother of Conchobar, king of Connacht (966–73), eponym of the Ua Conchobair kings of Connacht. Máel Sechnaill son of Tadc, king of Mag Luirg, who died in 1124, is the first of Clann Máel Ruanaid to be described as king of Mag Luirg, having displaced the Grecraige, a subject lineage of Uí Ailello, an instance of Síl Muiredaig expansion.[29] In 1159, when Ruaidrí Ua Conchobair's army suffered a heavy defeat at Ardee at the hands of Muirchertach Mac Lochlainn, king of Cenél nEógain, the slain included Gilla Críst mac Diarmata meic Taidc hUí Máel Ruanaig, 'king of Mag Luirg and the Aiccidecht'.[30] The Meic Diarmata took their name from Diarmait mac Taidc who died earlier in 1159 at his island residence in Lough Key.[31] In 1176, Conchobar Mac Diarmata acted as surety for Ruaidrí Ua Conchobair's grant 'to God and St Berach' of Tuaim Achaid near Termonbarry at Kilbarry (Co. Roscommon).[32] In 1187, lightning struck Conchobar Mac Diarmata's stronghold at Lough Key and, although he escaped, his wife, Dubessa, a daughter of Ruaidrí Ua hEidin, and his son's wife, a daughter of Domnall Ua Conchobair, lost their lives, as did three of the Uí Mannacháin.[33] In 1187, Muirges mac Taidc, king of Mag Luirg and Artech, died in his own house.[34] In 1190, Muirchertach, son of Conchobar Mac Diarmata, was drowned when a ship of Cathal Crobderg, brother of Ruaidrí Ua Conchobair, sank.[35] In 1196 Conchobar Mac

21 *ACott* 1196, 1197; *ALC*, 1196. **22** *ACott* 1197, 1199; *ALC*, 1197, 1199; *AFM* 1197. **23** *ALC*; *ACott*. **24** *ALC*; *AClon*, p. 215. **25** *AFM*; *AClon*, p. 218. **26** *AFM*. **27** *ALC*. **28** *ALC*; *AC* 1225.4, 10, 13, 16, 19, 22, 25, 26; *AFM*. In the same year Fedlimid, brother of Áed Ua Conchobair, captured a house of Domnall Ua Flaithbertaig and burnt him and his brother to death: *ALC*. **29** *AMisc* 1124.5; *AFM*; *ACott*. Cf. *AT* 1124.6 where his name has been incorrectly expanded. For the earlier Grecraige, see *Lebor na cert*, ll. 676, 706, 713, 813, 841. For the extent of Mag Luirg, see John O'Donovan's note (d) in *AFM*, 1187. **30** *AT* 1159.6; *ACott*; *AU*; *AFM*. For the identification of Aiccidecht, see Diarmuid Ó Murchadha, *The Annals of Tigernach: index of names*, ITS, Subsidiary Series 6 (London, 1997), p. 97. See also nos 1, 4, 9, 11 in this appendix. **31** *AT* 1159.2; *AFM*; *AU*; *ACott*. **32** *AFM* with identification as Toomaghy by John O'Donovan in note (g). Cf. below nos 3, 6, 9. For St Berach, see Pádraig Ó Riain, *A dictionary of Irish saints* (Dublin, 2011), pp 94–6. **33** *ALC* 1187, *ACott*; *AFM*; cf. nos. 9, 10 in this appendix. The burning of the rock, described as *rí port*, is also recorded in *ALC* 1184 which would appear to be a duplicate entry of the same event. **34** *ACott*; *AFM*. **35** *ACott*; *ALC*; *AU*;

Diarmata entered the Cistercian monastery of Boyle and his son, Tomaltach, assumed lordship in his stead;[36] Conchobar died in 1197 in the habit of a Cistercian monk in Boyle, of which he was a patron.[37] In 1200, in the dispute between Cathal Crobderg Ua Conchobair and Cathal Carrach Ua Conchobair for the kingship of Connacht, Cathal Carrach took the hostages of Tomaltach son of Conchobar Mac Diarmata resulting in the plundering in the following year by Cathal Crobderg of numbers of the people of Tomaltach.[38] In 1202, Diarmait son of Gilla Críst Mac Diarmata was killed fighting on the side of Cathal Carrach.[39] Tomaltach died in 1207 as king of Mag Luirg.[40] In 1208, Cathal son of Diarmait son of Tadc Ua Máel Ruanaid was taken prisoner by Cathal Crobderg but released under pressure from the bishops of Achonry, Elphin and Killala, who had extended their protection to him; he subsequently engaged in raiding and was overwhelmed by Cormac son of Tomaltach supported by Ua Conchobair dynasts; Cathal's son, Muirges, was killed and he himself was blinded by the sons of Tomaltach.[41] In 1210, Diarmait son of Conchobar Mac Diarmata, king of Mag Luirg, was given as a hostage for Cathal Crobderg Ua Conchobair, king of Connacht, to King John.[42] Diarmait died in 1218 and was succeeded by Cormac Mac Diarmata.[43] In 1224, Cormac, styled *comes* of Mag Luirg, witnessed a charter of Áed Ua Conchobair, king of Connacht, for the Cistercian abbey of Cîteaux.[44] In the revolt against Áed Ua Conchobair in 1225, Mac Diarmata remained loyal to him.[45] According to the prose tract on the inauguration of Ua Conchobair, Mac Diarmata was one of four *ríg-thoísig* of Síl Muiredaig required to be present at the inauguration of Ua Conchobair as king of Connacht and held the office of *ardmharusgál*, 'chief marshal'.[46]

3 **'Macherathi' > Mac Airechtaig** (Síl Muiredaig)

Mac Airechtaig was head of Muintir Roduib of Clann Tomaltaig, a branch of Síl Muiredaig descended from Tomaltach (d. 774) and located in the district immediately west of Roscommon.[47] In 1088, when Ruaidrí na Saide Buide Ua Conchobair, king of Connacht, plundered Corcu Mruad, among the nobles of Connacht who were killed was Cú Sinna son of Muirchertach, *toísech* of Clann Tomaltaig.[48] In 1133, during an attack by the men of Tethba on Síl Muiredaig, Amlaíb son of Airechtach Ua Raduib, *toísech* of Clann Tomaltaig, was killed.[49] In 1143, when land was ceded in perpetuity by Tairdelbach Ua Conchobair to the community of Roscommon, Murchad grandson of Airechtach Ua Raduib gave gold for the permanent alienation of the property.[50] In 1148, in the wake of an encounter at the Shannon between Tairdelbach Ua Conchobair and Tigernán Ua Ruairc, king of Bréifne, the son of Airechtach Ua Raduib was killed

AFM. Cf. nos 3, 9 in this appendix. **36** *AFM*. **37** *ALC*; *ACott*; *AU*; *AFM*. **38** *ALC* 1200, 1201. **39** *ALC*. **40** *ALC*; *AFM s.a.* 1206. **41** *ALC*; *AFM*. He died in 1215: *ALC*; *AU*. His wife may have been Dubessa, daughter of Ruaidrí Ua Conchobair, who died as a 'black nun', that is a Benedictine, in 1230: *ALC*; *AC* 1229.4. She had probably retired to the Benedictine nunnery of Kilcreevanty which was an Ua Conchobair foundation. **42** *ALC*, 1210, 1211; *AFM* 1209=1210, 1210=1211; *AU* 1211; *AClon* p. 223. Cf. above, p. 245, this appendix, no. 5. **43** *ALC*; *AU*; *AFM s.a.* 1217. **44** Flanagan, *Irish royal charters*, pp 350–1. **45** *ALC*, 1224, 1225; *AFM* 1225. **46** Dillon, 'Inauguration', pp 189–90, 197–8. At the inauguration of Fedlimid Ó Conchobair in 1310, Máel Ruanaid Mac Diarmata, Fedlimid's foster-father, waited upon the new king 'in the manner remembered by the old men and recorded in the old books': *AC* 1310.7. **47** Flanagan, *Irish royal charters*, p. 354. **48** *AT* 1088.2; *CS* 1084=1088; *AFM*. **49** *AT* 1133.5; *AFM*; *CS* 1129=1133. **50** *AT* 1143.9.

while pursuing Tigernán.[51] In 1153, Muirgius grandson of Muirchertach Odar, *ardtoísech* of Clann Tomaltaig, and Donn Catha son of Airechtach Ua Raduib died.[52] In 1176, Airechtach Ua Roduib was a surety for Ruaidrí Ua Conchobair's grant to the church of St Berach.[53] In 1181, Gilla Críst Mac Airechtaig was among those killed in battle between Flaithbertach Ua Máel Doraid, king of Tír Conaill, and the sons of the king of Connacht.[54] In 1190, Airechtach Ua Roduib was at Clonfert when Tomaltach Ua Conchobair, archbishop of Armagh, unsuccessfully sought to negotiate a truce between Cathal Crobderg and Cathal Carrach Ua Conchobair who were fighting for the kingship of Connacht.[55] Cathal Crobderg's party then proceeded to Clonmacnoise where they spent the night and early next morning the Síl Muiredaig embarked in their fleet and sailed up the Shannon to Lough Ree, but in a violent storm on the lake, the boat of Cathal Crobderg and his party got into difficulty and most of those on board were drowned, including Airechtach Ua Raduib, *toísech* of Clann Tomaltaig.[56] In 1200 Mac Airechtaig, supporting Cathal Crobderg Ua Conchbair, had to give hostages to his rival, Cathal Carrach.[57] In 1224 Donn Cathaig Mac Airechtaig, styled *dux* of Clann Tomaltaig, witnessed a Latin charter of Áed Ua Conchobair, king of Connacht, to the abbey of Cîteaux.[58] He died in the same year in Ballintubber abbey, which had been founded by Cathal Crobderg Ua Conchobair.[59] According to Dubhaltach Mac Firbisigh's *Leabhar Mór na nGenealach* Donn Cathaig Mór Mac Airechtaig had usurped the lordship of Clann Taidc (> Tadc son of Indrechtach (d. 723)).[60] In the prose tract on the inauguration of Ua Conchobair, Mac Airechtaig was one of four *ríg-thoísig* of Síl Muiredaig who assisted at the inauguration of Ua Conchobair and received *tuarastal* of sixty milch cows and sixty sheep on 1 May, and 240 beef cattle and 240 boars on 1 November, in addition to holding forty-eight townlands in virtue of his service in the household of Ua Conchobair.[61] The importance of Mac Airechtaig in the assembly of the Ua Conchobair kings is reflected in the appearance of their eponymous ancestor, Áed Rodub, in *Acallam na Senórach*, almost certainly composed during the reign of Cathal Crobderg Ua Conchobair (d. 1224), a key concern of the text being the conduct of the king's *airecht* or assembly.[62] In 1225 Donn Óc Mac Airechtaig supported Tairdelbach and Áed, sons of Ruaidrí Ua Conchobair (d. 1198) in their bid to challenge Áed, son of Cathal Crobderg Ua Conchobair, Donn Óc's motivation being revenge 'for the confiscation of his land and property'.[63]

4 'Okelli de Omani' > Ua Cellaig (Uí Maine)

The annalistic entries relating to the east Connacht kingdom of Uí Maine up to 1225 have been collated by John Kelleher and only a selected number are noted here.[64] In

51 *AT* 11411.1; cf. *AFM*. 52 *AT* 1153.11; *AFM*. 53 *AFM*, cf. nos 2, 6, 9 in this appendix. 54 *AFM*; cf. no. 1 in this appendix. 55 *AFM*. 56 *ACott*; *ALC*; *AU*; *AFM*. Cf. nos 2, 9 in this appendix. 57 *ALC*. 58 Flanagan, *Irish royal charters*, p. 354. 59 *AC* 1224.4; *AFM*. 60 *LMG*, i, p. 537, iii, p. 403, vi, p. 504, § 225.7; J.V. Kelleher, 'Uí Maine in the annals and genealogies', *Celtica*, 9 (1971), 61–112, at 111. 61 Dillon, 'Inauguration' pp 189, 197–8. 62 See Ann Dooley, 'The date and purpose of *Acallam na Senórach*', *Éigse*, 34 (2004), 97–106; Anne Connon, 'Plotting *Acallam na Senórach:* the physical context of the "Mayo" sequence' in Sarah Sheehan, Joanne Findon and Westley Follett, *Gablánach in scélaigecht*; *Celtic studies in honour of Ann Dooley* (Dublin, 2013), pp 69–102; eadem, 'The Roscommon *locus* of *Acallam na senórach* and some thoughts as to *tempus* and *persona*' in Aidan Doyle and Kevin Murray (eds), *In dialogue with the Agallamh: essays in honour of Seán Ó Coileáin* (Dublin, 2014), pp 21–59. 63 *AC* 1225.4, 10, 13, 25; *AFM*. 64 Kelleher, 'Uí Maine'.

1065, the son of Tadc Ua Cellaig, king of Uí Maine, was killed by Áed Ua Conchobair on the same occasion as Flaithbertach Ua Flaithbertaig.[65] In 1114, Domnall, son of Tairdelbach Ua Conchobair, was captured by the Uí Maine and 'delivered into Tairdelbach's hands'.[66] In 1135, when Murchad Ua Máel Sechnaill, king of Mide, put a fleet on the Shannon, the Síl Muiredaig 'with their king Conchobar, son of Tairdelbach Ua Conchobair', who was evidently placed in that role as successor-designate by his father and may also have been mediate lord of Uí Maine, was supported by Tadc Ua Cellaig, king of Uí Maine, though both were obliged to yield hostages to Murchad.[67] The Uí Maine also accompanied Conchobar on a raid on Cenél Forggo in 1142.[68] In 1145, during an expedition by the Munster army into Connacht, Tadc Ua Cellaig, son of Conchobar Ua Cellaig, king of Uí Maine, was killed on the same occasion as Ruaidrí Ua Flaithbertaig was taken prisoner.[69] In 1147, when Domnall, son of Tairdelbach Ua Conchobair, was defeated at Athlone by the men of Tethba, the Uí Maine were fighting alongside him.[70] In 1159, when Ruaidrí Ua Conchobair suffered a defeat at Ardee by Muirchertach Mac Lochlainn, king of Cenél nEógain, Murchad Ua Cellaig, king of Uí Maine, was among those slain on the Connacht side.[71]

The individual who accompanied Ruaidrí Ua Conchobair to Trim in 1174 may be identified as Conchobar Ua Cellaig, king of Uí Maine, who succeeded in 1159, built a *teampull* (church) in place of a *dearthach* (oratory) at Clonmacnoise in 1167,[72] and was killed in 1180 by Conchobar Máenmuige, son of Ruaidrí Ua Conchobair.[73] In 1163, Conchobar Ua Cellaig, alongside Conchobar Máenmaige, repulsed an attack by Niall, son of Muirchertach Mac Lochlainn, king of Cenél nEógain, who had crossed at Athlone into Uí Maine;[74] Conchobar Máenmaige was most likely deputed king of Síl Muiredaig under Ruaidrí Ua Conchobair at that time and thus successor-designate to the kingship of Connacht. Ua Cellaig is described as *toísech séd*, 'keeper of treasure', in the prose tract on the inauguration of Ua Conchobair.[75]

5 'Oharthire' > ? Ua hEgra Tíre [Luigne]

The identity of this individual is uncertain but it may refer to Ua hEgra for whom there is a sustained series of entries as kings of Luigne from the early eleventh century onwards.[76] In 1023, Domnall Ua hEgra, king of Luigne of Connacht, on campaign in Uí Briúin with Tadc in Eich Gil Ua Conchobair, king of Connacht (d. 1030), was killed.[77] In 1059,

65 *ALC*; *AU* 1065.6; *AT* 1065.1; *AFM*; see no. 1 in this appendix. **66** *AT* 1114.6; *AFM*. **67** *AFM*; *AClon*, p. 194; *ACott*. In 1141 it was Conchobar who restored goods that had been seized by Mac Cochláin and the Síl nAnmchada from Clonmacnoise to its abbot, Máel Mochta: *CS*; *AFM*; *AClon*, p. 192. **68** *AFM*. **69** *CS*; *AFM* 1145; see no. 1 in this appendix. **70** *AT* 1147.2; *CS*; *AFM*. Domnall is described at his death in 1176 in Mayo as king of Tuaiscert Connacht, an office that may have been delegated to him by his brother, Ruaidrí Ua Conchobair: *AFM*. In *ACott* he is named Domnall Midech and described as *tanaise Connacht*. Cf. *AT* 1176.9. **71** *AT* 1159.6; cf. *AU*; *AFM*; Kelleher, 'Uí Maine', 100. Cf. nos 1, 2, 9, 11 in this appendix. **72** *AFM*. **73** *AT* 1159.12; *AU*; *ALC*; *ACott*; *AMisc* 1180.4; *AI* 1180.4; *AFM*. **74** *AT* 1163.4; *AFM*; *AU* (secondary entry); cf. *ACott*. **75** Dillon, 'Inauguration', pp 190, 195, 198, 201. **76** Paul MacCotter, *Medieval Ireland: territorial, political and economic divisions* (Dublin, 2008), p. 140. **77** *AT* 1023.10; *CS* 1021=1023; *AFM*. Entries in *AU* and *ALC* record that he was killed by Ua Conchobair. There is also a death-notice in 1024 for Domnall Ua hEgra, 'king of Corann' in *AT* 1024.9, *CS* 1022=1024. For the identification of Corann with the bar. Corann, Co. Sligo, see Ó Murchadha, *Annals of Tigernach*, p. 126. For Corann as a sub-division of Luigne, see MacCotter, *Medieval Ireland*, p. 137.

Duarcán Ua hEgra, king of Luigne, was killed *a suis*.[78] Taichlech Ua hEgra, king of Luigne, 'with a slaughter of the Luigne about him', was killed by the Conmaicne in 1095.[79] Murchad Ua hEgra and his wife, significantly a daughter of Tairdelbach Ua Conchobair, king of Connacht and high-king, were killed in 1134 by Taichlech Ua hEgra.[80] Duarcán Ua hEgra was killed by Ua Gadra in 1147.[81] Conchobar Ua hEgra, king of Luigne, died in his bed in 1151.[82] Áed Ua hEgra, king of Luigne, died in 1155.[83] Domnall Ua hEgra, king of Luigne, died in 1177.[84]

If the identification of 'Oharthire' as Ua hEgra is correct, it would have been Domnall who accompanied Ruaidrí Ua Conchobair on campaign in Mide in 1174. In 1183, Bec Ua hEgra, king of Luigne, was killed treacherously in his own house.[85] In 1200 Ua hEgra, who was supporting Cathal Crobderg Ua Conchobair, had hostages taken by his dynastic rival, Cathal Carrach.[86] In 1202, Conchobar Got Ua hEgra, king of Luigne, took Tairdelbach, son of Ruaidrí Ua Conchobair, prisoner on behalf of Cathal Crobderg Ua Conchobair.[87] In 1210, Conchobar Ua hEgra, king of Luigne, was given as a hostage to King John by Cathal Crobderg Ua Conchobair, king of Connacht.[88] In 1225, Duarcán Ua hEgra, king of Luigne, Tadc Ua hEgra and Étaín, daughter of Diarmait son of Domnall Ua hEgra, died.[89] In the same year during the revolt against Áed Ua Conchobair, king of Connacht, Luigne was plundered for three nights by Áed's forces, obliging Ua hEgra to sue for peace for the sake of what little was left to him.[90]

6 'Ohinnathi' > Ua Fínnachta (Síl Muiredaig of Uí Briúin Aí)

The Uí Fhínnachta descended from Fínsnechtae, king of Connacht (d. 848). In 1135, Máel Ísu Ua Fínnachta, *comarba* of Roscommon, a church with close associations with the Ua Conchobair kings, died.[91] In 1140, when Tairdelbach Ua Conchobair constructed a bridge at Athlone, using it to raid into Tethba and Mide,[92] more than sixty of the men of Mide were killed by the 'Síl Muiredaig' but, in a counterattack, one of the Síl Muiredaig, Muiredach, grandson of Muiredach Ua Fínnachta, *toísech* of Clann Murchada and Clann Connmaig and 'foremost in sense and counsel of the whole Síl Muiredaig' was killed.[93] Clann Murchada derived from Murchad son of Indrechtach (d. 723) son of Muiredach Muillethan (d. 702, a quo Síl Muiredaig), while Clann Connmaig derived from Connmach, son of Muiredach Muillethan. Flann Ua Fínnachta acted as surety for Ruaidrí Ua Conchobair's grant to the church of St Berach in 1176.[94] He died in 1184, described as *toísech*, alias *dux*, of Clann Murchada.[95] In 1188, Flaithbertach Ua Fínnachta was killed.[96] In 1189, Conchobar Máenmaige was killed by his *lucht gráda* who included Magnus an Crosach Donn, son of Flann Ua Fínnachta.[97] In 1225, Tadc Ua Fínnachta, described as *fer gráda* of Áed, son of Ruaidrí

78 *AT* 1059.5; *ALC*; *AFM*; *AClon*, p. 223. **79** *AT* 1095.6; *CS* 1091=1095; *AI* 1095.10; *AFM*. **80** *AT* 1134.12; *CS* 1130=1134; *AFM*; *AClon*, p. 194. **81** *AT* 1147.4; *AFM*. **82** *AT* 1151.1. He is described as *tanaise* of Luigne in *AFM*. **83** *AT* 1155.3; *ACott*; *AFM*. **84** *AT* 1177.9; *AFM*. **85** *ACott*; *ALC*; *AFM*. **86** *ALC*. **87** *ALC*; *AU*. Cf. *AFM*. **88** *ALC* 1210, 1211; *AU* 1211; *AFM* 1209=1210, 1210=1211. Cf. above, p. 245; ses also no. 2 in this appendix. **89** *AC* 1225.35; *ALC* 1224; *AFM* 1225. **90** *ALC*; *AC* 1225.12. **91** *AFM*. **92** Above, p. 227. **93** *AT* 1140.4; *AFM*. 'Clann Muirchertaig' in *AT* should read Clann Murchada as in *AFM*. Cf. James Carney (ed.), *Topographical poems by Seaán Mór Ó Dubhagáin and Giolla-na-naomh Ó hUidhrín* (Dublin, 1943), ll. 567–8. **94** *AFM*; cf. nos 2, 3, 9 in this appendix. **95** *ACott*; *AU*; *ALC* 1185. **96** *ALC*; *AU*. **97** *ALC*; *AFM*; *AI* 1189.4. Cf. *AU*.

Ua Conchobair (d. 1198), was killed on a plundering raid; in the same year Muiredach Ua Fínnachta, variously described as *toísech* of Clann Fhínnachta and of Clann Murchada, died in a boat on Lough Corrib although he had been quite well on boarding it.[98] Ua Fínnachta was one of the four *ríg-thoísig* of Síl Muiredaig who were to be present at the inauguration of Ua Conchobair and to whom forty-eight townlands were allocated in right of the office of doorkeeper.[99] As in the case of Mac Airechtaig (no. 3), their eponymous ancestor, Fíndsnechtae, was of importance to the compiler of *Acallam na senórach*.[100]

7 'Ocarbri' > ? Ua Cairbre

The identity of this individual is not certain. By analogy with the other names in the list Ua Cairpre ought to be from Connacht and the name should represent a patronymic or surname rather than a territorial name. No Ua Cairpre patronymic or surname is attested in twelfth-century Connacht. Gilla Decair Ua Cairpre, *toísech* of Tuath Buadga, was slain in 1156 by Diarmait Ua Máel Sechnaill, king of Mide, during a conflict with his brother, Donnchad.[101] Tuath Buadga, however, was located in Mide. 'Ocarbri' could possibly refer territorially to Uí Cairpre, or Cenél Cairpre Mór, a district in Connacht in the northern Sligo/Leitrim area (represented by the later barony of Carbury in north Co. Sligo). The latest king of Cairpre Mór attested in the annals is Murchad mac Serraig, who died in 1033.[102]

8 'Oflannegan' > Ua Flannagáin (Síl Muiredaig of Uí Briúin Aí)

Ua Flannagáin was head of Clann Chathail (eponym, Cathal, king of Connacht, 728–35), a branch of Síl Muiredaig whose territory was located around Elphin (Co. Roscommon). In 1088 when Ruaidrí na Saide Buide Ua Conchobair, king of Connacht, attacked Corcu Mruad, among the nobles of Connacht who were killed in that encounter was the son of Cathal Ua Mugróin, *toísech* of Clann Chathail.[103] Muiredach Ua Flannagáin, '*toísech* of Clann Chathail', died at Cong in 1150, the first of that name to be recorded in the annals.[104] In 1184, Domnall Ua Flannagáin, *toísech* of Clann Chathail, died at Cong.[105] In 1189, Murchad Ua Flannagáin, '*dux* of Clann Chathail', died.[106] In 1208, Flaithbertach Ua Flannagáin was fighting in support of Cathal Crobderg Ua Conchobair against the rebellious Cathal Mac Diarmata.[107] Ua Flannagáin is listed as one of the four *ríg-thoísig* of Síl Muiredaig who participated in the inauguration of Ua Conchobair.[108] He was moreover described as his *ardmhaor* and received *tuarastal* of 240 beef cattle and 240 boars in right of that office. In the Ua Conchobair prose inauguration-tract Ua Flannagáin was accorded precedence over

98 *AC* 1225.30, 31 (Freeman suggests that Clann Muirthile should be Clann Murchada); *ALC*. Cf. *AU*; *AFM*. **99** Dillon, 'Inauguration', pp 189, 196, 197, 198, 202. See Simms, 'Gabh umad a Fheidhlimidh', 141, for a later duplication which lists Ua Fínnachta of Clann Chonnmaig and Ua Fínnachta of Clann Murthuile among the twelve chiefs of Síl Muiredaig who had to be present at Ua Conchobair's inauguration. **100** Connon, 'Plotting *Acallam na Senórach*', p. 73; eadem, 'Roscommon *locus*', pp 32–46. **101** *AT* 1156.3; *AFM*. Tuath Buadga was located in and around the par. Ballyloughloe, bar. Clonlonan, Co. Westmeath: Hogan, *Onomasticon*, p. 650; Ó Murchadha, *Annals of Tigernach*, p. 188; O'Donovan in *AFM*, ii, p. 1120. **102** *AFM*. **103** *AT* 1088.2; *AFM*. **104** *AT* 1150.4; *AFM*. In 1088 the son of the *toísech* of Clann Chathail lost his life in on campaign in Corco Mruad with Ruaidrí Ua Conchobair: *CS* 1084=1088. **105** *AFM*. **106** *ACott*; *ALC*. **107** *ALC*. **108** Dillon, 'Inauguration', pp 189–90, 195, 197, 201.

Mac Airechtaig, although in a charter of Áed Ua Conchobair, king of Connacht, in favour of the abbey of Cîteaux in 1224 Donn Catha Mac Airechtaig is listed before Flaithbertach Ua Flannagáin.[109] In 1225, following the death of Cathal Crobderg Ua Conchobair, Flaithbertach Ua Flannagáin, one of the *maithi inn arechta*, 'chief men of the assembly', was among those who supported Tairdelbach son of Ruaidrí Ua Conchobair against Áed son of Cathal Crobderg Ua Conchobair for the kingship of Connnacht and was delivered by Áed into the hands of his English supporters and they had to provide for their own ransom.[110] Flaithbertach died in 1231 in the Cistercian monastery of Boyle, his wife dying later in the same year.[111]

9 **'Omanathan'[112] > Ua Mannacháin** (Síl Muiredaig of Uí Briúin Aí)

Donnchad Ua Mannacháin, 'king of Uí Briúin na Sinne (Uí Briúin of the Shannon)', was killed in 1145 in an attack on a division of the fleet (*drem do coblach*) of Síl Muiredaig.[113] In 1159, when Ruaidrí Ua Conchobair's army suffered a defeat at Ardee at the hands of Muirchertach Mac Lochlainn, king of Cenél nEógain, among those slain was Muredach Ua Mannacháin, 'king of Uí Briúin Sinna', clear testimony to Ua Mannacháin's closeness to Ruaidrí Ua Conchobair.[114] In 1176, Ignaide Ua Mannacháin acted as surety for Ruaidrí Ua Conchobair's grant to the church of St Berach.[115] In 1187, the son of Donn Ua Mannacháin and two of Ua Mannacháin's daughters perished when the stronghold of Mac Diarmata at Lough Key was hit by lightning.[116] In 1190, the son of Ua Mannacháin was drowned when the ship of Cathal Crobderg Ua Conchobair got into difficulties and sank on Lough Ree.[117] In 1197 Ignaide Ua Mannacháin, king of Uí Briúin na Sinna, died.[118] In 1208, Gilla na nEch Ua Mannacháin, king of Uí Briúin na Sinna, was fighting on behalf of Cathal Crobderg Ua Conchobair against the rebel Cathal Mac Diarmata.[119] In 1216, Gilla Críst Ua Mannacháin died in Rome.[120] In 1224, the annalists described the accession of Áed Ua Conchobair as king of Connacht as peaceful other than that a robbery was committed on the road to Cruachain and a woman was violated by the son of Ua Mannacháin, who was 'blinded' as punishment.[121] In 1229, Lochlann Ua Mannacháin was killed by his father's brother,[122] and, in 1230, Máel Sechnaill Ua Mannacháin was killed by his own kinsmen,[123] and, in 1230, also Gilla na nEch Ua Mannacháin died in the monastery of Boyle.[124] In 1242, Áed Ua Mannacháin died in the habit of an Augustinian canon at Kilmore (Co. Roscommon).[125] Tadc Ua Mannacháin, 'king/*tigerna* of Uí Briúin na Sinna', died on 6 June 1249 and was interred in Kilmore.[126] In 1268, Domnall son of

109 Flanagan, *Irish royal charters*, pp 350–1, 354; cf. no. 2 in this appendix. **110** *AC* 1225.10, 18; *ALC*; *AFM*. **111** *AC* 1231.7, 10; *ALC*; *AFM* (his wife's name is given as Dub Themrach in *ALC* and *AFM*). **112** The name 'Omanethan' actually occurs twice in two consecutive lines in the poem. The most recent editor of the text, Dr Evelyn Mullally, considers this to be an accidental repetition on the part of the scribe. It is not possible to reconstruct what other name may have been omitted by that mistake; Ua Máel Brenainn, one of four *rígthoísig* who ought to be present at the inauguration of the king of Connacht, is a possibility; Dillon, 'Inauguration', pp 189, 197. **113** *AT* 1145.5; *CS*. Cf. *AFM*. **114** *AT* 1159.6; *AU* 1159.3; *AFM* 1159.13. Cf. nos 1, 2, 4, 11 in this appendix. **115** *AFM*. Cf. nos 2, 3, 6 in this appendix. **116** *ALC*. Cf. nos 2, 10 in this appendix. **117** *AFM*. Cf. nos 2, 3 in this appendix. **118** *AFM*. **119** *ALC*. **120** *ALC*. **121** *ALC*; *AFM*; *AC* 1226.3. **122** *AC* 1229.10; *AFM*; *ACott* which attributes his death to his own brother. **123** *AC* 1230.20; *ALC*; *AFM*. **124** *ALC*; *AC* 1237.12; *AFM*. **125** *ALC*; *AC* 1242.13. **126** *AC* 1249.12; *ALC*; *AFM*.

Tadc Ua Mannacháin and ten of his associates were killed by Tadc Ua Flannacáin and Gilla Críst Ua Birn.[127] The latest Ua Mannacháin whose death-notice is recorded in the annals is Gilla na nEch, 'king of the three Tuatha', who died on 7 September 1287.[128] Thereafter, lordship of Uí Briúin na Sinna passed to Ua Birn, whose ancestors had long served as hereditary officers in the household of the king of Connacht.[129] Ua Mannacháin was listed as one of the twelve *toísig* of Síl Muiredaig who participated in the inauguration of Ua Conchobair according to the portion of the prose tract that dates back to the twelfth or thirteenth century.[130]

10 'Odude' > Ua Dubda (Uí Fhiachrach Muaide)

There is an extensive series of entries related to the Uí Dubda in eleventh- and twelfth-century annals, many associating them with naval activity. In 1126, Domnall Finn Ua Dubda, 'king of Uí Amalgada, Uí Fhiachrach and Cera', was drowned while driving a prey out of Tír Conaill.[131] In 1135, the son of Domnall Ua Dubda slew Ua Máille but was subsequently killed himself by his own spear through a miracle of St Colum Cille.[132] Áed son of Muirchertach Ua Dubda, 'king of Uí Amalgada and Uí Fhiachrach', died in 1143.[133] In 1153, Brian Ua Dubda was killed at the battle of Fordruim fighting on the side of Ruaidrí, son of Tairdelbach Ua Conchobair, king of Connacht, along with 'West Connacht' against Muirchertach Mac Lochlainn, king of Cenél nEógain.[134] In 1154, An Cosnamach Ua Dubda was in command of a fleet of Tairdelbach Ua Conchobair on a plundering expedition against Tír Conaill and Inishowen and lost his life in a naval battle that ensued between the Connacht fleet and that of Muirchertach Mac Lochlainn.[135] Ua Dubda is named as *ceann do chabhlaigh*, head of Ua Conchobair's fleet, in the poem on the inauguration of Ua Conchobair.[136] In 1162, An Cosnamach Ua Dubda was killed by his own kin.[137] In 1187, the daughter of Ua Dubda was among those killed when Mac Diarmata's stronghold at Lough Key was struck by lightning.[138] In 1192, Taichlech Ua Dubda, king of Uí Fhiachrach, was slain by his grandsons;[139] his son Áed was killed in 1201.[140] In 1200, in the dispute between Cathal Crobderg Ua Conchobair and Cathal Carrach Ua Conchobair, Cathal Carrach took hostages from Ua Dubda.[141] In 1202 Tomaltach son of Taichlech Ua Dubda was slain alongside Cathal Carrach Ua Conchobair.[142] In 1202, Donnchad Ua Dubda was among the party who arrested Tairdelbach son of Ruaidrí Ua Conchobair on behalf of Cathal Crobderg Ua Conchobair.[143] In 1221 Máel Ruanaid Ua Dubda, king of Uí Amalgada, was among those with Diarmait son of Ruaidrí Ua Conchobair (d. 1198) who had gone to Inse Gall to assemble a fleet to challenge for the kingship of Connacht and was drowned on that expedition.[144] In 1225, Donnchad Ua Dubda killed Tigernán

127 *AC* 12611.11. **128** *AC* 1287.5; *ALC*; *AU*; *AFM*; Simms, 'Gabh umad a Fheidhlimidh', 141–2. **129** *Topographical poems*, ll. 587–8 Cf. *AT* 1133.3, 1153.7. **130** Dillon, 'Inauguration', pp 189, 197. Cf. Simms, 'Gabh umad a Fheidhlimidh', 141–2. **131** *AT* 1126.4; *AU* 1126.6; *AI* 1126.12; *CS* 1122=1126; *ALC*; *ACott*; *AFM*. **132** *AT* 1135.5; *CS* 1131=1135. Cf. *AFM*. **133** *AT* 1143.8; *AFM*. **134** *AT* 1153.7; *AFM*. **135** *AFM*; cf. *AT* 1154.6. **136** Dillon, 'Inauguration', pp 195, 202 (a role in the prose section assigned to Ua Flaithbertaig and Ua Máille when Ua Conchobair makes an expedition at sea). For subsequent chieftains, see Nollaig Ó Muraíle, 'Two lists of Ó Dubhda chieftains of Uí Fhiachrach' in Duffy (ed.), *Princes, prelates and poets*, pp 139–58. **137** *ACott*; *AFM*. **138** *ALC* 1184, *recte* 1187; cf. nos 2, 9 in this appendix. **139** *ACott*; *ALC*; *AFM*. **140** *ALC*. **141** *ALC*. **142** *ALC*. **143** *ALC*. **144** *ALC*; *AU*; *AFM s.a.* 1220.

son of Cathal Micuran son of Tairdelbach Ua Conchobair (d. 1156).[145] In 1235, Taichlech Ua Dubda, king of Uí Amalgada and Uí Fhiachrach, was killed by an arrowwound in the *longphort* of Fedlimid, son of Cathal Crobderg Ua Conchobair, king of Connacht, while intervening to quell a dispute.[146]

11 'Usathnessy de Poltilethban' > Ua Sechnusaig of Poll Toighe Líabháin (Uí Fhiachrach Aidne)

The two main branches of Uí Fhiachrach Aidne in south Connacht in the twelfth century were the Uí Eidin and the Uí Shechnusaig. Among those killed in 1159 at Ardee fighting in the army of Ruaidrí Ua Conchobair against Muirchertach Mac Lochlainn, king of Cenél nEógain, was Cellbuide Ua Sechnusaig, the first person of that surname noted in the annals.[147] Poll Toighe Líabháin, according to Geoffrey Keating, was in Uí Fhiachrach Aidne, 'which is now called the country of Ó Sechnassaigh'.[148] It is remarkable that this place-name is recorded in the late twelfth-century 'Song of Dermot and the earl' and in Geoffrey Keating's *Foras feasa ar Éirinn* but nowhere else.[149] In the fourteenth-century topographical poem of the Connacht poet, Seaán Mór Ó Dubhagáin (d. 1372), Ua Sechnusaig is described as one of two kings of Cenél nÁeda, that is, Cenél nÁeda na hEchtge,[150] the other being Ua Cathail.[151] These two lineages competed for the kingship of Cenél nÁeda during the twelfth and thirteenth centuries. In 1179, for example, Máel Sechnaill Riabach Ua Sechnusaig, *tigerna* of half of Cenél nÁeda, was killed by the son of Donnchad Ua Cathail.[152] In 1191 when Ruaidrí Ua Conchobair, having been deposed from his kingdom, unsuccessfully sought aid in Cenél Conaill, Cenél nEógain, Ulaid, among the Anglo-Normans in Meath and in Munster to recover the kingship, he eventually was recalled from Munster by Síl Muiredaig, and allocated lands in Uí Fhiachrach Aidne and Cenél nÁeda na hEchtge in south Connacht.[153] In 1221, the son of Gilla na Náem Ua Sechnusaig 'took a house upon Gillemochoynne O'Cahall prince of Kyneleagh, who killed him after his comeing forth'.[154] In 1240 Áed son of Gilla na Naem Crom Ua Sechnusaig was killed by Conchobar son of Áed son of Cathal Crobderg Ua Conchobair.[155] In 1242, Niall, son of Domnall son of Ruaidrí Ua Conchobair, 'was burned together with three Uí Shechnusaig in one house in Mayo' by a member of the household of Maurice Fitz Gerald.[156]

145 *ALC*; *AC* 1226.2; *AFM* 1226. **146** *ACott*; *AC* 1235.6; *ALC*; *AFM*. **147** *AT* 1159.6; *AFM*; *AU*. Cf. nos 1, 2, 4, 9 in this appendix. **148** *FFÉ*, ii, pp 324–7. **149** See Hogan, *Onomasticon*, p. 563. There is what appears to be a mention of the name – as Poltylebane – in the Elizabethan Fiants in 1602–3: *The Irish fiants of the Tudor sovereigns during the reigns of Henry VIII, Edward VI, Philip & Mary, and Elizabeth I*, with a new introduction by Kenneth Nicholls and preface by Tomás Ó Canann, 4 vols (Dublin, 1994), iii, no. 6765, p. 617. The location is uncertain but surrounding place-names occur in cos. Clare and Tipperary, and in one case possibly in the parish of Kilbeacanty, barony of Kiltartan, south Co. Galway. This would appear to be circumstantial evidence that the name Poll Tighe Liabáin still survived in or near the Ó Seachnasaigh territory in south Galway at the beginning of the seventeenth century (i.e., during the lifetime of Geoffrey Keating). I am very grateful to Dr Nollaig Ó Muraíle for this reference as well as for other comments on this paper. **150** MacCotter, *Medieval Ireland*, pp 144–5. **151** *Topog. Poems*, ll. 785–7. **152** *AFM*. For other references, see *AFM* 1154, 1222, 1224; *AClon*, 1221; *AC* 1224.6, 1240.4, 1248.3, 1248.4, 1249.4, 1251.3; *ALC* 1222. **153** *AFM*. **154** *AClon*, p. 229. **155** *AC* 1240.4; *AU*; *ALC*; *AMisc*, 1240.2; *AFM*. **156** *AC* 1242.12. For the later history of the Uí Shechnusaig, see John O'Donovan (ed.), *The genealogies, tribes, and customs of Hy-Fiachrach* (Dublin, 1844), pp 373–87.

Brian Bóraime's right to rule: an unfinished dialogue

LENORE FISCHER

INTRODUCTION

From the time when, after Brian Bóraime's death, Máel Sechnaill regained the sovereignty of Ireland, controversy began to rage as to how legitimate Brian's claim to rule had been. This contribution divides the participants in the controversy between the 'Uí Néillites' who supported the exclusive Uí Néill right to sovereignty, and the 'Dalcassians' who defended Brian's right to rule. The synthetic historians of Máel Sechnaill's court framed the initial Uí Néillite response to Brian's reign and Brian's Dalcassian successors responded with the *Cogadh Gáedhel re Gallaibh*. Gaelic poetry of post-Anglo-Norman Ireland kept the controversy alive and culminated in the 'Contention of the Bards'. Charles O'Conor and John O'Donovan later rowed in on opposite sides. The arguments made in the course of the dispute have significantly shaped our understanding of early Irish history and while the current trend among historians is to see Brian Bóraime in terms of a changing style of kingship, there are still entrenched Uí Néillites and Dalcassians among us today.[1]

Modern historical writing is often curiously tangled in paradoxes when it comes to assessing the importance of Brian Bóraime and his battle at Clontarf. Dáibhí Ó Cróinín in his *Early medieval Ireland*, for instance, states categorically that 'historians ... are almost unanimous in the verdict that the encounter [at Clontarf] was of no real political significance'.[2] Yet nevertheless he chooses 1014 as the break between the chapter on 'The Viking Age' and the following chapter 'Ireland 1014–1200'. In *A new history of Ireland i*, F.J. Byrne similarly has two chapters (XXIV–V), one entitled 'Ireland before the battle of Clontarf' followed by 'Ireland and her neighbours, *c.*1014–*c.*1072', yet his discussion of the battle is limited to a passing mention.[3] Why, if the battle was so unimportant, is its date repeatedly chosen as a major dividing point in early Irish history?

The answer to this may be that the significance of 1014 lies not in the battle that occurred in that year, but rather in Brian Bóraime's death in that battle, a death which terminated a reign that had marked a turning point in Irish kingship. For indeed Brian's kingship had been extraordinary, and not only

1 I am extremely indebted to Máirín Ní Donnchadha, Liam Irwin, Peter Smith, Catherine Swift and Alice Walsh all of whom made valuable suggestions and corrections in working through early stages of this paper. 2 Dáibhí Ó Cróinín, *Early medieval Ireland, 400–1200* (London, 1995), p. 266. 3 F.J. Byrne, 'Ireland and her neighbours, *c.*1014–*c.*1072' in *NHI*,

because he came of minor provincial stock. Curtis attributed to him 'the greatest moment in the history of native Ireland'; MacNeill credited him with 'ideas which in the Ireland of his time, were revolutionary';[4] Binchy called his reign 'a watershed in Irish history'.[5] Among more modern historians, Duffy goes so far as to call him 'the greatest of Ireland's high-kings';[6] Kathleen Hughes points out that 'Brian was the first king to control the forces of south and north', and Byrne even suggests that Brian's 'claim to be *imperator Scottorum* … may indeed have implied overlordship not merely of Ireland but also of the Gaelic realm in Britain'.[7] Tomás Ó Carragáin has suggested that Brian pioneered an innovative programme of church-building, possibly following a continental model;[8] William O'Sullivan gives evidence for a literary revival in Brian's era and quotes Pádraig Ó Riain who 'sees the famous lost "Psalter of Cashel" (a great compendium of genealogical and historical lore) as having been produced under the aegis of Brian'.[9]

Yet the paradox continues. Donnchadh Ó Corráin in *Ireland before the Normans*, a work that after more than forty years is still in many respects virtually a blueprint for our understanding of early Irish history today, had no difficulty assigning a prominent role to Brian's reign, devoting some ten pages to his career and its ending.[10] But *The New History of Ireland* and other modern texts tiptoe round the subject of Brian,[11] paying him a mere nodding recognition as they go, and Máire Ní Mhaonaigh, currently the main scholar of Brian material, hesitantly named her biography of him *Brian Boru: Ireland's greatest king?*[12] The reasons underlying this ambivalence towards Brian and his achievements would seem to go right back to the period immediately after his death.

UÍ NÉILLITES VERSUS BRIANITES: THE SYNTHETIC HISTORIANS AND THE UÍ BRIAIN ANSWER

Once the battle of Clontarf was over and Máel Sechnaill reinstated as king of Ireland, the work began to eradicate the traces of Brian's reign and prevent future similar disruptions to Uí Néill rule. This was not an initiative conjured

i, pp 862–98, at p. 862. 4 Edmund Curtis, *A history of Ireland* (London, 1936, repr. 1973), p. 29; Eoin MacNeill, *Phases of Irish history* (Dublin, 1919, repr. 1968), p. 269. 5 Daniel A. Binchy, 'Lawyers and chroniclers' in Brian Ó Cuiv (ed.), *Seven centuries of Irish learning 1000–1700* (Cork, 1971), pp 50–61, at p. 61. 6 Seán Duffy (ed.), *Atlas of Irish history* (Dublin, 1997, 2nd ed. 2000), p. 26. 7 Kathleen Hughes, 'The Irish church, 800–*c.*1050' in *NHI*, i, pp 635–55, at p. 647; Byrne, 'Ireland and her neighbours', p. 862. 8 Tomás Ó Carragáin, 'Patterns of patronage: churches, round towers and the Dál Cais kings of Munster (*c.*950–1050)' in Roger Stalley (ed.), *Limerick and south-west Ireland: medieval art and architecture*, British Archaeological Association Conference Transactions, no. 34 (Leeds, 2011), pp 23–41, at p. 27. 9 William O'Sullivan, 'Manuscripts and palaeography' in *NHI*, i, pp 511–48 at p. 539. 10 Ó Corráin, *Normans*, pp 120–31. 11 See, for example, Edel Bhreathnach, *Ireland in the medieval world, AD400–1000* (Dublin, 2014). 12 Ní Mhaonaigh,

up *de novo*, for an intimate connection between the Uí Néill, Tara and the sovereignty of Ireland had been formulated in the course of the ninth century, particularly in association with the reigns of Máel Sechnaill mac Máele Ruanaid and his son Flann Sinna. Genealogies at that stage were reworked, traditions synthesized and poetry produced to integrate an emerging view of social organization and in particular, to underpin a changing concept of kingship.[13] Nor does this ninth-century overhaul of received lore appear to have been the first of its kind, for it seems that the early 700s had also seen a flurry of activity in the coding of genealogy and laws,[14] as well as the production of works like *Baile Chuinn Chétchathaig* celebrating the Uí Néill's (specifically Síl nÁedo Sláine's) right to a supreme kingship based in Tara.[15] Irish society, then, experienced periodic bouts of self-assessment, as indeed, what society does not?

The wave of reassessment taking place after Brian's death was undertaken by a group of people dubbed by Eoin MacNeill the 'synthetic historians'.[16] Since MacNeill's day, the work of this 'mandarin class of monastic and secular scholars'[17] has been the focus of investigation showing how they reworked Ireland's mythopoetic background to fit a tightened concept of Uí Néill kingship at Tara. Recently scholars have begun drawing attention to the link between the work of these synthetic historians and the reign of Máel Sechnaill II. The core version of the *Dinnshenchas Éirenn*, for instance, promulgating the supremity of Tara is attributed to Cúán ua Lothcháin working under the

Brian Boru. 13 MacNeill identified the earliest known figure responsible for this work as Máel Muru, who died in 884 (*Phases of Irish history*, p. 39). For Máel Muru and Flann Sinna, see John Carey, 'In Search of Máel Muru Othna' in Emer Purcell et al. (eds), *Clerics, kings and Vikings: essays on medieval Ireland in honour of Donnchadh Ó Corráin* (Dublin, 2015), pp 429–39. A survey of the reigns of Máel Sechnaill and Flann Sinna can be found in Bart Jaski, 'The vikings and the kingship of Tara', *Peritia*, 9 (1995), 310–53, at 315–22. For Máel Sechnaill mac Máele-Ruanaid's claim to be the first *de facto* king of all Ireland, see Peter Harbison, 'A high cross base from the Rock of Cashel and a historical reconsideration of the "Ahenny group" of crosses', *PRIA*, 93C (1993), 1–20, particularly at 15. Objections raised to Harbison's thesis by Raghnall Ó Floinn, 'Patrons and politics: art, artefact and methodology' in Mark Redknap et al. (eds), *Pattern and purpose in Insular art: proceedings of the fourth international conference on Insular art* (Oxford, 2001), pp 1–14 (at p. 11), do not substantially alter the argument presented here. For the encoding of changing social conditions, see Charles Doherty's summary of material in 'The Vikings in Ireland: a review' in Clarke et al. (eds), *Ireland and Scandinavia*, pp 288–330, at p. 323. 14 For work on the genealogies, see Bart Jaski, 'The genealogical section of the Psalter of Cashel', *Peritia*, 17–18 (2003–4), 295–337, at 295, 317, 327. For a discussion of the dating of law tracts, see Liam Breatnach, 'Canon law and secular law in early Ireland: the significance of *Bretha Nemed*', *Peritia*, 3 (1984), 439–59, esp. at 456–7, 459; see also, Byrne, *Irish kings*, pp 254–60; Kim McCone, *Pagan past and Christian present in early Irish literature* (Maynooth, 2000), pp 242–3. 15 See Edel Bhreathnach, '*Níell cáich úa Néill nascatar géill*: the political context of *Baile Chuinn Chétchathaig*' in eadem (ed.), *The kingship and landscape of Tara* (Dublin, 2005), p. 50. 16 Eoin MacNeill, *Celtic Ireland* (Dublin, 1921), at p. 38. 17 Donnchadh Ó Corráin, 'Nationality and kingship in pre-Norman Ireland' in T.W. Moody (ed.), *Nationality and the pursuit of national independence* (Belfast, 1978), pp 1–35, at p. 35.

patronage of Máel Sechnaill;[18] the *Lebor gabála* was redrafted extensively;[19] mythologies and prophecies were reworked.[20] Peter Smith has suggested that 'at the beginning of the eleventh century several scholars set themselves the task of producing a compendium of the historical knowledge of the entire nation and its leaders',[21] a compendium designed to underpin the supremacy of Tara and the Uí Néill.[22]

The influence of the synthetic historians extended even to the editing of annals, the Clonmacnoise group of annals and in particular the Annals of Tigernach showing clear traces of revision and a distinct aversion to Brian Bóraime and his career and works.[23] Finally, in the poem 'Temhair III', Cúán ua Lothcháin makes the claim that Cormac mac Airt had compiled a Psalter of Tara outlining the rights and dues of each province towards the king of Tara and fixing the boundaries of provinces and baronies.[24] The existence of such a document has never been substantiated and it has been suggested that it was a

18 See work by Tomás Ó Concheanainn, 'A pious redactor of *Dinnshenchas Érenn*', *Ériu*, 33 (1982), 85–98, at 98; Pádraig Ó Riain, 'The Psalter of Cashel: a provisional list of contents', *Éigse*, 23 (1989), 105–30, at 109–10; Edel Bhreathnach, 'The topography of Tara: the documentary evidence', *Discovery Programme Reports* 2, RIA (Dublin, 1995), pp 68–76, at p. 68. In particular, see Máire Ní Mhaonaigh, 'A man of two faces: Máel Sechnaill mac Domhaill in Middle Irish sources' in Howard B. Clarke and Ruth Johnson (eds), *The Vikings in Ireland and beyond: before and after the battle of Clontarf* (Dublin, 2015), pp 232–52, at pp 249–51; Clodagh Downey, 'The Life and work of Cúán ua Lothcháin', *Ríocht na Midhe*, 19 (2008), 55–78, at 59 and 61. **19** See John Carey, *The Irish national origin-legend: synthetic pseudohistory*, Quiggin Pamphlets on the sources of Mediaeval Gaelic History, 1 (Cambridge, 1994), at pp 19 and 23; also Mark Scowcroft, 'The Leabhar Gabhála, part I: the growth of the text', *Ériu*, 38 (1987), 81–142; idem, 'The Leabhar Gabhála, part II: the growth of the tradition', *Ériu*, 39 (1988), 1–66; and Edel Bhreathnach, 'Cultural identity and Tara from *Lebor Gabála Érenn* to George Petrie', *Discovery Programme Reports* 4, RIA (Dublin, 1996), pp 85–98, at pp 85–6. **20** See Bart Jaski, 'The strange case of Ailill Mac Mágach and Cet mac Mátach' in Purcell et al. (eds), *Clerics, kings and Vikings*, pp 440–51, at p. 451. For prophecies, see Kevin Murray 'Introduction' in idem (ed.), *Baile in Scáil*; *'The phantom's frenzy'*, ITS (Dublin, 2004), esp. pp 4–5, 29; also idem, 'The reworking of Old Irish narrative texts in the Middle Irish period: contexts and motivations' in Elizabeth Boyle and Deborah Hayden (eds), *Authorities and adaptations: the reworking of transmission of textual sources in medieval Ireland*, DIAS (Dublin, 2014), pp 291–306. **21** Peter J. Smith, 'Early Irish historical verse: the evolution of a genre' in Próinséas Ní Chatháin and Michael Richter (eds), *Ireland and Europe in the early middle ages: texts and transmission* (Dublin, 2002), pp 325–41, at p. 340. **22** Byrne, *Irish kings*, p. 269. **23** See Ní Mhaonaigh, 'A man', esp. 239–45; Nicholas Evans, *The present and the past in medieval Irish chronicles* (Woodbridge, 2010), pp 230–1; David N. Dumville, 'The peculiarity of the Annals of Tigernach, AD489–766: the Clonmacnoise redaction of the "Chronicle of Ireland"' in Kathryn Grabowski and David Dumville, *Chronicles and annals of medieval Ireland and Wales: the Clonmacnoise-group texts* (Woodbridge, 1984), pp 109–52, at p. 115. A detailed comparison of the Annals of Tigernach with its companion annals was presented by Joseph Flahive in a paper misnamed 'The O'Clery Leabhar Gabhála', at the 21st Irish Conference of Medievalists, 28–30 June 2007. **24** 'Temhair III', Edward Gwynn's translation, downloaded 28 Oct. 2015 from ucc.ie/celt/published/T106500A; see Ó Conchennain, 'A Pious Redactor', p. 92 for the attribution to Cúán.

deliberate fraud 'created by Cúán to counter the existence of a real manuscript known as the Psalter of Cashel (now lost), which was part of the insignia of Brian Bórama'.[25] The Psalter of Cashel was reputedly compiled about a century previous to Brian, and since no copy of it exists any longer, it is difficult to form any firm conclusions regarding the context in which it was produced. Whether it was reworked in Brian's court or not must remain a moot conjecture, but it seems at any rate to have acted as a powerful charter on behalf of the southern half of Ireland (Leth Moga). Following on Brian's (i.e., Leth Moga's) extraordinary reign over both halves of Ireland it was evidently felt necessary to claim the existence of a similar charter for Leth Cuinn, the northern half.

Works such as the *Dinnshenchas* poems, produced for Máel Sechnaill's court within the decade after Brian's death, form the first place where we can put our finger securely on a controversy between what we may call the 'Uí Néillites' upholding the supposedly exclusive rights of the Uí Néill and Tara on the one hand, and the 'Dalcassians' who claimed that Brian Bóraime had a legitimate right to the kingship of Ireland.[26] The synthetic historians set the first wave of this debate going in the eleventh century but, as we shall see, the debate continues to this very day.

The synthetic historians' propaganda on behalf of the Uí Néill and the authority of Tara was not to go unchallenged. Brian's heirs were not content to sink back into obscurity: a riposte was issued in the form of a biography of Brian, the *Cogadh Gáedhel re Gallaibh*, and of a new charter, the *Lebor na Cert*. The *Cogadh* has been classed by some as an extremely late example of a king-tale,[27] while the suggestion has been made on the other hand that it is on the

25 Bhreathnach, 'The topography', pp 72–3; see also discussion in Ó Riain, 'The Psalter', 108–12. 26 Readers of this manuscript have been kind enough to offer a variety of possible terms for these concepts, including 'Temorians', 'Niallians', and 'pro-Uí Néill' for the one side and 'pro-Dál Cais', and 'Brianite' or 'Uí Briainite' for the other. 27 Ó Corráin, *Normans*, p. 78; he later defines it as a 'dynastic propaganda text', see Donnchadh Ó Corráin, 'Viking Ireland – afterthoughts' in Clarke et al. (eds), *Ireland and Scandinavia*, pp 421–52, at p. 443. Proinsias MacCana, on the other hand, saw the king-tales as ending with the death of Cathal mac Finguine in AD742 ('The influence of the Vikings on Celtic literature' in Brian Ó Cuív (ed.), *The impact of the Scandinavian invasions on the Celtic-speaking peoples* c.*AD800–1100*, DIAS (Dublin, 1983), pp 78–118 at p. 80); saying that the 'nearest approach [to a new historical cycle] came much later in CGG and its derivatives' ('The influence', p. 98). Ó Cuív seems less inclined to see any fundamental difference between the early king-tales and later semi-historical tracts such as the *Cogadh* ('Literary creation and Irish historical tradition', *Proceedings of the British Academy*, 49 (1963), 233–62, at 240–1). Byrne, however, sees a fundamental distinction between the earlier king-tales and the *Cogadh*. He describes the 'saga of the "Battle of Allen" where … the high king Fergal mac Máele Dúin fell in 722' as 'the latest historical event to be enshrined in saga literature … Later kings, indeed, such as Muirchertach of the Leather Cloaks, Cellachán Caisil, Cormac mac Cuilennáin or Brian Bóruma, become the protagonists of literary compositions, but these are no longer pure saga, but rather works of propaganda or historical fiction, based to some extent upon the annals or other historical documentation

contrary an extremely early example of an Irish *chanson de geste*.[28] This very diversity of interpretations points to its pivotal nature in Irish literature. The impact that it has had on subsequent generations has been phenomenal: its echoes have reverberated to such an extent down the centuries that in our own day Kathleen Hughes scarcely exaggerated when she said that it 'has probably shaped the public impression of Irish history more than any other single work'.[29] Its effect on the society of its own day has yet to be gauged. Certainly it spawned progeny: arguably in the case of a lost **Brjansaga* composed perhaps within the Dublin Viking community,[30] but indubitably in the case of the much later *Cath Cluana Tarbh* and *Leabhar Oiris*, (to be discussed below). Its theme and style were moreover imitated in works such as the *Caithréim Chellacháin Chaisil* and the later *Caithréim Thoirdhealbhaigh*. The disputed **Brjansaga* excepted, all of these were Leth Moga documents, carrying on in one form or another the theme of Leth Moga glory laid down in the *Cogadh*. It is notable that the Northern Half produced in response little in the way of such royal biographies other than the poem *A Mhuircheartaigh mhic Néill náir* describing the subject's supposed circuit of Ireland. Northern Uí Néillites favoured instead the more generalized works of synthetic scholarship cited above.[31]

This is not to be wondered at, perhaps, given the increasing fragmentation of the Uí Néill following the death of Máel Sechnaill. Uí Briain fortunes were on the rise again under Tairdelbach and his son Muirchertach, and the production of the *Lebor na Cert* may have hammered propaganda's nail into the coffin of the northern dynasties. *A Mhuircheartaigh mhic Néill náir*, produced most likely to enhance the career of the Uí Briain's rival, Muirchertach son of Niall Mac Lochlainn (d. 1166),[32] represents their swansong in this dynastic

against which records their veracity can be checked' (*Irish kings*, p. 146). Máire Ní Mhaonaigh classes the *Cogadh* and its ilk as 'royal biographies' and describes them as 'markedly different' from the earlier king-tales, pointing, like Byrne, to their greater reliance on 'annalistic packaging' ('The literature of medieval Ireland 800–1200: from the Vikings to the Normans' in Margaret Kelleher and Philip O'Leary (eds), *The Cambridge history of Irish literature* (Cambridge, 2006), pp 44–67, at p. 47). **28** Catherine Swift, 'Chivalry, Saracens and the *chansons de geste* of Brian Boru' in Seán Duffy (ed.), *Medieval Dublin XV* (Dublin, 2015), pp 119–40. **29** Kathleen Hughes, *Early Christian Ireland: introduction to the sources* (London, 1972), p. 288. **30** The main arguments in favour of a *Brjansaga written in Dublin are propounded by Donnchadh Ó Corrain, 'Viking Ireland – afterthoughts', pp 447–52. Benjamin Hudson, after an extensive review of the literature, provides qualified support for this thesis in 'Brjans Saga', *Medium Aevum*, 71 (2002), 241–68. Evidence supporting the theory has recently been produced by a former antagonist, see Gísli Sigurðsson, 'The saga map of Ireland and the British Isles' in Purcell et al. (eds), *Clerics, kings and Vikings*, pp 477–89, at p. 487n. **31** See also Ní Mhaonaigh, 'The literature', pp 45–8. **32** See Donnchadh Ó Corráin, 'Muirchertach Mac Lochlainn and the *Circuit of Ireland*' in A.P. Smyth (ed.), *Seanchas: studies in early and medieval Irish archaeology, history and literature in honour of Francis J. Byrne* (Dublin, 2000), pp 238–50; Byrne, 'Ireland and her neighbours', p. 896.

rivalry. As both parties were eclipsed by the growing power of Connacht, the debate over the specific figures of Brian and Máel Sechnaill and their claim to kingship waned. It was to rise afresh during the Gaelic Resurgence, as Gaelic Ireland struggled to reaffirm its roots. Like much else that was reasserted in the Gaelic Resurgence, however, it had changed in emphasis,[33] and was no longer aimed at justifying claimants to supreme power in the land. Rather, much of the new material produced seems to have been intended to frame specific views about the nature of Irish society and monarchy.

THE CONTENTION CONTINUES IN LATE MEDIEVAL GAELIC IRELAND

Given Cúán ua Lothcháin's major role in publicizing the rights of Máel Sechnaill and the Uí Néill, it is somewhat surprising that post-Anglo-Norman Gaelic tradition did not remember him as Máel Sechnaill's main poet, but instead assigned that role to Urard mac Coisse, a man described in the annals as Ireland's *príméces* or 'chief poet'.[34] Urard is credited with several poems celebrating the Uí Néill, including a quatrain beginning *Giamtis ghanna fir beatha* on the death of Máel Sechnaill's predecessor,[35] *Maoil Sechloinn sinnser Gaeoidhel* extolling Máel Sechnaill's rule,[36] and *Dursan mar taí, a Dhúin na Scíath*, an elegy on Máel Sechnaill's death.[37] The latter was certainly not Urard's own work, as he predeceased Máel Sechnaill by over three decades. There was at one time some debate as to whether Urard mac Coisse ever actually existed: both Colm O Lochlainn and Aideen O'Leary concluded that he was a figment of the Gaelic Resurgence;[38] but more recent historians take him more seriously.[39] As the debate surrounding Brian Bóraime and his rival developed momentum, Urard became a core figure, representing the honour

33 See Katharine Simms, *From kings to warlords: the changing political structure of Gaelic Ireland in the later Middle Ages* (Woodbridge, 1987), p. 29, for a cogent example of just such a modification of older tradition. 34 *AT* 989.1; *CS* 990.1; *AU* 990.2; *AR* §294 (=990). 35 Cited in *AU* 980.2; my thanks to Máirín Ní Donnchadha for clearing up some misinterpretations about this quatrain. 36 Surviving embedded in the foundation lore on kingship in the fourteenth-century *Leabhar Uí Mhaine*. 37 Recorded Stowe B.iv.2, a collection of poetry assembled by Mícheál Ó Cléirigh in 1627 while accumulating material for the Annals of the Four Masters. For more information on these and other mac Coisse poems, see Lenore Fischer, 'Two poets and Brian Bóraimhe', *NMAJ*, 49 (2009), 91–109 at 97, 95 and 98 respectively. 38 Colm O Lochlainn, 'Poets on the battle of Clontarf – I', *Éigse*, 3 (1942), 208–19, at 218, and 'Poets on the battle of Clontarf – II', *Éigse*, 4 (1944), 33–47, at 45; Aideen O'Leary, 'The identities of the poet(s) Mac Coisi', *CMCS*, 38 (1999), 53–71, at 68–9. 39 For Urard's outline of professional standards, see Proinsias Mac Cana, *The learned tales of medieval Ireland*, DIAS (Dublin, 1980), pp 36–8; also John Carey, 'The three things required of a poet', *Ériu*, 48 (1997), 41–58, at 50–2; Elva Johnson, *Literacy and identity in early medieval Ireland* (Woodbridge, 2013), pp 137–8, 143–4 and 154–5 examines how this affects our understanding of the artistic environment of the time.

of the Uí Néill. And just as tradition viewed Urard mac Coisse as Máel Sechnaill's poet, so a certain Muirchertach mac Liag, mentioned fleetingly in the *Cogadh*, became regarded as poet to Brian Bóraime. Mac Liag's death as *ardollam* of Ireland is recorded in 1016, and a poem of his figures in the *dinnshenchas* of the *Book of Leinster* recording lore of the borderlands between Uí Maine and Dál Cais. Poetry by him or attributed to him in later collections continued to associate him with this area.[40]

Both Urard mac Coisse and Muirchertach mac Liag appear as poets in the *Leabhar Oiris*. While there is no copy of this work preserved that is older than 1711/12, there is reason to suspect that a form of it must have already been in existence by *c.*1400.[41] This work has hitherto been regarded as an Uí Briain product engendered by the *Cogadh* and the *Cath Cluana Tarbh*, its author said to be a 'zealous partisan of Brian'.[42] Close examination of the text, however, shows that the author was not so much a zealous partisan of Brian as a zealous partisan of the Eóganacht Raithlind king Cian son of Máel Muad mac Brain, and the intention of the text was not to support the Uí Briain but to state Cian's (and by inference, his Eóganacht descendants') claim to succeed Brian as king of Munster. In making this claim, the text is careful to anchor itself firmly within an Uí Néillite framework: the text begins with Máel Sechnaill's accession and ends just after his death. The core message of the *Leabhar Oiris*, contained in the stories and poetry midway through the text, is introduced by Urard with a quatrain in praise of Cian. Mac Liag then tells a story of Cian's generosity and recites a poem praising the heroes of Dál Cais but also, in particular, of Cian. The climax of the threefold performance is rendered by a neutral poet who carefully maps out Cian's right to the kingship of all Munster.[43] In the *Leabhar Oiris* we thus see both Urard mac Coisse and Muirchertach mac Liag being employed to represent their respective courts; there is no discord between them, as it is in the interest of the author to create a harmonious balance: his patron (Cian's descendant) inherits the Uí Briain rule of Munster within an Uí Néill overlordship. That such a situation never existed, nor could exist given Anglo-Norman domination, is in keeping with the tenor of fourteenth-century Gaelic poetry which sought to envisage an imaginary Gaelic state *sans* an Anglo-Norman presence.[44]

A pair of poems involving the two poets was preserved by Mícheál Ó Cléirigh in a collection of poetry he compiled in 1627. These bring to a head

40 For a discussion of mac Liag and his poetry, see Fischer, 'Two poets', 93 and 103–6. 41 See Lenore Fischer, 'Brian's daughters, Cian mac Máel Muad, and the kingship of Munster', *JCHAS*, 121 (2016), 1–10. 42 See *CCT*, pp 77–8, at p. 78, and Meidhbhín Ní Úrdail, 'Observations on the text known as the *Leabhar Oiris*', *Studia Celtica Upsaliensis*, 9 (2013), 149–66, at 149–50. This quotation goes back to the text's original translator, Richard Best, in 'The Leabhar Oiris', *Ériu*, 1 (1904), 74–112, at 74. 43 See Fischer, 'Brian's daughters', for a more detailed analysis of the text and poems. 44 See, for instance, comments on Ó Dubhagáin's topographic poems in Simms, *From kings to warlords*, p. 17.

the antagonism between the rival factions. In *Marthain duit, a Iorairdfhéil*, Máel Sechnaill wins all the honours in a competition wherein Urard and his counterpart compare the generosity of their respective masters.[45] *Freiccari meisi, a meic Coissi* carries the theme to yet further lengths in a dialogue between Urard and Brian's son Donnchad.[46] In the surviving poems outlining this dogfight over patronage it is noticeable that Urard's (the Uí Néillite Leth Cuinn's) side consistently gains the upper hand. Nor is Urard's concern with patronage limited to the interchanges with Muirchertach mac Liag and with Donnchad described above, for apart from the doctrine on standards and patronage laid down in Urard's tale of *Airec Menman*,[47] the Annals of Clonmacnoise relate how he was granted the revenues of Ireland for an entire year by his patron, Máel Sechnaill, and how at the end of the year he fought Máel Sechnaill for the privilege of retaining them.[48] While Muirchertach mac Liag's side does not win the generosity stakes in these interchanges, the theme itself is far from absent in Dalcassian poetry, and we have seen it used in the poems of the *Leabhar Oiris*. More specifically, the poem *Bóraimhe Baile na Riogh* in which mac Liag is said to describe the tributes being brought into Cenn Corad (Kincora) from throughout Ireland, and in which Brian then bestows them all upon him,[49] appears to be a direct reply to the story of Máel Sechnaill granting the year's revenues to Urard mac Coisse.

These poems are listed below (table 1) along with the apologues referring to them.[50] We may see from the number of these apologues that these themes of Máel Sechnaill's generosity and of the unfavourable comparison between Máel Sechnaill and Brian Bóraime were very much part of the repertoire of backstories in use in the Gaelic literary world. Nor is the issue of patronage the only one wherein we see a theme being used as a poetic game of shuttlecock. Both of our protagonists, Brian and Máel Sechnaill, were at one stage or another lamented in an elegy: that on the death of Máel Sechnaill, *Dursan mar tái, a Dhúin na scíath*,[51] credited to Urard mac Coisse, uses the device of mourning the emptiness of the halls in which he dwelt. This same device is used in its better-known counterpart, *A Chinn Choradh, caidhi Brían?*, credited to Muirchertach mac Liag and translated by James Clarence Mangan as 'O, where, Kincora! is Brian the Great?'.

So far the poetry we have looked at has made no overt reference to actual poems produced by the opposition; but in the 'Contention of the Shannon' we see the antagonists squaring off against each other, each side, north and south,

45 *Marthain duit, a Iorairdfhéil* first appears in B.iv.2, a manuscript compiled by Mícheál Ó Cléirigh in 1627; see discussion in Fischer, 'Two poets', 97. 46 *Freiccari meisi, a meic Coissi* is likewise known from no manuscript older than the B.iv.2; see discussion in Fischer, 'Two poets', 98. 47 See n. 39 above. 48 *AClon* 983=990. 49 The name and contents of this poem appear in *FFÉ*, bk II, sect. XXV, but no actual copy of the poem occurs until RIA 23.G.8 from 1711; see discussion in Fischer, 'Two poets', 99 and 106. 50 I am indebted to Katharine Simms for supplying me with a list of these and other apologues. 51 Found in Mícheál O Cléirigh's collection known as Stowe B.iv.2 from 1628.

claiming the Shannon for their own. The dating of these poems is highly disputed, suggestions varying between the fourteenth and seventeenth centuries, with the latest contribution in the scholarly debate leaning towards an earlier date.[52] They must have been produced within a fairly short space of each other;

Table 12.1. Uí Néillite vs. Dalcassian poetry of the late medieval to early modern period

Uí Néillite	Dalcassian
PATRONAGE	
Urard mac Coisse fights Máel Sechnaill for Ireland's revenues;[53] *AClon* (*c.*1627) Apologues to this: a) '*Tánag d'Fhánad an einigh*', by Giolla na Naomh Ó hUiginn (mid-14c) b) '*Beith re dán dlighidh ollamh*', Cúchonnacht Ó Fialáin (mid-15c) c) '*Moghéanair ghabhas cairde*', by Domhnall Mac an Bhaird (late 16c) d) '*Ag seo chugat a Chormaic*', by Irial Ó hUiginn (late 16c) e) '*Mochean dot bhronnadh a Bhriain*', by Brian Ó Corcráin (early 17c)	'*Bóraimhe Baile na Ríogh*':[54] Brian grants Muirchertach mac Liag the year's tribute; cited in FFÉ (*c.*1635)
'*Marthain duit a Iorairdfhéil*':[55] Urard vs. Muirchertach; Stowe B.iv.2 (1628) Apologues to this: a) Gill Hwrsse [Giolla Íosa?] Ó Sléíbhín, '*Da sleigh ag Murchadh mac Floinn*' (early 16c) b) Giolla Íosa Ó Dálaigh, '*Damh fein coiglim an Cathair*' (late 16c) c) Tadhg Dall Ó hUiginn, '*Iomdha sochar ag Síol Néill*' (late 16c)	
'*Freiccari meisi, a Meic Coisi*':[56] Mac Coisse vs. Donnchad; Stowe B.iv.2 (1628)	

52 Edward O'Reilly, *Chronological account of nearly 400 writers*, Transactions of the Iberno-Celtic Society (Dublin, 1820), assigned *A Shionnainn Chuinn Chéadcathach* to the work of Tadhg Óg Ó hUiginn (d. 1448), a date which Brian Ó Cuív considers rash ('The poetic contention about the River Shannon', *Ériu*, 19 (1962), 89–110). Joep Leerson, *The contention of the Bards*, ITS, Subsidiary Ser. 2 (Dublin, 1994), p. 67, follows Eleanor Knott in identifying Tadhg Óg Ó hUiginn as the son of Tadhg Dall (*fl.* 1603), and therefore dates the poems to the seventeenth century. Katharine Simms, however, in 'Literacy and the Irish bards' in Huw Price (ed.), *Literacy in medieval Celtic Societies* (Cambridge, 1998), pp 138–258, believes that they are associated with a king of Thomond who died in 1364 (p. 249), and points out that the adjudicating poem appears in what seems to be an early sixteenth-century manuscript. 53 Published in *AClon* p. 121. 54 Only the first six out of the 33 quatrains of this poem have ever been published: see Kuno Meyer, 'Brian Bóromha', *Ériu*, 3 (1907), p. 72. 55 Published by Kuno Meyer, '*Mitteilungen aus irischen handschriften*', *ZCP*, 8 (1911–12), 218–22. 56 The text and translation of this poem appear in Osborn Bergin, 'A dialogue between Donnchad son of Brian and Mac Coisse', *Ériu*, 9 (1923), 176–9.

Uí Néillite	Dalcassian
ELEGIES	
'Dursan mar tái, a Dhúin na sciath':[57] Elegy on Máel Sechnaill; Stowe B.iv.2 (1628)	*'A Chinn Choradh, caidhi Brían?'*:[58] Elegy on Brian Bóraime; O'Gara MS, RIA 23.F.16, BB (1655)
SHANNON CONTENTION	
'A Shionainn Chuinn Chéadchathaigh',[59] by Tadhg Óg Ó hUiginn; *Book of the O'Conor Don* (1631) *'Bérad breath na himriosna'*,[60] by Tadhg an Ghadraigh Mac Aodhagáin, *Book of the O'Conor Don* (1631)	*'A Shionann Bríain Bhóroimhe'*,[61] by Diarmaid Ó Briain, *Book of the O'Conor Don* (1631)
CONTENTION OF THE BARDS	
II. '*Dáil catha idir Corc is Niall*', ascribed to Torna (date uncertain)	III. '*Olc do thagrais a Thorna*', by Tadhg (Mac Dáire) Mac Bruaideadha (early 17c)
IV. '*A Thaidhg ná tathaoir Torna*', by Lughaidh Ó Cléirigh (early 17c)	V. '*Éisd a Lughaidh rem labhra*', by Tadhg (Mac Dáire) Mac Bruaideadha (early 17c)
VI. '*Ro chuala ar thagrais a Thaidhg*', by Lughaidh Ó Cléirigh (early 17c)	
XV. '*Measa do thagrais a Thaidhg*', by Aodh Ó Domhnall (early 17c)	XVIII. '*Ní breith orm do bhreith a Aodh*', by Tadhg (Mac Dáire) Mac Bruaideadha (early 17c)
XVI. '*Gé saoile á Thaidhg nach dearnas*', by Roibeart McArtúir (early 17c)	

each of the original authors produced a second poem amplifying his arguments, but these appear to have been lost; they are mentioned, however, in *Bérad breath na himriosna*, an adjudicating poem produced by a third party. The first of the poems seems to have been *A Shionann Bríain Bhóroimhe* which in seven verses evokes the Shannon as running speedily through the lands of its origin and only reaching its full powers when reaching the realms of Brian Bóraime, his seat at Cenn Corad, the Falls of Dunass, the Limerick Estuary and Scattery Island. Ó hUiginn's reply in fourteen verses points out that

57 Kuno Meyer reproduced the text of this poem in *Archiv für celtische Lexikographie*, 3 (1907), p. 305; he furnished a translation in idem, *Selections from ancient Irish poetry* (London, 1959, repr. 1980), pp 78–9, in which, however, he omitted to translate verse 5. 58 James Hardiman published the text of this poem with accompanying translation by John D'Alton in *Irish minstrelsy, or bardic remains of Ireland*, 2 vols (London, 1831), ii, pp 196–201; James Clarence Mangan's translation appeared in his *Ballad-poetry of Ireland* (Dublin, 1845), and is readily accessible on www.ucc.ie/CELT. 59 The text and translations of both this and of *A Shionann Bríain Bhóroimhe* were published by Osborn Bergin, 'Two poems on the River Shannon', *Irish Review*, 25 Mar. 1913, 13–17. 60 See Ó Cuív, 'Poetic contention', 92–105. 61 See n. 59 above.

just because he, the poet, has been to West Munster does not make him a Munsterman, and that the Shannon was born in the land of Conn Cétchathach. The adjudicating poem decides in twenty-five verses in favour of the latter. In doing so it makes intriguing reference to a backstory which has been lost: evidently Máel Sechnaill was said to have caught a salmon whose belly contained a valuable jewel. A learned *Sean-Ghoill* [*sic*], presumably a man of the Hiberno-Norse community, granted the fish and the gem to Brian's people.

No such final arbitration was to appear in the vitriolic 'Contention of the Bards'.[62] This very large body of poetry takes as its origin a pair of poems said to have been produced by Torna Éices, a poet allegedly associated with the pre-Christian ruler Niall Noígiallach. There are five extant poems attributed to this Torna Éices. Two of these are in manuscripts pre-dating the Anglo-Norman conquest, and of these one uses language considered by Kuno Meyer as pre-ninth century. Our two poems, however, seem to make their first appearance with the rest of the Contention poetry. O'Curry was dubious as to their antiquity and McKenna has put on record a suggestion that at least one of the Torna poems in the Contention was written by a Torna Ó Maolchonaire who died in 1468.[63] Poem I of the Contention, Torna's *Mo dhá dhaltán níorsad liúm* has not been listed in Table 1 above, as it takes no sides. It merely states the north–south controversy in terms of Tara vs. Cashel, Niall Noígiallach vs. Corc, Torna proclaiming equal love for each. In Poem II, however, Corc claims the right to the kingship of Tara, but is eventually forced to submit to Niall. If we assume that these poems are of relatively late date, then it is apparent that the very real tenth-century challenge which Brian succeeded in winning against Máel Sechnaill is being restated here in the Gaelic Resurgence within a much broader framework of reference. There is however a serious danger here of circular logic, and an independent dating of these Torna poems would be needed to test the validity of this surmise.

Whatever the origin of the two poems attributed to Torna, in *Olc do thagrais a Thorna* (Poem III) Tadhg Mac Bruaideadha issued a vigorous rebuttal of the

62 The following discussion will use the numbering system established by Lambert McKenna in *Iomarbhágh na bhFileadh*, ITS (London, 1918). 63 See McKenna's introduction to *Iomarbhágh*; O'Curry discusses Torna Éices's poems in *On the manners and customs of the ancient Irish*, ed. K.W. Sullivan, 3 vols (London, Dublin, and New York, 1873), ii, pp 59–71, and *Dáil catha idir Corc is Niall* in particular on pp 61–4. For dating of Torna's *In tan theighmis don dáil*, see Kuno Meyer, 'Totenklage um König Niall Nóigiallach', *Festschrift Whitley Stokes um siebzigsten Geburtstage am 28. Februar 1900* (Leipzig, 1900), pp 1–6, at p. 2. McKenna incorrectly describes this as a poem on King Daithi, confusing it with *Atá fótsa rí fir find Fáil* (*Iomarbhágh*, p. ix). For further work on the Contention, see Bernadette Cunningham, 'Native culture and political change in Ireland, 1580–1640' in Ciaran Brady and Raymond Gillespie (eds), *Natives and newcomers: the makings of Irish colonial society, 1534–1641* (Dublin, 1986), pp 148–70; also Ann Dooley, 'Literature and society in early seventeenth-century Ireland: the evaluation of change' in Cyril J. Burne (ed.), *Celtic languages and Celtic peoples: proceedings of the second North American Congress of Celtic Studies* (Halifax, 1992), pp 513–34.

arguments presented in them, claiming that Corc was not a usurper but had an equal right in law to the kingship of Tara. Mac Bruaideadha is thus the first since the *Cogadh* to present the Dalcassian argument concerning Leth Moga's right to rule. Whereas the *Cogadh*, however, relied on a 'might makes right' approach, Mac Bruaideadha sought for legal precedents. Torna's two poems revolved around the two prominent pre-Christian figures of Niall Noígiallach and Corc of Cashel, but Mac Bruaideadha in *Olc do thagrais a Thorna* went yet further back into the origin-legends of Gaelic culture to the two sons of Míl who divided Ireland between them when they took the land from the Tuatha Dé Danann. Éber Finn, who got Leth Moga, was older than his brother Éremón, the ancestor of the Leth Cuinn ruling stock (verse 7). Mac Bruaideadha states:

> Not usurpers in strong Teamhair were the princes of the stock of Eibhear Fionn, but true princes … by good right and law (13). Five of Eibhear's sons held sway in strong Teamhair some time after their father … (14). Twenty-eight descendants of one of them flourished before Corc – an accurate statement – over Teamhair of the heroes (15).[64]

He further states it was from Éber that Ireland (Hibernia) was named (verse 9), and boasts of the great deeds that the descendants of Éber performed on behalf of Ireland (verses 16–20a), a train of argument that echoes that of the *Cogadh*.

The gauntlet thus thrown down was taken up by Lughaidh Ó Cléirigh in Poem IV, *A Thaidhg ná tathaoir Torna*. Ó Cléirigh stated that it was by fair judgment that Éremón was granted the kingship of Tara (verses 7–8); he states that the name 'Hibernia' in no way came from Éber Finn and cites several alternative derivations (verses 13–17). He counters Mac Bruaideadha's list of benefits by describing what Éremón's line had done for Ireland (verses 19–32) and states categorically that no Munster king descended from Corc had ever been king over Ireland, whereas 106 of Éremón's line were listed in the Roll of Kings (verses 45 & 46). Mac Bruaideadha's reply (Poem V, *Éisd a Lughaidh rem labhra*) brings in Brian Bóraime and the Dál Cais in verses 56–9: whereas Ó Cléirigh had credited his people with clearing the land of forests, Brian's people had shed their blood clearing the land of Danes: 'Count up slowly all the benefits of your kings down the ages. You shall not find in your kings of Éire the equal of the benefits conferred by Brian, son of Bébinn' (verse 71). The following nine verses are devoted to Brian and the cultural, economic and military advantages that he brought to Ireland, and Brian and his kin reappear in verses 85, 90, 139, 144–7.

64 Cited from McKenna's translation, *Iomarbhágh*, pp 13–15; numbers in the quotation refer to the verse numbers.

And so the argument raged on. Ó Cléirigh in Poem VI, *Ro chuala ar thagrais a Thaidhg* admits that four usurpers from Munster did briefly seize the sovereignty of Tara (verses 88–9). Of the 274 quatrains in this poem, nearly a quarter (67) are devoted either to a refutation of the Brian/Dál Cais claim or to support of Máel Sechnaill's superior right. The Contention eventually ran to some thirty poems, in which the Brian/Máel Sechnaill constellation and the Dál Cais claim appear in Poems XV (verses 66–7), XVI (verses 123–5, 131, 134, 135, 140 and 148–51), XVIII (verses 127 and 142). It should be stressed that the argument being presented here is not essentially a nationalist one. The north–south debate in which the poets of the Contention were engaged was not about creating a present sovereign nation, but about establishing their frame of reference, an 'overarching socio-cultural identity' or *mythomoteur*.[65] This concern with the history of kingship and the channelling of power within their society similarly informed the Annals of the Four Masters,[66] and, as we shall see, the work of Geoffrey Keating.

From the time when the *Cogadh* was composed up to the time when Keating wrote his *Foras feasa ar Éirinn*, the only significantly innovative arguments presented for the legitimacy and effectiveness of Brian's kingship were those put forward in the Annals of Clonmacnoise, as translated by Connell Mageoghagan in 1627. Mageoghagan's preface to his translation is devoted almost entirely to describing what might be called Brian's legislative achievements. Most of these are drawn from the *Cogadh*, but Mageoghagan also puts forward the unique claim that Brian caused the Psalter of Cashel to be compiled and distributed.[67] His annalistic section fully endorses Brian's takeover of the sovereignty, calling him 'well worthy of the place and government … the most famous king for his time that ever was before or after him of the Irish nation'.[68] The eulogy is a long one and compresses the entirety of Brian's reign and death into one entry, making a significant break, effectively a climax, in the overall text.

Bernadette Cunningham has outlined how the concept of Ireland as a kingdom underlay the basis of Keating's narrative. But while he 'characterised the nature of Irish kingship in considerable detail through the stories of the

65 See Marc Caball, 'The literature of later medieval Ireland, 1200–1600: from the Normans to the Tudors, part I: poetry' in Margaret Kelleher and Philip O'Leary (eds), *The Cambridge history of Irish literature* (Cambridge, 2006), pp 74–109. The term *mythomoteur* is defined in Anthony D. Smith, *The ethnic origins of nations* (Oxford, 1986) as 'fused and elaborated myths [which] provide an overall framework of meaning for the ethnic community' (p. 24). 66 Daniel Mc Carthy, *The Irish Annals: their genesis, evolution and history* (Dublin, 2008), pp 69, 301–2, draws attention to the fundamental change in perspective caused by the adoption of a regnal system of computation in which kingship becomes the framework on which chronology is hung; Bernadette Cunningham analyses *AFM*'s concern with kingship in *The Annals of the Four Masters: Irish history, kingship and society in the early seventeenth century* (Dublin, 2014), e.g. at pp 117–20. 67 *AClon*, pp 7–8. 68 *AClon*, p. 165.

individual exploits of successive kings of Ireland' he 'did not analyse the nature or sovereignty in any detail. Rather he focussed on the idea of a rightful king, under whom the country would prosper, and on the disaster that would befall if that rightful king was usurped'.[69] Keating laid great stress on Brian Bóraime's rightful claim to kingship by virtue of having shown himself the better man. He describes how 'the nobles of Leth Moga and of the greater part of Connaught' made the decision to depose Máel Sechnaill in favour of Brian (pages 246–9); he details the mechanisms by which the change of sovereignty was brought about (pp 248–57); and once more rehearses the arguments for Brian's genuine right to kingship in pp 264–5.[70] One might almost say he 'doth protest too much'. Just as Keating upholds Brian's right to rule, so does he blacken the image of his rival, Máel Sechnaill. Keating appears to have been the first to describe Máel Sechnaill as a man who 'gave himself up to luxury and comfort and ease' (p. 249). As a skilled orator, Keating must have perceived the advantage of denigrating his hero's rival in order to clinch his argument, but from where did he draw his description? We have seen that Máel Sechnaill had gained a reputation for being wealthy and open-handed. There are several references in the annals to his love of horsemanship.[71] The story told in the D-version of the *Cogadh* (dated provisionally by Máire Ní Mhaonaigh to the 1140s)[72] accuses Máel Sechnaill of having insidiously betrayed Brian at the battle of Clontarf. Finally, there is also the intriguing anecdote told by Gerald of Wales concerning Máel Sechnaill's earlier namesake, Máel Sechnaill mac Máele-Ruanaid, according to which he overcame Turgesius by deceit, disguising handsome young warriors as bridesmaids attending his daughter at her wedding to Turgesius. Taken together, these disparate rumours could be made to add up to a slightly effeminate individual who loved wealth and confined his daring to feats of horsemanship. Certainly this view of Máel Sechnaill was to pervade literature on the subject well into the twentieth century.

THE DEBATE CONTINUES IN PRINTED HISTORIES

Keating's model of Irish kingship seems to have fairly quashed opposition to Brian, at least within the ranks of the Irish-speaking world. Such works as the *Cath Cluana Tarbh* built very much on the substrate laid down by Keating and the *Cogadh*, and became widely disseminated.[73] Once printing came into fashion, this Dalcassian stance continued to inform the works of early Gaelic

69 Bernadette Cunningham, *The world of Geoffrey Keating: history, myth and religion in seventeenth-century Ireland* (Dublin, 2000), pp 142–3. 70 *FFÉ*, vol. iii. 71 See *AU* 1004.10; *AClon* 983 (=990). 72 'Bréifne bias in *Cogad Gáedel re Gallaib*', *Ériu*, 43 (1992), 135–58, at 148; see also 150–3 for a discussion of D's depiction of Máel Sechnaill. 73 See Meidhbhín Ní Úrdail's masterly exposition in *CCT*.

historians such as MacCurtin and O'Halloran.[74] Opposition to this model was confined solely to rather fleeting references in Ware, Hanmer and the like.[75] Not until Charles O'Conor's *Dissertations on the antient history of Ireland*, published in 1753, was the seesaw set in motion again and Máel Sechnaill restored to the sovereign heights, Brian cast down as the encroaching usurper. Charles O'Conor, described by Leerssen as 'one of the most important cultural mediators between native and ascendancy Ireland',[76] was in a unique position to appreciate the Uí Néillite versus Dalcassian arguments, for he himself was descended from the Uí Chonchobair kings of Connacht; he had been raised within the aristocratic Gaelic community and, significantly, one belonging to Leth Cuinn. A copy of the *Contention of the Bards* which he had been given as a boy still exists: it contains inscriptions by him both in English and in Irish.[77] In a letter to the Chevalier Thomas O'Grady he remarks:

> I shall send you the Conaght [*sic*] Annals ... But ... I doubt that you have a man in France or Ireland who can decipher the contractions; in my province of Conaght I know of none, I am sure there is not one, myself

74 Hugh MacCurtin, *A brief discourse in vindication of the antiquity of Ireland* (Dublin, 1717); Sylvester O'Halloran, *An general history of Ireland, from the earliest accounts to the close of the twelfth century, collected from the most authentic records, in which new and interesting lights are thrown on the remote histories of other nations as well as of both Britains* (Dublin, 1778); discussion of these works can be found in Lenore Fischer, 'Brian Boru and the Vikings: a historiographic study' (MA, MIC Limerick, 2008), pp 51–4, 59–62; see also, Joep Leerssen, *Mere Irish and Fíor-Ghael: studies in the idea of Irish nationality, its development and literary expression prior to the nineteenth century* (Notre Dame, 1997; first pub. Amsterdam, 1986), at pp 316–18, 357–8; also Clare O'Halloran, 'The triumph of virtuous liberty', *Eighteenth-Century Ireland*, 22 (2007), 151–63, esp. at 157–60, and eadem, 'Brian Boru and his afterlife', *History Ireland*, 22 (2014), 38–41. 75 Sir James Ware, *De Hibernia et antiquitatibus eius disquisitones* (London, 1654), later expanded and reissued by Walter Harris as *Antiquities and history of Ireland* (Dublin, 1705); Meredith Hanmer, *The chronicle of Ireland*, Society of Stationers (Dublin, 1663); see also Richard Stanihurst, 'A plain and perfect description of Ireland' in Raphael Holinshed (ed.), *The firste volume of the chronicles of England, Scotlande, and Irelande: conteyning the description and chronicles of England, from the first inhabiting vnto the Conquest: the description and chronicles of Scotland, from the first originall of the Scottes nation, till the yeare of our Lorde 1571: the description and chronicles of Yreland, likewise from the first originall of that nation, vntill the yeare 1547* (London, 1577). Some discussion of these will be found in Fischer, 'Brian Boru', with references there and Lenore Fischer, 'How Dublin remembered the Battle of Clontarf' in Seán Duffy (ed.), *Medieval Dublin XVIII* (Dublin, 2013), pp 70–80. 76 Joep Leerssen, '"Why sleeps O'Conor"? Charles O'Conor and the Irish nationalization of native historical consciousness' in Luke Gibbons and Kieran O'Conor (eds), *Charles O'Conor of Ballinagare, 1710–91: life and works* (Dublin, 2015), pp 244–5, at p. 248. 77 For details of his background, see Catherine A. Sheehan, 'The contribution of Charles O'Conor of Belanagare to Gaelic scholarship in eighteenth-century Ireland', *Journal of Celtic Studies*, 2 (1958), 219–237, at 220–2. A selection of O'Conor's letters has also been published by Robert E. Ward, John F. Wrynnn and Catherine Coogan Ward (eds), *Letters of Charles O'Conor of Belanagare* (Washington, 1988); see also, Gibbons and O'Conor (eds), *Charles O'Conor of Ballinagare*.

> excepted, who can read those annals or explain many of the terms, though he could read them.[78]

O'Conor thus had an insider's appreciation for Irish history which was wholly foreign to such contemporaries as Warner and Leland, and differed in its northern perspective from K'eogh [*sic*], the Abbé Ma Geoghegan [*sic*] and O'Halloran, all of whom subscribed to Keating's Dalcassian argument.[79] O'Conor's emotional assessment of Brian is entirely at odds with Keating's, and clearly derives directly from the arguments presented by Ó Cléirigh and other Leth Cuinn poets of the Contention.

Constitutionality provides the structural background for Charles O'Conor's argument: Wrynn describes him as influenced by Montesquieu, Locke and Hobbes.[80] O'Conor himself, moreover, came from a background dominated by legal wrangles to recover property lost through the Penal Laws.[81] His personal experience and philosophical background thus predisposed him to a concern for law. In his *Dissertations* he is at pains to establish that ancient Ireland was a civilized society ruled by constitution. Brian Bóraime, he declared,

> deposed Malachy II, set aside the Niallian Succession, which governed Ireland for 600 Years before, and thrust himself into the Throne, although incapacitated by law and although none of his Race sat there before him for a thousand and fifty Years … This violent Step produced a fatal Change in the Constitution. But that is not all: the Son (Donogh by Name) to obtain the usurped Authority of the Father, made a journey to Rome, laying there the Crown of Ireland at his Holiness's Feet, making, at the same Time, a vile Composition with the great Pontiff; to subject to him a People, who, hitherto, for two thousand Years, owned no sovereign jurisdiction … The several Provincial Sovereigns of Ireland easily entered the gap, made by Brian Borovey. Following his Example they set themselves up for Candidates to the Throne of Ireland … for more than a hundred Years, while every such petty Prince contended to be King, none was admitted to be one.[82]

78 Ward, Wrynn and Ward (eds), *Letters*, p. 429. **79** See Fischer, 'Brian Boru', pp 51–70; Ferdinando Warner, *The history of Ireland* (London, 1763); Thomas Leland, *The history of Ireland from the invasion of Henry II with a preliminary discourse on the antient state of that kingdom*, 2 vols (Dublin, 1773), vol. i; John K'eogh, *A vindication of the antiquities of Ireland* (Dublin, 1748); L'Abbé Ma'Geoghegan, *Histoire de l'Irlande ancienne et modern* (Paris, 1758). For O'Halloran's *A general history of Ireland,* see n. 74 above. General discussions of these will be found in Leerssen, *Mere Irish*; Clare O'Halloran, *Golden ages and barbarous nations: antiquarian debate and cultural politics in Ireland,* c.*1750–1800* (Cork, 2004); and Norman Vance, *Irish literature: a social history: tradition, identity and difference* (Dublin, 1990). **80** John Wrynn, 'Charles O'Conor as a "philosophical historian"' in Gibbons and O'Conor (eds), *Charles O'Conor of Ballinagare*, pp 72–80, at p. 74. **81** See Sheehan, 'The contribution', p. 220, and Ward, Wrynn and Ward (eds), *Letters*. **82** Charles O'Conor,

Charles O'Conor appears to be the first to claim that Brian Bóraime caused subsequent political anarchy. Keating had traced a stable kingship through a further hundred years of Brian's descendants, only gradually admitting to such a thing as 'kings with opposition'. Hostile writers such as Peter Walsh may have attributed the Anglo-Norman invasion directly to the inability of the Irish to govern themselves, but though Walsh treats in some detail of both Brian's reign and the subsequent political disharmony, he nowhere blames the one upon the other, having seen no evidence of stable government in the preceding eras either.[83]

O'Conor's formulations became hugely influential. His concern with constitutionality was taken up by Thomas Moore who, during the course of his 47-page description of Brian's exploits, uses the term 'usurper' in one form or another thirteen times, in one instance employing it four times on the pair of facing pages. He states that

> in his usurpation of the supreme power he was impelled evidently by motives of selfish ambition; nor could he have entailed any more ruinous evil upon the country, than by thus setting an example of contempt for established rights and thereby weakening, in the minds of the people, that habitual reverence for ancient laws and usages which was the only security afforded by the national character for the preservation of public order and peace. The fatal consequences of this step, both moral and political, will be found but too strikingly evolved in the course of the subsequent history.[84]

When the young government of independent Ireland decided to put together an *Official handbook* of Ireland's history, it was O'Conor's Uí Néillite line that they followed:

> Brian had broken the prestige of the two chief dynasties of Ireland, which had lasted for more than half a millennium, and had left nothing to replace them ... For the next century (1075–1175) there was a succession of kings of Ireland 'with opposition' ... each having an authority based on no tradition, but wholly on the amount of force, local, not national, that he was able to command: so that the monarchy itself, instead of being an element of stability and order, became the prize of mutability and violence.[85]

Dissertations on the antient history of Ireland, wherein an account is given of the origine, government, letters, sciences, religion, manners and customs of the antient inhabitants (Dublin, 1753), p. 83. 83 Peter Walsh, *A prospect of the state of Ireland, from the year of the world 1756 to the year of Christ 1652* (London, 1682), pp 160–3 (Brian's reign), pp 167–70 (later anarchy). 84 Thomas Moore, *The history of Ireland*, 4 vols (London, 1835–46), ii; pp 82–129, quotation from p. 120. 85 Saorstát Éireann, *Official handbook*, Talbot Press (Dublin,

This view of Brian's effect on Irish history was repeated in *Early Christian Ireland*, the hugely influential volume by Máire and Liam de Paor:

> The high-kingship had been usurped by the minor sept of the Dál Cais, most of whose leaders were killed at Clontarf. From then until the Anglo-Norman invasion, the most powerful families of the country were engaged in a futile struggle for the high-kingship … Almost every summer provincial kings were marching into the territory of their neighbours, seeking not only cattle but the kind of power that Brian Boru had commanded.[86]

It is O'Conor's formulation, therefore, that confirmed the consistent break that characterizes Irish history texts of the nineteenth and twentieth centuries. The battle of Clontarf is viewed as a significant turning-point in history not only because it supposedly exterminated Norse independence (following the *Cogadh* and Keating), but also because the intrusive nature of Brian's rule meant that his death was necessarily followed by anarchy.

Brian's rule as such, however, whatever about its aftereffects, was not so easily dismissed. A particularly influential piece on this was an article by a very young John O'Donovan, purporting to be a translation of the *Cath Cluana Tarbh*. In fact, it contains much material from the 'Dublin Annals of Inisfallen', Ademar of Chabannes and other sources, but it was widely cited in popular literature as a true account of the battle and of Brian's reign.[87] The hero-worship evident in O'Donovan's account continued to be a feature not only of the popular press, but even subliminally of later scholars such as John Ryan.[88] The de Paors, while accepting O'Conor's overall assessment of Brian's career and its effects, were sufficiently astute historians to point out that the nature of kingship itself was changing at the time. This theme has been taken up by many historians since and continues to be a fertile field for investigation.[89] But the Uí Néillite versus Dalcassian debate continues. Within the last decade, three major works on the subject of Brian Bóraime have been published. Seán Duffy's is overtly Dalcassian, drawing extensively upon the *Cogadh* for information and inspiration. Darren McGettigan's work is heavily permeated by the northern Uí Néillite perspective. Máire Ní Mhaonaigh's attempted objectivity in examining sources fails to bring her to any decisive conclusion.[90]

1932), p. 51. **86** Máire and Liam de Paor, *Early Christian Ireland* (London, 1958), p. 161. **87** John O'Donovan, 'The battle of Clontarf', *Dublin Penny Journal*, 1:17 (2 Oct. 1832), 133–6; for an assessment of his sources and influence, see Fischer, 'Brian Boru', pp 75–80. **88** See, in particular, John Ryan, 'Brian Boruma, king of Ireland' in Etienne Rynne (ed.), *North Munster studies: essays in commemoration of Monseignor Michael Moloney*, Thomond Archaeological Society (Limerick, 1967), pp 355–74. **89** See in particular, Byrne, *Irish kings*, which is in essence a 300-page exposition on the subject. **90** Duffy, *Brian Boru*; Darren McGettigan, *The Battle of Clontarf: Good Friday 1014* (Dublin, 2013); Ní Mhaonaigh, *Brian Boru*.

One can certainly appreciate the Uí Néillite efforts through the centuries to beat off the challenge to their sovereignty. Both sides put out literature which today continues to mould our understanding of pre-Anglo-Norman Ireland: the Uí Néillite synthetic historians entirely recast their foundation lore in order to prove their point, the Dalcassians composed Ireland's first great romantic biography. What with those posthumous works and with Brian's own achievements during his reign, his influence on Irish history has been profound. But the battle of Clontarf is entirely miscast in its role as a pivotal point in Irish history: it was not primarily a fight against a Viking threat, and it was not the precursor to anarchy on the political scene. The pivotal point in Irish history was in 1002, when Máel Sechnaill ceded the kingship of Ireland to Brian Bóraime. The nature of kingship had been changing for some time but Brian was the first to exercise a new form of sovereignty, and the arguments for and against his work continue today to shape our view of his times.

The battle of Clontarf in later Irish tradition

MEIDHBHÍN NÍ ÚRDAIL

In considering the battle of Clontarf in later Irish tradition, an obvious starting point is a tale known as *Cath Cluana Tarbh* ('*The battle of Clontarf*') (*CCT*) which, as the present writer has discussed elsewhere, was one of the most popular Irish prose texts to have come down to us in eighteenth- and nineteenth-century Irish manuscripts.[1] Its popularity may be ascribed in part to two reasons. First, at the heart of the tale's message is the fact that the battle of Clontarf amounted to Brian Bóraimhe's victory over centuries of foreign heathen oppression, a message which, as will emerge below, appealed to Irish scribes. Second, rather than being a laconic record of events, *CCT* presents the historical battle as a story in which 'heroes shine and villains play their sinister parts and dramatic incidents are invented or exaggerated for the benefit of the reading public'.[2] These two reasons are not exceptional to this prose tale, of course, as the same could be said (and indeed has been said) about the earliest literary account we have in Irish concerning the battle, that in the early twelfth-century Irish text *Cogadh Gáedhel re Gallaibh*. Many of the plot details in the Modern Irish story, in fact, ultimately derive from those forming part of the account of the battle in the latter Middle Irish text.

Two further factors have ensured the popularity of *CCT* among eighteenth- and nineteenth-century scribes. Given in the first instance that most of the tale's manuscript sources are of Munster provenance, we can hardly be surprised that a Clontarf story presenting Brian Bóraimhe and the O'Briens of Munster as heroes *par excellence* should find favour with scribes from that province in particular. Added to that is a second factor, namely the influence on the tale's transmission of *Foras feasa ar Éirinn* (*FFÉ*) which Geoffrey Keating, alias Séathrún Céitinn (*c.*1580–*c.*1644), compiled *c.*1634. Keating's prose and style of presenting events in Ireland's past in an intelligible idiom found great favour with Irish native men of letters. When we consider, for example, that about sixty copies of this work form part of the manuscript collection of the Royal Irish Academy alone, we may be confident that, within the parameters of scribal texts, *FFÉ* was very popular among eighteenth- and nineteenth-century scribes. It will become apparent presently, moreover, that it was Keating's particular interpretation of events at Clontarf that would

1 Meidhbhín Ní Úrdail, in *CCT*. 2 John Ryan, 'The battle of Clontarf', *JRSAI*, 68 (1938), 1–50, at 3.

resonate with Irish scribes when they turned their hands at compiling their own transcripts of *CCT*.

* * *

What, we may ask, of the scribal evidence itself regarding the transmission of this Modern Irish prose tale as we have it in eighteenth- and nineteenth-century Irish manuscripts? We do not know exactly when *CCT* was first composed and by whom, but it certainly was in existence as an independent text in the first half of the seventeenth century when it appeared as part of the contents of an anthology of prose tales relevant to Munster, all of which were interlinked by a series of annals beginning at AD174 and coming down to AD1138.[3] While the original compilation has not survived, six eighteenth-century copies of it tell us that its title was *Leabhar Gearr na Pailíse* ('The Short Book of Pallas') (*LGP*).[4] The present writer has suggested that An Phailís incorporated into this title refers to the townland of Pallas, Co. Kerry, Pallas Castle being the chief residence of Mac Carthaigh Mór, which was located near Beaufort Bridge, Killarney.[5] The following colophon incorporated into the two earliest transcripts of *LGP* by the Co. Meath scribe Seón Mac Solaidh, alias John Solly (*fl.* 1715), provides further information:

> Ag sin foras feasa clainne Mhīleadh Easpāinne, 7 ar ghabh lánrīghe Ēireann dīobh 7 rīghe dhā chōigeadh Mum[h]an fo leith. Sgriptum per me Eugenium Carti Baile an Oilēin aedibus Domini Tadei Dermisi Cormaci Carti anno domini 1648 undesimoque Januarii. Arna athsgrīob[h]adh le Seón Mac Solaidh a mBaile Hardaman a bporraisde Thighthe Callain a cCondae na Mid[h]e 7 a mbarūntacht Shlāinghe da charaid ionm[h]uin Risdard Tiubear, an t-ochtmhadh lā .x. dho m[h]ī Feab[h]ra an b[h]liadhain d'aois an Tig[h]earna 1715/16. Is gach duine dā lēighfidh nō dā ccluinnfid[h]e dā lēaghadh ē tugadh beannacht ar anmoinn na dēisi rēimhrāidhte madh beo marbh iad.[6]
>
> ('That is the basis of knowledge about the descendants of Míl Easpáinne, and those of them who assumed the full kingship of Ireland and the kingship of the two provinces of Munster in particular. Written by me Eugenius Carti Baile an Oiléin in the house of Lord Tadeus son of Diarmaid son of Cormac Carti anno domini 1648 and on the eleventh of January. Having been rewritten by Seón Mac Solaidh in Harmanstown

3 *CCT*, pp 37–8, 40–1. 4 Ibid., pp 42–7. 5 Ibid., p. 44. 6 BL Egerton MS 106, fo. 132v; a similar colophon in RIA MS 23 K 37 (p. 172) is dated 24 Feb. 1715/16. Unless otherwise stated, this and other accompanying translations below are by the present writer; the macrons in this passage and elsewhere represent a length mark which is not visible in the

> in the parish of Stackallan in Co. Meath and in the barony of Slane for his dear friend Richard Tipper, the eighteenth day of the month of February the year of our Lord 1715/16. And everyone who will read or will hear it being read let him give a blessing on the soul of the two aforenamed be they alive [or] dead.')

The prose anthology, then, was completed in 1648 by one Eugenius Carti who resided at Baile an Oiléin – probably the same as Oileán Ciarraí (Castleisland), Co. Kerry – thereby suggesting that he probably belonged to the Coshmang branch of Clann Charthaigh. Munster genealogies in the eighteenth-century *Leabhar Muimhneach*, in fact, specify three separate septs within this Coshmang branch, i.e., Molahiffe (Maigh Laithimh), Fieries (Na Foidhrí) and Cloonmealane (Cluain Maoláin), and the same source traces the Molahiffe branch in descending order from Eoghan son of Cormac, king of Desmond (d. 1359), down to the aforementioned 'Lord Tadeus son of Diarmaid son of Cormac'.[7] Moreover, one 'Teige M'Dermod M'Cormac', lord of Coshmang, is named in the patent rolls of Elizabeth I for the year 1589 and, according to the Annals of the Four Masters, this same Tadhg of Molahiffe died in 1581 in a skirmish at Aghadoe during the Desmond wars.[8]

It cannot be claimed with certainty, of course, that Eugenius Carti was the original compiler of *LGP*, but the above colophon, copied subsequently by Seón Mac Solaidh into his early eighteenth-century transcripts, leaves no doubt that, by the late 1640s, *CCT* existed as an independent tale when it formed part of this anthology's contents. Indeed, the compiler of *LGP* may have been guided in his work by his contemporary, Geoffrey Keating. We may note, for example, the reference in the same colophon above to a *foras feasa* of the descendants of Míl Easpáinne, which recalls the title of Keating's history, *FFÉ*. Equally, the distinction between the two provinces of Munster (*dhá chóigeadh Mumhan*) is also significant, as this may have been inspired by *FFÉ* where the place-names Cúigeadh Eochaidh Abhradhruaidh and Cúigeadh Chonraoi mic Dáire designate east and west Munster, respectively.[9] Furthermore, Keating stated that the battle at Clontarf was fought on the Friday before Easter (*an Aoine ria gCáisc*), 1034, a conclusion he reinforced with an accompanying quatrain on the death of Brian Bóraimhe, beginning *Cheithre bliadhna tríochad* ('Four years and thirty'). The date 1034 for the battle occurs not only in the earliest extant sources of *LGP*, but it was also

manuscript source. 7 *LM*, pp 209–10. 8 James Morrin, *Calendar of patent and close rolls of chancery in Ireland from the 18th to the 45th of Queen Elizabeth*, 2 vols (Dublin, 1861–2), ii, p. 170; *AFM* 1581 [v, 1756]. 9 *FFÉ*, i, pp 120 (l. 16)–122 (l. 39); cf. Meidhbhín Ní Úrdail, '*Foras feasa ar Éirinn*: establishing a literary canon' in Pádraig A. Breatnach et al. (eds), *Léann lámhscríbhinní Lobháin. The Louvain manuscript heritage* (Dublin, 2007), pp 139–67, at p. 145; Meidhbhín Ní Úrdail, 'The literary legacy of Keating's *Foras feasa ar Éirinn*' in Pádraig Ó Riain (ed.), *Foras feasa ar Éirinn. The history of Ireland by Geoffrey Keating*, ITS

reproduced in most sources of the text of *CCT* which once formed part of the anthology's contents.[10]

What contemporary relevance would *LGP* have for a member of the Coshmang branch of the McCarthys in the 1640s? The prose tales that seem to have comprised its contents celebrate a glorious era in Munster's past. The source originally concluded with the death of Cormac Mac Carthaigh in 1138, one of the ablest and most widely esteemed rulers in the province. By contrast, the end of the sixteenth century was marked by much division and political restiveness. We have noted above that in the particular case of the Coshmang branch, Tadhg, lord of Coshmang, died in 1581 while serving with the earl of Desmond against his overlord, Mac Carthaigh Mór, and the English forces. It appears, then, that *LGP* was essentially a prose compilation of Mac Carthaigh interest, but it gathered together prose tales focussing on the triumphs of a glorious past, from which the intended seventeenth-century reader may have inferred that such glory could be retrieved through unity of purpose rather than by division of loyalties. Fortuitously, the source itself, or a subsequent copy, reached Dublin in the early decades of the eighteenth century and transcripts of its contents (including *CCT*) were made by scholar-scribes based in the capital city.[11] That this should be so, of course, tallies with an overall feature of Irish literary scholarship at that time, whereby many primary sources were becoming available via a network of exchange practised by scribes who had begun to gravitate towards Dublin.[12]

* * *

Turning now to *CCT* itself, ninety transcripts, dating from the period between 1701/2 and 1890, have survived.[13] A further 'incomplete' text in a manuscript 'in handwriting, presumably, of John Browne, of Waterford' and described in the early years of the last century is now missing.[14] The tale's title recalls the historical battle that occurred at Clontarf near the city of Dublin on Good Friday, 1014, and two of its main protagonists, namely Brian Bóraimhe and his son Murchadh. We have to do here, however, with a literary re-enactment of the historical battle at Clontarf, whereby the main characters are cast as foils to heathen Viking invaders who are eventually overthrown and expelled from Ireland. *CCT*, then, belongs to the genre of Irish romantic tales (*scéalta*

Subsidiary Series, 19 (London, 2008), pp 52–67, at p. 57. **10** *CCT*, pp 12–13, 38–9. **11** Ibid., pp 2–3, 46–7. **12** Nessa Ní Shéaghdha, 'Irish scholars and scribes in eighteenth-century Dublin', *Eighteenth-Century Ireland. Iris an Dá Chultúr*, 4 (1989), 41–54. **13** For a description of eighty-nine surviving sources, see *CCT*, pp 226–54. In 2013, two years after the publication of the latter, a further manuscript came to light. It was acquired by the Royal Irish Academy, now RIA MS 12 K 50, and was written by 'E[a]dbhard Ó Troith' (p. 325), who gives no date or place of transcription. **14** Patrick Power, 'Irish MSS in Waterford', *Irisleabhar na Gaedhilge*, 14 (1904–5), 647–9, 692–5, 707–9, 728–9, at 729; cf. Pádraig de Brún,

rómánsaíochta) that presents virtually interchangeable heroes (in this case Brian Bóraimhe and his son Murchadh) and details their exploits, adventures and encounters with the marvellous and the Otherworld.[15]

Notwithstanding the extraordinary number of manuscript sources for the tale, certain literary embellishments and innovations are evident in this substantial amount of material which makes a division into the following manageable textual groups possible:

		Version 2A
		Version 2B
Version 1	← CORE NARRATIVE →	Version 2C
		Version 2D

The core narrative relates to that part of the narrative common to *all* transcripts of *CCT*. It has also been preserved as a text in its own right in twenty-four manuscripts, written between 1715/16 and 1853, and this too is the text that once formed part of the contents of the aforementioned *LGP*.[16] Material added to the opening passage of the core narrative yielded a variant text, named Version 1 above, which has been transmitted in thirteen manuscripts written between 1701/2 and 1859. Version 2 refers to a separate text, of which there are four variants, 2A, 2B, 2C and 2D, preserved in fifty-three manuscripts written between 1702/3 and 1890. Unlike Version 1, Version 2 differs considerably from the core narrative in that its compilers derived passages, sometimes almost verbatim, from *FFÉ*. We find these passages from Keating's history spliced onto the core narrative of our text, and the result of such scribal cutting and pasting is a separate version, the Version 2 narrative.

The main incidents making up the content of the core narrative may be divided into the following sections:

> §1–3 An army, led by Brian Bóraimhe and his son Murchadh, gathers at Clontarf to do battle against Maol Mórdha son of Murchadh, king of Leinster, and his Viking allies.
> §4 Unwilling to spill blood on Good Friday, Brian Bóraimhe remains apart from the battle at prayer in his tent.
> §5 Maol Seachlainn Mór, king of Meath and ally of Brian Bóraimhe, abandons the battlefield.

Lámhscríbhinní Gaeilge: treoirliosta (Dublin, 1988), p. 87, no. 405. **15** On Irish romantic tales in general, see Gerard Murphy, *The Ossianic lore and romantic tales of Medieval Ireland* (Dublin, 1961), pp 37–55; Alan Bruford, *Gaelic folk-tales and mediaeval romances. A study of the Early Modern Irish 'romantic tales' and their oral derivatives* (Dublin, 1969); Joseph Falaky Nagy, 'In defence of rómánsaíocht', *Ériu*, 38 (1987), 9–26. **16** Twenty-three manuscripts are discussed by Ní Úrdail, in *CCT*, pp 2, 36, 37, 38, 226–35, at a time when the existence of RIA MS 12 K 50 was not known (see above, n. 13). The core narrative of *CCT* in the latter manuscript is on pp 110–28.

§6 Murchadh encounters a friend (Dubhlaing Ó hArtagáin) on the battlefield and follows him to the Otherworld where a supernatural woman (Aoibheall of Craglea) foretells their deaths and that of Brian Bóraimhe.
§7 Murchadh and Dubhlaing return to the fray, but Murchadh must quench his insatiable thirst by drinking regularly from the well of Clontarf.
§8 Those guarding the well on Murchadh's behalf are killed by a Viking band and once their blood mingles with the water of the well Murchadh is unable to drink it.
§9 Murchadh dies at the hands of a Viking warrior.
§10–11 Brian Bóraimhe is killed by a fleeing Viking but his death marks the end of Viking oppression in Ireland.
§12–13 Toirdhealbhach son of Murchadh dies at the weir of Clontarf and the opposing armies suffer heavy losses.
§14 The bodies of Brian and Murchadh are transported for burial to Ireland's primatial church in Armagh.
§15 Maol Seachlainn Mór describes to his kinsmen the horrors of the battle which he witnessed.
§16 As instructed by his father, Donnchadh son of Brian pays twelve score cows to the primate of Armagh on Easter Sunday.
§17–18 While Donnchadh returns homewards to Thomond with his wounded army, tensions are already beginning to erupt within Munster.

The characterization of Brian Bóraimhe as summarized at section four as a pious bystander is one which finds its primary parallel in the account of the battle of Clontarf in the Middle Irish *CGG* text, where we learn that he 'opened his psalter and he began to clasp his hands and to pray after the battle had commenced (*ro oslaic a shaltair, ocus ro gab i clasecul allam, ocus ic airnagi dar eis na cath*)'.[17] According to the Modern Irish *CCT* narrative, however, Brian Bóraimhe's absence from the battle-scene is not so much motivated by his advanced years, but by his unwillingness to shed blood during the Lenten season. The text tells us that he retires from the fray to his tent, complete with 'his psalter before him and his crucifix in his hand while chanting his psalms (*a psaltair ina fhiadhnaise agus a chrosfhighil ina láimh agus é ag gabháil a psalm*)'.[18] According to sources for Version 2A, moreover, he prays with 'his rosary beads in his hand (*a phaidrín ina láimh*)'. It will be clear from the above that Brian Bóraimhe does not appear again until further down in the narrative at sections ten and eleven. We find him at this point refusing a request by his servant that he flee from the battle on horseback at the height of the ferocious battle. His bravery, according to the text, costs him his life when he falls prey to a

17 *CGG*, pp 196–7, §113; the accompanying translation here and elsewhere from *CGG* is that of its editor, J.H. Todd. 18 *CCT*, pp 110–11.

retreating Viking who cleaves Brian Bóraimhe's head with an axe, but not before Brian himself manages to overcome his enemy.[19]

Sections five to nine present the main protagonist of the core narrative of *CCT* – undoubtedly Murchadh son Brian Bóraimhe – not only because of his heroic contribution on the field of battle, but because a series of motifs is attached to him, which highlights the supernatural and valorous aspects of his character. We find him, for instance, encountering a supernatural friend, Dubhlaing Ó hArtagáin, who has abandoned the magical Otherworld to bolster the cause of Brian Bóraimhe's troops on the battlefield. This mysterious intervention derives ultimately from an interpolated passage in the Middle Irish account in *CGG*, which tells of one Dúnlaing Ua hArtagáin who appears to Murchadh and describes the delights of his paradisiac homeland. Unlike the passage in *CGG*, in which Murchadh recognizes his supernatural visitor on the battlefield, Dubhlaing in the narrative of *CCT* is not immediately visible to the Dál gCais hero. This is because he is wearing what is called 'the magic veil', or *féig(h) fia(dh) / fé fia*,[20] a protective magic veil or cloak given to him as a gift by the supernatural Aoibheall to ensure his safe passage from the Otherworld by keeping him invisible from the mortal world. On discarding his protective cloak, Dubhlaing becomes visible to Murchadh who, in turn, follows his friend into the Otherworld where the heroes learn of their terrible fate from Aoibheall in an ensuing metrical dialogue between the trio.[21]

Prophecy is without question an important part of the narrative of *CGG* and involves this otherworldly woman foretelling the death of Brian Bóraimhe when she appears to him on the eve of the battle. Her role in *CGG* is less pronounced, however, whereas Aoibheall plays a significant part in *CCT*. As Dubhlaing's very powerful lover (*leannān lánchumhachtach*), we are told that Aoibheall initially managed to entice Dubhlaing away from the mortal world to her magic dwelling.[22] She recalls the well-informed supernatural helper of Irish romantic tales when, in this instance, she tries to avert the catastrophe awaiting Murchadh and Dubhlaing in Clontarf by convincing them to remain with her in the Otherworld and not return to the fray. She fails in this, but Murchadh's encounter with Aoibheall forms part of an overall development concerning him in later tradition where we find him in other romantic tales entering the Otherworld through a dark magical mist, for example, and confronting supernatural beings there, or where in another instance he is sought out at the court of his father by a mysterious ambassador from the Otherworld in the form of a druid (*draoi*). Journeying to the Otherworld by means of a lake, Murchadh's encounters with the supernatural are predominantly adversarial.[23] Essentially, then, this particular son of Brian Bóraimhe who was killed in the historical battle of 1014 has, by the later medieval period, become

19 Ibid., pp 118–23. **20** *DIL* s.v. *féth*; see also, *CCT*, pp 53–4, 136. **21** *CCT*, pp 52–4, 112–19. **22** Ibid., p. 54. **23** Ibid., pp 54–5.

Murchadh the universal ahistorical hero who confronts the marvels of the Otherworld.

Sections seven to nine of the core narrative of *CCT* present us with another important motif: that of the hero's insatiable thirst, which he must slake at regular intervals by drinking water. The hero in this instance is once again Murchadh son of Brian Bóraimhe, whose downfall is unavoidable once his Viking enemies realize the importance of the well and that of the warriors guarding it. A summary execution of the appointed guards results in their blood mingling with the water of the well, rendering it undrinkable when Murchadh next arrives to quench his thirst. This motif of the well in the core narrative of *CCT* finds parallels elsewhere in Irish and Scottish Gaelic traditions, and is an important plot detail that adds to the central role accorded Brian Bóraimhe's heroic son in our tale.[24]

Sections twelve to thirteen focus on yet another character, Toirdhealbhach son of Murchadh, who, according the narrative, is 'the most accomplished 15-year-old man in his own time (*fear cúig mbliadhan ndēag dob fhearr lāmh ina aimsir féin*)'. This young man also emerges as a key character who relentlessly pursues his Viking foes as far as the Irish Sea. His valour costs him his life for 'he was found on the morrow with a Viking beneath him and a Viking in each hand and a stake from the weir of Clontarf through him having been drowned by the torrent of the full tide (*frīoth ē arna mhārach agus Lochlannach faoi agus Lochlannach is gach lāimh dho agus cuaille do choraidh Cluana Tarbh thrīd arna bhāthadh don bhuinne rabharta*)'.[25]

There is one final character who is also of importance in the core narrative of *CCT*, namely Maol Seachlainn Mór or Maol Seachlainn son of Domhnall of Meath. We know from the annals that, on coming to power in 978 as ruler of the midland territory of Midhe, he was Brian Bóraimhe's primary opponent in the northern half of Ireland, but that he lent his support to the Munster king at Clontarf. His characterization as presented in section five of *CCT* is very much that of friend turned foe, albeit one who acts as a foil to the heroic Brian Bóraimhe in abandoning the battlefield. And, when Maol Seachlainn reappears in section fifteen as part of the post-battle section of the narrative, we find him delivering in direct speech an eyewitness report of events on the battlefield at the request of his kinsmen.[26] Now, while the early twelfth-century *CGG* narrative was the inspiration for this dramatic monologue, in that work the speech underlines the savage nature of the conflict itself rather than drawing attention to Maol Seachlainn's inactivity. Maol Seachlainn in *CCT* morphs into a betrayer who withdrews his support for Brian Bóraimhe at Clontarf with the result that his speech amounts to the specious delivery of a cunning traitor.

* * *

24 Ibid., pp 55–7, 116–19. **25** Ibid., pp 49, 122–5. **26** Ibid., pp 112–13, 126–9.

The foregoing overview of the main incidents of the core narrative of *CCT*, together with the tale's important plot details concerning its main protagonists, alerts us to a central aspect of Irish-language tradition: the one-time historical event at Clontarf has been remoulded into a fictionalized fight complete with rhetorical flourishes. Any discussion of the battle of Clontarf in later Irish tradition, however, must acknowledge the profound effect of Geoffrey Keating's *FFÉ*. The fact that we find passages taken almost verbatim from this history of Ireland points to the work's canonical influence on subsequent narrative tradition. Specifically, it was Keating's particular understanding of pre- and post-battle events which caught the fertile imagination of the successive compilers of *CCT*, and resulted in the Version 2 narrative mentioned above. Even in matters of style, the opening section of the Version 2 narrative of *CCT* contrasts with the annalistic-style of the opening both in the core narrative and in Version 1 of the tale. Version 2, then, begins not just by drawing particular attention to the exalted status of Brian Bóraimhe in his campaign to consolidate his political power in Munster and beyond, but, more importantly, it includes a colourful plot detail explaining how the battle of Clontarf came about in the first place. Taking this plot detail from Keating's *FFÉ*, scribes grafted it onto the core narrative of the romantic prose tale and produced thereby a different version of events, namely the Version 2 narrative of *CCT*.

The plot detail itself sets the scene in Brian Bóraimhe's residence at Kincora (Ceann Cora), and it is Gormfhlaith, wife of Brian Bóraimhe, who emerges as an ambitious woman who castigates her brother, Maol Mórdha son of Murchadh and king of Leinster, for bowing down in vassalage to the O'Briens of Munster. Gormfhlaith persists in rebuking her brother for not being like his father and grandfather, and warns that Brian's son would demand vassalage of Maol Mórdha's offspring. We find a somewhat sober depiction of this already in the Middle Irish *CGG* text, and while Keating reproduces this characterization of Gormfhlaith as an ambitious woman who promotes her Leinster connections he embellishes it as follows:

> Agus ar rochtain dóibh go Ceann Choradh, cuiris rí Laighean a ionar dhe is tug da shiair, do Ghormfhlaith, inghin Mhurchadha, .i. bainchéile Bhriain, an t-ionar do chur chnaipe ann. Do ghlac an ríoghan an t-ionar is tug urchor de san teinidh do bhí 'n-a fiadhnaise, is do ghabh ag iomcháineadh ar a dearbhráthair tré bheith fá mhoghsaine ná fá dhaoirse do neach san domhan, 'an ní', ar sí, 'nar fhaomh th'athair ná do sheanathair'; is do ráidh go sirfeadh mac Briain ar a mhac an ní céadna. Acht cheana fá cuimhin lé Maolmórdha comhrádh na ríoghna [...] .
>
> ('And when they reached Ceann Choradh the king of Leinster took off his tunic and gave it to his sister Gormfhlaith, daughter of Murchadh (that is Brian's wife), to fix a clasp in it. The queen took the tunic and

> cast it into the fire that was in front of her, and proceeded to reproach her brother for being in slavery or subjection to anyone on earth, "a thing," said she, "which neither thy father nor thy grandfather brooked"; and she added, that Brian's son would make the same demand of his son. Now Maolmórdha kept in mind the queen's remarks [...].').[27]

The cumulative effect of Gormfhlaith's remarks, together with a subsequent quarrel between Maol Mórdha and Murchadh son of Brian Bóraimhe during a game of chess, moves Maol Mórdha to seek allies in war against Thomond. Accordingly, the role of Keating's Gormfhlaith is that of instigator of open warfare at Clontarf. Version 2 of *CCT* reproduces Keating's interpretation of what caused the outbreak of the battle, namely the words spoken by an ambitious woman and inciter of violence, who sought the downfall of her own husband, but this text goes further in embellishing Keating's own embellished presentation. One example will suffice here, that contained in a footnote to a translation of *CCT* which was intended for publication by the Celtic Society in the late 1840s:

> The flimsy pretext used by the Queen of Ireland to pick a quarrel with her brother was only assumed; and her anger was only the outpouring of the mind of an ambitious woman, who seeing that her own children by Brian had no chance of the crown of Ireland while his sons by a former marriage stood in the way, resolved to stir up a revolution in the hope that her son, the King of Dublin, or her brother might chance to succeed instead of her step-children, in case her own other children would be set aside.[28]

The other aspect of Keating's influence on the battle of Clontarf story in eighteenth- and nineteenth-century Irish manuscripts was his contrastive representation of Brian Bóraimhe and Maol Seachlainn of Meath. In the account of kingship, for example, Brian Bóraimhe, so Keating in *FFÉ*, succeeded to power 'by the strength and bravery of his feats of valour and championship, driving the foreigners and the Danair out of the country, and not by treachery (*lé calmacht is lé cródhacht a ghníomh goile is gaiscidh, ag ionnarbadh eachtrann is danar as an gcrích, agus ní go cealgach*)'. The tenure of Maol Seachlainn Mór, however, was one given 'to luxury and comfort and ease, a line of action that was useless for the defence of Ireland at that juncture (*do shádhaile is do sheascaireacht is do shuaimhneas, inneall fá héadtarbhach ré cosnamh Éireann an tráth soin*)'.[29] As such, then, Keating cleverly succeeds in

27 *FFÉ*, iii, p. 268 (ll. 4208–16) with accompanying translation on p. 269. 28 RIA MS 23 E 4, p. 48. The project to have the text published was subsequently abandoned by the Celtic Society; cf. *CCT*, pp 5–6. 29 *FFÉ*, iii, p. 256 (ll. 4020–2) with accompanying translation on p. 257, and p. 248 (ll. 3888–90) with accompanying translation on p. 249, respectively; cf. Bernadette Cunningham, *The world of Geoffrey Keating. History, myth and religion in*

contrasting Brian Bóraimhe, the resolute protector of territory and honourable sovereign who revered the church as well as its vocation to learning, with his predecessor, Maol Seachlainn, who forfeited his claim to the kingship of Ireland. Now, while it is true that the theme of Maol Seachlainn as friend turned foe is central to the core narrative of *CCT*, as mentioned above, both Keating – and the scribes of the Version 2 narrative after him – go even further in presenting Maol Seachlainn as the consummate traitor, a depiction that encouraged certain Munster scribes to add their own condemnation to that already found in Keating's history. Let us look first at Keating's *resumé* of Maol Seachlainn's character as presented in this damning clarification to the reader:

> Féach, a léaghthóir, bíodh gurab ar sluagh Briain do bhí Maoilseachlainn is fir Mhidhe ag teacht go láthair an chatha, maseadh do bhí do cheilg idir sé féin is Lochlonnaigh nach táinig san ordughadh i measc shluagh Briain, acht is eadh do rinne é féin is a shluagh d'anmhain do leathtaoibh an chatha, amhail ro orduigheadar Lochlonnaigh dó.
>
> ('Observe, O reader, that though it was as part of the host of Brian that Maoilseachlainn and the men of Meath came to the field of battle, still through a plot between himself and the Lochlonnaigh, he did not come into the battle array amongst Brian's host, but what he did was to remain with his host beside the battle, as the Lochlonnaigh had directed him.')[30]

Not only do we find this negative characterization of the Meath king in the Version 2 narrative, but we also find that Keating's withering sentiments aroused further expressions of provincial loyalty among certain Munster scribes. Sources for Version 2A, for example, describe how Maol Seachlainn's perfidy in standing idly by was brought to Brian's attention before the battle of Clontarf commenced:

> Ro fhág Maol Seachlainn Rígh Midhe an cath faoi Mhurchadh agus faoi Dhál gCais óir do bhí do cheilg idir é agus Lochlannaigh gan teacht san gcath, agus ro chuir gort treabhtha idir a mhuintir agus an cath, agus an tan do hinseadh san do Bhrian do thuig gur le ceilg do sheachain an cath agus a-dubhairt gurab a n-éagmais do-rin sé féin gach áthas riamh dá ndearna riamh.
>
> ('Maol Seachlainn King of Meath left the battle to Murchadh and Dál gCais since there was a plot between him and the Vikings not to enter the battle, and he placed [a distance of] a ploughed field between his people and the battle, and when Brian was told that he understood that it was because of a conspiracy that he [Maol Seachlainn] avoided the battle and

seventeenth-century Ireland (Dublin, 2000), pp 145, 176. **30** *FFÉ*, iii, p. 284 (ll. 4474–9) with accompanying translation on pp 285, 287.

he said that every victory that he [Maol Seachlainn] himself ever achieved was futile.')[31]

Versions 2C and 2D likewise highlight the perfidious aspect of Maol Seachlainn's character:

> Cuireas Maoilseachlainn fios ós íseal go Rígh Laighean an oidhche roimh an ccaith dá rádh leis teacht do chur an chatha do bhrígh gur chuir Brian Donnchadh mac Briain agus trian an tsluaigh Mhuimhnigh mo chreacha Aoíbh cCinnsiolla, agus do gheall féin go ttréigfeadh Brian san ccaith.
>
> ('Maol Seachlainn sent word secretly to the King of Leinster on the eve of the battle telling him to come to fight the battle because Brian sent Donnchadh son of Brian and a third of the Munster host to plunder Uí Chinnsealaigh, and he himself promised that he would abandon Brian in the battle.')[32]

In some sources for Version 2B, moreover, the reader is addressed with the rhetorical question: *(ó) nach truadh a léightheoir an cheilg sin do bhí ag Leath Cuinn chum Muimhneach*? ('(o) reader is that plot which Leath Cuinn had against Munstermen not a pity?').[33] A particularly striking example is the reaction by the scribe Diarmuid Ó Maolchaoine (*fl.* 1764–87) from near Sixmilebridge, Co. Clare, who finished his text of *CCT* in 1787 with a direct address to his reader:

> Bíodh a fhios a léightheóir [...] gurb[h]o tré fheall agus chum fealla air Bhrían Bhóirbhe mac Cinnéide chum teacht asteach ionna Árdrígh Ēirionn do-rinne Maoilseachluinn Mór, agus fir Mhídhe, an tarang úd as cath Chluana Tairbh tarsna guirt béatála agus claídhe, agus as íad do thug túarusgabháil úatha 7 dob é a mían lingneamh uim thráthnóna air a mbíodh beó do chaithibh Bhríain, Mhurchaidh, Thoirdhealb[h]aigh, Dhubhlainn, agus Dáil gCais, agus a mbīodh beó díobh do mharb[h]adh air an láithir sin, ag sin Cath Chluana Tairbh.[34]
>
> ('Know O reader [...] that it was because of treachery and with a view to treachery against Brian Bóraimhe son of Cinnéide becoming High King of Ireland that Maol Seachlainn Mór, and the men of Meath, drew back from the battle of Clontarf across a lea-burned field and ditch, and it is they who gave a report and it was their desire to jump in the evening on all the survivors of the battalions of Brian, Murchadh, Toirdhealbhach, Dubhlaing, and Dál gCais, and kill all those alive there, that is the Battle of Clontarf.')

31 *CCT*, p. 72. 32 Ibid. 33 Ibid., p. 73. 34 RIA MS 24 C 14, pp 27–8; see fig. 13.3.

Another compelling example is that completed *c.*1813 by the Waterford scribe Uilliam Breathnach (*fl.* 1812–18) who concluded that Maol Seachlainn's treachery amounted to a conspiracy against the men of Munster:

> Ionus gurab ē sinn Catha Cluana Tarbh 7 feall Rígh Laighion 7 Mhídhe do shaoil Gaoidhil do thabhairt fa d[h]aorsmacht 7 moghsaine Lochlainig. Acht faraoir trēim[h]se g[h]airid 'na dhíagh sinn do-rin Mac Mhurchadh Laighionn 7 Laighionnac[h]aibh sinn do thabhairt fa d[h]aorsmacht Gall, acht tiocfa[i]dh an lā a ionna mbeidh Ruagadh na Loc[h]lannach aig Muimhneachaib[h] ortha is náirbho fada uat[h]a ē.[35]
>
> ('So that that is the Battle of Clontarf and the treachery of the Kings of Leinster and Meath who thought to bring the Gaels under submission and bondage to the Vikings. Unfortunately however a short while after that Mac Murchadh of Leinster and the men of Leinster brought us under the slavery of Foreigners, but the day will come when they will suffer [a fate similar to] the Banishing of the Vikings by the Munstermen and let it not be far from them.')

This and much more evidence besides in eighteenth- and nineteenth-century Irish manuscripts tells us that the scribes (especially those in Munster) were undoubtedly influenced by Keating's negative depiction of the Meath king in *FFÉ*. Crucially, however, their presentation of Maol Seachlainn as one attempting to excuse his lack of involvement in the battle of Clontarf shows a certain literary sensibility to characterization on their part, and this sensibility, in turn, further enriches the overall plot of *CCT* itself. It is also important to note that the evidence of such engagement with the material that they set about transcribing suggests that the scribal text carried with it an intimacy for them that allowed them to project their individuality onto it. When we consider, then, the overall transmission of *CCT* with its extraordinary number of transcripts, we are reminded that the scribes worked as copyists on the one hand, of course, but as inventive authors on the other, whose creative sense was provoked by their activity in dealing with their texts. Indeed, the present writer has argued that the variety of transmission of *CCT* calls into question the fixity or permanence of the scribal text in eighteenth- and nineteenth-century Ireland. In other words, instead of dealing with an authoritative, fixed or uniform text, we have to do here with a variety of texts, each with a potential for uniqueness.[36]

* * *

35 Dunnington MS 1, p. 356. This manuscript is one of two which belonged to Michael Dunnington, Lexington, Kentucky, described by Edgar M. Slotkin, 'Two Irish literary manuscripts in the Mid-West', *Éigse*, 25 (1991), 56–80. 36 For further discussion, see *CCT*, pp 90–101.

It was noted at the outset of this paper that an obvious starting-point for any treatment of the battle of Clontarf in later Irish tradition is *CCT*. This prose tale is but one example, albeit an important one, as four other literary re-enactments of Clontarf, the historical event, have also been transmitted in eighteenth- and nineteenth-century Irish manuscripts. They too form part of the story that evolved around the actual events of 1014. Three discrete sets of annals, mainly concerned with Munster affairs, present their own particular encomium of the O'Briens of Thomond, and they accord the battle of Clontarf and events surrounding it a central place in their respective narratives. The first in this post-classical triad of annals is known as the Dublin Annals of Inisfallen, while the remaining two are described in the manuscript sources as extracts *d'Annálaibh Innis Faithlionn* ('from the Annals of Inisfallen').[37] The fourth example is that referred to in the manuscripts as *Leabhar Oiris agus annála ar chogaibh na hÉireann* ('Book of History and annals concerning the battles of Ireland'). The intent here again is to praise the O'Briens of Thomond and the heroic age with which this dynasty is associated.[38]

We may briefly touch on just one of the foregoing texts, the Dublin Annals of Inisfallen, which came to be thus known because of a Latin ascription given to it by the Revd Charles O'Conor (d. 1828) to distinguish it from the Bodleian Annals of Inisfallen in excerpts he printed of both in 1825.[39] The main thrust of these annals, now part one of TCD MS 1281 (fos 14r–78v), is the recording of historical events mainly relevant to Munster from AD 250 down to AD 1320. The work was commissioned by Dr John O'Brien, Roman Catholic bishop of Cloyne and Ross (1748–69), who was particularly interested in the role played by his eponymous ancestors in Irish history. In light of this, it should come as little surprise that the most substantial entries in this set of annals focus on matters relating to the O'Briens of Thomond. Seventeen transcripts in all of this compilation have survived.[40]

The description of events for the year 1014 is the work's first considerable entry. Brian Bóraimhe, at this point, is depicted as Ireland's gallant sovereign who, together with his heroic son Murchadh, leads the native Irish to victory.

37 Cormac Ó Cuilleanáin, 'The Dublin Annals of Inisfallen .i. na hannála i MS H.1.7, TCD' in Séamus Pender (ed.), *Féilscríbhinn Torna. Tráchtaisí léanta in onóir don Ollamh Tadhg Ua Donnchadha, D.Litt., in am a dheichiú bliana agus trí fichid, an ceathrú lá de mhí Mheán Fhómhair, 1944* (Cork, 1947), pp 183–202; Meidhbhín Ní Úrdail, '*Annála Inse Faithleann* an ochtú céad déag agus cath Chluain Tarbh', *Eighteenth-Century Ireland. Iris an Dá Chultúr*, 20 (2005), 104–19; Meidhbhín Ní Úrdail, 'Some observations on the *Dublin Annals of Innisfallen*', *Ériu*, 57 (2007), 133–53; *CCT*, pp 82–90. 38 *CCT*, pp 77–81; Meidhbhín Ní Úrdail, 'Observations on the text known as the *Leabhar Oiris*' in Ailbhe Ó Corráin and Gordon Ó Riain (eds), *Celebrating sixty years of Celtic Studies at Uppsala University: proceedings of the eleventh symposium of Societas Celtologica Nordica. Acta universitatis Upsaliensis.* Studia Celtica Upsaliensia, 9 (2013), 149–66. 39 *Annales Inisfalenses, ex duobus codicibus, Dubliniense et Bodleiano*, Rerum Hibernicarum Scriptores Veteres, 4 vols (London, 1814–26), ii, pp 1–83, 1–122. 40 *CCT*, pp 267–71.

As paragons of Christian virtue, father and son are portrayed as foils to the heathen Viking invaders, but the striking feature of the entry for the year 1014 is the shift from a laconic and somewhat lacklustre style of presentation characterizing the narrative before this point, to one that is animated in tone. As with *CCT*, we find a battle of Clontarf story opening with a catalogue of the opposing forces converging to do battle at Clontarf. The narrative swiftly moves on to a duplicitous Maol Seachlainn of Meath, a motif which, as mentioned already, ultimately derives from Keating's colourful interpretation of the Meath king's role at Clontarf:

> 1014 Kl Sluag[hadh] mór le Brian Borúmha mac Cinnéide Rígh Éireann et le Maolseachluinn Rígh Mídhe go hÁith Cliath ag tabhairt catha do Ghallaibh et do Laighnibh um a ttaoiseacha Lochlannach[a] et um Maol Mórdha mac Murchadh Rīgh Laighean gona rīog[h]ra et go [t]trí catha uime, gur chuir Maolseachloinn teachta chuige ós ísiol dā inisin gur chuir Brian Don[n]chadh mac Briain go nglasláith Dháil cCais et go [t]trían shlúagh sleachta Eōghain Mhōir air cheann chreach Laigheann et Ó cCinnsealach, et geallas féin go bhfúigfeadh Brian et deich ccéad do Mhídheachaibh leis. Ó 'd-choncadar Gaill et Laighnig Brian air uathadh sochuídhe air faithche Áith Cliath a n-oireachtas, tángadar féin seacht ccatha 'na choinne, et do roinneadar a ttrí iad féin .i. sluag[h] Lochlannach lán d'arm is d'éide ó mhullach go lár um Caralas mac Eibhricc et um Anrudh mac Eibhric, dā mhac rīgh Fionnlochlanach, et um Dolat et Conmhaol, dá thréinmhíleadha, et Gaill Áith Clíath mar aon reo. An dara slúagh .i. Maol Mórdha mac Murchadh Rīgh Laighean gona Laighnibh, et an treas sluagh le Gallaibh na nOileán um Luadar Iarla Inse hOrc, et um Bruadar taoiseach Danair, et Gaill Innse Céad, et Manainne, et Sgiticc, et Leodhasa, et Cinn Tīre, et Oirear Gaedhil [*sic*], et Coirbhreathnaicc et Breathnaicc Cille Minne [*sic*] et Coir na Liogóg gona rīoghaibh uile, et fós Gaill ó Thíre an tSneachta et ó na Gaothloíghibh Meódhanach[a].
>
> ('1014 Kl. A great hosting by Brian Bóraimhe son of Cinnéide King of Ireland and Maol Seachlainn King of Meath to Dublin fighting the Foreigners and the Leinstermen, led by their Viking rulers and Maol Mórdha son of Murchadh King of Leinster together with his chiefs and three battalions along with him, and Maol Seachlainn sent a message to him [Maol Mórdha] secretly telling that Brian had sent Donnchadh son of Brian with the young champions of Dál gCais and a third of the hosts of the descendants of Eóghan Mór to plunder Leinster and Uí Chinnsealaigh, and he himself promised that he along with ten hundred Meathmen would leave Brian. When the Foreigners and Leinstermen saw Brian with a diminished host in a gathering on the outskirts of

Dublin, they themselves advanced as seven battalions against him and divided themselves into three, i.e. a Viking host equipped with arms and armour from head to toe led by Carolus son of Eibhric and Anrudh son of Eibhric, two sons of the king of the Norwegians, and led by Dolat and Conmhaol, two strong warriors, and the Foreigners of Dublin with them. The second host, i.e. Maol Mórdha son of Murchadh King of Leinster with his Leinstermen, and the third host with the Foreigners of the Isles led by Luadar Jarl of the Orkney Islands, and Bruadar ruler of the Danes, including the Foreigners of Inis Céad, and Man, and Shetland, and Lewis, and Kintyre, and Argyll, and the Corr-Britons and Britons of Ceall Mhuine and Coir na Liogóg with all their kings, and also Foreigners from Tír an tSneachta and the Maeotian marshes.')[41]

The record continues with a passage reiterating Maol Seachlainn's duplicity, while Brian Bóraimhe, by contrast, is exalted as a warrior-king:

> Ar riaradh a shluaighte amhla san do Bhrian, do luidh féin mar aon le Murcha mac Briain 'na measg ón cceann go roile dá ndúsgadh chum crōdhachta a n-aighidh na n-allmhúrach, et ró fhoillsicc dóibh gan luighid meanma do ghabháil tré Dhonnchadh mac Bríain go [t]trian sluagh Muímhnicc d'imtheacht uatha ōir is ag creachadh Laighean et Gall do bhí; iar san nochtas dóibh gur fada bhādar fir Ēirionn fá anbhruid na Lochlannach n-allmhúrdha ag marbhadh iomad ríghthe et príomhthaoiseacha et ag sīorargain 's ag losgad[h] dúnta et cealla et eaglaise Dé go mionnaibh Naomh; et ró ráidh sé do ghuth árd: 'A cháirde, ró thug an Coimdhe cómhachta et calmachta díbhse aniúgh chum an annfhlathas Lochlannach fór fhearaibh Éirionn do shríanadh go bhruinne [*sic*] an bhrátha, et chuim na n-iomad feall et ceallairgthe sin do dhīog[h]ailt fhorra an lá so 'nar fhuilling Críost féin bás ar bhúr soin.' Et taisbeánas dóibh an tan san an chros-fhighil ina láimh chlídhe et a chloídheamh go ndornchlainn óir ina láimh dheis, dá fhoillsiúghadh dóibh go bhfúigheadh féin bás mar aon leó dá cosnamh.
>
> Iar san gabhas Brian et Murchadh go sluagh Dáil cCais ag ionnsaighe lucht na [n]deich ccēad lúithreach um dhís m[h]ac rīgh Fionnlochlanach, ach d'ēalaigh Maolseachloinn gona Mhidheachaibh, mar do gheall an oidhche roimhe sin, et do chuir gort eatartha et an chath; acht nír luíghdig sin meanmain Bhriain ná an Dáil cCais, ōir do chosnamhadar an cath go ró dhásachtach.[42]

('After Brian arranged his hosts thus, he himself went together with Murchadh son of Brian amongst them from one to another encouraging

41 TCD MS 1281, part one, fo. 22v. 42 Ibid., fo. 23r–23v.

> them to valiant deeds against the foreigners, and he indicated to them that they should not lose heart at the departure from them of Donnchadh son of Brian and a third of Munster hosts for they were plundering the men of Leinster and the Foreigners; after that he [Brian Bóraimhe] revealed to them that the men of Ireland were for a long time under the oppression of the foreign Vikings killing many kings and chief leaders and constantly plundering and burning fortresses and monasteries and churches of God containing saints' relics; and he said in a loud voice: 'Friends, the Lord granted you powers and strengths today to curb the Viking oppression of the men of Ireland till Doomsday, and to exact vengeance for those many treacheries and church-plunders this day on which Christ himself died on your behalf.' And he showed them then the crucifix in his left hand and his gold-hilted sword in his right hand, revealing to them that he himself would die together with them protecting it.
>
> After that Brian and Murchadh and the Dál gCais host set about attacking the ten hundred armoured men led by the two sons of the king of the Norwegians, but Maol Seachlainn absconded with his Meathmen, as he promised the night before, and established a distance of a field between them and the battle; but this did not diminish Brian's courage nor that of Dál gCais, for they contested the fight very fiercely.')

Clearly, Brian Bóraimhe, as depicted here, is not only a source of strength for his men, but he is also protector of the crucifix (*crosfhighil*). Rather than adopting the more passive role of an elderly king who opts to remain in prayer apart from the combat, he is a king pitted against foreign oppression and plundering at Clontarf, one who above all else is an active defender of the cross. Valiantly brandishing a crucifix in one hand and wielding a sword in the other, this is a portrayal of the Munster king that would undoubtedly have appealed to his descendant, he who commissioned the work, the aforementioned Dr John O'Brien. Indeed, it would also have engaged the same reader whose episcopate was one of vigilance and steadfastness in the defence of the liberties of the Catholic church in eighteenth-century Ireland.[43]

These annals' dramatic description of Brian Bóraimhe circulating among his troops does not, it seems, occur in other Irish-language sources. However, it does appear in English-language tradition, for example, in that nationalist ballad by William Kenealy (1828–76) 'Stand ye now for Erin's glory!', which is essentially a poetic paraphrase of the above passage.[44] Sylvester O'Halloran (1728–1807) also reproduces his version of this vivid description in his *A general history of Ireland*:

43 For Dr O'Brien's episcopal difficulties, see James Coombes, *A bishop of penal times. The life and times of John O'Brien, bishop of Cloyne and Ross, 1701–1769* (Cork, 1981), pp 40–69.
44 Edward Hayes, *The ballads of Ireland*, 2 vols (London, 1855), i, pp 81–3.

> Brian rode through the ranks with a crucifix in one hand, and his drawn sword in the other. He exhorted them as he passed along, 'to do their duty as soldiers and Christians, in the cause of their religion and their country. He reminded them of all the distresses their ancestors were reduced to, by the perfidious and sanguinary Danes, strangers to religion and humanity! That these their successors waited impatiently to renew the same scenes of devastation and cruelty, and, by way of anticipation, (says he), they have fixed on the very day on which Christ was crucified, to destroy the country of his greatest votaries; but that God, whose cause you are to fight this day, will be present with you, and deliver his enemies into your hands.' So saying, he proceeded towards the centre to lead on his troops to action; but the chiefs of the army with one voice requested he would retire from the field of battle, on account of his great age, and leave the gallant Morrogh the chief command.[45]

Given the similarity between this account and that in the Dublin Annals of Inisfallen, it is difficult to imagine that O'Halloran did not consult the Irish-language source for his own history. Besides, Brian Bóraimhe thus presented would have resonated with O'Halloran, a Limerick native with an abiding interest in Irish history.

The respective accounts by Kenealy and O'Halloran remind us, of course, that any discussion of the battle of Clontarf in later Irish tradition must also incorporate the important parallel world of English-language accounts. Even though it is true that the importance which Keating's *FFÉ* attached to the Uí Bhriain in Ireland's history finds parallels in subsequent Irish-language tradition, as outlined above, the evidence holds equally true for the work's influence on English-language tradition concerning the battle of Clontarf. In fact, most of these accounts, that by Sylvester O'Halloran included, follow Keating in representing an ineffectual and duplicitous Maol Seachlainn on the one hand, and an honourable Brian Bóraimhe on the other, one acclaimed as a pious ruler and tenacious protector of territory.[46] Moreover, English-language writers concentrated on the issue of the high-kingship, although some softened their characterization of Maol Seachlainn as the disgraceful and disgraced sovereign. Charles O'Conor of Belanagare (Béal Átha na gCarr), Co. Roscommon, for instance, is unusual among eighteenth-century writers for his somewhat ambivalent presentation of Brian Bóraimhe in his *Dissertations on the history of Ireland*. O'Conor devotes little attention to the conflict itself at

45 Sylvester O'Halloran, *A general history of Ireland*, 2 vols (London, 1778), ii, pp 262–3, with italics here and in the subsequent passages in English reproduced from the original; cf. Clare O'Halloran, 'The triumph of "virtuous liberty": representation of the Vikings and Brian Boru in eighteenth-century histories', *Eighteenth-Century Ireland. Iris an Dá Chultúr*, 22 (2007), 151–63, at 161. 46 *CCT*, pp 25–36.

Clontarf, except to emphasize its internecine character, rather he takes particular exception to the negative portrayal of Maol Seachlainn:

> Some writers, who drew most of their materials from modern *Romances*, accuse him of a malicious Desertion at the Battle of *Clontarfe*: But this account being irreconcilable with the whole Tenour of his Life and Conduct, and not in the least supported by *Tigernach*, or any other Writer who lived near the Period in Question, must be deservedly rejected.[47]

The specific passage in the Annals of Tigernach intended by O'Conor here is that part of Maol Seachlainn's obituary where he is hailed as 'the tower of supporting generosity and nobleness of the whole of the world (*tuir chongbala einigh 7 uaisle iarthair domain uile*)'.[48] Interestingly, although O'Conor was guided by Keating in comparing the qualities of both rulers, Maol Seachlainn emerges as the principled one who deserves recognition for honouring the title of high-king by gracefully relinquishing it; and, Brian Bóraimhe remains for him a provincial king and usurper of the title:

> He gave the Title of *Brian* the best Colour it could bear, that of conferring his own upon him. He hereby preserved an able and virtuous Prince from the Odium of open Usurpation; and he supported him afterwards, as he engaged to do, by his whole Interest, which was still very considerable. The World was amazed at such a Conduct, and may be so still; because Mankind, unworthy of so exalted a Character, seldom frame a proper Judgement of it.[49]

O'Conor's argument continues by undermining the notion of a disgraceful, and disgraced, reign of Maol Seachlainn as advanced by Keating, and attributes instead the success of Brian Bóraimhe's rule to the benevolent support of his predecessor:

> MALACHY II, well deserved the Crown he resigned, and *Brian* departed from his Magnanimity in accepting it. By leaving it where it was, he might have the Merit of establishing a more orderly Form of Government in the royal *Hy-Niall* Family, and of laying the Foundations

47 Charles O'Conor, *Dissertations on the history of Ireland* (Dublin, 1766), pp 264–5. The work was first published under the title *Dissertations on the antient history of Ireland* (Dublin, 1753), and a new and heavily reworked second edition appeared in 1766; cf. Clare O'Halloran, *Golden ages and barbarous nations: antiquarian debate and cultural politics in Ireland* c.*1750–1800* (Cork, 2004), pp 24–7, 87, 147; and Flanagan, in this volume, above. 48 *AT* 1022, accompanied by Whitley Stokes's translation. 49 O'Conor, *Dissertations on the history of Ireland*, p. 259.

> of a new Monarchy, which might have preserved the Nation from its approaching Destruction. *Brian* had not the Glory of doing this, and, perhaps, he had not the Power.
>
> On this great Man's Elevation to the Throne, he was rather to be pitied than envied. Without the Co-operation of the Prince who resigned to him, he would probably be obliged himself to resign in Favour of some other powerful Oligarch, or reign with his Faction in the Places subservient to his Government. With *Malachy*'s Assistance, he actually governed over most of the Provinces.[50]

O'Conor's is a conflicting view to that of O'Halloran: the latter highlighted the military and heroic aspects of medieval Ireland, and, as such, countered O'Conor's view of a society severely weakened by factionalism among its provincial kings and lesser chiefs.[51]

* * *

To summarize, then, it is clear from the evidence in Irish-language sources that the battle of Clontarf became a literary creation – or, indeed, a re-creation – in later Irish tradition. Imaginative compilers formulated their own enhanced interpretation of the historical battle of 1014. The result of one such imaginative approach, and the main focus of this paper, was the Modern Irish prose tale *CCT*. As pointed out in the concluding discussion, however, this text is but one of a cluster that forms part of a greater story about the battle of Clontarf, both in Irish- and in English-language sources. Taking this material in its entirety, it developed and promoted what the present writer has termed elsewhere an 'O'Brien Saga', whereby the O'Briens of Thomond emerge as key figures in Ireland's glorious past.[52]

50 Ibid., pp 261, 262. **51** Their conflicting view of Irish history in general led to their disagreement over the value of James Macpherson's *Ossian*, as discussed by O'Halloran, *Golden ages*, pp 108–11. **52** Ní Úrdail, '*Foras feasa ar Éirinn*: establishing a literary canon', p. 148; Ní Úrdail, 'The literary legacy of Keating's *Foras feasa ar Éirinn*', p. 52; *CCT*, p. 77.

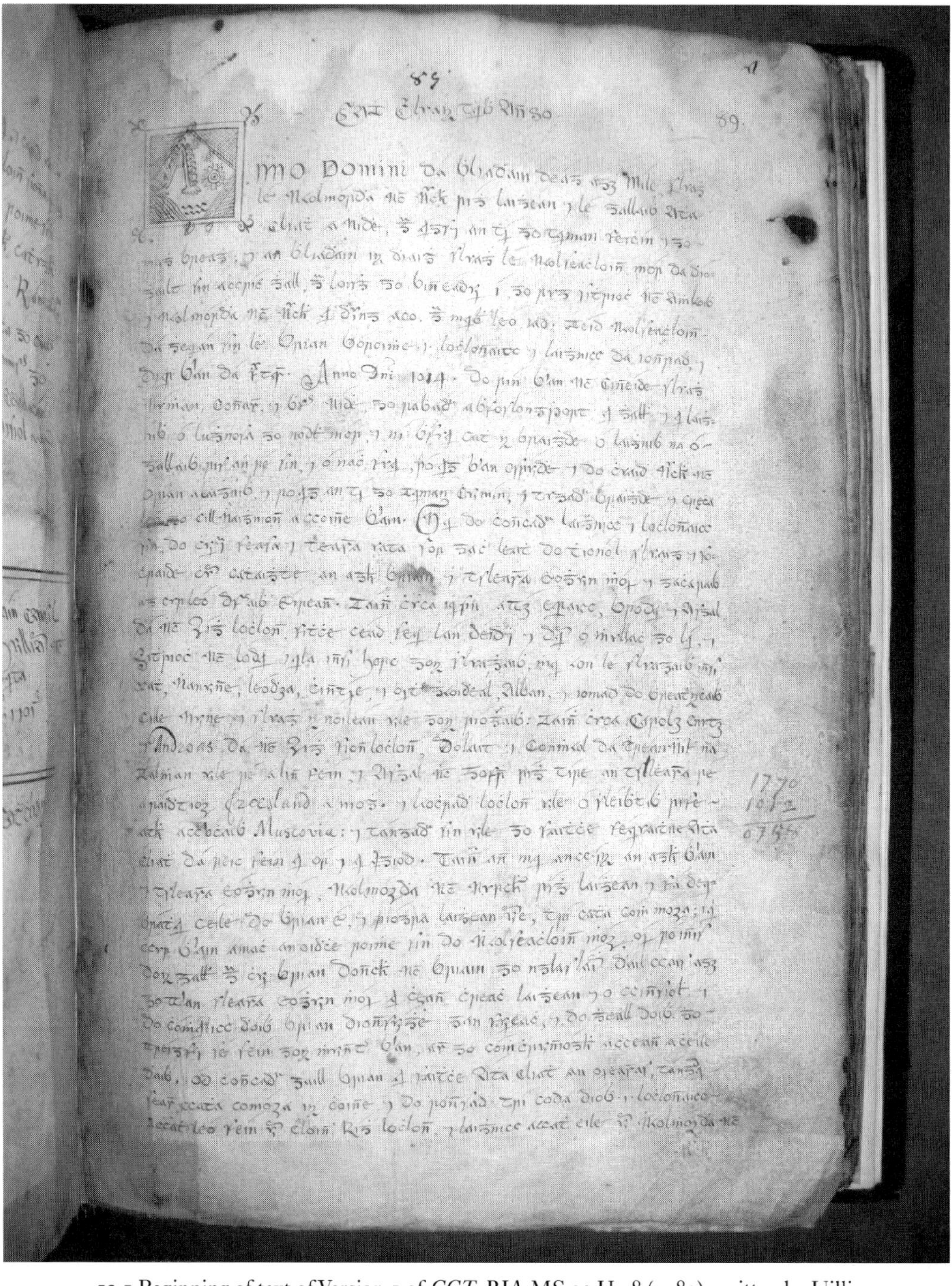

13.1 Beginning of text of Version 1 of *CCT*, RIA MS 23 H 18 (p. 89), written by Uilliam Mac Cairteáin, Co. Cork, 1701–2 (By permission of the Royal Irish Academy. © RIA)

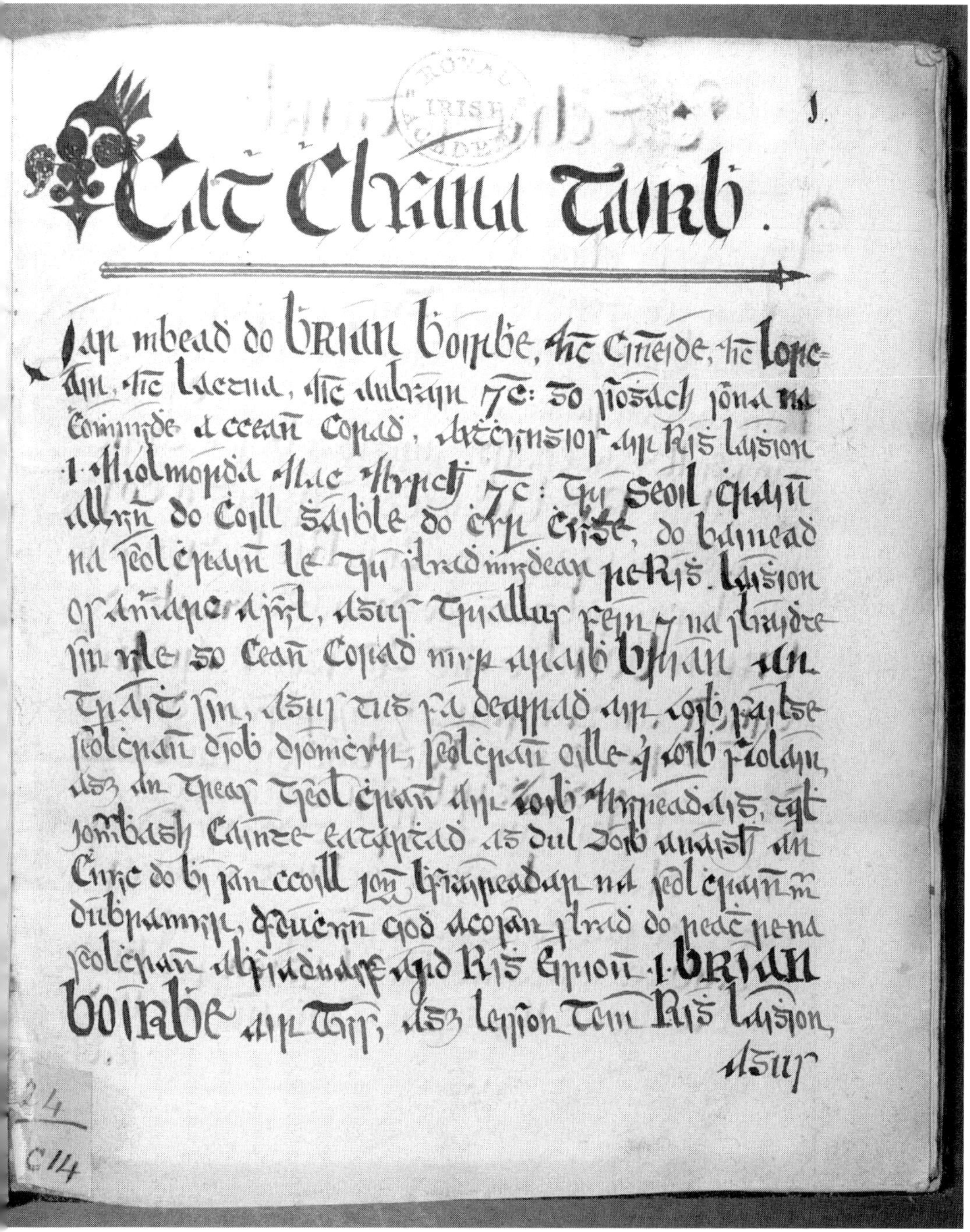

13.2 Beginning of text of Version 2B of *CCT*, RIA MS 24 C 14 (p. 1), written by Diarmuid Ó Maolchaoine, Co. Clare, 1787 (By permission of the Royal Irish Academy. © RIA)

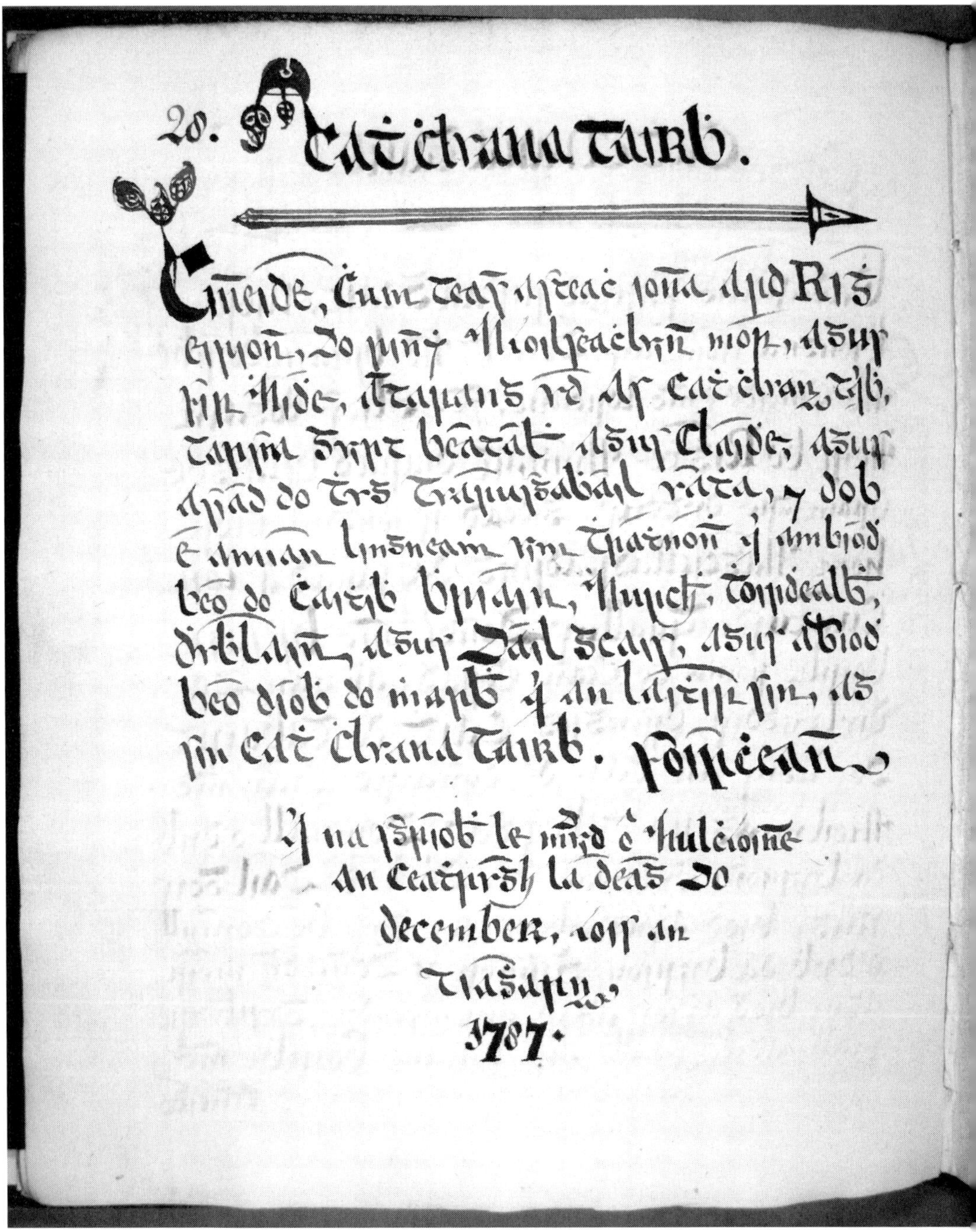

13.3 Part of an address to his reader by Diarmuid Ó Maolchaoine, concluding his text of Version 2B of *CCT*, RIA MS 24 C 14 (p. 28), 1787 (By permission of the Royal Irish Academy. © RIA)

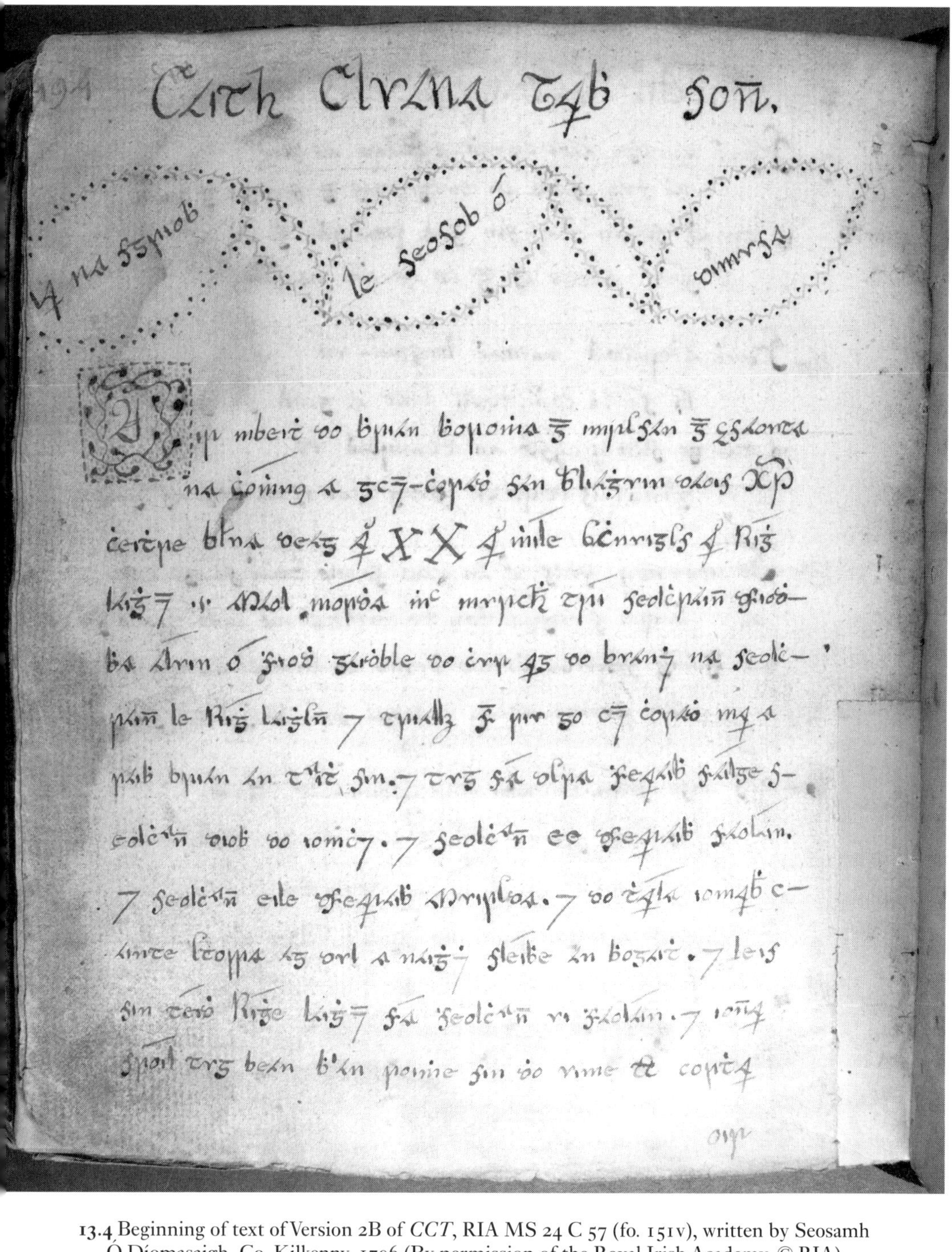

13.4 Beginning of text of Version 2B of *CCT*, RIA MS 24 C 57 (fo. 151v), written by Seosamh Ó Díomasaigh, Co. Kilkenny, 1796 (By permission of the Royal Irish Academy. © RIA)

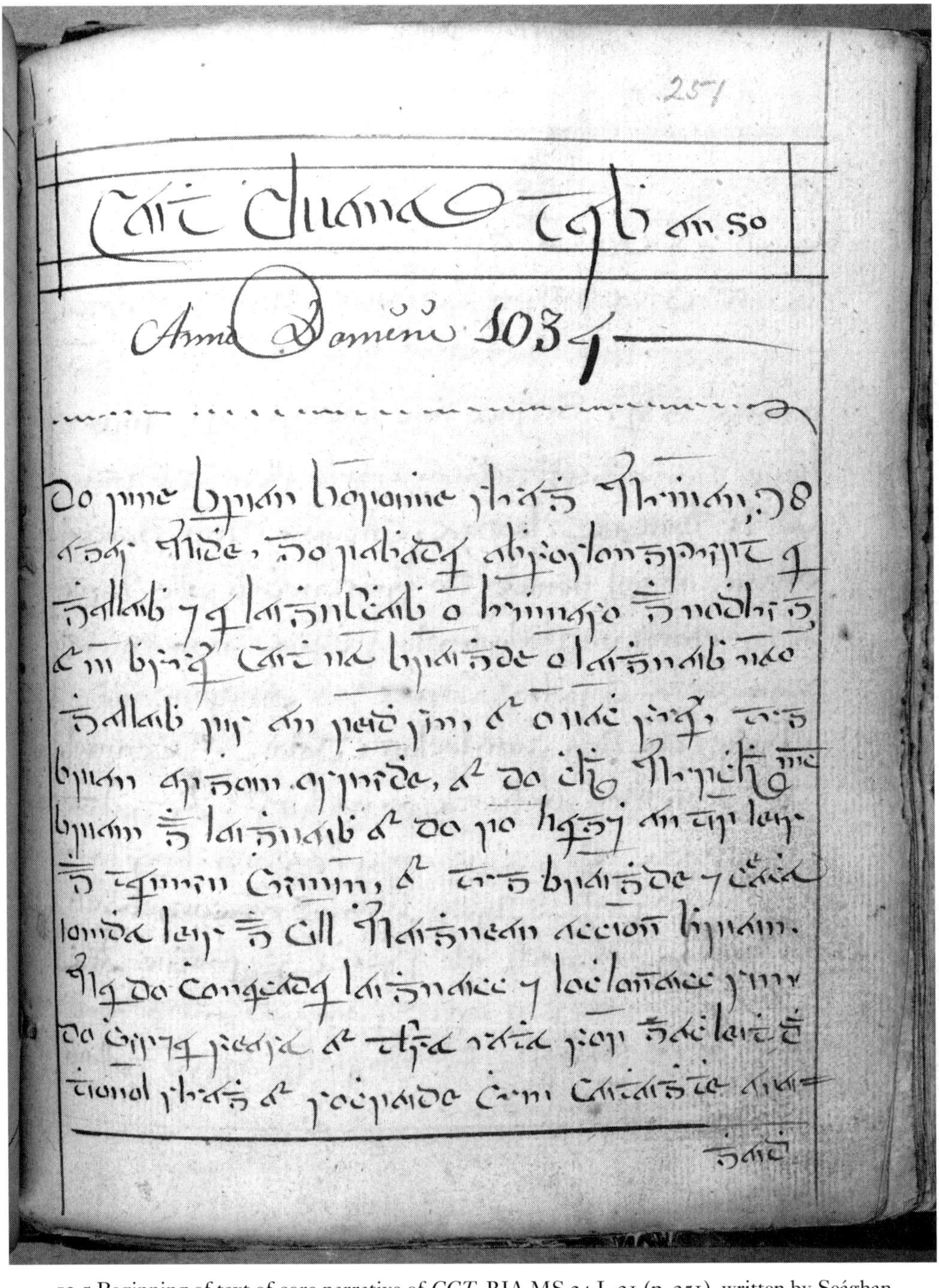

13.5 Beginning of text of core narrative of *CCT*, RIA MS 24 L 21 (p. 251), written by Seághan Ua Dóghbhuir, Co. Limerick, 1811-12 (By permission of the Royal Irish Academy. © RIA)

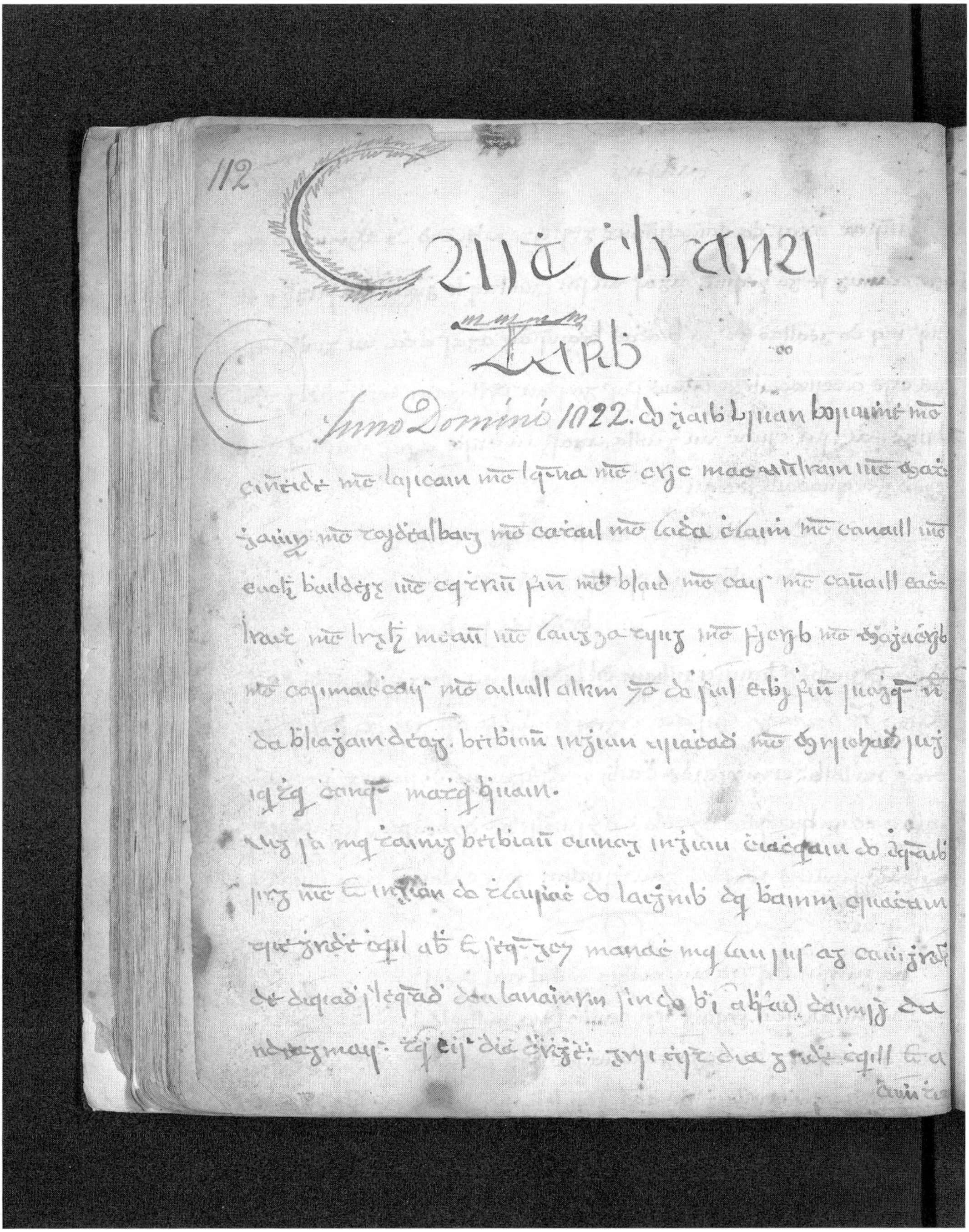

13.6 Beginning of text of Version 2A of *CCT*, UCD-Ferriter MS 25 (p. 112), written by Uilliam Ó hAodha, Co. Cork, 1816 (By permission of University College Dublin. © UCD)

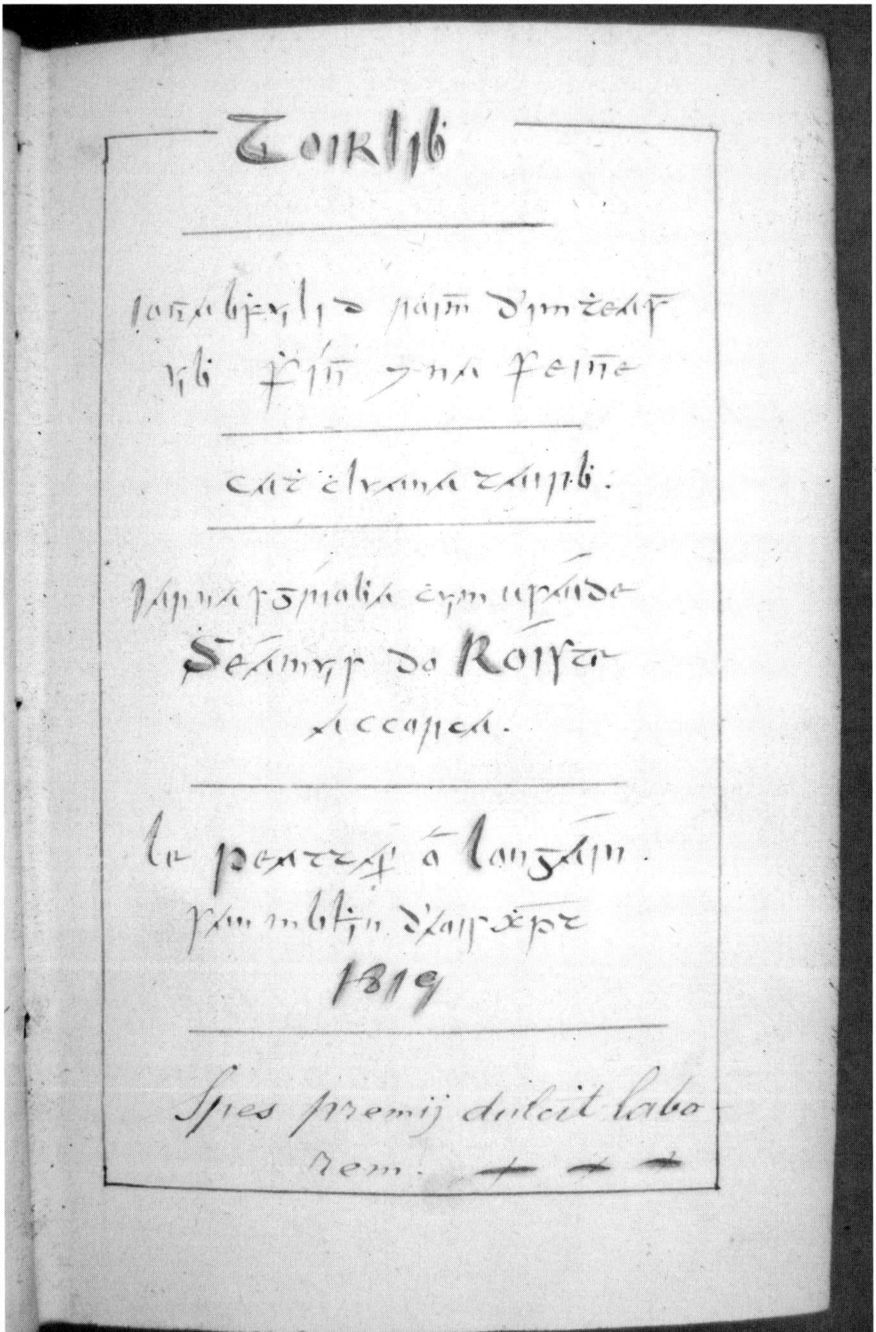

13.7 Title-page of RIA MS E vi 3, written by Peadar Ó Longáin, Co. Cork, 1819, containing Version 2D of *CCT* (By permission of the Royal Irish Academy. © RIA)

Writing history in the digital age: the battle of Clontarf goes online

ROMAN BLEIER, SPARKY BOOKER, EOIN O'FLYNN, CHERIE N. PETERS, CHRISTINA WADE, CAOIMHE WHELAN

INTRODUCTION

This article reflects on the process of creating a website – available at https://dh.tcd.ie/clontarf/ – about the battle of Clontarf from the perspective of the Humanities researcher. It will also consider issues that the development team encountered during the project. We hope that a discussion about the problems we encountered and the solutions we arrived at may be of use to future researchers embarking on similar projects.[1]

The battle of Clontarf is arguably one of the most significant events of Irish history and, consequently, its millennial anniversary in 2014 was extensively commemorated by numerous books, articles, conferences and re-enactments. These ways of marking the event were augmented by various digital projects launched during the year, such as the aptly titled *Battle of Clontarf* videogame where a gamer could control Brian and his forces fighting the Vikings at the battle of Clontarf.[2] While the historical accuracy of some of these products leaves a lot to be desired – such as the anachronistic Viking horned helmets of the videogame – they are nevertheless interesting artefacts of remembrance, and reflect the important and increasing role of the digital medium as a repository of historical memory. In recent years, an increasing number of academic institutions have developed digital platforms to make their research available to the wider public. Indeed, some aspects of medieval Irish history, such as the migration of early missionaries to and from Ireland,[3] the writings of St Patrick,[4] and various manuscript databases,[5] are well-served by online

1 We would like to thank the following people for their assistance during the creation of the website: Yan Bourke, Stephen Harrison and Simon Tompkins. 2 'Eyesodic: Game Studios' (http://www.eyesodicgames.com/the-battle-of-clontarf.html) (21 Jan. 2015). During the writing of this article, the above link was removed striking fear into the hearts of all of us regarding the transience of the internet. 3 'Converting the Isles: An International Network for the Study of Conversion to Christianity in the Insular World' (http://www.asnc.cam.ac.uk/conversion/) (16 Jan. 2015); Méadhbh Nic an Airchinnigh (ed.), 'The Foundations of Irish Culture: Irish Manuscripts on the Continent AD600–AD850' (http://foundationsirishculture.ie/) (16 Jan. 2015). 4 Franz Fischer and Anthony Harvey (eds), 'The Saint Patrick's Confessio Hypertext Stack' (2011) (http://www.confessio.ie/about/hyperstack) (16 Jan. 2015). 5 'Irish script on screen', Dublin Institute for Advanced Studies (http://www.isos.dias.ie/english/index.html) (24 Apr. 2015).

resources. Nevertheless, in 2013 it was astonishingly difficult to learn about Brian Boru and the battle of Clontarf through digital resources. It was not that primary and secondary sources were unavailable online, rather, the issue was the huge amount of available data scattered across the internet: editions of primary sources (mostly translated), could be accessed via UCC's Corpus of Electronic Texts (CELT), an online resource containing hundreds of medieval and early modern sources for Irish history,[6] the Internet Archive, and similar online repositories.[7] Furthermore, good academic papers were available, but found side-by-side with outdated information and unreliable articles. A maze of information with no guide to help locate and identify reliable sources left the non-expert in need of help to determine just how far the often complicated primary sources could be trusted.

As this volume demonstrates, establishing the 'facts' of the battle is often contentious, creating a variety of arguments and conflicting narratives. Online resources offered a variety of media through which a general audience could access this complex dataset, including blogs and Wikipedia pages. In 2013, Wikipedia was the main provider of information about the battle and key figures around the event. The information available, however, was sometimes inaccurate. On 19 April 2014, a Battle of Clontarf Wikipedia 'Edit-a-thon' (in which some of the authors of this article were involved) was held in the Science Gallery of Trinity College Dublin.[8] The goal of this event was to improve Wikipedia articles about the battle and related key figures like Brian Bóraime (Boru), Gormlaith, Sitric Silkenbeard, and Máel Sechnaill. Over the course of 2014, the quality of many Wikipedia articles connected with the battle improved. The crowdsourcing nature of Wikipedia ensures that it remains a problematic and unstable secondary source.[9] Furthermore, Wikipedia and other online resources often simplify complex historical information for the sake of an overarching narrative, and provide limited contextual information about primary sources. The sources for the battle of Clontarf include annalistic, literary and ecclesiastical texts that must be problematized before they are used. While some existing websites provide thought-provoking insights into modern perceptions of and mythology surrounding the battle, many fail clearly to distinguish perception from fact. In short, before 2014, it was difficult for interested members of the public to find

6 'Corpus of Electronic Texts' (http://www.ucc.ie/celt/) (13 Jan. 2015). 7 *CGG* is available through Google Books as well as Internet Archive: J.H. Todd, Cogadh Gaedhel re Gallaibh https://books.google.ie/books?id=TgMGAAAAQAAJ&pg=PR16#v=onepage&q&f=false) (23 Mar. 2015); J.H. Todd, Cogadh Gaedhel re Gallaibh (https://archive.org/details/cogadhgaedhelregootodd) (23 Mar. 2015). 8 'Wikipedia: WikiProject Ireland/Battle of Clontarf Edit-a-thon April 2014' (http://en.wikipedia.org/wiki/Wikipedia:WikiProject_Ireland/Battle_of_Clontarf_Editathon_April_2014) (21 Jan. 2015); 'Wikipedia Edit-A-Thon' (http://1014retold.com/wikipedia-editathon/) (23 Jan. 2015). 9 Wikipedia: Academic use (http://en.wikipedia.org/wiki/Wikipedia:Academic_use) (15 Mar. 2015).

reliable online resources that allowed for in-depth engagement with the battle and the fascinating sources and characters connected to it. The millennial anniversary changed this and, in addition to the Edit-a-thon (above), prompted several academic web projects about the battle of Clontarf, including the online exhibition of the Trinity College Dublin Library (to complement the Trinity College Dublin Battle of Clontarf exhibition in the Long Room Library), and, of course, our project, the Battle of Clontarf website.[10]

Preparations for the Battle of Clontarf project began in 2013 when Seán Duffy (Professor in medieval history at Trinity College Dublin) and Dermot Frost (of the Trinity Centre of High Performance Computing or TCHPC, now the Research IT unit) determined to develop an online resource about the battle, and brought together a team of medievalists and web developers tasked with creating this new digital resource. The medieval researchers – Roman Bleier, Sparky Booker, Eoin O'Flynn, Cherie N. Peters, Christina Wade and Caoimhe Whelan – were responsible for content production and design, while Juliusz Filipowski and Paddy Doyle from the Research IT unit were responsible for the implementation of the web-design and the server side web-development. The project was, from the beginning, a collaborative project between medieval historians based in the Trinity Medieval History Research Centre and IT experts within Trinity College Dublin, and the team functioned in a non-hierarchical structure, contributing to the website in various ways. While initial preparation began in late 2013, the main research and the development of the website happened between January and April 2014, a very narrow timeframe. Appropriately, the website was launched on 12 April 2014 (during the 16th Medieval Dublin Symposium in Trinity College Dublin, which served as the national conference to mark the millennium of the battle of Clontarf) by David Ditchburn, the Head of the School of Histories and Humanities at Trinity.

AUDIENCE AND WEBSITE-DESIGN

The first, and perhaps most critical, step in the creation of any website is choosing your target audience. We initially thought we could best contribute to the commemoration by designing a website aimed at primary-school children. This perhaps could have been linked to their existing Irish primary-school curriculum, as there is a dearth of information on the battle aimed specifically at children. Our initial inspiration was the BBC website design for their primary history section.[11] We liked how the user could easily interact with the website and access data in a variety of formats. We also liked the crisp graphics,

10 'Emperor of the Irish', (http://www.tcd.ie/Library/about/exhibitions /bru/) (21 Jan. 2015). 11 'Schools Primary History' (http://www.bbc.co.uk/schools/ primaryhistory/) (Accessed 7 Apr. 2015). This website has now been archived and is no longer being updated.

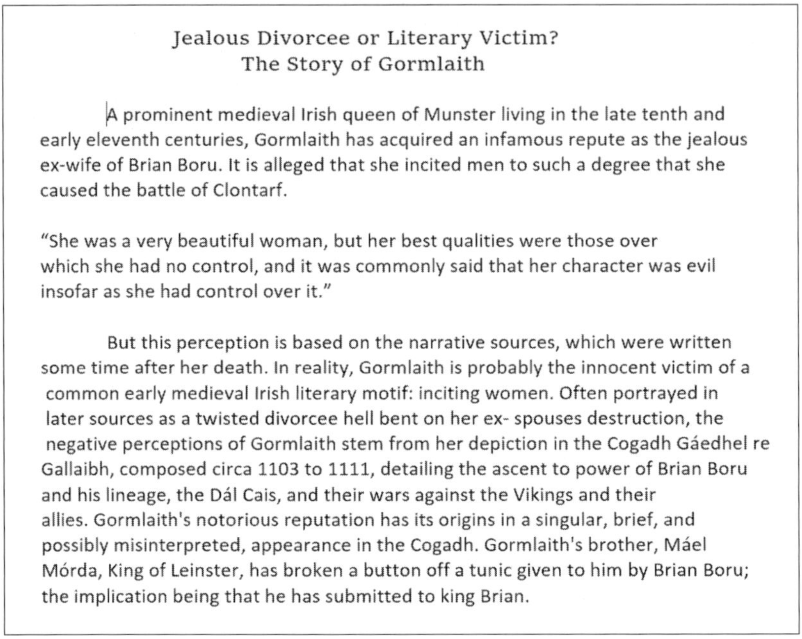

Jealous Divorcee or Literary Victim?
The Story of Gormlaith

A prominent medieval Irish queen of Munster living in the late tenth and early eleventh centuries, Gormlaith has acquired an infamous repute as the jealous ex-wife of Brian Boru. It is alleged that she incited men to such a degree that she caused the battle of Clontarf.

"She was a very beautiful woman, but her best qualities were those over which she had no control, and it was commonly said that her character was evil insofar as she had control over it."

But this perception is based on the narrative sources, which were written some time after her death. In reality, Gormlaith is probably the innocent victim of a common early medieval Irish literary motif: inciting women. Often portrayed in later sources as a twisted divorcee hell bent on her ex- spouses destruction, the negative perceptions of Gormlaith stem from her depiction in the Cogadh Gáedhel re Gallaibh, composed circa 1103 to 1111, detailing the ascent to power of Brian Boru and his lineage, the Dál Cais, and their wars against the Vikings and their allies. Gormlaith's notorious reputation has its origins in a singular, brief, and possibly misinterpreted, appearance in the Cogadh. Gormlaith's brother, Máel Mórda, King of Leinster, has broken a button off a tunic given to him by Brian Boru; the implication being that he has submitted to king Brian.

14.1a An early version of our 'Gormlaith' page.

animation, and friendly, inviting atmosphere for learning. Children respond better to graphic-heavy websites with a great amount of interaction and play, as opposed to more text-focussed designs.[12] Therefore, we planned on building our website with this target-audience in mind and this type of design. This idea, however, had to be jettisoned quite quickly. The BBC website used complex graphics and, not having access to a designer, we tried to generate comparable graphics using open source programs, such as Inkscape. After several attempts at creating characters, we quickly learned that a graphic-centred website was beyond both our skill-set and the time-limitations of the project. This realization necessitated a change in our target market from young children to a more general audience. This could include older children of 12 years and up, and also support school projects, although it was not designed to tie in with any particular curriculum. In the end, we kept some of the original features that we found so successful in the BBC site, such as the appealing design and interactive elements, while leaving behind the animation, games and characters.

After determining our audience and the way in which the data would be presented, we could finally begin to design the website layout. Web-design is critical for history-based websites, as the average user decides in ten seconds whether or not he/she will continue to use it.[13] Therefore, a website should not

12 Blowers and Bryan 2004, esp. pp 60–3. **13** Nielsen 2011; Haile 2014.

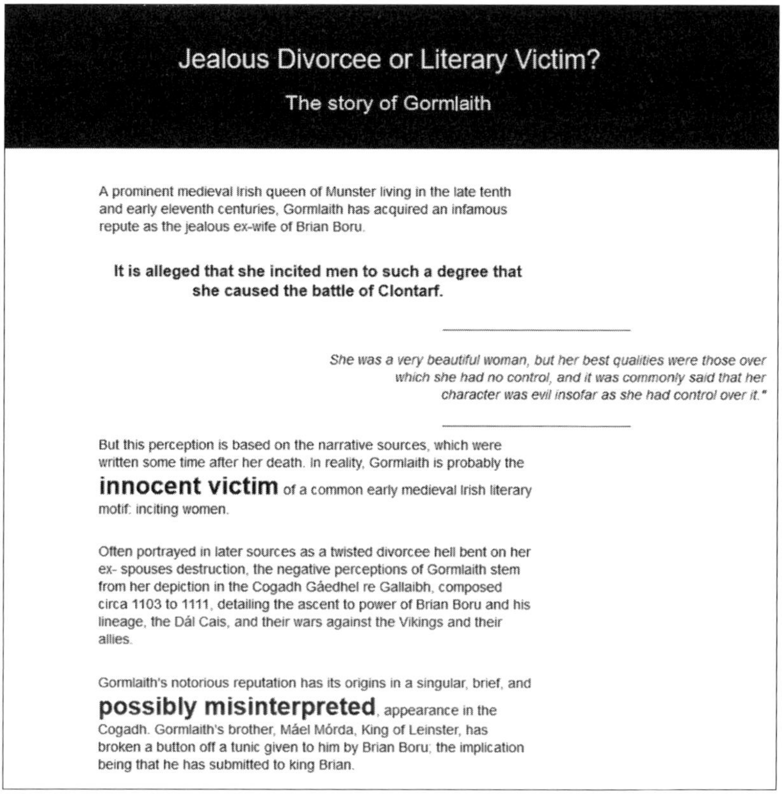

14.1b Another early version of our 'Gormlaith' page.

only be functional and well-researched, but also visually attractive.[14] Some scholars who have investigated online material, such as Constantinos Coursaris and Konstantinos Kripintris, argue that it is crucial to generate a visually-stunning website, as a user's judgment of the attractiveness of the site may subconsciously influence their experience and use of the site.[15] Rebecca Hagen has also made the case for the importance of images, and white space in web-design in order to make online pages more visually appealing and attractive to a user.[16] This attention to design, however, is not always acknowledged as being integral to the use of scholarly websites. Some researchers, such as Daniel Cohen and Roy Rosenzweig, have argued that scholarly website and blogs should be less concerned with graphics and design, and focus on offering long well-written and engaging texts.[17] Jakob Nielsen's 2011 study supported this theory, and established that people will read a long text online if the article holds their interest.[18]

14 Cohen and Rosenzweig 2006. 15 Coursaris and Kripintris 2012, p. 36. 16 Golombisky and Hagen 2010. 17 See Cohen and Rosenzweig 2006, chap. 4. 18 Nielsen 2011.

Given that our audience would be a mix of novice and expert, we wanted to lessen the possibility of a 'textual overload' for the general public, and generate a striking and memorable page. Aiming for both an approachable and interesting narrative, we decided to create a visually dynamic website with ample white space, images to attract the broadest audience, and a clear and accessible prose. We determined that one of the critical features in creating a website was to balance white space, the blank space in between paragraphs, images, or other blocks of text. According to Keith Robertson, white space can 'make or break the effective transmission of image and text'.[19] A large block of text is a quick way to alienate your audience. The more space and less text that appears on a page, the less overwhelming the information will be. Thus, the webpage transforms the printed word to a dynamic text (see figs 14.1a and 14.1b). Sometimes even the smallest of things can make a big difference. We sought to add interest to the pages through changing fonts (a seemingly simple design-element that took two meetings, four hours and an unhealthy quantity of coffee to determine), adding quotes, shifting margins, and including relevant and eye-catching images. Something as 'simple' as font can have a significant impact on the users' experience of a website. Goran Bidjoviski argued that fonts actually impart values to the reader, and different fonts evoke differing 'desires, ambitions, attitudes'; thus font choice is an integral component of our overall design-scheme.[20]

One of the central difficulties with building an image-dense website is copyright privilege. It was extremely useful (and much appreciated) that, by the time we started constructing our website, a number of institutions had made their images freely available in the public domain, and we were thus free to use them as long as they were accompanied by the proper attribution. In some cases, however, image rights did have to be requested.[21] This gave us a rich selection of relevant images to use on our pages, and undoubtedly contributes to the appeal of the website. We were able to utilize photographs of contemporary artefacts and while occasionally, we used later, anachronistic depictions of relevant events or people, we always provided a context for the image.

19 Robertson 1993. **20** Bidjovski 2013. **21** We would like to thank the following for allowing us to use their images: Linzi Simpson, Edmund O'Donovan, Tomás Ó Brógáin, National Library of Ireland, National Museum of Ireland, Marsh's Library, Trustees of the British Museum, British Library, National Museum of Scotland, Árni Magnússon Institute for Icelandic Studies, National Museum of Iceland, Getty Images, Ballyhoura Failte, Board of Trinity College Dublin, The National Gallery, London, and the University of Manchester. We would also like to thank all the contributors to Wikimedia Commons for making their images part of the public domain.

ACADEMIC INTEGRITY

While endeavouring to make the website both accessible and engaging, we also wanted to respect the principles of academic transparency and integrity. Indeed, as time went on it became apparent that the very nature of this project and the digital resources upon which it would draw were well suited to combining these goals of general accessibility and academic integrity. We deliberately avoided presenting a singular narrative of the battle that might gloss over the complexity of the sources and of opinion among historians. Instead, the user of the website is encouraged to discover why such a singular narrative is problematic if not impossible, by learning about the agendas, biases and problems associated with the historical sources that tell us about the battle. In short, while those new to the topic will find an account of the battle of Clontarf sketched out for them in a broad outline on the website, they are encouraged to decide for themselves where the colour and shade should be added, and why.

A critical task was to create a consistent and professional writing-style across the website and to avoid any jarring changes in style or tone. With this in mind, we regularly edited one another's content to ensure cohesiveness across the website. A common approach to referencing was also crucial and was standardized early in the project. The clear signposting of the sources used was a central tenet in maintaining academic standards in the Battle of Clontarf project. Indeed, the digital format of the project was ideally suited to achieve this goal. Such is the wealth of resources available online or in electronic format that it was perhaps easier to integrate references than in a traditional publication.[22] Whereas a reader might find it hard to access some primary resources in print, it was possible to refer the website user to online editions of the original sources and translations of them via hyperlinks embedded throughout the website.[23] By layering information through a series of links and bibliographies, a reader can chose to read only a brief discussion of a topic related to the battle, or can delve deeper, linking to scholarly works on the subject, or to the original documents. For example, in the section of the website at which reference is made to the capture and execution of Brian Boru's older brother Mathgamain (fig. 14.2), we also provide the record of this event in the *Annals of Inisfallen*, an important contemporary source. By clicking on the hyperlinked text below the quotation – *AI* 972.3 – the user is taken to an electronic edition of the Annals of Inisfallen freely available at CELT. Every effort was made to provide access to the original source materials

22 For the value and potential of 'hypertextual history' that Edward L. Ayers anticipated back in 1999, see Ayers 1999; Gilbert 2005, esp. pp 422–3. **23** For instance, the editions of the various Irish Annals available at the Corpus of Electronic Texts (CELT, www.ucc.ie/celt) or J.H. Todd's edition of *Cogadh Gaedhel re Gallaibh* and George Webbe Dasent's edition of *Njal's Saga*, both available at the Internet Archive (www.archive.org).

It was not long before Máel Muad had Mathgamain summarially executed 'in violation of the guarantee and despite the curse of the elders of Munster', according to the *Annals of Inisfallen:*

> "*The capture of Mathgamain son of Cennétig, king of Caisel. He was treacherously seized by Donnuban and handed over to the son of Bran in violation of the guarantee and despite the interdiction of the elders of Mumu, and he as put to death by Bran's son.*"
> *— AI972.3 on CELT*

14.2 Section of the page 'Death of Mathgamain mac Cennétig, 976 AD'.

for the user. This, it is hoped, will help to facilitate further independent study and research. We were also keen to direct readers to further secondary material on the topics, and to this end, a bibliography is included at the bottom of each page via a 'Sources' button which lists a number of important secondary works relating to each subject-page as well as relevant primary material.

We wanted to offer users not just signposts to these primary and secondary texts, but to put some of these important sources in context. For example, the twelfth-century text known as the *Cogadh Gáedhel re Gallaibh* ('The War of the Irish against the Foreigners') is a key source for the battle, but enormously problematic. Viewed as 'reliable' by scholars into the twentieth century, more modern research has argued that it is a heroic biography of Brian Boru commissioned by his descendants a century after his death.[24] While drawing on earlier sources, this early twelfth-century text cannot be relied upon to provide an accurate account of the early eleventh-century battle. In order to inform its readers, the Battle of Clontarf website offers a critical examination of the problems this pivotal source presents to modern readers. In this way, the user can engage with the *Cogadh* directly and with greater awareness of what drove its author or authors and influenced its depiction of Brian and the battle.

THE WEBSITE STRUCTURE AND NAVIGATION

The overall structure of the website enabled us to capitalize on the range and strength of our own research. Our team includes experts on the battle of

24 The inspiration for this text and the agenda of its authors has generated debate among scholars. Máire Ní Mhaonaigh, among others, argues that the *Cogadh* can be regarded as a product of the court of Brian Boru's great-grandson, Muirchertach Ua Briain (d. 1119). More recently, Denis Casey argues that versions of the *Cogadh* may have been in existence from the later eleventh century. See Máire Ní Mhaonaigh, '*Cogad Gáedel re Gallaib* and the annals: a comparison', *Ériu*, 47 (1996), 101–26; eadem, 'The date of *Cogad Gaedel re Galliab*' *Peritia*, 9 (1995), 354–77; Denis Casey, 'A reconsideration of the authorship and transmission of *Cogadh Gáedhel re Gallaibh*', *PRIA*, 113C (2013), 139–61. See also discussion in this volume, above, passim.

14.3 Screenshot of our Homepage.

Clontarf, the Vikings, and daily life in early medieval Ireland, but also incorporates scholars whose expertise lies in later periods, and focusses on the ways that history is reinterpreted and utilized by historians. Playing to our strengths and allowing each team member to contribute based on their various areas of expertise permitted us to present the battle of Clontarf in its myriad contexts. With this in mind, we created seven main sections for the website: 'Social Context', 'People', 'Politics', 'Maps', 'The Battle', 'Remembering' and 'Timeline'. The Homepage (or landing page) is the entry page to our website (fig. 14.3), and is usually the first page that new visitors will encounter.

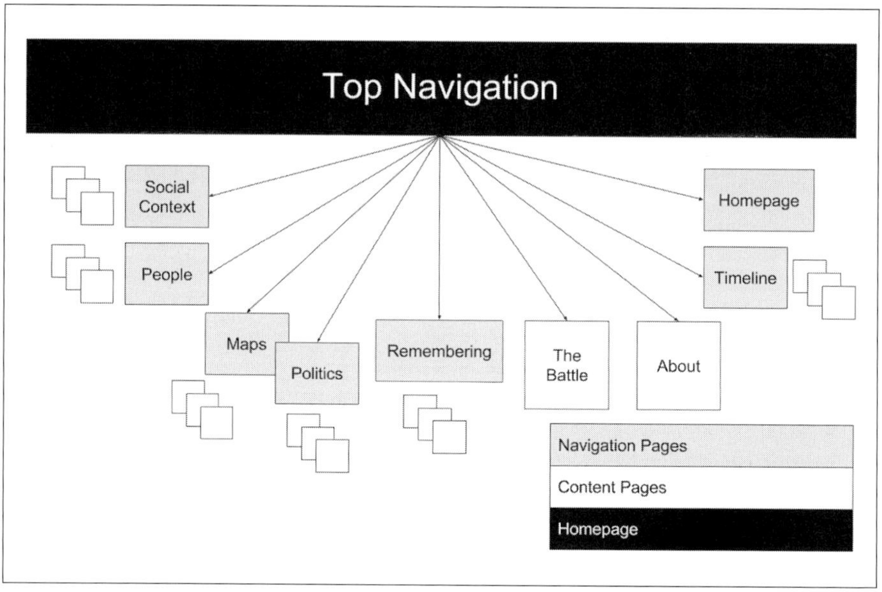

14.4 Navigation structure of the Battle of Clontarf website.

Consequently, its purpose is to interest the user and motivate them to stay on the site and explore it further. It is also a navigation hub from which the user can easily navigate to other sections of the website. As with most websites today, we provide access to these different sections through the main or top navigation bar. Our top navigation bar has two additional links, one which returns users to the Homepage, and another to an 'About' page. The About page provides additional information about the project and the individual team members that are responsible for creating the site.

The website itself was built on Drupal, a very successful open source web framework and content-management system. Our colleagues from the Trinity High Performance Computing created the Drupal website, and provided basic templates on which we could add timeline and page content. Without a well-designed website structure, a potential user is lost in a maze of pages. Thus, it is important to plot the website structure early in the creation process and determine how a user can access the individual web pages and how they will be related to each other.[25] All of the pages were originally created as content pages, meaning that they contained the content that the user would be interested in, such as text, images, links or maps. Since some of our sections had several content pages, it was necessary to create intermediary pages that could act as a gateway through which pages about the same topic could be accessed together.

25 On the importance of website structure in general, see Morville and Rosenfeld 2006, pp 41–144. In the context of writing history online, see Cohen and Rosenzweig 2006, pp 133–40.

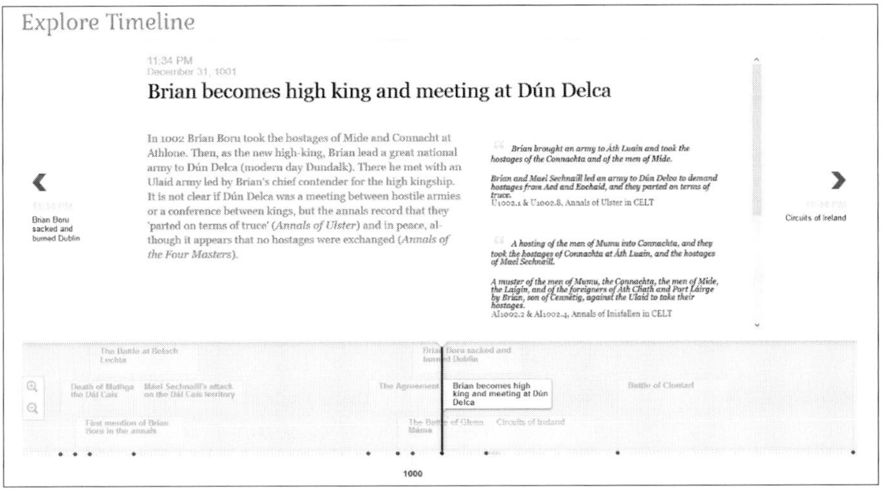

14.5 Entry for the year 1002 in our 'Timeline'.

These 'linking' or 'navigation' pages are crucial, because they guide the user through content pages. The graph shows the website structure and distinguishes between the different types of web pages (fig. 14.4).

We also included four special design-elements that provide an alternative way to navigate and explore our website. Rather than being forced to follow the website structure outlined above, a user can browse the content based on personal interest via the 'Trivia' and 'Did You Know' sections as well as the 'Timeline' and 'Maps' pages which are available via the Homepage. Image links are provided to each of the six main content sections, and direct links are offered to content pages via the 'Trivia' content on the right side (under the title 'Explore the Hidden History of Clontarf'). The 'Trivia' section selects interesting facts related to each of the pages that are randomly generated on the 'Homepage'. The hope is that each time someone visits this page, even if only for a minute or two, they can learn something new. Memorable information is also highlighted through the 'Did you know' elements of each page. These facts serve a design purpose as well, making the pages appear more visually attractive: the sections are offset from the regular text and coloured in red. Unlike the 'Trivia', which appear at the bottom of content pages, these appear throughout. The 'Timeline' contains snippets of information on various important events leading up to the battle; this information is then augmented with hyperlinks to the relevant sections in the primary material. The arrows to the left and right of the timeline allow the user to browse chronologically, while a navigation tool below the timeline allows them to skip straight to whatever event they want to read about (fig. 14.5). The maps allow the user to engage with the likely events of the battle and Brian's rise to power

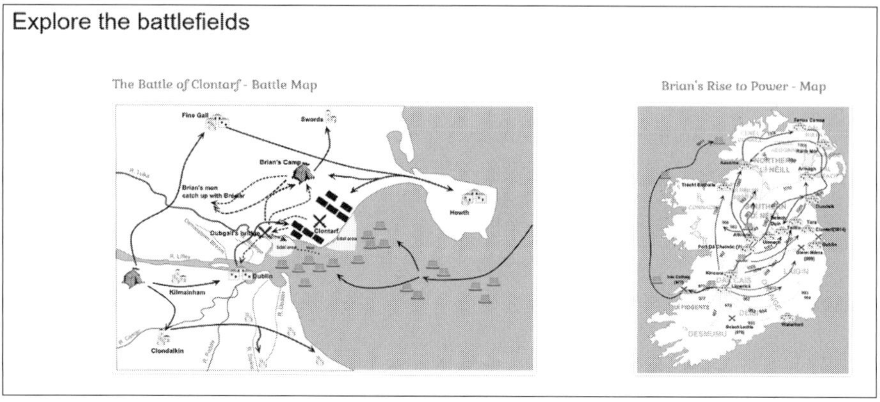

14.6 The 'Maps' section of the Battle of Clontarf website.

in a visual format. While the maps are based on the information in those same written sources discussed elsewhere, and therefore come with the same health warnings, it is hoped that they provide both a useful supplement to the site's written account of the battle, and perhaps also a different, visual perspective which may be attractive to some users (fig. 14.6). This enables users with different learning styles to get the most from the website, and ensures that it is as accessible as possible.

The sections 'Trivia', 'Did You Know', 'Timeline' and 'Maps' are part of our overall strategy to provide users with as many interesting and useful ways of accessing relevant information as possible in an effort to make the Battle of Clontarf website accessible and enjoyable for users, and to help them with their own research and reading.

BATTLE PAGE WALK-THROUGH

A brief walk-through of the 'Battle of Clontarf' page demonstrates how the disparate elements and features of the website come together in practice. The 'Battle' page provides users with a basic account of the events leading up to the battle of Clontarf and what scholars think is likely to have happened at the famous clash itself. Throughout this page a good deal of thought has been given to providing users with easy and transparent access to the sources and texts available for the battle. For example, clicking on the *Njál's Saga* hyperlink on the 'Battle of Clontarf' page takes the user to another internal page discussing the historiography of the source. Returning to the 'Battle' page itself, the user will find the account of the battle presented using a visual style which clearly distinguishes between what the medieval sources say and what we as authors and commentators are saying. For instance, indentation, italicization

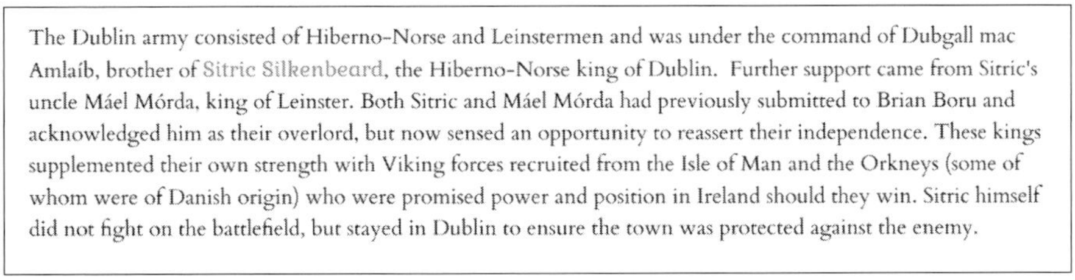

The Dublin army consisted of Hiberno-Norse and Leinstermen and was under the command of Dubgall mac Amlaíb, brother of Sitric Silkenbeard, the Hiberno-Norse king of Dublin. Further support came from Sitric's uncle Máel Mórda, king of Leinster. Both Sitric and Máel Mórda had previously submitted to Brian Boru and acknowledged him as their overlord, but now sensed an opportunity to reassert their independence. These kings supplemented their own strength with Viking forces recruited from the Isle of Man and the Orkneys (some of whom were of Danish origin) who were promised power and position in Ireland should they win. Sitric himself did not fight on the battlefield, but stayed in Dublin to ensure the town was protected against the enemy.

14.7 Section from The Battle of Clontarf page with embedded link to biography of Sitric Silkenbeard.

and other visual cues guide the user to the primary source. As key players at the battle are introduced, they are highlighted, and embedded links lead to detailed biographies in the 'People' section of the website. By clicking on Sitric Silkenbeard's name in the above part of the 'Battle' page, for example, the user is taken to his biographical entry (fig. 14.7).

While most of the key players in the battle are well known, the details of their lives are shrouded in the myths which surround the battle. With the use of these hyperlinks, we have attempted to provide as much information about these people as possible from the extant sources. We were keen to ensure that women's involvement in the battle was fully realized, and included two women, Gormlaith and Sláine, among the eight historical persons discussed. We also look at the mythical female characters – the Babh, Valkyrie and Aibhell – who were important to medieval understandings and literary renderings of the battle. Citations and contextualization are always provided to help the user distinguish between contemporary sources, later romantic imaginings of the battle, and modern study tools. Furthermore, while various maps are included on the 'Battle' page itself, users also have the option to navigate via internal links to the website's dedicated pages on maps.

In addition to our section about what historians know about the battle itself, and our different tools for visualizing information about it, we have also provided several other avenues for engaging with the battle. In our political context section, we provide a discussion of the politico-military background to the conflict. Brian fought a number of battles in his quest for the high-kingship, and accounts of what we know about these are included to show how the battle of Clontarf follows on from and relates to the events that preceded it. Overall, the sections concentrating on 'The Battle', 'Politics' and 'People' offer the most traditionally narrative material about the battle, but the way we present it is, we hope, somewhat more innovative. We seek to provide this information in a way that is dynamic and interactive, and try not to impose a 'correct' version, but rather give tools for users to find out things for themselves and challenge our and other historians' interpretations, trusting the public readership with the uncertainty and nuance of historical research.

SOCIAL CONTEXT

One of the more unusual elements of the website is its inclusion of information not only about the events of the battle, but also about religion, weaponry and daily life at the time of Clontarf. This is a resource for those interested in how the battle fits into its wider context. For example, the battle has often been interpreted in popular culture as a contest between the Christian Irish and pagan Vikings. This is not particularly accurate in an eleventh-century context, as both sides comprised Irish and Viking forces (and most Vikings had by this time converted). However, this representation is based on one of the oldest known accounts of the battle – the previously mentioned *Cogadh* – and anti-Viking religious propaganda was a feature of contemporary Irish literature. Thus, to understand what the battle meant for contemporaries and succeeding generations, an understanding of religious life in Viking-Age Ireland is essential. This information is central to understanding the gulf between the representations of religion in the historiography of the battle and how people in early eleventh-century Ireland actually worshipped and thought about their God or gods.

The information about clothing, diet and weaponry included on the site takes advantage of our team's expertise, and means that users can visualize the combatants as well as those affected by the battle who were living at that time in Dublin and its hinterlands. Dublin, the most significant urban settlement on the island in that period, is examined to allow users to understand why it was of such strategic importance for Brian and his enemies. It is no coincidence that the battle (reputedly) took place within sight of the city's walls; control of the port was essential to the high-kingship, and the city was contested many times by rival claimants, both before and after this most famous contest.[26] The website's exposition of Dublin's material culture and society allows users to understand why both sides were a mix of Viking and Irish. The Viking towns were *loci* of cultural exchange and key to the forging of transcultural alliances of the type that were so evident at the battle of Clontarf. This social and cultural background informs any understanding of the battle, but this section of the website can also act as a stand-alone resource for those interested in Viking-Age Ireland rather than the battle *per se*.

THE (AFTER)LIFE OF BRIAN: THE REMEMBERING SECTION

The battle has long had a significant place in the Irish historical imagination. Our 'Remembering' section provides snapshots of the ways in which the battle

26 See, for example, Clare Downham, 'The battle of Clontarf in Irish history and legend', *History Ireland*, 13:5 (2005), 19–23; Duffy, *Brian Boru*.

and Brian Boru have been interpreted in the past 1000 years, and the combination of historiographical alongside historical material is one of the most unusual aspects of the website. It was important to us to make this a significant part of the site because the project was triggered by commemoration – so, from its inception, the myth of Clontarf was a key aspect of the website. Modern historians differ in their interpretation of the significance of the battle on eleventh-century Irish political life, and some argue that it was not particularly important politically.[27] However, in historiographical terms, this does not matter – what matters is that, from the eleventh century to the present day, it has been seen as a key event in this island's history.

Indeed, given that our most useful literary account of the battle, the *Cogadh*, is a twelfth-century text compiled for one of Brian's descendants, interrogating how later sources recall the battle is hugely significant. Our key goal in the 'Remembering' section was to explore a range of interpretations which were offered for this medieval battle stretching from the medieval (such as the *Cogadh*) to the modern era (for instance, to give just one among many, the popular musical version of the legend known as 'Brian Boru's March'). Far from dismissing these later 'unhistorical' accounts of the battle, we embraced the new versions of the story and later adaptations and legends as a significant legacy of the battle. Gabrielle Spiegel's approach to understanding the material past involves embracing the 'social logic' of a source (in our case, a story), and argues that one must understand the 'historical purposiveness' of such material in order to recognize that each 'interpretively reconstituted' version has significant value.[28] This way of considering the enduring and evolving memory of events helps us to acknowledge the multiplicity of 'truths' about the battle. Thus, far from limiting our focus to 'what actually happened' at the battle and what this meant for the wider society, we were keen to engage in an exercise of recovery, gathering a number of these later variations of the story and presenting them as valid ways of remembering the past. This allowed us to engage with the many ways in which the legend of Brian Boru and his final battle impinged on Irish historical memory.

The historiography of the battle includes different conclusions and understandings often influenced by the political and social environment of individual commentators. The *Book of Howth* contains an imaginative sixteenth-century account of the cause of the battle (supposedly due to a liaison between Brian's son and a Dublin woman and the resulting anger of her husband, the 'White Merchant'). This may have been reflective of a local Dublin tradition that sought to link the battle closely with events in the city.[29] Elsewhere, Sylvester O'Halloran, an eighteenth-century scientist and historian,

27 See, for example, Etchingham in this volume, above. 28 Gabrielle Spiegel, 'History, historicism, and the social logic of the text in the middle ages', *Speculum*, 65:1 (1990), 85. 29 See Lenore Fischer, 'How Dublin remembered the battle of Clontarf' in Seán Duffy (ed.), *Medieval Dublin XIII* (Dublin, 2013), pp 70–80.

presented Brian as a modern, enlightened and pious leader, defending Ireland against heathen Danes. This portrayal owes much to O'Halloran's own political and religious agenda, as a patriotic Catholic Irishman who agitated against the penal laws.[30] Similarly, Geoffrey Keating's historical masterpiece *Foras feasa ar Éirinn* (1643) uses the battle as a way to glorify Ireland, and emphasizes Brian's success as a peacekeeper and lawgiver.[31] There are many other examples of the ways in which the story was adapted in the early modern period, and these offer a rich source of fascinating material that can reveal the ways history is used to craft and celebrate Irish identity.

Brian's legacy has continued into the modern period. Brian was included (as part of an Irish historical trinity of St Patrick and the Virgin Mary) among the carved heads representing the great men and women of Ireland sculpted by the Smyth brothers at the Chapel Royal of Dublin Castle. Those agitating for greater independence for Ireland from the United Kingdom in the modern era, like the poet Thomas Davis, presented the battle as a clash of united 'Irish' forces led by a pious and charismatic leader against a foreign invader. In another medium, the battle of Clontarf was deemed worthy of commemoration in the series of murals painted between 1914 and 1919 on Dublin's City Hall rotunda by James Ward. Ward's depiction has a similarly Christian flavour, one scene showing Brian holding a crucifix aloft before his assembled troops. This echoes the pro-Christian propaganda present in some of the medieval sources, but with new religious implications relating to the religious divide that arose after the Reformation. Oftentimes, what is not articulated can be hugely significant, and the absence of any depiction of British rule in Ireland in the wider mural series in City Hall perhaps makes Brian's victory over other 'invaders' all the more striking.

The impact of the battle has long been and will continue to be debated. However, it is clear that the enduring memory of the battle has exerted influence on perceptions of Ireland and her past. In this way, the story of Brian Boru and the battle of Clontarf was truly significant. The modern presence of Brian in songs, graphic novels, video games, and possibly on the silver screen in the near future, suggests that the legend of this Munsterman and his most famous battle will endure for some time to come.

CONCLUDING REMARKS

As this article has demonstrated, the Battle of Clontarf project was a highly collaborative effort that involved a multitude of variables typically not

30 See Clare O'Halloran, 'The triumph of "virtuous liberty": representation of the Vikings and Brian Boru in eighteenth-century histories', *Eighteenth-Century Ireland. Iris an Dá Chultúr*, 22 (2007), 151–63. **31** See Ní Úrdail in this volume, above.

considered by historians. Electronic editing, blogging, and social media have become increasingly important as publishing media, especially for public outreach, and historians are not only engaged in delivering content, but also increasingly in the planning and design of websites, blogs and other forms of online publication. This requires us to use different skills and to think about content delivery in new ways. Collaboration was an important aspect of our project. This included collaboration among us as historians, but also interdisciplinary collaboration with our colleagues from the Centre for High Performance Computing. We had to learn about each other's work and find a way to communicate effectively. In our first meeting it became clear that while we were speaking 'Historian', our collaborators were speaking 'Computer Scientist', but over the course of the project both sides adapted and learned the language of our collaborating partners. The success of this collaboration is manifest, we hope, in our website. The flexibility and patience of our IT colleagues was essential in making this a success, and the presence of a Digital Humanities specialist among the historians was also enormously helpful in allowing us to communicate effectively.

While collaborative publishing is very common in science disciplines, it is still relatively uncommon in the Humanities, and the experience was new to all of us who work primarily in a historical context. Despite this, we encountered remarkably few problems between collaborators, possibly because we are all at a similar career-stage, and without any clear hierarchy we were encouraged to respect and consider one another's ideas more readily. Many of us share office space in the Medieval History Research Centre at Trinity and this enabled us to talk through problems in person and in detail, to revisit questions each day and deal with issues together as they arose. This real-world interaction and connection (perhaps paradoxically) is key to a successful online project. Even this article was designed and written in a collaborative way using Google Docs. Contributors were assigned a section to draft and then individually or in teams of two they presented their text, which was then edited by all members of the team. Online text editors such as Google Docs, online publishing such as Wordpress or Drupal, and the myriad other online services that allow scholars to connect with each other make this collaboration much easier, and are already transforming research in the Humanities. In that light, our project and this article are experiments in new ways of writing history, both collaboratively and digitally.

Finally, much like the way the battle has been remembered, the digital format of the Battle of Clontarf website means that it is not finished or static, nor indeed does it ever have to be. Hosted by the Research IT unit at TCD, it will remain accessible on a secure server, and can, with continued support, function as a dynamic tool that will evolve as modern interpretations of Clontarf change.

APPENDIX 14.1

Things to consider when doing a Digital History project

Many of these suggestions are common sense, but we think they are worth listing here. We thought about some of these issues from the start, while others came to us as the project developed.

1. Enter the digital world wholeheartedly – do not try to reproduce a monograph or article online as a resource. The format changes the way you present content, and this is a good thing, not to be resisted. To this end, some initial research on online publishing styles and how users view content online is definitely recommended.

2. Embrace the unique elements available in digital publishing. Make good use of hyperlinks. Take advantage of the fact that you can use colourful high-resolution images without the costs associated with traditional colour printing.

3. Think about the sustainability of the website from the start. Does the hosting cost money? If so, make sure you have funding in perpetuity. Will the server be around in five years? Who will update content? Nothing is worse than putting work into a project and then having it lost through a variety of heart-stopping disasters such as formatting/platform changes or other vagaries of the digital world.

4. If possible, involve a Digital Humanities specialist. They can help translate between different partners on the project.

5. Match your audience and skill-set. On this point we suffered an early setback and needed to reassess and readjust our approach. Think carefully about what other resources already exist on the topic and how yours can make the greatest impact.

6. Know and like the other members of your team – this may not always be possible, and we got lucky here, but the collaboration required for a project such as this requires much more cooperation and give-and-take than historians are used to, so a team that gets along is essential. We found that having regular meetings in person as well as using online platforms was useful in maintaining harmonious relationships and aided effective communication.

Digital Project Bibliography

Ayers, Edward L., 'The pasts and futures of digital history' (1999) (http://www.vcdh.virginia.edu/PastsFutures.html).

Bidjovski, Goran, 'Interpretation of selected text fonts with their typographic features from the websites of computer users', *International Journal of Image, Graphics and Signal Processing*, 5:2 (2013), 71–8.

Blowers, Helene, and Robin Bryan, *Weaving a library web: a guide to developing children's websites* (Chicago, 2004).

Cohen, Daniel J., and Roy Rosenzweig, *Digital history: a guide to gathering, preserving, and presenting the past on the web* (Michigan, 2006), pp 108–13.

Coursaris, Constantinos K., and Konstantinos Kripintris, 'Web aesthetics and usability: an empirical Study of the effects of white space', *International Journal of E-Business Research*, 8:1 (Jan. 2012), 35–53.

Fischer, Franz, and Anthony Harvey (eds), 'The Saint Patrick's Confessio hypertext stack' (2011) (http://www.confessio.ie/about/hyperstack) (16 Jan. 2015).

Golombisky, Kim, and Rebecca Hagen, *White space is not your enemy: a beginner's guide to communicating visually through graphic, web and multimedia design* (Burlington, 2010).

Haile, Tom, 'What you think you know about the web is wrong', *Time magazine*, 9 Mar. 2014 (www.time.com/12933/what-you-think-you-know-about-the-web-is-wrong/) (21 Mar. 2015).

Morville, Peter and Louis Rosenfeld, *Information architecture for the world wide web*, 3rd ed. (Sebastopol, 2007).

Nic an Airchinnigh, Méadhbh (ed.), 'The foundations of Irish culture: Irish manuscripts on the continent AD600–AD850' (http://foundationsirishculture.ie/) (16 Jan. 2015).

Nielsen, Jakob, 'How long do users stay on web pages?', 12 Sept. 2011 (www.nngroup.com/articles/how-long-do-users-stay-on-web-pages/) (21 Mar. 2015).

Patterson Gilbert, Stephanie, 'Harrisburg's old eighth ward: constructing a website for student research', *Pennsylvania History*, 72:4 (Autumn 2005), 419–27.

Robertson, Keith, 'On white space in graphic design' (1993) (www.logoorgane.com/white-space.php) (23 Mar. 2015).

'Wikipedia Edit-A-Thon' (http://1014retold.com/wikipedia-editathon/) 'Wikipedia: WikiProject Ireland/Battle of Clontarf Edit-a-thon April 2014' (http://en.wikipedia.org/wiki/Wikipedia:WikiProject_Ireland/Battle_of_Clontarf_Editathon_April_2014) (21 Jan. 2015).

ONLINE DATABASES

Converting the Isles: an international network for the study of conversion to Christianity in the insular world (http://www.asnc.cam.ac.uk/conversion/) (16 Jan. 2015).

Corpus of Electronic Texts (http://www.ucc.ie/celt/)

Internet Archive (www.archive.org)

Irish script on screen, Dublin Institute for Advanced Studies (http://www.isos.dias.ie/english/index.html)

OTHER ONLINE RESOURCES

Emperor of the Irish (http://www.tcd.ie/Library/about/exhibitions/bru/)

'Eyesodic: Game Studios' (http://www.eyesodicgames.com/the-battle-of-clontarf.html) (Accessed 21 Jan. 2015 but no longer online).

'Schools Primary History' (http://www.bbc.co.uk/schools/primaryhistory/) (7 Apr. 2015).